SHADOW AND SUBSTANCE

ReFormations

MEDIEVAL AND EARLY MODERN

Series Editors:
David Aers, Sarah Beckwith, and James Simpson

RECENT TITLES IN THE SERIES

Against All England: Regional Identity and Cheshire Writing, 1195–1656 (2009)
Robert W. Barrett, Jr.

The Maudlin Impression: English Literary Images of Mary Magdalene, 1550–1700 (2009)
Patricia Badir

The Embodied Word: Female Spiritualities, Contested Orthodoxies, and English Religious Cultures, 1350–1700 (2010)
Nancy Bradley Warren

The Island Garden: England's Language of Nation from Gildas to Marvell (2012)
Lynn Staley

Miserere Mei: The Penitential Psalms in Late Medieval and Early Modern England (2012)
Clare Costley King'oo

The English Martyr from Reformation to Revolution (2012)
Alice Dailey

Transforming Work: Early Modern Pastoral and Late Medieval Poetry (2013)
Katherine C. Little

Writing Faith and Telling Tales: Literature, Politics, and Religion in the Work of Thomas More (2013)
Thomas Betteridge

Unwritten Verities: The Making of England's Vernacular Legal Culture, 1463–1549 (2015)
Sebastian Sobecki

Mysticism and Reform, 1400–1750 (2015)
Sara S. Poor and Nigel Smith, eds.

The Civic Cycles: Artisan Drama and Identity in Premodern England (2015)
Nicole R. Rice and Margaret Aziza Pappano

Tropologies: Ethics and Invention in England, c. 1350–1600 (2016)
Ryan McDermott

Volition's Face: Personification and the Will in Renaissance Literature (2017)
Andrew Escobedo

SHADOW
and
SUBSTANCE

*Eucharistic Controversy and English Drama
across the Reformation Divide*

Jay Zysk

UNIVERSITY OF NOTRE DAME PRESS

NOTRE DAME, INDIANA

University of Notre Dame Press
Notre Dame, Indiana 46556
undpress.nd.edu

Copyright © 2017 by the University of Notre Dame

All Rights Reserved

Published in the United States of America

Library of Congress Cataloging-in-Publication Data

Names: Zysk, Jay, 1983– author.
Title: Shadow and substance : Eucharistic controversy and English drama across the Reformation divide / Jay Zysk.
Description: Notre Dame : University of Notre Dame Press, 2017. | Series: ND reformations: medieval & early modern | Includes bibliographical references and index. | D
Identifiers: LCCN 2017024312 (print) | LCCN 2017036418 (ebook) | ISBN 9780268102319 (pdf) | ISBN 9780268102326 (epub) | ISBN 9780268102296 (hardback) | ISBN 0268102295 (hardcover) | ISBN 9780268102302 (paper)
Subjects: LCSH: Lord's Supper in literature. | English drama—Early modern and Elizabethan, 1500–1600—History and criticism. | English drama—17th century—History and criticism. | Religion and literature—England—History—16th century. | Religion and literature—England—History—17th century. | Christianity and literature—England—History—16th century. | Christianity and literature—England—History—17th century. | BISAC: RELIGION / Christianity / Literature & the Arts. | DRAMA / English, Irish, Scottish, Welsh. | LITERARY CRITICISM / Medieval.
Classification: LCC PR658.R43 (ebook) | LCC PR658.R43 Z97 2017 (print) | DDC 822/.3093823--dc23
LC record available at https://lccn.loc.gov/2017024312

∞ *This paper meets the requirements of ANSI/NISO Z39.48-1992 (Permanence of Paper).*

For Courtney

CONTENTS

List of Figures ix

Acknowledgments xi

Introduction: Many Reformations   1

ONE. Eucharistic Semiotics:
The Body of Christ and the Play of Signs   19

TWO. Words and Wounds:
Christ Crucified and *Coriolanus*   53

THREE. Sacramental Signs and Mystical Bodies
in Lydgate, Bale, and Shakespeare   83

FOUR. Father Faustus? Confection and Conjuration
in *Everyman* and *Doctor Faustus*   119

FIVE. Relics and Unreliable Bodies in the Croxton
Play of the Sacrament, *The Duchess of Malfi*, and *The Changeling*   155

SIX. Conjured to Remembrance: Emmaus Plays,
Jack Juggler, and *The Winter's Tale*   191

Afterword   225

Notes   230

Bibliography   323

Index   359

FIGURES

Figure 3.1. Woodcut from John Foxe's *Actes and Monuments* (London: John Day, 1563) depicting the murder of King John. Reproduced by permission of Folger Shakespeare Library.   103

Figure 4.1. Frontispiece woodcut from Christopher Marlowe, *The Tragicall Historie of the life and death of Doctor Faustus* (London: John Wright, 1631). Reproduced by permission of Folger Shakespeare Library.   127

Figure 4.2. Historiated initial T in the "Te igitur" prayer. *Missale ad usum insignis ac preclare Ecclesie Sarum* (London: Richard Pynson, 1520), Houghton f Typ 505.20.262, fol. lxxxvii. Reproduced by permission of Houghton Library, Harvard University.   133

Figure 4.3. Historiated initial T in the "Te igitur" prayer. *Missale Romanum ad usum sacrosancte Romane ecclesie* (Venetiis, 1546), Houghton f Typ 525 46.262, fol. 127r. Reproduced by permission of Houghton Library, Harvard University.   134

Figure 4.4. Historiated initial T in the "Te igitur" prayer. *Missale Romanum* (Saragossa, 1511), Houghton Typ 560.11.262, sig. O3r. Reproduced by permission of Houghton Library, Harvard University.   135

Figure 4.5. Blessing crosses as used in the words *corpus* and *sanguis*. *Missale Romanum ad usum sacrosancte Romane ecclesiae* (Venetiis, 1546), Houghton f Typ 525 46.262, fol. 127v. Reproduced by permission of Houghton Library, Harvard University.   136

Figure 4.6. Funeral liturgy depicted in the Knollys Family Psalter [Winchester?], vellum, ca. 1430, fols. 28v–29r. Reproduced by permission of Transylvania University Library, Lexington, Kentucky.   153

Figure 5.1. Foldout illustration from B. G. [Bernard Garter], *A newyeares gifte* (London: Henry Bynneman, 1579). Reproduced by permission of Folger Shakespeare Library. 160

Figure 5.2. "O sacrum convivium," from *A Manual of Prayers*, ca. 1685. Folger Shakespeare Library MS V.a.488, fol. 38r. Reproduced by permission. 173

ACKNOWLEDGMENTS

Eucharistic discourse bears witness to both the strains of controversy and the bonds of community. Much of this book focuses on the former, and in that context I hope the chapters and notes that follow adequately record my debts to the work of those who have sustained vibrant debates about drama and religion in recent critical circles. In these opening pages, however, I would like to express my heartfelt thanks to those who have, by dint of their generosity and friendship, fostered communities that have sustained and supported me as I wrote this book.

Shadow and Substance began as my doctoral dissertation at Brown, where I was privileged to work under the guidance of a gracious and involved committee. Coppélia Kahn, my director, offered the right balance of enthusiasm and skepticism, and always delivered both with characteristic wit and style. Coppélia inspires me not only for her scholarship but also for her integrity; she models all that is right with our profession. Jean Feerick steadily encouraged me to work on religion and helped me develop and hone my ideas before they were ready to hit paper. Stephen Foley shared his knowledge of sixteenth-century religious controversy with me over many lunches and conversations. I have benefited enormously from Kristen Poole's insights into Reformation culture and her unflagging commitment to this project. She continues to find untapped potential in my work, responding to drafts and queries with rigor and curiosity.

Historically, religious controversy tends to drive people apart. In my case, however, shared interest in such a topic forged two wonderful friendships. Katie Brokaw read the manuscript many times and weathered far too many complaints, questions, and anxieties with energy and brilliance. Though we work on opposite coasts and our communications are almost always virtual, Katie has offered this book a most real presence throughout. Rachael Deagman has directed her acute attention to many chapter drafts and engaged me in many spirited conversations, offering sound advice at crucial moments. On matters of drama and theology, she let me get away with nothing; her commitment to the success of this book has meant everything.

My arguments have transformed in surprising and delightful ways because of the innovation and influence of the "ReFormations" series, in which my book has been fortunate to find a home. I am grateful to the series editors—David Aers, Sarah Beckwith, and James Simpson—for supporting this project and helping to shape its development at various stages. Their own scholarly work has been pivotal in cultivating my interests in theology and literature across periodic divides.

It has been my pleasure to work with the University of Notre Dame Press, particularly Stephen Little, who has invested much time and energy in this project from its initial submission. I also wish to thank Rebecca DeBoer, Elisabeth Magnus, and Nicholas Koenig, along with the production team at the Press, for patiently and gracefully guiding the book through its final stages. An earlier version of chapter 4 and brief parts of the Introduction appeared in the *Journal of Medieval and Early Modern Studies* 43, no. 2 (2013): 335–67, reproduced here with permission of Duke University Press. A shorter version of chapter 5 was published in *English Literary Renaissance* 45, no. 3 (2015): 400–424, and is reproduced by permission of Wiley Blackwell.

The Folger Shakespeare Library has always been an ideal place to work, in large part because of its collegial atmosphere and dedicated staff. A short-term Folger Fellowship, supported by the Mary and Eric Weinmann Fellowship Fund, helped me advance research on this project significantly. I am very grateful to Michael Witmore, Gail Kern Paster, Kathleen Lynch, Owen Williams, Daniel DeSimone, Georgianna Ziegler, Melanie Leung, and Carol Brobeck, and to the always capable, ever cheerful reading room staff: Meghan Carafano, LuEllen DeHaven, Denise Dolan, Alan Katz, Rosalind Larry, Rachael Mueller, Camille Seerattan, Betsy Walsh, and Abbie Weinberg. I also thank the librarians at the British Library and Trinity College Library, Dublin; James Capobianco, Susan Conant, and Mary Haegert of the Houghton Library at Harvard University; and B. J. Gooch, of Transylvania University Special Collections, all of whom lent their able assistance.

Gail McMurray Gibson and Kent Cartwright, the external readers for the Press, offered sensitive queries and generous suggestions for strengthening the book's global claims and local details. My work could not have found better reviewers, and I hope the final version repays their keen attention. I am also grateful to those who read portions of the manuscript in draft and offered helpful comments and bibliography: Sarah Beckwith, Katharine Cleland, Theresa Coletti, Alice Dailey, Sara Deats, Nicole Discenza, Doug Lanier, Kat Lecky, Nora Peterson, Kristen Poole, Jennifer Rust, James Simpson, and Claire Sponsler. For stimulating conversation, suggestions, and advice at various points along the way, I thank Sari Altschuler, Tamara Atkin, Giovanna Benadusi, Claire Bourne, Dennis Britton, Devin Byker, Bill Carroll, Holly Crocker, Jane Hwang Degenhardt, Helga Duncan, Derek Dunne, Sarah Eron, Thomas Fulton, Kate Gillen, Elizabeth Hageman, Hunt Hawkins, Megan Heffernan, Anne Koenig, Thomas Lay, John Lennon, Carole Levin, Erika Lin, Catherine Loomis, Fabio Luppi, James Mardock, Craig Martin, Cameron McNabb, Heather Meakin, Karen Newman, John Pfordresher, Amy Rodgers, Laura Runge, Nancy Serrano, Sarah Stanbury, Lisa Starks-Estes, Rachel Trubowitz, Kyle Vitale, Christina Wald, and Janet Yount. I am also grateful to the Humanities Institute at the University of South Florida, and particularly Elizabeth Bird, for a summer fellowship during which I completed some of the research for this book. This book is better for the perceptive comments and insights of many students over the years, especially Mike Frederickson, Ariana Gunderson, Lynnette Macomber, Elan Pavlinich, and Rachel Tanski,

While a graduate student at Brown I was surrounded by many people whose friendship, encouragement, and intellectual curiosity have enriched this project. I want to thank especially James Beaver, Lindy Brady, Khristina Gonzalez, Chris and Katie Holmes, Nora and Andy Peterson, Corey McEleney, Jennifer Schnepf, Cristina Serverius, Brian Sweeney, and Jessica Tabak. For sound advice and engaging seminars, I thank Nancy Armstrong, Paul Armstrong, Elizabeth Bryan, Geoffrey Russom, Barbara Herrnstein Smith, and Len Tennenhouse. As an undergraduate at Stonehill College, I had the pleasure of studying with Barbara Estrin and Katie Conboy, whose warm mentorship and personal investment in my work and career continue to this day. I am grateful as well to Molly Benjamin, Warren Dahlin, Bob Goulet, Jared Green, Ron Leone, Maurice Morin, and Wendy Peek. To Rita Green and James J. Izzo I am likewise grateful.

I am truly delighted to work in the English Department at the University of Massachusetts Dartmouth, where I find myself in the company of generous, dedicated colleagues and curious, energetic students. I am grateful to the chair of the English Department, Christopher Eisenhart, and to the dean of the College of Arts and Sciences, Jeannette Riley, along with Anupama Arora, Shari Evans, Laurel Hankins, and Mary Wilson. My thanks are due also to Anthony Arrigo, Jerry Blitefield, Elisabeth Buck, Katie DeLuca, Sue Demers, Karen Gulbrandsen, Tracy Harrison, Stanley Harrison, Joan Kellerman, Elizabeth Lehr, Ellen Mandly, Lucas Mann, Bill Nelles, Morgan Peters, Matthew Roy, Judy Schaaf, Thomas Stubblefield, Alexis Teagarden, Tim Walker, and Bob Waxler.

I am a better person and this is a better book for the support and encouragement of my friends, who have offered good food, good wine, and good company, along with a wealth of enthusiasm, as I have worked on this project. I especially want to thank Mike and Amy Maslauskas (along with Tyler and Katie), Katie and Chris Hanscom, Lauren McCoy, Andrew Leahy, Greg Bradford, Fr. Joseph Kane, and Susan Ferzoco.

My family has always encouraged me to be curious—and has patiently followed me where my curiosity has led. My parents, Craig and Marylee, have made all things possible for me. They have been this book's greatest champions, supporting my efforts in innumerable ways over the years (including trips to the tombs of saints and the shrines of relics!). Their friendship, selflessness, and boundless love are gifts I cannot fully repay. My sister, Jenn, and my brother, Craig, are two of the most loyal people I know, and their sharp wit keeps me in good humor. Tim and Mary McKinney are to me so much more than "in-laws," and their genuine interest in this book has been a source of comfort and encouragement. I thank Laura and Drew Cardona (along with Ava and Natalie); Tim McKinney; Krista Corso; and my grandparents, aunts, uncles, and cousins.

The book's dedication records my life's greatest blessing: my wife, Courtney, who is the best teacher I know. She has seen many more plays, attended many more conferences, and endured many more drafts of these pages than she probably bargained for. As our lives have moved us up and down the Eastern Seaboard, Courtney has brought into my world more kindness and beauty, more wisdom and laughter, than I ever could have fathomed. But for the substance of her great love, this book would be only a shadow of what it is.

Introduction

Many Reformations

> *As there were many reformers,*
> *so likewise many reformations.*
>
> —Thomas Browne, *Religio Medici* (1643)

This is a book about bodies and signs in theological debates over the Eucharist and dramas staged in their wake. In it I show how several early English dramas, including biblical dramas; early Tudor comedies and histories; and commercial playhouse dramas by Marlowe, Shakespeare, Webster, and Middleton, stage volatile semiotic struggles that stem from controversies over Christ's body—both his physical body and its presence in the sacramental signs of bread and wine. Riddled with paradox and ambiguity, Christ's Eucharistic body produces an excess of meaning as well as a profound loss thereof. It beggars all description and exhausts interpretive labor. This is why theologians find the Eucharist so controversial as a point of doctrine; this is also why dramatists find it so productive as a literary resource.[1]

Shadow and Substance advances current critical conversations about the influence of the Eucharist on literary representation.[2] These conversations, however stimulating, tend to rely on a medieval/early modern historical periodization that creates chasms between the religious and the secular, the word and the flesh, the plays of Shakespeare and those that came before. By contrast, *Shadow and Substance* crosses the periodic borders of medieval and early modern, and charts the intersection of theological controversy, semiotic representation, and early English drama along a trans-Reformational course.³ Across the Reformation divide, I argue, questions about physical embodiment and textual interpretation raised by drama—how words relate to things and signs to bodies, how the literal relates to the figurative and the worldly to the otherworldly—are also drawn together in the sacrament of the Eucharist. In turn, this sacrament not only constitutes a devotional object or doctrinal crux but also forges a working theory of semiotics.⁴ The controversies over the Eucharist, which give rise to vehement and enduring theological debates, also shape ways of thinking about how bodies human and divine are interpreted through dramatic and sacramental signs. By taking a *longue durée* approach to the Eucharist's literary and theological histories, this book does not support a narrative that runs from transubstantiation to trope. Rather, it demonstrates that regardless of one's confessional position—traditional or reformed, orthodox or evangelical—to speak of the sacrament is to speak of the body's unstable relationship to language.⁵

While Christ's real presence creates a semiotic situation that is categorically unique, it also provides a way of thinking about cultural protocols of interpretation outside a religious context. One of those contexts is early English drama.⁶ Even when they do not address religious matters explicitly, the dramas studied in this book stage difficult interpretive acts that call to mind the theological and hermeneutic debates waged over the Eucharist from the late Middle Ages through the seventeenth century. As sacramental theology and semiotic theory, the Eucharist provides an apt way of thinking about dramatic bodies that are broken or fragmented; bodies that vanish or mysteriously come to life; and bodies whose signs are disrupted, resignified, or dissimulated. From *quem quaeritis* to London's public theaters, many English dramas powerfully reimagine the strenuous, often violent acts of embodiment and interpretation that characterize the Eucharist. In play as in sacrament, body and sign sometimes work in concert; more often than not, however, they are rendered out of joint.

In reimagining the semiotic problems created by the Eucharist, the dramas studied in this book demonstrate that categories such as "word" and "flesh" do not divide into neat oppositions between traditional and reformed religion but rather are deeply and often problematically entangled. In the biblical dramas of the Crucifixion and the Resurrection, for example, Christ blazons his wounds and translates his body into readable signs.

In the post-Resurrection dramas of Emmaus, the disciples recognize Christ's divine body only after grappling with these signs; the entire episode, rich in Eucharistic content, is as much semiotic as it is sacramental. Though they were prohibited from staging the sacred outright, later playwrights such as Shakespeare and Marlowe repurpose these representational strategies, often at moments of highest dramatic tension. When Faustus's blood stops his contractual signature, when Leontes discovers Hermione's warm flesh beneath the appearance of cold stone, and when the Duchess of Malfi misreads wax heads as the relics of her dead kin, drama exploits the instability of semiotic reference that characterizes the Eucharist. In commanding attention to such instances of interpretive failure, misreading, and deception, these dramas reprise the Eucharist's call to interpret the body through the sign and the sign through the body—and they do so with no guarantee that the work of interpretation can pluck out the heart of the mystery.

In bringing Eucharistic theology to bear on late medieval and early modern drama, *Shadow and Substance* argues that the shifting semiotics of the Eucharist create gaps in doctrine, confessional identity, and dramatic representation that are extremely difficult to bridge. In England and on the Continent, for defenders of traditional religion as well as any number of reformers, Christ's body and its sacramental signs are ruptured and conjoined, renamed and redefined in debates known as the Eucharistic Controversies, which originated as early as the ninth century and continued well into the seventeenth century.[7] As I demonstrate in chapter 1, these debates unfold within a wide dissemination of texts characterized by biblical exegesis, theological argument, and literary craft. They illustrate how the Eucharist, perhaps more than any other sacrament, typifies Richard Hooker's claim that "sacraments, by reason of their mixt nature, are more diversely interpreted and disputed of than any other part of religion besides."[8]

These diverse interpretations and disputes bear out the point that every theology of the Eucharist—from transubstantiation to memorialism—grounded its understanding of sacramental doctrine and liturgy on various, often contentious, semiotic positions. "The dominant form of Eucharistic ritual, iconography, and theology in the late medieval Church," David Aers argues, "was organized around a particular version of Christ's presence in the sacramental sign."[9] While many different theological positions emerged in the centuries that followed, the crucial connections between sacraments and semiotics only intensified. As Stephen Greenblatt writes, "Most of the significant and sustained thinking in the early modern period about the nature of linguistic signs, and particularly about figuration, centered on or was deeply influenced by Eucharistic controversies."[10] The sacrament of the Eucharist and its attendant controversies were both complex and consequential for the reformation of doctrine, ecclesiastical organization, and liturgical practice. The Eucharistic Controversies also raised critical questions that challenged prevailing understandings of language, embodiment, and representation. How do the sacramental signs of bread and wine make the divine body of Christ manifest? Do bread and wine symbolize Christ's sacrifice, such that *est* in "Hoc est corpus meum" means *significat*, as Zwingli argued? Do the Eucharistic signs cease to be bread and wine at the level of being so that they can be transformed, fully and completely, into the substance of Christ's body and blood, as Thomas Aquinas asserts? Or do the signs communicate participation in Christ's mystical body—what Hooker calls "a transubstantiation in us"—by which the recipient becomes what he receives?[11] *Transubstantiation* and *trope*, *figure* and *flesh*, *representation* and *reality*: these terms define both theological controversy and dramatic practice in the long history of England's religious reformations. They also unleash a range of fraught interpretive possibilities that are neither simple nor harmonious.

While it is improbable that dramatists and audiences studied the formal theological debates over the Eucharist intensely, it is hard to imagine that they would have been unaware of the sacramental controversies or their import.[12] Hardly mere intellectual exercises, the Eucharistic Controversies stirred up conflict over theology, politics, and identity. They also created hermeneutic crises of the highest consequence. For Catholics as well as reformers, there was much at stake in one's interpretation of a piece of bread and cup of wine. As James Simpson reminds us, "Questions of semiotics," when analyzed in the context of the Eucharist, "are no academic matter.... Both interrogators and victims, all with full consciousness that the answers mean life or death, sort out what is real from what is figurative; one side is prepared to kill and the other to die for the 'right' answers."[13] Anne Askew, for example, was interrogated, tortured, and killed for her refusal to affirm the doctrine of transubstantiation, still upheld as the orthodox position under Henry VIII. The reformers William Tyndale and Thomas Cranmer met a similar fate, as did the Catholics Edmund Campion and Robert Southwell, who died for their faith at Tyburn. Religious violence could even resurface posthumously, as when the Council of Constance (1415) ordered that the remains of John Wyclif be exhumed and scattered away from consecrated ground. Such acts of violence waged in the name of religious politics would have been hard to forget, and they suggest that even as the Eucharistic sacrament organized the ecclesial community of the church—the mystical body of Christ—the controversies over it often led to discord and death.

At a specifically literary level, even if Shakespeare did not see biblical dramas that may have passed through the surrounding towns of Stratford-upon-Avon, he joins other playwrights in echoing the verbal and iconographical representations of Christ's body that define both incarnational drama and Eucharistic controversy.[14] As Thomas Bishop writes, "All through Shakespeare's career, questions of embodiment framed in relation to the sacramental model are central to his thinking through of the meaning of theatrical performance."[15] Anthony Dawson argues a similar point, namely that "theatrical representation was understood and deployed in terms that derive from Eucharistic controversy," not least because the material conditions of staged performance and audience response experimented with simulated presence as a condition of the interplay between body and word.[16]

Shakespeare's first tragedy, *Titus Andronicus* (1594), which is set in a pagan Rome that knew nothing of Christian sacramental ceremony, creates a particularly arresting engagement between Eucharistic theology and dramatic representation at the level of the interpretive act itself. Shakespeare figures Lavinia's bloody and dismembered body as a set of "martyr'd signs," a phrase that evokes the Eucharist's dual emphasis on the materiality of texts and the semiotics of bodies.[17] Lavinia's "martyr'd signs" also recall the wounded body of Christ as represented in biblical drama, particularly plays of the Passion and Resurrection. In the York *Crucifixion*, for example, the soldiers fix Christ to the cross "so all his bones / Are asoundre nowe on sides seere," and after the Resurrection, Christ commands Thomas to "Behalde and se myn handis and feete, / And grathely gropes my woundes wette . . . And se that I have flessh and bone."[18] Like Christ, Lavinia is represented as a collection of wet wounds, gaping flesh, and broken bones; like his body, hers evokes shock and pity in those who gaze on it. Moreover, Lavinia's status as "martyred sign" echoes Christ's self-representation as a martyr in the Towneley *Crucifixion*: "To whome now may I make my mone / When thay thus martyr me, / And sakles wille me slone / And bete me bloode and bone?"[19] Unlike the lamenting Christ, however, Lavinia cannot speak. Her body can be considered "Eucharistic" not only because of its Christological analogue but also because, like the consecrated host, it confounds relations between body and sign.[20]

Titus Andronicus, like the dramas studied in this book, does not simply testify to the imbrication of body and sign that defines Eucharistic theology; rather, the play imagines anew the semiotic problems and debates that such an imbrication precipitates. If Christ's physical and symbolic bodies defy interpretation for everyone from Doubting Thomas to late medieval and Reformation era theologians, Lavinia's mutilated body puzzles the characters and audiences who behold it. Her body, like Christ's, stands at the center of a strenuous, nearly impossible public act of interpretation. Shakespeare stages these interpretive difficulties when, after Lavinia's rape, Titus struggles to make sense of her dismembered body—her "martyr'd signs"—which the Goths have rendered unreadable through acts of physical violence. As he labors to put her wounds into words, Titus positions Lavinia at the nexus of the semiotic and the somatic. First he calls her a "map of woe that thus dost talk in signs" (3.2.12); then he figures her body as a text, claiming, "I can interpret all her martyr'd signs" (3.2.36); and he concludes by rendering this body a readable surface from which he will forcibly "wrest an alphabet / And by still practice learn to know thy meaning" (3.2.44–45). Titus's words fail him, however. Lavinia frustrates her father's "still practice" as her wounds obscure rather than clarify the body's meaning, thereby illustrating what Coppélia Kahn calls "the problematics of Lavinia as signifier."[21] Titus is so thwarted by Lavinia's corporeal signs that in the process of groping for meaning he loses the capacity to differentiate signifier from signified to the point that he verges on madness. As Marcus describes it, "Grief has so wrought on him, / He takes false shadows for true substances" (3.2.80–81). Titus is baffled not so much by the horror of Lavinia's dismemberment as by her inaccessibility to language. Stopped by the shadow of Lavinia's inscrutable body, Titus cannot ascertain the substance of his daughter who, as "Rome's rich ornament" (1.1.55), also represents the body politic.

Marcus's antithetical pairing of "shadow" and "substance" in Titus Andronicus, which inspires the title of this book, is familiar to English drama and appears no fewer than eighteen times in Shakespeare's corpus alone.[22] Shakespeare uses the antithesis to differentiate real from representational, appearance from truth. For example, Sonnet 53 begins, "What is your substance, whereof are you made / That millions of strange shadows on you tend?"[23] Richard III, waking from a dream in which all his victims curse him, remarks, "Shadows tonight / Have struck more terror to the soul of Richard / Than can the substance of ten thousand soldiers / Armed in proof."[24] When Bassanio opens the lead casket in *The Merchant of Venice*, moreover, he says to Portia, "Yet, look how far / The substance of my praise doth wrong this shadow / In underprizing it, so far this shadow / Doth limp behind the substance."[25] And in *Richard II*, Bushy consoles the Queen upon Richard's departure for battle by saying, "Each substance of a grief hath twenty shadows / Which shows like grief itself, but is not so."[26]

The antithetical pairing of "shadow" and "substance" also strikes to the heart of theological controversy, where *substantiam* functions as what Judith Anderson calls "a code word in Eucharistic debate."[27] Both Catholics and reformers employ the terms *shadow* and *substance* to negotiate the meaning of Christ's body and its sacramental signs. Thomas More, for example, is charged with taking "every shadowe and symylytude representynge the bodye" as though it "were a bodyly substaunce."[28] Stephen Gardiner, bishop of Winchester, refers to Christ as the fulfillment of Old Testament promises—"the body of al the shadowes & figures of the law"—and says that Christ's words at the Last Supper are to be understood "without figure in the substaunce of the celestiall thyng of them."[29] In the seventeenth century, the bishop of Norwich, Edward Reynolds, defines sacraments as "nothing else but Evangelicall Types or shadows of some more perfect substance," and the Protestant cleric Edmund Gurnay dismisses Papists as those who "cannot perceive a difference betwixt His remembrance, and His very reall presence; betwixt the signe and the thing, the shell and the kernel, the shadow and the substance."[30]

Situated at the crossroads of shadow and substance, Christ's Eucharistic body is shattered in its signage and rich in its materialism. As such, Christ's body demands that Catholics and reformers alike wrest an alphabet from its martyred signs. The words spoken by Christ at the Last Supper—translated in the Latin liturgy as "Hoc est corpus meum" (This is my body)—confounded interpretive efforts for centuries after their original utterance and have "attracted a more fearsomely complex commentary than perhaps any words in history."[31] At one level, Christ replaces the Old Testament Passover with a new covenant in his passion. At another, he forever changes the relation of word to body, text to flesh, and becomes what Rowan Williams provocatively terms "a sign-maker of a disturbingly revolutionary kind."[32] In this regard, the Last Supper constitutes not only a soteriological event tied to Christ's sacrifice but also a watershed semiotic intervention that challenges ideas about language and signification, being and essence, space and time.

What makes the Eucharist a *mysterium tremendum*—a "terrible mystery" or "mystery that repels"—is its paradoxical claim to materialize Christ's divine body in the most ordinary of earthly elements: bread and wine. "What is a great mystery," Stephen Greenblatt says, "is a great banality, a prime piece of the everyday."[33] By materializing Christ's sacramental body in visible and tangible forms of matter, the Eucharist introduces new questions about what signs and bodies are, what they do, and how they signify. As a body that does not resemble a "body" and a sign that claims to be more than a "sign," the Eucharist illustrates how the delicate fibers of signification unravel or come undone. The "coincidence of sign and body" that Catherine Pickstock says "is most manifest in the event of the Eucharist" is rarely neat.[34] Rather, as Sarah Beckwith argues, "It is in the Eucharist that the tension between the visible and the invisible, between palpable presence and ineffable mystery is at its most difficult."[35] Whereas the many different forms of Eucharistic doctrine attempt to delimit the relation between signifier and signified according to a determinate grammar of meaning, the Eucharist continually tests the limits of body and sign. What many theological writers cast in terms of semiotic closure almost always creates semiotic fissures.

By looking to the Eucharist as a way to consider the semiotics of bodies and the materiality of signs in early English drama, *Shadow and Substance* brings together critical interests in Reformation history, the history of the body, and periodization studies. While the Eucharist shaped a central (if not *the* central) discourse for thinking about language and representation in many late medieval and early modern contexts, its literary applications have been most pronounced in several recent studies of sixteenth- and seventeenth-century religious poetry. These studies argue that John Donne, Richard Crashaw, and George Herbert (among others) facilitate a form of sacramental encounter, devotion, or presence through the lyric's formal properties and religious content.[36] Additionally, the Eucharist has been a perennial topic in studies of drama, which tend to analogize the material conditions of theatrical performance—the embodiment of a dramatic character by an actor, the participation of an audience, and the role of costume and disguise—to sacramental idioms, namely the Catholic theology of transubstantiation and reformed theologies of Eucharistic participation.[37] In these and other studies, the Eucharist serves as a convenient signpost of the political, religious, and social changes brought about by the Protestant Reformation.[38] Within such readings, which have shaped a robust "turn to religion" in early modern studies, Christ's body has been evacuated and disenchanted, recovered and resurrected.[39]

Shadow and Substance takes a different argumentative line. When dramas take up religious materials (including source texts and props, liturgical acts and ritual practices, biblical citations and theological concepts), they do not simply "memorize another Golgotha" (*Macbeth*, 1.2.40) or suggest that "miracles are past" (*All's Well That Ends Well*, 2.3.1). Rather, the dramas studied here—from biblical dramas, many of which capture a long narrative of salvation history in local space and time, to the commercial playhouse dramas staged after the institution of a vernacular liturgy—all engage with aspects of the sacrament that we today would designate as literary, textual, or theoretical. What emerges in this book is a way to think about drama and theology such that, as Theresa Coletti says in the context of dramatic representations of Mary Magdalene, "sacramentality involves not a prescriptive set of dogmas that drama is either for or against, but the understanding and reading of signs."[40] In looking to Eucharistic discourse as a way to think about dramatic representation in general, as well as the interplay of body and sign in particular, this book also responds to David Scott Kastan's charge to consider "what the religious language, values, practices, spaces, and personnel are doing in the plays [and] what the plays do to and with them."[41] Drama reinvigorates the spirit of Eucharistic controversy and continues to pose its key semiotic questions by reimagining the interpretive problems created by a sacrament that is at once textual and material.

In working across the domains of physical embodiment and textual representation, this book also makes an intervention in the well-established field of early modern embodiment studies, which have landed solidly in the secular terrains of anatomy, physiology, historical phenomenology, and ecocriticism.[42] This work has remapped the field according to pre-Cartesian understandings of the body differentiated from post-Enlightenment theories of emotion, cognition, gender and sexuality, race, trauma, and disability. Yet this renewed interest in the body's physical materiality tends to underemphasize two key discourses deeply related to the study of early modern embodiment: religion and hermeneutics. *Shadow and Substance* addresses this gap, looking to Eucharistic discourse as a way to think about "embodiment" not only as a state of lived physical experience but also as a process of textual interpretation. The body of Christ, which is arguably the most contested body and sign in Western history, constitutes a rich aesthetic resource for exploring this interplay of flesh and language in religious and dramatic contexts—an interplay that can be synchronous, contrapuntal, or wildly dissonant.

The history of the Eucharist, its semiotics, and its dramatic representations spans many centuries and confessional stances, many reformers and many reformations. While the sacrament of the altar provided a locus for thinking about theological difference, it was also retained as one of two official sacraments by the Church of England and many of the reformed confessions. Thus the Eucharist itself calls into question periodic categories of "medieval" and "early modern" as well as confessional designations like "traditional" and "reformed" that have long governed assumptions about literary and religious history.[43] *Shadow and Substance* puts pressure on these temporal and confessional periodizations. To see late medieval theology and drama as a residue, leftover, or nostalgic remainder is to insist on a teleological progression from an antiquated and retrograde past to a more progressive reformist present.[44] The Protestant Reformation does not inaugurate a secular age so much as it opens issues of sacramental efficacy, liturgical and dramatic performance, and textual interpretation to new scrutiny. By the same token, the Eucharistic Controversies shape a religious reformation that does not remove God from the world but instead places the body of Christ at the center of cultural debate.

Given the Eucharist's own trans-Reformational history, then, it does not make sense to organize this book according to a trajectory that runs *from* the medieval *to* the early modern. Doing so would risk tidying the very periodic ruptures and categorical back-formations I intend to unsettle.[45] Instead, each chapter brings together earlier and later forms of Eucharistic theology and English drama so as to illustrate that what has been routinely labeled "medieval," "early Tudor," or "early modern" defies the sweeping literary, cultural, and religious histories suggested by such periodic markers. After an initial chapter that focuses on the semiotics of Eucharistic theology from multiple historical, religious, and literary perspectives, I proceed to five chapters centered on drama's engagement with these semiotics, each organized around a key Eucharistic topos: Christ's wounds; the king's sacred body; liturgical books and language; relics and devotional objects; and sacramental presence.

In chapter 1, "Eucharistic Semiotics: The Body of Christ and the Play of Signs," I work through four semiotic concepts that define Eucharistic controversy: (1) body and sign; (2) flesh and spirit; (3) literalism and figuralism; and (4) words and deeds. These concepts, which are vital to dramatic representation, also unfold in the writings of Augustine and the patristic fathers; scholastics such as Peter the Lombard and Thomas Aquinas; dissenters from orthodoxy, especially John Wyclif; and the long cast of figures who shaped the religious reformations of the sixteenth century, from Thomas More, John Jewel, and Richard Hooker to Martin Luther, Ulrich Zwingli, and Jean Calvin. These writings have often been cited independently as part of a grand narrative about the development of Eucharistic thought from its origins in early Christianity through to the Reformation. Since the thrust of such controversy is best understood in terms of ongoing dialogue, however, I read these texts as part of the polemical exchanges and textual debates in which they emerged. By emphasizing the robust dialogue through which Eucharistic controversy unfolded (a good deal of which was disseminated in printed books and pamphlets), I show how Eucharistic writing constitutes a key discursive domain for thinking about questions of interpretation and embodiment in both religious and nonreligious drama written and performed across the Reformation divide.

In its dramatic representations from crucifix to Eucharist, the body of Christ demands visual devotion and interpretive labor. These complementary acts are the subject of chapter 2, "Words and Wounds: Christ Crucified and *Coriolanus*." In biblical dramas of Christ's passion, Christ is represented not simply as a passive recipient of physical torture and pain but also as an active interpreter who blazons his wounded body and puts those wounds into words. These plays make reading, speaking, and gazing on Christ's body central to an ecclesiological vision of social community forged by linguistic bonds. In Shakespeare's play, the wounded body performs the opposite function, as Coriolanus shuts down the Romans' enthusiasm to view and read his battle wounds during the ceremony of election. Resistant to civic ceremony and linguistic community, Coriolanus removes his body from semiotic systems and civic performances. His iconoclasm is ultimately punished when Aufidius and the conspirators tear him to pieces and render him a wounded, fragmented body.

Since the early church, Christ's Eucharistic body was thought about in relation to both his Galilean body and the mystical body of the church, otherwise known as the *corpus mysticum*. Chapter 3, "Sacramental Signs and Mystical Bodies in Lydgate, Bale, and Shakespeare," discusses sacred kingship in the context of both liturgical and civic representations of the *corpus mysticum*. In *Henry VI's Triumphal Entry into London* and in *A Procession of Corpus Christi*, the fifteenth-century poet John Lydgate connects royal and sacramental bodies in terms of social communities, both the civic body of London and the ecclesial community of the church, in ways that open out a complex semiotics of the Eucharist. In a different register, Bale and Shakespeare figure the *corpus mysticum* in terms of regicide; in scenes that parody Eucharistic liturgy, the body politic is both vulnerable and incoherent. Bale's polemical aim is to purify the church of Catholic ritual and forge an alternative semiotics of kingship based on scriptural truth. King Johan's murder, executed by a Catholic monk who serves the king a poisoned chalice, highlights the dangers of a sensuous liturgy founded on a carnal understanding of the Eucharist. But it also leads to the ascension of Imperial Majesty, who restores the body politic by enacting the aggressive liturgical reforms that his predecessor could not achieve. Shakespeare takes a more moderate stance in representing the *corpus mysticum* in *Macbeth*. Duncan's murder ruptures the seemingly inviolable body politic in terms that disjoin the king's mystical body from Christ's Eucharistic body. Whereas *King Johan* attempts to divest the *corpus mysticum* of its Eucharistic symbolism (a symbolism also evident in Lydgate's verses), *Macbeth* figures the rejection of sacramental kingship as a catalyst for Scotland's political chaos. If Duncan's sacred body was assaulted in ways that parody Eucharistic ritual and the sacramental foundations of *corpus mysticum*, the political unrest brought on by regicide generates semiotic confusions of real and representational presence that signal Macbeth's linguistic and political dissolution.

In chapter 4, "Father Faustus? Confection and Conjuration in *Everyman* and *Doctor Faustus*," I show how the priest's capacity to make (or confect) Christ through the words pronounced over the host informs Faustus's fascination with clerical agency and liturgical ritual. I begin with *Everyman*, which in its exposition of eschatological matters such as reckoning and final judgment affirms episcopal power as the conduit for spiritual health.

Much of Everyman's spiritual education—not to mention his hope for salvation—rests on his understanding the priest's authority to administer the sacraments. Faustus, by contrast, vies for a priestly power over language that a lay doctor of theology can think about but not possess. I focus first on Faustus's attraction to the necromantic books, the textual features of which are similar to those of the missal, or liturgical book used by the priest during Mass. I then turn to Faustus's attempted conjurations, which trope on sacramental lexicons and performances; to his signing the deed of gift; and to the eleventh-hour vision of Christ's blood in the firmament. Drawing on Eucharistic theology and speech-act theory, I show how these scenes demonstrate the appeal of sacramental performativity to Marlowe's drama of supernatural knowledge.

Chapter 5, "Relics and Unreliable Bodies in the Croxton *Play of the Sacrament*, *The Duchess of Malfi*, and *The Changeling*," extends the semiotics of the Eucharist to the domain of devotional objects, specifically relics. Relics posit problematic connections between part and whole, real presence and simulated presence. In the *Play of the Sacrament*, the contested sign in question is the consecrated host, which is resignified as false relic, exotic commodity, and common "cake" before it is ritually tortured and revealed as the body of Christ. The play dramatizes several acts of misreading born out of the semiotic deceit that reformers located in the Eucharist and the cult of relics. This deceit is also the hallmark of Jacobean tragedies, which use wax heads, discarded gloves, and severed fingers to willfully (and fatally) skew the relation between body part and bodily whole. By appropriating the semiotics of holy matter for unholy purposes, *The Duchess of Malfi* and *The Changeling* show that true and false relics are not all that different from one another, for both offer versions of real presence predicated on tricks of representation.

If the consecrated host posits a body present in substance but inaccessible to the senses, the final chapter, "Conjured to Remembrance: Emmaus Plays, *Jack Juggler*, and *The Winter's Tale*," considers the converse idea: How does one come to know a body that is present in the flesh but obscured by the sign? In the dramas of Christ's post-Resurrection appearance at Emmaus, Christ disguises himself as a stranger, reveals himself in a sacramental breaking of bread, and then vanishes. The disciples can make sense of this absence only by interpreting the body's relation to the sacramental sign. The early Tudor comedy *Jack Juggler* (attributed to Nicholas Udall) stages a similar process of semiotic rupture but refuses a final act of repair; it ends in social disharmony rather than social community. By wearing Careaway's clothes and taking his name, Jack the Juggler dislocates Careaway's body from its outward signs and thereby creates a semiotic crisis that leads to psychosomatic dissolution. Only in *The Winter's Tale* are such semiotic and somatic rifts fully transformed through participatory acts of interpretation that foster remembrance and reconciliation. Leontes comes to see the wrinkles, veins, flesh, and blood in Hermione's "statue" as vital signs of her virtue; in so doing he bridges the gap between body and sign caused by his prior misnaming of Hermione as an adulteress. Unlike Careaway, Leontes physically reunites with the body he seeks; unlike the disciples at Emmaus, moreover, he finds—and keeps—the living flesh among the seeming dead.

These chapter outlines should make clear that while *Shadow and Substance* pursues many connections across disciplines and historical periods, remapping English drama's engagement with the Eucharist from a trans-Reformational perspective initiates a conversation about different kinds of drama written for different kinds of theatrical institutions. After all, the early modern commercial playhouse emerged in England well after the suppression of the feast of Corpus Christi in 1548 and religious drama in the 1570s.[46] In addition, official injunctions prohibited playwrights from representing biblical content or calling God by name on the stage.[47] These important differences in dramatic performance and religious history will play out in more detail over the course of this book. It is important to recognize, moreover, that the differences in these dramas do not parse out neat confessional divisions or shifts in religious thought. The dramas of Shakespeare and his contemporaries do not empty out religious ritual or replace a longing for divine enchantment with the artistic power of theater. Nor do they endorse a particular theological sensibility or belief system. Instead, they draw with great verve on the Eucharist's semiotic energies in negotiating the possibilities and limits of verbal and nonverbal representation. And they do so within the decidedly secular domain of the commercial playhouse.[48]

What is more, just as the rise of a secular theater does not spell the end for dramatic engagements with sacramental discourse (and sacramental semiotics), so the reformation of liturgical practice does not quell the controversy over the Eucharist. While the Mass was officially replaced in England first by a vernacular Order of Holy Communion (1548) and a year later by the official liturgy of the first *Book of Common Prayer*, the semiotics of the sacrament were far from stable, as evidenced by significant revisions to the 1549 liturgy in 1552 and 1559.[49] In the following century, the same prayer book initially hailed as a departure from the Roman Church was criticized by Puritans who felt that its liturgy (especially under the administration of Archbishop William Laud) was too Papist.[50] The Eucharist also remained a prominent subject of biblical commentary well into the seventeenth century, and the contested interpretations of the sacrament unfolded within the glosses, annotations, and textual apparatus of English Bibles themselves. This conjunction of sacramental controversy and scriptural hermeneutics is exemplified by William Fulke's confutations to the Rheims New Testament, published in four editions from 1589 to 1633.[51] Fulke's parallel-text edition featured the Rheims translation of the Vulgate in one column and the Bishop's Bible translation in the other, along with copious annotations in which Fulke refutes Catholic interpretations. Finally, as late as 1673, the Test Act demanded that English subjects not only profess the confessional creeds of the Church of England but also explicitly reject the doctrine of transubstantiation. While specific doctrinal arguments about the Eucharist changed, the sacrament's semiotic richness never diminished.

In its final assessment, then, *Shadow and Substance* endeavors to correct widespread misrepresentations of the Protestant Reformation as a decisive shift from the flesh to the word, the theological to the poetic, and the sacred to the secular.[52] It sees religious reformation not as a fixed epistemological shift but rather as a constellation of diverse theological and semiotic positions asserted and interpreted over time. The creation of a vernacular liturgy, the rise of iconoclasm, and the insistence on *sola scriptura* should not be seen as a univocal clarion call for a disenchanted modernity fully divested of the long history of textual controversy sparked by the Eucharist. Moreover, traditional religion should not be seen as the standard bearer of the body any more than reformed religion should be aligned exclusively with the text.[53]

Certainly the Protestant Reformation did not invent representation, nor did it put an end to bodily habitation by replacing transubstantiation with tropes. Seeing textual representation as a singularly reformist innovation ignores the ways in which body and sign converge in Eucharistic theology, liturgy, and ecclesiology across England's long Reformation. Such an approach also irons out the sacramental and semiotic differences within

Catholic and reformed Eucharistic theologies themselves. Instead, the Eucharistic debates gain theological, political, and literary urgency precisely because they provoke an ongoing conversation about what Christ's Eucharistic presence is and how it can be made manifest in sacramental signs. Thus to assimilate the whole of traditional or reformed religion to any uniform semiotic or theological position is to misconstrue the argumentative tenor of the debates, for as Andrew Cole reminds us, "Sacramental theology is a matter of emphasis."[54] A Tyndalean view of the sacrament is not exactly commensurate with a Hookerian view, just as Thomas More's writings on the Eucharist adopt different stances from those of earlier thinkers such as Aquinas and later defenders of Catholic orthodoxy such as Thomas Harding and Stephen Gardiner. And even the *Book of Common Prayer*, though it authors a new liturgy in a new language, does not settle the sacrament's interpretive problems but renders the tensions between body and sign all the more fraught.

An example of this tension, and a fitting point on which to conclude this introduction, comes from Thomas Cranmer, who in his description of spiritual eating writes, "The bread and wine be called examples of Christes fleshe & blud, and also thei be called his very flesh and blud, to signify unto us that as thei feede us carnally, so do thei admonish us that Christ with his flesh & blud doth feed us spiritually and most truly unto everlasting life."[55] Bread and wine, spirit and flesh, and heaven and earth are all dynamically related here. Rhetorically, the spiritual sacrament as Cranmer describes it cannot be understood except as analogized to flesh: as bread and wine feed the body carnally, so does Christ feed the faithful recipient spiritually. Theologically, this is no poetic sacrament; spiritual eating is not merely figurative eating, for Cranmer sees it as a real encounter with Christ, albeit one that does not accede to the terms of transubstantiation. Cranmer does not oppose word to flesh; that would be too simple. Rather, he casts these categories into more complex and mutual contact.

In the pages that follow, *Shadow and Substance* offers a new way of thinking about drama, language, and embodiment in the context of the Eucharist. These relationships are inherently contentious. Because of the imaginative worlds it creates, drama can straddle the boundaries of representational play and sacramental ritual. But speaking in Eucharistic terms or reimagining liturgical ceremonies does not amount to performing a sacrament. By the same token, when a dramatist parodies the sacraments he does not necessarily desacralize them, strip them of meaning, or push them to the cultural margins. Even though dramas are performed within particular social institutions, they do not themselves reproduce religious ideologies, intervene in theological controversies, or endorse confessional creeds. The dramaturgy is too delicate and its semiotics too multivalent for such neat arguments to hold. Moreover, given ubiquitous arguments concerning Shakespeare's Catholicism or Marlowe's atheism, dramatic engagements with Eucharistic discourses do not disclose the religious beliefs of these playwrights. Nor do they indicate on the part of this critic a suggestion that the sum of English drama or premodern semiotics is singularly derived from the Eucharist. But these dramas do suggest that the Eucharist matters to medieval and early modern literary practice. Whatever one's opinion—then or now—of the Mass, the host, or the real presence, the controversies over the sacrament raise pressing questions about textual representation and physical embodiment that outreach a purely theological context. Christ's Eucharistic body becomes a construct by which to consider the dynamics of body and sign, shadow and substance, the idea of a thing and the thing itself, in English drama and the religious reformations that defined the stages of its emergence.

ONE

Eucharistic Semiotics

The Body of Christ and the Play of Signs

The anxiety, the desire to see, touch, and eat the body of God,
to be that body and be nothing but that,
forms the principle of Western (un)reason.
That's why the body, bodily, never happens,
least of all when it's named and convoked.
For us, the body is always sacrificed: eucharist.

—Jean-Luc Nancy, *Corpus*

What bread does one eat?
What wine does one drink?

—Wallace Stevens, "The American Sublime"

The hallmark events in the life of Christ—from the Incarnation through the Eucharistic institution to the Passion and Resurrection—are the foundation of Christian creeds and doctrines. They shape ecclesiastical communities as well as constitute the origin and terminus of liturgical worship. These same events also witness an incisive rupture in how signs, bodies, and their meanings are interpreted. When the Son of God takes human flesh, breaks bread and shares wine as his body and blood, and overcomes a bloody crucifixion by rising from the dead, he transforms the signs of the

Old Law into new wonders. Such transformations, however astonishing in their uniqueness, generate confusion and controversy over the meaning of Christ's body and its sacramental signs.

The Eucharist produces many interpretive possibilities, all of them difficult. This chapter threads together from a range of theological writings a narrative about the semiotics of the Eucharist and its influence on the religious culture, intellectual history, and dramatic production of late medieval and early modern England. While Eucharistic controversy dwells on the intricacies of metaphysics (form and essence, substance and accident, being and time), it also precipitates arguments about semiotic interpretation—particularly how the sacramental signs relate to the body of Christ and how their meanings were understood, revised, and contested at a time when one's interpretation of the word and the flesh was a matter of life or death.[1] For clergymen and churchgoers as well as dramatists and audiences, the sacrament of the altar seizes on the space between sign and referent; it casts into conflict the unstable meanings of a divine body one cannot see and the material signs by which it is made known. The great twentieth-century theologian Henri de Lubac captures this semiotic difficulty in his description of the Eucharist as "that indeterminate place . . . between shadow and truth, nearer the shadow because of the form of knowledge with which we are left—*through a mirror and in enigmas*—but how much nearer the truth because of its profound substance."[2]

The Eucharistic Controversies show us that the sacrament of the altar means many different things to many different people. One person's sign is another's body; one's shadow is another's substance. In the *Apologie of the Church of England* (1562), John Jewel surveys these differences with remarkable economy and bracing clarity:

> There be some among them that say the body of Christ is present in the supper naturallye: again there be some even of their owne company also that deny it: that there be some that saye the body of Christ in the holy Communion is torne and ripped with the teeth: againe there be some that deny it: that there be some that write that the body of Christ in the sacrament hath quantitie and bygnesse, on the other syde ther be some that denye it: that there be some that saye, Christ did Consecrate by a certaine power of divinitie, some that by blessing, some by five specially prescribed wordes: some by repetting of the self same five wordes, some also

that in those five wordes, by the pronoune demonstrative, Hoc, that is to say, This, thinke that the bread of wheate is pointed to.... there be also some that say, that the accidentes of bread and wine may nourishe, some that say the substance retourneth againe. What nedeth any more? It were too long and over tedious to rehearse all, so uncertayne and so full of controversye is the whole platt of these mens religion and doctrine.[3]

Jewel recognizes that any attempt to impose a fixed meaning onto the Eucharist is almost impossible. What is even more striking is that Jewel does not simply differentiate Catholic and reformed Eucharistic theologies but rather surveys the diverse theological and semiotic possibilities debated among Catholics themselves. For example, Jewel refers to the doctrine of transubstantiation, which holds that Christ is made "present in the Supper naturalye," meaning that after the consecration the bread and wine become Christ's Galilean body and blood at the level of substance.[4] Moreover, such an ontological change is said to occur when the priest speaks "five specially prescribed wordes"—"Hoc est enim corpus meum"—and through God's power confects Christ's body and blood in the consecrated host and wine. Some accede to these terms, Jewel says, while others deny them. Jewel also raises the distinction between spiritual and carnal eating. Is Christ's body "torne and ripped with the teeth," or is it received as food for the soul? Furthermore, he speaks to linguistic issues, asking whether Christ speaks literally or figuratively when he employs the "pronoune demonstrative" (*this*, or *hoc*) at the Last Supper. Does Christ use ordinary words, or does he institute a new kind of language to establish a new sacramental covenant?

The Eucharistic Controversies address such philosophical, theological, and linguistic questions from a wide range of perspectives. Though it is not my intention to rehearse a comprehensive history, I want to offer at least a brief survey, if only to illustrate how any study of the Eucharist demands a trans-Reformational approach.[5] The remainder of this chapter will offer several close readings of the various texts that shape such debates. Historically, these arguments unfolded dialogically in texts that advanced different Eucharistic positions. All too often, however, the textual intricacies of such discussions are reduced to a series of exempla that round out a conventional narrative from early Christian writers to the rise of Scholasticism and then on to the English and Continental reformers of the sixteenth century. Taking a different approach, I will draw out of Eucharistic discourses—scriptural writing and exegesis, sermons, polemics, and conciliar decrees—a working vocabulary for thinking about language, interpretation, and the body in drama. Considering these claims as part of ongoing controversies rather than as isolated examples of fixed theological positions enables us to appreciate how, despite significant differences in doctrine and practice, those who write about the Eucharist shape an ongoing semiotic debate about bodies and signs that conditions the landscape in which drama is written and performed in late medieval and early modern England.

The Eucharistic Controversies: A Brief Survey

Though disagreements over the Eucharist emerged in early Christianity, the first formal controversy is said to originate in the ninth century at the Abbey of Corbie in France, where Paschasius Radbertus (a defender of Catholic orthodoxy) and Ratramnus (one of the first to question those orthodox positions) disagreed over the nature of Christ's presence in the sacrament. The two monks offered divergent interpretations of Augustine, Ambrose, Origen, John Chrysostom, and other patristic authorities.[6] Similar controversies continued in the eleventh century, when Berengar of Tours said that the body of Christ received in the sacrament was not the same body born of the Virgin Mary and crucified on Calvary. He was forced to retract his position and confess before Popes Nicholas II and Gregory VII that what was received in the sacrament was indeed the Galilean body of Christ.[7]

The rise of Scholasticism in the twelfth century introduced a new articulation of orthodox Eucharistic theology based on particular applications of Aristotelian metaphysics, especially in the writings of Thomas Aquinas. Aquinas's doctrine of transubstantiation held that the sacramental signs of bread and wine become Christ's body and blood at the level of substance. This position would come to define the orthodox doctrine of the Roman Church and, as the centuries wore on, would be sharply contrasted especially with the sacramentarian positions advanced by sixteenth-century Continental reformers including Andreas Karlstadt, Johannes Oecolampadius, and Ulrich Zwingli. These theologies of memorial symbolism suggest, at their most basic level, that the sacrament of the altar was a figure and memorial rather than a repetition of Christ's original sacrifice. For Zwingli especially, the bread and wine represented Christ's covenant but did not re-create his sacrifice or manifest his real presence in either ontological or mystical terms. Zwingli thus marked out considerable distance between the sacramental bread and wine and Christ's Galilean body and blood. Zwingli, as Kimberly Johnson notes, "postulates the sign as crucial because it is the material object of encounter, because it must be confronted as the apprehensible term of a hermeneutic act distinct from but assistive to its content."[8] In the Marburg Colloquy of 1529, Martin Luther famously debated Zwingli on these points, holding fast to the version of real presence that he termed "consubstantiation," as set against Zwingli's arguments for sacramental commemoration and remembrance.[9]

Between the extremes of metaphysical conversion and memorial symbolism lie a number of spiritualist theologies in which the Eucharist was regarded as both a holy sign and a manifestation of Christ's real presence. In the fourteenth century, John Wyclif dissented from orthodoxy in arguing for a theology of real presence that was not contingent on an ontological change of substance.[10] In centuries following, the English reformers Thomas Cranmer and John Jewel also developed theologies of spiritual eating in which Christ's real presence could be understood apart from the Scholastic emphasis on metaphysics. They sparred over transubstantiation with the likes of Stephen Gardiner, the orthodox bishop of Winchester; Richard Smith, who was stripped of his title as Regius professor at Oxford under Edward VI and was restored to it under Mary I; and Thomas Harding, a convert to Catholicism under Mary I who along with the Catholic clergyman Dr. Henry Cole debated Bishop Jewel in the 1560s.[11]

As this chorus of theological voices suggests, it is difficult to conceive a theology of the Eucharist independent of a semiotics of the Eucharist. One does not have to read far in theological discourse to see how sacraments are described in terms of sealing and signing, representing and witnessing, promising and confessing. Peter the Lombard devotes the entire fourth book of his *Sententiae* (ca. 1150) to a "doctrine of signs," which, following Augustine, rests on the principle that "a sacrament is a sacred thing which designates the sacred thing which is designated."[12] Thomas Aquinas describes sacraments as both secrets and signs and, following Augustine, states that man is to "be led by things corporal and sensible to things spiritual and intelligible."[13] This connection between sacraments and signs continued to mark sixteenth-century writings, as demonstrated by Bishop Jewel's reference to sacraments as "figures, signes, markes, or badges, printes, copies, formes, seales, signettes, similitudes, patterns, representations, remembraunces and memories . . . certaine visible words, seales of righteousness, tokens of grace."[14] Thomas Cranmer likewise emphasizes the affinity between the sacramental and the semiotic: "Although the scripture be full of Schemes, tropes, and figures, yet specially it useth them when it speaketh of sacramentes."[15]

If sacramental theology iterates a theory of signs, the converse is also true: sign theory is, at least during the years covered in this book, related to sacramental theology. At a moment in history that did not yet know structuralism, poststructuralism, and speech-act theory as we do today, questions about language—namely how words relate to bodies, how texts construct and convey meaning, and how signifying systems operate—unfolded in the context of theological discourse. As Judith Anderson claims, "The most perceptive ideas about metaphor, as about close reading in the Renaissance, are often to be extracted from the theologians, rather than from the rhetoricians (if the distinction is tenable)."[16] While I do not wish to posit a theological origin for literary theory, I do want to make the point that just as literary critics today would readily cite passages from Saussure, Lacan, Barthes, Freud, or Derrida to interpret a text or make a metacritical argument about reading, writing, or interpretation, so did medieval and early modern readers and writers quote from Augustine, Aquinas, Jerome, and Origen for similar purposes. Conversely, contemporary theorists such as J. L. Austin put forth ideas about the efficacy of words that, we will see later in this chapter, had their origin in Eucharistic theology.[17]

How, then, does Eucharistic theology construct an approach to semiotic thinking? Keeping in mind the important differences in doctrine and devotional practice that arise over the *longue durée*, the various theologies of the Eucharist attempt, in one way or another, to control and delimit the interpretation of Christ's body and the signs of bread and wine. In doing so, these theologies also disseminate Christ's body and its sacramental signs into vast interpretive networks. Hence the paradox of a Eucharistic semiotics: the Eucharist is deeply entrenched in signifying systems at the same time that it pushes ideas about language and the body toward new horizons. The Eucharistic sacrament is, as Greenblatt writes, "the thing which at once precedes and exceeds symbolization, the intertwining of intense pleasure with equally intense grief or lack, the coincidence of opposites."[18] Across the Reformation divide, the Eucharist emerges as sacramental mystery and a semiotic crux—a crux described variously as a "symbolic surplus," a "plenitudinous presence," a "simultaneity of signification and immanence," a "sign that exceeds the sign," and one of "the very densest sites of signification."[19]

While the paradoxes of a Eucharistic semiotics are particularly well suited to literature, and especially drama, they are also evident in conciliar decrees and official injunctions. The official texts of church and state routinely attempted to impose doctrine on a community of believers at the same time that they respond to (and provoke) alternative interpretations. Take, for example, the first documented use of *transubstantiation*, in the Fourth Lateran Council in 1215: "Jesus Christ is both priest and sacrifice. His body and blood are truly contained in the sacrament of the altar under the forms of bread and wine, the bread and wine having been changed in substance [*transsubstantiatis*], by God's power, into his body and blood, so that in order to achieve the mystery of unity we receive from God what he received from us."[20] Within the sixteenth-century Counter-Reformation, moreover, the Council of Trent (1545–63) not only upheld Lateran IV's decree as the orthodox doctrine but also imposed excommunication on dissenters: "If anyone says in the venerable sacrament of the eucharist the substance of the bread and wine remains together with the body and blood of our lord Jesus Christ and denies that marvelous and unique change of the whole substance of the bread into the body, and of the whole substance of the wine into the blood, while only the appearance of bread and wine remains, a change which the catholic church most aptly calls transubstantiation, let him be anathema."[21] Lateran IV and Trent both advance a Eucharistic theology based on a particular interpretation of sacramental signs and bodies, and they bind the believer to it. The penalty for dissent is excommunication. To read the Eucharist against the grain of orthodoxy, as promulgated first by Lateran IV and then reiterated centuries later by the Council of Trent, is to effectively remove oneself from Roman Catholicism's interpretive and ecclesiastical communities.

The same determination to fix the meaning of the Eucharist is evident in the Church of England, namely in the Six Articles issued by Henry VIII in 1539; the Thirty-Nine Articles (1563) that authorized the liturgy, doctrine, and ecclesiastical politics of the Elizabethan Settlement; and the *Book of Common Prayer* itself. The Six Articles reveal the doctrinal conservatism of Henry VIII, who defended a Eucharistic theology that, while not called "transubstantiation" outright, is strikingly similar to the orthodox doctrine as established in the Lateran decrees: "First, that in the blessed Sacrament of the altar, by the strength and efficacy of Christ's mighty word (it being spoken by the priest) is present really, under the form of bread and wine, the natural body and blood of our Saviour Jesus Christ, conceived of the Virgin Mary; and that after the consecration there remaineth no substance of bread and wine, nor any other substance, but the substance of Christ, God and man."[22] As in the context of Lateran IV, here too in the Six Articles: Christ's Eucharistic presence is predicated on a dogmatic assertion of the semiotics of the sacrament. There is no provision for ambiguity or multivalence.

And yet, while Eucharistic doctrines articulate and authorize such relations between Christ's body and its sacramental signs as an unassailable truth, the Eucharistic Controversies show that the relation of body to sign in the sacrament was anything but fixed. If, as Sophie Read argues, "different ways of understanding the mode of Christ's presence in the Eucharist are founded on different ways of reading, and on competing symbolic economies," it is equally true that the Eucharist interrupts the bonds between signifier and signified and thus pushes language to its limits.[23] What Michael O'Connell says about religious images and Reformation iconoclasm helps to explain how the Eucharist establishes a semiotic context apart from ordinary applications. "When we use *sign, signifier, and signified* on the analogy of Saussurean linguistics," O'Connell suggests, "we swerve from its usage there in denying that the relation is simply an arbitrary one, based on an agreed upon semiotic system." When it comes to religious or theological operations of the sign, he continues, "the form of the subject appears recognizably in a way that exceeds conventional systems of representation of language or culturally constructed systems of sign or symbol."[24] Thus even as the sacrament of the Eucharist inheres in semiotic systems, it calls accepted theories of the sign—as well as the sign's relation to the body—into question.

If we trace a Eucharistic semiotics back to its scriptural origins, we can appreciate how Christ's institution of the Eucharist is itself a semiotic interruption. At the Last Supper, Christ takes bread and wine and calls these ordinary elements his body and blood. He revises the Old Law and reinterprets the ancient rites. But what, exactly, does Christ mean when he says, "This is my body" and "This is my blood"? While Christ's words of institution are recorded in the Last Supper narrative of the three synoptic gospels

(Matthew, Mark, and Luke), the gospels do not settle the issue of whether Christ refers to the bread or his natural body when he uses the demonstrative pronoun *this*.[25] The absence of concrete scriptural evidence produces a gap in signification that generates keen curiosities about how the semiotics of this pivotal sacramental event might be read.

Many Reformation era debates focused on interpreting this very semiotic difficulty. In his *Assertion and Defence of the Sacrament of the Aulter* (1546), for example, the Catholic academic Richard Smith reimagines the scene of the Last Supper, particularly the relationship between the words Christ speaks and the gestures he makes. Smith says that when Christ points to the bread, he points to that which becomes his body in substance: "Christ at his last supper, toke bread, blessed it, brake it, and gave it unto his disciples, saieng, Take, and eate, this is my body, not poyntynge (as some folish fantasticall fooles do fantasye) to his visible body, then sittynge at the table (which had ben a fond triflying and jugglyng) but poyntyng, and meaning of that his body, which was then really conteined under the forme of bread, then given to his apostles."[26] Stephen Gardiner, a stalwart defender of Catholic orthodoxy, especially when it came to Eucharistic doctrine, states that "Christ was makynge demonstration of the bread, when he says, This is my body, by the myghte of whyche wordes of Christe that was demonstrate by the demonstration (this) which was the bread, was altered and changed into his body, wherby the substaunce of brede was converted in to the substaunce of his moste precious body."[27] On the reverse side of the argument, Thomas Cranmer interprets Christ's same gesture in a markedly different way. He charges, "No man that was there present was so fond, but he knew well that the bread was not Christes body, nor the wine his bloud. And therefore they might well know that Christ called the bread his body, and the wine his bloud for some figure, similitude, and property of the bread and wine unto his flesh and bloud. For as bread and wine be foodes to nourish our bodies, so is the flesh and bloud of our Savyour Christ (being annexed unto his Deity) the everlasting food of our soules."[28] Here Cranmer disavows Smith's and Gardiner's arguments, which locate Christ's body in the bread itself at the level of substance. Christ, says Cranmer, calls the Passover bread by a new name at the Last Supper but does not actually make it into his body and blood in an ontological sense. Instead, Cranmer posits that the sacrament makes Christ present as a spiritual reality, "in deede, yet not corporeally and carnally, but spiritually and effectually."[29]

The exacting detail in which these texts reimagine the scene of the Last Supper shows that in the Eucharist an understanding of Christ as sign, word, and symbol confronts an understanding of Christ as body, flesh, and sacrifice. Regardless of the particular theological positions taken by Smith, Gardiner, or Cranmer, the episode demonstrates how the Eucharist challenges the hermeneutic closure on which its doctrines are based. As these churchmen vie for the right understanding of the Last Supper, they further disseminate Christ's words, the sacramental signs, and the ritual actions into vast interpretive networks.

In the sections that follow, I work through a variety of semiotic positions produced by Eucharistic discourse in contexts both medieval and early modern, traditional and reformed. To lend coherence to a set of debates that are hard to pin down conceptually, I will focus on the following four concepts: body and sign; flesh and spirit; literal and figurative; and words and deeds. Though for the sake of clarity I present these aspects of Eucharistic semiotics as conceptual pairs, they are not meant to be seen as mutually exclusive. In fact, the controversies I am about to investigate will sufficiently frustrate any attempt to set such concepts in strict opposition and will thereby dismantle the narrative of progress from body to text and from corporeality to trope that has governed many recent literary histories of the Reformation.

(1) *Body and Sign*: How do the elements of bread and wine signify the body and blood of Christ? How is the relationship between sacramental signs and divine thing signified interpreted? What is the nature of Christ's Eucharistic body, in what manner is it made present to and received by the believer, and what are the effects of such reception?

(2) *Flesh and Spirit*: Is one to receive the Eucharist carnally (with the teeth and jaws) or spiritually (with the heart and soul)? If the signs of bread and wine are not merely figures, how do they constitute a spiritual reality in the sacrament? What role does faith play in effecting sacramental grace? And how does Christ's sacramental body connect to his mystical body, the church?

(3) *Literal and Figurative*: How does Eucharistic theology relate to and complicate scriptural translation and exegesis? When Christ spoke the words "This is my body" and "This is my blood" at the Last Supper, was he speaking literally or figuratively? Did he use plain words or metaphors? How does the interpretation of the Eucharist relate to debates over the "literal sense" of scripture?

(4) *Words and Deeds*: Where can we locate the efficacy, or "work," of the sacrament—in the priestly words of consecration, in the act of Eucharistic reception, or in the spiritual bonds forged there? What power do words have in the sacramental liturgy? Is the language of the Eucharist efficacious or referential? And how is sacramental efficacy inflected by liturgical ritual and ecclesial formations?

These four interrelated concepts illustrate a dynamic relationship between theology and semiotics, a relationship that drives Eucharistic controversy as it takes shape across the *longue durée*. For example, when Wyclif dissents from orthodoxy, he does not simply reject transubstantiation as a point of doctrine but also targets the signifying function of the sacramental signs on which the doctrine is based. Similarly, when Thomas More, William Tyndale, and George Joye present different arguments about scriptural hermeneutics, especially as concerns the interpretation of scriptural texts on which Eucharistic doctrines are founded, they are concerned not only with biblical truths but also with the interpretive acts by which such truths are iterated.

Body and Sign

The sacrament of the Eucharist confounds the categories of body and sign. As a sign—a piece of bread and cup of wine—the Eucharist claims some aspect of Christ's real presence whether through a metaphysical change in substance or a spiritual conversion achieved by the communicant's faithful participation. As a body that can be really present but also imperceptible, the Eucharist ruptures sign systems and troubles interpretive acts. Regardless of the particular theological position one adopts, one must always consider the operation of body and sign in the sacrament as well as the distance set between them. The doctrine of transubstantiation cannot get around a discussion of the sacramental sign any more than a more symbolic interpretation of the Eucharist can dispense with a consideration of the body.[30]

In the *Summa theologiae*, Thomas Aquinas predicates his discussion of Eucharistic physics (how Christ is made present in the sacrament, under what forms, and with what effect) on a discussion of Eucharistic semiotics (how sacramental signs manifest or represent these divine realities). As

David Aers argues, "All realms of orthodox discourse, in their different disciplinary modes, shared a commitment to closing the gaps between the sacramental sign of Christ's presence and the bodily presence it signifies."[31] For Aquinas, sign becomes body in the most real sense. What appears as ordinary bread and wine at a physical level is transformed into the substance of Christ's divine body and blood at an ontological level. Even though the Eucharistic signs do not look, feel, or taste like the body they contain, Aquinas nonetheless asserts that "the Eucharist contains something which is sacred, absolutely, namely, Christ's own body."[32] Peter the Lombard, who wrote his *Sententiae* (ca. 1150) just over a century before Aquinas wrote the *Summa*, likewise states that Christ's body and blood are contained within the sacramental signs: "The thing contained and signified is the flesh of Christ, which he derived from the Virgin, and the blood which he shed for us."[33]

Aquinas and the Lombard both suggest that the sacramental sign transcends ordinary signifying capacities. For them bread and wine do not simply signify Christ's body and blood at the level of reference but become Christ's body and blood in essence. The Eucharist thus realizes what Aquinas sees as the incarnational foundation of all sacraments: "The word of God is joined to the sensible sign just as in the mystery of the Incarnation, the word of God is united to sensible flesh."[34] Christ, himself the fleshly embodiment of an otherwise ineffable, invisible God, is miraculously made present in the sacramental signs.

Aquinas distills both his Eucharistic theology and his Eucharistic semiotics in the hymn "Lauda Sion Salvatorem," which he wrote for the Mass of Corpus Christi. "Lauda Sion" opens with an extensive typological reading of Christ's Eucharistic institution in the context of the Old Testament Passover and then proceeds to a meditation on Christ's real presence in the sacrament of the altar. In its final verses, the hymn focuses intently on the sacramental signs of bread and wine:

> Sub diversis speciebus,
> signis tantum, et non rebus,
> latent res eximiae;
> caro cibus, sanguis potus,
> manet tamen Christus totus
> sub utraque specie.

[Here beneath these signs are hidden
priceless things, to sense forbidden;
signs, not things, are all we see.
Flesh from bread, and Blood from wine,
yet is Christ in either sign,
all entire confessed to be.][35]

For Aquinas, the signs of bread and wine translate an inscrutable sacramental mystery into legible, visible, and tangible terms.[36] These signs also crucially eliminate the burden of ingesting actual flesh and blood, which would result in cannibalism.[37] Christ, who assumes the substance of God (and also partakes of the flesh of man), offers that very substance in the Eucharist: "Yet is Christ in either sign, / all entire confessed to be." The Eucharistic signs therefore have two operations. While the bread and wine enable the communicant to make sense of the mystery, the signs also claim to house Christ's divine body and blood within themselves. "We do not understand that Christ is there only as in a sign, although a sacrament is a kind of sign," Aquinas writes in the *Summa*, "but that Christ's body is here after a fashion proper to this sacrament."[38] Though they are sacramental signs, bread and wine are transformed into a higher reality; in turn, the communicant must believe in something his senses deny, namely that Christ is actually contained *in* the sign.[39] What emerges, says Andrew Cole, is "Aquinas's own sacramental semiotic in which sacraments are signs but not just any signs fusible with others."[40] Thus, while Aquinas defines a Eucharistic theology according to the convergence of sign and referent, he also creates a perplexing semiotic situation whereby one cannot see the body contained in the sign. Sacraments are signs, yes, but they are signs of a radically different kind.

In the sixteenth century, English writers such as Smith and Gardiner defended Aquinas's Eucharistic theology, which had become enshrined as the orthodox doctrine within Roman Catholicism. In particular, Smith and Gardiner promoted a Thomistic understanding of Eucharistic signs as unique in their capacity to manifest Christ's presence; these sixteenth-century apologists for Catholic orthodoxy subscribed to the belief that the Eucharistic signs contained the body and blood of Christ wholly and substantially within themselves rather than merely signifying or memorializing such a reality. Smith, for example, claims that an ordinary sign like a badge or a token "doth not really conteine in it self the thing that is signified and represented by it," whereas the bread and wine in the Eucharist, "beynge diverse respects but a sygne, and also a veritie, conteyn[e] in it the very thinge which is represented and signified."[41] Smith concludes by saying that "there muste be putte an othermaner difference between a figure or a badge, and a sacrament," demonstrating that the sacrament of the altar demands a unique semiotics.[42] The Eucharist is a sign but not merely a sign: it is also a "veritie," or truth.

Bishop Gardiner makes a similar argument: "The speache hath not been abhorred to call the sacrament of the aulter a figure, and to call it a signe, and a memorial, for so it is, but not only a figure, not onlye a signe, not onlye a memorial, but there with the thynge it selfe."[43] When it comes to explaining this convergence between "signe" and "thynge it selfe," however, Gardiner cautions his readers not to resort to reason alone in probing the divine mysteries: "And although, to mans reason it semeth straunge, that Christ standyng or sittyng at the table, would deliver them his bodie to be eaten: yet when we remember Christ to be verie God, we muste graunt him omnipotent, and by reason thereof, represse in oure thoughtes, all imaginacions how it might be, and considre Christes intent, by his will preached unto us by scriptures, and beleved universally in his church."[44] Smith and Gardiner both defend the Scholastic position that the consecrated host joins signifier to signified; the sacramental signs do not merely point toward but actually contain the body and blood of Christ they signify, so that heaven meets earth in a very real way. Christ's Galilean body is thus present in the consecrated host with all its immensity but without physical dimension.[45]

The semiotics of transubstantiation that underwrite Catholic orthodoxy creates an unavoidable discrepancy between the signs perceived by the senses and the divine body they contain. What looks, feels, tastes, and smells like bread is distinctly not so at the level of being. Thus the conversion of bread into body and wine into blood demands that one ignore what one perceives.[46] What appears as bread and wine is only an accident; it ceases to exist (really and truly) as bread and wine after the consecration.[47] As Aers describes it, "The doctrine of transubstantiation with non-remanence is the only way of getting the Galilean body into the sign without Christ's body undergoing changes of motion in an interstellar odyssey from its location in heaven to diverse altars on earth."[48] The idea that after the consecration bread and wine are accidents without substance—a signal departure from a key principle of Aristotelian metaphysics—is regarded by many opponents to transubstantiation as a falsehood or deception that is incompatible with the sacred operation of the sacraments.[49] Aquinas denies such a proposition when he asserts, "The accidents [of bread and wine] which are discerned by the senses, are truly present. But the intellect, whose proper object is substance . . . is preserved by faith from deception."[50] Such a position suggests that the recipient's faith directs the senses to the mystery of the sacrament: Christ's body consists in substance, which transcends physical matter and is hidden beneath the sensible signs. The substance of bread and wine is not merely taken away, voided, or "annihilated" (the word Aquinas takes issue with) but is miraculously converted into the very substance of Christ's body and blood by God's power acting through the words of the priest.[51]

Early reformers, notably John Wyclif, respond to the claims of Lombard and Aquinas by positing a different Eucharistic theology grounded on a different Eucharistic semiotics. Throughout *De Eucharistia* (*Tractatus maior*), Wyclif rehearses many points of contention that continue to define controversy over the Eucharist for centuries following. These include the problematic assertion of accidents without substance; the difference between carnal and spiritual eating; the idea that Christ's body cannot be in multiple places at the same time (referred to as "multilocationism" in later debates); the interpretation of Christ's original words of institution; the threat of idolatry posed by Eucharistic veneration; and the ethical aspects of the Eucharist as related to the cardinal virtues of faith, hope, and charity. Wyclif dismisses as a great error Aquinas's teaching that after the consecration bread and wine can be regarded as accidents without substance. Such a proposition violates natural reason, he argues, because just as a substance is made known through its accidents, so must an accident inhere in a substance ("Docet enim racio naturalis quod non potest esse accidens sine subjectum, quia non potest esse subjectum sine suo accidente, ergo multo magis econtra").[52] Furthermore, if Aquinas suggests that faith leads the recipient to understand the substance hidden behind the sensible signs, Wyclif argues that the signs remain as bread and wine. In fact, Wyclif challenges those who claim that Christ's body is present in flesh and blood to disclose specific details about that body, such as whether Christ stands or sits ("Item, quererem ab istis fictoribus, si in sacramento vident sensibiliter corpus Christi, uturum inibi stat vel sedet").[53] He concludes that Christ's presence in the host cannot be understood in terms of physical dimensions (*dimensionaliter*) because Christ's body can be present as such only in heaven. In the host, by contrast, Christ is virtually present (*virtualiter*), meaning that though Christ is not present in physical or substantial form, his presence is still more than symbolic or metaphorical.[54]

Wyclif's theology unfolds according to a semiotics of the sacrament that accommodates neither the metaphysical burdens of transubstantiation taken up by the Scholastics nor the metaphorical preoccupations set forth by later sacramentarians like Zwingli and Karlstadt, who set greater distance between divine body and sacramental sign. Wyclif develops a Eucharistic theology that allows Christ's real presence in the sacrament without insisting on an ontological change in the elements. "The line taken by Wyclif," Aers argues, "included a reverent belief in the real presence of Christ, a sacramental, spiritual presence in which the communicating faithful participated but which included neither the presence of the Galilean and risen body of Jesus nor the annihilation of bread and wine."[55] Bread and wine can remain as bread and wine at the same time that Christ can be truly present. In a profession of faith written just years before his death, Wyclif draws on Christ's hypostatic union to defend his position: "Right as hit is heresye to trowe that Crist is a spirit and no body, so hit is heresye to trowe that this sacrament is Gods body and no bred; for hit is bothe togedir."[56] By taking a position that allows for body and sign to exist independently but coterminously, Wyclif moves beyond the semiotic deceit he locates in transubstantiation and offers what he sees as a sacramental theology more in keeping with the church fathers as well as a liturgy and ecclesiology more aligned with the early Christian Church.[57] In keeping with such a focus, Wyclif also yokes the sacrament of the Eucharist to Christian virtue, concluding that sacramental reception is of little worth if it does not engender acts of faith, hope, and charity. The bread of the Eucharist, Wyclif says, must be "kneaded in charitable works."[58]

Wyclif's theology reminds us that all "late medieval" Eucharistic theology should not be assimilated to transubstantiation, which was a single position (that of orthodoxy) among many others.[59] By the same token, Wyclif's reformist stance is different from a Zwinglian symbolism, for Wyclif holds fast to the real presence and the sanctity of the sacramental signs. He also emphasizes the participation of the faithful within Christ's mystical body, the church. Wyclif's theology of real presence, which foregrounds spiritual reception and participatory communion, lays the foundation for the arguments of Cranmer, Jewel, and Hooker, which come to organize the Eucharistic positions of the English church in the sixteenth century. Here too the sacramental signs are seen not as mere symbols or metaphors alone. Rather, these theologies draw the lines between flesh and spirit carefully in describing the nature of the Eucharistic body and its relation to the worshipping community of Christ's mystical body, the church.

Flesh and Spirit

"Howe, saith he, shal I holde him that is absent? Howe shall I reache forthe my hande into heaven, that I might holde hym there sitting? Reache out, saith he, [in] faithe, and thou haste caught him."[60] Here Bishop John Jewel paraphrases Augustine, who says that the communicant accesses Christ's Eucharistic body through the grasp of faith. This way of thinking about sacramental presence is different from the ontological literalism of the Scholastics. It constitutes a spiritualist theology of the Eucharist in which Christ is made present not by means of a metaphysical transformation but through a mystical bond forged with the faithful recipient. As Thomas Cranmer writes, "The breade is not made reallye Christes bodye, nor the wine his bloud, but sacramentally. And the myraculous workyng is not in the bread, but in them that duely eate the bread, and drynke that drynke."[61] For Cranmer, the term *sacramental* suggests a spiritual or mystical form of presence predicated not on transubstantiation but on faithful reception. Yet as for Hooker after him, this presence is still considered to be real: "The reall presence of Christs most blessed body and blood," Hooker says, "is not therefore to be sought for in the sacrament but in the worthie receiver of the sacrament."[62] This form of dynamic sacramental participation sees real presence not as a miracle effected in the hands of a priest but as a mystical communion by which the believer becomes what he receives.[63]

Though the Church of England's Eucharistic theology ultimately departs from transubstantiation (which was still, by and large, upheld as the orthodox position during the reign of Henry VIII), it nonetheless accommodates corporeality within its semiotics of spiritual reception and sacramental presence. As Anthony Dawson puts it, "The Anglican view is rifted—it insists on both presence and representation. The sacrament is not simply a *memorial* representation, not just a ritual designed to commemorate the Last Supper and the passion.... At the same time, 'presence'... is not, as in the Catholic view, absolute and unquestioned, masked only by the *appearances* of bread and wine, but rather is itself troubled or mediated—unreal but also efficacious."[64] While Cranmer, for example, stresses the fruits of the spirit rather than accidents without substance, he does not evacuate the body from his Eucharistic theology. In an oft-quoted passage from the *Defence of the True and Catholike Doctrine of the Sacrament of the Body and Blood of Our Saviour Christ* (1550) Cranmer writes, "Christ ordained this sacrament in bread & wyne ... to the intent that as surely as we see the bread and wyne with our eyes, smell them with our noses, touche them with our hands, and tast them with our mouthes, so assuredly ought we to believe, that Christ is our spiritual life and sustenaunce of our soules, like as they sayd bread and wyne is the food and sustenaunce of our bodies."[65] Cranmer analogizes flesh to spirit at a rhetorical level in order to express the spiritual conversion that takes place at a sacramental level. The bread and wine, which signify bodily eating, express in comprehensible terms the spiritual sustenance provided by the Eucharist. Even though he argues that Eucharistic reception is the province of the heart rather than the mouth, Cranmer maintains that Christ is present nonetheless.[66] Thus the term *spiritual* does not suggest "metaphorical" or "figural," as we might assume, but instead signifies a dynamic relation between flesh and spirit that creates a distinct form of sacramental presence.

A fine example of such dynamism is evident in Hooker's description of sacramental efficacy in terms of Christ's crucified body:

> The very letter of the word of Christ giveth plaine securitie these misteries doe as nayles fasten us to his verie crosse, that by them we draw out, as touching, efficacie, force and virtue, even the bloude of his goared side, in the wounds of our Redeemer we there dip our tongues, wee are died red both within and without, our hunger is satisfied, and our thirst for ever quenched, they are things wonderful which he feeleth, great which hee seeth, and unheard of which he uttreth whose soule is possest of this pascall Lambe and made joyfull in the strength of this new wine, this bread hath in it more than the substance which our eyes behold. This cup, hallowed with solemne benediction availeth to the enlesse life and wel-fare both of soule and body, in that it serveth as well for a medi-

cine to heale our infirmities and purge our sinnes as for a sacrifice of thanksgiving, with touching it sanctifieth, it enlighteneth with beliefe, it truly conformeth us unto the image of Jesus Christ.[67]

Rather than sweep corporeality away, Hooker unfolds his theology of Eucharistic participation according to a semiotics of Christ's crucified body. In emphasizing Christ's corporeality, however, Hooker does not advocate affective piety or transubstantiation but rather resignifies the crucifixion wounds as vehicles in an elaborate conceit meant to convey the reality of spiritual reception. He sees flesh and spirit not as inimical but as analogical, and he shifts attention from the physical flesh to the spiritual reality it signifies. The Eucharist cannot be separated from the Word of God, which fastens the mystery of the sacrament in the hearts of those who receive it worthily. We do not simply see with our eyes or eat with our mouths, Hooker argues, but when we participate in the Lord's Supper we "draw out as touching" the efficacy of the sacrament; we "dip our tongues" into Christ's wounds; and we are "died red both within and without" by Christ's blood. Debora Shuger notes Hooker's emphasis on Christ's body in this particular passage, suggesting, "There is only one *body* in these texts, the wounded body of Christ; the prose always becomes concrete, vivid, dramatic in depicting that body, making it present—not only as an object beheld, but touched, tasted, embraced."[68] As Shuger suggests, Hooker's characterization of Christ's body in spiritual terms does not wholly reject Christ's real sacramental presence. "Christes flesh is meate and his blood drinke, not by surmised imagination," Hooker goes on to declare, "but truly, even so truly that through faith we perceive in the body and blood sacramentally presented the very tast of eternall life. The grace of the sacrament is here, as the foode which we eate and drinke."[69] The truth of Christ's Eucharistic food is activated by and grounded in faith, and the semiotic logic is one defined by analogy and simile. The sacramental "presentation," moreover, is no mere "surmised imagination" or symbolism. Rather, sacramental grace is as real and tangible as the bread and wine received.

Hooker's Eucharistic theology bears out a dynamic relationship between flesh and spirit, a position derived in part from John Calvin, who devotes long passages of the *Institutes of the Christian Religion* (1536, rev. 1559) to describing the spiritual fruits of the Eucharist in corporeal terms.[70] Calvin writes, "That sacred consumption of flesh and blood by which Christ transfuses his life into us, just as if it penetrated our bones and marrow, he testifies and seals in the Supper, and that not by presenting a vain or empty sign, but by there exerting an efficacy of the Spirit by which he fulfills what he promises."[71] This passage vividly sets forth a theology of the Eucharist according to a semiotics of the body, right down to the bones and marrow. Yet in characterizing the sacramental conversion according to the metaphor of "transfusion" (as opposed to the miracle of transubstantiation), Calvin uses the language of corporeality to limn the sacrament's spiritual fruits. Yet, as we saw in Cranmer's theology (and Wyclif's earlier), Calvin does not present his spiritualist theology of the Eucharist as strictly figurative. While he sets critical distance between sign and referent, he also emphasizes the sacramental reality of the Eucharistic signs: "Truly the thing there signified he [Christ] exhibits and offers to all who sit down at that spiritual feast.... I admit, indeed, that the breaking of the bread is a symbol, not the reality. But this being admitted, we duly infer from the exhibition of the symbol that the thing itself is exhibited.... The rule which the pious ought always to observe is whenever they see the symbols instituted by the Lord, to think and feel surely persuaded that the truth of the thing signified is also present."[72] Such a theology, Read argues, "occupies a conceptual middle ground in early Protestant thought," one that "combines a clear rejection of the notion that consecration can transform the elements into body and blood with an equally clear assertion that the body and blood are indeed in some way received by the elect believer."[73] Calvin goes on to claim that Christ's body is not to be collapsed into the sign as in transubstantiation, for "they are greatly mistaken in imagining that there is no presence in the flesh of Christ in the Supper unless it be placed in the bread." Those who see the sacrament this way "leave no room for the operation of the Spirit which unites Christ himself to us."[74] Instead, though bread and wine do not become body and blood at the level of substance, they are different from ordinary signs insofar as they allow the recipient to "think and feel surely persuaded" that Christ is really present.[75]

To understand the importance of Eucharistic presence to the theology of Calvin, Cranmer, and Hooker, we might contrast their positions with the Zwinglian views expressed by William Tyndale and George Joye in a series of texts (both pamphlets and books) printed during the Henrician Reformation. Joye, for example, divests the sacrament of all fleshly connotations:

> It is ther called the body of our Lorde not that ther is anything wheryn his very natural body is contained so longe and brode as it hanged on the crosse, for so it is ascended into heaven and sitteth on the right hande of the father: but that thinge that is there done in the souper as the breaking & dealing & eting of the brede, and the wholl lyke action of the wyne, signifieth representeth and putteth into our hertis by the spirit of faithe the commemoracion, joyful remembraunce, and so to give thanks for that inestimable benefit of our redempcion.[76]

The organizing terms of Joye's argument—*signifieth, representeth, commemoracion, remembraunce*—are to be read as more Zwinglian than Calvinist, and while Joye recognizes that faith activates grace in the recipient, he does not see the relation of flesh to spirit as more than analogical. It is not surprising, then, that Joye contextualizes the description of the Lord's Supper in the figurative terms adopted by Zwingli: "Neither let it not offende thee, o crysten reader, that Est is taken for significat, for this is a comen maner of speche in many placis of scripture."[77] For Joye, the signs are strictly representational and memorial, as are Christ's words of institution; less a real presence, they function more as tokens of remembrance.

Joye's emphasis on the interpretation of *est* introduces to our discussion of Eucharistic semiotics a question about hermeneutical practice, particularly as it pertains to the reading of scriptural and patristic texts. In analyzing debates over body and sign as well as flesh and spirit, I have thus far focused on the nature of Christ's body in the Eucharist and how that body is interpreted in the sacramental signs. These are primarily questions about *what* (or even *who*) is present in the Eucharist. In the final two sections, I want to consider two related matters taken up in medieval and early modern writings on the sacrament: first, the conflicts over literal and figurative interpretation; and second, the doctrine of Eucharistic confection, which posits that Christ's body is made present by the words of consecration spoken by the priest during the Mass.

Literal and Figurative

The English Jesuit Thomas Wright, perhaps best known for *The Passions of the Minde in Generall* (1604), a text often cited in studies of humoral physiology, also wrote a text on the Eucharist titled *A Treatise, shewing the possibilitie, and conveniencie of the reall presence of our Sauiour in the blessed Sacrament* (1596). In this text, Wright launches a defense of Catholic orthodoxy: "The Catholikes from these foure wordes *Hoc est corpus meum* deduce their dreadfull, reverent, majesticall, and deified sacrifice, the light of paradice, the foode of angels. The Heretikes their common-table communion, their prophane supper, their schismaticall cup, their tipicall bread, their unblessed breakfast."[78] Wright flippantly rejects the reformers' metaphorical interpretation of the sacrament as heresy, claiming that "Christ ... had sufficient occasion to conceive through his infinite wisdom, that here was no place for metaphoricall figures, symbolicall senses, or harsh speeches subject to sundry interpretations."[79] Wright's text bespeaks a delightful irony, however: though he dismisses figures of speech in writing about the sacrament of the altar, Wright cannot escape using such "metaphoricall figures" to deride reformed theological positions.

Wright demonstrates that the controversies over the Eucharist focused not only on what the sacrament was (or was not) but also on the criteria for what constituted a doctrinally valid interpretation of the sacrament. Wright's was just one of many voices on the matter. In his *Confession Concerning Christ's Last Supper* (1528), Martin Luther rejected Zwingli's figurative interpretation of the sacrament as a perversion of the gospels, which are "unambiguous, simple, sure, and certain in every word, syllable, and letter."[80] Decades later, the Council of Trent (1551) asserted that transubstantiation presents the literal sense of Christ's Eucharistic institution, claiming that Christ "bore witness in express and unambiguous words that, after the blessing of the bread and the wine, he was offering to them his own body and his own blood. Since those words, recorded by the holy evangelists and afterwards repeated by St. Paul, bear that proper and very clear meaning which the fathers understood them to have, it is surely a most intolerable and shameful deed for some base argumentative persons to twist them to false and imaginary meanings that deny the reality of Christ's flesh and blood, against the universal understanding of the church."[81] The definitive sense of the Eucharist—its "proper and clear meaning"—is, according to the decree, nonfigurative. Dissenting views are deemed heretical and dismissed as the fictions of apostates.

The Eucharistic doctrine asserted by the Council of Trent as unassailably literal was exposed by reformers such as Cranmer as unfounded by scriptural authority. Consider Cranmer's charge to Gardiner on this point: "If you can prove that your Transubstantiation, your fleshly presence of Christes body and bloud, your carnall eatynge and drinkynge of the same, your propiciatory sacrifice of the masse, are taught us as plainly in the scripture, as the sayd articles of our faith be, then I will beleve that it is in dede."[82] In the context of the Elizabethan Settlement, moreover, Article 28 of the Thirty-Nine Articles states, "Transubstantiation (or the change of the substance of Bread and Wine) in the Supper of the Lord, cannot be proved by holy writ; but is repugnant to the plain words of Scripture, overthroweth the nature of a sacrament, and hath given occasion to many superstitions."[83] In distinguishing church tradition from biblical authority, the Articles, like Cranmer's text, argue that sacramental theology cannot be valid if it is not corroborated by scripture.

The crux of such hermeneutic disputes were the words uttered by Christ at the Last Supper, translated in Latin as "Hoc est enim corpus meum." Was Christ speaking literally, in the "plain sense," or was he speaking metaphorically in parables? "The fundamental indeterminacy of that little shifter 'hoc,'" writes Sarah Beckwith, "is seen either as the laughably reductive literalism, the merely stupid equation of a debased popular piety, or as an attack on the mendacious subtlety of scholasticism's exclusive, precise, fanatically, and fantastically defensive logic."[84] Thomas Harding strikes to the heart of such a debate over literal and figurative reading when he writes in answer to Bishop Jewel, "For if Christ spake plainely, and used no tropes, figures, nor metaphor, as the scripture it selfe sufficiently declareth to an humble beleever, and would his disciples to understand him, so as he spake in manifest terms, when he sayde, 'This is my body which is geven for you': then may we say that in the sacrament his very body is present, yea really, that is to saye in dede, substantially, that is in substance, and corporally, carnally, and naturally."[85] Christ, says Harding, speaks "plainly" (that is, literally) when he shares bread and wine as his body and blood. It is on the grounds of this literal interpretation that Harding asserts his understanding of real presence.

When Calvin takes up a similar issue in his *Institutes*, he lambastes Scholastics for willfully misconstruing *est* as a verb of being. "In interpreting the particle *is*, as an equivalent to being transubstantiated," he argues, "[they] have recourse to a *gloss*, which is *forced*, and violently wrested. They have no ground, therefore, for pretending that they are moved by a reverence for the words."[86] John Foxe, too, asserts that "the olde Doctors dooe call thys speakyng of Christe tropical, figurative, anagogical, allegoricall, whiche they dooe interpret after this sorte, that althoughe the substaunce of bread and wyne dooe remayne, and bee received of the faythfull, yet not withstandyng Christe changed the appellation thereof, and called the breade by the name of hys fleshe, and the wyne by the name of hys bloude, *non rei veritate, sed significante mysterio*. Not that it is so in verye deede, but signified in a mysterie."[87] For Foxe, the Eucharist witnesses a change of "appellation"—a shift in naming and, by extension, in interpretation—rather than a change in substance. At the same time, Foxe employs words such as "tropical, figurative, anagogical, [and] allegorical" not to construct an opposition between real and representational presence but rather to indicate that one must "understande the Sacramente, not carnallye but spirituallye" and "shoulde looke up to the bloude of Christe wyth oure fayth."[88]

These examples illustrate how what appears to be a contest between literal and figurative interpretations of the Eucharist is actually an ongoing debate over what constitutes the literal sense of the sacrament and its scriptural texts. Writers from a range of confessional positions all strive to fix their particular interpretation as itself the uniquely literal sense of the Eucharist. I want to examine such claims in the context of two formative debates over the literal sense in the English Reformation: Thomas More's disputation with John Frith and William Tyndale in the 1530s and Thomas Cranmer's disputation with Stephen Gardiner in the 1550s.

More engaged in a number of debates over scriptural interpretation, particularly the passage in John 6 where Christ refers to himself as the bread of life and says that those who eat his flesh and drink his blood will live eternally: "Verily, verily I say unto you, Except ye eat the flesh of the Son of man, and drink his blood, ye have no life in you. . . . Whosoever eateth my flesh, and drinketh my blood, hath eternal life, and I will raise him up at the last day. For my flesh is meat indeed, and my blood is drink indeed. He that eateth my flesh, and drinketh my blood, dwelleth in me, and I in him" (John 6:53–57).[89] The passage was a chief subject of contention in More's disputes with George Joye, which constitute More's *Answer to a Poisoned Book* (1533), as well as in a set of related arguments with the English reformer John Frith.[90] More, who asserted that the Eucharistic sacrament joins the sacramental figure and its divine reality, argued against the Zwinglian readings of the passage adopted by Joye and Frith, which saw the comparison of Christ to bread as no different from other instances in the gospels where Christ compares himself to a vine, door, salt, or light.

More has a habit of rejecting not only his opponents' theological views but also their exegetical methods. For example, he characterizes Frith as one who "flyt[s] in conclusion fro the faith of playne and open scripture & so farre falle[s] to the newe fangled fantasyes of folysshe heretykes, that he will for the allegorye dystroye the trewe sense of the letter."[91] More claims that just because Christ speaks allegorically elsewhere in the gospels one must not conclude that Christ's every word should be interpreted in the same manner. In fact, he argues that Christ's teaching on the Eucharist itself introduces a new way of reading, one in which Christ "spake of hys very body and very bloud besyde all allegories."[92] As More would have it, Christ (in addition to the patristic fathers whom he routinely cites) always speaks the plain, literal, and true sense, and this sense predictably accords with More's defense of Catholic Eucharistic doctrine. It is on this basis that More derogates Frith as a foolish interpreter: "This yong man taketh away now from the Blessed Sacrament the very body & blood of Christ, by expounynge hys playne words wyth an allegory under colour of some other places where such allegoryes must nedes have place & were none otherwise ment."[93] Though More recognizes that allegory has a place in biblical interpretation, he cautions his reader not to reduce Christ's teaching on the Eucharist to allegory alone. Frith, he charges, fails to appreciate that distinction.

More's rejection of allegory must be situated within a broader debate over scriptural reading in the Reformation. Medieval exegetes subscribed to a fourfold biblical hermeneutics that recognized allegorical, tropological, and anagogical understandings of scripture in addition to the literal sense.[94] Allegory, for example, could be seen as one way that God reveals the divine mysteries in scriptural texts. Surprisingly, More's resistance to allegory seems at odds with medieval exegetical models providing for its hermeneutic validity; by the same logic, it seems to align with evangelical arguments in favor of the literal sense of scripture, such as those made by William Tyndale and Martin Luther in the early sixteenth century.

This stunning reversal of theological and hermeneutic positions with respect to allegory, the literal sense, and the Eucharist demands further commentary, especially given the quite complex history of evangelical reading practices in the sixteenth century. James Simpson has gone a long way to show how the evangelical commitment to the literal sense of scripture, despite its dual promise of transparency and liberty, brings about a violent and unstable form of religious politics, especially among sixteenth-century evangelicals. Part of this instability, he argues, has to do with the fact that a literalist hermeneutics is not singular, simple, or plain but inherently contradictory. Another part has to do with the fact that reading in the vernacular, far from providing liberation from institutional pressures, is bound up in institutional authority.[95] In an illuminating essay on William Tyndale's *A Briefe Declaration of the Sacrament of the Altar* (1533–35), Simpson explains that these contradictions are readily apparent in Tyndale's Eucharistic theology, which creates friction between the literal and allegorical senses. When it comes to Christ's "This is my body," Simpson argues, "almost everything Tyndale says elsewhere about the literal sense of Scripture would persuade him to read Christ's 'is' literally."[96] Yet Tyndale settles on an interpretation of the sacrament in line with Zwingli's understanding of the bread and wine as memorial signs. In Tyndale's Eucharistic theology, Simpson explains, "two extremely powerful evangelical commitments come into outright collision . . . and the repudiation of idolatry wins over commitment to the literal sense."[97] Lest he maintain that Christ is present in bread and wine at the level of substance (which would imply that the signs are effectively more than signs), Tyndale must somehow accommodate allegory to his sacramental theology.

In the specific context of Eucharistic theology, as Simpson suggests, the reversal of hermeneutic positions by both More and Tyndale appears contradictory, so much so that when it comes to the interpretation of Christ's words of institution, "More sounds like an evangelical, Tyndale like a Catholic."[98] However striking this reversal of hermeneutic positions is, it makes logical sense, especially in the context of Tyndale's charged polemic. In *A Briefe Declaration*, which is Simpson's focus, Tyndale stresses the reality of the covenant forged by the Lord's Supper, not the reality of Christ's presence in the sacramental signs. "Chryste wrote the covenaunt of hys bodye and bloud in bread and wyne, gevynge them that name that ought to kepe the covenaunt in remembrauns," Tyndale writes. "And hereof ye se[e] that our sacraments are bokys of storyes only, and that there is none other vertu in them then to thestyfye the covenaunts and promyses made in Chrysts bloud."[99] In speaking of the sacraments as textual signs or "books of stories," Tyndale argues that the Eucharist is not to be interpreted literally, as in carnally or substantially, but that these sacramental signs are themselves capable of iterating the plain sense of the sacrament. A literal reading, in other words, need not coincide with a literal eating.

In so rejecting the literal sense of the Eucharist, however, Tyndale does not simply make a clear-cut choice between "literal" and "figurative," nor does he understand the terms according to the strict opposition between them favored by modern readers. Instead, he presents his figurative interpretation *as itself the literal sense*—and in fact, the only sense—in which to understand the Eucharist. While he may well do so to ward off the threat of idolatry, as Simpson suggests, it also seems that there is no plausible theological alternative for Tyndale than to read Christ's words in a nonliteral way. In doing so, Tyndale suggests that when Christ said, "This is my body," he meant that bread and wine represent (rather than contain) his body and blood. By dint of this nonliteral reading, which stresses the remembrance of Christ's original sacrifice and the covenant it establishes, Tyndale arrives at the plain sense of both the scriptural text and the sacramental theology it supports. Recollection and memory of Christ's sacrifice triumph over its reenactment and real presence. What emerges from this subtle parsing of the Eucharistic sacrament, then, is that both the hermeneutic and theological operations of "literal" and "figurative" are far more complex than they appear, especially when it comes to such a delicate matter as the Eucharist.

The issues debated between Catholics and evangelicals over the literal sense of the Scriptures, and especially the sacrament of the Eucharist, in the 1530s recur in a later set of debates between Thomas Cranmer and Stephen Gardiner during the Edwardian Reforms of the 1550s. Cranmer holds that the Eucharist is called the sacrament of Christ's body and blood not because Christ is physically present but because it is conventional for signs to take the name of the things they signify. Cranmer predicates his theological interpretation on metonymy, which Anderson says "is the figure invoked by reformers of different stripes and with different intentions perhaps more often than any other to explain the words of institution."[100] Cranmer reasons, "As all sacraments be figures of other thynges, & yet have the very names of the thynges which thei do signifie, so Christ institutying the sacrament of his most precious body and bloud, did use figurative speaches, calling the bread by the name of his body, because it signifieth his body: and the wyne he called his bloud, be cause it represented his bloud."[101] Cranmer's metonymic reading of Christ's words works against the literalism of the Scholastics. "In plaine speech," Cranmer writes, "it is not true that we eate

Christes body and drynk his bloude. For eatyng and drynkyng in their proper and usual signification is with the tong, teeth, and lyppes, to swallow, divide, and chawe in peeces: which thinge to do to the flesh and bloud of Christe, is horrible to be hearde of any Christian."[102]

We have already seen in the debates between More and Tyndale how the literal sense could be accommodated to different arguments about the Eucharist. In *Detection of the Devils Sophistrie* (1546), Gardiner argues that it is reformers such as Cranmer and not defenders of transubstantiation who abuse the literal sense and speak of the Eucharist in carnal terms. As his title suggests, Gardiner adds that they commit such errors under the devil's influence.[103] Gardiner reasons that since reformers reject transubstantiation on the grounds that Christ's body and blood cannot be proven to exist in physical form within the consecrated host, it is *they* who fixate on a carnal interpretation.[104] Like More, Gardiner argues that the plain sense of scripture authorizes the doctrine of transubstantiation and that sensory proof is not necessary. He writes, "For as muche as the plaine wordes of Scripture, declare, and testifie unto us the presence of the most preciouse bodye and bloud of our Savior Christ, in the sacrament of the aulter, we should not be shaken or altered from that byleef, what so ever oure sense or carnal understanding should barke to the contrary."[105] Gardiner marshals the scriptures toward his own understanding of the literal sense, which he aligns with transubstantiation.

As these controversies illustrate, the literal sense is hardly stable in a Eucharistic context. The tension between literal and figurative interpretations of the Eucharist represents the attempt of both Catholics and evangelicals to arrest the signification of the sacrament and, more importantly, to authorize that signification as its singular literal sense. As Harding writes to Bishop Jewel, "Christ gave not a figure of his body, but his owne true body in substance, and likewise not a figure of his bloude, but his very pretiouse bloude it self. . . . The words of the institution of this sacrament admitte no other understanding, but that he geveth unto us in these holy mysteries, his self same body, and his selfe same bloude, in truth of substance, which was crucified and shedde forth for us."[106] Harding articulates one particular interpretation of the sacrament to the exclusion of all others. This compulsion to fix the meaning of the sacrament is frustrated by the fact that the sacrament itself calls semiotic closure into question by creating new possibilities for the operation of language itself. Arguments about what words can do in a sacramental context are the focus of the last section of this chapter, in which we turn to the notion, widely accepted in Catholic sacramental doctrine, that the words spoken by the priest during the Mass can make God present in the consecrated host.

Words and Deeds

How do words operate? What can words do? These are basic questions about linguistic efficacy that originate in sacramental discourse, particularly the Catholic doctrine of Eucharistic confection. According to this doctrine, Christ's body and blood are made present in substance after the priest pronounces the words of consecration, "Hoc est enim corpus meum." These five words challenge standing assumptions about the power of language in the world; indeed, they bear out Brian Cummings's claim that "the Reformation, among other things, involved an intense anxiety about how to do things with words."[107]

Eucharistic confection operates according to a theory of performative language (similar to the speech-act theory of J. L. Austin) in which words do not merely refer to, but bring about, the divine realities they signify. As Giorgio Agamben writes, "The paradox of sacramental theory . . . is that it presents us with something that is inseparable from the sign yet irreducible to it, a character or signature that by insisting on a sign makes it efficacious and capable of action."[108] The sacrament of the altar manifests not only a divine transformation in bread and wine but also an astonishing revaluation of the effects that words can achieve. Insofar as sacrament "signifies that which sanctifies," as Aquinas writes, it is regarded as an *opus operatum*—a work or act that is done or accomplished.[109] Peter the Lombard states that sacramental signs are far from ordinary because of their performativity. Therefore the words pronounced by the priest during the Mass are not ordinary words. "The sacraments were not instituted only for the sake of signifying," he writes in the *Sententiae*, "but also to sanctify."[110] What is performed at a sacramental level manifests a spiritual truth, and the sacramental signs and actions are themselves considered efficacious.

In the Eucharistic context, the words of consecration act with particular force, and because these words bring about the body of Christ in the world as a substantial reality, it is a force like no other. In speaking the words "This is my body," the priest does not simply recall Christ's sacrifice but re-creates it on the altar. "When these words are pronounced," writes the Lombard, "the change of the bread and wine into the substance of the body and blood of Christ occurs."[111] These words of consecration, Bishop Gardiner maintains, are "believed to be of effecte and operatorie, and they set forth lively unto us the communicacion of the substance of Christes most precious bodie in the Sacrament, and the same to be in dede delivered."[112] The doctrine of transubstantiation, in both its Scholastic origins and its sixteenth-century defenses, inheres not only in a miraculous transformation of the bread and wine but also in a specialized operation assigned to the words of consecration, which behave differently and achieve different effects than do ordinary words.

According to Catholic doctrine, the unique powers of sacramental language are firmly located within the auspices of the ordained priesthood, which is indispensable to the sacramental life of the church (a point discussed at greater length in chapter 4). As stated by the Fourth Lateran Council, "Nobody can effect this sacrament except a priest who has been properly ordained according to the church's keys, which Jesus Christ himself gave to his apostles and successors."[113] Though the words of consecration are actually quite ordinary words ("This is my body," "This is my blood"), they operate differently when used during the Mass. While the priest says these words, it is not his power that confects the Eucharist; rather he is the instrument through which Christ works. "The sacrament is confected by the word of Christ," says Lombard (following Ambrose), "because it is Christ's word that changes the created thing; and so from bread is made the body of Christ, and the wine mixed with water in the chalice, at the consecration of the divine word, becomes his blood."[114] Thus it is *God* who confects the sacrament; the words are his, not merely the priest's.

Many reformers reduced the doctrine of Eucharistic confection to a laughing matter.[115] They likewise rejected the doctrine of the keys, which authorized priestly authority, and regarded the priest as the consummate black magician. It was proverbial in anti-Catholic polemic for the Mass to be derogated as mere *hocus pocus* (a pejorative distortion of the words *Hoc est corpus meum*). But other objections were made on more technical grounds. In his *Defence*, for example, Cranmer specifically refutes the notion that upon the pronunciation of the words of consecration the substances of bread and wine are miraculously transformed so that the substance of Christ's body and blood can become present in them. While Cranmer acknowledges that the sacrament of the Lord's Supper is spiritually effective, he rejects previously held ideas about Eucharistic physics and semiotics, especially the assumptions about linguistic efficacy on which transubstantiation is based. In one of the most arresting linguistic analyses in the Eucharistic debates, Cranmer divides words of consecration into syllables in order to expose transubstantiation as an ontological impossibility:

> For (saye they) as soone as these wordes be fully ended, there is no bread lefte, nor none other substance, but only Christis body, Whan Christe sayd (this,) the bread (say they) remayned. And whan he sayde (is) yet the breade remained, and also when he added (my) the bread remayned stylle. And whan he sayd (bo-) yet the bread was there styll. But when he had finished the hole sentence, This is my body, than (say thei) the bread was gone, and there remayned no substance but Christes body as though the breade could not remaine, when it is made a sacramente, But this negative, that there is no bread, they make of their owne braynes, by theyr unwritten verytees.[116]

How, Cranmer reasons, could God's body be made present whole and entire in a piece of bread? How could such a momentous transformation occur in the short breath between syllables? Cranmer rebuts Aquinas's contention that the change in substance occurs instantaneously rather than successively. The change, says Aquinas, "is wrought by Christ's words, which are spoken by the priest, so that the last instant of pronouncing the words is the first instant in which Christ's body is in the sacrament; and that the substance of the bread is there during the whole preceding time."[117] In other words, bread remains bread until the priest has uttered the very last syllable of the words of consecration. At that instant, however, bread ceases to be bread and Christ's body is miraculously present. As his sardonic mimicry of Eucharistic confection suggests, Cranmer subscribes to none of this. Instead, as Anderson suggests, he "noticeably shifts the issue from being to calling, from object to language, truth to interpretation."[118] What transubstantiation declares to be true at the level of metaphysics is, for Cranmer, a manipulation of semiotics; what Aquinas regards as an extraordinary, miraculous change in substance, Cranmer sees as a renaming of bread as body. Gardiner says as much in his reply to Cranmer: "After the breade is consecrate by the prieste, goddess minister, and by the omnipotencie of Christes myghtye worde is converted into the body of Christ, the name that signifieth the substaunce of that sacramente is the body of Christ."[119] Is this a change in substance or a change in name? Gardiner seems to prove Cranmer's point.

The debates over Eucharistic confection and a confecting priesthood raise additional questions: What is the source of sacramental grace, and where is it located—in the sacramental words and acts or in the mystical reality they signify? As much as reformers rejected the premises of a confecting priesthood, they did not dispense with a notion of sacramental efficacy. The sacrament of the altar is indeed efficacious insofar as it brings about a spiritual reality, but its efficacy is not to be understood in terms of transubstantiation or confective language. As Calvin writes, "The sacrament . . . does not make Christ become for the first time the bread of life; but while it calls to remembrance that Christ was made the bread of life that we may constantly eat him it gives us a taste and relish for that bread and makes us feel its efficacy."[120] For Calvin, the sacramental effect is produced in the believer as a result of faithful reception rather than confection. Likewise, Richard Hooker argues, "The grace which we here receive doth in no way depend upon the naturall force of that which we presently behold." Instead, the liturgy recalls Christ's original words of institution and unites them to the sacramental action so that "one might infallibly teach what the other do most assuredly bring to pass."[121] Hooker distinguishes between the sacramental activity, which mortals perform, and its divine promise, which God fashions. "The use whereof is in our hands," he says of the Lord's Supper, "the effect is his."[122]

Hooker, like Calvin, shifts the focus of sacramental efficacy from the priest and the elements to the recipients who participate in the church's public worship. This is a shift away from Catholic theology, which held that Eucharistic reception was a vicarious act performed by the priest. During the Mass, the priest speaks the words of consecration silently in Latin, holds the host and chalice up for public adoration, and then communicates on behalf of the people. Eucharistic reception was in this sense dominantly visual; Christ's body and blood were most often received with the eyes at the moment of elevation rather than the mouth. When the laity did receive for themselves, they received the bread only; otherwise, they held fast to the belief that gazing on the host accomplished the same sacramental effect as eating it.[123]

With their theologies of sacramental participation, Hooker and Jewel revise the semiotic field in which Eucharistic reception was understood. In his description of the Eucharistic table, Jewel articulates the shift from priestly confection to a dialogic vernacular liturgy that emphasized not only the linguistic accessibility of an English text but also individual reception and participation in Christ's mystical body, the church. Jewel opens sacramental communion to all. "Unto this basket ought all the people to be bidden," he says, "that altogether might be partakers one with another, and might yelde an open signification and testimony of the fellowship thei have amongst them selfe, and of that same hope which thei have in Christ Jesus."[124] This mutual partaking, both of the sacrament and with one's neighbor, models a new form of sacramental conversion—one predicated not on a change of substance but on an act of faith. "Christ is present in the supper that by faith and in spirite we might eat him," says Jewel, "and out of hys passion and bloode we myghte drynke lyfe everlasting. And all this we say: is done not faynedly and coldely, but in very dede and truly. Albeit we touche not the body of Christ with our teeth and jawes, yet with faith, mynde, and spirite we take holde of hym and crushe hym."[125] Cranmer makes a similar point: "For as Christe is a spirituall meate, so is he spiritually eaten & digested with the spiritual part of us, & gyveth us spirituall & eternall lyfe, and is not eaten, swallowed, & digested with our teeth, tunges, throtes, & bellies."[126] Even in the absence of metaphysical transformation, the sacrament is no less efficacious. When he receives in faith, the recipient participates in and is changed by the divine realities in which he believes. "We knowe most assuredly that we are now become fleshe of his fleshe and bone of his bones: and that Christ dwelleth in us and we in him," says Jewel.[127] Jewel's chiasmus beautifully encapsulates at a rhetorical level the threefold incorporation of Christ, recipient, and church that occurs at a sacramental level.

This chapter has shown that Eucharistic discourse should not be reduced to a series of esoteric debates about substance and accidents. Its reach was far greater. The Eucharist opens up a space between declaration and interrogation, a space between the idea that a piece of bread can become the body of Christ and the confusion surrounding how (or whether) that body is really present. These controversies over the sacrament do not simply die out after the Elizabethan Settlement. While it can be argued that the 1559 *Book of Common Prayer* reaches a compromise position that alleviates some of the doctrinal and liturgical instability that characterized England during the reigns of Edward VI and Mary I, the Eucharistic Controversies—particularly the semiotic problems they generate—are invigorated anew in both religious and secular dramas. The remainder of this book discusses how a Eucharistic semiotics, which often emphasizes the rifts between flesh and text, inflects dramatic representations of body and sign at a time when both religion and drama were subject to ongoing reformations.

TWO

Words and Wounds

Christ Crucified and Coriolanus

In a Good Friday sermon preached in or around 1533, the Catholic bishop of Rochester, John Fisher, compares Christ's body to a book, his blood to ink, and his wounds to textual inscriptions. Christ's crucified body becomes a surface so penetrated and gashed that "there was no margent lefte in all thys booke, there was no voyd place, but every where it was eyther drawne with lynes, or els written with letters, for these scourges fylled not onely his most precyous bodie with lynes drawne every where, but also left many small Letters, some blacke, some blewe, some reade."[1] In limning Christ's wounds this way, Fisher draws on the affective piety tradition of the late Middle Ages.[2] This tradition was constructed in a range of vernacular literatures including religious lyrics and prayers; the *Stanzaic Life of Christ* and the *Northern Passion*; Nicholas Love's *Mirror of the Blessed Life of Jesus Christ*; and especially the biblical dramas of Christ's crucifixion and resurrection.[3] In making books, ink, and letters the vehicles of his metaphor, Bishop Fisher figures Christ's body as a textual surface and thus draws the affective response toward semiotic interpretation. Fisher suggests that the act of seeing Christ's wounds involves a reciprocal act of reading those wounds. As a physical aperture, the wound acts as a portal into the body of Christ. As a fleshly sign, it is the primary means by which Christ's body can be put into words and interpreted.[4]

This chapter focuses on such a connection between wounds and words in biblical dramas of Christ's passion and Shakespeare's Roman tragedy *Coriolanus* (1608–9). The plays all but defy comparison. The biblical dramas are built on scriptural, theological, and liturgical narratives and traditions.

They focus on incarnational topoi, particularly the body of Christ. By contrast, *Coriolanus* is based on the classical Roman histories of Plutarch and Livy and focuses on a martial hero's conquest of enemy powers, his refusal of political participation, and his eventual exile and death. Despite their differences, however, these dramas pivot on a wounded body situated at the center of a public gaze. Naked and dying, Christ is described in the York cycle with "his flessh al beflapped" and as one who "schalle be flaied," ultimately left "ragged and rent on this roode."[5] After defeating the Volscians, Coriolanus "does appear as he were flayed" (a linguistic echo of the "flaied" Christ in the York plays) and is described, like Christ, as "a thing of blood."[6] In addition to their shared dramatic representations, the wounded bodies of Christ and Coriolanus signify the formation of social communities. In the biblical dramas, Christ's body galvanizes public devotion and interpretation; in Shakespeare's tragedy, Coriolanus's body figures forth the nationalist ideology of *pietas* in ancient Rome.[7] In both plays, the capacity to behold and interpret wounds, which renders the body a readable text and part of a semiotic system, is a pivotal condition on which these related aesthetic and social dynamics turn.

This chapter does not pursue an allegorical reading of Coriolanus as a Christ figure but rather demonstrates how Shakespeare reimagines the semiotics of Christ's wounds as represented in biblical dramas both performed and compiled in manuscript well into the sixteenth century. *Coriolanus* exemplifies how Shakespeare "was notably open-ended and flexible in his religious thinking as he worked creatively in a multifaceted Protestant culture that not only destroyed but assimilated vestiges of its Catholic past."[8] At the same time, however, Shakespeare reimagines biblical drama with a crucial difference—a difference that has everything to do with how Coriolanus's wounded body is constructed semiotically and interpreted by the Roman citizenry. In biblical drama, Christ exposes his body to the passersby who behold it hanging on the cross; he then reveals his glorified body to the disciples after the Resurrection. Moreover, in those biblical dramas performed as civic cycles, namely the York and Chester plays, Christ's body was acted by members of artisan guilds and performed for a witnessing public audience in the city streets. By contrast, Shakespeare writes Coriolanus as an insular character who refuses to participate in the drama of the commons. Rather than allow the public to see his wounded body as Christ does, Coriolanus makes his wounds unavailable, his body unreadable, and participation in civic performance impossible. In effect, he removes his body from the language of the people.

In the first section below, I survey recent arguments about the periodization of early English drama in order to lay additional groundwork for my subsequent discussion of the semiotics of wounds in biblical dramas and *Coriolanus*. The vast body of scholarship made possible by the Records of Early English Drama (REED) has challenged prevailing assumptions about what early English drama (especially religious drama) was; how, when, and by whom it was performed; and in what contexts these performances and manuscripts were received.[9] In surveying some of these arguments, I hope to illustrate, particularly for those who remain skeptical about the critical import of biblical drama for Shakespeare and his contemporaries, how so-called "medieval" dramas have important sixteenth-century afterlives. The interplay of medieval and early modern, as well as religious and secular drama, suggests a history of dramatic compilation, performance, and reception that is more complicated than once assumed. It also opens up a new route by which to chart Shakespeare's engagements with important dramatic forms, texts, and traditions written and staged before the rise of the commercial theater in 1576.

Shakespeare and Biblical Drama

Regardless of whether he saw biblical dramas performed firsthand, Shakespeare refers to them on more than one occasion. The most explicit description of Christ's body in the Shakespearean corpus occurs at the start of *1 Henry 4* (1598), where King Henry draws on the familiar iconography of Christ's wounds in describing his intended crusade to the Holy Land: "Forthwith a power of English shall we levy . . . To chase these pagans in those holy fields / Over whose acres walked those blessed feet / Which fourteen hundred years ago were nailed, / For our advantage, on the bitter cross."[10] Shakespeare cites conventional emblems of the Passion—the nails, Christ's "blessed feet," the "bitter cross"—that not only signify religious crusade and penitential pilgrimage but also recall the Crucifixion and Resurrection plays in which Christ's wounded body was dramatized over a span of two hundred years—plays that continued to be compiled and read in manuscripts through the early seventeenth century.[11]

Despite the richness of such textual interactions, critics have for too long derogated biblical drama as blandly allegorical if not also aesthetically deficient. Its suppression has been seen as a welcome achievement of the Protestant Reformation and its supersession by a secular commercial theater hailed as nothing short of a triumph.[12] Yet as we now know, religious dramas were not formally suppressed until well into Elizabeth I's reign (as late as 1569 in York, 1575 in Chester, and 1579 in Coventry). And while biblical drama originated with the *quem quaeritis* tradition in the tenth century and reached its apex in the late Middle Ages, such drama was revised, compiled in manuscripts, and restaged throughout the sixteenth century and into the early seventeenth. What is more, the sixteenth century also saw John Bale's reformed religious dramas as well as the creation and performance of distinctly Protestant Resurrection plays, such as the anonymous *Resurrection of Our Lorde* (ca. 1530–60), which I discuss in chapter 6.

The endurance of biblical drama into the sixteenth century sufficiently complicates long-standing histories of English drama by revealing a complex negotiation of traditional and reformed doctrines, devotional practices, and hermeneutics across the periodic borders of "medieval" and "early modern." It also requires a revision of terminology. In this chapter and throughout the book, I employ the terms *biblical drama* and *religious drama* as alternatives to the more familiar (but also misleading) terms *cycle plays* and *Corpus Christi plays*. Recent scholarship has shown that not every biblical drama is a "cycle play" or "Corpus Christi play" and that cycle plays were not the dominant form of drama in late medieval England.[13] Both Lawrence Clopper and Paul Whitfield White argue that biblical dramas were part of a much larger network of urban, professional, and folk drama.[14] Moreover, Alexandra F. Johnston trenchantly interrogates the term *Corpus Christi play*, suggesting that evidence does not support a stand-alone drama that emerges out of, and is unique to, the liturgical feast. Johnston asserts that "Corpus Christi drama as a genre simply did not and does not exist except as a scholarly construct as old as the first commentators on English biblical drama."[15] In fact, the York cycle now appears to be the only surviving medieval cycle of biblical plays performed specifically for the Corpus Christi feast, which has long been noted for the town-wide processions that made Christ's Eucharistic presence visible to a social community. Despite the association between some civic cycle plays and the liturgical feast of Corpus Christi, Johnston reminds us that "medieval England had an important tradition of biblical plays of all shapes and sizes designed for presentation at Easter or at one of the seasonal festivals." There was more to medieval drama than the cycle play, and there were more occasions for dramatic performance than just the Corpus Christi feast, she argues: "These plays could be prophet plays, plays on Old Testament themes, passion plays, resurrection plays, 'Creation to Doomsday' sequences, plays on the Creed or the Pater Noster . . . or plays on the sacrament itself, such as the Croxton *Play of the Sacrament*. They could have protestant leanings or be staunchly catholic. . . . There were also saints plays, morality plays, and folk plays, particularly the ubiquitous Robin Hood plays."[16]

Rethinking such familiar terms as *cycle plays* and *Corpus Christi plays* also suggests the need to reconsider the periodic categories by which biblical drama has been conventionally understood. Just as all late medieval religious drama is not associated with Corpus Christi (and conversely, not all Corpus Christi plays are cyclical or even religious), many of the plays long categorized as "late medieval" exhibit histories of performance, compilation, and reception that suggest pervasive and consequential postmedieval afterlives. In a recent essay entitled "The Tudor Origins of Medieval Drama," Theresa Coletti and Gail McMurray Gibson testify to the importance of such afterlives, arguing that "much medieval English drama survives today because Tudor and Stuart antiquarians and recusants compiled, collected, and preserved these texts from an imperiled past."[17] They go on to critique "prevalent assumptions regarding radical distinctions between medieval and early modern dramatic traditions, distinctions often articulated through binary categories that characterize medieval drama as communal, sacred, and Catholic and its early modern counterpart as professional, secular, and Protestant."[18] Crossing these categorical borders complicates the assumptions underlying a teleological history of early English drama and suggests that this history can no longer be read as an uncomplicated progression from the religious to the secular or from the medieval to the early modern. As Clopper argues, "A history of the drama that encourages in any way an evolutionary model—medieval to early Tudor to Renaissance or Elizabethan drama—or that ignores the persistence of medieval drama in the sixteenth century is an intellectual scam to maintain a distinction between us, we moderns, and them, those medieval people."[19]

Rather than homogenize the diverse range of English drama before Shakespeare, then, we must approach each biblical drama—particularly the four extant "Creation to Doomsday" plays (York, Chester, N-Town, and Towneley)—as "a unique literary collection which holds its own manuscript history, performance history, provenance, and developmental circumstances."[20] Work on such issues is now in full bloom, but a short summary of critical positions and working hypotheses can provide useful grounding, especially to readers unfamiliar with these important critical developments.

Both the York and the Chester plays were performed as civic cycles, but only York can be properly regarded as a late medieval cycle play performed for the feast of Corpus Christi. The York cycle was staged by artisan guilds as early as 1377, and the date of its final performance is most likely 1569. The only extant text of these plays is contained in the York Register (British Library MS Additional 35290), which dates to the middle of the fifteenth century (ca. 1463–77) and was used as an official document against which the words spoken during a performance of the plays were compared. The dating of the Register, Richard Beadle explains, helps us to understand that the surviving text of the plays is nearly a century later than the earliest possible date of their performance. "The script as preserved," Beadle says, "reflects for the most part a version of the cycle current in the third quarter of the fifteenth century, already much revised from earlier forms, and itself subject to substantial alteration until the religious drama was fully suppressed in York about a century later."[21] Before the late fifteenth century, Beadle goes on to note, there was no complete text of the York Corpus Christi play. It was the Register itself that gave a textual form to "the impressively unified cycle"; until then, such unity "existed solely on the occasion of performance."[22]

In addition to York, Chester sponsored the civic performance of religious drama, and we know that the five surviving manuscript texts of the Chester cycle were copied between 1591 and 1607.[23] Clopper has traced the documentary evidence to show that as early as 1422 Chester had a Corpus Christi play, but these earlier versions were likely short Passion plays rather than complete cycles.[24] The shorter play developed into a longer, more complete cycle only after the Passion play was moved from the feast of Corpus Christi to Whitsunday (Pentecost) in or near 1521; thus, as Clopper maintains, the Chester cycle "was largely an invention of Tudor times."[25] May games, morris dances, and other folk dramas were commonplace during Whitsuntide, a well-known period of festivity in England's civic calendar. Whitsun dramas, it is worth pointing out, were well known to Shakespeare, who refers to them at least twice. In *The Winter's Tale*, Perdita says, "Methinks I play as I have seen them do / In Whitsun pastorals"; in *Two Gentlemen of Verona*, moreover, Julia mentions "Pentecost / When all our pageants of delight were played."[26]

In contrast to York and Chester, the N-Town and Towneley plays are not civic cycle plays (as was long assumed) but rather are manuscript compilations of biblical dramas that may also have been performed before or after their compilation.[27] As Clopper writes of the N-Town play, "It is obvious that the manuscript is a compilation of plays originally of separate and earlier origin that were brought together by the scribe-compiler no earlier than the last decade of the fifteenth century."[28] In addition to the N-Town play, critics have devoted significant attention to the compilation of the Towneley plays, formerly regarded as the "Wakefield cycle." The name for this collection of religious drama derives from the Towneleys, a prominent English recusant family from Lancashire who long possessed the manuscript. The Towneley plays have often been studied in relation to the York Cycle, and as Beadle posits, similarities in theme, language, and content suggest that Towneley could even be considered a variant of York.[29] Yet as Barbara Palmer has influentially argued, the Towneley manuscript does not constitute the record of a civic cycle play from Wakefield, a Yorkshire town she suggests was too small to support such an undertaking.[30] Instead it was nineteenth- and twentieth-century antiquarians and historians who created this narrative about the plays contained in the Towneley manuscript. In 1814, Palmer explains, the manuscript was included in the sale of items from John Towneley's library. In his catalog description for that auction, the antiquarian Francis Douce described the manuscript as "a Collection of English Mysteries or Theatrical Pageants . . . formerly belonging to the Abbey of Widkirk, near Wakefield, in the county of York. It contains several *mysteries* or theatrical *pageants*, constructed from incidents in the Old and New Testaments."[31] At the turn of the twentieth century, moreover, the historian John Walker and a grammar school headmaster named Matthew Peacock characterized the plays in the Towneley manuscript as a large-scale "Wakefield cycle."[32] This characterization was not supported by credible evidence; rather, as Palmer writes, it "was pieced together of fragmentary historical information, other towns' records, anachronistic generalizations, and at least one serious misreading of a Burgess Court record which [Walker] used to construct an entire performance history of a Wakefield

Corpus Christi professional guild cycle."[33] In fact, Palmer shows that Walker was so intent to prove that the Towneley manuscript was the record of a biblical cycle that he not only misread or wrongly transcribed but also outright forged much of his evidence.[34] Palmer thus underscores the point that the received history of the Towneley manuscript—as well as the terms used to think about that history—is based not on contexts indigenous to the play's compilation or possible performance but rather on the conjectures (if not forgeries) of later historians, antiquarians, and local enthusiasts.

The range of critical arguments over the Towneley manuscript provenance has only intensified since the publication of Palmer's influential essay in 1988. Many recent studies have been keen to focus on the manuscript's sixteenth-century afterlives, a topic pertinent to the present chapter. In one such study, Coletti and Gibson work from Malcolm Parkes's conclusion that the Towneley manuscript was written during Mary I's reign (1553–58) to posit that the plays could have been compiled for the occasion of the marriage of Mary and John Towneley in 1556.[35] In this context, the manuscript would pay "unifying homage to sacred history of both biblical and Catholic past" as well as provide "a fitting symbol of that occasion and of both Marys—Mary Towneley and Mary Tudor—whose very names celebrated the Mary invoked in the opening inscription of the Towneley manuscript."[36] In addition to marking the marriage, moreover, the manuscript as textual object could index a local history of early modern English Catholicism, for "the Towneley manuscript's compilation of biblical plays once presented all over Lancashire and Yorkshire—including Wakefield—into a chronological sequence seems a response to the short-lived return to official Catholicism under Mary Tudor."[37] Far from a record of a late medieval "Wakefield cycle," the Towneley manuscript could well play a distinct role in enabling an ardent English Catholic family to maintain traditional devotional practices through the act of reading biblical drama in the mid-sixteenth century.[38]

Coletti and Gibson's hypothesis represents but one of several recent claims put forward about the Towneley manuscript's compilation, provenance, and reception.[39] At the very least, such an argument for the early Tudor contexts of the Chester and Towneley plays encourages us to reconsider commonly held assumptions about biblical drama and its afterlives. Sixteenth-century revisions and compilations demonstrate the adaptability of biblical drama to England's shifting religious landscape, a point I will consider in the next section. Such adaptability is likely one reason for the endurance of biblical drama across different stages of religious reform in Edwardian, Marian, and Elizabethan England.[40] What is more, the sixteenth-century circulation of biblical drama, both in performance and in manuscript compilation, presents sufficient cause to break down prevailing oppositions between late medieval biblical drama and early modern secular drama. While local disagreements about the provenance and compilation of early English drama remain, the debate shows that it is now shortsighted, if not impossible, to cordon off "Shakespearean" or "post-Reformation" drama as an entity independent from the texts, performances, and reception histories of earlier dramatic forms—both the biblical dramas studied in this chapter and many other nonreligious festive performances—that extend across the medieval/early modern divide.

In what follows, I will consider dramas of Christ's passion and resurrection, paying particular attention to how these dramas—both the civic performances of York and Chester and the N-Town and Towneley manuscript compilations—engage the semiotics of Christ's wounded body in a Eucharistic context and in so doing give voice to various strands of theological controversy across the medieval/early modern divide. That discussion will ground my reading of *Coriolanus*, in which I argue that Shakespeare stages a failed leader who cuts his wounds off from public viewing and removes himself from both the performance of political ceremony and the formation of interpretive community. Shakespeare's reworking of material from biblical drama constitutes not simply a set of thematic parallels or literary allusions but something more akin to a theoretical refashioning of the semiotics of wounds and words set forth in dramatic representations of Christ's body.

Signs on the Cross

In the York *Crucifixion*, staged by the Pinners, Christ's body is contorted, stretched, and wrenched about so that it will fit an ill-measured crossbeam. The boisterous din of the soldiers, conveyed in hasty monosyllables, translates Christ's sacrifice into a day's labor and his divine body into that of an ordinary criminal. "Faste on a corde / And tugge hym to, by toppe and taile" (113–14), says one soldier; "Heve uppe! / Latte doune, so all his bones /

Are asoundre nowe on sides seere" (222–24), say two others.[41] As Peter Travis notes, images of fleshly wounds so dominate these dramas that we see Christ's body "gradually transformed into a pulpy mass of welts, lacerations, bruises, and open sores."[42] In the Towneley *Resurrection*, for example, Christ refers to his "woundes . . . weytt and alle blody," his body "Alle to-rent and alle-toshentt," and the work of the soldiers who "with cordes enewe and ropys toghe . . . / felle my lymmes out-droghe."[43] In the Chester *Passion*, moreover, the Virgin Mary finds her "sonne here me before, / tugget, lugget, and all totorne / with traytors nowe this tyde, / with nayles thrast and crowne of thorne."[44] And in the N-Town *Crucifixion* Mary laments her "swete sone with peynes stronge," while in the *Harrowing of Hell* play Anima Christi discloses, "My body is ded — the Jewys it slew — / That hangyth yitt on the rode, / Rent and torn, all blody red."[45]

While the physicality of Christ's wounds resonates with the late medieval affective piety tradition, I want to move beyond affective piety to demonstrate that these dramas make sacramental encounters into semiotic encounters, a dynamic that also plays out in the sixteenth-century afterlives of these biblical dramas.[46] More specifically, in foregrounding the interplay between body and language, these dramas reproduce many of the semiotic issues raised in the Eucharistic Controversies. That is, these dramas not only reflect familiar scriptural, liturgical, or devotional iconographies but re-create, and in many cases intensify, the interpretive debates occasioned by the sacrament of the altar. Sarah Beckwith says of incarnational drama, "Since God cannot be understood propositionally, it is in the reach and resource of a symbolic language that he has to be not so much understood, as approached."[47] The biblical dramas of the Passion and the Resurrection demonstrate how such an approach requires Christ's wounds to be understood as both flesh and sign. In turn, the plays do not simply make Christ's body the center of a dramatic spectacle: they reproduce the curious semiotics of the Eucharist itself.

What is particularly striking about many biblical dramas, moreover, is that Christ himself emerges as the author of the semiotic system within which his wounded body can be read and interpreted. The questions about semiotic representation and interpretation not only constellate around Christ's body but also take shape in Christ's own speeches. In this regard, Christ becomes less a passive recipient of physical torture and more a catalyst of hermeneutical struggle. He gives voice to his wounded body, putting it into words and inviting those who look upon it to link flesh to sign. For example, in the York *Death of Christ*, staged by the Butchers (who dealt with flesh, blood, and broken bones as part of their daily labor), Christ describes his wounds in three separate complaints before he dies (118–30, 183–95, 248–60). In each speech he draws attention to his body "ragged and rente" (120, 253), to the breaking and bending of his bones (123–24, 186), and to the "bittirfull bale" (183) that he suffers for the sake of humankind.[48] In the York *Last Judgment* pageant, moreover, Christ repeats this catalog of torments almost verbatim (253–300) and ends with a pointed challenge: "Say, man, what suffered thou for me?" (276). In all these contexts, Christ suggests that his wounds are significant not on account of their brute physicality but because of their salvific function. Those who behold Christ's crucified body both within and without the play must interpret that body in terms of their own sinfulness and the salvation Christ's passion wins for them.

In the York cycle, Christ's wounded body is publicly displayed both to the onlookers in the play and to the spectators watching on the city streets. The elevation and presentation of Christ's body, which has direct liturgical antecedents in the *elevatio* of the Mass, is the climax of the whole cycle.[49] This spectacular gesture fixes a city's collective gaze on Christ's body and mobilizes its interpretive activity. Christ, who has erstwhile been silent amid the chatter of the bumbling soldiers, addresses the people directly as he blazons his wounds:

> Al men that walkis by waye or strete,
> Takes tente ye schalle no travayle tyne.
> Byholdes myn heede, myn handis, and my feete,
> And fully feele nowe, or ye fyne,
> Yf any mournyng may be meete,
> Or myscheve mesured unto myne.
> My fadir, that alle bales may bete,
> Forgiffis thes men that dois me pyne.
> (*Crucifixio*, 253–64)

In hailing "Al men that walkis by" (253), Christ fashions his self-blazon as a public address in which he figures his wounds as signs of salvation. The speech echoes the *O vos omnes* hymn, based on Lamentations 1:12. This hymn is adapted in late medieval religious lyrics, sung during the Easter

Triduum liturgy, and even recalled in many Good Friday sermons preached in the Church of England.[50] Christ makes a similar speech, also evocative of *O vos omnes*, in the Towneley *Crucifixion*:

> I pray you pepylle, that passe me by
> That lede youre lyfe so lykandly,
> Heyfe up youre hertes on highte,
> if ever ye saw body
> Suffer and bett thus blody.
>
> (86v)

If this play was indeed read in manuscript by a recusant family like the Towneleys (as Coletti and Gibson suggest), then the *O vos omnes* could function in this context as a call to devotional contemplation of the wounds—a call also predicated on an understanding of Christ's body as the sign of sacrifice and salvation.[51] The play figures wounds in such a context when Christ consoles the Virgin Mary, who is overcome with grief at the fact that Christ's flesh, which she figures Eucharistically as "the foode that I have fed," has been so mangled. Christ reminds her that this sacrifice is intended for the salvation of all humankind: "Blo [blue] and blody / thus am I bett, / Swongen wit swepys & all to-swett, / Mankynde, for thi mysdede!" (86v).

Both York and Towneley suggest that in displaying his wounds Christ demands more than "an onlooker's silent complicity";[52] in addition, he requires an active semiotic response. In the *O vos omnes* speech, Christ shapes a reading practice that tethers visual devotion to semiotic interpretation. (He reprises the invitation during his post-Resurrection appearances to Mary Magdalene, discussed below, and to Doubting Thomas and others in the Emmaus plays discussed in chapter 6.) Christ initiates this reading practice with the imperative "Behold," which functions repeatedly as a call not only to gaze upon but also to interpret his body: "Byholdes myn heede, myn handis, and my feete" (York *Crucifixion*, 255); "Behold if ever ye saw body / Suffer and bett thus blody" (Towneley *Crucifixion*, 86v). In the Towneley *Resurrection*, moreover, Christ uses the same verb at least six times after he rises from the dead. He enjoins the disciples to "Behald how dere I would thee buy! / My wounds are wet and all bloody," to "Behald my body, in each place / How sore a sight; / Torn in this depe disgrace," and to

"Behald my shankes and my knees, / Myn armes and my thees, / Behold me well, loke what thou sees" (103v–104r). These commands anticipate a final catalog of tortures:

> Behold my body how Jues it dang
> With knottes of whyppys and scorges strang,
> As stremes of welle the bloode out sprang
> On every side;
> Knottes where thay hyt, welle may thou wytt,
> Maide woundes wyde.
>
> (104r)

Christ anatomizes his broken body part by part and wound by wound. Not only does he offer the image of his broken body to the reader, but he also supplies the textual apparatus—the words, the figures of speech, the linguistic and corporeal signs—by which it can be made legible. Such a transformation of body into sign is particularly evident in the York *Road to Calvary* play, where the Third Mary pleads, "A, lorde, beleve lete clense thy face." Left with Christ's image on her cloth (a miracle frequently attributed to Saint Veronica) she says, "Behalde, howe he hath schewed his grace, / Howe he is moste of mayne! / This signe schalle bere witnesse / Unto all pepull playne, / Howe Goddes sone here gilteles, / Is putte to pereles payne" (183–89).[53] This cloth crosses the interpretive categories of flesh and text. Christ's image impressed on Mary's cloth not only leaves a physical trace of Christ's real presence but also functions as a sign of his passion and the salvation it wins for humankind.

The rhetorical conventions of the *O vos omnes* trope—specifically the delineation of Christ's wounds, the call to behold them, and the beholder's need to connect those wounds to his own sinfulness—are reproduced across historical and confessional divides, particularly in the Church of England's Good Friday sermons. In one such sermon preached before James I in 1604, Lancelot Andrewes writes, "Our very eye will soone tell us, No place was left in his Body, where he might bee smitten, & was not. His Skin and flesh rent with the whips & scourges, His hands and feet wounded with the nailes, His head with the thornes, His very Heart with the speare point; All his senses, all his parts loden with whatsoever wit or malice could invent. His blessed Body given as an Anvile to bee beaten upon, with the violent hands of those barbarous miscreants, til they brought him into this case."[54] Andrewes's sermon, which suggests comparisons with both biblical drama and John Fisher's Good Friday sermon discussed at the chapter's outset, is remarkable for its intense focus on the wounds of Christ. Because the sermon is verbal rather than visual, however, Andrewes relies on anaphora and zeugma—"His skin and flesh rent with the whips & scourges, His hands and feet wounded with the nails, His head with the thorns, His very Heart with the speare point"—to elaborate the emotional intensity of Christ's crucifixion wounds. His rhetorical repetition is meant to evoke a keen penitential response in the auditor.

A similar focus on Christ's wounded body is evident in an Elizabethan *Homilie for Good Friday*. The same imperative verb, *behold*, used in the biblical dramas now compels the congregation to acknowledge Christ's sacrifice and repent their sins:

> Call to mynde, O sinfull creature, and set before thine eyes Christ crucified. Thinke thou seest his body stretched out in length upon the crosse, his head crowned with sharpe thorne, his hands & his feete pearsed with nayles, his hart opened with a long speare, his fleshe rent & torne with whyppes, his browes sweating water & bloud. Thynke thou hearest hym nowe crying in an intolerable agonie to his father, and saying: My God, my God, why hast thou forsaken me. Couldest thou beholde this wofull syght, or heare this mournefull voice, without teares, considering that he suffered all this not for any desert of his owne, but onely for the greevousnes of thy synnes?[55]

Like Andrewes's sermon, the *Homilie* blazons the body of Christ with phrases that echo the dramas of Christ's passion. The homily delineates various stages of torment ranging from the stretching of Christ's body on the cross to the crowning with thorns to Christ's final utterance. This blazon, offered here not by an actor personating Christ on the cross but by a priest in the pulpit, makes a similar demand on the laity: to "behold this woefull syght" is to recognize one's own sin and thereby to see the Passion as a sign of one's salvation.[56]

To "behold" Christ in both the biblical dramas and the Reformation era homilies is at once to see, to read, and to acknowledge; it is also to contemplate, interpret, and confess. These semiotic and sacramental energies are carried over from the Passion sequence itself to Christ's Resurrection and post-Resurrection appearances staged in subsequent plays. One such episode occurs in the York *Christ's Appearance to Mary Magdalene*. The Magdalene models the interpretive response the Passion plays are meant to achieve: she first recognizes the glorified Christ according to the wounds marked on his body and then reads these wounds as signs of her own sinfulness, and thus her need for salvation won by Christ's passion.[57] During his encounter with Mary, Christ repeats the command to interpret his wounds set forth during his *O vos omnes* speech in the York *Crucifixion*: "Beholde my woundes wyde, / thus for mannys synnes I schedde my bloode ... / thus was I rased on the roode, / With spere and nayles that were unride" (*Mary Magdalene*, 63–64, 66–68). The Magdalene responds by reaching out to touch Christ's body but meets a stern reproof: "Goo awaye, Marie, and touche me nought / But take goode kepe what I schall saie: / I ame hee that all thyng wroght, / That thou callis thi lorde and God verraye" (72–75).[58] Christ's *noli me tangere* redirects an encounter initially based on physical contact to an encounter that foregrounds semiotic interpretation. Mary cannot touch the glorified body of Christ, so Christ himself puts that body into words, disclosing his identity as the risen Lord by linking the divine body she sees to its significations of salvation. The Magdalene's understanding of the Resurrection is thus contingent not on corporeal proof (of the sort demanded by Doubting Thomas) but on reading Christ's body as a sign of her salvation.

In redirecting a physical encounter between Christ and Mary Magdalene toward a more complex semiotic encounter, this poignant scene models an interpretive response to the Resurrection in Eucharistic terms. When Mary reads Christ's wounds, she does so according to the specific terms Christ set forth earlier when he blazoned his body on the cross. "Mi lorde Jesu, I know nowe the, / thi woundes thai are nowe wette" (80–81), she says. Later, when Christ commands her, "Marie, in thyne harte thou write / Myne armoure riche and goode" (94–95), she answers,

> A blessid body that bale wolde beete,
> Dere haste thou bought mankynne.
> Thy woundes hath made thi body wete,
> With bloode that was the withinne.
> Nayled thou was thurgh hande and feete,

> And all was for our synne ...
> To se this ferly foode,
> Thus ruffuly dight,
> Rugged and rente on a roode,
> This is a rewfull sight;
> And all is for our goode,
> And nothyng for his plight.
> Spilte thus is his bloode,
> For ilke a synfull wight.
> (110–15, 118–25)

Mary Magdalene acknowledges Christ's passion and resurrection by, in effect, blazoning Christ's wounded body again. She further connects Christ's resurrected body to the Eucharist by figuring Christ as as "frely foode," an idiom common to biblical drama.[59] This figuration recalls Mary Magdalene's earlier lament over the loss of Christ's body: "For it wolde do my sorowe to slake / Whe[n] Goddis body founded myght be" (45–46).[60] Richard Beadle reads the phrase "Goddis body" as "an overtly eucharistic expression" that also echoes the levation prayers recited by the laity when the priest elevated the host and chalice.[61] The encounter between Christ and Mary Magdalene concludes with Christ asking her to further disseminate his body in language. In one of the foundational acts of preaching after the Resurrection, Mary must go to Galilee and "Tell thame ilke worde to ende, / that thou spake with me here" (146–47).

Christ's Appearance to Mary Magdalene frames an interpretive and sacramental response to the wounded body of Christ that gestures toward the semiotic problems posed by the Eucharist in both late medieval and sixteenth-century controversies. Such a position is articulated with greater verve in the Towneley and Chester plays, where it is often difficult to pin down the precise sort of Eucharistic language that is used or the precise theological claims it organizes. Presenting the link between Christ's resurrected body and his Eucharistic body according to conflicting theological and semiotic positions offers one example of what Theresa Coletti sees as the play's more general pattern of "toggling back and forth between traditionalist and reformist possibilities for interpretation."[62] The different sacramental modalities by which Christ's Eucharistic body is represented enrich, because they complicate, each other.

One example of such complication is evident in the Towneley *Resurrection* when, at the very instance of his resurrection, Christ launches into an exposition on the Eucharist and the Mass:

> I grauntt theym here a measse [Mass]
> In breade myn awne body.
> That ilk veray brede of lyfe
> Becomys my fleshe in wordes fyfe,
> Who so it resaves in syn or stryfe
> Bese dede for ever;
> And who so it takes in rightwys lyfe
> Dy shalle he never.
>   (104v)

Christ identifies himself as the Eucharistic bread by linking his resurrected body specifically to the Mass, in which the "wordes fyfe" spoken by the priest ("Hoc est enim corpus meum") make, or confect, Christ's body in the host.[63] Christ's direct reference to transubstantiation—specifically the lines running from "Becomys my fleshe" to "Dy shalle he never"—would appeal to recusant families like the Towneleys, who stood fast to the old faith and would likely have relished (if not commissioned) such Eucharistic material in the manuscript.[64] The same passage, however, is crossed out in red ink in the single extant manuscript of the Towneley plays (Huntington MS HM 1), which suggests a later revision intended, perhaps, to make the play acceptable to reformed audiences. Such revision is not, as Murray McGillivray argues, violently iconoclastic, for "The methods used to cancel the passage are notable for their lack of ferocity, since they all leave the text perfectly legible . . . and it is difficult to avoid the conclusion that the person or persons who did this work were not so offended by these references as to attempt to obliterate them."[65]

The theological ambiguity evident in this emendation to the Towneley manuscript is embedded more deeply in the Chester *Resurrection*. The Chester cycle as a whole does not dwell extensively on Christ's bloody body and broken bones as do the York cycle and Towneley plays. Instead, the Chester cycle presents Christ's death as what Peter Travis calls "a tolerable aesthetic experience," an experience grounded in scriptural texts rather than liturgical conventions like the *O vos omnes* hymn or the levation prayers.[66]

Yet the Chester *Resurrection* witnesses a critical emphasis on Christ's body, namely the semiotic link between Christ's glorified body and his Eucharistic body. The Chester *Resurrection* engages Eucharistic controversy head on when, in a manner similar to Towneley, Christ uses the occasion of his resurrection to articulate multiple semiotic and theological interpretations of the Eucharist:

> I grant them peace trulye
> And therto a ful rych messe [Mass]
> In bread, my owne bodye.
> I am verey bread of liffe.
> From heaven I light and am send.
> Whoe eateth that bread, man or wiffe,
> Shal lyve with me withowt end.
> And that bread that I you give,
> Your wicked life to amend,
> Becomes my fleshe through your beleeffe
> And doth release your synfull band.
> (167–77)

This is the only time Christ speaks in the *Resurrection*. Here he teaches about Eucharistic theology and liturgy in the didactic manner of Chester's Expositor, a figure absent in the Passion sequence.[67] Over the course of his post-Resurrection exposition, Christ does not define the sacrament as much as disseminate it into multiple theological and semiotic positions.

Christ begins his post-Resurrection speech by referring to the Eucharistic ritual as a "ful rych messe," or "Mass," a term that refers explicitly to the Catholic liturgy.[68] As the speech continues, it echoes the controversial passage in John 6 (discussed in the previous chapter), where Christ calls himself the bread of life and says that whoever eats his flesh and drinks his blood will live forever: "Whose eateth that bread, man or wiffe / Shal lyve with me withowt end" (172–73). Christ further connects the "bread of liffe" (170) offered in the Eucharist to his own body risen from the grave. With that said, however, the Chester play does not contain the kind of explicit reference to transubstantiation found in the Towneley *Resurrection*, where Christ states outright that the bread "Becomys my fleshe in wordes fyfe" (104v).[69] The absence of such a reference allows for a possible shift toward both a theology and a semiotics of the sacrament consistent with the Church of England's positions, especially when Christ says that the bread "Becomes my fleshe through your beleeffe" (176).[70] The emphasis on "your beleeffe" reflects the importance of worthy, faithful reception—a point shared by both traditional and reformed theologies but emphasized especially in the Order of Communion for the *Book of Common Prayer* as well as in the theological writings of John Jewel and Richard Hooker discussed in chapter 1.[71] Thus the episode does not reflect "a significant suspension of the drama of sign," a pattern David Mills identifies throughout the Chester cycle, but rather draws attention to the complicated relations (both dramatic and theological) between Christ's body and its sacramental signs.[72]

While the York, Towneley, and Chester plays represent Christ's Eucharistic body according to different devotional iconographies and doctrinal emphases, they all figure that body and its wounds as semiotically available. The body of Christ can be accessed and read in the context of an interpretive process that is at the same time a dramaturgical, social, and devotional act. More specifically, citizens of towns like York and Chester come together to represent salvation history in dramas that celebrate and forge social community. These two attributes of the Passion dramas—a wounded body disclosed to the witnessing public and a form of civic drama produced by working citizens—come under attack in Shakespeare's *Coriolanus*. Whereas Christ puts his body into signifying systems, Coriolanus takes his wounds out of language, out of legibility, and out of community. Moreover, like the York and Chester cycles, which were civic performances as well as biblical dramas, the Roman ritual of election is produced by the citizens and coheres around a wounded body emblematic of Rome's political integrity. The plebeians desire access to the bodily signs of *virtus* inscribed on Coriolanus's battle-tested flesh; seeing the wounds is necessary for the people to seal Coriolanus's election as consul. In restricting his wounds to the private domain, however, Coriolanus rejects the civic spectatorship and ceremony that defined early English drama long before the rise of the early modern commercial playhouse. Shakespeare ultimately punishes this iconoclastic stance by sending Coriolanus not to a martyr's death but to a traitor's butchery.

Private Wounds

As the preceding discussion has shown, the biblical dramas of the Passion do not just emphasize Christ's body and blood at a thematic or iconographic level; they also focus on Christ's semiotic construction of his body at the nexus of the word and the flesh. By putting his wounded body into language—first from the cross, then at the tomb, and again in the context of the Mass—Christ makes his wounds (and his body) into a readable text that also forges the bonds of social community. The biblical dramas provide a point of reference—if not also a critical point of difference—for thinking about Shakespeare's representation of Coriolanus's wounds, a representation that departs significantly from Thomas North's translation of Plutarch's *Lives*, which Shakespeare otherwise follows consistently.[73] A willingness to see the biblical dramas as sites of textual appropriation is crucial to understanding the connection between words and wounds in *Coriolanus*, however differently Shakespeare manifests it.[74] In *Coriolanus*, wounds signify martial victories on earth rather than the paschal mysteries of heaven. Yet in representing the threats to political community posed by a consul-elect who fails to reveal his wounded body to the masses, *Coriolanus* draws widely on biblical dramas of Christ's passion not only for the bloody violence they represent but also for the semiotics of the body they iterate.[75]

Wounded bodies—of the Roman warrior as well as the crucified Savior—organize particular versions of social community. Stanley Cavell places Coriolanus's rejection of both language and the body in the context of Eucharistic idioms such as food, sacrifice, and community. "If," Cavell proposes, "you accept the words as food, and you accept the central figure as invoking the central figure of the Eucharist, then you may accept a formulation of the effect (not that the play is the ritual of the Eucharist, but to the effect) that the play celebrates, or aspires to, the same fact as the ritual does, say the condition of community."[76] To enter one's body and wounds into language is to enact a form of social communion that has obvious sacramental implications. As Cavell goes on to say, "A community is thus identified as those who partake of the same body, of a common victim," and such a community is built on the exchange of words: "Language is metaphysically something shared, so that speaking is talking and giving in your mouth the very matter others are giving and taking in theirs."[77] Sacramental theater, Sarah Beckwith argues, brings the liturgical valences of the sacrament into similar terms of communal incorporation: "In its complex resemioticization of the sign, the sacrament is no longer the little wafer held aloft between priestly hands but strives to fulfill and point toward the host's most ardent and outrageous claims—its most generously utopian aspirations to cause what it signifies, to perform a bond of love in the community of the faithful."[78]

Christ's charitable sacrifice, so represented in biblical drama, provides a counterpoint to Coriolanus's narcissistic insularity. What Christ gives freely to the people—both his wounded body on the cross and the bread of life in the Mass—is reconfigured as both the grain and the battle wounds that Coriolanus keeps to himself. The Romans' hunger to see Coriolanus's wounds recalls their hunger for real food expressed at the outset of the play by the Third Citizen: "I speak this in hunger for bread, not in thirst for revenge" (1.1.22–23). In denying the Romans both political and semiotic access to his wounded body, Coriolanus, who earlier denies them literal nourishment, effectively starves them again. In doing so, he not only rejects the sort of communitarian bonds iterated by the Eucharist but also severs the crucial connection between word and wound that organizes a corporate body, whether civic or sacramental.

At a semiotic level, Coriolanus's wounds (like Christ's) are fleshly gashes as well as textual signs; their visual appeal likewise requires a hermeneutic response. In the context of ancient Rome, moreover, wounds distinctly signify *virtus*, or masculine valor, which is linked to nationalist ideologies of *pietas* and *paterfamilias*. Coppélia Kahn shows that in *Coriolanus* it is Volumnia, the martial mother, who inscribes and maintains this semiotics of the battle wound. "Poised, as it were, between 'warriors' (men locked in agonistic structures of rivalry), and 'women,'" Kahn argues, "the wound in these texts is always a site of anxiety and indeterminacy."[79] Volumnia creates such anxiety and indeterminacy by defining the semiotic relation between martial wound and *virtus*. She is not simply a participant in patriarchy but its principal spokesperson. When Coriolanus returns from battle, for example, Volumnia exclaims, "Oh, he is wounded, I thank the gods for it" (2.1.118). Menenius likewise sees the wound as a signifier of *virtus* when he urges the people, "The warlike service he has done, consider. Think / Upon the wounds his body bears, which show / Like graves i'th'holy churchyard" (3.3.48–50).

By urging the people to "consider" and "think" on Coriolanus's wounds, Menenius suggests that the wounded body of the Roman warrior must be made available to a public community, and an interpretive community at that. Not only must these wounds be viewed and counted, but also they must be allowed to circulate as signs interpretable by members of the body politic. In this sense, the wound requires the wounded to make himself vulnerable not only physically but also semiotically, thereby bearing out the etymology of *wound* as derived from the Latin *vulnus* ("vulnerable").[80] This vulnerability is particularly evident when Volumnia and Menenius anatomize Coriolanus's battle wounds:

> MENENIUS: Where is he wounded?
> VOLUMNIA: I'th' shoulder and i'th' left arm. There will be large cicatrices to show the people when he shall stand for his place. He received in the repulse of Tarquin seven hurts i'th' body.
> MENENIUS: One i'th' neck and two i'th' thigh—there's nine that I know.
> VOLUMNIA: He had, before this last expedition, twenty-five wounds upon him.
> MENENIUS: Now it's twenty-seven; every gash was an enemy's grave.
>
> (2.1.142–51)

This dialogue constitutes the only moment in the play when Coriolanus's body is publicly blazoned. Volumnia and Menenius put Coriolanus's wounds into words in order to persuade the Romans to elect Coriolanus as consul. In addition to translating the wounds, they count them, so as to suggest that quantity signifies valor. (In *Julius Caesar*, for example, Octavius counts "three and thirty wounds" on Caesar's body, suggestive not only for its impressive number but also for its symbolic correspondence to the reputed age of Christ at his crucifixion.) For that matter, in the Towneley *Resurrection*, Christ counts his own wounds in a self-authored blazon, in which he describes his body publicly as vulnerable to physical torture:

> And therefor thou shall understand
> In body, heed, feete, and hand,
> Four hundrethe woundes and five thowsand
> Here may thou see.
>
> (104r)

By inviting the reader to reflect on his body—"Here may thou see"—Christ emphasizes his initial act of vulnerability, the Incarnation, by which he took human flesh. In enumerating his 5,400 wounds, he then compels onlookers to admit that their salvation is purchased by his passion, itself the most gruesome illustration of Christ's humanity, especially as dramatized in the Passion plays. Christ makes this point plain in a brief lament during the Towneley *Crucifixion*: "Bot Goddes son, that shuld be best, / Has not where apon his hede to rest, / Bot on his shulder bone" (87r). This intimate detail of the Son of God resting his head on a single exposed bone that tears through his flesh makes Christ's vulnerability legible in decidedly physical terms.

Whereas Volumnia and Menenius see wounds as seals of *virtus* that necessitate public exposure and acknowledgment, Coriolanus rejects both the wound's capacity to signify valor and the social process by which those wounds enter into language. Coriolanus's uneasy relationship to language and signification has been noted by many critics, including Cynthia Marshall, who suggests that in refusing to make himself vulnerable by rendering his wounds readable signs, Coriolanus "attempts to halt the process of signification."[81] Moreover, Coppélia Kahn writes, "Though he seeks wounds with unparalleled zeal, he cannot bear to have them spoken of, not only before the people but among the patricians as well. . . . In battle he could avoid confronting language as a symbolic order, a system of sounds that are signs; he could speak with his body, in a pre-linguistic code of representation."[82] In addition to the public display of his wounds, Coriolanus rejects the ceremony of election staged by the Roman plebeians. As a civic performance, the election ceremony confirms the participation of the people in their government, even if such elections were historically a foregone conclusion.[83]

As we have seen in biblical drama, Christ makes his wounded body available in the vernacular, and his body evokes both the ecclesial body of the church (Christ's mystical body, a concept discussed in chapter 3) and the sacramental body at the center of Eucharistic ritual. By contrast, Coriolanus is an iconoclast: he removes his body from a semiotic system and divorces it from civic rituals. While he accepts a new name upon his return to Rome— "Martius Caius Coriolanus! / Bear th'addition nobly ever" (1.9.64–65)—he refuses to put his body on display before the people. When Coriolanus speaks of his wounds, he does so only to shut down their signifying capacity and thereby remove his body from public discourse. He says that his wounds will "smart," or teem again with blood, "to hear themselves remembered" (1.9.28–29). He would "rather have my wounds to heal again / Than hear say how I got them" (2.2.67–68). And while Coriolanus appears to relent in saying, "I have wounds to show you which shall be yours in private"

(2.3.75–76), he concludes just a few lines later, "I will not seal your knowledge with showing them. I will make much of your voices, and so trouble you no farther" (2.3.106–8), thereby echoing the pervasive use of *seal* to describe the sacraments in both traditional and reformed contexts. The need to exchange such verbal and visual signs is paramount to the Roman electoral process, especially for the plebeians who not only crave grain at their own rates but also seek to have their voices heard within the republic.[84] Coriolanus refuses to convert his wounds into tangible signs of *virtus* and thereby achieve social reciprocity with the plebeians. He also rejects outright the material excesses of political spectacle. I will now examine both strands of Coriolanus's iconoclasm, beginning with language and then turning to drama.

As suggested at the start of this chapter, wounds shape an invitatory gesture to know the body through the fleshly aperture. For Coriolanus to show his wounds, suggests John Plotz, is tantamount to "asking the *polis* to enter, but enter fully, unabashedly, into the theater of Coriolanus's spectacular body" by means of a public act of signification, an act by which "the citizen imagines becoming part of Coriolanus's wounded body, and so coming to speak, not against him, but both for him and from him."[85] The Third Citizen describes the verbal and physical communion forged by such an interpretive act: "We have power in ourselves to do it, but it is a power that we have no power to do. For, if he show us his wounds and tell us his deeds, we are to put our tongues into those wounds and speak for them. So, if he tell us his noble deeds, we must also tell him our noble acceptance of them" (2.3.4–9).

This image of the Roman citizens putting their tongues into Coriolanus's wounds evokes similar images used to describe Eucharistic reception familiar to early modern audiences from the ongoing theological controversies discussed in the previous chapter. While Shakespeare's image of putting tongues into wounds may call to mind dangers of cannibalism and carnality routinely raised by opponents of transubstantiation, it may also recall Richard Hooker's analogy between the word of God and the wounds of Christ. For Hooker, we will recall from chapter 1, the reading of scripture is itself so efficacious that "in the wounds of our Redeemer we there dip our tongues, wee are died red both within and without, our hunger is satisfied, and our thirst for ever quenched."[86] By putting wounds into words, the scriptures manifest not Christ's Galilean body (his natural flesh and blood) but his mystical body, the corporate entity in which the faithful members are united through a sacramental reception predicated on faith and participation.

Hooker's ecclesiology relates to the figuration of political community put forth by the Third Citizen's use of *tongues* as a metonymy for language. For the citizens to put their tongues into Coriolanus's wounds is both to ratify his election and to achieve linguistic reciprocity with him. Such a collective vision is flatly refused by the consul-elect. If Coriolanus eschews the fleshly vulnerability shown by Christ in the Crucifixion and Resurrection plays, he is no more enthusiastic about the prospect of the Roman people— a mob he describes as "dissentious rogues" (1.1.159), "curs" (1.1.163), and "fragments" (1.1.217)—speaking of his body or its battle wounds. He resists subjecting his body to the "tongues o'th'common mouth" (3.1.22). As Anne Barton argues, "The image of citizens, men who do not themselves wield swords, mere opinion personified, intruding their tongues into the scars and cicatrices of honor, becomes, in this context, oddly strained and unpleasant."[87] For Coriolanus to show his wounds, he would have to insert his body into a semiotic system authored by the commons and thus subject that body's meaning to their voices. In response, Coriolanus retorts, "I had rather have one scratch my head i'th'sun ... / Than idly sit / To hear my nothings monstered" (2.2.73, 75). That final verb, *monstered* (from the Latin *monstrare*, "to show"), suggests that Coriolanus will not show the wounds for fear of having them barbarized by the mob. It also puns tellingly on *monstrance*, the vessel used to expose the Eucharistic host to public adoration during Corpus Christi processions.

I want to turn now from Coriolanus's rejection of the wound's linguistic implications to the second aspect of his iconoclasm: dramatic spectacle. Contrary to Christ, who in many biblical dramas is a character who relishes actorly spectacle, Coriolanus professes an ardent antitheatricalism.[88] "It is a part," he says, "That I shall blush in acting, and might well / Be taken from the people. ... To brag unto them 'Thus I did, and thus,' / Show them th'unaching scars which I should hide, / As if I had received them for the hire / Of their breath only" (2.2.143–45, 146–49). Coriolanus overlooks the fact that political spectacle is, for ancient Rome as well as Jacobean England, crucial to executing political authority. During his progress to York in 1603, for example, James I rejected travel by coach and walked on foot so as to be more visible to the people: "I will have no Coach, for the people are desirous to see a King, and so they shall, for they shall as well see his body as his face."[89] King James writes elsewhere of the same need for the monarch to make his body accessible to the people. Of political ceremony he says, "A King must looke to have that action performed in publique, and in a publique place; that the love of his people may appear in that solemne action. Two things a King hath specially to looke unto at his inauguration; first, that his title to the croune be just, and next that hee may possesse it with the love of his people.... It is a great signe of the blessing of God when he enteres in it with the willing applause of his subjects."[90] The ceremony both legitimates the king's appointment and signifies his divine right. By making the monarch's body accessible to his people, such a ceremony also mobilizes a form of civic participation by which the citizens are incorporated into the mystical body of the monarch. It is this form of civic participation that, as Cavell argues, Coriolanus cannot achieve, for he "cannot imagine, or cannot accept, that there is a way to partake of one another, incorporate one another, that is necessary to the formation rather than to the extinction of a community."[91]

For the Romans in *Coriolanus*, the election ceremony signifies such social incorporation because such a ceremony centers on the physical presence of the consul-elect. As Brutus describes it, "All tongues speak of him, and the bleared sights / Are spectacled to see him.... Stalls, bulks, windows / Are smothered up, leads filled and ridges horsed / With variable complexions, all agreeing / In earnestness to see him" (2.1.199–200, 204–7). This entire dramatic ceremony teems with sensory overload. The Messenger likewise admits that the crowd seizes not on the political signification of election but on its dramatic spectacle: "I have seen the dumb men throng to see him, and / The blind to hear him speak. Matrons flung gloves, / Ladies and maids their scarves and handkerchiefs upon him as he passed. The nobles bended / As to Jove's statue, and the commons made / A shower and thunder with their caps and shouts. / I never saw the like" (2.1.256–62). In a Reformation context, this is the stuff of which idolatry is made, and it is partially on the basis of such idolatry that Coriolanus refuses to participate. Moreover, the ceremonial processions, sightings, costumes, and props are the ancient Roman equivalent of *adiaphora*, the "things indifferent" that reformers deemed inconsequential to liturgical practice.[92] The commons threaten to obscure the valor signified by the wounds with sensuous ceremony.

Coriolanus has only one alternative: he must try to kill the spectacle.[93] "Let me o'er leap that custom," he says (referring to showing his body), "for I cannot / Put on the gown, stand naked and entreat them, / For my wounds' sake, to give their suffrage. Please you / That I may pass this doing" (2.2.135–38). Coriolanus initially refuses to wear the gown of election, which would first mark his body out as the center of the political spectacle and then be removed so as to reveal his wounds. In doing so Coriolanus reverses a well-known scene in biblical drama: the stripping of Christ's garments prior to the Crucifixion. In the York *Road to Calvary* pageant, the soldiers stage such a scene of ritual humiliation that emphasizes the vulnerability of the wounded body: "He muste be naked, nede. / All yf he called hymselffe a kyng, / In his clothis he schall nought hyng, / But naked as a stone be stedde." In what follows, the soldiers cast lots for Christ's clothes and one of them says, "Take of his clothis beliffe, latte see—Aha, this garment will falle wele for me, / And so I hope it schall" (309–12, 320–22). Whereas Christ allows his gown to be stripped and his wounds displayed, Coriolanus puts on the "gown of humility" (2.3.39) only reluctantly and still refuses to show his wounds.[94] "I heard him swear," says Brutus, "Were he to stand for consul, never would he / Appear i'th'market-place nor on him put / The napless vesture of humility, / Nor, showing, as the manner is, his wounds / To th'people, beg their stinking breaths" (2.1.225–30).

In addition to linguistic disclosure and dramatic spectacle, there is a third element to Coriolanus's iconoclasm. Coriolanus is not simply opposed to showing his wounds, participating in public discourse, or playing the role of consul-elect. Rather, he takes aim at the very *form* of civic drama centered on the wounded body and produced by working-class citizens. Insofar as the election ceremony is a drama of the people, and insofar as that drama takes as its pivotal focus the wounded body of a civic leader who embodies the corporate body of the people, the Roman election ceremony is of a piece with the biblical dramas staged as civic performances in the streets of York and Chester. Viewed from such a perspective, Coriolanus's iconoclasm, not to mention his endeavor to kill dramatic spectacle, targets not just the political election ceremony but also the very form of civic religious drama and all that it signifies.

The York and Chester cycles were part of a lay devotional tradition that "gave the laity the opportunity to interpret and express church doctrine and liturgy, as well as biblical narrative, in their own terms, thereby shaping and developing popular religious practice."⁹⁵ But these dramas also represented civic community to itself.⁹⁶ The members of lay guilds—carpenters, pinners, bakers, sausage makers, tapsters, and the like—funded the plays, constructed the pageants, and performed the roles. The very body of Christ presented to the public gaze in these Crucifixion pageants was, in the context of its performance, a civic creation. The York Memorandum Book provides some insight into the civic dimensions of the "Creation to Doomsday" cycle plays:

> In accordance with a certain custom followed for many years and times, all the craftsmen of the city of York at their own expense have caused a certain sumptuous play of the Old and New Testaments compiled in different pageants to be performed every year, and put on at diverse sites of the aforesaid city on the feast of Corpus Christi; likewise, making a certain solemn procession then for reverence of the sacrament of the body of Christ, by beginning at the great doors of the Priory of the Holy Trinity of York and so going processionally to the cathedral church of York and thence to the Hospital of St Leonard at York, the aforesaid sacrament having been left there, with the light of many torches and a great multitude of priests dressed in surplices preceding.⁹⁷

Christ's body, both the Eucharistic body carried in the Corpus Christi procession and the theatricalized body performed in the plays of the York cycle, is mobilized by the efforts of York's civic guilds. The civic dimensions of the biblical dramas are transferred on another level to representational parallels between biblical places and personages and those in the city, as Beckwith explains: "The fictive localities of Calvary, Jerusalem, Herod's palace, Pilates dais, and Lazarus's tomb are held in active tension with the public spaces of the city, and that tension is animated every time an actor assumes a role in the streets of York."⁹⁸ *Tension* is the operative word, since plays such as the York cycle did not always foster civic harmony; in some cases, they fomented the sort of factional unrest witnessed in the grain riots at the start of *Coriolanus*.⁹⁹ The civic production of a biblical drama does not necessarily unify the citizens but exposes the friction at play in York's urban economy.¹⁰⁰

Whatever social tensions are at play in the York cycle, they do not amount to the kind of discord that results from Coriolanus's iconoclasm in ancient Rome. While his rejection of ritual ceremony, dramatic spectacle, and corporeal piety resonates with the iconoclastic reforms of the sixteenth and seventeenth centuries in England, Coriolanus is eventually punished on account of his refusal to communicate physically and verbally with the people. The price for trying to suppress the drama of election is exile followed by death. "He should have showed us / His marks of merit, wounds received for's country" (2.3.160–61), says the Second Citizen; in the formal scene of banishment, Brutus says, "The people cry you mocked them, and of late, / When corn was given them gratis, you repined, / Scandalled the suppliants for the people, called them / Time-pleasers, flatterers, foes to nobleness" (3.1.43–46). Coriolanus is then exiled: "Banish him our city / In peril of precipitation / From off the rock Tarpeian," Sicinius says, "never more / To enter our Rome gates. / I'th'people's name / I say it shall be so" (3.3.100–103). This is the commoners' response to a consul-elect who encloses his body from the public gaze and shields his wounds from the people's voice—a consul-elect who makes his body unreadable, placing it outside the realm of interpretive activity.[101] The Romans acquire a newfound sense of authority when they banish Coriolanus, which anticipates his murder at the hands of Aufidius and the Volscian conspirators.

By keeping to himself that which must be shared with the people—both the corn and his wounds—Coriolanus throws the Roman body politic out of joint. His iconoclasm, especially as it pertains to the body, is not rewarded as a political strategy because it gives rise to factionalism rather than social cohesion, starvation rather than nourishment. By the play's end, moreover, Coriolanus becomes a version of the very bleeding body exposed in the Crucifixion dramas—a body that, by the play's end, is displayed publicly to spectators as bloody, gashed, and dismembered. Almost on cue from his taunt, "Cut me to pieces, Volsces men and lads; / Stain all your edges on me" (5.6.112–13), Coriolanus is turned into a fragment of flesh, his body spattered with blood and dotted by incalculable gashes. "Tear him to pieces! Do it presently! He killed my son! My daughter! He killed my cousin Marcus! He killed my father!" (5.6.121–23), chants the angry mob, landing on "Kill, kill, kill, kill, kill him!" (5.6.131). Coriolanus, who earlier derided the Roman citizens as "scabs" (1.1.161), "fragments" (1.1.217), and a "common cry of curs" (3.3.119), now becomes a discarded remnant both in his physical flesh and in his relation to the social body. His dismemberment is a sign of political failure, as compared to Christ's, which is a sacramental sign of salvation. Christ's Eucharistic body, which is intimately tied to the mystical body of Christ in the Church, signifies ecclesiastical cohesion;

Coriolanus's body signifies political cohesion only as a result of its being first exiled and then murdered. As Aufidius says to the people, "You'll rejoice / That he is thus cut off" (5.6.139–40). Aufidius's words prove slightly ironic, for a few lines later he declares that, despite his exile and murder, and despite his narcissistic withdrawal of his body from the people, Coriolanus "shall have a noble memory" (5.6.155). This suggestion of an honorable legacy is double edged, however. For Coriolanus to enjoy a "noble memory," his deeds must be put into narrative form (as they are in Plutarch's *Lives* and Shakespeare's play); what is more, Coriolanus's deeds may well be remembered by means of a tangible burial memorial that will be accessible to the public. The point here is that Aufidius's promise of a "noble memory" (5.6.155) carries with it his capacity to control—and to disseminate—Coriolanus's posthumous image within an enduring civic spectacle, which is precisely the type of public performance that the consul-elect eschewed.

In the Crucifixion and Resurrection dramas, wounds are linked to Christ's sacrifice and the devotional piety that such a sacrifice is meant to stir in response. They also open out the contested and multiple semiotic positions that define the Eucharist. In *Coriolanus*, wounds signify martial sacrifice as well as the ideologies of *pietas* and *virtus* on which the Roman republic is founded. While its pre-Christian setting has little to do with the sacrament of the Eucharist, *Coriolanus*'s controversy over the public exposure of wounds as a sign of Roman political integrity takes up the representational tensions that were articulated in both biblical dramas and Eucharistic controversies. By making Coriolanus's body a problematic crux of political spectacle and relating Coriolanus's rejection of public exposure to an iconoclastic defiance of drama, Shakespeare evokes the semiotics of Christ's body as worked out in earlier biblical dramas, which treat the relation of word to wound in the context of social community and make social community contingent on the interpretability of that body.

The concept of a social body—more specifically, the political and theological iterations of a *corpus mysticum*, or "mystical body"—is the subject of the next chapter. There we will examine different representations of the king's sacred body and the kinds of social community and discord that it signifies in three different contexts: performative verses for a civic entry as well as a sacramental procession, both written by the fifteenth century poet-monk, John Lydgate; John Bale's polemical drama, *King Johan*; and a second Shakespearean tragedy, *Macbeth*.

THREE

Sacramental Signs and Mystical Bodies in Lydgate, Bale, and Shakespeare

In both late medieval and early modern England, the bodies of kings and queens were regarded as sacred entities. So sacred were these bodies that the king's "royal presence" was often analogized to Christ's real presence in the Eucharist.[1] The rituals of kingship, furthermore, were themselves couched in sacramental liturgy. During the coronation ceremony, kings and queens were anointed with consecrated oil and (at least until the coronation of Elizabeth I) crowned during Mass, when they held Edward the Confessor's chalice and swore an oath on the Blessed Sacrament. As Alice Hunt describes the coronation of Henry VIII and Katherine of Aragon, "After both Henry and Katherine were anointed and crowned, the ceremony closed with the celebration of Mass, encasing the coronation in the logic of the Eucharist: the consecration of the monarch and his regalia pre-empt the consecration—and transformation—of the bread and wine."[2] In addition to sacramental ritual, the theory of divine right, which saw monarchs as God's appointed deputies on earth, was given scriptural support in Romans 13.[3] Many subjects also believed that the monarch had the divine power of healing, often referred to as the "royal touch."[4] Finally, the king's "mystical body"—the body that transcends time and continues uninterrupted through the royal genealogy—derives in large part from the theology of the *corpus mysticum*, which in its early Christian inflections stressed the relations between Christ's Galilean or physical body; his sacramental or Eucharistic body; and his ecclesial body, the church.[5]

In this chapter, I focus on the relationship between the king's body and Christ's body as represented in John Lydgate's verse transcriptions of a royal entry, *Henry VI's Triumphal Entry into London* (1432), and a sacramental procession, *A Procession of Corpus Christi* (late 1420s); John Bale's *King Johan* (ca. 1538); and William Shakespeare's *Macbeth* (1606). Whereas Lydgate draws on Eucharistic imagery and ceremony to forge a salient connection between *corpus mysticum* and *corpus Christi*, Bale and Shakespeare reimagine such a relationship both theologically and politically. While in theory the king's mystical body was sacred and eternal, as expressed in the metaphysical continuity of royal genealogy and sacramental ceremony, both Bale and Shakespeare represent the vulnerability of the monarch's mystical body in staged acts of regicide that parody Eucharistic ritual. Before turning to these dramatic texts, I will first offer a brief history of the *corpus mysticum* in its early Christian theological contexts.

Corpus Mysticum and Corpus Christi

The concept of sacred kingship derives from early Christian understandings of the *corpus mysticum*, which stressed the mutual relation of sacramental theology, liturgy, and ecclesiology. Christ's "mystical body" signifies the participation of the Christian faithful gathered together as the church; this is a metaphysical incorporation that transcends space and time. In this sense, the *corpus mysticum*, as Jennifer Rust aptly describes it, "is not exactly an 'institution' but the performative, sacramental condition of possibility for socially meaningful institutions in the premodern Christian world."[6] The earliest theologies of the *corpus mysticum* situate these institutional significations of Christ's body—the body of Christ incorporated within the church's sacramental, liturgical, and ecclesial community—within the debates over flesh and spirit that define Eucharistic controversy. Thus the concept of *corpus mysticum*, especially as it relates to the concerns of the present chapter, is contextualized by both ecclesiastical and semiotic concerns.

Building on the doctrine of Christ's hypostatic union (which asserted against the Arian heresies that Christ was fully human as well as fully divine), the *corpus mysticum* comprises three understandings of Christ's body that were seen by the church fathers as mutually constitutive. They are (1) the Galilean body (the natural body that took flesh and was born of the Virgin); (2) the Eucharistic body (the sacrament of the altar, which according to orthodox doctrine of transubstantiation made the Galilean body present in substance); and (3) the ecclesial body (the Christian faithful incorporated mystically as church).[7] This tripartite definition was formatively advanced by Amalarius of Metz and Paschasius Radbertus in the ninth century.[8] This is the same Radbertus who debated Ratramnus at the Abbey of Corbie in the earliest controversies over the Eucharist, as discussed in chapter 1. Radbertus saw the Galilean, sacramental, and ecclesial bodies as "three different accepted interpretations of *corpus Christi*," though he regarded all three as equally Christ's body.[9] According to this understanding of *corpus mysticum*, the body of Christ was simultaneously human and divine, natural and spiritual, ecclesial and sacramental.

The most extensive study of the Eucharistic origins of *corpus mysticum* is Henri de Lubac's *Corpus Mysticum: The Eucharist and the Church in the Middle Ages* (1963). De Lubac, a formative participant in the Second Vatican Council (1962–65), deeply influenced Ernst Kantorowicz's historical study of the king's two bodies, which drew the theology of Christ's mystical body toward a theory of secular kingship centered on the body politic.[10] According to de Lubac, one could not separate Christ's physical, sacramental, and mystical bodies. In the writings of Origen, Ambrose, and other church fathers, the mystical body and the Eucharistic body are "not so much used to describe two successive objects as two simultaneous things that make one whole, for the body of Christ that is the Church is in no way *other* than the body and blood of the mystery."[11] Against the argument that the mystical body replaces the Eucharistic body (and that the spirit likewise replaces the flesh), de Lubac reminds us that theologically the two are coequal. "In the same way that sacramental communion (*communion in the body and blood*) is always at the same time an ecclesial communion (*communion within the Church, of the Church, for the Church . . .*)," he says, "so also ecclesial communion always includes, in its fulfillment, sacramental communion."[12] In receiving Christ's sacramental body, then, the communicant tethers himself to Christ's ecclesial body; conversely, incorporation within the ecclesial body has no meaning outside the Eucharistic sacrament.

At a certain point, however, the theology of *corpus mysticum* was reconceptualized according to a different semiotics, one that created a dichotomy between flesh and spirit. Beginning in the ninth century and gaining firmer traction in the twelfth century, *corpus mysticum* gradually came to signify the spiritual reality of the ecclesial body over against the corporeality of the Eucharistic body. What emerged, argues Rust, was "a substantial new opposition between two terms (Eucharist, church) that *mysticum* had effectively linked, even in their distinctness."[13] In the High Middle Ages, both Ratramnus and Berengar of Tours challenged the belief that Christ's Galilean body was received in the sacrament, which in turn prompted a reconsideration of the relations between flesh and spirit not only in terms of Eucharistic presence and sacramental reception but also in the theological formulations of *corpus mysticum*. Once the term *mystical* was used to signify "spiritual," with the express purpose of rejecting the doctrine of transubstantiation, the three reciprocal categories of Galilean, Eucharistic, and ecclesial bodies were driven apart.

As time wore on, the terms *mystical* and *sacramental*, once united in early Christian theologies of *corpus mysticum*, came to mark out disparate views of sacramental theology and ecclesiology. Scholastics privileged transubstantiation, while their opponents emphasized spiritual reception and ecclesial community. For many dissenters from orthodoxy, the church as Christ's mystical body was seen as the correct signification of the sacrament of the altar as well as its fullest realization. John Wyclif, we recall from chapter 1, appeals to Augustine and other patristic authorities in using Christ's mystical body to argue against the doctrine of transubstantiation. In the sixteenth century, moreover, the *Book of Common Prayer* opposes Christ's mystical body to his physical body in delineating its Eucharistic theology. The penultimate prayer in the Order of Communion, for example, situates the Lord's Supper in the context of the "very membres incorporate in [Christ's] misticall body, whiche is the blessed compaignie of all faithful people." The priest then asks God to "knit together thy elect in one Communion and felowshyp in the misticall body of thy sonne Christ our lord."[14] While the *Book of Common Prayer* does not make the mystical body inimical to the sacrament of the altar, it expresses Christ's real presence in terms of a spiritualist theology of the Eucharist grounded not on the metaphysics of transubstantiation but on the ecclesiology of the body of Christ as church. The sacramental body and the ecclesial body can be reciprocal here, but only on the condition that Christ's Galilean body is removed from a theology of Eucharistic presence.

In their long history from early Christianity through the Protestant Reformation, the theological debates over the *corpus mysticum* centered on a key question. To what extent does the ecclesial community of the church as Christ's mystical body depend on the Eucharistic body of Christ in the sacrament of the altar? Must they be reciprocal and simultaneous, or should they be seen as having different theological implications? These theological reconsiderations prompt similar reconsiderations of a more contemporary use of *corpus mysticum* as a political term. To what extent is the king's royal body modeled on Christ's sacramental and ecclesial bodies? Is the body politic necessarily akin to the *corpus mysticum* as "church," or is it more properly conceived as a secularized *corpus politicum*?[15]

In *The King's Two Bodies*, Ernst Kantorowicz sees the theological distinctions within the discourses of *corpus mysticum* as "the beginning of the so-called secularization of the mediaeval Church."[16] Stressing a separation between individual and collective as well as church and world, Kantorowicz argues that "the expression, 'mystical body,' which originally had a liturgical or sacramental meaning, took on a connotation of sociological content."[17] Once the liturgical becomes juridical, as Kantorowicz would have it, the sacramental dimensions of mystical kingship become secularized. Rust argues that Kantorowicz "flattens out what de Lubac presents as an originally dynamic situation which involves a fluid relation between *ecclesia* and *Eucharist*, to further his own idea of a genealogy of secular polity." She further expounds Kantorowicz's secularizing vision: "As theological tropes become sociological in *The King's Two Bodies* they tend also to be tamed into pliable fictional material for representing specific political, very human interests, evacuated of all but the barest hint of transcendent content."[18] Thus, by converting the Eucharistic foundations of the early Christian theology of *corpus mysticum* into a secularized *corpus politicum*, Kantorowicz suggests that sacrament is replaced by metaphor, church by corporation.

The texts I study in this chapter all reject such a secularized narrative of political theology whereby sacramental energies are evacuated by metaphorical figures. Like Lydgate, the subject of the first section that follows, Bale and Shakespeare each figure the king's royal presence in terms of a mystical body. Yet *King Johan* and *Macbeth* emphasize the chasm evident between a theory of sacred, metaphysical kingship and the reality of violent, conspiratorial threats against the monarch's body and office. These plays do not draw on Eucharistic idioms, as Lydgate does, to praise the king or incorporate him within the collective civic body. Rather they stage regicide, which is the most grievous assault on the king's sacred body, by means of Eucharistic parodies that undermine both sacramental and political foundations of the *corpus mysticum*.

"Crystes Bred, Delicyous unto Kynges": Lydgate's *Procession of Corpus Christi* and *Henry VI's Triumphal Entry into London*

John Lydgate, the fifteenth-century English poet and monk from Bury St. Edmunds, provides an apt context in which to begin a discussion of literary representations of the *corpus mysticum*.[19] Illustrative of Lydgate's remarkably prolific and diverse career, the two texts studied here—*Henry VI's Triumphal Entry into London* and *A Procession of Corpus Christi*—demonstrate the symbolic convergences between Christ's Eucharistic body and the king's royal body in Lydgate's imagination of the *corpus mysticum*. In the *Triumphal Entry*, written on the occasion of the young Henry VI's return to England from France in 1432, Lydgate fashions the king's royal presence in scriptural and liturgical terms, often keying in on specific aspects of Eucharistic theology and ceremony to emphasize both the sanctity of the king's office and the integrity of the city. In *A Procession of Corpus Christi*, Lydgate performs the converse operation: by employing images of kingship to describe the majesty of the Eucharistic sacrament, Lydgate figures the Eucharist in terms of a mystical body, the church, which coheres around the sacrament's spiritual fruits. These mutual representations of royal and sacramental bodies not only shape a theocratic vision of "messianic kingship," as Gordon Kipling has argued, but also suggest the fluid semiotics by which Lydgate figures sacred bodies and social communities.[20] At some junctures, the sacramental and mystical converge in ways that recall the early Christian theologies of *corpus mysticum* discussed above; at others, they split apart in ways that highlight the instability of sign and body that characterizes a Eucharistic semiotics more generally.

Both the *Entry* and the *Procession* are, strictly speaking, poetic verses rather than staged dramas. Yet as Claire Sponsler has shown, Lydgate is known for negotiating embodied performance and written text, rendering the boundaries between image and word quite permeable.[21] Henry VI's entry, which comprised seven pageants beginning at Blackheath and terminating at Westminster, was officially recorded in a Latin letter written by the London clerk John Carpenter.[22] Lydgate's version was commissioned (in all likelihood by London's mayor, John Welles) after the event; as such, the verses "reinterpret the public event of the entry through inscription into the cultural field of vernacular poetry" and create a text that "is active, capturing more vividly than Carpenter does a sense of the processional movement."²³ The *Procession*, written some years before the 1432 entry, similarly crosses the borders of embodied performance and readable text.²⁴ While the verses may be linked to a historical Corpus Christi procession organized by the Skinners guild, there is no documentary evidence to support the claim that Lydgate's *Procession* is an actual performative script.²⁵ By comparison to the *Entry*, the *Procession* focuses less on the Eucharist's ceremonial acts than on its textual contexts and controversies (scriptural, theological, and liturgical). Aware of its own status as text, the *Procession* functions as what Sponsler calls "a gloss on Eucharistic devotion" and, as Andrew Cole argues, offers Lydgate a way to "explore alternate versions of the Real Presence, versions notably different from, and more flexible than, those in the fifteenth century that follow the Lateran line."²⁶ Cole demonstrates how Lydgate not only negotiates orthodox and nonorthodox theologies of real presence but also locates in patristic writers like Jerome and Peter the Lombard (who are often assimilated to the orthodox side) support for nonorthodox views.²⁷ Thus the complexity of Lydgate's Eucharistic semiotics provides a context in which to situate his equally complicated representation of the *corpus mysticum*.

While royal entries and Corpus Christi processions are no doubt civic rituals, and while Lydgate is no doubt a civic poet (even a "civic mouthpiece," as C. David Benson suggests), Lydgate often tethers the civic to the religious in his representation of a mystical body, whether the royal body of Henry VI or the Eucharistic body of Christ.²⁸ The pageants that comprise the 1432 *Triumphal Entry*, for example, feature biblical inscriptions intended to instruct the king on matters of civic administration. These "written mottoes," Sponsler argues, also "linked the unique event of the royal entry to a broader context of church ritual, grounded in biblical history."²⁹ The most notable example of such a link occurs in the *Triumphal Entry* when Lydgate situates Henry VI within the biblical genealogy of David, from whose lineage Christ descended: "And lyke for David, after his victorie, / Rejoyssed was alle Jerusalem, / So this Cittee with laude, pris [praise], and glorie, / For joye moustred lyke the sonne beem."³⁰ Lydgate further represents Henry as a civic authority blessed by God when the Old Testament prophets Enoch and Elijah pray that "God conserve thee and kepe thee evermore, / And make him blessid, here in erthe levyng / And preserve him in alle manere thyng" (379–81).³¹ This is a prayer for the health and prosperity of the king as well as London's body politic. Such a connection between royal body and civic body likewise runs through "A Prayer for King, Queen, and People," where Lydgate writes, "And Christ Jesu, by mercy us conveye, / Whiche on the crosse liste for our sake blede, / Fortune this Realme, and make it wel to spede, / Benigne Jesu, preserve eke with thin hande, / The kynge, the quene, the peple, and thy londe."[32]

Enoch and Elijah's benediction occurs during the fourth pageant's Wells of Paradise scene, where Henry VI witnesses the figure of a Eucharistic miracle:

> The Kyng forth rydyng entryd Chepe anoon,
> A lusty place, a place of alle delycys,
> Kome to the Conduyt, where, as cristall stoon,
> The watir ranne like welles of Paradys,
> The holsome lykour, ful riche and of grete prys,
> Lyke to the water of Archedeclyne,
> Which by miracle was turned into wyne.
>
> (307–13)

Against the glut of Cheapside's carnal pleasures stands this visual and textual representation of Christ's first public miracle: the changing of water into wine at Cana as recorded in the Gospel of John.[33] Kipling reads the miracle, itself a prefiguration of the Eucharistic institution, as a displacement of Christ's transformative powers onto the young monarch: "By virtue of this sign, Henry appears to the people of London as the Christ who changes water into wine, and in so doing he manifests his regal divinity once again."[34] What Kipling regards as a manifestation of divine kingship linked to Christ's divinity, as expressed in both the epiphany and the Eucharistic institution, must also be read in the communitarian context of the *corpus mysticum*. As the community of the faithful is gathered into the ecclesial body of the church, so the London citizenry is united in the royal body of the king. Thus the episode does not simply affirm royal divinity or the royal person of the king but describes the symbolic incorporation of London's citizens within the king's mystical body. As the pageant proceeds, wine itself embeds this mystical signification. First figured as a "holsome lykour, ful riche and of grete prys," wine is then described by Lydgate as "a likour of recreacioun" (311, 321). Here Lydgate figures wine as a restorative liquor, implying that the health of the physical body corresponds to the health of the civic weal: "Out of the londe he putte away alle trouble," Lydgate writes of Henry, "And made of newe oure joyes to be double" (326–27).

Lydgate's symbolic connection of Eucharistic wine to the *corpus mysticum* echoes a similar figure in *A Procession of Corpus Christi*, where Lydgate references an iconographic representation of Jeremiah's chalice with grain rising out of it:

> Beholde this prophete called Jeremye,
> B'avisyoun so hevenly devyne
> Tooke a chalyce and fast cane him hye
> To presse owte lykoure of the rede vyne
> Greyne in the middes, which to make us dyne,
> Was beete and bulted floure to make of bred,
> A gracyous fygure that a pure virgyne
> Should bere manna in which lay al our speede.[35]

Here the grain and wine in Jeremiah's chalice prefigure Christ's incarnation and passion. As the grain is "beete and bulted" to make bread and the wine is pressed from the "rede vyne," so does the Virgin Mary bear forth Christ. Moreover, Lydgate characterizes Christ as "manna," the Old Testament bread that finds its typological fulfillment in Christ's Eucharistic institution.[36] As with the royal entry, Lydgate tethers this image of Christ's Eucharistic body to his mystical body. Christ's manna takes the form not of the transubstantiated host but rather of a sacrificial body tied to the collective *ecclesia*. In emphasizing that this sacrifice is for the entire Christian community— the sacrifice "in which lay al our speede" (88)—the procession verses instate a sacramental vision that "sutures social divisions and hierarchies in the name of a sacrament of unity and community."[37]

Taken in tandem, the Eucharistic symbolism of the Wells of Paradise scene and the iconography of Jeremiah's chalice gesture toward the vision of sacramental and political community that punctuates the *Triumphal Entry*. In those stanzas, King Henry arrives at St. Paul's, "the chirche cathederall" (423), where he is greeted by bishops and clergy before he beholds the Trinitarian scene in the final pageant. Then, moving toward Westminster Abbey, he is invested with the scepter of Edward the Confessor, an instrument of monarchy figured as one of the saint's "relikes" (478), which suggests that the holy presence of England's ideal sacred king is vitally transmitted through the material objects touched to his royal body. This relic likewise figures the mystical continuity of the king's sacred office as it is passes from one member of the royal genealogy to the next. Finally, moving "Into the mynstre," Henry approaches the "hyh awtere [altar]" (482–83) to the ringing of bells and communal singing of the *Te Deum*, a hymn that praises the Trinity and signifies ecclesial unity. This laudatory hymn, which Lydgate himself translated, was sung in many liturgical contexts including the Divine Office, Corpus Christi processions, and royal coronations.[38] In this, the entry's final movement, civic pageantry meets sacramental liturgy in a figuration of London as the mystical body that coheres in the royal presence of its king: "And the peple, gladde of looke and chere, / Thanked God with alle here hertes entere" (485–86).

The convergence of the civic and sacramental in the *Triumphal Entry*'s final scene recalls a similar episode in the *Procession of Corpus Christi* where Lydgate uses images of kingship to figure the Eucharistic sacrament. In an early stanza devoted to Jacob, Lydgate moves from the biblical text of Genesis 28, which describes the familiar vision of angels ascending and descending a ladder (41–43), to a detailed description of the Eucharistic host:

> The whete glene crowned above the greyne,
> Forged of golde an Hoost thereinne eseyne;
> This Crystes bred, delicyous unto kynges,
> With goostly gladnesse, gracious and sovereyne,
> Gayve forreyne damage of alle eorthely thinges.
> (44–48)

Here Lydgate describes the Eucharistic host in terms of sacred kingship. The bountiful head of wheat grows so plentiful that it crests into a crowned shape; the crown becomes a host fashioned of gold (recalling the earlier reference to the wheat rising out of Jeremiah's chalice as well as the gilded monstrance in which the host would be carried during a Corpus Christi procession); and the host is finally figured as "Crystes bred, delicyous unto kynges" (46). If in the *Entry* Christ's Eucharistic wine signifies the health promised subjects by their monarch, here in the *Procession* Eucharistic bread is described as food fit for kings, suggesting the health promised to the church as Christ's mystical body.

By describing the host in terms of sacred kingship, Lydgate does not simply interleave political and sacramental figures of the *corpus mysticum*. He also unfolds a complex semiotics whereby the transubstantiated host collides with a spiritualist sacramental theology that emphasizes Christ's mystical body. For Cole, such a transposition is typical of the *Procession*, in which "we find Lydgate espousing a model of real presence that is strikingly distinct from those versions that characterize anti-Wycliffite orthodoxy."[39] Whereas Cole focuses exclusively on the patristic material in Lydgate's verses, the *Procession*'s biblical stanzas perform a similarly complex theological argument. The Jacob stanza moves from the host (which simultaneously points to the doctrine of transubstantiation; serves as the material object of Eucharistic devotion; and marks out the convergence of Christ's Galilean, sacramental, and mystical bodies in the Mass) to the final iteration of "goostly gladnesse, gracious and sovereyne" (47)—that is, the sacrament's spiritual succor, which transcends "alle eorthely thinges" (48), including flesh and blood. This shift in emphasis, engineered by the accompanying references to the king's body, suggests a Eucharistic theology predicated on Christ's mystical body more than his transubstantiated body and thereby illustrates the rift between Galilean, Eucharistic, and mystical bodies discussed by Henri de Lubac. In the context of fifteenth-century Eucharistic controversies, moreover, the passage casts Lydgate as one who, according to Cole, "takes the contemporary issue of Christ's indivisible, fleshly body as it inheres in the host and frames it within a Hieronymian understanding of Christ's body as a social body."[40] The Jacob stanza rounds out this ecclesial vision by describing Christ's passion not in more conventional terms of affective piety but in terms of redemption and sacrifice: Christ "gayve forreyne damage" (48), or made public reparation, for the members of the Christian community incorporated as his church.[41]

It is indeed tempting to argue that Lydgate's emphasis on the mystical body supersedes the more orthodox rendering of the Eucharistic host with which the Jacob stanza begins. Yet I want to suggest that this stanza accommodates different Eucharistic signs and theologies rather than marks out a shift from one Eucharistic position (transubstantiation) to another (an emphasis on Christ's mystical body). The Jacob stanza offers the most overt connection between sacramental and royal bodies in the *Procession*, and in so doing it brings us back to the early Christian theologies of *corpus mysticum*, which saw Christ's Galilean, sacramental, and mystical bodies as mutually constitutive.[42] While Lydgate may well adopt a more spiritualist stance on the Eucharist elsewhere in the *Procession*, in the Jacob stanza he collapses multiple theologies—and hence multiple semiotics—of the Eucharist. In this reading, the initial image of the host signifies Christ's substantial body as transformed in the sacramental signs; these sacramental signs, in turn, point toward the assimilation of Christian believers to an ecclesial community, which itself constitutes a focal point of the Corpus Christi procession that lends a thematic frame to Lydgate's verses. What we have, then, is a reflection on the mutual interaction of Christ's Galilean, Eucharistic, and mystical bodies. What appears as a movement from one Eucharistic theology to another may be better understood as a nuanced figuration of the early Christian theologies of *corpus mysticum*, which assimilated all three bodies of Christ. If such a reading is at odds with Lydgate's rejection of orthodoxy elsewhere in the text, this oddity may well reflect the complex semiotics that govern a text that readily negotiates figure and reality, performative procession and written inscription.[43]

In expressing such conflicting attitudes toward the Eucharist and the *corpus mysticum*, Lydgate's *Triumphal Entry* and *Procession of Corpus Christi* do not merely advertise "the medieval mind at its characteristic work" (whether we are speaking in literary or theological terms) but limn the interpretive tensions and complex textual accretions that define debates over the *corpus mysticum* and the Eucharist across the Reformation divide.[44] In the context of the present chapter, the complicated political, theological, and semiotic positions staked out by Lydgate are negotiated further in two plays that situate the king's mystical body in terms of violence and vulnerability: Bale's *King Johan* and Shakespeare's *Macbeth*. Turning first to Bale, I discuss the transformation of the negative chronicle portrayals of King John (r. 1199–1216) in a play that figures this monarch positively as a royal reformer. Such a move is unsurprising given Bale's anti-Catholic bite, which is as sharp in this drama as it is in his polemical prose. *King Johan* divests sacred kingship of its Eucharistic symbolism and articulates instead a new understanding of *corpus mysticum* founded on the authority of scripture. After King Johan is fatally poisoned by a Catholic monk, Imperial Majesty ascends to the throne, regains control of the clergy, and confirms England's integrity as a Protestant nation.

"From Ceremonyes Dead to the Lyvynge Wurde of the Lorde": *King Johan*

John Bale's *King Johan*, often recognized as the first English history play, is influenced by both the allegorical structure of the morality plays and contemporary religious laws, including the 1534 Act of Supremacy (which authorized Henry VIII's break with Rome) and the conservative-leaning Six Articles of 1539 (which preserved traditional Eucharistic doctrine and auricular confession).[45] While the play's editors agree on 1538 as a probable date of composition, evidence also suggests that *King Johan* was revised during the Edwardian Reforms and again after 1558.[46] The play was also performed under the patronage of Thomas Cromwell, notably in the home of Archbishop Thomas Cranmer at Christmas in 1538.[47] While the play's textual and performance histories encompass several phases of England's religious reformations, the play consistently defends the monarch and the royal supremacy by figuring England's king as the sole authority on religious matters.[48] Moreover, the play rails boisterously against the papacy, reduces clergy to mere actors, and dismisses Catholic ceremony as mere pageantry inimical to scriptural truth.[49]

Bale marshals his antipapal and antiliturgical satire toward a new vision of the *corpus mysticum*. For him, liturgical reform is essential to maintaining a reformist stronghold against the ever-present threat of Rome, which saw itself as its own governmental polity. In *King Johan*, Bale does not secularize the *corpus mysticum* in the way that Ernst Kantorowicz suggests, but he does assert the opposition between the mystical and the sacramental that Henri de Lubac critiques. Bale, who was a Carmelite monk before he became a reformer, shapes his political theology according to scriptural authority and vernacular worship as set against the Latin Mass and its sacramental rituals, particularly those associated with the Eucharist. For him, the king's mystical body derives its sanctity from the Word of God rather than the Eucharistic body of Christ, which he rejects in *King Johan* as "that bred so hard ther gald gummes may yt not byght."[50] (Such an image contrasts with Lydgate's description of "Crystes bred, delicyous unto kynges," in *A Procession of Corpus Christi* [46].) King Johan emerges as a religious reformer, a monarch appointed by God to chart a new vision of the *corpus mysticum* by defeating the papacy and turning Protestant England "from ceremonyes dead to the lyvynge wurde of the Lorde" (1119).[51]

Bale advances a reformed political theology by emphasizing King Johan's divine election and situating that godly appointment in distinctly anti-Catholic (and antipapal) terms. At the end of act 1, Interpretour informs the audience that King Johan "was of God a magistrate appoynted / To the governaunce of thys same noble regyon, / To see maynteyned the true faythe and relygyon" (1088–90). As Greg Walker claims, "The twin principles which govern the actions of Bale's John are the certainty of his own divine ordination, with the responsibilities attendant upon it, and a resolve to base all spiritual life upon the text of the Scriptures."[52] The scriptural foundations of King Johan's reign are further evident in Veritas's words to Nobylyte and Clergye: "Learne of the scriptures to have better undrestandynge. / The harte of a kynge is in the handes of the Lorde" (2236–37). Bale upholds this conjunction of royal and scriptural authority in his polemical prose. Answering Bishop Edmund Bonner, he writes: "Kinges, Princes, Magistrates ... had neade to be very circumspecte, what letters, lawes, articles, statutes, or proclamacions they put fourth, specially in causes of religion. They ought nothing to bring in to the Christen church, much lesse to enforce or compelle, that is not conteyned in Christes Gospell."[53] King Johan figures himself as such a king sent by God "to reforme the lawes and sett men in good order" (20); he does so by commanding the Catholic clergy to "Take to ye yowre traysh, yowre ryngyng, syngyng, and pypyng, / So that we may have the scryptures openyng" (1391–92).

However robust its enthusiasm for the royal supremacy, *King Johan* negotiates a delicate balance between approbation and critique of the Henrician program. While Henry VIII broke with the papacy on political grounds, he also retained Catholic doctrines and liturgical practices in spite of contrary positions taken up by Cromwell and Cranmer. As Thomas Betteridge writes, "The Henrician Reformation created a complicated situation in which the process of confessionalization was embraced, but without any proper confessions. Injunctions, examinations, and statements of doctrinal orthodoxy were established parts of Henrician government, but the confession they were designed to enforce was terrifyingly vague to all but the King himself."[54] Bale cautions against Henry VIII's liturgical and doctrinal conservatism by satirizing the material practices of Catholic liturgy, usually in copious catalogs of Popish trinkets: "All your ceremonyes, your copes and your sensers, doubtlesse, / Your fyers, your waters, your oyles, your aulters, your ashes, / Your candlestyckes, your cruettes, your salte, with suche lyke trashes" (1828–31).⁵⁵ Bale himself felt that many bishops of the English church were too accommodating of the Roman rites, and suggests in *King Johan* that if Roman doctrine and liturgy go unchecked, Rome can regain its power. Thus he mocks liturgical ceremonies not only to reduce them to *adiaphora* (things indifferent) but also to signify them as a political threat. As Rainer Pineas argues, "To Bale and his co-religionists, the Henrician church was merely popery without the pope, and Bale's works militantly advocated an English church completely purged of Roman influence."⁵⁶ For this reason, Bale sets the material superfluities of traditional worship in strict opposition to a liturgy based on scripture. King Johan must abolish the former in order to institute the latter, and only by doing so can he steel the reformed church against the encroaching power of Rome.

Particularly threatening to Bale and Cromwell was Henry VIII's affirmation of transubstantiation and auricular confession in the Six Articles of 1539. The first article addresses the Eucharist: "First, that in the most blessed Sacrament of the altar, by the strength and efficacy of Christ's mighty word (it being spoken by the priest) is present really, under the form of bread and wine, the natural body and blood of our Saviour Jesus Christ, conceived of the Virgin Mary and that after the consecration their remaineth no substance of bread and wine, nor any other substance but the substance of Christ, God and man."⁵⁷ Given Henry's retention of Catholic doctrine as expressed in the Six Articles, it stands to reason that, as Peter Happé claims, Bale "wanted to nudge or persuade Henry to go further along the way towards Bale's own brand of Protestantism, bearing in mind that Henry was rarely consistent in the religious changes and that he acted sometimes from personal caprice as well as from a spirit of opportunism."⁵⁸ While there is no evidence that Henry VIII disapproved of the play (in fact, critics suggest that the king would have liked what he saw), Bale's zeal for more aggressive doctrinal and liturgical reform is clear and may explain why, upon the fall of his patron Cromwell, he went into exile.⁵⁹

While the Eucharist remains a key target for Bale's satire, one of the most trenchant liturgical parodies in *King Johan* concerns auricular confession, also upheld by the Six Articles of 1539. The sixth article mandates that "auricular confession is expedient and necessary to be retained and continued, used, and frequented in the Church of God."⁶⁰ In the play, Sedicyon, acting on the pope's behalf, uses the sacrament of penance as a political—and antimonarchical—strategy. He manipulates church-authorized penance in order to turn King Johan's subjects against him and thereby stage his deposition.[61] In a scene that closely resembles the Catholic *forma confidendi*, Nobylyte confesses his sins to Sedicyon (1144–89), who assigns Nobylyte a penance. Rather than having Nobylyte perform the conventional mortifications, prayers, or pilgrimages, however, Sedicyon (acting in the capacity of priestly confessor) demands that he turn against the king:

> Ye know that Kyng Johan ys a very wycked man
> And to Holy Chyrch a contynuall adversary.
> The Pope wyllyth yow to do the best ye canne
> To his subduyng for his cruell tyranny;
> And for that purpose this prevylege gracyously
> Of clene remyssyon he hath sent yow this tyme
> Clene to relesse yow of all yowre synne and cryme.
> (1169–75)

The sacrament of confession, when manipulated for the purpose of advancing the papacy's political agenda, does not foster spiritual health but instead organizes political overthrow; in the words of David Coleman, it is "used as a means to foment treason and sedition within and between political realms."[62] In a sardonic echo of the church-authorized form of absolution, Sedicyon says, "I assoyle [absolve] the[e] here from the kynges obedyence / By the auctoryte of the Popys magnifycence" (1184–85). The sonic play on "obedience"/"magnifycence" suggests how one mystical body (the Catholic Church assembled under the jurisdiction of the pope) displaces another (the reformed church united as an ecclesial body under the authority of the king). Sedicyon forces Nobylyte—with nothing less than salvation hanging in the balance—to reject his obedience to the king in order to support the pope. Such manipulation is an apt example of how liturgical rites could be used to advance Rome's political authority.

While the scene might provoke laughter or contempt for the clergy, it also reveals the pope's political program, which threatens King Johan's reformed political theology. For this reason, Bale's parody of confession charts a related shift in the semiotics of the *corpus mysticum*. We have seen how the concept of *corpus mysticum* emerged out of a Eucharistic context in the early church, so it is not surprising that Bale calibrates his political theology according to a reformed understanding of the sacrament. This connection is evident in two key examples from his polemical prose. First, in *The Epistle Exhortatorye of an Englysshe Christiane* (1544), Bale posits the Last Supper as an origin for the reformed idea of the mystical body. He sees Christ's Eucharistic institution as forging a spiritual collective set in opposition to sacramental transubstantiation: "For a contynuall remembraunce of Christes death in his congregacion was that heavenly supper fyrst ordained / & for a universall thankesgevyng for the most frutefull benefyght of the same. In that sacred supper are the mutual members of Christes mysticall bodye there gathered / perfightlye knyt togyther to their head with the joyntes of fayth and synowes of love / where as it is truly ministered. In youre Popish Masse was never yet soche godlye ordre."[63] The Last Supper joins together "the mutual members of Christes mysticall bodye" through "joyntes of fayth" and "synowes of love." Sacramental efficacy thus lies in the communitarian vision of a spiritual polity that contrasts markedly with what Bale sees as the fleshly spectacle of the Mass. This is precisely the kind of split between sacramental body and mystical body that de Lubac traces in his history of the *corpus mysticum*. For Bale, *spiritual* or *mystical* does not connote "individual," as has been often assumed by those who see the Reformation as a turn toward interiority and private prayer. Instead, it signifies what Bale calls "godlye ordre"—a public, ecclesial collective "knyt togyther" by the word of God as opposed to the transubstantiated host.[64]

In a second example, from Bale's answer to Bishop Bonner, Bale differentiates between his reformed version of the *corpus mysticum* and one predicated on the fleshly trappings of the Eucharistic sacrament: "Blessed is that sacrament of God of their late creacion, called here, not for that it hath Gods blessinge or yet allowaunce, but for that it hath their manifolde blessinges, crossinges, calkinges, and breathinges, with *Hoc est corpus meum*, as they understande it.... So grossely do not we take it in our ministracions, but for a sacrament of Christes bodye, a signe to remembraunce of his payneful suffringes, and a certentie, that we are his misticall members."[65] In place of the ritual actions associated with the Mass, Bale offers a "signe to remembraunce" that reminds the faithful of their membership in Christ's mystical body, the church. Bale does not advocate a thorough eradication of sacramental Communion, but he resignifies the sacrament—and with it the *corpus mysticum*—as the perfected ideal of the ecclesial body in heaven.

King Johan does not live long enough to realize this new vision of political theology. Despite his divine election and his attempt to reform liturgical ceremony, he cannot protect England against papal encroachment. The pope, to whom Bale gives the allegorical name "Usurped Power," conspires with Sedicyon, Dissymulacyon, and Privat Welth to stage King Johan's overthrow: "We four by owre craftes Kyng Johan wyll so subdwe / That for three hundred yers all Englond shall yt rewe" (775–76).⁶⁶ As the tensions between king and pope escalate, Usurped Power formally charges King Johan with heresy and then excommunicates him: "Kynge Johan of Englande bycause he hath rebelled / Agaynst Holy Churche usynge it wurse than a stable, / To gyve up hys crowne shall shortly be compelled" (1005–7).

King Johan's confrontation with Sedicyon is not so much a simple contestation for power between king and pope as it is a debate over the political and theological understandings of *corpus mysticum*. When King Johan finally decides to relinquish the crown—ostensibly to save the English people from the crusade threatened by Rome—he says, "To hym I resygne here the septer and the crowne / Of Ynglond and Yrelond, with the powre and renowne, / And put me wholly to his mercyfull ordynance" (1729–31).⁶⁷ In submitting to Catholic authority, King Johan implicitly incorporates himself into the mystical body of the Roman Church—pope, sacraments, transubstantiation, and all. Moreover, he becomes not a communicant but a supplicant: "Unto Holy Churche ye are now an obedyent chylde" (1805) says Sedicyon, who next directs the clergy to "laye yokes upon hym, more than he is able to beare; / Of Holy Churche so he wyll stande ever in feare" (1934–35). In a public profession of faith to Rome, King Johan is forced to declare, "Agaynst Holy Churche I wyll nomore speake nor loke" (1972), taking on a new identity as a "commen slave" who "shall do nothynge but as we [the Church] byd hym do" (1989–90). As if his self-articulated transformation from reformist monarch to papal servant were not enough, King Johan's incorporation into the Roman Church is marked by the collective singing of *Te Deum* (1974), a liturgical hymn that, we recall from Lydgate's *Triumphal Entry*, signifies the integrity of the Church as mystical body.⁶⁸ Bale appropriates the hymn's late medieval sacramental and ecclesial functions in order to emphasize King Johan's forced shift from a reformed vision of the *corpus mysticum* to a Catholic one.

The conversion of King Johan in the context of royal deposition is punctuated by his eventual murder at the hands of Catholic monks in a scene that unfolds as a Eucharistic parody.[69] While Lydgate's *Triumphal Entry* and *Procession of Corpus Christi* employ the Eucharistic symbolism of wine to suggest the restorative powers of both royal and sacramental bodies (recall, for example, the figuration of wine as "likour of recreacioun" [321] in the 1432 royal entry), *King Johan* inverts that symbolism to signify political and religious fissures. While King Johan himself advocates a reformed understanding of the mystical body as an ecclesial collective grounded in the text of scripture rather than the Eucharistic body of Christ, his murder not only strips the reigning king of monarchical authority but also profanes his sacred body and office. While a new king's coronation would be coupled to the reception of Holy Communion during the coronation ceremony, the deposition of King Johan is cast in terms of a symbolically profaned Eucharist. He meets his death in a cup filled not with restorative sacramental wine but with poison concocted and administered by "bloudsuppers" (1098), a pejorative term used to deride the Catholic clergy in Simon Fish's *Supplicacyon for Beggars* (ca. 1529), a source for Bale's play.[70]

Assuming the role of the monk from the chronicles, Dissymulacyon concocts a drink made from the venom of toads and then obtains sacramental absolution from Sedicyon (who, we recall, performed a similar service for Nobylyte) along with the promise that monks "wyll daylye praye for the sowle of Father Symon, / A Cisteane monke whych poysened Kynge John" (2044–45). Sedicyon figures his "marvelouse good pocyon" (2104) as choicest wine—"a better drynke never was" (2110)—and he enjoins the king to "suppe it of[f] and make an ende of it quycklye" (2115). He then partakes of the poisoned drink with King Johan in a perverse act of communion that promises not life but death. Thus the reforming king dies from poison served to him in a vessel akin to a chalice, which functions as a metonymy for both the Catholic liturgy and the Eucharistic foundations of the mystical body. This ritualized death scene proves that King Johan cannot disassociate *corpus mysticum* from *Corpus Christi*. Because he tries to do so, the monks (acting on the authority of Rome) murder him. This murder inverts the very sacrament of the altar King Johan denies, and it is staged by members of the very clergy he rebukes.

The anti-Eucharistic parody in this murder scene is made more explicit when viewed alongside a woodcut illustration of King John's murder from John Foxe's *Actes and Monuments* (1563) (figure 3.1). "*The description and manner of the poysoning of king John*" captures in six panels the major events of the murder, all of which correspond to events staged in Bale's play. While there is no evidence that the woodcut is based directly on *King Johan*, the panel depicting the poisoning itself includes a caption that reads, "Wassail, my lige," which corresponds to Dissymulacyon's "Wassayle, wassayle," sung offstage while he prepares the poison (2086–91). The woodcut also foregrounds the anti-Eucharistic iconography and liturgical parody exactly as represented in Bale's play. The poisoned cup is figured as a chalice; the monk carries a candle; he presents the chalice of wine to the king as the priest would elevate the chalice during Mass; and he does so while standing behind an altar-like structure. Taken together, these images figure the Eucharist negatively as an instrument of murder rather than salvation—a murder executed by a Catholic monk against an anointed king. The anticlerical sentiment is intensified in the woodcut's adjacent panel, which shows a "perpetuall Masse sung daylye in Swinstead for the Monk, that poysoned the king." With parodic Mass set against real Mass, the scene depicted in the woodcut (like the scene staged in Bale's play) suggests that ritual and anti-ritual are one and the same. This is why, at the end of *King Johan*, Nobylyte calls the pope a "bloudy bocher" who "with hys pernycyouse bayte / Oppresse Christen princes by frawde, crafte, and dissayte" (2407–8). As we shall see, Shakespeare reprises such a characterization at the end of *Macbeth*, when Macduff, holding Macbeth's severed head, declares that Scotland is free from "this dead butcher, and his fiend-like Queen."[71]

Though Bale's blasted Mass puts pressure on a reformed vision of the *corpus mysticum*—a vision that asserts Christ's mystical body over against the Galilean and Eucharistic bodies—King Johan's murder is not the last word on the issue. Upon King Johan's death, Imperiall Majestye assumes the crown, steadies England's reformist course, and brings about its "godly reformacyon" (1401). Working with Veritas, he rescues England from papal control and resignifies the *corpus mysticum* as a distinctly Protestant *ecclesia*. At the same time, both characters posthumously memorialize King Johan not as a weak reformer but as a "proto-Protestant martyr."[72] As Veritas says, "I assure ye, fryndes, lete men wryte that they wyll / Kynge Johan was a man both valeaunt and godlye" (2193–94), which is followed by a lengthy exhortation on King Johan's "godlynesse" (2207) and "noble actes" (2218). Veritas then reasserts the biblical truth of divine kingship and enjoins the Catholic clergy to recognize royal supremacy, in anticipation of Imperiall Majestye's ascension to the throne:

Sacramental Signs and Mystical Bodies in Lydgate, Bale, and Shakespeare 103

Figure 3.1. Woodcut from John Foxe's *Actes and Monuments* (London: John Day, 1563) depicting the murder of King John. Reproduced by permission of Folger Shakespeare Library.

> For in hys owne realme a kynge is judge over all
> By Gods appoyntment, and none maye hym judge agayne
> But the Lorde hymself. In thys the scripture is playne.
> He that condempneth a kynge condempneth God without dought
> He that harmeth a kynge to harme God goeth abought ...
> All subjectes offendynge are undre the kynges judgement:
> A kynge is reserved to the Lorde Omnypotent.
> He is a mynyster immedyate undre God,
> Of hys ryghteousnesse to execute the rod.
> I charge yow therfor as God hath charge me
> To gyve to your kynge hys due supremyte
> And exyle the Pope thys realme for evermore.
>   (2347–51, 2354–60)

Responding to Veritas's demand that the Catholics "gyve to your kynge hys due supremyte" (2359), Imperiall Majestye redresses the deposition and excommunication of King Johan by abolishing papal power and subjecting the people of England to the sovereignty of a reformed king: "He sayth that a kynge is of God immedyatlye. / Then shall never pope rule more in thys monarchie" (2385–86). This time, Clergy responds affirmatively: "If it be your pleasure we wyll exyle hym cleane, / That he in thys realme shall nevermore be seane, / And your grace shall be the supreme head of the Churche. / To brynge thys to passe ye shall see how we wyll wurche" (2387–90). In effect, these passages figure a benediction for Imperiall Majestye that corresponds to the prayers for the king in royal entries, such as the one described by Lydgate in his verses for Henry VI.

Imperiall Majestye assimilates England's political and ecclesial bodies to his own royal person. He then confirms this new status with a final flourish of reformist rhetoric in which he replaces the famous Catholic martyr, Thomas Becket, with the reformist martyr, King Johan:

> Kynge Johan ye subdued for that he ponnyshed treason,
> Rape, theft, and murther, in the holye spirytualte.
> But Thomas Becket yet exalted without reason
> Because that he dyed for the Churches wanton lyberte,
> That the priestes myght do all kyndes of inyquyte
> And be unponnyshed.
>
> (2595–99)

Imperiall Majestye scripts the death of King Johan in a martyrological context and represents the king's death as the harbinger of a new reformation. Yet in re-creating King Johan as the reformed counterpart to Thomas Becket, Imperiall Majestye also hits on an ineluctable truth: it is *he* and not King Johan who shores up England's identity as a Protestant nation. What Johan could not accomplish in deed during his reign, Imperiall Majestye must now recount in words. The fact that King Johan fails to achieve the political and liturgical reformation he promises is evident in his own meek apology to the nation at the time of his death: "Farwell, swete Englande, now last of all to the; / I am ryght sorye I coulde do for the nomore" (2178–79).

The extant 1538 manuscript of *King Johan* breaks off at the scene of King Johan's death, though editors are agreed that the original play continued beyond this point. However, editors cannot agree on whether Imperiall

Majestye was part of the original play in performance or whether this character was added later, perhaps in an Edwardian or Elizabethan revision. In the absence of conclusive evidence, it is anyone's guess whether Imperiall Majestye represents Henry VIII, Edward VI, or Elizabeth I. Peter Happé sees this character as a new addition who continues Johan's reformist agenda, while Greg Walker argues that Imperiall Majestye refers in his speeches to specifically Henrician matters like the Pilgrimage of Grace, and that through him Bale "presents Henry dramatically as the ardent reformer in an attempt to persuade him to adopt the role in reality."[73] The precise historical referent of Bale's political allegory perhaps matters less than the relationship Bale creates between the two monarchs in the play. Imperiall Majestye is a different kind of reformer—because a more aggressive iconoclast—than King Johan. He leads England toward a new horizon of reform and resignifies the *corpus mysticum* according to scripture and the reformed church.[74] This narrative may well play out in a Henrician context, for it was not until the reign of Edward VI that England's liturgical reform took firm hold, not least through the publication of the *Book of Common Prayer* in 1549, two years after the death of Henry VIII, and its significant revision in 1552.[75]

The ambiguity of *King Johan*'s religious politics also raises the issue of the play's place in dramatic history, especially since Bale's play is one of several sixteenth-century dramas written about the historical King John. Two others, written almost six decades later, are the anonymous *The Troublesome Raigne of King John* (1591) and Shakespeare's own history play *King John* (1596).[76] While it is not impossible to suggest that Shakespeare knew Bale's play, recent editors including A. R. Braunmuller suggest that Shakespeare's principal sources were Holinshed's *Chronicles* and *The Troublesome Raigne*.[77] Unlike Bale's *King Johan* and the anonymous *Troublesome Raigne*, Shakespeare's play does not stage King John's death as a Eucharistic parody. Rather, it conveys the death through Hubert's one-line report: "The King, I fear, is poisoned by a monk" (5.6.23). At the start of the next scene, Prince Henry confirms this: "It is too late. The life of all his blood / Is touched corruptibly" (5.7.1–2). Curiously, what Shakespeare reduces to an offstage event related in short, matter-of-fact lines in *King John* he stages explicitly and with abandon in *Macbeth*. The travestied Eucharist staged in Bale's *King Johan* and the anonymous *Troublesome Raigne* is refashioned in Shakespeare's staging of Duncan's regicide in *Macbeth*, which unfolds in the context of a new set of religio-political pressures at the turn of the seventeenth century: the Gunpowder Plot of 1605.

Macbeth's Blasted Mass

Despite the sanctity of the monarch's body and office, kings and queens both faced deposition and weathered conspiracy. Such threats to the body politic were often motivated by religion and in the context of the Reformation were displaced specifically onto Catholicism. This anti-Catholic attack is especially evident in *The Troublesome Raigne of King John*, where the king's bastard son laments the murder of his father at the hands of the clergy: "See how he strives for life, unhappy Lord, / Whose bowels are divided in themselves. / This is the fruit of Poperie, when true Kings / Are slaine and shouldred out by Monkes and Friers" (L4r).

The identification of regicide with the "fruit of Poperie" is a common refrain in anti-Catholic polemic, which frequently blames the murder of the historical King John on the pope and, by extension, the Roman Church. John Bale himself brands the pope as the "troblouse termagaunt of Rome which a fore made all Christen kynges his common slaves." He then presents the pope as the obvious answer to the following questions: "Who subdued and poisoned kynge Johan? Who mourthered kynge Edwarde the seconde / and famished kynge Rychard the seconde most unsemyngly?"[78] In his *Apologie of the Church of England* (1562), moreover, John Jewel suggests that these murders took shape in the context of travestied Eucharistic rituals: "Of what religion I pray you were thei that poisoned Henry the Emperour in the consecrated bread? That poisoned Pope Victor in the holy Chalyce? That poisoned John our King here in Englande, in a drinking cuppe?"[79] Invectives like Bale's and Jewel's lost none of their urgency in the context of the Gunpowder Plot, the foiled conspiracy of Robert Catesby, Thomas Percy, Guy Fawkes, and other English Catholics to murder James I in Parliament on November 5, 1605.[80] The reign of the medieval King John was no less relevant in this early modern context, as suggested by Thomas Spencer in *Englands Warning-Peece* (1659): "His Holiness ... and his Parasites will command bloody Massacres, will commend Treason and Rebellion; Pope Innocent the third, who lived in the time of our King *John*, and was his great and troublesome Enemy, decreed an immortal war against the poor Christians ... charging them with all kindes of Heresies, because they blamed and detested the Vices and Errors of the Popes and Clergy."[81]

The Gunpowder Plot not only fomented anti-Catholic sentiment but also presented an opportunity to shore up arguments for divine kingship as a way to defuse threats to the king's body. In a speech before Parliament following the conspiracy, James I claimed that "God hath so miraculously delivered us all . . . [from] the horrible and fearful cruelty of their Device, which was not only for the destruction of my Person, nor of my Wife and Posterity only, but of the whole Body of the state in general."[82] James I's ascription of his deliverance to God's providence would become a common theme in sermons given on the November 5 anniversary of the Gunpowder Plot. One of the most memorable, at least for its imagery, was delivered by John Donne in 1622:

> They made that whole house one Murdring peece: and having put in theyr powder, they chargd that peece with Peers, with people, with Princes, with the King, and meant to discharg it upward at the face of heaven, to shoote God at the face of God, Him, of whome God hath said, *Dii estis*, you are Gods, at the face of that God who had said so: as though they would have reprochd the god of heaven, and not have been beholden to him for such a king, but shoote him up to him and bid him take his king a gaine.[83]

Divine kingship is not merely metaphorical for Donne, who fashions king and deity as homologous entities. Thus the Catholic plotters commit both deicide and regicide when they threaten to kill the king, an act that Donne figures as "shoot[ing] God at the face of God." Lancelot Andrewes shapes a similar argument around the trope "Nolite tangere Christos meos" (Do not touch mine anointed) and warns the king's subjects against dissent and uprising in a sermon preached in the presence of James I himself: "*See you touch them not*. . . . Whom God hath Anointed, Let no man presume to touch."[84] Andrewes recontextualizes this idiom in the context of the Gunpowder Plot, implying that the conspiracy to touch (by which he means harm or kill) the king was stopped by divine providence. He concludes the sermon with the suggestion that the king's protection is essential for the spiritual and political integrity of the realm: "Whereby, Gods *Anoynted* are endangered, mens soules are poisoned, Christian Religion is blasphemed, as a murtherer of her owne Kings, God in his Charge is openly contradicted, and men made believe, they shall goe to heaven, for breaking Gods Commandements."[85]

James I, Donne, and Andrewes all assert the divine authority of kings in the theological context of the *corpus mysticum*. While their admonitions are intensified by the historical contingencies of the Gunpowder Plot, they also replay similar directives launched in earlier literary discussions of the *corpus mysticum*, such as Lydgate's *Henry VI's Triumphal Entry into London*. When Henry VI comes to the end of his ceremonial entry, Lydgate cites a "precept in scripture" by which angels constantly assure the king's health and safety against threats of violence and conspiracy both foreign and domestic: "To kepe the Kyng from alle damage / In his lyf here, duryng alle his age, / His hyh renoun to sprede and shyne ferre" (436–38). The king's divine protection must also be matched with the subjects' vigilance for his welfare, not least because the king's consecrated body is, according to the theology of *corpus mysticum* (as both polity and *ecclesia*), inherently tethered to the body of Christ. As Henri de Lubac writes, "To say mystical body, is also and at the same time to say sacred body—consecrated body: sacrosanct body, brought forth in the course of a sacred ceremony, through the mystery of sacred prayer, received, as holy nourishment, at a holy table."[86] The mystical body, for de Lubac, is inextricable from the sacramental or Eucharistic body and the communal ritual practices in which it is made present. It is in this Eucharistic context of the *corpus mysticum* that I would like to situate my reading of Shakespeare's *Macbeth*, for many of de Lubac's terms apply to Shakespeare's figuration of King Duncan. As Duncan is a holy king, his body is "sacred," "consecrated," and "sacrosanct"; it has been anointed in the context of the "sacred ceremony" of coronation; and its violation is contextualized in the play by a parodic travesty of "holy nourishment, at a holy table." While Shakespeare does not stage a direct conflict between crown and papacy as Bale does, he does figure Macbeth's murder of Duncan as a desecration of the king's sacred body. By committing such an act, Macbeth jeopardizes the integrity of the *corpus mysticum* on both religious and political levels.[87]

While Harry Berger Jr. stresses Duncan's political weakness—he is "memorialized but not remembered; sanctified as a gracious king, but hardly mourned for as a man"—Duncan's human foibles must not obscure the sanctity of his office. Berger deflates Duncan's sacred kingship on account of his "poor judgments of character" and weak political governance, concluding that "his kingdom is no less shaky than his control of the facts or of his subjects' loyalty."[88] By contrast, Richard McCoy notes that "Duncan is generally seen as a holy king" and "[his] killing is an act of religious desecration."[89] Shakespeare figures Duncan's sanctity by symbolically conflating the categories of physical body, sacramental body, and mystical body—categories Bale labors to separate in *King Johan*. Before Duncan's murder, for example, Macbeth lauds the king, saying that Duncan is "clear in his great office" and that his "virtues / Will plead like angels" (1.7.18–19)—angels, to recall Lydgate's verses for Henry VI, who are biblically charged to protect the king from danger. After the murder, moreover, Macbeth refers to Duncan as "the Lord's anointed temple" (2.3.70) and cites his "silver skin laced with his golden blood" (114); he also concludes that, upon Duncan's murder, "renown and grace is dead" (2.3.96). Macbeth's figurations of Duncan parallel those attributed to Edward the Confessor, whom Malcolm hails as both the paragon of English kings and the perfect embodiment of sacred kingship. Edward can "solicit Heaven" (4.3.149), offer "healing benediction" (4.3.156) with his royal touch, and demonstrate a "heavenly gift of prophecy" (4.3.157), not to mention that "sundry blessings hang about his throne / That speak him full of grace" (4.3.158–59).[90]

Macbeth's murder of Duncan not only violates the monarch's consecrated body but also unfolds as a symbolic profanation of the sacramental and liturgical foundations of *corpus mysticum*. Macbeth's two principal murders—the first of Duncan, the second of Banquo—are contextualized by two royal banquets of state that are figured as parodies of Eucharistic liturgy, especially the Mass. In the first, King Duncan is invited to ostensibly celebrate Scotland's military victory over Norway. During the second, which follows on the murders of Duncan and Banquo, the Ghost of Banquo returns and displaces Macbeth from the table. These banquets not only invert Eucharistic symbolism but, in doing so, also re-create the semiotic tensions between flesh and spirit that define Reformation era debates about the *corpus mysticum*.

Prior to the first staged banquet, Macbeth hesitates to commit regicide for two reasons: first, it would lead to his temporal punishment and eternal damnation; second, it would compromise his double duty to Duncan as both subject and host. He says:

> But in these cases
> We still have judgement here, that we but teach
> Bloody instructions, which being taught, return
> To plague th'inventor. This even-handed justice
> Commends th'ingredience of our poisoned chalice
> To our own lips. He's here in double trust:
> First, as I am his kinsman, and his subject,

> Strong both against the deed; then as his host
> Who should against his murderer shut the door,
> Not bear the knife myself.
>
> (1.7.7–16)

Macbeth admits that killing Duncan amounts not to an ordinary murder but to a direct, treasonous assault on the king's sanctified body. Citing the "double trust" (1.7.12) to which he is bound, Macbeth admits that murdering Duncan would not only constitute treason but also violate well-established protocols of hospitality.[91] Duncan acknowledges these protocols in the previous scene when he calls Lady Macbeth "our honored hostess" (1.6.11) and a "fair and noble hostess" (1.6.25), when he refers to himself as "your guest" (1.6.26), and when he asks Lady Macbeth to "Conduct me to mine host" (1.6.30).

Macbeth's violation of hospitality rituals also unfolds symbolically as a travesty of sacramental rituals, especially the Eucharistic liturgy in which the early Christian theologies of *corpus mysticum* originate. When Macbeth recognizes that murder tends to redound upon the murderer, he reasons that "the ingredience of our poisoned chalice" will likely return "to our own lips" (1.7.11–12). By using the figure of a "poisoned chalice" to represent regicide, Macbeth not only recalls the poisoned drink served by the monk to King Johan at Swinstead Abbey (dramatized in Bale's play and depicted in Foxe's woodcut) but also employs a negative metonymy for the Eucharist—one that runs counter to the more positive association of restorative wine with civic health expressed by Lydgate. The term *chalice* does not require a sacramental connotation, for going back as far as the Anglo Saxon period it applies to any drinking vessel.[92] But as situated in the context of Macbeth's assault on Duncan's consecrated body, it calls to mind the sacred cup used to hold the sacramental wine during the Mass.[93] The chalice's Eucharistic signification becomes clearer after the murder, when Macbeth describes Duncan's blood in Eucharistic terms: "The wine of life is drawn, and the mere lees / Is left this vault to brag of" (2.3.96–98). Duncan's royal blood, McCoy suggests, "is clearly seen as the Eucharistic 'wine of life,' now irretrievably spilt, staining the hands and faces of guilty and innocent alike."[94]

Shakespeare couples the Eucharistic signification of the "poisoned chalice" to Macbeth's use of *host* in the same soliloquy from 1.7. While *host* signifies the secular protocols of hospitality, it also calls to mind the sacramental bread consecrated during the Mass as well as the identification of Christ as the sacrificial victim, or *hostia*.[95] The blood of the *hostia* is, in the Old Testament, that of the slaughtered lamb associated with Passover; in the New Testament, moreover, it is the body of Christ that typologically fulfills God's promise to the Israelites and establishes a new covenant in his blood. In this Eucharistic context, says Caroline Walker Bynum, the blood of Christ is sacramentally efficacious because it comes from "Christ the *hostia* who both remains with God and yet spills out onto humankind."[96] This is the sense in which Thomas Aquinas uses the term in "O salutaris hostia," a hymn written for the liturgy of Corpus Christi, which begins: "O saving victim opening wide, the gates of heaven to all below."[97]

When read in the symbolic context of Eucharistic blood, chalice, and host, the murder of Duncan calls the political and theological integrity of the *corpus mysticum* into question. As an unhospitable host, Macbeth turns the body of his guest (which is also the body of the king) into the *hostia*, or slain victim. He thus separates the king's body from Christ's body and thus realizes in himself a further connotation of *host,* one derived from the Latin *hostem/hostis* (enemy, stranger).[98] Such a characterization makes Macbeth's own Eucharistic figurations of Duncan's murdered body all the more ironic:

> Confusion now hath made his masterpiece:
> Most sacrilegious murder hath broke ope
> The Lord's anointed temple, and stole thence
> The life o'th'building.
>
> (2.3.68–71)

As "the Lord's anointed temple," Duncan embodies the *corpus mysticum*. He is represented symbolically in Eucharistic and Christological terms, which reinforce his status as an anointed king whose royal body incorporates the members of the realm. Moreover, the image of a broken temple connotes not only the king's bodily frame and political office but also the *pyx,* or tabernacle, in which the reserved hosts were kept after the consecration in order to protect them against theft, decay, and desecration. The murder of Duncan is thus tantamount to the seizure of Christ's sacramental body from the church, an episode staged over a century earlier in the Croxton *Play of the Sacrament,* discussed in chapter 5.

Eucharistic images such as "poisoned chalice," "host," "anointed temple," and "wine of life" resonate even more vividly when contextualized by James I's own writings on the divine right of kings, which draw on images of Christ's body to advance such a position. In *Two Meditations of the Kings Majestie* (1618–19), James I offers a thorough exegesis of the Passion narrative in Matthew 27, where Christ is mocked by the Roman soldiers, dressed in a scarlet robe, and crowned with thorns. King James presents this narrative as a context in which to situate royal coronation. He writes, "Here have we in these three Verses, set doune the forme & patterne of the Inauguration of a King, together with a perfect description of the cares and crosses that a King must prepare himself to indure.... The Person was our Saviour Jesus Christ, who was humbled for our exaltation, tortured for our comfort, despised for our glorie, and suffered for our salvation."[99] King James furthers the point by analogizing the king's purple raiment to Christ's death as well as his sacramental blood: "This purple or scarlet dye may also admit a metaphoricall allusion to the blood of *Christ*, that was shed for us. For the robes of his flesh were dyed in that true purple and scarlet dye of his bloud, whose bloud must wash our sinnes, that we may appear holy and unspotted before him in our white robes, washed in the blood of the *Lambe*."[100] Washed in Christ's blood, the king must not only mystically incorporate the realm but also safeguard it, a task that is not without suffering: "That King therefore, who will take his paterne from this heavenly King, must not thinke to weare a croune of gold and pretious stones onely, but it must be lyned with thornes, that is, thorny cares: for he must remember that hee weares not that croune for himself but for others; that he is ordained for his people, and not his people for him."[101] Such sufferings were nearly realized on the royal body of King James himself in the Gunpowder Plot. In *Macbeth* they are meted out on Duncan, who spills his blood as a consequence of Macbeth's treason.

If the king's mystical, quasi-sacramental blood, which James analogizes to Christ's own, flows continuously within the metaphysical line of royal succession, *Macbeth* complicates James's own defense of kings, even those kings who are tyrannical.[102] Moreover, in "opposing the demonic Macbeths with sanctified kingship," as Rebecca Lemon puts it, Shakespeare renders vulnerable what political theology upholds as inviolate.[103] Duncan's murder brings forth a legitimate successor (legitimate, at least, according to the Scottish system of tanistry) who nonetheless obtains the crown by means of treason.[104] The "wine of life" that once flowed in the body of a holy king now flows in a tyrant. This paradoxical transfusion of royal blood from Duncan to Macbeth instates a reciprocal translation of a sacred *corpus mysticum* into a debased *corpus politicum*. Shakespeare's play exhibits a representational pattern in which, as Jennifer Rust writes, "the political is mysticized in new and sometimes frightening ways as relations between the mystical body and the political body are reconfigured."[105] As a traitor, Macbeth enacts such a reconfiguration by murdering a holy king and travestying the sacramental symbols of his investiture, a rupture evident in Duncan's "gashed stabs" that "looked like a breach in nature / For ruin's wasteful entrance" (2.3.115–16). Now that Duncan lies dead, his consecrated body "laced with his golden blood" (2.3.114), Scotland is subject to the rule of a "butcher" (5.7.99).[106] The spilled blood of the holy Duncan, once analogized to the salvific blood of Christ, becomes more akin to the blood of Judas that no baptism can cleanse: "I am in blood / Stepped in so far," says Macbeth, "that should I wade no more, / Returning were as tedious as go o'er" (3.4.137–39).[107]

In murdering Duncan, Macbeth iterates a semiotics of kingship that emphasizes not the king's sacred body but the raw carnality of "vaulting ambition" (1.7.27) and "bloody business" (2.1.49). Grossly realizing the opposition of flesh to spirit in the theology of *corpus mysticum*, Macbeth reduces Duncan's mystical body to a mere representational figure, thereby contrasting it with his own carnal appetites. Moreover, by severing the bond between king and Christ (and, by extension, the mystical and the sacramental), Macbeth forges a "breach in nature" (2.3.115), which manifests itself as the semiotic rift between real and representational presence activated by Banquo's Ghost and extended to the final sequence of equivocated prophecies. In the play's second banquet, to which we now turn our attention, the seemingly formless, yet vital, ghost of the murdered Banquo proves that the absence of a body does not an empty figure make.

This second banquet unfolds, like the first, as a parody of both hospitality ritual and Eucharistic liturgy. The Macbeths identify Banquo as "our chief guest" (3.1.11) and invite him, as they did Duncan, to "solemn supper" (3.1.15). This last phrase recalls an analogy between the king's banquet and Christ's banquet expressed widely in Eucharistic discourse, such as in this passage from Thomas Cranmer:

As in a princes house the officers & ministers prepare the table, and yet other (aswell as they) eate the meate and drynke the drynke: So do the priestes and ministers prepare the Lordes supper, reade the Gospell, and reherse Christes woordes, but all the people say therto: Amen, All remembre Christes death, all geve thankes to God, all repent and offer them selfes an oblation to Christ all take him for their Lorde and saviour, and spiritually feade upon him, and in token therof they eate the bread and drynke the wyne in his mistical supper.[108]

Likewise, the Elizabethan *Homilie of the worthie receyvyng and reverent esteemyng of the Sacrament* characterizes a royal feast as a prelude to the heavenly banquet: "When thou syttest at an earthlye kinges table, to take diligent heede what thynges are set before thee: So now much more at the kyng of kynges table, thou must carefully search and knowe what dainties are provided for thy soule, whyther thou are come . . . not to feede thy senses and belly to corruption but thy inward man to immortalitie and life, not to consider the earthly creatures which thou seest, but the heavenlye graces which thy fayth beholdeth."[109] Set in the context of these analogies between royal supper and mystical supper, Macbeth's banquet emerges more as the tragic inverse of Christ's heavenly banquet than its earthly analogue. Unlike Cranmer's worthy congregants who, gathered into Christ's mystical body, "say thereto: Amen," Macbeth "could not . . . pronounce 'Amen'" (2.2.30). At the moment of Duncan's murder, he admits, "I had most need of blessing, and 'Amen' / stuck in my throat" (2.2.31–32). Macbeth not only travesties the *corpus mysticum* in killing Duncan but also speaks himself out of the ecclesial community.[110]

Macbeth's linguistic excommunication is duplicated when Banquo occupies Macbeth's seat at the banquet and prompts the king to acknowledge, "The table's full" (3.4.46). This is the king's seat, but it is now occupied by a usurping tyrant. By taking the seat of state from Macbeth, Banquo attempts to redress Duncan's murder, not to mention his own. Moreover, by physically unseating Macbeth, Banquo removes the reigning king from full participation in a ritual meal that signifies the integrity of the body politic. As Daniel Swift suggests, "Beginning with the murder of Duncan, the play banishes Macbeth: he is exiled from the community of shared experience."[111] Even though Macbeth urges Banquo to "fail not our feast" (3.1.27), it is Macbeth who, as both host and king, fails his guest once again.

The displacement of Macbeth from the table has both political and liturgical connotations. In particular, it throws light on a key sticking point in sixteenth-century Eucharistic controversies, which centered on communal participation in the liturgy and worthy reception of the sacrament. In the *Book of Common Prayer* (from the original 1549 edition forward), the Order of the Lord's Supper begins with the suggestion that anyone who receives Communion in a state of sin profanes the sanctity of the sacrament and risks his own damnation: "If we receive the same unworthely... we become gilty of the body and bloud of Christ our savior, wee eate and drinke our awne dampnacion, not considering the lordes body.... Therefore if any here be a blasphemer, adouterer, or bee in malice or envie, or in any other grievous crime... let him bewayle his synnes, and not come to that holy table, lest after the taking of that moste blessed bread: the devel entre into him as he did into Judas."[112] By refusing Communion to those in a state of grave sin, the reformed Eucharistic liturgy sees worthy reception of the sacrament as essential to preserving the ecclesial body in terms of the charity and thanksgiving it signifies. Macbeth commits nearly every sin listed in the Order of Communion: blasphemy, malice, envy, and the "grievous crime" of regicide. His murder of Duncan violates not only the king's anointed body but also the mystical body of the realm. This assault on monarchy, which Shakespeare represents as a parody of Eucharistic ritual, evinces Rust's claim that in post-Reformation dramas "ritual confusion is insistently shown to disintegrate (rather than knit together) the corporate body."[113] Macbeth destroys the sacramental and political functions of mystical dining by turning them toward murder. In turn, by excommunicating Macbeth, Banquo's Ghost literalizes Macbeth's prior metaphor and makes Macbeth himself into the "gap in our great feast" (3.1.12).

This gap is registered not only politically but also semiotically, particularly in terms of the representational gap between corporeality and incorporeality that vexes Macbeth in the final acts of the play. Banquo's Ghost, for example, overtakes a ritual banquet in such a way that, as Swift aptly says, "a thwarted feast dramatizes the collapse of shared comprehension."[114] As a "sweet remembrancer" (3.4.37), moreover, the Ghost not only calls to mind the Eucharistic connotation of "Do this in remembrance of me," which was included in the Canon of the Mass and retained in all editions of the *Book of Common Prayer*, but also ironizes Macbeth's earlier invitation, "I'll request your presence" (3.1.15).[115] Like the consecrated host, Banquo is simultaneously presence and absence, sign and thing signified, a "horrible shadow" (3.4.107) and that which is "alive again" (3.4.104).

In turn, the banquet scene presents Macbeth as a failed reader. Lady Macbeth says as much: "When all's done / You look but on a stool" (3.4.67–68). The reference to an empty stool reiterates the point that Macbeth, himself a king in flesh and blood, is politically displaced and sacramentally excommunicated, effectively unseated by an illusory (but no less real) presence. Such chaotic spectacles underscore Lady Macbeth's accusation of Macbeth as one who has "displaced the mirth, broke the good meeting, / With most admired disorder" (3.4.110–11). The disorder, like the displaced mirth, is not so much psychological (the effect of hallucination) as it is semiotic (the effect of dissimulation). Banquo's Ghost proves that regicide renders the world unreadable, as Macbeth can no longer link words to things or spirit to flesh. This gap between sign and thing signified manifests itself in other instances including Macbeth's "dagger of the mind" (2.1.39), the spirits that Lady Macbeth calls "sightless substances" (1.5.48), and the weird sisters who "seemed corporal" but then "melted / As breath into the wind" (1.3.81–82).

The semiotic gap between presence and absence, especially as it plays out in the banquet scene, reprises the dagger soliloquy from act 2, where Macbeth contemplates assault on one sacred body (Duncan's) through the idioms used to explain another sacred body (Christ's). He asks, "Is this a dagger which I see before me, / The handle toward my hand? Come, let me clutch thee" (2.1.34–35). Macbeth's interrogative "Is this?" inverts the most controversial linguistic utterance of the period: "This is my body." Like the consecrated host, moreover, this illusory dagger riddles the relation of sign to referent, substance to shadow. Any explanation ends in paradox: "I have thee not, and yet I see thee still" (2.1.36); the dagger is "sensible / To feeling as to sight" but also a "a dagger of the mind" (37–39); it is both a "fatal vision" (2.1.37) and a "form as palpable / As this which now I draw" (2.1.41–42). As he does with the dagger, so Macbeth attempts to fix the signification of Banquo's Ghost. "Thou canst not say I did it— never shake / Thy gory locks at me" (3.4.50–51), Macbeth charges, before baiting the Ghost further: "If thou canst nod, speak too" (3.4.70). For as much as Macbeth insists on seeing the Ghost as a lifeless illusion, the Ghost retains its agency by which it can, as Macbeth says, "push us from our stools" (3.4.83).

The Ghost, like the dagger, illustrates that by manipulating the semiotics of the *corpus mysticum* Macbeth finds himself confounded by similar semiotic fissures between flesh and spirit. Such figures, which characterized theological debates over the mystical body from early Christianity through the Protestant Reformation, figure at a representational level the political upheaval caused by Macbeth's desacralization of Duncan's kingship. They are particularly evident in the sequence of equivocated prophecies that lead Macbeth to his final defeat. The first apparition, an armed head, warns Macbeth to "beware Macduff" (4.1.85); the second, a bloody child, offers the infamous statement that "none of woman born / Shall harm Macbeth" (4.1.94–95); and the last, a crowned child carrying a branch, assures Macbeth that he "shall never vanquished be, until / Great Birnam Wood to high Dunsinane Hill / Shall come against him" (4.1.107–9). What Macbeth interprets as a triple assurance of his royal security proves to be no more than a set of equivocations. What the prophecies represent on one plane of signification they dissimulate on another. In this final movement, Macbeth's treasonous uprooting of Duncan's royal genealogy is redressed by an ironic, but no less real, breach in nature. Malcolm and his army "bid the tree / Unfix his earth-bound root" (4.1.110–11) and carry before them individual branches that, by means of synecdoche, bring Birnam Wood to Dunsinane Hill indeed.

The coronation of Malcolm that concludes the play does not bring political integrity to Scotland, nor does it reaffirm the sacramental dimensions of the *corpus mysticum* that Macbeth has assailed. This point signals a key difference in Shakespeare's handling of the *corpus mysticum* as compared to Bale's in *King Johan*. Bale condemns the death of a monarch at the hands of the Roman clergy, but he also rectifies the regicide of King Johan with the ascension of Imperiall Majestye, who is a more ardent reformer and one better suited to preserving a political theology based on scripture and the royal supremacy. England emerges as stronger and more integral, because more Protestant, by the play's end. Shakespeare, by contrast, offers no such redemption. Malcolm gains the throne through the same act of regicide committed by Macbeth—an act of treason that makes no improvement on the past. Unlike the Eucharistic parody in Bale's *King Johan*, moreover, the assault on the *corpus mysticum* staged in *Macbeth* symbolically severs the king's royal body from Christ's Eucharistic body. If the play's end puts an end to Macbeth's villainy, it "marks as well the vulnerability of sacred kingship," as David Kastan argues.[116] Such vulnerability is mirrored by a world in which "the frame of things disjoint" (3.2.17). Signs are broken apart from their referents such that "nothing is / But what is not" (1.3.142–43). The "fantasy of uncontested restoration" that Lemon locates in the play's ending is as illusory as a dagger of the mind, hollow as a shapeless substance.[117]

The comparison between *King Johan* and *Macbeth* illustrates that Shakespeare does not accede to a Balean agenda of dramatic or religious reform. He is not writing under the patronage of Thomas Cromwell, nor is he using drama to advance reformed doctrine and politics; his attitude is far more heterodox. *Macbeth* affirms sacred kingship as well as its representation in the context of Eucharistic ritual. The rejection of the sacramental foundations of *corpus mysticum* in *Macbeth* does not pave the way for the rise of an Imperial Majesty figure but rather figures the political upheaval brought about by regicide.

The chasm between flesh and spirit in the fifteenth-, sixteenth-, and early seventeenth-century literary representations of the *corpus mysticum* examined in this chapter reveals that the Eucharist cannot be reduced to either a thematic construct or a religious allusion even in overtly reformist dramas like Bale's. Rather, the body of Christ exerts political, sacramental, and dramatic power on account of the semiotic rifts that it limns—rifts exposed at the outset of this chapter in the early Christian theologies of *corpus mysticum* and in Lydgate's apparent conjunction of multiple Eucharistic idioms in *A Procession of Corpus Christi*. The next chapter transposes this discussion of sacramental power, embodied action, and semiotic representation into a different key: the efficacy of words and gestures as contextualized by the liturgy of the Mass and the linguistic acts of the priest. These powers are recounted by *Everyman*'s emphasis on the priestly administration of the sacraments; they are also the powers that captivate Marlowe's protagonist, Doctor Faustus, and impel him toward black magic.

FOUR

Father Faustus?

Confection and Conjuration in Everyman *and* Doctor Faustus

It has been a central claim of this book that Christ's body is as much a semiotic as a theological construct. We have gauged how, in theology and drama as well as in liturgical ceremony and ecclesiastical organization, the Eucharist produces unresolvable tensions between word and flesh. This chapter considers such tensions in the context of sacramental efficacy, particularly the texts, speech acts, and gestures used by the priest to confect, or make present, Christ's body and blood during the Mass. Eucharistic confection carries with it a unique power over language by which the words spoken by an ordained priest during the Mass accomplish what ordinary words cannot: they make God manifest in the world.

I will begin by considering the relationship between efficacious language and a confecting priesthood in the play *Everyman* (early 1500s), which upholds the ecclesiastical adjudication of the sacraments and emphasizes the priest's role in helping the laity achieve salvation through the church's devotional praxis. More specifically, the play draws attention to the priest's authority over words—particularly the words of the Mass—by which he makes Christ's body and blood present in bread and wine. These words are set forth in liturgical books called missals, which were used by the priest to celebrate the Mass from the High Middle Ages forward. These books, which contain the authorized scripts for the Mass's performative ritual, provide a framework for my reading of Christopher Marlowe's *Doctor Faustus* (A text 1604; B text 1616). When read alongside the missals, Marlowe's play reveals a protagonist who approximates the roles of magician and priest in trying to make his words work efficaciously in the world.

While *Doctor Faustus* has been read as a religious drama about predestination, a psychological drama about salvation anxiety, and a humanist drama about skepticism and the appetite for knowledge, its engagement with sacramental language and rituals has not been sufficiently addressed.[1] By attending to the semiotics of the Eucharist in an otherwise anti-Eucharistic play, I argue that in *Doctor Faustus* black magic fronts for the priestly power over language that Faustus (as a lay theologian) can know about but not himself possess.

In dramatizing such a relation between liturgy, magic, and drama, *Doctor Faustus* unleashes a critical paradox: the books Faustus reads, the language he speaks, and the conjuring acts he performs all depend on the sacramental rituals he purportedly rejects. Yet Faustus does not parody the liturgy in order to desecrate it. Instead, he executes a series of failed performative rituals that bespeak his fascination with priestly power. Faustus's attraction to necromantic books, spells, liturgical acts, and fleshly inscriptions represents what I call his "priest-envy." This term does not indicate Faustus's desire to *become* a priest; rather, it suggests his fascination with the specialized language of Eucharistic ritual used uniquely by Catholic priests.

Keith Thomas notes that the medieval church "acted as a repository of supernatural power" and that transubstantiation was regarded as a "magical notion" by which "the mere pronunciation of words in a ritual manner could effect a change in the character of material objects."[2] By claiming to make Christ present at the level of substance, transubstantiation stands as one of the most controversial supernatural acts and may well constitute what Faustus himself calls "the uttermost magic can perform."[3] What brand of transformation could eclipse producing a deity in one's hands? Set in this context, Eucharistic confection marks out the absolute limit of Faustus's knowledge and power. Not even necromancy can grant Faustus the unique powers over language that a priest can wield.

To understand Faustus's fascination with liturgical rituals, priestly power, and sacramental speech acts, we must consider the fundamental place of Eucharistic confection and clerical authority in Catholic Eucharistic theology. For this we can turn to *Everyman*, a text that highlights the importance of a confecting priesthood to the sacramental life. In *Doctor Faustus*, Marlowe does not simply improvise the dramatic structure of the morality play but also repurposes claims about liturgical language on which *Everyman*'s spiritual didacticism is founded. Rather than reject Eucharistic ritual outright, *Doctor Faustus* combines the spiritual and the skeptical, the magical and the sacramental. As Euan Cameron argues, "When a dramatist could play on the different theological readings of magic and sorcery, as Marlowe did in *Doctor Faustus*, he testified to the currency of a religious and intellectual conundrum to the public mind of his era."[4] Marlowe meditates on such a conundrum by relating magical conjuration to Eucharistic confection in the context of the sacrament's efficacious language and performative texts.

Making God in *Everyman*

The English play *Everyman*, largely modeled on an earlier Dutch play, *Elckerlijc*, has long been heralded as a touchstone medieval morality play.[5] While *Everyman* engages with ideas about reckoning, final judgment, good works, and the afterlife, all of which are conventions of the morality play tradition, there is no extant late medieval dramatic manuscript of the play, nor is there evidence of a late medieval performance. (The earliest record of performance is from London, in 1901.)[6] In fact, *Everyman* may be more properly regarded as a printed playbook from the early 1500s as opposed to a performance script, which is the form taken by other English morality plays such as *Mankind* and *The Castle of Perseverance*.[7] In fact, *Everyman* draws attention to its own status as a printed book in the *incipit*, which states, "Here beginneth a treatise how the High Father of heaven sendeth Death to summon every creature to come and give account of their lives in the world, and is in manner of a moral play."[8] A play that styles itself as a moral treatise—a formal printed text intended to provide religious instruction (in this case, instruction about eschatological matters)—*Everyman* offers a salient account of the necessity, authority, and majesty of the ordained priesthood, which is crucial to Everyman's spiritual education.[9] It is this aspect of the play that commands our attention in the present chapter.

Everyman upholds the priest's power to cure souls and locates this power in the sacramental rites he is authorized to administer by virtue of his episcopal ordination. Since only ordained priests can confect the Eucharist, it follows that only by means of clerical authority can the laity receive the spiritual benefits of the sacrament. For this reason, priests possess both spiritual and political power, and these powers were strengthened in the post-Gregorian reforms of the liturgy. As Caroline Walker Bynum explains, "In the course of the twelfth century, canon law was elaborated, the sacraments were defined, the penitential system and theory that functioned in the later Middle Ages were established, and higher education was brought firmly under the control of the church with the result that advanced theological training became by definition the preserve of the clergy."[10] In *Everyman*, Five Wits affirms clerical authority by praising the priest's importance to the secular world: "There is no emperor, king, duke ne baron, / That of God hath commission / As hath the least priest in the world being" (713–15). Why is the priest so superior to a secular monarch? The answer lies in the priest's adjudication of spiritual matters and his administration of the sacraments: "For of the blessed sacraments pure and benign / He beareth the keys and thereof hath the cure / For man's redemption" (716–18). The "keys" are the keys of the church, referring to the authority of the priesthood that goes as far back as Christ's appointment of Peter as the first pope.[11] The doctrine of the keys grants the priest the power to absolve sins and assign penance, confect the Eucharist, and administer the last rites of confession, communion, and unction. Priestly authority is thus grounded in the Petrine ministry and the belief in apostolic succession, both of which are the ecclesiastical foundations on which the Roman Church is built.

Everyman demonstrates the importance of clerical authority at several junctures, not least of which involves the administration of the protagonist's last rites. The priest is the one who grants Everyman absolution, extreme unction, and the sacrament of the Eucharist prior to his death. As Everyman remarks, "I have received the sacrament for my redemption / And then mine extreme unction. / Blessed be all they that counselled me to take it!" (773–75). Without these sacraments, which provide Everyman with a clear conscience and a proper burial, the fate of Everyman's soul would be jeopardized; with them, however, he apparently dies in a state of grace, as, according to the Angel, his "reckoning is crystal clear" (899). Of course, only a priest could administer these sacraments, which is why Five Wits declares, "No remedy may we find under God / But all only priesthood" (745–46).[12]

The authority of the clergy, however expressed in the administration of Everyman's last rites, is nowhere more evident than in the play's discussion of Eucharistic confection. The priest holds the power to administer sacraments that actually perform what they signify. Unlike mere symbols, these signs are holy unto themselves. As Thomas Aquinas writes, "The corporeal sacraments by their operation, which they exercise on the body that they touch, accomplish through the Divine institution an instrumental operation on the soul."[13] The capacity of the sacramental signs of the New Law to themselves confer God's grace differentiates them from the sacraments of the Old Law (circumcision or the Passover meal, for example), which did not. The pouring of water in baptism; the anointing in confirmation, orders, and extreme unction; and the absolution granted in penance are all sacred signs that, instituted by God and executed by the priest, create a real and holy encounter between heaven and earth.

Such an encounter reaches its fullest expression in the sacrament of the Eucharist. *Everyman* suggests that, because the Eucharist is cardinal within Catholic sacramental theology and hence necessary to achieve salvation, the priests who confect the sacrament eclipse even the power of the angels:

> For priesthood exceedeth all other thing.
> To us Holy Scripture they do teach,
> And converteth man from sin, heaven to reach.
> God hath to them more power given
> Than to any angel that is in heaven.
> With five words he may consecrate,
> God's body in flesh and blood to take,
> And handleth his maker between his hands.
>   (732–39)

As Five Wits makes clear, while God is the primary agent in confecting the sacrament of the altar, the priest is the minister authorized to speak the words of consecration and perform the gestural acts necessary for transubstantiation to occur. As Charles Zika puts it, "To hear mass was 'to see God,' but to see God in the hands of the priest."[14] Indeed, the result of the priest's confection is that he "handleth his maker between his hands" (739) in a real, substantial manner. The priest's centrality to the sacrament also embodies the central connection between the Eucharist as the sacramental body of Christ and the church as the ecclesiastical body of Christ, or *corpus mysticum*, as discussed in the previous chapter.

Eucharistic confection not only emphasizes priestly authority but also asserts the uniqueness of sacramental language, which is unlike ordinary language because of its divinely authorized agency and its power to realize divine mysteries materially in the world. Ecclesiastical power is hereby predicated on a particular form of linguistic power. The words uttered almost silently by the priest during the Canon of the Mass behave differently than do other words.[15] They do not merely refer to Christ's once completed sacrifice but rather make that sacrifice anew on the altar. The priest's words are thus performative in J. L. Austin's sense of the term.[16] For the priest to utter the words "This is my body" and "This is my blood" is for him to *do* something and, in the case of sacramental rites, to do something spiritually and ontologically transformative. When he recites the words of consecration, makes the sign of the cross over the host and chalice, and elevates them for public adoration, the priest turns ordinary bread and wine into Christ's body and blood.

It is important to emphasize, as Aquinas does in the passages devoted to Eucharistic confection in his *Summa theologiae*, that the ultimate power to consecrate lies with God. "God alone works the interior sacramental effect, but that effect is in part manifested through the words and actions of an ordained priest," Aquinas says.[17] In other words, if God is the principal agent in bringing about sacramental grace, then the priest acts in the capacity of an instrumental cause, "not by reason of its own form but by the power of the one who moves it."[18] As Aquinas states later, "The dispensing of the sacraments belongs to the Church's ministers; but their consecration is from God Himself."[19] While Eucharistic transformation happens principally through God's agency, the priest's words and gestures play a crucial part in facilitating the liturgical actions that enable heaven to touch earth. The divine source of sacramental confection is further emphasized in the doctrine of *ex opere operato*, which held that while the priest's words and gestures were essential for consecration, his human frailties had no bearing on the sacrament's validity. The idea of *ex opere operato* ("from the work worked") originated in the Donatist Controversies of the fourth century and was upheld as official doctrine at the Council of Trent (1547). The doctrine held that sacramental grace is conferred by the act itself and does not depend on the moral bearing of the celebrant: "If anyone says that grace is not conferred by the sacraments of the new law through the sacramental action itself [*ex opere operato*], but that faith in the divine promise is by itself sufficient for obtaining the grace: let him be anathema."[20]

For as much as *Everyman* insists on the importance of sacramental action, Eucharistic confection, and clerical authority, myriad reformers derogated the clergy as superfluous and lambasted the act of confection as illogical. For example, in the satiric poem *Concerning the Holy Eucharist and the Popish Breaden-God* (1625), Thomas Tuke argues that a mere mortal, regardless of his episcopal status, cannot create the being that created him: "Never Cake could make a Baker, / And shall a Priest make his Maker?"[21] Tuke excoriates what Five Wits extols and suggests that Eucharistic confection amounts to an ontological impossibility at best and blasphemy at worst. This Protestant polemicist cannot countenance a priest who, in Five Wits's view, "handleth his maker between his hands" by virtue of the words he speaks (*Everyman*, 739). Elizabeth I makes a similar remark in her *Opinions Concerning Transubstantiation*: "And if the Art of Man can make his Maker, / The Smith may do as well as do's the Baker."[22] The emphasis on artistic creation evident in both Tuke's and Elizabeth I's satires suggests that Eucharistic confection not only makes for bad theology but also makes for bad art insofar as it violates the protocols of *poiesis*.

One did not have to satirize the Eucharist in order to challenge the doctrine of transubstantiation, however. From its original 1549 edition forward, the Order of Communion in the *Book of Common Prayer* retains the words of Christ's Eucharistic institution but insists that they call to mind Christ's sacrifice without making his Galilean body present or repeating Christ's sacrifice on the altar.[23] Within the Church of England's Communion liturgy, the words spoken by the priest are seen as referential rather than performative. Thus the revision of the sacrificial function of the Mass inheres within a reciprocal revision of liturgical speech acts. We recall from chapter 1 that while the Church of England did not reject the real presence outright, it redefined Holy Communion in terms of spiritual eating and the faith of the communicant, so that the sacramental transformation was said to occur not at the level of bread and wine but within believers themselves. In like manner, the effects of the sacrament are materialized not by God working through the priest's words but by God working through the heart of the recipient. "The participants in the sacrament of the altar," write David Aers and Sarah Beckwith, "are transformed into the source of life, assimilated to become the body of Christ."[24] As the Elizabethan *Homilie of the worthie receyvyng and reverent esteemyng of the Sacrament* (1563) puts it, "Thou nedest no other mans helpe, no other sacrifice or oblation, no sacrifysyng priest, no masse, no meanes established by mans invention. That faith is a necessary instrument in all these holy ceremonies, we maye thus assure ourselves."[25] The efficacy of the sacrament is no longer tied to the priest's specialized speech act but rather assigned to a collective act of faithful reception contextualized by an ecclesial body at worship. Eucharistic participation therefore replaces Eucharistic confection.

From Wycliffite dissents from orthodoxy to the Elizabethan Settlement, many reformers argued against the version of priestly authority put forward in *Everyman*, where the priest is characterized as compulsory for spiritual administration, not to mention salvation. While the history of the Reformation suggests a prolonged attack on clerical power and Eucharistic confection, English dramatic history suggests that the idea of priestly confection was not so fast to fade. This particular linguistic power returns in the context of Doctor Faustus's pursuit of the black arts. What does a Catholic doctrine of sacerdotal authority and sacramental confection have to do with a drama written by a reputed atheist about an over-reacher who rejects God in the name of Lucifer? The answer, it turns out, is quite a bit.

Magic Books and Mass Books

Doctor Faustus is a play about books, a point illustrated by the well-known frontispiece woodcut that appears in printed editions of the play beginning in 1616 (figure 4.1). Faustus, arrayed in robes and holding a book in his hands, presides over a conjuror's circle. The book is meant to be a book of spells—more specifically a book of necromancy—that Faustus seeks as a replacement for the more legion tracts on law, philosophy, theology, and scripture that he discards in his opening speech. While the necromantic book commands attention unto itself, I want to read it in relation to another book that contains performative scripts for transformative actions: the missal, or Mass book, used by the priest to confect Christ's body in the Eucharistic host. The Mass book is one of several liturgical books that, Bruce Holsinger notes, attracted wide attention in medieval and early modern England. "English print culture was in many ways organized around liturgical production," he writes, adding that the books associated with the liturgy "constitute as much as a third, in many cases half, or more of the surviving attributable books from the vast majority of medieval English libraries." Holsinger goes on to say that in the *Short Title Catalogue* itself, "more editions of

Figure 4.1. Frontispiece woodcut from Christopher Marlowe, *The Tragicall Historie of the life and death of Doctor Faustus* (London: John Wright, 1631). Reproduced by permission of Folger Shakespeare Library.

liturgical books are listed there than those of Ovid, Virgil, Horace, Chaucer, Gower, Lydgate, Shakespeare, Sidney, Marlowe, Jonson, Spenser, and Milton combined."[26] This claim is consequential for literary history during the English Reformation, for it illustrates just how influential religious texts were in shaping the reading habits of English subjects.

The link between these quite popular Mass books and Faustus's magic book relies not simply on an overarching theme of supernatural transformation but more specifically on the efficacy of sacramental words and gestures. This link also illustrates how Marlowe's play creates a space of contested rites in which Faustus negotiates the roles of magician and priest.[27] Read this way, *Doctor Faustus* does not defiantly replace or nostalgically recall Catholic rituals and doctrines. Instead, the play stages the uneasy conjunction of demonic necromancy and priestly confection, thereby eliciting the interpretive difficulties that arise with respect to sacramental language in the Eucharistic Controversies.

For Doctor Faustus, magic presents the opportunity to conjure spirits, raise bodies, and transform landmasses through the power of his words. But these effects of secular magic are not enough. Faustus seeks to obtain "the uttermost magic can perform" (A 1.3.15) and to "try thy brains to gain a deity" (A 1.1.63).[28] Secular magic permits Faustus "to gain a deity" in the sense that he can become godlike. Yet there is another form of magic that allows a mortal man "to gain a deity" in a more literal sense. This is the act of Eucharistic confection, whereby the priest, through the power of God, makes Christ's body and blood present during the Mass. In his sense, the priest acts as the magician par excellence, for as Five Wits reminds us in *Everyman*, "with five words he may consecrate / God's body in flesh and blood to take / And handleth this Maker between his hands" (737–39). All of this is to the point that occult knowledge alone does not satisfy Faustus. "Yet art thou still but Faustus, and a man," he says a mere twenty lines into the play, before he pivots toward greater powers: "Wouldst thou make men to live eternally / Or, being dead, raise them to life again" (1.1.23–25). While necromancy would allow Faustus to raise spirits from the dead, it does not compare with the priest's ability to turn bread and wine into Christ's body and blood. Furthermore, by making Christ present miraculously in the host, the priest also "make[s] men to live eternally" in the sense that the Eucharist was essential for one's spiritual health and ultimate salvation. Again, while Doctor Faustus does not desire to become a priest, he wants to participate in a linguistic economy in which to say something is to do something. Discontented with being a mere everyman, Faustus seeks to arrogate the linguistic powers of a confecting priesthood to himself. The problem is that Faustus, as a theologian and not an ordained minister, can never attain the powers of linguistic confection he seeks.[29]

In the play's first scene, Faustus is attracted to the textual and visual features of necromantic books. The necromantic book is different from the legal, medical, biblical, and philosophical texts Faustus discards in his opening soliloquy because it contains performative scripts for bringing about worldly transformations through the power of words:

> These metaphysics of magicians
> And necromantic books are heavenly;
> Lines, circles, scenes, letters, and characters—
> Ay, these are those that Faustus most desires.
> (A 1.1.49–52)[30]

As both script and spectacle, the necromantic book compels Faustus at the levels of both word and flesh. Before Faustus lands on an actual spell, he is arrested by the "lines, circles, scenes, letters, and characters" that pique his curiosity and attract his sensory response.[31] Faustus then transposes the necromantic books into a religious register and encodes them as "heavenly" (50). He also concludes that "a sound magician is a mighty god" and sets out to "try thy brains to gain a deity" (A 1.1.62–63). Valdes further links the book to sacred powers when he says, "Faustus, these books, thy wit, and our experience / Shall make all nations to canonize us" (A 1.1.119–20). Later, Faustus says to Mephistopheles, "Yet fain would I have a book wherein / I might behold all spells and incantations, / That I might raise up spirits when I please" (A 2.1.161–63).

As a compilation of profane texts used to perform conjuring tricks, the necromantic book calls to mind enchanted books of a secular nature, such as the *grimoire*, which contained various recipes, spells, and cures.[32] Marlowe also displaces onto this secular book of spells the properties of a unique liturgical book, the missal, which has a direct link to sacramental confection. The missal is a specialized book used solely by the priest, and it contains all of the ritual scripts necessary to celebrate Masses for every feast in the liturgical calendar. Chief among these ritual scripts is the *Canon Missae*, or "Canon of the Mass," which comprises the consecratory prayers necessary for the priest to transubstantiate bread and wine. Insofar as the missal contains the words used in the act of Eucharistic confection, it can be regarded as a supernatural book. In fact, in the B text, Mephistopheles speaks of the extraordinary properties of liturgical books when he directs Faustus to "Follow the cardinals to the consistory, / And, as they turn their superstitious books, / Strike them with sloth and drowsy idleness" (B 3.1.112–14). The cardinals' books are superstitious because, as the liturgical equivalent of the secular book of spells, they contain the verbal and gestural formulas necessary for the priest to transubstantiate bread and wine.[33] If the missal compiles the official scripts for the liturgical rites of the Mass, and the Mass was thought to be the most controversial yet most powerful of all ritual enchantments, why wouldn't Faustus want to crack its cover?

Faustus's attraction to the necromantic book is doubly coded, for the book crosses the categories of divine miracle and demonic magic. The necromantic book is the play's first indication that the boundaries between liturgy and magic are hard to demarcate. As Leah Marcus argues, "There is no clear line of distinction between the acts of conjuring performed by the Doctor of Wittenberg and the play's other ritual and doctrinal forms."[34] Though Marcus restricts this observation to the B text of *Doctor Faustus*, the necromantic book operates similarly in the A text, as do the quasi-liturgical rituals that Faustus enacts over the conjuror's circle, which we will examine a bit later. Granted, Marlowe does not characterize the necromantic book as explicitly liturgical, and liturgical books are not included in Faustus's initial catalog of texts at the play's outset. Yet the secular book of magic exhibits several of the formal and textual features of the missal. The formal similarities of these books, combined with the extraordinariness of their contents, further evince Faustus's "priest-envy," which is directed at the most supreme form of supernatural transformation: that which will enable him to "gain a deity" (A 1.1.63). Let us briefly examine some of these similarities.

First, the necromantic books and the missal both contain words that, when spoken in the proper way and the right order, can effect material transformations in the world. The secular magic books provide the performative scripts necessary to raise spirits from the dead; likewise, the liturgical Mass books compile the performative prayers required to make God truly present on the altar. Second, both books display an arresting textual materiality. They contain elaborate illuminations, ornaments, and rubrics that cross the planes of textual representation and physical embodiment. Third, both books belong to a specialized class of reader, whether the ordained priest or the trained magician.[35] Finally, both books are copious. Sarah Wall-Randell reads the necromantic book as nothing short of encyclopedic, claiming that it transcends the limits of its codex, so that Faustus finds "in one volume every spell that [he] could ever need."[36] The missal is likewise encyclopedic. From Advent to Pentecost, Christmas to Corpus Christi, the missal includes every prayer that any priest would ever need. And at its center lies the most essential liturgical script, the Canon of the Mass, which comprises the words and gestures necessary to confect the Eucharist.

Both the necromantic books and the missal display shared textual, phenomenological, and performative features. Thus the "lines, circles, scenes, letters, and characters" (A 1.1.51) that Faustus observes in the secular magic books correspond to the ornate textual presentation of the missal. Three brief examples will suffice to further bear out the correspondences between the two books at the specific level of the material text. These include a folio-sized portrait of the Crucifixion that introduces the Canon of the Mass; the historiated *T* initial that begins the *Te igitur*; and colored blessing crosses that direct the priest to complement his verbal recitations with bodily gestures. These visual features illustrate the correspondence between the mise-en-page of the liturgical book and the mise-en-scène of the Mass. As Eric Palazzo notes, "Certain illustrations may have been the occasion for the creation of a theological discourse through images."[37] These images transcend mere ornamentation, for they show how in the Canon of the Mass body and text work together to efficaciously transform bread and wine into Christ's body and blood.

The first example, the image of Christ crucified, indicates the beginning of the *Canon Missae* and separates this set of prayers from the propers pertaining to specific feasts. Many of these Crucifixion images are reproduced in black and white with some red floriation along the margins, while others are more vividly illustrated. In the latter, for example, the five wounds on Christ's body stand out in resplendent red ink against a backdrop of darker blues and greens.[38] In *An Anatomi, that is to say a parting in Peeces of the Mass* (1556), the Italian reformer and pamphleteer Agostino Mainardi displays a keen understanding of the image's function within liturgical action even though he objects to the Mass itself: "In certen bokes, that is to say the masse bokes . . . the image of the crucifix is paynted, to the intent that the priest might see (as it were presently) him that he calleth on, and with whom he speaketh, saying *Te igitur* &c. At that the passion which is here represented may pearce in to the eye of the heart."[39] Mainardi acknowledges that the image offers a visual cue or instruction to the priest intended to signal the miraculous ritual he is about to perform. The image allows the priest to "see (as it were presently)"—that is, to experience Christ's image as though Christ were really present before him.[40] Far from mere ornament, the Crucifixion image provides a visual cue that connects the priest's verbal and gestural actions at the altar, as well as Christ's Eucharistic body transubstantiated during the Mass, to Christ's sacrifice on the cross. In this respect, the missal's textual materiality coincides with its affective piety.

The connection between the missal's textual and liturgical forms is further illustrated by the historiated *T* initial that introduces the *Te igitur* on the facing page. Mainardi calls this prayer "the most holy and chefe part of the masse" because it is here that transubstantiation occurs.[41] Commenting on the *T* initial, Mainardi notes that "Scholasticus saith . . . that the first letter of this canon should be *T* . . . which in his shape sheweth and expresseth the signe and mistery of the crosse."[42] Figure 4.2 displays one such *T* initial, which not only recalls the shape of the cross but actually uses the cross to form the letter *T*. Thus the image of Christ crucified is itself the first letter of the first word of the Canon of the Mass. In addition, many European editions of the *Missale Romanum* as well as some printed in the Americas contain a *T* initial that circumscribes a Eucharistic scene.[43] The historiated initial *T*, shown in figures 4.3 and 4.4, features an image of the priest consecrating or elevating the host, and this initial is the first letter of the first word of the consecratory prayers. These three historiated initials are related at once to visual devotion, liturgical action, and textual representation. In each instance, the initial unites Christ's body, the priest's body, and the words of the Mass within a poignant liturgico-textual drama.

In addition to the *T* initial, several missals contain red or blue blessing crosses that signal to the priest the places at which he must make the sign of the cross on his body, over the altar, or over the elements of bread and wine as he recites the accompanying text. Figures 4.2 and 4.4 both depict the blessing crosses in the words *hec dona*, *hec munera*, and *hec sancta sacrificia illibata*, which refer to the bread and wine as sacramental gifts as well as holy, unblemished offerings. The crosses are used again during the consecration prayers in the words *cor* ✠ *pus* and *san* ✠ *guis*, as illustrated in figure 4.5. The sign of the cross marked out on the page breaks these words apart with a

Te igitur clementissi=
me pater: per iesum
christū filium tuum
dñm nostrū: suppli=
ces rogamus corpo=
re inclinato donec dicat. ac petim9
Hic erigens se sacerdos osculetur
altare a dextris sacrificiu dices. vti
accepta habeas et benedicas. Hic
faciat sacerdos tres cruces: super
calicem et panem dicendo. Hec ✠
dona. hec ✠ munera. hec ✠ sancta
sacrificia illibata. Factis signacu=
lis super calicem eleuet manus su=
as ita dicens.

In primis que tibi offerimus
p ecclesia tua sancta catho=
lica: quā pacificare: custodire: adu
nare: et regere digneris toto orbe
terrarū vna cuz famulo tuo papa
nostro. N. et antistite nostro. N.

Figure 4.2. Historiated initial *T* in the "Te igitur" prayer. *Missale ad usum insignis ac preclare Ecclesie Sarum* (London: Richard Pynson, 1520), Houghton f Typ 505.20.262, fol. lxxxvii. Reproduced by permission of Houghton Library, Harvard University.

Figure 4.3. Historiated initial *T* in the "Te igitur" prayer. *Missale Romanum ad usum sacrosancte Romane ecclesie* (Venetiis, 1546), Houghton f Typ 525 46.262, fol. 127r. Reproduced by permission of Houghton Library, Harvard University.

Figure 4.4. Historiated initial *T* in the "Te igitur" prayer. *Missale Romanum* (Saragossa, 1511), Houghton Typ 560.11.262, sig. O3r. Reproduced by permission of Houghton Library, Harvard University.

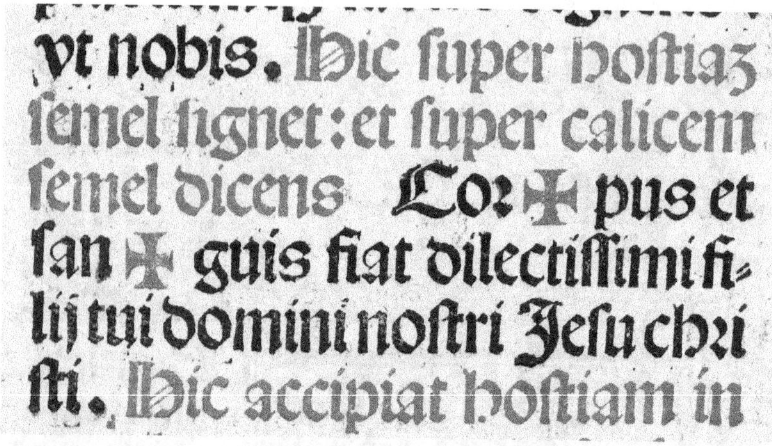

> vt nobis. Hic super hostiaȝ
> semel signet: et super calicem
> semel dicens Cor ✠ pus et
> san ✠ guis fiat dilectissimi fi-
> lij tui domini nostri Jesu chri-
> sti. Hic accipiat hostiam in

Figure 4.5. Blessing crosses as used in the words *corpus* and *sanguis*. *Missale Romanum ad usum sacrosancte Romane ecclesiae* (Venetiis, 1546), Houghton f Typ 525 46.262, fol. 127v. Reproduced by permission of Houghton Library, Harvard University.

typographical signal for a bodily gesture. As the priest utters these words, he makes the sign of the cross over the elements. In doing so he transforms ordinary bread and wine into Christ's body and blood. At a textual level, moreover, the blessing crosses reflect the semiotic tension between body and sign both in the presentation of the words on the page and in the ritual of the Mass enacted at the altar, to which the words correspond. These crosses are not ordinary linguistic signs but textual iterations of Eucharistic sacrifice. They direct the priest to make a gesture that, by virtue of its context in the liturgical rites of the Mass, confects the Eucharist. Robert Sokolowski writes that such a gesture constitutes "an analogue to the verbal citation; it is a kind of quotation of the bodily movement. The citation of the words and the quotation of the gesture allow the things taken up and spoken about—the bread and wine—to become the same in substance as those that were taken up by the Lord."[44] Thus the blessing crosses not only draw the priest's eye to the words of consecration but also represent the Eucharistic sacrifice. The physical breaking of Christ's body on the altar, which repeats the breaking of his body on the cross, is further represented textually by the words *cor ✠ pus* and *san ✠ guis*, which are broken apart visually on the page.[45]

Beyond their local liturgical function in the Mass, the blessing crosses index critical shifts in liturgical practice during the English Reformation. As

Timothy Rosendale has shown, the earliest edition of *The Book of Common Prayer* (1549) displays several correspondences with the Roman liturgy, including the use of blessing crosses in a Communion rite that looked remarkably Catholic in its early iterations. The 1549 edition, Rosendale argues, "provides an equivocal midpoint between Protestant and Catholic, and moves between the Latin liturgy it replaced and the more radical liturgy that would soon follow." The 1552 edition, by contrast, sought to "clear up the doctrinal vagueness" with "the removal of all traces of transubstantiation and propitiatory sacrifice."[46] As a result, any textual rubrics that pointed to the priest's confective powers—the blessing crosses chief among them— were expunged. Rosendale writes, "The words of consecratory Invitation are now free of manual acts—as [Martin] Bucer referred to them, 'those little black crosses'—which might suggest a conjuration of divine presence."[47] In a prefatory letter to Jean Calvin's *A Faythful and most godlye treatyse concernynge the most sacred sacrament of the blessed body and bloude* (1548?), Miles Coverdale makes a point similar to Bucer's, charging that when Christ took bread at the Last Supper "he blessed [it], not crossynge the breade wyth the hinder fyngers, havynge the forefinger and the thombe faste joined together.... No he made no sygne of the crosse at al."[48] As the physical presence of Christ's Galilean body is removed from the liturgy proper, gone too are the textual iterations of fleshly sacrifice.

The removal of the blessing crosses from the *Book of Common Prayer* is a direct reaction to the perceived efficacy of the liturgical language included in the missal. The rubrics of the missal, like the words, lines, circles, and letters of Faustus's necromantic books, suggest that the missal text surpasses ordinary language and therefore constitutes a supernatural script used by the priest to confect God during the Mass. This is a key point of contention among reformers from Wyclif through the sixteenth century, all of whom challenged not only the act of Eucharistic confection but also the clerical authority it signified. What was dangerous from a reformed perspective was not simply the Eucharistic ritual but the presumed efficacy of its words— the force of its priestly performatives. When the priest speaks the words *Hoc est enim corpus meum* and elevates the host and chalice, something actually happens: Christ's real body and blood become really present as substance overcomes sign and heaven touches earth. The missal contains what Regina Schwartz calls "effective" or kinetic utterances; they script the sacramental rites and "make something happen" in a real, indeed ontological way.[49]

As the repository of the liturgical scripts for Eucharistic confection, the missal may be regarded as the prototypical magic book from which Faustus's necromantic rituals derive. Indeed, from the congregant's perspective, the Latin Mass was both a secret conjuration and what Piero Camporesi calls a moment of "highest liturgico-magical tension."[50] The priest, says Camporesi, "had to turn into a necromantic mediator and transform two inanimate substances into bread and wine, into supernatural food."[51] The stakes of the proper execution of the missal's ritual script were high: "Any infraction, however involuntary, in the rigorous ritual of the consecration of bread and wine was seen as particularly serious. The delicate moment of transubstantiation ... had to involve a faithful replica and precise repetition of both liturgical formulas and ceremonial prescriptions."[52] Drama, magic, ritual, sacrifice: the Mass requires a precise execution of gestures and speech acts. Any aberration could have disastrous consequences, the gravest of which was that Eucharistic confection would not be accomplished and the Mass would be invalid.

It is about time we work through the similarities that Eucharistic confection bears to contemporary speech-act theory, for while our working ideas about language and the power of words to bring about material effects in the world stem from the works of J. L. Austin and others interested in the philosophy of language, they can be traced back to questions raised by theological discourse, specifically the Eucharistic Controversies. In *How to Do Things with Words*, Austin discusses several "infelicities" in which speech acts can go wrong because certain protocols are not followed. In addition to the articulation of a set of words, Austin says, "A good many other things have to be right and go right if we are to be said to have happily brought off our action."[53] In Lectures II and III, Austin speaks of various "misfires," utterances in which "the procedure which we purport to invoke is disallowed or is botched: and our act (marrying &c.) is void or without effect, &c."[54] In the specific kind of misfire known as a "flaw," moreover, "we attempt to carry out the procedure but the act is abortive" because of "wrong formulas" in which "there is a procedure which is appropriate to the persons and the circumstances but it is not gone through correctly."[55] In the Eucharistic context, saying the wrong words, omitting words from the consecratory prayers, neglecting to make the sign of the cross over the elements, as indicated by the blessing crosses printed in the missal text, and failing to raise the host at the proper time all constitute misfires that can invalidate the act of sacramental confection. For example, while the priest is the designated minister to say the Mass, if he utters the wrong words or omits a key part of the missal's script (like the crucial "Hoc est enim corpus meum"), he could well bring about what Austin terms "a flaw in the ritual" by which the speech act (and the sacrament) could not hold.[56] In the *Summa theologiae*, Thomas Aquinas meditates on similar errors in the ritual utterances and actions of the Mass (III.60.8–10). For example, if an omission, addition, or alteration destroys the sense of the sacrament, the sacrament is rendered invalid: "If anything is subtracted of those things which are of the substance of the sacramental form the required sense of the words is taken away and, consequently, the sacrament is not accomplished."[57]

The missal's rubrics are designed to ward off such errors in the performance of liturgical ceremony. To confect Christ in the sacrament, the priest must hover over, speak to, touch, and then elevate the bread and wine in a certain manner. The missal's rubrics convey these directions "in the order in which it is required in the service," and they "give texts, music, and instructions where it is necessary that [the priest] should speak, sing, or act."[58] For example, at the beginning of the consecration prayers the priest is instructed, "Hic accipiat hostiam in manibus: et elevat sursum oculis benedicat eam dicens: ..." (Here he takes the host in his hands, lifts up his eyes, and blesses it, saying: ...).[59] Another rubric reads: "Tenens ambabus manibus Hostiam inter indices & pollices, profeit verba consecrationis secrete, distincte, & attente: Hoc est enim corpus meum" (He holds the host in his hands between the fingers and thumbs, says the words of consecration secretly, distinctly, and attentively: This is indeed my body).[60] These rubrics and others like them script a series of liturgical protocols and instructions so as to prevent even the most minor infractions that could invalidate the sacrament.

What the missal deems necessary for the proper confection of the Eucharist many reformers reduce to idle histrionics, typified by the proverbial derogation of the Mass as "hocus pocus," a pejorative conflation of the words of consecration, *Hoc est corpus meum*. George Joye derides the Catholic clergy as "fleshly papists" and "juggelers [who] sleyghly [slyly] can conveye him [Christ] wyth a fewe wordis into a syngyng lofe ... so that they shulde eate hys fleshe & drynke his blood after their owne carnal understanding."[61] The term *juggler* was used in both reformist polemic (notably by William Tyndale and John Jewel) and drama (such as the early Tudor play *Jack Juggler*, discussed in chapter 6) to characterize the priest as a deceptive trickster. Jean Calvin charges that priests delude the faithful with "the erroneous idea that the body of Christ included under the bread is transmitted by the bodily mouth into the belly" and concludes that "the cause of this brutish imagination was, that consecration had the same effect as magical incantation."[62] In a separate treatise on the Lord's Supper, Calvin flatly rejects the efficacy of the priest's words: "Theyr consecration differeth nothinge from a kynde of inchauntment. For after the maner of an inchaunter, they thynke that with whysperynges and diverse gestures they bringe Christe out of heaven into theyr handes."[63] And, exasperated with the full-blown theatrics of the Mass, Mainardi states, "Another abuse is so gret a varietie of gestures, of strange dedes, now this, now that, now the priest stoupeth, now he standeth up.... Oh there be made I can not tell how many crosses, and how much adoo."[64] Joye, Calvin, and Mainardi analogize the Mass to magic in order to emphasize the material excesses of the liturgy as well as the deceptive acts performed by its central conjuror, the priest.

Doctor Faustus echoes such derision. At the same time, however, Faustus gravitates toward liturgical words and actions as a way to "try [his] brains to gain a deity" (A 1.1.63). This resolution suggests that Faustus not only wants to possess divine knowledge but also wants to harness the linguistic power of the priest who makes God on the altar. What Faustus lacks in the capacity of priestly confection he locates in magical conjuration, which offers him a means by which to rule the world as his own empire, span the air with bridges, alter the flow of rivers, cloak the schoolrooms in silk, and reconfigure geographical boundaries (A 1.1.82–99). But the lack of Faustus's true priestly power is displayed at the start of act 4, where even Faustus's secular magic fails him. When Charles V requests Faustus to summon Alexander and his paramour, Faustus can only admit, "It is not in my ability to present before your eyes the true substantial bodies of those two deceased princes which long since are consumed to dust" (A 4.1.45–47). Tellingly, Marlowe expresses the limits of Faustus's power in the Eucharistic context of "substance" so as to underscore the point that a greater form of magic eludes Faustus's grasp.

Indeed, Faustus cannot present a true substantial body to anyone's eyes, yet alone confect the true substantial body of Christ that the priest can make present in the host. What Faustus can do, however, is parody the sacraments he cannot administer and mimic the powers over language he cannot wield. It is to these scenes of liturgical parody—the conjuror's circle, the interlude at Rome, the signing of the deed of gift, and the final vision of Christ's blood in the firmament—to which we will now turn. Before we do so, however, it is worth stating the obvious: nowhere in the play does Marlowe stage a literal Mass. The setting of ritual acts in the theater rather than the church and the placement of liturgical words and gestures in the hands of an actor rather than a priest would not under any circumstance lead to an efficacious sacrament. (Austin himself says that any performative "uttered by an actor on stage" is "in a particular way hollow or void.")[65] However failed his speech acts may be, Faustus speaks secular spells that mock their liturgical correlatives. Hence parody's appeal to both character and playwright: the botched ritual is the only means by which Faustus can assimilate sacerdotal power to himself and Marlowe's only way by which to stage it.

Faustus, the Host, and the Mass

This section treats two related sacramental parodies in *Doctor Faustus*: Faustus's spell over the conjuror's circle (1.3) and the interlude at Rome (3.1), where he mocks the pope and steals the dish and cup. Both scenes throw light on Faustus's attraction to liturgical language and instruments, which itself further manifests his priest-envy. Faustus turns to magic in the play's first scene to "resolve" himself "of all ambiguities" (A 1.1.80). Yet both scenes of liturgical parody are ambiguous. The conjuror's circle and the interlude at Rome not only bring together traditional and reformed texts and rites but also demonstrate the futility of Faustus's magical powers.

Turning first to the conjuror's circle, we see how Faustus presides over his first spell as both aspiring magician and pseudopriest. The clerical connotations are evident in a detail of performance history, for it has been noted that the Elizabethan actor Edward Alleyn may have worn a white surplice and cross during this scene, which signals visually the clerical powers Faustus approximates in this first act of black magic.[66] In addition to the surplice, the spell itself indicates Faustus's attempt to experiment with the efficacious language of sacramental rituals. This experimentation, which is ostensibly an act of black magic, unfolds in a liturgical context:

> Now that the gloomy shadow of the earth,
> Longing to view Orion's drizzling look,
> Leaps from th'Antarctic world unto the sky
> And dims the welkin with her pitchy breath,
> Faustus, begin thine incantations
> And try if devils will obey thy hest,
> Seeing thou hast prayed and sacrificed to them.
> [*Draws a circle.*]
> Within this circle is Jehovah's name
> Forward and backward anagrammatized,
> The 'breviated names of holy saints,
> Figures of every adjunct to the heavens,
> And characters of signs and erring stars,
> By which the spirits are enforced to rise.
> Then fear not, Faustus, but be resolute
> And try the uttermost magic can perform.
> *Sint mihi dei Acherontis propitii! Valeat numen triplex Jehovae! Ignei, aerii, aquatici, spiritus, salvete! Orientis princeps Beelzebub, inferni ardentis monarcha, et Demogorgon, propitiamus vos, ut appareat et surgat Mephistopheles! Quid tu moraris? Per Jehovam, Gehennam, et consecratam aquam quam nunc spargo, signumque crucis quod nunc facio, et per vota nostra, ipse nunc surgat nobis dicatus Mephistopheles!*
> (A 1.3.1–22)

In its content, Faustus's spell desacralizes sacrament and liturgy; in its form, however, it partakes of the rites it travesties. Thus the spell is at once a debasement of Catholic ritual and a reiteration of sacramental materiality in the Reformation world.

The most obvious expression of such religious polysemy is the combination of liturgical Latin and vernacular English in the text of the spell itself. The spell proper is spoken in Latin, which, as John Parker notes, "would have sounded like a version of the Roman liturgy."[67] Faustus's Latin calls to mind the words of consecration spoken silently by the priest as he hovers over the elements placed on the altar. In this sense, conjuration looks a bit like confection. In addition to liturgical Latin, the spell occasions Faustus's use of holy water ("*consecratam aquam*") and the sign of the cross ("*signum crucis*").[68] It also conjoins the secular arts of astrology and necromancy and sets the name of Jehovah "forward and backward anagrammatized" against "[t]he 'breviated names of holy saints" (A 1.3.9–10).[69] The spell is itself an anagram, if not also a messy conjunction of sacred and profane emblems. Yet Faustus does not merely cite the litany of the saints, make the sign of the cross, and sprinkle holy water (all actions that reformers rejected as *adiaphora* at best and idolatrous at worst). He also employs these gestures as part of a spell he thinks is efficacious.[70] While these liturgical props shape sacramental parody, they are also the very instruments by which Faustus imitates priestly confection. In a sense, if Faustus cannot turn a round wafer of bread into the body of Christ, he can use an analogously enchanted circle to try priestly power on for size. This paradoxical connection between conjuration and confection makes the circle at once sacred and demonic, Eucharistic and iconoclastic. This unresolvable ambiguity accounts for the scene's gripping dramatic power. It also prompts a revaluation of Marlowe's religious parody.

John Parker and Catherine Belsey both suggest that the liturgical valences of the conjuror's circle indicate Marlowe's rejection of Catholic ritual. "Latin," Parker says, "once the sacred tongue of the English church, was fast becoming hocus pocus."[71] Belsey agrees, suggesting that Faustus "perform[s] the ceremonies and Latin invocations which constitute a travesty of the signifying practices of Christian knowledge."[72] But must Faustus's spell thoroughly evacuate liturgical ritual and travesty sacramental thought? On the one hand, Faustus conveys through a sacramental semiology the mechanisms of demonic transformation. So religious parody is indeed operative here. On the other hand, Faustus uses demonism as a way to step into the role of priest and mimic the liturgical spells contained in the missal and performed over the host. Far from casting magic as that which dismantles sacrament and liturgy, the spell offers Faustus the chance to play the role of the priest, whose powers of confection he seeks to replicate. In this regard, the conjuror's circle and the spell proclaimed over it may be better regarded as what Jonathan Gil Harris calls a "palimpsest": a material object that conjoins rather than bifurcates temporalities and makes possible "an explosive memory of the past that shatters the present."[73] Seen as such a palimpsest, the conjuror's circle allows a character who outwardly travesties sacramental rites to reveal his implicit fascination with the Roman liturgy, chiefly the powers of a confecting priesthood that he cannot possess.

Faustus's parody of the liturgy not only expresses his priest-envy but also exposes the limits of his linguistic efficacy, even in the secular context of necromancy. Parodies of the sacraments, like any staged representation of them, can never be efficacious because they lack authorized actors, words, gestures, and intentions. The fact that Faustus can only ever employ a parodic blessing or exorcism as opposed to an authorized one underscores the point that he is a lay person and not a priest, or even a competent magician. To use Austin's terms, the best Faustus can arrive at is an "infelicity" rather than a valid performative because he is not an authorized agent (whether a priest or a necromancer) for the actions he wishes to carry out. The entire conjuration over the circle is a failure because Faustus's speech acts do not produce tangible effects in the world.[74]

Faustus's express intention in uttering the spell over the conjuror's circle is to use words to do something—for example, to make Mephistopheles appear in the flesh. Yet nothing he pronounces is ever fulfilled. Faustus himself admits such a failure when he asks halfway through his spell, "Quid tu moraris?" (A 1.3.19; Why do you delay?). Mephistopheles clearly does not come on cue, which causes Faustus to resort to the liturgical acts of sprinkling holy water, reciting the botched litany, performing mock exorcisms, and making the sign of the cross. When Mephistopheles does appear, Faustus congratulates himself: "I see there's virtue in my heavenly words" (A 1.3.27), with *virtue* connoting linguistic efficacy (while also punning ironically on moral probity). A few lines later, Faustus asks, "Did not my conjuring speeches raise thee? Speak" (A 1.3.45). Mephistopheles's reply undercuts Faustus's presumed verbal efficacy: "That was the cause, but yet *per accidens*, / For when we hear one rack the name of God, / Abjure the Scripture and his Savior Christ, / We fly in hope to get his glorious soul" (A 1.3.46–49). Thus it is not Faustus's speech act as much as his blasphemy that causes Mephistopheles to appear.[75] Over the course of his conjurations, then, Faustus cannot do things with his words. His language ultimately goes nowhere.

The connection between liturgical parody and Faustus's priest-envy evident in the conjuror's circle extends deeper into the play, namely the interlude at Rome (3.1), where Faustus taunts the pope and steals his dish and cup. It remains a critical commonplace that the interlude at Rome is aesthetically inferior to the rest of the play. While David Bevington is correct to note that Faustus "uses evil powers to embarrass the pope and his cardinals," the scene extends beyond its entertaining travesty of clergy and sacraments.[76] At one level it combines the literary conventions of farce with the liturgical symbols of the Mass.[77] At another, it serves as the comic prefiguration of Faustus's tragic end. The Eucharistic instruments of dish and cup that Faustus snatches from the pope's table are resignified in the play's final scenes as more serious vehicles (especially the blood of Christ streaming in the firmament) through which Faustus recognizes the prospect of salvation and its devastating loss.

The scene at Rome begins when Faustus and Mephistopheles (both invisible) occupy the pope's "privy chamber" (A 3.1.24) following a fantastic tour of Prussia, France, and Italy.[78] Having landed in "bright splendent Rome" (A 3.1.47), they "take some part of holy Peter's feast" (A 3.1.50). The private banquet attended by the ecclesiastical hierarchy both inverts the Eucharistic meal and satirizes papal decadence. The pope's "dainty dish" (A 3.1.64), like Mephistopheles's sardonic characterization of "a troop of baldpate friars, / Whose *summum bonum* is in belly cheer" (A 3.1.51–52), indicates the ease with which the clergy move from the altar (where they confect the sacrament in bread and wine) to the banqueting hall (where they gorge their bodies on mundane food and drink). Marjorie Garber sums up the scene as an "anti-Mass" that shows how the pope "approaches the meat and wine in an epicurean rather than a sacramental manner."[79] This "anti-Mass" slips into an anticlerical farce when Faustus boxes the pope on the ears and steals his dish and cup at the scene's climax. Here Marlowe doubtless relies on anti-Catholic parody to generate effective comedy. Faustus's antics anger the pope, who exclaims, "How, now! Who's that which snatched the meat from / me?" (A 3.1.68–69). The friars follow with a mock litany in which they chant, "*Maledicat Dominus!*" and curse the invisible agents who engineer the mishaps (A 3.1.89–100).[80]

In spite of its anticlericalism, the scene at Rome also reveals Faustus's fascination with the Eucharist, especially given the ritual significance of the dish and cup as props that refer to the sacrament and the priest's power to confect it. The dish and cup are symbolic analogues to the paten and chalice, the official vessels used by the priest to contain the consecrated bread and wine. Because they are handled only by the priest, they also indicate the priest's singular authority to confect and administer the Eucharist. Therefore, by stealing the pope's dish and cup, Faustus really does "take some part of holy Peter's feast" (A 3.1.50). He becomes a participant—not only a dramatic actor but also a sacramental communicant—at the pope's table.

He also figuratively unseats the pope, who is regarded as Peter's successor and thus the church's highest priest. Nowhere does Marlowe suggest that Faustus desecrates or disposes of the vessels, however. By stealing the dish and cup, Faustus reveals his desire not simply for secular magic but for the supreme power of Eucharistic confection. In this sense, while the dish and cup betray Faustus's priest-envy, they also emphasize his nonpriestly status. Even if he gains the symbolic equivalent of the Eucharistic instruments, Faustus cannot celebrate the Mass or serve himself the sacrament, which also means that he cannot renege on his pact with Lucifer by usurping the priestly power necessary for him to achieve salvation. That salvation, if not already determined according to the Calvinist doctrine of predestination, is gained only through faith combined with the church's sacraments and the priests who administer them. Faustus, this parodic scene reminds us, is not one of them.

The conjuror's circle and the interlude at Rome show how, in his dramatization of a parodic Mass, Marlowe calls the audience's attention to the Mass outright. Transgressive through they may be, these scenes grant stage presence and stage time to Eucharistic ritual and a confecting priesthood on the post-Reformation stage. The sacramental instruments that figure both Faustus's spell over the conjuror's circle and the interlude at Rome inform a second set of related episodes: Faustus's writing of the deed of gift (2.1) and his final gazing upon Christ's blood streaming in the firmament (5.2).

Faustus, Flesh, and Text

In signing the deed of gift, Faustus employs his body and blood—his own *corpus* and *sanguis*—to author the pact with Lucifer. The primary condition for making this demonic contract is an act of bloody inscription that not only has Eucharistic antecedents but also exhibits the semiotic instability of the Eucharist itself. In the deed of gift, flesh and text converge in what Sara Munson Deats calls a "stigmatic script": Mephistopheles, providing his own rubrical instructions, directs Faustus, "Then stab thine arm courageously / And bind thy soul, that at some certain day / Great Lucifer may claim it as his own" (A 2.1.49–51).[81] Mephistopheles situates the pact in the contractual typologies of Hebrew and Christian scripture. The Old Testament topos of "cutting a covenant"—sealing an agreement between two parties with the blood of a sacrificed animal—finds its New Testament analogue in Christ's sacrifice of his own body and blood on the cross.[82] Moreover, within the propitiatory context of the Mass, the priest re-creates Christ's passion by confecting Christ's body and blood and offering it anew as Eucharistic food.

Signing the deed of gift in flesh and blood constitutes yet another attempt by Faustus to use sacramental efficacy for demonic purposes. In a recent study of the religious significations of blood, Caroline Walker Bynum suggests that late medieval and early sixteenth-century writers saw the shedding of blood in terms of sacrifice: "The characteristics of *cruor*, which can pour out yet remain (at least for a little while) red and living, are appropriate representations of Christ the *hostia* who both remains with God and yet spills onto humankind. But the blood of sacrifice . . . is an act—a 'something done.'"[83] Bynum's emphasis on the kinesis of sacrificial activity foregrounds the function of efficacious language to sacramental theology and, in the context of the play, urges us to see Faustus's bodily signature as a "deed" in the dual senses of both legal agreement and physical act. The contractual deed is enacted when Faustus signs it corporeally in his flesh and blood, making his body the textual surface on which the promise is authorized. In the final scene of the A text, Faustus refers to the binding consequences of the deed when he says, "Gush forth blood instead of tears! . . . / I writ them a bill with mine own blood," an exclamation that echoes Christ sweating blood at Gethsemane (A 5.2.30–31, 40). By making Faustus's pact conditional on both a verbal speech act and a physical inscription, Marlowe represents the contract scene according to a semiotic crux that evokes the Eucharistic tension between word and flesh.

Faustus twice inscribes the bond into his flesh: once after he speaks with the Good and Evil Angels (2.1) and again just before he encounters Helen of Troy (5.1). During the first staging, Faustus cuts into his flesh after he pronounces the deed verbally, making the contract sacramental in its use of efficacious language and liturgical in its visual representation. "View here the blood that trickles from mine arm, / And let it be propitious for my wish," he says (A 2.1.57–58). Faustus then elevates his bloody arm for Mephistopheles's observation. The imperative *view* recalls the widespread practice of host elevation and Eucharistic gazing in the Middle Ages, for like the priest who speaks over, blesses, and elevates the host, Faustus makes a pronouncement, effects a change in his flesh, and presents his bloody body to the public gaze. Moreover, Faustus's desire for his blood to be "propitious" echoes one of the key sticking points in the Reformation: Is the Mass a propitious sacrifice—that is, a real re-creation of Christ's passion and crucifixion?[84] If we read Faustus as one who envies the powers of a confecting priesthood, we can see him doing with his own flesh and blood a version of what the priest does during the Mass. Faustus situates his body and his words in the context of sacramental efficacy, using both word and gesture to make his corporeal signature do something in the world.[85]

In our examination of the missal, we saw how the act of Eucharistic confection depends on the coordination of the priest's words and gestures during the Mass. However evocative of Eucharistic sacrifice is the representation of Faustus's blood pact, Faustus's words and deeds do not achieve their intended effects. Writing of the "textuality of the blood" in *Doctor Faustus*, Lowell Gallagher says, "What puzzles Faustus is the evidence that the physical substance of his blood is not consistent with the simple, instrumental function he intends."[86] No sooner does Faustus articulate his will and stab his arm than his blood stops, enacting a corporeal interruption that results in textual failure. He says, "Ay, so I will. [*Writes.*] But, Mephistopheles, / My blood congeals and I can write no more" (A 2.1.61–62). The speaking subject, "I," becomes indistinguishable from "ay," the signifier of Faustus's consent to Lucifer. At the same time, the verb *will* signifies Faustus's intention and also calls to mind the nominal sense of *will* as his official contract. In the B text, Faustus says, "Ay, so I do" (B 2.1.59) instead of "Ay, so I will." The replacement of *will* with *do* confirms the attempted performativity of his speech act and suggests, as evident in his earlier experimentation with magic books and spells, the importance of efficacious language in making his oaths. In his attempt to sign the contract, however, Faustus confronts the rupture of word and flesh that results in a temporarily botched ritual.

Marlowe further marks out this discrepancy between word and flesh in Faustus's verbal transition from "Ay, so I will" (or "Ay, so I do"), which signifies confirmation, to "But . . . / . . . I can write no more," which signifies failure. Faustus's "but" redirects his "ay." At the linguistic level, he is prevented from completing the act of inscription. His utterance, "I can write no more," casts the entire speech act into doubt. At the corporeal level, moreover, the conjunction *but* ruptures flesh from text, which leads Faustus to question the efficacy of his own bloody signature: "Is it unwilling I should write this bill? / Why streams it not, that I may write afresh[?]" (A

2.1.65–66). Faustus desires to cut a contract by writing words into his body. But he is also bound to the flesh and blood that obstruct both his verbal promise and his physical inscription. The liturgical ritual of the legal signing thus goes awry. Both language and body thus become radically unstable in Faustus's signing of the deed of gift, and such instability reflects Faustus's ongoing negotiation of divine and demonic allegiances.

While signing the contract is fraught with difficulty and delay, Faustus ultimately seals the deed when Mephistopheles procures hot coals to spur the flow of his blood. In this respect, body and blood (which assume Eucharistic connotations throughout the scene) come together to author the demonic pact. In the play's final scene, Faustus displaces the physical terms of the contract onto a different bond, which he makes with a mystical vision of Christ's salvific blood. Before his death, Faustus looks upward and exclaims, "See, see where Christ's blood streams in the firmament!" (A 5.2.74), a line omitted from the B text. Faustus then says, "One drop would save my soul, half a drop. Ah, my Christ!" (A 5.2.75). The B text alters the line as follows: "One drop of blood will save me. O, my Christ!" (B 5.2.145). By replacing "soul" with "me," the B text conflates body and spirit; by replacing "Ah" with the vocative "O," it also gives "O, my Christ!" the devotional force of an exasperated prayer. Such an utterance could be performative, in such a way that Faustus's recognition of Christ's salvific blood becomes a formal acknowledgment of his sin and a petition for forgiveness. In this sense, Faustus would exchange word and body for the redemption of his soul. In his subsequent promise to burn his books, moreover, Faustus would in effect offer two corpuses in exchange for Christ's redemptive body and blood.

Given all we have said about the shifting liturgical and sacramental practices in the wake of the Reformation, it is possible to read the play's final scene according to the Eucharistic tensions of word and flesh evident in the contract scene. Sacrament, sacrifice, and semiotics come together in this final moment when, gazing on Christ's blood streaking the sky, Faustus contemplates the Crucifixion: "See, where God / Stretcheth out his arm and bends his ireful brows" (A 5.2.79–80), a point of emphasis omitted from the B text. Faustus's blood, which initially frustrated his signing of the deed of gift, now connects him to the salvific powers of Christ's blood, which according to Thomas Aquinas is the source and summit of all the sacraments.[87] Aquinas writes, "The sacraments of the Church derive their power from Christ's Passion, the virtue of which is in a manner united to us by our receiving the sacraments. It was in sign of this that from the side of Christ hanging on the Cross there flowed water and blood, the former of which belongs to Baptism, the latter to the Eucharist."[88] Such sacramental efficacy is the subject of the spiritual counsel offered by the Old Man, described in a passage unique to the A text: "Break heart, drop blood, and mingle it with tears / Tears falling from repentant heaviness / Of thy most vile and loathsome filthiness" (A 5.1.39–41). Suggesting redemption through charitable works and sacramental grace, the Old Man points Faustus toward a Christological terminus: "But mercy, Faustus, of thy Savior sweet, / Whose blood alone must wash away thy guilt" (A 5.1.45–46). Read in the context of the Old Man's sacramental significations, this blood is akin to the blood that streams in the sky. This is the blood of Christ's passion, and it is not only Eucharistic but also baptismal and penitential in its capacity to cleanse Faustus of his sins. Faustus incorporates the Old Man's sacramental signification of Christ's blood into his final plea in the A text, where he calls out, "O God, if thou wilt not have mercy on my soul, / Yet for Christ's sake, whose blood hath ransomed me, / Impose some end to my incessant pain" (A 5.2.92–94).

Marlowe's focus on Christ's redemptive blood calls to mind the figure of God in *Everyman*, who laments, "My law, that I showed when I for them died, / They forget clean, and shedding of my blood red. / I hanged between two, it cannot be denied; / To get them life, I suffered to be dead" (29–32). When Everyman steps into his grave, he echoes the words of Christ on the cross: "Into thy hands, Lord, my soul I commend; / Receive it, Lord, that it be not lost" (881–82). At the end of the contract scene, Faustus also echoes the words of Christ on the cross when he says, "*Consummatum est*; this bill is ended" (A 2.1.73). Of course, Faustus transposes Christ's last words into the register of a demonic pact. At the same time, however, that pact has biblical and sacramental connotations. This paradox is emblazoned through the sacramental topos of blood—both the salvific, Eucharistic blood of Christ streaming in the firmament and the mortal blood of Faustus used to sign the deed of gift. Marlowe's version of the Faust legend not only foregrounds the familiar saga of a scholar who sells his soul for divine knowledge but also provokes necessary questions about the fate of the soul that is sold. What does Faustus's final sacramental vision of the incarnate God made flesh suggest about the fate of this perplexed protagonist? Does Faustus, like Everyman, find any redemption in Christ's saving blood?

"Due Burial" and Faustus's Return to Church

In a final episode unique to the B text, the Second Scholar says of Faustus's violently dismembered corpus, "See, here are Faustus's limbs / All torn asunder by the hand of death" (B 5.3.6–7). This scene enacts an ironic inversion whereby Faustus becomes the body broken and the blood outpoured, offered to the collective gaze of the scholarly congregation in the play as well as the theatrical audience watching it. Prior to Faustus's death, the Second Scholar enjoins him to "look up to heaven and remember mercy is infinite" (B 5.2.39–40). After Faustus dies, the same scholar provides additional evidence for Faustus's possible salvation through the liturgical rites of the church. He declares, "We'll give his mangled limbs due burial, / And all the students, clothed in mourning black, / Shall wait upon his heavy funeral" (B 5.3.17–19). The liturgical rites of "due burial" and "heavy funeral" enable the physically dismembered Faustus to be spiritually reassembled through the rites of the Requiem Mass, which would be offered by the very priest whose powers Faustus envies.

While Marlowe's play ends with a scene of apparent damnation, it is also punctuated by the prospect of salvation. As Leah Marcus argues, "The 1604 text presents a man in the throes of psychic torment; the 1616 text enacts his literal dismemberment and encodes that bodily condition with ritual significance."[89] Despite the "ritual significance" she ascribes to the B text, Marcus concludes that it is the A text that "leaves open . . . the (admittedly faint) possibility of salvation even at the very last instant," while "in B [Faustus's] damnation is sealed through outward ceremonies."[90] Marcus presumably refers to the "pageant of heavenly throne and hell mouth that shows Faustus his infernal destiny in hideously graphic form," an aspect of the B text's staging that cannot be ignored (and one that recalls the Harrowing of Hell pageants from biblical drama). Yet such a distinction may be too pat, and Faustus's salvation, like so much else in the play, is ultimately ambiguous in both the A and B texts. In the A text, the Good Angel says, "Never too late, if Faustus can repent" (2.3.76), whereas the B text reads slightly differently: "if Faustus will repent" (2.3.80), which suggests the reality of free will and makes Faustus's damnation a matter of choice. These invitations to conversion echo the Good Angel's earlier command in both the A and B texts: "Faustus, repent; yet God will pity thee" (2.3.12).

The B text provides greater insight into the possibility for salvation by alluding to an additional ceremony—the rite of Christian burial—that complicates any neat alignment of the 1616 text with Faustus's damnation. By admitting the possibility of "due," or proper, burial, the Second Scholar complicates a reading of Faustus as unequivocally damned. Those who die in a state of sin would be denied the church's official burial rites, as illustrated by the controversy surrounding Ophelia's truncated burial obsequies in *Hamlet*.[91] We cannot say where Faustus goes at the end of time, but at the end of the B text we know that his body will be brought back to church. Ironically, the Requiem Mass that precedes the "due burial" includes the same liturgical instruments that Faustus mocks when, during the scene at Rome, he chants, "Bell, book, and candle; candle, book, and bell. / Forward and backward, to curse Faustus to hell!" (A 3.1.84–85).[92] Tolling bells indicated death and sacring bells were rung when the host and chalice were elevated so as to alert worshippers to gaze on them; the liturgical book, as we have seen, includes the prayers and rubrics of the Mass; and candles would normally surround the funeral bier at the foot of the altar. Figure 4.6 depicts such a scene as illustrated in a fifteenth-century English psalter whose likely original owner was none other than John Welles (the London mayor who commissioned John Lydgate to write the verses on Henry VI's 1432 royal entry discussed in chapter 3).[93] This is the sort of scene Faustus travesties when he converts "candle, book, and bell" into a curse, which indicates his backslide toward moral turpitude at the same time that he gazes on Christ's blood. Such a tension reprises an earlier scene in which Lucifer reminds Faustus to redirect his attention toward his necromantic pursuits. "We come to tell thee thou dost injure us," says Lucifer. "Thou talk'st of Christ, contrary to thy promise. / Thou shouldst not think of God. Think of the devil" (A 2.3.87–89). Faustus asks pardon, vows "Never to name God, or to pray to him," and says he will "burn his Scriptures, slay his ministers, / And make my spirits pull his churches down" (A 2.3.93–95). When Faustus then reacts to a pageant of the Seven Deadly Sins by saying that such a "sight will be as pleasing unto me as Paradise was to Adam," Lucifer must remind him, "Talk not of Paradise nor creation. . . . Talk of the devil and nothing else" (A 2.3.100–103). Here Marlowe sets sacred and profane, sacramental and satanic in conflict as a way to show that Faustus cannot abandon religious language. Faustus, like Marlowe, thinks on Christ, names God even as he promises not to, and compares a demonic drama to a paradisal experience. *Doctor*

Figure 4.6. Funeral liturgy depicted in the Knollys Family Psalter [Winchester?], vellum, ca. 1430, fols. 28v–29r. Reproduced by permission of Transylvania University Library, Lexington, Kentucky.

Faustus, despite its liturgical parodies, is no iconoclastic play. Like its protagonist, the play talks of Christ, contrary to its purpose.

Such contrariety admits the possibility of a more dynamic relationship between post-Reformation drama and sacramental rites. While the Eucharist and its attendant devotions were contested in church, this does not mean that they could not provide an aesthetic resource for playwrights to explore different dimensions of religious reform or semiotic representation in the theater. We shall see such a reworking of religious material in chapter 5, which focuses on religious objects such as relics and images that reproduce the semiotics of the Eucharist. For now, it is worth noting that the end of *Doctor Faustus* reaffirms its central paradox, for we find Faustus situated between good and evil (allegorized by the Old Man and Bad Angels of the morality tradition, who make a cameo appearance in the play). We cannot know whether Faustus is saved with any greater certainty than we can conclude that he is damned. And by the play's end, Faustus never acquires the priestly powers of confection and consecration he envies. But he does experience a sacramental encounter set in the context of Eucharistic gazing and Crucifixion piety. And, at least in the B text, Faustus's broken limbs are returned not to his study but to the church, with the implication that he (like Everyman) will be given some version of the last rites. The play sounds a final, ambiguous liturgical note by entertaining the possibility of "due burial" for a demonic necromancer who rejected God even as he vied for divine power. There is no more contested a rite than that.

FIVE

Relics and Unreliable Bodies in the Croxton *Play of the Sacrament*, *The Duchess of Malfi*, and *The Changeling*

On January 8, 1522, in the maritime village of Cannobio, Italy, an iconoclast's worst fear was realized: a painted image came to life. According to accounts of this miracle, an icon of the *pieta* that hung in the home of the Tommaso Zacchei family began to spout droplets of blood from Christ's hands and feet. The next day, a piece of rib bone fell out from Christ's side.[1] This miracle, known as *sacra costa* (holy rib), organizes Cannobio's devotional culture to the present day. Every January, the village holds a candlelight procession during which the rib relic is carried from the Church of S. Vittore, where it is housed in an elaborate reliquary above the tabernacle, to the Sanctuaria della Pietà, where the miraculous icon is encased beneath the reredos at the main altar. The latter church was built in 1578 at the command of the archbishop of Milan, San Carlo Borromeo, to commemorate the miracle.

The *sacra costa* miracle fits within an established tradition of Eucharistic *miracula*. In many miracles of this kind, notably the Mass of Bolsena in 1263, the consecrated host bleeds or congeals as flesh in order to shore up the faith of a doubting priest or skeptical communicant.[2] What makes the *sacra costa* miracle different, however, is that it witnesses a shift from iconic likeness to fleshly presence. When a painted icon of the pietà spouts blood and ejects bone, it blurs the very boundary between devotional object and

155

divine body. In addition, the *sacra costa* miracle shows how the semiotics of Eucharistic presence extends to holy objects such as relics, which, like the consecrated host, are physical matter charged through with divine force.

This chapter focuses on such relics as a way to think about Eucharistic semiotics in the context of devotional objects. Like host miracles, saints' relics play a key part in the lay piety of the late Middle Ages because they make divine presence tangible and transportable. They create a material afterlife for the saints, capturing in the smallest fragment of bone or flesh the wholeness of the saint's glorified body. In addition to their devotional functions, relics are the most literary of all religious objects. If in the context of religious devotion relics keep the bodies of saints present after death, in the context of literary representation they work according to patterns of fragmentation, substitution, and dissimulation evident in tropes such as synecdoche and metonymy. Thus what Caroline Walker Bynum calls the "theology of holy matter" cannot be divorced from the semiotics of holy matter.[3] These religious and literary contexts show how the relic's relation to the body is notoriously hard to pin down. Relics not only bring heaven down to earth but also encode the semiotic discrepancies between part and whole, presence and absence, truth and deceit that characterize the controversies over the Eucharist we have been examining throughout this book.

Over the course of this chapter I chart the semiotics of holy matter in three plays: a fifteenth-century Eucharistic miracle play, the Croxton *Play of the Sacrament* (ca. 1461); John Webster's *The Duchess of Malfi* (1613–14); and Thomas Middleton and William Rowley's *The Changeling* (1622). The *Play of the Sacrament* pivots on a series of Eucharistic miracles that bring about spiritual and semiotic conversions. The consecrated host, initially treated as a false relic, ultimately reveals Christ's body as a fleshly image. This climactic miracle corrects the skepticism of the Jews, whose sacramental initiation into the Roman Church rests on their assertion of a Eucharistic semiotics commensurate with transubstantiation, regarded as the orthodox position within fifteenth-century Christianity.[4] By contrast, both *The Duchess of Malfi* and *The Changeling* refigure holy relics into horrifying body parts that signify erotic fantasy, misogyny, and murder. By employing wax heads and discarded gloves that spuriously index real bodies, these plays demonstrate the relic's own instability of semiotic reference. They remind us that the relic's own claim to contain the presence of a saint in the smallest tangible object opens wide the door to religious abuse and semiotic deceit.

Before turning to these plays, I want to consider the semiotics of relics as evident in both Roman Catholic devotion and Reformation iconoclasm. Within Catholic doctrine (as established at the Fourth Lateran Council and upheld at the Council of Trent), a fragment of flesh, a piece of bone, or an article of clothing is seen as an efficacious piece of heaven scattered across the earth. On the other side of the debate, reformers see relics as specious signs that deceive the faithful into idolizing a bone rather than worshipping God. When the smallest bits of mundane matter can stand in for the grandest of divine realities, relations between part and whole as well as body and sign can be easily dissimulated, if not forged outright.

The Semiotics of Holy Matter

Whether a weighty object like a heart or skull, a smaller body part like a tooth, finger, or drop of blood, or even "a bracelet of bright hair about the bone," relics are bits of the body left behind.[5] Far from mere fragments of flesh and bone, however, these sacred remains capture the totality of a saint's glorified body—not only its physical matter but also its metaphysical essence—in its fragments. In doing so, relics contain the saint's *praesentia*, which Peter Brown defines as the "physical presence of the holy."[6] By harnessing the saint's real presence, relics were seen as tangible markers of saintly intercession. As such, they occasioned widespread veneration and were often touched, kissed, and gazed upon by those eager to receive grace, favors, and blessings.

Insofar as they contain the fullness of a saint's holy presence, relics are never mere symbols or icons (just as for Catholics the Eucharist is not a symbolic sacrament). Rather, relics provide a material trace to a glorified body and also carry this trace of real presence across space and time, even transmitting sacred *praesentia* to other objects. In this sense, their semiotic function is primarily indexical. An "index," as C. S. Peirce defines it, is "a sign which refers to the object that it denotes by virtue of being really affected by that object."[7] Relics are "really affected" by the saint's body because they locate the essence of the whole in the physical part. As an indexical sign, the relic posits some propinquity between the saint's body and itself such that the "relationship is concrete, actual, and usually of a sequential, causal kind."[8] Traditional religion regards relics are such "concrete, actual" fragments of bodily matter that bear a physical and natural trace to the body proper, and this is what distinguishes them from ruins, icons, and fetishes.[9]

Relics derive their spiritual power and semiotic logic from the Eucharistic doctrine of *pars pro toto*, which holds that the whole of Christ's body—"not just the flesh, but the entire body of Christ, that is, the bones, the nerves, and the like" (totum corpus Christi, idest ossa et nervi et alia huis modi), as Thomas Aquinas writes—is contained in every particle of the consecrated host.[10] Even though it could not be seen with the sensible eye, Christ's entire body is no less present in a fragment of the host than in a larger piece, no more present in the whole contents of the chalice than in a single drop. The sacramental recipient finds "whole Christ in every crumme," as the seventeenth-century poet Richard Crashaw puts it in "Lauda Sion Salvatorem," a poem based on Aquinas's hymn for Corpus Christi.[11] Relics bear out the synecdoche that defines the semiotic logic of *pars pro toto*. Since the time of the early church, the remains of saints were considered holy in such a way that "every part [of the body], like every morsel of Christ's body eaten at the altar, was a whole."[12] Even the smallest relic—a drop of blood or saliva, a bit of skin, a follicle of hair—made a saint really present on account of its making tangible contact with a single body part that could be translated across time and space.[13] If relics operate like the Eucharistic host in this regard, the converse is also true. Margaret Aston suggests that the creation of the Corpus Christi feast in 1264 was intended, in part, "to provide a focus for popular devotion to the sacrament by making it comparable to the worship of saints and relics."[14] And many late medieval thinkers, says David Aers, "show how the consecrated host could work as the most powerful of relics."[15]

The doctrine of *pars pro toto* lost no urgency in the sixteenth-century Eucharistic Controversies. Thomas Cranmer, for example, protests that the Papists "say that in the Sacrament the corporall membres of Christ, be not distant in place on[e] from another, but that whersoever the hede is, there be the feete, & whersoever the armes be, there be the legges, so that in every parte of the bread and wyne is all together, whole heade, whole feete, whole fleshe, whole bloud, whole hearte, whole longes, whole breaste, whole backe, and al together whole, confused and mixte without distinction."[16] Cranmer suggests the impossibility of locating Christ's body in the host in terms of physical dimension. His hyperbole suggests that when the synecdoche implied by *pars pro toto* is literalized the doctrine becomes "a folishe and an abhominable invencion," not to mention an anatomical mess.[17] By contrast, Stephen Gardiner upholds the logic of synecdoche in the Catholic doctrine of of *pars pro toto*. "As in one loofe of bread broken, every piece broken, is a piece of that bread," he says. "[And] every piece of the bread broken is in it selfe a whole piece of bread, for every piece hath a hole substaunce of bread in it. So we truely speake of the hooste consecrate . . . each one pece is christis hole body."[18] Richard Smith, who also debated Cranmer, deems it heretical to say "that so much is not of the body of Chryst in a part of the hoste, which is consecrate, as in the hole hoste, nor so moche under a little hoste as under a greate hoste."[19] Gardiner and Smith accede to the semiotic terms of synecdoche by which the part of the host is said to contain the whole.

The semiotics of *pars pro toto* is further evident in a key detail of church architecture. Relics, notes Elizabeth Williamson, were to be "embedded in [altars] to sanctify them as the holiest places in the church" so that the very altar on which Christ's body and blood were confected during the Mass would also contain the holy remains of the saints. In cathedrals, moreover, it was customary to find the entire body of a saint entombed under an altar or within a shrine.[20] The altar relics were encased in a slab of stone called a superaltar, which the anti-Catholic polemicist Bernard Garter defines as "a quadrant or stone, four square of Marble," that "hath at every corner, and in the middest, a Crosse, and is halowed."[21] The superaltar was used particularly by recusants during secret Masses. "These stones are portable," Garter writes, "and serve to say Masse on in any secrete place, where there is no Altare, and to that purpose are they sent over into Englande."[22] The superaltar, which contained the sanctified parts of saints' bodies, was itself a part of the altar that stood in for the whole structure. As such, it could be used as a substitute altar on which the Mass could be offered in recusant homes. In a foldout included in Garter's book, the superaltar takes its place among a range of Catholic trinkets (figure 5.1). Garter says that the Papists "sende into this Realme of Englande, Bulles, Pardons, Beades, Latin Primers, Papisticall Books, Superaltares, Pictures of Sainctes, hallowed Graynes, Crosses, *Agnus Dei*, wyth Sainct Johns Gospell in them: and three or four droppes of Balme, font water, and of a hallowed candle," all of which Garter characterizes as "holy Reliques."[23] Garter dismisses all of these items as superstitious superfluities, as does John Foxe,

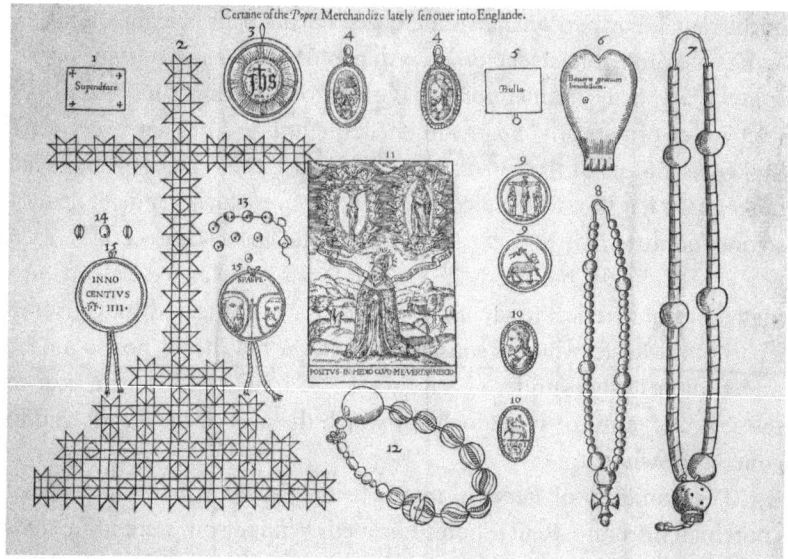

Figure 5.1. Foldout illustration from B. G. [Bernard Garter], *A newyeares gifte* (London: Henry Bynneman, 1579). Reproduced by permission of Folger Shakespeare Library.

who in *A Sermon of Christ Crucified* (1570) describes "the holywater stocke to the hangyng pixe on the high altar. Whiche all beyng packt in one fardell, as in Pandoras boxe together, make but a heape or chaos of phantasticall trifles, procedyng onely of the ignorance of Christ Jesus crucified."[24]

Whereas Catholics saw relics as efficacious matter that bridged earth and heaven, reformers saw them as fleshly distractions. So long as relics were present on earth, the laity (who were attracted to the relic's materiality) could ignore the divine referents properly located in heaven. As Alexandra Walsham puts it, "The notion that the body parts and possessions of Christ and the saints were sources of supernatural power and conduits of heavenly grace ostensibly flew in the face of a system of faith that powerfully re-emphasized the transcendence of the sacred and the incorporeality of the divine."[25] The Catholic teaching that the body parts of a saint could free souls from purgatory, cure sickness, bleed at will, and secure favors was to the reformed mind both implausible and idolatrous. "Bones are bones, not gods," charged the German reformer Martin Bucer.[26] Arguing that devotion to the saints should focus on their charitable example rather than their enchanted relics, William Tyndale writes that "the true worshepynge of saintes is their memorial / to follow them as they did christe."[27] Over a century later Titus Oates (the leader of the infamous anti-Catholic Popish Plot of 1678–79) reduces relics to popish trash: "Instead of worshipping God, and honouring him, they worship and honor Reliques; and instead of trusting in God through Christ, they trust in old rotten rags, and worm-eaten chairs."[28]

Beyond their threatening materiality, relics could be forged and used by the clergy to deceive the laity. As Sebastian Mayer charges, "The laity may have thought that they were venerating holy relics ... but all they were probably doing was kissing the bones of dogs and asses."[29] These false relics manipulate the laity by means of semiotic deceit. They skew the gap between sign and referent by substituting an ordinary bone in place of a saint's body part. Because ossification obscured fine distinctions between human and animal bones, relics were all too easy to forge, counterfeit, and disperse. One need only think of Chaucer's Pardoner, who deceives the faithful with his "large cristal stones / Ycrammed ful of cloutes and bones," which he passes off as "Relikes."[30] The Pardoner turns a profit because the average member of his audience cannot ascertain the difference between a sheep's bone and the Lamb of God. Two centuries later, Jean Calvin addresses the spiritual, semiotic, and economic deceit promoted by false relics when he says, "It is a thing notorious & knowen, that the most part of the reliques that are shewed throughout al places are false and counterfeite, and have been set forthe and preferred by deceyvers, who impudently have abused the world."[31] Devotion very clearly emerges as a front for deception. The relic, which threatens to replace its divine referent, becomes a supplement (in Jacques Derrida's sense of the term) that dangerously stands in for the saint's body. Derrida characterizes the *supplement* as "an addition to the whole that intervenes or insinuates itself *in-the-place-of*" and, Derrida says, "*takes-(the)-place [tant-lieu]*" of its host.[32] What Derrida sees as a productive semiotic plenitude, however, reformers saw as idolatry.

If the Pardoner uses false relics to allure susceptible congregants, another strand of medieval sermon exempla suggests that if a faithful Christian unwittingly took a false relic for a true one, God would miraculously transform the false relic into an authentic relic. In *Dialogus miraculorum* (The dialogue of miracles), written between ca. 1220 and 1235, the Cistercian monk Caesarius of Heisterbach (ca. 1170–1240) asserts, "In my judgment ignorance in such matters excuses the fault; and piety always wins grace. It is certain that this seems to be true, since sometimes the Lord works miracles through false relics to the honour of the saints to whom they are ascribed, and for those who do honour to them in good faith."[33] Caesarius then relates to his novice an anecdote concerning a false relic of Thomas Becket in which "a certain knight who ardently loved the aforesaid blessed martyr Thomas of Canterbury, sought everywhere if he might find any relic of his."[34] Caesarius describes how a guileful priest presented the knight with a bridle purportedly possessed by Becket. "I have in my possession a bridle which the blessed Thomas used for a long time, and I have often experienced its virtues," the priest says to the knight, who unwittingly takes the false relic for an authentic relic and pays the priest for it. Caesarius sums up the account saying, "God to whom nothing is impossible, willing to reward the faith of the knight, deigned to perform many miracles in honour of his martyr by means of this bridle."[35] Caesarius suggests that one kind of semiotic transformation—a divine miracle that turns an ordinary object into a sacred object—can correct another, the deceitful marketing of false relics. The fact that such a provision for divine miracles was commonplace in many medieval sermon exempla suggests how formatively false relics factored into discussions about late medieval material devotion.

A particular kind of relic known as a "contact relic" made this proliferation of false relics even easier to achieve. While not literal body parts, contact relics were objects or articles of clothing touched to the saint's body or even the saint's tomb and thereby imbued with the saint's *praesentia*.[36] The contact relic thus brought about a secondary or tertiary transferal of holy presence. As such the contact relic intensified the relic's own unique materiality, demonstrating that relics were not fixed in a particular location or historical moment (or even to an actual saint's body) but rather were objects that could powerfully displace holy presence infinitely across space and time. The contact relic created for its saintly referent an afterlife that was always expanding, owing mainly to the fact that sacred presence could be transferred and multiplied by means of the slightest touch. But what exactly constituted such contact? If an ordinary object—a piece of cloth, a rosary, an article of clothing—was touched to a follicle of the saint's hair or piece of her skin, was there a transfer of sacred presence? If that same secondary relic touched another object, did it transmit *praesentia*? Was there ever a limit to this multiplication of presence, or could it extend across space and time forever? One can appreciate just how precarious were the relic's claims to real presence grounded on physical contact. These claims inform many additional reformist arguments about relics, which objected not only to the obvious danger of idolatry but also to the semiotic deceit embedded in this devotional practice.

For reformers, the most controversial (because most ubiquitous) contact relics were the pieces of Christ's true cross, which was purportedly discovered by the mother of Constantine, Saint Helena. This contact relic illustrates the semiotic properties of synecdoche. It was assumed that because Christ died on the cross, and made physical contact with the wood, the pieces of the cross were imbued with his real presence (*praesentia*). Following the logic of *pars pro toto*, this real presence would be contained in every splinter of the cross, just as it would be contained in a fragment of bone or in the smallest particle of the Eucharistic host.[37] Whereas traditional believers saw no problem with such a synecdochic claim to divine presence, reformers saw it as suspect. "There is not so litle a town where there is not some peece thereof," says Calvin. "To be short, yf a man would gather together all that hath bene founde of thys crosse, there would be inoughe to fraighte a great ship. . . . What audacitie then was this to fyll the earth with peeces of wo[o]d in such quantitie that thre hundred men can not carry them?"[38] Calvin speaks in similar terms about Christ's crown of thorns: "We must nedes saye that the peeces therof wer planted again for to grow & wexe greene: otherwise I can not tell howe it coulde have bene so augmented."[39] The rampant augmentation of relics shows that the plenitude of relics gives the lie to their authenticity. The unsuspecting laity, allured by this proliferation of holy matter, could not differentiate specious sign from sacred referent.

When reformers like Calvin associate relics with idolatry and superfluous materiality, they implicitly point out the specious semiotics by which all relics operate. Earlier I characterized relics as indexical signs that bear a real, physical, and causal trace to the body of the saint from which they are taken. While entire corpses offer an iconic likeness to the saint's body, smaller fragments do not have to visually resemble that body. Just as the consecrated host contains Christ's body at the level of substance but does not look like Christ's body at the level of physical dimension, relics—as indexes rather than icons—do not have to resemble their bodily referent. After all, while a fragment of bone or drop of blood may be divinely charged at an ontological level, it is decidedly *not* the same as the saint at an empirical level. "In honoring bits of saints," Bynum explains, "we revere physical stuff that will be reassembled, resurrected, animated, and glorified at the end of time. In other words, the relic both is and is not the saint. Insofar as it is, what matters is its matter."[40] The relic's status as a supplemental form of presence—as that which is the body but also is not the body, or, in the Derridean sense, as that which adds to and also replaces its referent—makes it a thoroughly paradoxical form of matter. At the same time that the relic draws the believer into greater physical and spiritual intimacy with the saints, it also differentiates the bodily fragment remaining on earth from the saint's glorified body in heaven.

Holy remains—true relics and false relics, bone relics and contact relics—elicit troubling relations between sign and referent, visible matter and invisible reality. These sacred remains also forge a wide gap between the body and its parts. In the three dramas to which we now turn, relics function as powerful symbolic vehicles for representing fragmented bodies and the signs by which they are dissimulated. In the *Play of the Sacrament*, a consecrated host is stolen, reduced to a false relic, and submitted to a test for real presence. In *The Duchess of Malfi*, wax heads are taken for real bodily remains in an act of misinterpretation that proves fatal to the Duchess. And in *The Changeling*, gloves and a ring are eroticized and taken as real body parts, again with fatal consequences. All three plays—one a late medieval Eucharistic miracle play contained in a single extant sixteenth-century manuscript, the others Jacobean tragedies written for the secular stage—draw on the semiotics of relics as related to Eucharistic doctrine in order to stage episodes of misreading the body and its signs.

"To Prove in Thys Brede Yf Ther Be Eny Lyfe": The Croxton *Play of the Sacrament*

The Croxton *Play of the Sacrament* is a late fifteenth-century miracle play from East Anglia. Its subject is a host miracle that, according to the play's banns, purportedly took place in Heraclea (a fictional city in Aragon) in 1461 and was presented in Rome during that same year.[41] Like its Continental analogues such as the French *La Misterie de la sainte hostie*, the *Play of the Sacrament* centers on a group of Jewish merchants who steal and torture a consecrated host in order to disprove the doctrine of transubstantiation.

While the play was likely performed in the late fifteenth century, both Seth Lerer and Tamara Atkin posit that its single extant manuscript (Trinity College Dublin MS 652 [F.4.20]) is more likely an early sixteenth-century text.[42] I want to build on the play's own trans-Reformational history by suggesting that the physical violence inflicted on the host, which is figured in the play as a relic, has a great deal to do with both late medieval and early modern ideas about reading Eucharistic signs and relating them to the flesh and blood of Christ. The ongoing endeavor to prove the identity of the consecrated host, which propels the play dramatically and theologically, cannot be pinned down to any single theological strain, whether orthodox or nonorthodox, late medieval or sixteenth century. Yet insofar as the play's performance and manuscript histories invite us to cross confessional and historical divides, they also suggest how critical the semiotic interpretation of the host—as body and sign, object and text—was to a number of the intellectual and theological movements that shaped England's long reformation.

Discussion of the Croxton play has focused on physical violence, anti-Jewish stereotypes, critiques of Lollardy, and the negotiation of theatrical and sacramental forms of presence.[43] The majority of these readings emphasize the status of the Eucharistic host as both a theatrical and a sacramental object. As Sarah Beckwith writes, "The miracle in a miracle play is overtly, explicitly, and outrageously theatrical, drawing attention histrionically to its sense of show. The host, the little biscuit, is a mere stage prop. Even the Christ who appears, as the stage directions state, is an image."[44] The host's alluring materiality is especially evident in the play's scenes of physical violence. As John T. Sebastian, the play's most recent editor, writes, "Awash in blood and bedecked with wounded flesh, the Croxton *Play of the Sacrament* places bodies and bodily things center stage" in such a way that "human flesh is everywhere in the play."[45] James Simpson likewise says that in this play "the Eucharist brims with a terrible violence," for it is "an unbreakable body that breaks bodies."[46] In just one thousand lines, we see the host pricked, poked, beaten, and nailed to a wall; we see one of its abusers dismembered; and at the play's climax, we confront the bloody image of Christ bursting out of an oven.

My reading of the Croxton *Play of the Sacrament* relates these physical tortures—the "new passyoun" and "new turmentry" inflicted violently on the host—to a complementary pattern of semiotic violence by which the significations attributed to the sacrament by the doctrine of transubstantiation are called into question and submitted to bloody proof.⁴⁷ In so doing, it shifts critical emphasis on the host's physicality to the violent verbal abuse by which it is translated from sacred relic to secular object.

The connection between physical violence and semiotic violence may be best expressed in the play's figuration of the host as the relic of all holy relics. The host, which is arguably the most controversial sacred object in medieval and early modern Christianity, organizes scenes of interpretation and misinterpretation that dramatize many of the semiotic problems posed in the Eucharistic Controversies. As the host changes hands—moving from the Catholic merchant Aristorius to the Jewish merchant Jonathas and finally to the bishop Episcopus—it not only undergoes a sequence of physical abuses but also changes significations from an enchanted object to a trivial cake and then to a sacramental body. By attempting to impose a new signification on the host, the Jews strive to unsettle a semiotic paradigm in which the sign constitutes Christ's divine body at the level of substance. However, the final religious conversion of the Jews involves a compulsory semiotic conversion: the repentant Jews must call the host by a new name—the body of Christ—and must publicly acknowledge a Eucharistic semiotics predicated on transubstantiation.

For much of the play, the host is hardly treated like a holy relic, and surely not as the *hostia*, or sacrificial victim offered on the altar. The violence inflicted upon the host takes two forms: before the host is physically assaulted, it is verbally abused. By wresting the host from its signification as Christ's body in substance, Jonathas endeavors to prove that it is an ordinary piece of bread. He first reduces the consecrated body of God to a mere commodity, calling it a "maner of marchandis" (284) that he can "bey and sell" (252).⁴⁸ Then, after obtaining the host from Aristorius, Jonathas says he "shall kepe thys trusty treasure, / As I wold doo my gold and fee" (381–82). *Treasure*, a term used in reference to relics and shrines in the late Middle Ages, now connotes a vendible good that Jonathas inserts into his *wunderkammer* of exotic objects.⁴⁹ The consecrated host thus takes its place in a rhetorical catalog of commercial goods that includes an "abunddaunce of spycys" and "saphyre seemly" as well as "perlys precyous" and "curyous carbunclys" (159, 163, 169, 172).⁵⁰

In addition to commoditizing the host, Jonathas verbally mocks it as a "cake," or common bread.⁵¹ This act of renaming constitutes a semiotic perversion of a sacramental object. *Cake* was not always a derisive term, for in devotional lyrics it is written that "Gods body is hed / In a cake ybakenne fresche."[52] Jonathas, however, uses the term pejoratively at least ten times. "The beleve of thes Cristen men ys false, as I wene," he says, "For they beleve on a cake" (199–200). By resignifying the host as a trivial cake and thereby as the opposite of Christ's Eucharistic body, Jonathas reduces the elevation of the host (which was the climax of the Mass) to idol worship, concluding that for Christians, "Yowr God . . . ys full mytheti in a cake" (285).[53] The term *cake* overdetermines the host's materiality and aligns it with the relics, statues, and icons proverbially reduced to "dead stocks and stones" in the polemical attacks on orthodoxy leveled by Wycliffites.[54] To claim that God can be found in a cake, as Jonathas would have it, is no better than saying that the fullness of a saint's presence can be located in a shard of bone or drop of blood. However alarming his violent treatment of the Eucharistic object (both verbally and physically), Jonathas hits on the fundamental semiotic paradox of the host itself: How can the body of God be contained in ordinary bread?

Jonathas's verbal debasement of the host—what I have referred to as his semiotic violence—prepares us for the sequence of physical tortures that comprises an arresting piece of stagecraft.[55] In addition to its vibrant theatrics and suggestions of religious hostility, the violence of host desecration organizes an extended inquiry into the semiotics of the Eucharist, if not also a staged version of Eucharistic controversy.[56] After all, the Jews' torture of the host pivots on the discrepancy between visible sacramental sign (the host) and invisible referent (the body of Christ). This semiotic discrepancy elicits a range of questions that stem from the earliest theological controversies over the sacrament: How can such a small piece of visible matter contain a body that is physically and metaphysically larger than it? How can one bridge the gap between the visible host and the invisible body of Christ? Is this discrepancy a fundamental deception in orthodox Eucharistic teaching or is it a matter of faith? Eucharistic controversy exerts considerable dramatic and theological energies in this seemingly orthodox Eucharistic miracle play.

The strands of Eucharistic debate taken up in the *Play of the Sacrament* all address the critical gap between Christ's Eucharistic body and its sacramental signs, which opens out a related distinction between what faith asserts and what the senses can perceive. By situating the response of Jonathas and the Jews in the wider context of Eucharistic controversy, we can see that the physical violence for which the play has been noted unfolds in direct relation to the host's vexing semiotics. For example, Jonathas calls the doctrine of transubstantiation "onkynd" (200), which Sebastian glosses as unnatural and therefore irrational. He also reduces the doctrine to a "conceyte" (203)—a trick or device—invented by priests and unsupported by scripture. Jonathas also rejects the host's semiotics, claiming that so long as the host is a piece of bread it cannot also "be He that deyed upon the Rode" (204). Masphat reiterates the point when he says, "I dare sey feythfulli that ther feyth ys false: / That was never He that on Calvery was kyld / Or in bred for to be blode: yt ys ontrewe als[o]" (213–15).

Jonathas and Masphat cannot countenance the lack of visual resemblance between host and Christ on which the doctrine (and semiotics) of transubstantiation rests. Neither could John Wyclif and other opponents of orthodoxy. As David Aers notes, Wyclif mounts a counterargument that "concerns seeming, semblance, and deception in the sacramental sign."[57] Wyclif writes, "I knowleche that the sacrament of the auter is verrey Goddus body in fourme of brede. But it is in another maner Godus body than it is in heven. For in heven it is seve[n] fot [feet] in fourme and figure of flesshe and blode. But in the sacrament Goddus body is be miracle of God in fourme of brede, and is he n[ei]ther of seven fote, ne in mannes figure."[58] Wyclif makes the basic point that Christ's Eucharistic body is not the same as the Galilean body, and he suggests the impossibility of locating Christ's physical dimensions in a small wafer of bread.[59]

The host torture in the Croxton *Play* operates along a similar line of argument, for the Jews torture the host in order to prove that it is only bread and not God's body. If in Eucharistic miracles like the Mass of Bolsena the host bleeds in order to correct a believer's doubt, Jonathas inverts the semiotic logic of a Eucharistic miracle. He treats the host like a real body in order to disprove its vitality and thereby conclude that it is nothing more than a false relic or ordinary object. In this respect, I agree with John Parker that "the very test that the Jews devise to discredit the real presence ... fully depends on the assumption that the host *is* Christ." Yet I do not find that the torture "amounts to a secret longing that the host *not* be a fraud."[60] Instead, the Jews need the host to be fraudulent. So long as they can prove that the host is not Christ's body, they can dismantle the semiotic system on which transubstantiation (and other devotional practices such as the cult of relics) is based. If they torture the host and it does nothing, then the Jews can prove that it is a common cake—and thus ordinary sign—after all.

The ritual torture of the host brings together physical and semiotic forms of violence in the context of Jonathas's parody of both the Crucifixion and the Mass. Twice echoing the priest's "Hoc est" (This is), Jonathas says, "Thes Crysten men carpyn of a mervelows case: / They say this ys Jhesu that was attayntyd in owr lawe, / And that thys ys He that crwcyfyed was" (394–96). He then garbles Christ's words of Eucharistic institution before deciding that "thys bred I wold myght be put in a prefe" (442). The Jews resort to the language of proof (*prefe*) in order to test the relation between sign and body from which both host and relic derive their devotional force. Jason seeks to determine "yf that thys be He that on Calvery was made red" and concludes that "with clowtys we shall know yf He have eny blood" (449, 452). Masphat likewise resolves "to prove in thys brede yf ther be eny lyfe" (460). The bodily proof figures a parody of the Crucifixion that recalls the wounded Christ represented in biblical drama. "Thys syde I hope for to sese," says Jason, and Jasdon adds, "And I shall with thys blade so bryght / Thys other syde freshely afeze!" (470–72). The host is then punched, buffeted, struck, and stabbed until it starts to bleed when Jonathas strikes it "in the myddys" (480). The host's vitality shocks the Jews: "Yt bledyth as yt were woode, iwys!" (483), cries Jonathas, who then runs mad with the host in his hand, nails it to a post, and soon after finds himself bereft of an arm. This combination of madness and miracle anticipates the play's memorable climax, during which "*the owyn [oven] must ryve asunder and blede owt at the cranys and an image appere owt, with woundys bledyng*" (712 s.d.). At least in the idiom of the play, the host's semiotic deceit is corrected as the seemingly false relic betrays its true identity as the fleshly image of Christ. Whole Christ is indeed shown to be present in every crumb.

Much has been said about the metatheatricality of this climactic scene, particularly insofar as Christ appears as an "image," albeit the image of a bleeding body. Yet the play does not force us to oppose image to body or to set theatrical representation against Eucharistic presence. Rather, the very semiotic tensions between play and sacrament strike to the heart of the interpretive issues raised by the sacrament itself and render this climactic scene a dramatic representation of Eucharistic controversy. While Christ's image is indeed theatrical, the term *image* as used in the stage direction may also suggest that the fully divine Christ appears to the Jews in the form of human flesh—flesh made in the image and likeness of God—and thereby bears out the essential link between Eucharist and Incarnation. With an arresting, terrifying transformation of host into body, Christ corrects the Jews' attempt to resignify the host as commoditized good, false relic, and common cake. By appearing in the form of a gory physical spectacle, moreover, Christ also resignifies the physical tortures the Jews have enacted on his Eucharistic body in the host.[61]

The astonishing dramaturgy of the scene is not to be restricted to its own theatrics, for it leads into a scene of instruction during which Christ teaches the Jews how to read the relationship between body and host. The Christ of incarnational drama is not just a physical Christ but a didactic Christ; he does not restrict his Galilean or Eucharistic bodies solely to the plane of flesh and blood but is equally interested in how those bodies are signified and interpreted. Recall that in chapter 2 we saw Christ instruct the faithful how to read his wounds in the Crucifixion plays, and in the next chapter we will see Christ's similar form of instruction on display in the post-Resurrection appearances at Emmaus. In the Croxton play, the "grete wondere" (713) concerns not only the histrionic revelation of Christ's physical body from the oven but also Christ's reinscription of the host in terms of orthodox Eucharistic theology and especially the semiotics that governs it. At this point, the Jews must acknowledge the host's sacramental significations, profess them in public, and then convert at the hands of Episcopus.

The play's twinned semiotic and sacramental conversions begin when Christ heeds Episcopus's plea and transforms from speaking image back into consecrated host. In so doing, Christ not only demonstrates that the host contains his true body but also corroborates the doctrine of priestly confection discussed in the previous chapter. What is more, Christ compels the Jews to rename the host by retracting the pejorative *cake* and imposing the proper name *Lord* onto the sacred object that they must also recognize as Christ's sacramental body. "O Thu, Lord, whyche art my defendowr" (741), says Jonathas. Jasdon likewise refers to Christ as "Thow blyssyd lord of mykyll myght" (750), and Malchus pleads, "Lord, by the water of contrycion lett me aryse" (760). The ultimate act of resignification occurs some forty lines later when Jonathas refers to the host not as a cake but as "The Holy Sacrament, the whyche we have done tormentry" (802). The host, once discredited and disregarded as a common cake, is now restored to its proper signification as divine body. Following this semiotic conversion, Episcopus summons Jonathas and the Jews to sacramental conversion:

> No[w], Jonathas, on thyn hand thow art but lame,
> And ys thorow thyn own cruelnesse,
> For thyn hurt thu mayest thiselfe blame:
> Thow woldyst preve thy powre Me to oppresse.
> But now I consydre thy necesse:
> Thow wasshest thyn hart with grete contrycion.
> Go to the cawdron—thi care shal be the lesse—
> And towche thyn hand to thy salvacion.
> (770–77)

Jonathas's physical re-membering, which is achieved sacramentally through penance and baptism, coincides with his incorporation into Christ's mystical body as figured in the character of Episcopus, its local ecclesiastical head.

The semiotic conversion of the host itself is also represented by the play's concluding liturgical procession, which redefines the host as both sacramental body and sacred relic. Earlier in the play, Jonathas mocked this liturgical procession and parodied the Mass when he placed the stolen host under an ordinary cloth, took it into his home, and set it on a table (381–84). Now, at the play's end, Episcopus says,

> Now wyll I take thys Holy Sacrament
> With humble hart and gret devocion,
> And all we wyll gon with on[e] consent,
> And beare yt to chyrche with solempne processyon.
> Now folow me, all and summe,
> And all tho that bene here, both more and lesse,
> Thys holy song, *O sacrum convivium*,
> Lett us syng all with grett swetnesse.
> (834–41)

As the authorized minister of the sacraments, Episcopus not only converts the Jews but also reaffirms an understanding of Eucharistic signs, bodies, and objects consistent with the orthodox doctrine of transubstantiation and the ritual practices that shape traditional Eucharistic devotions. The host is processed back to church, perhaps, as Gibson has argued, to the church at Bury St. Edmunds, which was associated with its own host miracle in 1464.[62] Episcopus emphasizes the mystical incorporation of Christian community when he invites "all and summe" (838)—both the crowd in the play and the audience members watching it, "all tho that bene here, both more and lesse" (839)—to sing the Eucharistic hymn "O sacrum convivium" (O sacred banquet) written by Thomas Aquinas for the liturgy of Corpus Christi.[63] This hymn outreaches a late medieval devotional context, as evidenced by its inclusion in a seventeenth-century manual of prayers (figure 5.2). Here we see the Latin text of the hymn accompanied by an English translation of the first stanza, set alongside other Eucharistic prayers by Aquinas, Bonaventure, and Ambrose.[64]

In the play's final liturgical movement, the host is not only restored to its proper signification—"Whoys name ys callyd Jhesus" (1005)—but also returned to the church from which it was stolen.[65] As Beckwith writes, "The play . . . must return us to the consecrated space of the church, as it forms into an episcopal procession, its Jews and merchants, and its actors converted and banished or transformed into the participants of ritual, its theatricality dispelled."[66] During such a movement into consecrated space, the host would be treated like a holy relic and placed in an ornate vessel like the monstrance donated by York's Corpus Christi guild in 1432:

> [They presented] at their own expense a certain shrine of sumptuous work, lately both carved and moreover painted with gold, which henceforth [is] to be enriched and ornamented more preciously with the purest silver and gold with the Lord's help, which they wish also to be carried each year in the hands of priests on the feast of Corpus Christi . . . with the body of Christ enclosed in it and in crystal or beryl or some other thing open to the sight of men more suitably for the sacrament, always preceded by the light of the torches of the good citizens of the aforesaid fraternity, so that from this, faith and devotion may be increased among the present people.[67]

Just as the host was carried processionally in a monstrance, so too were other relics carried in reliquaries and other gilded vessels. A 1465 inventory from York suggests that among other religious objects were provided "1 silver jewel with a crystalline stone containing precious relics, viz., part of the cross of the lord, part of the vestment of St. Thomas, bishop of Canterbury, and part of the habit of St. Francis . . . and 2 precious stones taken from the little wheel of St. Katherine."[68] Both host and relic make divine *praesentia* accessible to the laity at worship and in doing so make tangible the connection

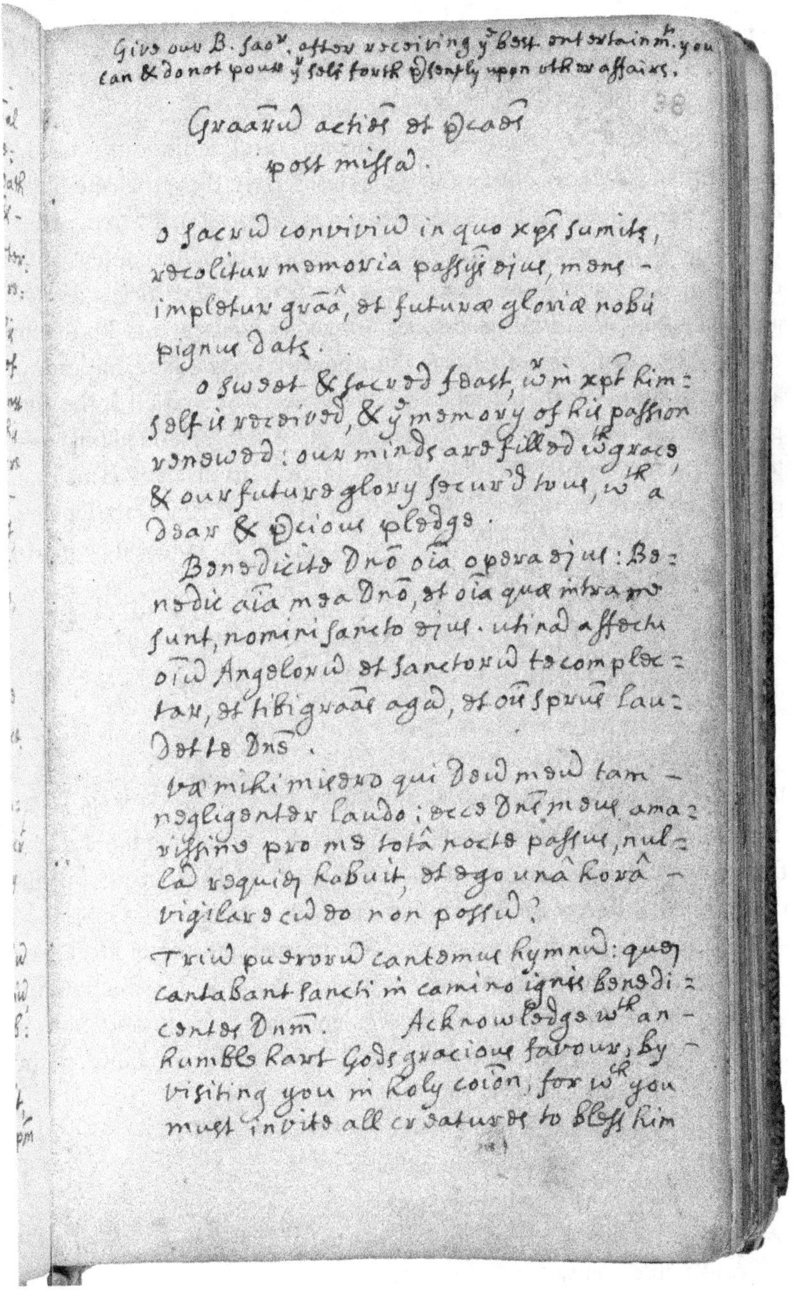

Giue our B. Sav.r after receiuing y.e best entertainm.t you
can & do not poure y.e selfe forth instantly upon other affaires.

Gratiarum actio et Laus
post missam.

O sacrum convivium in quo xp̄s sumit?,
recolitur memoria passij eius, mens
impletur grā, et futurae gloriae nobis
pignus dat?.

O sweet & sacred feast, w.ch xp̄t him=
self is receiued, & y.e memory of his passion
renewed: our minds are filled w.th grace
& our future glory secur'd to us, w.th a
dear & precious pledge.

Benedicite Dn̄o oīa opera ei9: Be=
nedic aīa mea Dn̄o, et oīa quae intra me
sunt, nomini sancto ei9. utinā affectu
oīū Angelorum et Sanctorum tecomplec=
tar, et tibi gratias agā, et oīs spūs lau=
det te Dn̄s.

Vae mihi misero qui Deum meum tam
negligenter laudo: ecce Dn̄s meus ama=
tissim9 pro me tota nocte passus, nul=
lā requiem habuit, et ego una horā
vigilare cū eo non possū?

Trium puerorum cantemus hymnum: quem
cantabant sancti in camino ignis Benedi=
centes Dn̄m.   Acknowledge w.th an
humble hart Gods gracious fauours, by
visiting you in holy co̅ion, for w.ch you
must invite all creatures to bless him

Figure 5.2. "O sacrum convivium," from *A Manual of Prayers*, ca. 1685. Folger Shakespeare Library MS V.a.488, fol. 38r. Reproduced by permission.

between ecclesial community and Eucharistic body. This is the connection that the *Play of the Sacrament* figures in its final conversions that are at once liturgical and semiotic, ecclesial and theatrical.

In the *Play of the Sacrament*, sacramental and semiotic conversions correct the fissures of body and sign that result from the verbal and physical violence performed on the host when it is treated as a false relic. These fissures, which in the late Middle Ages are generated in the context of the consecrated host and saints' relics, are reproduced in *The Duchess of Malfi* and *The Changeling*. In these Jacobean tragedies, Webster and Middleton repurpose the semiotics of relics to show how the body is false, misleading, and dangerous even when it appears as the subject of adoration or the signpost of virtue. They use relics—wax heads, gloves, rings, severed fingers— to link the body's unreliability to its discontiguity, its dismemberment, its piecing into parts. In Webster's drama, relics first prove fatal to the Duchess but then organize her resurrection and redemption. For Middleton, by contrast, they lead to a point of no return.

"Cased Up Like a Holy Relic": *The Duchess of Malfi*

John Webster draws on the semiotics of relics in *The Duchess of Malfi*, a play in which a seemingly substantial body is revealed as nothing more than a figure in wax. Represented as a physical fragment and displayed as an artificial icon, the body emerges here at the crossroads of shadow and substance, with the relationship between sign and referent manipulated and realigned at will. Webster's horrifying "waxworks" scene in act 4 demonstrates one of the most sustained and perverse engagements with the semiotics of holy matter on the early modern English stage.[69] Before that scene, however, the Duchess herself introduces the term *relic* in act 3:

> Why should only I,
> Of all the other princes of the world,
> Be cased up like a holy relic? I have youth
> And a little beauty.[70]

The Duchess's problem is not so much with the relic itself as with the reliquary's hermeticism. Reliquaries, or gilded vessels in which relics were encased, provided a means for visual devotion while also protecting the sacred remains from decay and theft. These containers also created several degrees of separation between the saint's remains and those who venerated them, sometimes even making it impossible to see the physical remains at all.[71] The Duchess uses the reliquary as part of a simile to expresses her refusal of political conscription and bodily regulation.[72] If she were to allow her brothers to arrange her marriage in accordance with their plans to expand the family dynasty, the Duchess would forfeit her sexual agency and become, like the enshrined relic, an object available to visual devotion but removed from physical contact.[73]

The Duchess's relic simile overturns the image of the "virtuous widow" put forth by Thomas Overbury in *Newe and Choice Characters* (1615), a text Webster expanded after Overbury's death and likely had in mind when writing *Duchess*.[74] Overbury's "vertuous Widow" "is like the Palme-tree, that thrives not after the supplanting of her husband. . . . No calamity can now come neere her, for in suffering the losse of her husband, she accounts all of the rest trifles: she hath laid his dead body in the worthyest monument that can be: She hath buried it in her owne heart. To conclude, she is a Relique, that without any superstition in the world, though she will not be kist, yet may be reverenc't."[75] By making "her owne heart" into her husband's "worthiest monument," the virtuous widow preserves her husband's memory specifically by remaining chaste. The widow is defined not by fleshly allurement but as a "Relique" removed from the physicality of the wooing world. (Overbury may also pun on *relict*, which meant "widow" in the seventeenth century.)[76] Bound to her chastity like a relic encased in glass, the Overburian widow can be gazed upon but not touched.

If the virtuous widow figures her chaste body as a monument to her husband's memory, the Duchess sets her bodily vitality against such a figure of cold, subservient mourning. Her relic simile is of a piece with her wholesale rejection of artifice—effigies, graves, images, reliquaries—in the name of fleshly vitality. In place of artificial likeness, the Duchess insists on real presence. Perhaps the most memorable instance occurs when she proposes marriage to Antonio by offering him nothing less than her living body. After presenting him with a ring during a private ritual that results in marriage lawfully contracted *per verba de presenti*, she says, "This is flesh and blood, sir: / 'Tis not the figure cut in alabaster / Kneels at my husband's tomb" (1.2.363–65). The Duchess's language is patently Eucharistic. Not only does she offer Antonio her real body and blood, but she also employs her own version of the Eucharistic words *Hoc est* ("This is flesh and blood" [1.2.363]), in defying her brothers' mandate, arranging her own remarriage, and giving her sexualized body to Antonio. Neither encased relic nor stony image, the body of the Duchess is living flesh.

For all her resistance to the relic's circumscription and its connotations of chastity, however, the Duchess stands to be deceived with relic-like objects that stand in not for the living God but for the corpses of her dead kin. This is the severe, often horrifying irony that typifies Jacobean tragedy. Ferdinand uses artificial body parts made out of wax not only to implicate the Duchess within a representational trick but also to reinvent the semiotics of holy matter for a punishing purpose. Webster's "waxworks" scene operates according to the specious semiotics of relics discussed in the previous two sections. Ferdinand bears out Robyn Malo's claim that "relics and relic discourse are interesting precisely because they draw our attention to falsehood, artifice—to assumption, to what remains unsaid."[77] Ferdinand reminds us that every relic, whether true or false, forges a gap in signification between itself and the body it references. In the "waxworks" scene, Ferdinand relates two kinds of matter—wax and flesh—to two kinds of signs—iconic and indexical. Unto themselves, the wax head and hands are simply artificial likenesses. As iconic signs, the wax heads resemble the bodies of Antonio and his sons visually, but they bear no ontological relation to them. In this sense, they may be regarded as symbolic inverses of the consecrated host, which does not look like Christ's physical body but contains it at the level of substance. Yet as Ferdinand presents them and as the Duchess interprets them, the wax figures are taken for vital remains—relics, in fact—that trace real presence.

Ferdinand redraws the fragile boundaries between wax and flesh in two related movements, each centered on a deceptive misrepresentation of the iconic sign as an indexical trace. Ferdinand's trickery rests on the confusion between visual resemblance and physical presence, which is what makes the wax figures analogous to holy relics. The first movement begins with an ostensible gesture of reconciliation in which Ferdinand offers the Duchess what she initially thinks is his own hand. "I come to seal my peace with you," he says. "Here's a hand / To which you have vowed much love. The ring upon't / You gave. (*Gives her a dead man's hand.*)" (4.1.42–44). When the Duchess kisses the hand she observes, "You are very cold" (4.1.50). She thereby concludes that it is not the hand of Ferdinand after all:

"What witchcraft doth he practice that he hath left / A dead man's hand here?" (4.1.53–54).[78] The living hand that initially signifies familial reconciliation (if not also a grotesque parody of the marriage rite) now becomes the false relic meant to confirm Antonio's death.[79] Should the cold hand fail to persuade, Ferdinand moves to the second phase of his deceit, in which he reveals the wax heads of Antonio and his sons. Again, Ferdinand conceives of these wax figures as relics by which the Duchess will "know directly they are dead" (4.1.57).

The stage directions go a long way to capture Ferdinand's semiotic deceit and the misinterpretation it engenders. We read, "*Here is discovered, behind a traverse, the artificial figures of Antonio and his Children, appearing as if they were dead*" (4.1.53 s.d.). This stage direction is available to the reader of the play but not to members of the audience, who share in the Duchess's shock by experiencing the revelation of dismembered heads from her vantage.[80] The semiotics of the scene operates in such a way that the Duchess first appreciates the iconic resemblance of the dead heads to her kin and then, by virtue of that resemblance, concludes that the heads are true relics of their corpses. It is all too easy for the Duchess to misinterpret the relation between sign and referent. Not only do the wax figures visually resemble the bodies of Antonio and the Duchess's children, but also wax appears soft and malleable like flesh. Leah Marcus notes that while wax limbs may well have been used as props in the seventeenth-century staging, it is just as likely that "the actors playing Antonio and the children could easily have stood in the discovery space to be revealed when the traverse was drawn."[81] If this is the case, then the play confounds the relations between wax and flesh all the more. Members of Webster's audience witness real bodies performing wax artifices, which the Duchess then takes for dead limbs.

These complicated relations between wax and flesh in *The Duchess of Malfi* recall the semiotics of host and body as represented in the *Play of the Sacrament*. In the earlier play, an unconsecrated wafer (or *oble*) functions in the idiom of the play as the sacramental body of Christ. When this host miraculously turns into Christ's speaking image, we know that the body we see is ever only the body of an actor, even though it is presented as the real body of Christ in the play. Ferdinand elicits a similarly fragile boundary between prop and body when he uses wax limbs as relics of dead bodies. Whereas Jonathas and the Jews submit the host to a test for real presence, however, the Duchess does not view the wax heads with such skepticism.

Instead, she takes false shadows for true substances. In this sense, *The Duchess of Malfi* repurposes the semiotics of relics evident in late medieval religious drama in order to confound distinctions between flesh and wax, representation and reality, life and death. Furthermore, whereas the *Play of the Sacrament* ends with the conversion of the Jews and their integration into an ecclesial body, Ferdinand's waxworks reduce the Duchess to a still-life, stone-cold semblance of the vitality she previously celebrated. As Cariola remarks, the effect of the despair caused by the waxworks scene renders the Duchess "like to your picture in the gallery, / A deal of life in show, but none in practice" (4.2.30–31). Once vital flesh, the Duchess now becomes a still image.

The Duchess becomes entangled in the gap between iconic and indexical signs forged by false relics. False relics, as I suggested earlier, were tangible objects—pieces of wood, stone, or animal remains—passed off deceitfully as holy matter.[82] Ferdinand discloses his reliance on this kind of semiotic deceit when he reveals to the audience (but not to the Duchess) the fact that he deploys the wax heads as false signs of real presences:

> Excellent! As I would wish: she's plagued in art.
> These presentations are but framed in wax
> By the curious master in that quality,
> Vincentio Lauriola, and she takes them
> For true substantial bodies.
> (4.1.109–13)

Ferdinand reverses the devotional function of relics as signs of comfort, intercession, and grace. If the relic forged a bond between heavenly saint and earthly pilgrim, Ferdinand employs the wax heads in a representational scheme by which to punish the Duchess. Using the terms *presentation* and *true substantial bodies*, Ferdinand also employs Eucharistic idioms in describing his representational trick. Such terms were ubiquitous in the Eucharistic Controversies. John Frith, for example, writes that the consecrated host "is not the verye bodie of our lorde / but onely a sacrament / signe memorialle / or representation of this same."[83] Conversely, Richard Smith explicates Christ's words of institution with an emphasis on the substantial reality of the sacrament: "Take ye breade, geve thankes to God for al his benefites geven to man, blesse it, consecrate it, turning the substaunce of it into my flesh."[84] And Edmund Gurnay begins his treatise *Corpus Christi* with these words: "That this then is the body of our Saviour, it is without al question: Yea, not onely his body, but even Himself (a part being put for the whole) it may be affirmed; by whether it bee His body indeed, and substance; or onely by way of Sacrament, that is the terrible and unappeaseable question at this day."[85] Insofar as Ferdinand explains his trick in Eucharistic terms, Huston Diehl is correct to say that "in presenting the counterfeit as the real, the cruel Ferdinand imitates the playwright as well as the priest."[86] By displacing real presence onto wax figures, Ferdinand reiterates the semiotic deceit associated with false relics. It does not matter whether Antonio and the children are actually alive so long as the wax heads can effectively persuade the Duchess otherwise. If one cannot interpret the difference between sign and thing signified, one becomes, like the Duchess, "plagued in art" (4.1.109). This is as true for wax figures as it is for relics.

As if Ferdinand's plot were not appalling enough, the very medium he uses to deceive the Duchess—wax—bears a connection to the devotional cult of relics, for wax was used to preserve saints' remains from destruction and decay. This was the case with the Saxon leader Byrhtnoth, who defeated the Danes at the Battle of Maldon in 991, as recounted in the twelfth-century *Liber Eliensis* (Book of Ely). Byrhtnoth was eventually beheaded by the Danes, who carried off his head as a token of their victory, but his body was reconstructed for veneration using a wax mask. The abbot from the Church of Ely recovered Byrhtnoth's headless body, returned it to church, and buried it. Before the burial, "in place of the head he put a round lump of wax."[87] The *Liber Eliensis* hardly criticizes the hybrid state of Byrhtnoth's body or ascribes it to idolatry. To the contrary, it suggests that the wax fronted unproblematically for flesh as Byrhtnoth "was recognized by this sign, and was honourably entombed among the others."[88]

The reformist response to such wax reconstructions was less sparing. In *A Very Profitable Treatise on Relics*, Jean Calvin rails against a church in Marseilles, which claimed to hold the head of Mary Magdalene. This head, however, was created "wyth the morsel of past[e], or waxe that is fastened upon her eye." Calvin says that "men do make a treasure of her, as it were a god descended from heaven: but if a trial wer made of things men might clearly find the deceyt and craft."[89] He cites a further example of such "deceyt and craft" in which animal and mineral matter are passed off as sacred relics:

Thei had (as men say) in times passed, an arme of S. Anthony that which when it was inclosed in a glasse they kissed and worshipped: but at such time as it was taken out & shewed forth, it was found to be the member of an hart [deer]: there was also on the high auter hangyng the braine of Sainct Peter. As long as it was inclosed men did not doubte thereof. For it had been blasphemie not to believe the superscription. But when as the neste was pulled out, and that men did better beholde it, it was found to be a marble stone.[90]

The Duchess of Malfi, as we have seen, registers such attitudes toward false relics by showing how easily the signs of the body can be manipulated for profit and pleasure. In passing off wax likenesses as true relics, Ferdinand echoes the manipulations of the laity who, overwhelmed by the relic's materiality and anxious about their own salvation, were led to idolatry through such deceit and craft. He also reminds a post-Reformation audience of the implicit dangers (both theological and semiotic) that constitute a devotional cult of relics.

But Ferdinand's false relics only go so far. Webster ultimately redeems his heroine, who directs the scene of her death toward her own apotheosis. At her execution she commands Bosola (who assumes the role of the hangman), "Pull and pull strongly; for your able strength / Must pull down heaven upon me" (4.2.222–23). She then kneels and embraces a martyr's death.[91] But death does not silence her. Webster allows a momentary return to consciousness so that the Duchess can know definitively that her family is alive. In a telling echo of Hermione's reanimation in Shakespeare's *The Winter's Tale* (discussed in the next chapter), the converted Bosola says, "She stirs! Here's life.— / Return, fair soul, from darkness, and lead mine / out of this sensible hell.— She's warm, she breathes!—" (4.2.330–33). When the Duchess asks if Antonio lives, Bosola says, "Yes, madam, he is living. / The dead bodies you saw were but feigned statues" (4.2.339–40). Bosola thus corrects the previously skewed relation between relic and body, wax and flesh. With that knowledge in hand, the Duchess dies on the word "Mercy!" (343).

Webster also writes a Duchess whose real presence transcends the grave. Just as she promised Antonio her "flesh and blood" (1.2.363) in marriage, the Duchess offers her lively body once again in the form of her echo, which returns to haunt Antonio in the graveyard (5.3). There are a total of ten echoes, three of which change the language, grammar, and meaning of Antonio's initial utterances. These echoes do not confirm the Duchess's death but rather mark the return of the Duchess's physical and linguistic agency.[92] For example, when Antonio says of the echo, "'Tis very like my wife's voice," the echo volleys back a different statement: "I, wife's voice" (5.3.26). Translating the adjectival *my* into the speaking subject *I*, the echo purports to turn the representational (a sound that is *like* the Duchess's voice) into a real presence (that which *is* her voice). Though relics are conventionally concrete objects or body parts that manifest the sacred through sight or touch, Webster reimagines the relic as an auditory phenomenon that works according to the logic of a tangible relic. As Bynum writes, relics "must carry beyond the grave the power of the living saint [and] must lift up (not erase) the experience they have borne in life."[93] In similar fashion, the Duchess's echo carries her voice (and thus her presence) beyond the grave. The voice acts like a relic primarily because it provides a physical, indexical trace to the Duchess's presence after her death.

While the echo keeps the Duchess present in earthly space and time, it does not make that presence visible or manifest it in terms of physical dimension. Rather, it partakes of the semiotics of the consecrated host, which contains Christ in substance but does not render his body and blood perceptible to the senses. Catherine Belsey reads the echo as "insubstantial," by which she means that it lacks bodily form.[94] But "substance" (at least in a Eucharistic context) is more complicated than this opposition between corporeal body and incorporeal voice suggests. Substance does not itself have physical dimensions; rather, as Aquinas says, "the matter of the substance is known by its accidents."[95] Surely the Duchess's echo lacks bodily form, but it does not lack substance, for Antonio recognizes the Duchess through the accident of sound. If we read the echo in Eucharistic terms, we can see it less as a void and more as a material accident that makes the Duchess present at the level of substance. The Duchess's voice is an essence heard but not seen. It thus partakes of the tensions between the physical and metaphysical iterated by both host and relic. Transformed into a vital echo, the Duchess corrects Ferdinand's semiotic abuses through the invisible materiality of her speech, which triumphs over wax.

Reimagined by Webster as wax limbs and a disembodied echo, the relic represents the fragmented and dismembered body as a site of somatic and semiotic unreliability. If in *The Duchess of Malfi* relics deceive the heroine while also pointing toward her redemptive death, in *The Changeling* Thomas Middleton and William Rowley stage the Duchess's inverse in Beatrice-Joanna. Their heroine, who resists the patriarchal mandates of an arranged marriage by employing a deformed malcontent to murder her betrothed, hardly dies a martyr's death. In this play, dismembered fingers and hands, along with gloves and rings, structure a drama in which semiotic deceit abets murder, adultery, and abjection.

"I Could Not Get the Ring without the Finger": *The Changeling*

Spectacles of bodily fragmentation in *The Changeling* have often been set in the context of anatomical discourse, yet such representations also draw significantly on the religious cult of relics.[96] *The Changeling* exploits the differences between relic and body to reveal the criminality and deceit that could be concealed beneath the semblances of sanctity and honor. By skewing relations between bodies and signs, Beatrice-Joanna and DeFlores turn the spiritual power of the relic into the deceptive power of the antirelic in order to achieve monetary profit, erotic pleasure, and political advancement, all of which are tied to cold-blooded murder. Much of the play's tragedy, which centers on sexual deviance unleashed in the name of patriarchal resistance, stems from the fact that the body's semiotic and somatic contours are manipulated at will and thus are notoriously hard to pin down. While they never lose their religious significations in this play, relics connect physical dismemberment to semiotic rupture, the performance of virtue to the discovery of vice. My analysis focuses on four related scenes: the glove scene in act 1; DeFlores's presentation of Piracquo's ringed finger, which confirms Beatrice-Joanna's as an accomplice to murder, in act 3; the chastity test of act 4; and Alsemero's and DeFlores's revulsion toward Beatrice-Joanna's polluted body in act 5.[97]

Beatrice-Joanna's initial encounter with DeFlores in act 1 pivots on a pair of gloves, which DeFlores quickly turns into substitute hands. Initially, DeFlores kneels down to retrieve one of these discarded gloves, which falls from Beatrice-Joanna's hand. Coming from a malcontented, disfigured social subordinate, this gesture of courtesy can be regarded as a point of ironic humor. Yet it soon turns into idolatry as DeFlores kneels before his beloved and returns the glove as a sign of affection. His idolatry resembles that of

Alsemero, who in the play's first line figures Beatrice-Joanna as a sacred body: "'Twas in the temple where I first beheld her."[98] To Alsemero, Beatrice-Joanna is a compliant saint; to DeFlores, she is a deviant temptress. She construes DeFlores's touch as dangerous and meets his gesture with a brusque retort:

> Mischief on your officious forwardness!
> Who bade you stoop? They touch my hand no more.
>   [*Removes the other glove*]
> There! [*Throws it down*] for t'other's sake I part with this—
> Take 'em and draw thine own skin off with 'em.
>   (1.1.220–23)

Beatrice-Joanna not only refuses DeFlores's advances but also returns the relic to the worshipper and resignifies it. In doing so she instates a "politics of touch," Laura Gowing's term for social codes meant to separate subordinates from their masters in seventeenth-century England.[99] Beatrice-Joanna uses the glove to suggest that DeFlores, on account of his physical deformity and social inferiority, is untouchable. By touching one glove, she reasons, DeFlores pollutes the other.

Beatrice-Joanna's "politics of touch" not only draws on the logic of contact relics but also reverses the customary pattern of devotion between pilgrim and saint. Thomas More defends the charitable intercession of saints when he says, "Were it likely that sayntes than being so full of blessyd charyte in hevyn / wyll nothynge care for theyr bretherine in Cryst / Whom they se[e] here in this wretched worlde?"[100] If pilgrims seek out relics in the hope of obtaining spiritual succor, Beatrice-Joanna becomes the saint who refuses the pilgrim's prayer.[101] Whereas holy relics forge an intimate bond between saint and pilgrim, moreover, Beatrice-Joanna turns her relics into agents of physical mutilation. Returning the gloves to DeFlores, she says, "Take 'em and draw thine own skin off with 'em" (223). As Peter Stallybrass and Ann Rosalind Jones write, "On DeFlores's hands, she wishes that they will be a physical reminder of her hatred for him, eating his skin with poison, so that when he takes them off, he will strip off his own skin."[102] If bits of flesh and bone were taken from the bodies of saints in order to disseminate their real presence, Beatrice-Joanna directs DeFlores to further disfigure his already unhandsome body. Her *noli me tangere*, however, is not without an accompanying ironic invitation to make physical contact.[103]

If DeFlores's touch can pollute the gloves, as Beatrice-Joanna argues, it stands to reason that the gloves must somehow contain the physical trace of Beatrice-Joanna, whose hands they enclose. In this sense, the gloves exhibit the indexical and metonymic logic of the contact relic. That is, gloves, which contain the hands, harness the presence of the very hands they contain.[104] Such metonymy is further supported by early modern physiology. DeFlores's skin, which comprises real matter and spirit (what in Galenic physiology was termed *spiritus*) would rub off on the gloves and thus leave a corporeal trace.[105] The gloves thus capture the physical matter—*spiritus* in physiological terms, *praesentia* in religious terms—of the hands they enclose. Once the gloves are in DeFlores's hands, DeFlores eroticizes their link to Beatrice-Joanna's body. He takes them as real hands by literalizing their indexical function and turning them into penetrable parts. The gloves, he reasons, provide him ready access to an otherwise unavailable body. Moreover, the gloves, like relics, make Beatrice-Joanna's real presence tangible in a way similar to how relics make the *praesentia* of a saint tangible.

By so uncritically reading the relationship between sign and referent, DeFlores falls into a pattern of idolatry that soon becomes a full-blown erotic fantasy. At the end of act 1, DeFlores figuratively penetrates Beatrice-Joanna's body by forcing his hands inside her gloves. He eventually appreciates no difference between glove and hand, relic and body:

> Here's a favour come—with a mischief! Now I know
> She had rather wear my pelt tanned in a pair
> Of dancing pumps than I should thrust my fingers
> Into her sockets here.
>
> (1.1.224–27)

DeFlores metaphorically transgresses the politics of touch by making contact with the gloves. When he literalizes the metaphor, DeFlores allows the gloves to take on the physical dimensions of Beatrice-Joanna's body. As Stallybrass and Jones write, "Insofar as the single glove condenses Beatrice-Joanna's own body, DeFlores handles her when he handles her glove."[106] By locating the whole body in the detachable part, *pars pro toto*, DeFlores imagines the "thrust" of his "fingers" in the "sockets" of the glove in a self-generated symbolic sex act that eradicates the social and physical boundaries imposed on him by Beatrice-Joanna.

DeFlores's sexual fantasy is fleetingly realized when, in the next act, Beatrice-Joanna actually touches his face. "Her fingers touched me" (2.2.81), he exclaims. For him, Beatrice-Joanna's fingers stand in synecdochically for her whole body. "O my blood! Methinks I feel her in my arms already," De-Flores fantasizes, "Her wanton fingers combing out this beard, / And, being pleased, praising this bad face" (2.2.146–49). Consigned to the hypothetical "methinks" and goaded by the proleptic "I feel her in my arms already," De-Flores sees Beatrice-Joanna's touch as part of this scene of sexual fulfillment. What he does not realize is that throughout the scene, his own hands perform the erotic work, making the sexual contact self-imposed if not also self-fulfilled. Even though Beatrice-Joanna touches him, DeFlores is ultimately locked in his own embrace and caught in the physical and semiotic gap between relic and body. He is unaware of the fact that he effectively makes love to an illusory presence, a body that is not there.

DeFlores's transformation of gloves into relics signals wider debates over idolatry and iconoclasm within various reform movements. In the fourteenth century, Wycliffites charged that no bodily remain or image could encompass the grace of God received spiritually in the heart: "Oure lord God dwellis by grace in gode mennus soulis, and without comparesoun bettere than all ymagis made of man in erthe, and better than alle bodies of seyntis, be the bones of hem never so gloriously shreynyd in gold."[107] Centuries later, William Tyndale makes a similar point: "For yf we care more to cloth the deed [dead] image made by man and the pryce of silver then the lively image of God and the price of chrystes bloude / then we dishonor the image of god and hym that made hym and the price of chrystes bloude and hym that brought hym."[108] In a more flippant passage, Tyndale quips, "When thou stekest upp a candle before the image / thou mightest with as good reason make an hollow bely in the image and pouer in meate and drincke. For as the saynt nether eateth ner drincketh so hath he no bodily eyes to delyte in the light of a candle."[109] Jean Calvin also observes how earthly signs can obscure heavenly referents when the laity "by a most execrable sacrilege have worshipped dead and insensible creatures in steade of the onely livyng God."[110] Of the various responses to the cult of relics, the Royal Injunctions of 1538 resonate most clearly with *The Changeling* because they cast relic worship in erotic terms. The faithful are ordered "not to repose their trust of affiance in any other works devised by men's phantasies besides Scripture; as in wandering to pilgrimages, offering of money, candles, or tapers to images or relics, or kissing or licking the same."[111] It is worth noting that the Council of Trent also decreed that "all superstition must be removed from invocation of the saints, veneration of relics, and use of sacred images; all aiming at base profit must be eliminated; all sensual appeal must be avoided; so that images are not painted or adorned with seductive charm."[112] Both the Henrician Injunctions and the Counter-Reformation decrees resist the sexual allure that DeFlores finds in the gloves, which he transforms into erotic relics.

The interplay of semiotic and somatic manipulations in the glove scene informs the rest of the play, where DeFlores and Beatrice-Joanna mark out further distance between part and whole, sign and body. In the final three acts, however, these manipulations redound negatively to Beatrice-Joanna. DeFlores ultimately seizes on the powers of both true and false relics in order to leave Beatrice-Joanna no choice but to surrender her maidenhead to him. He forces her to give up her chastity, ruin her marriage, and compromise her honor. This shift in the power play between master and servant unfolds in the context of the play's only literal relic: the ringed finger of Alonzo de Piracquo, whom Beatrice-Joanna hires DeFlores to kill.

Unlike Ferdinand's wax heads in *The Duchess of Malfi*, the ringed finger is represented in *The Changeling* as a physical body part that stands in, *pars pro toto*, for the whole. DeFlores claims, "I cannot get the ring without the finger" (3.3.28), and he describes his physical struggle in Eucharistic terms: "I was loath to leave it . . . / He was as loath to part with it, for it stuck / As if the flesh and it were both one substance" (3.3.35–38). The fusion of ring to finger as "one substance" expresses the relic's claim to harness real presence. As we have seen in the doctrine of *pars pro toto*, the sanctified part (whether of the host or the saint's body) contains the entire substance of the sanctified whole. DeFlores not only echoes but also ironizes this logic when he says of the severed member, "Why, is that more / Than killing the whole man?" (3.3.29–30). He suggests not only that one part of Piracquo's body contains the essence of the whole but also that the ring, which is attached to Piracquo's flesh, has become one with it. Bone relic and contact relic meld together in DeFlores's account of the murder.[113]

DeFlores capitalizes on the implicit sexual metaphor of the ringed finger to remind Beatrice-Joanna of his desired recompense for the murder. He says, "Why are not you as guilty, in (I'm sure) / As deep as I? And we should stick together" (3.3.83–84), and concludes, "Nor is it fit we two, engaged so jointly, / Should part and live asunder" (3.3.88–89). Despite her aristocratic birth, Beatrice-Joanna is no less guilty than the servant she employs. As Maurizio Calbi puts it, DeFlores, by reminding the heroine that her aristocratic rank does not exonerate her, makes Beatrice-Joanna "see herself through the eyes of the other as a guilty identity inhabiting the difference between herself and her class and gender ideal."[114] "You're the deed's creature" (3.3.137), DeFlores charges, and in doing so redraws the lines between master and servant that Beatrice-Joanna first established in the glove scene. Thus the ringed finger not only signifies Beatrice-Joanna's complicity in Piracquo's murder but also figures symbolically the consequences of a reneged bond. "If I enjoy thee not," says DeFlores, "then thou ne'er enjoy'st: / I'll blast the hopes and joys of marriage, / I'll confess all—my life I rate at nothing" (3.3.147–49). Stuck to the deed like the ring stuck to Piracquo's cold finger, Beatrice-Joanna realizes that she can no longer use her body, its parts, and its signs to manipulate DeFlores. In the hollow darkness of the offstage, she must grant him her maidenhead, thereby realizing DeFlores's fantasy, which is galvanized by a figuration of her body as both animated glove and penetrated socket.

Such sexual repayment intensifies rather than curbs Beatrice-Joanna's dissimulation of her bodily signs, however. Having compromised her virtue, she must spend the final two acts of the play convincing Alsemero she is chaste. At the start of act 4, she unlocks Alsemero's closet and finds there a manuscript of Antonio Mizaldus's *De arcanis naturae* (Secrets of nature) opened to a formula for testing chastity: "How to know whether a woman be a maid or not" (4.1.40). The test states that after drinking from a vial called "glass M," a virgin will gape, sneeze, and laugh in that order (4.1.46–50). Intent to "beguile / The master of the mystery" (4.1.37–38), Beatrice-Joanna studies the symptoms and first tests them on her chaste servant, Diaphanta, so that she can dissimulate the expected bodily reactions and prove her virginity to Alsemero. While the chastity test does not involve a literal relic, it creates a gap between the body's surface and its interior—that is, a gap between physical signs and spiritual virtues—that evokes the substitution, fragmentation, and semiotic deceit associated with relics. By performing outward symptoms that indicate a virtue she does not possess, Beatrice-Joanna turns her entire body into a relic and hence into an unreliable sign system. If Alsemero sees Beatrice-Joanna's body as an interpretable surface, Beatrice-Joanna upsets his reading practice by feigning the symptoms of chastity and concealing the truth of her spoiled maidenhead.

Beatrice-Joanna's masterful performance during the staged chastity test in act 4, scene 4, unfolds as one of the more memorable episodes of semiotic deceit in all of early modern English drama. She situates the test in such a performative context when she says, "I'm put now to my cunning: th'effects I know, / If I can now but feign 'em handsomely" (4.2.137–38). Beatrice-Joanna effectively feigns chastity by divorcing sign from body in a thoroughly metatheatrical performance.[115] Beatrice-Joanna beguiles Alsemero with signs of sanctity, yet the body she presents to him is itself a false relic. Like Ferdinand in *The Duchess of Malfi*, she plagues her beholders in art. While one should acknowledge Beatrice-Joanna's cunning in trying to wrest herself away from patriarchal constraint, one cannot ignore the fact that at the play's end she is reinscribed by DeFlores and Alsemero as a defiled and polluted woman. Furthermore, she is presented to the audience's collective gaze as a body that must be completely removed from familial and social structures in order to preserve the integrity of Alicante's body politic.

Having learned from DeFlores that Beatrice-Joanna is unchaste, Alsemero casts her into his closet, which acts as a countersite to the temple in which he first saw her (1.1.1). Idolized as a saint in the play's opening line, Beatrice-Joanna is now condemned: "You are a whore" (5.3.32), Alsemero declares, and then metaphorically razes the temples of courtly love and religious devotion with which he formerly associated her:

> I'll all demolish and seek out truth within you,
> If there be any left. Let your sweet tongue
> Prevent your heart's rifling—there I'll ransack
> And tear out my suspicion.
>
> (5.3.37–40)

Like Jonathas in the *Play of the Sacrament*, Alsemero resorts to figures of physical violence in order to discern the semiotic relation between sign and body. Jonathas, we recall, subjects the host to physical tortures, which then culminate in the Eucharistic miracle that convinces him of Christ's bodily presence contained within the sign. Alsemero limns a violent dismemberment in which he analogizes Beatrice-Joanna's ruined body to a penetrable space that he will "ransack," "demolish," and "tear out." He lands on a final resignification of Beatrice-Joanna's body as a ruined space:

> Oh, the place itself e'er since
> Has crying been for vengeance, the temple
> Where blood and beauty first unlawfully
> Fired their devotion, and quenched the right one—
> 'Twas in my fears at first; 'twill have it now.
> Oh, thou art all deformed!
> (5.3.73–78)

Recall that, at the end of the *Play of the Sacrament*, Episcopus bridges the gap between Christ's body and its signs and restores the host to its proper sacramental significations. At the end of *The Changeling*, by contrast, there is no intervening figure to provide such remedy; there is no sacramental conversion and certainly no mystical communion. Instead there is only the abjection of Beatrice-Joanna's polluted body:

> O come not near me, sir, I shall defile you:
> I am that of your blood was taken from you
> For your better health; look no more upon't,
> But cast it to the ground regardlessly,
> Let the common sewer take it from distinction.
> (5.3.149–53)

Beatrice-Joanna's body and blood will not be contained in a reliquary, altar, or shrine. Nor will it produce noble offspring. Rather, it will trickle into a "common sewer" (5.3.153). Relocated from the pedestal of devotion, her body becomes a blasted temple, a shattered image, a discarded relic. Inverting her own *noli me tangere* from earlier in the play, Beatrice-Joanna makes her body into an object of defilement rather than devotion when she says, "O come not near me, sir" (5.3.149). Unlike the Duchess of Malfi, Beatrice-Joanna dies "regardlessly" (5.3.152). Her body loses its aristocratic distinction, its purity thoroughly dis-tincted by the bloody signs of murder and adultery marked out upon her. The deified "Beatrice" who initially embodies her namesake in Dante's *Vita nuova* is reduced to the common whore signified by the second half of her compound name. She becomes a "greasy Joan" who "doth keel the pot."[116]

However separated by time, theatrical conventions, and religious politics, the three plays studied in this chapter all illustrate how relics bring the semiotics of the Eucharist into the context of devotional objects. Michael O'Connell argues that "Reformation iconoclasm brought to an end a semiotic and symbolic field for apprehending and imagining the sacred," and concludes that by the seventeenth century, "what was lost was a visual aesthetic that had materialized religious concepts and experience in traditions of painting, sculpture in stone and alabaster, wood carving, stained glass, and theatrical performance."[117] In terms of the present discussion, however, the question is not whether relics (and their semiotics) disappear but rather to what uses they are put in post-Reformation drama. While they invoke Reformation iconoclasm at various turns, *The Duchess of Malfi* and *The Changeling* both suggest that relics, their devotional cults, and particularly their deceptive semiotics are revivified rather than abolished. These plays locate the power of the relic not in its divine agency but in its semiotic instability. Here bodies can be real and representational, vehicles for devotion and agents of deceit.

In shaping a semiotics of the body predicated on the relic's logic of fragmentation and wholeness, the three plays studied here suggest the precariousness of the relic's own claim to real presence. On the stage as in the reliquary, the body's signs can be wrested away from their proper significations. Whereas the Duchess of Malfi is deceived by relics and thus misreads wax as flesh, Beatrice-Joanna uses one set of relics (the gloves) to deceive DeFlores, who then uses another relic (Piracquo's ringed finger) to bring her down. These Jacobean tragedies transpose the semiotic issues presented in the *Play of the Sacrament* into another register, one in which bleeding hosts, speaking images, and bits of divine bone and flesh are reimagined as eroticized gloves, wax heads, haunting echoes, and severed fingers. The efficacious bones of saints said to make intercession for devout believers are remade into unreliable bodies that lead to sexual deviance and death. When DeFlores refers to Beatrice-Joanna as "that broken rib of mankind" (5.3.146), he alludes to God's creation of Eve from the rib of Adam as recorded in Genesis 2:21 in order to reduce her to a mere relic and remnant of a man's body. (And, to recall this chapter's opening anecdote, the rib is at the center of the sixteenth-century *sacra costa* miracle, in which the image of Christ crucified miraculously ejected a piece of rib bone.) Indeed, in the Jacobean underworld, where blood repays blood and every hired deed demands a reward, the body of a recalcitrant woman proves even more specious than the bone of a dead saint.

SIX

Conjured to Remembrance

Emmaus Plays, Jack Juggler, *and* The Winter's Tale

In the York *Incredulity of Thomas*, Christ says to the skeptical apostle, "Beholde my woundis are bledand, / Here in my side putte in thi hande, / And fele my woundis, and undirstande / That this is I."[1] Echoing the Eucharistic idiom "This is my body," Christ yokes physical apprehension to a hermeneutic process by which Thomas must work to understand the relation between signifier and signified—that is, the relation between "this" (the body he beholds and probes) and "I" (the resurrected Christ). By the end of this sacramental encounter, which is at the same time an act of interpretive labor, Thomas's initial skepticism gives way to his renewed faith. He learns to believe because he learns to read.

As we have seen throughout this book, the Eucharist generates many semiotic possibilities. The doctrine of transubstantiation posits that in the consecrated host Christ's Galilean body is present at the level of substance but cannot be seen, tasted, or touched as such. Moreover, the theologies of sacramental participation adopted by the Church of England suggest that Christ's real presence is to be found in the worthy recipient who becomes what he receives. In both cases, Christ is made present sacramentally through visible, tangible, and edible signs but his physical and mystical bodies remain inaccessible to the senses. This final chapter explores the inverse position. How does one come to know a body that *is* physically present but cannot be recognized by means of its outward signs? How do we read a body whose signs do not reliably point to what they signify? What is required to understand, like Doubting Thomas, "That this is I" (178)?

I situate such questions in three different dramatic contexts: biblical dramas of Christ's post-Resurrection appearance at Emmaus; the early

Tudor comedy commonly attributed to Nicholas Udall, *Jack Juggler* (ca. 1553–55); and William Shakespeare's romance *The Winter's Tale* (1610–11). In these plays, bodies are physically present but their signs do not readily convey the body's meaning. Words, names, clothes, broken bread, and a stony posture all dissimulate the bodies to which they refer in such a way that characters cannot comprehend the flesh and blood really present before them. In the Emmaus plays, the disciples do not recognize Christ until he reveals himself in the breaking of bread and then disappears. In *Jack Juggler*, the daft page Jankyn Careaway believes that his identity is actually stolen when Jack Juggler disguises himself in Careaway's clothes and calls himself by Careaway's name. And in *The Winter's Tale*, Leontes rashly brands his wife Hermione an adulterer and traitor, accusations that bring on her apparent death. He corrects these false significations when, after sixteen years of repentance, he interprets her anew. Against Paulina's protestations to the contrary, Leontes ultimately recognizes that his wife is alive, her flesh and blood pulsing beneath a stony front. By the end of *The Winter's Tale*, as at the end of the Emmaus plays, sign and body are put right by means of interpretive acts in which ruptures between sign and signified are repaired at the same time that social communities (whether the church as the body of Christ or the state as the body politic) are restored. In *Jack Juggler*, by contrast, bodies remain thoroughly dislocated from their signs and characters from their social bonds. Careaway never comprehends the Juggler's trick for what it is and thus remains confounded by a semiotic gap (not to mention a psychosomatic crisis) that he never overcomes.

While both *Jack Juggler* and *The Winter's Tale* are secular plays, they reproduce the semiotic problems posed in both biblical dramas and Eucharistic controversies. To recognize real presence, one must repair the broken bonds between sign and body by engaging in acts of naming and renaming, interpretation and recognition. No biblical drama displays these frustrating semiotics of bodily presence more compellingly than the Emmaus plays. Let us begin, then, by examining how the disciples read (and misread) the signs of Christ's real presence as he stands among them, before their very eyes.

Body, Sign, and Story:
The Biblical Dramas of Emmaus

The Emmaus story, as recorded in the Gospel of Luke, is presented as itself a drama of concealment and recognition, of the body's inscrutability and its eventual discovery.² Luke writes, "And it came to pass, whiles he [Christ] sat at table with them, he tooke bread and blessed and brake, and did reach to them. And their eies were opened and they knew him: and he vanished out of their sight. And they said one to the other: Was not our heart burning within us, whiles he spake in this way and opened unto us the scriptures?"³ At a scriptural and theological level, Emmaus is a story about knowing the risen Christ and confirming this knowledge by faith. At a semiotic level, it is a demonstration of how Christ's body relates to its sacramental signs and how the disciples labor to interpret this relation. In a dramatic scene that borrows much from the literary genre of romance, Christ initially confronts the disciples in disguise and then the stranger on the road is ultimately revealed as a friend. The disciples, who presume Christ dead and entombed in stone, come to know him as living flesh in the breaking of bread. An otherwise mundane supper unfolds as the first post-Resurrection Eucharist as well as the first Mass of the early church.

The story of Emmaus has a long dramatic history that extends from the tenth-century *quem quaeritis* trope to sixteenth-century reformed Resurrection dramas. The liturgical trope of the *peregrini* ("pilgrims" or "travelers") was performed at Vespers on either Easter Sunday or the day following.⁴ The trope also recalls the dramas of the sepulcher, during which a consecrated host was buried in a replica of the tomb on Maundy Thursday and then was "resurrected" during the singing of "Christus resurgens" during the Easter Sunday liturgy.⁵ If these liturgical tropes focus on the revelation of Christ's sacramental body in the host, the biblical dramas make the discovery of Christ's real presence contingent on a shared act of interpretive labor. The Emmaus episode is staged as one of several post-Resurrection encounters (the others feature Peter, Mary Magdalene, and Doubting Thomas) in the York and Chester cycles, the N-Town and Towneley plays, and sixteenth-century Resurrection plays such as the anonymous *Resurrection of Our Lorde* (ca. 1530–60).⁶

Without neglecting the well-documented details of dramatic performance in the Emmaus plays, I want to examine the semiotics of the sacramental encounter they stage.⁷ In the Emmaus episode, Christ's body is present but unrecognizable, inscrutable but eventually interpretable. What is more, interpreting Christ's body proves to be as consequential as encountering its physical presence. To know Christ, the disciples must confront him in disguise, witness his disappearance, and then discern the relation between Christ's physical body and its sacramental signs. Such interpretive labor conditions the disciples' newly formed faith. In this regard, the Emmaus plays draw out the semiotics of presence and absence that characterize the Eucharist so that, as Sarah Beckwith writes, "God is neither dissolved into absence or nothingness, nor fetishized as a dead body contained and constrained to concealment and burial. He is rather endlessly disseminated in strenuous and difficult encounters."[8] These encounters, which are paramount in the Emmaus plays, also demonstrate the use of scriptural material to set forth a semiotics of the body, as Theresa Coletti suggests: "The resurrection and the biblical scenes marking its aftermath (the Supper at Emmaus, the doubt of Thomas) provided medieval English dramatists with the most direct occasions for probing the material fact of divine carnality."[9] For Thomas Bishop, moreover, the dramatic trajectory of the post-Resurrection plays "comes to rest in a hermeneutic moment, the object of which is the incarnate Word transfigured at once under its aspect of the knowable and the unknowable, the representable and the unrepresentable."[10]

That "hermeneutic moment" can be said to reach its climax in the Emmaus plays, which bring the scriptural, theological, and dramatic contexts of Christ's Passion and Resurrection together in an extended meditation on the semiotic difficulties that characterize the Eucharist. They do so according to three interrelated movements, each of which ties Christ's bodily presence to an act of interpretation. First, Christ appears in disguise to the pilgrims on the road to Emmaus. Second, he breaks bread with them, his identity revealed only at the point of his vanishing. Finally, faced with the body's absence, the disciples must undertake the labor of interpreting Christ's glorified body in the sacramental signs that remain.

At the outset of the Emmaus story, Christ's resurrected body is already divorced from its signs. When Christ first approaches the disciples on the road, he appears in pilgrim's garb, which identifies him outwardly as an ordinary man walking among men. Consequently, the disciples cannot know the substance of their friend through the shadow of the stranger. In the Chester *Emmaus* play, Cleophas surmises, "A, syr yt seemes to us here / a pylgryme thou art, as can appeare."[11] In the N-Town *Cleophas and Luke*, the same character says, "Sere, me thynkyth th[o]u art a pore pylgrym / Here walkyng be thiselfe alone."[12] By disguising himself in a pilgrim's humble weeds, Christ manipulates the semiotics of his body to great effect. Here, as in the consecrated host, the outward sign does not look like the body it signifies. Such obfuscation bears out Beckwith's point that "the resurrected

Christ is a disseminated Christ, a gift who must be received to operate as such, a stranger who always judges the church who represents him, a Christ who travels."[13] This itinerant, disguised Christ so manipulates the semiotics of his body that he feigns ignorance about the very details of his own passion and resurrection. Rather than reveal his sacred presence immediately or outright, Christ first instructs the disciples to put the narrative of his Paschal Mystery into their own words. In the York *Emmaus*, he asks, "What are these mervailes that ye of mene, / And thus mekill mournyng in mynde that ye make, / Walkyng thus wille by these wayes?" (67–69). The N-Town play captures Christ's linguistic turn particularly well: "Qwat is youre langage to me ye say / That ye have togedyr, ye t[w]o? . . . Why, in Jerusalem, what thynge is wrought? / What tydyngys fro thens brynge ye?" (45–46, 57–58). These questions are, of course, superfluous: Christ is the principal character in the stories he asks the disciples to rehearse, and he has undergone all of the travails they go on to recount (cf. York *Emmaus*, 33–43 and 104–12; Towneley *Peregrini*;[14] and N-Town *Cleophas and Luke*, 9–24).

The post-Resurrection appearances both obscure and defer the meaning of Christ's resurrected and sacramental bodies. So effective is Christ's semiotic play that the disciples go so far as to reprove the pilgrim's apparent ignorance. In the York cycle, the Second Pilgrim says, "Why, arte thou a pilgryme and haste bene / At Jerusalem, and haste thou noght sene / What dole has been done in these daies?" (67–69). In the Towneley *Peregrini*, Luke makes a similar query and then scolds the pilgrim for his lack of mourning: "Me thynk thou shuld make mone, / And wepe here in thi ways" (109r). Readers and spectators would recall the Crucifixion plays and know that Christ has already "ma[d]e mone" in the extended scenes of the Passion discussed in chapter 2; they would also know that Christ has already fulfilled the promise of Resurrection that the disciples do not yet comprehend. Yet Christ appears to the disciples as an unwitting pilgrim in order to engage them in the ongoing process of sacramental interpretation that organizes these dramas. By suspending the revelation of his glorified body and deferring it to a later moment in the play, Christ enables the disciples to speak about him as a character within a narrative (a move that also works metatheatrically, drawing attention to the play's own construction of Christ as such). From the disciples' vantage, Christ's body is physically gone; as such it can only be recalled by words. In this sense, Christ becomes a textual sign that cannot be linked to a physical, bodily referent in the flesh. The irony, of course, is that, as the disciples deliver their account of the Passion, the very body signified by these storied signs—the glorified, resurrected body of Christ—is really present in their midst and hears their words as the living Word made flesh. Yet Christ deliberately confounds the disciples not simply to test their faith but to involve them in a process of interpreting his body by means of sacramental signs. To know that body the disciples must first put it into words. On the road to Emmaus they participate in story so that later, when Christ disappears from the table, they might participate in sacrament.

Having tasked the disciples with the burden of describing his passion, Christ next "becomes his own expositor," as he does earlier in the Crucifixion plays, in demonstrating to the disciples how to interpret the Paschal Mystery.[15] The disciples, who react with skepticism to Mary Magdalene's initial report of the Resurrection, grow despondent in their disbelief. "A mystie thinge yt is to mee," says Cleophas in the Chester *Emmaus*, "to have beleyffe yt should so bee, / howe hee should ryse in dayes three— / such wonders never was wyst" (25–28). To correct their disbelief, Christ does not launch into theological platitudes or homiletic aphorisms. Rather, he teaches the disciples how to read and interpret scriptural texts. Thus before Christ reveals his body in sacramental breaking of bread he first breaks open the word of scripture. In like manner, the disciples must interpret Christ's revelation during the Eucharistic meal using the protocols of reading that he teaches them on the road.

The Resurrection, Christ argues, must be read as the typological fulfillment of Old Testament signs and prophecies. The disciples will not understand the mystery until they learn how to read scriptural and sacramental signs accordingly. The conjunction of scripture to sacrament is a crowning element of the Emmaus story, as Henri de Lubac writes: "The supper at Emmaus made possible an identical and more natural bringing together of the two, given the explanation of the Scriptures which had preceded the moment of recognition."[16] While several of the Emmaus plays emphasize the typological reading of scripture and sacrament, the N-Town play elaborates Christ's lesson in biblical hermeneutics with greatest emphasis.[17] In the N-Town *Cleophas and Luke*, Christ says, "For to beleve in Holy Scrypture, / Have not prophetys with wurdys smerte / Spoke be tokenys in signifure / That Cryste shulde deye for your valure / And syth entre his joye and blys?" (90–94). The "tokenys in signifure" refer to the Old Testament signifiers that now must be linked to their New Testament signifieds. Christ offers many such examples, including Moses, David, Melchizedek, and Isaiah, as well as Aaron's rod, the subject of the following explication:

> Take hede at Aaron and his dede styk
> Which was ded of his nature,
> And yit he floryschyd with flowrys ful thyk
> And bare almaundys of grett valure.
> The ded styk was signifure
> How Cryst, that shamfully was deed and slayn.
> As that ded styk bare frute ful pure,
> So Cryst shuld ryse to lyve ageyn.
> (N-Town *Cleophas and Luke*, 129–36)

Here Christ offers a basic lesson on interpreting scriptural signs typologically. Aaron's rod, previously a "ded styk" in the context of the Old Testament, acquires its fullest signification when read in terms of Christ's incarnation, passion, and resurrection in the New Testament, at which point it becomes a flourishing plant that bears pure fruit.

Christ's role as biblical expositor and semiotic practitioner (already exhibited in the biblical dramas of the Crucifixion and Resurrection examined in chapter 2) is intensified in the sixteenth-century Protestant play *The Resurrection of Our Lorde*. This parish drama, which survives only in fragments of a single scribal copy (Folger MS V.b.192), was likely written for a two-day performance.[18] The first day included a scene at the tomb (not dissimilar to *quem quaeritis*), and the second focused on Christ's appearances to Peter, the disciples at Emmaus, and Doubting Thomas.[19] During the Emmaus scene, Christ argues that the disciples misunderstand his resurrection because they interpret it in carnal terms rather than understand it as a spiritual mystery:

> Thought you that Christ should be a worldlye conqueror
> And that his kingdome stands not rather by invisible power
> Then am I a better scoller (I perceave) then you be
> And did take better heede, to his Doctryne Daylye
> For you myght have perceived, yf you had not byne carnall
> That his kingdome ys to be understood spirituall.
> (47)

Because *The Resurrection of Our Lorde* is a reformed Resurrection play that issues a pointed polemical response to Catholic theology, Christ frames his call to interpretation by styling himself a "better scoller" who argues for a properly spiritual understanding of the Resurrection as opposed to a reading that emphasizes the physical body alone. Christ does not reject the body or the flesh outright but rather criticizes an interpretive practice that fails to appreciate how bodily signs signify spiritual realities.

In addition to Christ, the expositiory figure Appendix comes on stage several times to instruct the audience how best to interpret dramatic representations of the Resurrection. In this regard, Appendix functions in a manner similar to John Bale's "Baleus Prolocutor," though as his name suggests he speaks at the end of scenes rather than at the beginning.[20] At the end of the Emmaus scene, Appendix cautions the audience not to overdetermine Christ's physical body: "Though we see Christ eate in sight of his Disciples yt argues not theirfore, that our immortall bodyes shalbe susteigned with meate, or other carnal tryfles" (47). Appendix uses the Resurrection as an occasion to defend reformed theologies of spiritual eating against the orthodox Eucharistic doctrine of transubstantiation, which many reformers reduced to gross carnality. As *The Resurrection of Our Lorde* illustrates, the Resurrection and post-Resurrection appearances provided a neutral ground on which these hermeneutic challenges posed by the Eucharist could be expressed and debated. One possible reason for the endurance of such a Resurrection play into the sixteenth century is that unlike transubstantiation the Resurrection is an uncontested creedal tenet of Christianity. Catholics and reformers may have disagreed over Christ's body in the sacrament of the altar, but there was little if any dispute over the Resurrection.[21] Thus the play seizes on the Resurrection as a less contested theological tenet on which to ground a more controversial debate over the Eucharist.

The arguments presented by both Christ and Appendix concerning Eucharistic interpretation gain more urgency when situated in the context of the debates over spiritual and carnal eating waged between Stephen Gardiner and Thomas Cranmer in the early 1550s, contemporaneous with *The Resurrection of Our Lorde*.[22] Gardiner goes so far as to cite the Emmaus story in his defense of transubstantiation: "Christe appearing to his disciples going in to Emmaus opened the scriptures to them, for the prouf of his death . . . and yet he used also in some parte to preache to there senses, with sensible exhibition of himself unto them, and so all Christes doings which were most true, do beare testimonie to the truth."²³ Rejecting Gardiner's claim about the sensory apprehension of Christ's body, Cranmer writes,

> The Papisticall doctrine is also agaynst al our outwarde senses, called our five wittes. For our eies say thei se ther bread & wine, our noses smel bread & wine, our mouthes tast[e], and our handes feele bread and wyne, and although the article of our faith be above all our outward senses, so that we beleve thinges which we can neither se, fele, here, smell, nor taste, yet they be not contrary to our senses at the leste so contrary, that in suche thynges whiche we from tyme to tyme do seem smell, fele, here & taste we shall not trust our senses, but beleve clean contrary.²⁴

Such an argumentative line was ubiquitous in Cranmer's writing, which emphasized the spiritual reality of Christ as ascertained through the physical signs: "For as there is a carnall generation, and a carnal fedyng, and nouryshment, so there is also a spirituall generation, and a spirituall fedyng. . . . And as every man is carnally fedde and nouryshed in his body by meate and drynk, even so is every good christen man spiritually fed and noryshed in his soule by the fleshe and bloud of oure Savior Christ."²⁵ As we recall from chapter 1, Cranmer does not reject a notion of Eucharistic presence outright but rather revises its semiotics, suggesting that physical food is an analogy by which Christ's spiritual presence in the sacrament might be understood and received. By echoing Cranmer's arguments, Appendix may well literalize his own textual function, presenting *The Resurrection of Our Lorde* as itself a participant—and a reformed one at that—in both Eucharistic debates and biblical dramas.²⁶

The endurance of the Emmaus play well into the sixteenth century illustrates the salient connection between Eucharistic theology and Eucharistic semiotics evident in the historical controversies over the sacrament. I now want to discuss two additional aspects of the semiotic encounters staged in the Emmaus plays: first, the disciples' recognition of Christ in the breaking of bread, which the church fathers read in the context of the Eucharist; and second, the interpretive process by which the disciples connect Christ's resurrected body that disappears to the Eucharistic signs that remain. When Christ appears as a pilgrim, his body is there but its identity cannot be known. Conversely, after Christ links body to sign in the meal at Emmaus, that body is recognized but cannot be physically grasped. In the first instance, the disciples cannot read the body because of its outward signs; in the second, they have signs without the body. In both cases, they must grapple with the undefined space between signifier and signified opened up by Christ's revelation and subsequent disappearance—a space of semiotic instability that defines the sacrament of the Eucharist itself.

On the whole, the Emmaus plays make Christ's absence more productive than evacuative. At one level, Christ's disappearance catalyzes the disciples' struggle to interpret his body semiotically. Ascertaining the real presence requires such hermeneutic labor—that is, a tireless process of first dealing with the absence of the physical body and then struggling to interpret the mystery of that body through its sacramental signs; thus only when Christ disappears can the disciples repair the link between bread and body and translate it into words. At another level, Christ's disappearance opens out the play's paradoxical stances relative to the sacrament of the altar in the historical context of the Eucharistic Controversies, especially since the biblical dramas span late medieval and early Tudor contexts of performance and compilation. The Emmaus plays shape a semiotics of the sacrament that, on one hand, does not align with the doctrine of transubstantiation and, on the other, evokes reformed theologies of Eucharistic participation and communitarian reception as put forth by John Wyclif in the fourteenth century and by John Jewel and Richard Hooker in the sixteenth. Before turning to the play's engagement with these various aspects of Eucharistic theology, let us first consider the disciples' semiotic struggle staged in the plays.

The absence of Christ's physical body is the primary condition required for the disciples to understand both the Resurrection and the Eucharist and to put into practice the hermeneutic instruction Christ gave them on the road to Emmaus. In the York *Emmaus*, Christ sits at table, blesses the bread, breaks it, and shares it: "Nowe blisse I this brede that brought is on the borde. / Fraste theron faithfully, my frendis you to feede" (157–58).[27] But then he vanishes: "Ow! I trowe some torfoyr is betidde us! / Saie, where is this man?" says the First Pilgrim, to which his companion replies, "Away is he wente— / Right now satte he beside us" (160–62). In the Towneley *Peregrini*, Luke reacts with similar astonishment: "Wemmow! where is this man becom, / Right here that sat between us two?" He then remarks, "A, dere God, what may this be? / Right now he was here by me, / Now is this great vanyte, / He is away; / We are begyld, by my letwe, / So may we say" (110v). Beckwith captures the disciples' disappointment fittingly: "It is as if, here, when they offer to share food with him [Christ], he shares himself with them. The bread is the token of this exchange and the precipitate of it. But what begins as a typical eucharistic scene—the breaking of bread that provokes acknowledgment—ends in the vanishing of the stranger, leaving the bread broken, the supper disrupted."[28] The disciples' joy turns quickly to despair, for their moment of recognition engenders yet another instance of loss—the second in three days. The Christ initially lost to crucifixion vanishes at the moment the disciples begin to comprehend the Resurrection.

Why does Christ reveal himself and then vanish? Why does his bodily absence follow fast on the disclosure of his bodily presence? Christ disappears from the table for the same reason he disguises himself and feigns ignorance on the road: to draw the disciples into a sacramental encounter that takes the shape of a semiotic act, if not a dramatic iteration of Eucharistic controversy. Christ's vanishing is a temporary interruption that, paradoxically, advances the disciples' comprehension of the relationship between physical body and sacramental sign. While the theatrical splendor of the scene gives the impression that the disciples immediately recognize Christ when he vanishes, this recognition materializes only after some painstaking hermeneutic work.[29] In fact, when compared to the scriptural narrative in Luke 24, the plays extend and intensify this interpretive struggle so as to emphasize how the disciples labor together to repair the link between Christ's physical body that has vanished and the sacramental signs that remain.[30] They must likewise connect Christ's Eucharistic body to his ecclesial body, the church. Thus Christ's revelation and disappearance are less fixed material events than a fluid semiotic process.

The disciples, like participants in the Eucharistic Controversies, must grapple with the exasperating disconnect between body and sign that accompanies Christ's vanishing. As Lucas remarks in the Chester cycle, "With us he was a longe fytt / and undyd his holy wrytt; / and yett our wyttes were so knytt / that him we might not knowe" (152–55). The disciples can untangle their knotted wits only by reading the relation of sign to body in Eucharistic terms, and they can do so only once Christ has left the scene: "We no knowledge had him upon / tyll he was passed awaye" (142–43). To know Christ, the disciples must interpret Christ in the signs he leaves behind. And only by interpreting these signs can the disciples eventually name the divine body they signify. Their dynamic and dialogic acts of interpretation are expressed in the York *Emmaus*, where the First Pilgrim says, "Beside us we both sawe hym sitte, / And by no poynte couth I parceyve hym passe," to which the Second Pilgrim replies, "Nay, be the werkis that he wrought full wele myght we witte / Itt was Jesus hymselffe—I wiste who it was" (163–66). Over the course of their dialogue, the disciples emphasize further how Christ's body is made known through, or by means of, the sign of bread: "We saugh hym in sight, nowe take we entent, / Be [by] the brede that he brake us so baynly betwene" (179–80). In the Chester cycle, Cleophas declares, "This was Jesus in this place. / By breakinge the bread I knew his face / but nothinge there before" (129–31). These passages refer to the scriptural phrase "in breaking of bread" (*in fractio panis*; Luke 24:35). Grammatically, this phrase is prepositional; so too are the theological and semiotic logics of Emmaus. The prepositionality of the sacramental encounter as staged in the Emmaus plays—coming to know Christ *by* or *in* the sacramental signs—shows that Christ is revealed, not through a metaphysical conversion of substance, but through a process of communal reflection and interpretation. Through such a process, the disciples come to understand the relation between sacramental signs and resurrected body as the expression of Christ's mystical body, the church.

The communal acts of interpretation by which the disciples finally appreciate the connection between divine body and sacramental sign evoke many of the theological, ecclesiological, and semiotic concerns raised in the historical Eucharistic Controversies. The Emmaus plays draw attention to these vexed issues by expressing somewhat contradictory readings of the Eucharist that cross traditional and reformed stances on the sacrament. In short, the plays assert Christ's real presence in the sacrament, but they do not provide explicit evidence for the doctrine of transubstantiation as is commonly assumed. Bread does not become Christ's body in substance; rather, Christ's presence is made known through first through the disciples' collective interpretation of the sacramental signs and then by their collective reception of Christ's body. While the plays do not necessarily reject the physical reality of Christ's flesh and blood in the sacrament upheld by Catholic orthodoxy, they register certain aspects of reformed Eucharistic theology, namely the tenets of sacramental participation and communitarian reception that are written about by John Wyclif in the fourteenth century and, centuries later, define many aspects of the Church of England's

Eucharistic theology. Both play and sacrament are thus disseminated into a range of historical, theological, and literary interpretations.

Recall that in the late medieval church it was customary for the priest to consume the consecrated host and wine on behalf of the laity. With the exception of an annual reception commonly regarded as one's "Easter Rights," the average communicant received the Eucharist with the eyes rather than the mouth.[31] John Wyclif rejected the priest's solitary, vicarious reception as well as the laity's visual adoration, and for this reason "attention was shifted from the metaphysics of consecration . . . to the faithful's reception of Christ."[32] John Jewel advanced a Eucharistic theology in the mid-sixteenth century grounded in a similar understanding of faithful reception. In *A Sermon Pronounced at Paul's Cross* (1560), Jewel connects the breaking of the bread during the liturgy to the breaking of the bread at Emmaus. "For that end," he says, "the breade is broken, that it may be divided amonge the people. And therefore, the supper of the Lorde is called *Fractio panis*, that is the Breakyng of Breade."[33] Jewel sees the breaking of bread not in terms of transubstantiation but as an indication of sacramental participation and, beyond that, as grounds for abolishing private Masses. The Eucharist is to be realized in the body of the faithful gathered at a common sacramental table. Such communal reception reiterates the emptiness of visual and vicarious communion. Jewell challenges his reader to ask, should he find himself at the Mass, "What make I here? What profite have I of my doynges? I have nothyng: I understand nothing: I am taught nothyng: I receive nothynge: Christ bad me, take: I take nothynge. Chryste bade me, eate: I eate nothynge. Christ bad me drynk: I drynk nothing. Is this the Institucion of Christ? Is this the Lordes Supper? Is this the right use of the holy misteryes?"[34]

The Eucharistic encounter represented in the Emmaus plays satisfies all of Jewel's objections, not least because the disciples model the sacramental participation Jewel envisions by eating with and then receiving the risen Christ. In the N-Town version, Christ bids all to the table by transmitting the sacramental bread directly from his hands to the disciples: "With myn hand this bred I blys / And breke it here as ye do se. / I geve yow parte also of this, / This bread to ete and blythe to be" (213–16). The Towneley play contains a similar reference: "Fro he tooke breede fulle welle I wyst, / And brake it here with his awne fyste, / And laide it us at his awne lyst, / As we it hente, / I knew hym then" (111r). Just as he earlier instructed the disciples in the typological reading of scripture, here Christ visibly and tangibly connects bread to body. The burden to interpret and believe is then left to them.

In both the N-Town play and the Chester cycle, the road to Emmaus terminates with the physical revelation of Christ's body in the Doubting Thomas episode, which further dramatizes communal reception and participation.[35] The Christ who earlier dissimulated his body with signs, stories, and broken bread now unfolds himself in the flesh as the divine thing signified:

> Beholde wele, Thomas, my woundys so wyde
> Which I have sufferyd for all mankynde.
> Put thin hool hande into my ryght syde,
> And in myn hert blood, thin hand that thu wynde.
> So feythffful a frend, were mayst th[o]u fynde?
> Be stedfast in feyth, beleve wel in me.
> (N-Town *Cleophas and Luke*, 337–42)

Christ offers a similar invitation in the Chester *Emmaus* in order to offset Peter's skeptical objection that Christ appears merely as a "ghooste" (175). In response, Christ invites the disciples to handle his body. If, as Richard Hooker writes, "the fruite of the Eucharist is the participation of the bodie and bloud of Christ," the disciples truly receive what they behold at Emmaus.[36] They participate in Christ's body and blood, which Christ offers to them personally and physically:

> Handle me, both all and one,
> and leeve well this everychone:
> that ghooste hath neyther fleshe ne bonne
> as you see nowe on mee.
> (Chester *Emmaus*, 184–87)

To further prove that he is no ghost, Christ eats fish and honeycomb: "Eate we then in good manere, / Thus nowe you know withowt were / that ghooste to eat hathe no powere / as you shall see anon" (196–99). Christ then makes a point of identifying the body the disciples see in Emmaus with the natural, Galilean body crucified on the cross: "I am that same bodye / that borne was of meeke Marye / and on a crosse your sowles did bye / upon

Good Frydaye" (256–59). Christ gives to the disciples his fleshly presence, something they cannot receive as such in the consecrated host. They become "ghestes and not gasers, eaters and not lookers," to quote the Elizabethan *Homily of the Worthy Receiving of the Sacrament*.[37] As participants at the table rather than lookers on the altar, the disciples receive Christ in the flesh *appearing as the flesh*.

Coming to know Christ's body through the sacramental signs also forges an ecclesial community, and the Emmaus plays end with such a vision of the church united as the mystical body of Christ (discussed in chapter 3). So many of the sacramental and scriptural elements in the Emmaus story point toward a communitarian vision realized as the *corpus mysticum*. The Christ who initially appeared as a pilgrim in disguise and then revealed himself in breaking of bread before vanishing from the table is now fully received as Galilean, sacramental, and mystical body. Having interpreted the relation of Christ's body to its sacramental signs, the disciples must put Christ's body into words yet again and share the mystery with the entire Christian community. Their reach extends outward as they leave Emmaus for Jerusalem:

> Ryse, go we hens fro this place,
> To Jerusalem take we the pace,
> And telle our brethere alle the case,
> I red right thus;
> From ded to lyfe when that he rase
> He apperyd till us.
>
> (111r)

A similar summons to evangelization is found in the Chester *Ascension* play, where Christ calls the disciples to traverse the world and preach his message: "My wytnesse all ye shalbee, / In Jerusalem and Judee, / Samarye also, and eych countree / to the worldes end. / Goe yee all the worlde, and through my grace / preach my word in eych place" (69–74). The repair of Christ's body and the sacramental signs thus occasions the first act of public preaching in the early church.

The pattern of semiotic rupture and repair, which forges sacramental encounter as well as sacramental community in the Emmaus plays, is further displaced onto the different but related topic of dramatic representation in the sixteenth-century *Resurrection of Our Lorde*, which I introduced earlier in this discussion. In this play, Appendix teaches the audience members how to negotiate dramatic representation and scriptural text:

> That we gather this, even of the circumstance
> Both of St Luke his wordes, and of St Paules together
> Which both doth write that Christ appeared unto Peter
> But with what words, or when, or where, doubtles, the scripture
> Shewes not; but that by conference of place, we conjecture ...
> Then where we have in Scripture, but two words of the matter
> The rest you must then attribute, unto our invention
> And though about the thynge, we can noe more but smatter
> Lett judgement passe of us, as we with good intention
> Upon the circumstances, have shewed our ymaginacion.
>
> (45)

Appendix issues his own call to interpretation in which he instructs the audience members to differentiate actor from Christ, dramatic fiction from scriptural truth. Like Christ's character in the same play, Appendix warns against a carnal understanding in order to resist idolatry. Yet Appendix, who outs himself as the play's scriptural expositor, is himself a product of dramatic "ymaginacion." Despite his didacticism, Appendix cannot escape the physical, theatrical medium he cautions against: he is, after all, a dramatic figure brought to life and embodied on stage. Rather than severed apart, body and text are dynamically related once again.

I began this chapter with a reference to York's *Incredulity of Thomas*, where Christ reveals his wounded body in order to help the doubting apostle bridge the gap between body and sign. "This is I," Christ says to Thomas when he reveals the glorified body (178). While the Emmaus plays dramatize a tortuous dislocation of "This" and "I," they ultimately reconcile presence and absence, earthly sacrament and divine referent. In what follows, I show how *Jack Juggler* and *The Winter's Tale* generate a similar pattern of semiotic rupture and repair. In the former play this pattern is contextualized not by matters divine but by those ridiculously mundane. In the latter play, the semiotics of real presence crosses the enchanted and the ordinary. In *Jack Juggler*, to which I turn first, Jack muddies the relation between "this" and "I" so that Careaway is absented from the communitarian vision achieved in the Emmaus plays and, at a later stage in the history of English drama, in *The Winter's Tale*.

"Bringe Me to Me Againe": *Jack Juggler*

Jack Juggler is an early Tudor play based on the Italian *commedia dell'arte* tradition and Plautus's Roman comedy *Amphitruo*. It has been commonly attributed to Nicholas Udall.[38] If the play, which has been called "a shrewdly executed satire on Marian Catholicism," is indeed Udall's, it strikes a different religious and political tone than Udall's earlier, more moderate dramas, *Ralph Roister Doister* (ca. 1552) and *Respublica* (ca. 1553–54).[39]

The plot of *Jack Juggler* is simple enough. To settle an unspecified "great debate," Jack Juggler "requites" an unsuspecting page, Jankyn Careaway, by counterfeiting his (Careaway's) identity.[40] While on an errand for Master Buongrace, Careaway becomes distracted by dice games, minor theft, and sex—the very vices that educational dramas like *Jack Juggler* inveigh against—and comes upon a person who resembles himself.[41] This is none other than Jack Juggler, who has disguised himself in Careaway's clothing. Jack successfully persuades Careaway that he (Jack) is the real Careaway. When the page finally returns to his master and says that his identity has been usurped, Buongrace beats Careaway, rejects his fanciful notion that one body can be in two places, and dismisses him from the household. Although Jack Juggler suggests that he will "let Careawaye be Careawaye agayne" (770), he does not make this disclosure known to Careaway himself.

In addition to following the Plautine plot of confused identities (which Shakespeare takes up in *The Comedy of Errors* and elsewhere), *Jack Juggler* echoes the semiotic problems posed by real presence and representational presence set forth both in the Eucharistic controversies and, more specifically, in the Emmaus plays just discussed. Like the Emmaus plays, which have not as yet been read alongside secular early Tudor drama, *Jack Juggler* pivots on disguise and sets the rupture of signifier and signified in the context of a meal—not Christ's Eucharistic supper but the unremarkable supper to which Careaway must summon his choleric mistress, Dame Coy. Both plays also use dramatic irony to implicate the audience in these tricks of disclosure and revelation. Though *Jack Juggler* exhibits a pattern of semiotic rupture similar to that seen in the Emmaus plays, it refuses a final act of repair. Whereas the disciples eventually recognize the disguised pilgrim as Christ, Careaway never bridges the gap between name and body. Instead, he finds himself entangled in what Kent Cartwright calls a "comic epistemological nightmare of having his identity stolen from him by Jacke."[42] Moreover, while the disciples struggle to read a body other than their own,

Careaway struggles to read the signs and referents of his own identity. Such a struggle reaches its climax when the desperate Careaway pleads, "Bringe me to me againe" (595). What is most crushing in *Jack Juggler*—and what most contradicts the Prologue's advertisement of a play about "mirthe and joye" (13)—is that sign and thing signified are driven apart without ever being put back together. Careaway is put back on the road as though, in *Jack Juggler*'s rewriting of the Emmaus plays, he is the pilgrim who fails to correctly understand the relation of sign to body. As a result, he is left without a sense of either personal identity or social community.

In its language alone, *Jack Juggler* indexes the theological debates over the Eucharist, especially as they played out in the Edwardian and Marian reforms in England from 1547 to 1558. Words such as *debate, substantial, presence, shadow, flesh, God's body, remembrance, thing it selfe, receive, confess, supper, grace,* and *passion of Christ* all call to mind the theological and semiotic issues pertaining to Christ's sacramental body and its interpretations. Most critics address the play's religious matter in the context of the disputed theological idea of multilocationism, which holds that Christ's body can be present in two places, as the glorified body in heaven and as the consecrated host on the altar.[43] With the exception of Martin Luther, all reformers reject the idea, which is referenced explicitly in *Jack Juggler* when Master Buongrace rebuffs Careaway's foolish belief that "on[e] man may have t[w]o bodies and two faces / And that one man at on[e] time may be in two placys" (786–87).[44] In what follows, I move beyond the play's engagement with multilocationism to examine Careaway's false belief that calling something by a new name can make it so. This dubious relation between words and deeds amounts to a dramatic critique of Eucharistic confection, which, as we recall from chapter 4, asserts that the words pronounced by the priest at Mass make Christ's body and blood present at the level of substance in the bread and wine.

Jack Juggler dupes Careaway by skewing the semiotic bond between the servant's body and his name. This trick functions as what Tamara Atkin calls "a dramatic illustration of the semiotic process at work in drama."[45] Certainly *Jack Juggler* uses the mechanisms of theater—costumes, actors, disguise, dramatic irony—to open up distance between sign and thing signified. The term *juggler* refers to a trickster, jester, or magician known for deceit (*OED*, 2, 3). It was used in this sense by reformers to debase Catholic priests and the histrionics of the Mass.[46] John Jewel, for example, derogated the Papists' "juggeling toyes"; in a similar vein, Udall's contemporary John Bale describes the Roman clergy as "playeng suche popishe and jugling partes" and thus deceiving the "good playne people" with what reformers saw as the superstitious drama of the Mass.[47] Moreover, Thomas Cranmer writes of Catholics that they make Christ into "a craftie jugler, that made thynges to appeare to mennes sightes, that in dede were no such thynges, but fourmes only, figures, & apparaunces of them."[48] Like Bale, Cranmer also locates this juggling act in the Mass, which he further associates with the devil, who "hath so craftily juggled herein, that of nothing riseth so much contention as of this holy sacrament."[49]

As Cranmer makes clear, the term *juggler* does not refer solely to dramatic performance (religious or otherwise) but also points to a second strand of the play's critique, which concerns interpretation, namely the interpretation of scripture and sacrament. Throughout the English Reformation, but particularly in its Henrician phase, *juggler* was used to refer to someone who deliberately distorted the scriptures, as evident in the writings of both the evangelical William Tyndale and the Catholic Thomas More. In *The Obedience of a Christian Man*, Tyndale characterizes priests as "false prophets that shall juggle / with the scripture and begile the people with false interpretacions."[50] He also says that "the falseheed of the bysshopes & jugglige of the Pope . . . have with sotyll wyles tamed the obedience that shuld be geven to Gods ordinaunce unto them selves."[51] On the other side of the debate, More says that his Zwinglian opponent George Joye "maketh Christes holy word serve hym for his juggling boxes and layeth them forth upon the borde afore us / and byddeth us to loke on this texte/ and than loke so upon this/ and when he hath shewed forth thus two or thre textes and byd us loke upon them he telleth us not wherefore/ nor what we shall fynde in them."[52] In More's characterization, Joye emerges as both a deceptive juggler and a failed exegete. Not only does Joye wrest the words of scripture from their proper meaning, but he also fails to correctly explicate the meaning of the scriptural texts.

With such debates over scriptural hermeneutics at the vanguard of sixteenth-century evangelical reforms, *Jack Juggler* can be said to draw one meaning of *juggler* (which suggests dramatic performance) toward a second, complementary meaning (which suggests semiotic distortion). Jack "juggles" Careaway through theatrical disguise, yes, but he also steals his name and compromises the semiotic system in which Careaway grounds his self-identity. Like the Vice character from the morality plays, Jack states that his aim is to deceive: "My purpose is / To make Jenkine bylive if I can / That he is not him selfe, but an other man" (177–79).[53] For Jack, this is an innocent joke; for the dullard Careaway, it unleashes severe consequences. Careaway accepts too readily the idea that dissimulative tricks involving disguise and renaming can constitute someone's actual identity. At the lowest point of his plot, Jack adds to Careaway's identity confusion the suggested loss of cognitive agility that arises when the signifying bond between name and person dissolves: "Thou art noo poynte Careawaye, thy witts do the[e] faylle" (482). Careaway endeavors to resolve this semiotic crisis—the splintering of "thou" and "Careaway"—by initially rejecting Jack's ruse. "And yf thou woll strike me and breake thy promise, doo!" he says. "And beate on me tyll I stinke and tyll I dye / And yet woll I stiell saye that I am I" (495–97). Whereas many critics have identified Careaway's statement as echoing the Yahwist declaration of identity in the Old Testament (Exod. 3:14), the lines also echo Christ's New Testament "Hoc est" in asserting a link between Careaway's body and his name. After all, Careaway aims to offset the dubious claims of Jack Juggler by declaring that "this is his body" and "this is his name." In a telling echo of Christ's presentation of his hands and feet to Doubting Thomas, moreover, Careaway resorts to bodily proof: "Doo not I speake now? Is not this my hande? / Be not these my feet that on this ground stande? . . . / For surely my name is Jenkin Careawaye" (514–15, 521). The Juggler will not have it. "I woll make thee say otherwise ere we depart if wee can" (522), he says, and later declares his new identity outright: "Looke well upon me and thou shalt see as now / that I am Jenkyne Careawaye, and not thou" (564–65). Of course, while Jack Juggler can pretend to assume an identity that is not his own (a pretension further illustrated by the fact that he is already an actor performing a dramatic role), he cannot actually usurp Careaway's identity simply by stealing his name. The statement is thus verbally and dramatically ironic. At the theatrical level, Jack Juggler is Careaway. At an ontological level, he is decidedly "not thou."

Not only does Careaway fail to appreciate these ironies, but he also participates in the crisis of identity Jack Juggler brings about. In doing so, he intensifies semiotic rupture and makes the kind of semiotic repair witnessed in the Emmaus plays (and, as will be discussed below, in *The Winter's Tale*) impossible. Rather than strengthen his protestation, Careaway renames himself using compound pronouns like "*I thou,*" "*he I,*" and "*I he*."⁵⁴ By articulating his identity according to this new grammar, Careaway tethers himself to his fictitious double. Already socially subordinate to Master Buongrace, Careaway now becomes semiotically subordinate to Jack Juggler. Consequently he can only surmise, "I must go sike me a nother name" (541). Careaway finds this other name in the confused pronouns, which render him a floating signified, a body without a name to make it meaningful. Careaway then introduces an even more damaging prospect: that Jack Juggler is a *better* Careaway than is Careaway himself. Careaway says of Jack, "Who so in England lokethe on him stedelye / S[h]all perceive plainelye that he is I. / I have sene my selfe a thousand times in a glasse / But soo lyke myselfe as he is, never was" (570–73). Not only does Careaway perpetuate Jack Juggler's semiotic deceit, but he now asserts that the fictional version of himself is more authentic than the real version. Careaway thus turns himself into a psychological and textual "voyde" (590) and confirms his fractured identity when he pleads to the Juggler, "Then, maister, I besiche you hartylye take the paine, / Yf I be found in any place, too bringe me to me again" (594–95).

In the Emmaus plays, Christ suggests that the disciples do not understand the Resurrection because they do not understand how to interpret it. Christ founds such interpretation on the typological reading of scripture. In the reformed drama *The Resurrection of Our Lorde*, moreover, Christ insists that the mystery of the Resurrection (and by extension the sacrament of the Eucharist) be interpreted in spiritual rather than carnal terms. Jankyn Careaway displays a hermeneutic deficiency similar to the disciples' in his inability to understand the trick played on him by Jack Juggler. In particular, he believes too uncritically in the performativity of Jack's language and thus attributes to the act of naming a reciprocal act of being. As Careaway says of Jack, "And he woll depose upon a boke that he is I. / And I dare well say you woll saye the same / For he called hym selfe by my owne name" (892–94). To say something, to depose something, to call one thing by the name of another is, in Careaway's limited understanding of signs, to make it so. Because Careaway cannot distinguish the representational act of naming from the ontological state of being, he can never repair the rift between his body and his name.

In calling attention to the dangers of deceptive performatives, if not also to the dissimulative properties of language itself, *Jack Juggler* turns Careaway's hermeneutic failure toward a critique of priestly confection, which (to recall chapter 4) was at the core of Catholic Eucharistic theology. Does saying make it so? Can the declarative act constitute a new identity? Does calling bread by the name "body" or wine by the name "blood" make any more sense than Jack Juggler calling himself Jankyn Careaway? Can superiors—whether ordained priests or lay masters—enforce compulsory belief in such things? The relationship of naming to being, which *Jack Juggler* dramatizes as trivial farce, directly echoes these questions as raised in the Eucharistic Controversies. For example, Cranmer argues that while the bread is called by a new name, this act of renaming does not result in the change of substance: "There is no man of anye discretion, that understandeth the English tongue, but he maye well knowe by the order of the speech, that Christ spake those wordes of the bread, callynge it his body, as al the olde authors also do affirm."[55] Cranmer submits that Christ calls bread by the name of his body, but Cranmer does not see in this renaming a reciprocal ontological transformation. Careaway errs because he fails to appreciate such a distinction.

Unlike the disciples at Emmaus, Careaway does not resolve his confusion about what signs are, how they work, and how they can be manipulated. When Jack Juggler tells the audience that the joke is up—"I woll go do of this myne apparell. / And now let Careawaye be Careawaye agayne" (769–70)—Careaway is never informed and thus cannot ever return to himself. While this disclosure could be achieved offstage, nothing in the text or its performance history suggests that the play ends with such a revelation. Moreover, Careaway never countenances a basic fact of representation—that identities and appearances can be mirrored or feigned without constituting an ontological identity—as explained by Master Buongrace: "Plainelye it was thy shadow that thou didest see" (880). Unable to differentiate shadow from substance, Careaway can define himself only in terms of "that other I" (949) he references in his last speech. In the world of the play, sign and body, like name and person, are taken apart without being put back together. What is more, this lack of semiotic repair brings about social consequences. Not only does Careaway lose his linguistic and social identity, but he also loses his position as page in Buongrace's household.

I opened this chapter by suggesting that if the consecrated host contains Christ's body in substance without making it accessible to the senses, the dramas I study here take up the opposite problem. As we have seen, both the Emmaus plays and *Jack Juggler* deal with bodies that are present in the flesh but cannot be known through their external signs. *The Winter's Tale* also works through a version of this semiotic problem, but it ultimately bridges the gap between body and sign that Careaway cannot correct. Leontes labors to comprehend what Careaway cannot read and what the disciples cannot initially see. In cooperation with Paulina, he learns to read the relation of body and sign anew, and by doing so he receives the fleshly Hermione who has been really present all along. This act of reception, which restores political, linguistic, and familial harmony, is contingent on difficult acts of interpretation. In staging Leontes's process of reading body and sign, Shakespeare engages with semiotic issues raised by both the doctrine of transubstantiation and the doctrines of Eucharistic participation adopted by the Church of England. While *The Winter's Tale* evokes these theologies and semiotics, it accedes to the terms of neither and sufficiently complicates the notions of presence posited by each.

"Warm Life as Now It Coldly Stands": *The Winter's Tale*

In a relatively unremarked line in act 5, scene 2, of *The Winter's Tale*, the Steward recounts the reunion of Leontes and Perdita that has occurred offstage. The recovery of Sicilia's living heir is not enough to offset the sadness of Hermione's presumed death. At the mention of such a loss the Steward says, "Who was most marble there changed colour. Some swooned, all sorrowed."[56] (Sadly, nobody speaks of Mamillius or Antigonus, the play's unremembered dead.) The Steward uses *marble* metaphorically, suggesting that Hermione's death is so tragic it softens even the stoniest heart. Obviously, nobody is actually marble here; rather, they are already flesh to begin with. Shakespeare places the Steward's metaphor just prior to the revelation of Hermione's statue so as to set a precedent for reading stone in a metaphorical sense. In like manner, while it appears that stone is transformed into flesh in the final scene, we discover with Leontes that such a transformation is representational, for Hermione's body has been really present in flesh and blood all along.

Shakespeare did not find a resurrection scene in his principal source, Robert Greene's *Pandosto, or the Triumph of Time* (1588). Rather, he likely added Hermione's "resurrection" to the play after its early performances in

1610–11. The scene then went relatively unexamined until the eighteenth century.[57] More recently, the scene has attracted much critical interest in the play's religious engagements, ranging from transubstantiation and iconoclasm to the cult of the Virgin Mary and *quem quaeritis*.[58] While Resurrection plays foreground the issues of corporeality, performance, and representation evoked by the final scene of *The Winter's Tale*, the Emmaus plays discussed earlier in this chapter provide an even more robust context in which to situate Shakespeare's engagement with the semiotics of sacramental presence. Like the Emmaus plays, *The Winter's Tale* attends less to the bodily event of resurrection and more to the interpretive labor by which an elusive body comes to be recognized, interpreted, and received. Yet in a signal point of contrast, Hermione does not vanish as Christ does but rather reveals herself as fully present in the flesh, completing the restoration of the familial and political communities once threatened by Leontes's rash jealousy. In this reading, Hermione is the revealed living rather than the resurrected dead; Leontes, by extension, is an active participant in a semiotic struggle rather than the passive witness of a divine miracle.

Certainly the prospect of Hermione's statue being transformed into a living body invites an analogy to transubstantiation—an invitation that has been readily accepted in recent readings of *The Winter's Tale*.[59] Yet what Shakespeare renders "Eucharistic" in *The Winter's Tale* is not so much a scene of fleshly resurrection or transformation as the process of repairing the rift between body and sign. In other words, it is the semiotics rather than the metaphysics of the Eucharist that is most relevant to Shakespeare's play. Hermione is not made flesh in any ontological sense; rather, she reveals herself to Leontes as the living body that she already is. What is marvelous at the end of this play—what induces us to "more amazement" (5.3.87)—is not the miracle of stone becoming flesh but rather the hermeneutic process by which bodies are reconnected to their outward signs. Leontes, his "evils conjured to remembrance" (5.3.40) by Hermione's statue, eventually acknowledges that the statue is simply a front for Hermione's vital body.[60] Hermione's cold stoniness is the material sign of the false identities Leontes has imposed on her. Yet by recognizing Hermione as living flesh—and implicitly as pure, loyal, and just—Leontes corrects these near-tragic ruptures in an interpretive act that tethers spiritual conversion to semiotic repair.[61] Leontes needs to embrace in the flesh—and as a living body—that which was denied to the disciples in the Emmaus story and, in the sixteenth-century *Res-*

urrection of Our Lorde, met with skepticism by Christ and Appendix. Yet rather than take sides on matters of confessional politics, *The Winter's Tale* makes Eucharistic theology (of many confessional persuasions) a crucial resource for creating fissures between flesh and sign that organize the debate over Hermione's real presence in the play's final scene.

Shakespeare renders Leontes's initial encounter with the statue not just as a verbal description or as an act of visual gazing but also as a dynamic interpretive argument with Paulina over the relations between body and sign. This exchange embeds into the play arguments about the semiotics of the body similar to those raised in the historical Eucharistic Controversies. Paulina directs Leontes to see the statue as a figurative and symbolic likeness, a memorial image of the deceased Hermione. Leontes, by contrast, sees the statue more vitally and more literally, ultimately recognizing flesh pulsing beneath the appearance of stone. Their tightly structured interchange unfolds as a succession of rapid, yet controlled, antitheses. In three related movements, Paulina identifies as a stony likeness that which Leontes sees as living flesh. Every time Leontes argues for the statue's vitality, Paulina halts such a reading with an appeal to visual representation.

At the outset of their debate, Paulina refers to the statue as a "dead likeness" (5.3.15) and "life as lively mocked as ever / Still sleep mocked death" (5.3.19–20). Here she sets the statue in a representational cast: as she would have it, the statue's relation to real life is mimetic. Furthermore, she attempts to dictate Leontes's interpretive response: "Behold, and say 'tis well" (5.3.20), echoing Christ's own imperative "behold" issued to Doubting Thomas in the Emmaus plays. But Leontes does not accept Paulina's assertions; by contrast, he focuses on the physical conditions of Hermione's "natural posture" (5.3.23). He then apostrophizes the statue: "Chide me, dear stone, that I may say indeed / Thou art Hermione" (5.3.24–25). Calling out to the stone in penitential guilt, Leontes seeks its stern reproof. Only by admitting his own hardness of heart can he eventually "say" that this is Hermione "indeed"— that is, really, truly, and in the flesh. In the second movement, Leontes turns to the statue's physical features once again: "Hermione was not so much wrinkled, nothing / So aged as this seems" (5.3.28–29). Paulina explains the wrinkled face by appealing to Giulio Romano's artistic mastery: "So much the more our carver's excellence, / Which lets go by some sixteen years and makes her / As she lived now" (5.3.30–32). Here Paulina reaffirms her figurative hermeneutics. In the final phase of the debate, Leontes draws

Polixenes into the fray, dwelling again on the statue's vitality: "Would you not deem it breathed, and that those veins / Did verily bear blood?" (5.3.64–65), he asks, to which Polixenes responds, "The very life seems warm upon her lip" (5.3.66). Leontes then concurs: "The fixture of her eye has motion in't, / As we are mocked with art" (67–68). Here Leontes asserts that the statue is not figural but real. Paulina rejects such a claim as idolatrous: "I'll draw the curtain. / My lord's almost so far transported that / He'll think anon it lives" (68–70). In a gesture of exasperation, Paulina threatens to conceal the statue and evacuate the gallery.[62]

It is instructive that the debate between Leontes and Paulina is set within Paulina's gallery, or "chapel" (5.3.86). This is where Hermione's statue is located and where Leontes, Perdita, and the others "intend to sup" (5.2.101).[63] Unlike the disciples who encounter Christ in the supper at Emmaus, Leontes seems to understand from the start that what presents itself as a visible likeness is actually vital life. He does not simply look at Hermione's statue; he interprets it. Unlike Jankyn Careaway, moreover, Leontes does not merely accept Paulina's description of the statue but rather labors to arrive at a different interpretation of sign to body, one by which he gleans flesh beneath the appearance of stone. Leontes thus transposes the manual labor assigned to Giulio Romano's artistic excellence into the readerly activity of resignifying Hermione as living, loving, and chaste. In this sense, Leontes is the lead character in a play that Gillian Woods has characterized as "the reformation of a bad reader."[64] Leontes's hermeneutic labor is necessitated by Paulina's refutation of his interpretive claims, for her antagonism forces Leontes to shore up his conviction that Hermione is really present. In responding to such antagonism, Leontes puts Hermione's fleshly body into words—words that restore Hermione to a state of virtue and thus repair the rifts in signification (and reputation) that Leontes previously caused. All of this has to happen before Hermione can descend from the pedestal.

The semiotic investments hereby evident in Shakespeare's statue scene suggest an analogy between Shakespeare's dramatic transformation of Hermione and the Eucharistic transubstantiation of bread and wine only to complicate it. Once we begin to ponder the theological criteria required for such an analogy to work, we recognize that the transformation of the statue differs markedly from the transformation of the host at Mass. There are three specific reasons why transubstantiation fails to explain Hermione's transformation in the final scene. The first has to do with the relationship between transubstantiation and "real presence"; the second with sacramental confection; and the last with the relation of substance to accident in scholastic theology. I will keep these discussions brief, but I find it necessary to engage with the theology on its own terms in order to appreciate the complexity of transubstantiation as it informs Shakespeare's play.

Real Presence. At the end of *The Winter's Tale*, Leontes receives the real presence of Hermione when she reveals herself as a living body rather than a statue. In this respect, the real presence staged in the play recalls the disputes over Christ's real presence in the Eucharist, namely how his body and blood are manifested in or through the sacramental signs of bread and wine. It is indeed tempting to see real presence (if not the Eucharist itself) as synonymous with the doctrine of transubstantiation. But it is not. Nonetheless, a critical shorthand has developed in which all non-Catholic Eucharistic theology is essentially assimilated to a single, uniform doctrine set in opposition to real presence. What stems from this reductive view is a polarized alternative between transubstantiation or trope, real presence or metaphorical memorial. This too is not the case. We learned in chapter 1 that many reformed Eucharistic theologies subscribed to a belief in the real presence without predicating it on the ontological requirements of transubstantiation or priestly confection. The uncritical elision of real presence with transubstantiation ignores this fact and creates a set of unhelpful binaries that lead to oversimplified narratives about both Eucharistic theology and Shakespeare's engagement with it. By contrast, we should regard transubstantiation as one available position (that of Catholic orthodoxy) used to explain Christ's real presence. That said, even orthodox theologies were by no means univocal. As Paul Strohm explains, "Whatever artificial or imagined unity might be brought to the theory of the eucharist, the inner diversity of the debate guaranteed that it was never—and in fact could never be—concluded or closed."[65] In *The Winter's Tale*, we get a version of real presence without transubstantiation, and while such presence seems to fit the model of sacramental participation that defined the Church of England's position, this too falls short in explaining Hermione's transformation, for reasons we shall see momentarily.

Sacramental Confection. The doctrine of transubstantiation also requires a complex ontological change brought about by God's power working through the priest's words. We recall from chapter 4 that when the priest utters the words of consecration the substance of bread and wine is changed into the substance of Christ's body and blood. This change is ontological; it alters states of being. By contrast, when Paulina speaks to Hermione prior to the climactic descent in *The Winter's Tale*, she speaks words that are declarative, not performative. Paulina's words may direct Hermione, but they do not confect her:

> Music, awake her; Strike!
> Tis time, descend; be stone no more; approach.
> Strike all that look upon with marvel.
> (5.3.98–100)

Despite their imperative force, Paulina's charges—"awake," "descend," "be stone no more," "Strike"—are verbal cues that signal to Hermione when and how she is to shift from one dramatic role (stone) to another (body).[66] Rather than a miraculous transformation, Hermione's revelation unfolds as what Thomas Bishop calls a "verbal process" of "negotiating the transition between impression and expression, between silence and speech, between stone and flesh." Bishop goes on to stress the declarative rather than performative: "Apart from 'Tis time'—a kind of declarative command—only one utterance before Hermione's stirring is not an imperative. Each seems to punch itself into being against a resistance, a resistance registered in the strange sense of violence and blockage in the lines, as if Paulina's call had somehow to bore through or chisel away layers of deafness to reach its target ear."[67] Indeed, Paulina's penultimate command, "Be stone no more" (which may be the closest approximation of a priest's "Hoc est" in this play), brings about a change that is dramaturgical rather than ontological. During his earlier debate with Paulina, moreover, Leontes characterized the statue as "warm life, / As now it coldly stands" (35–36). Hermione realizes such an interpretation. She *is* "warm life" (as is the boy actor who plays her), but at this moment she stands coldly, performing a stony exterior until Paulina directs her to move. No supernatural miracle is necessary. All Hermione has to do is move her feet.

Substance and Accidents. The fact that Paulina's language does not change the substance of Hermione suggests the most obvious reason for why transubstantiation fails to explain Hermione's revelation in *The Winter's Tale*: there is no change of substance because there is no actual stone available to change into flesh. The flesh is already there. This is, in part, why Paulina defends herself against the assistance of "wicked powers" (5.3.91). The basic premise of transubstantiation is that the substance of ordinary bread and wine is miraculously changed into the substance of Christ's body and blood. After this change, what looks, tastes, feels, and smells like bread and wine at the level of sensory perception is not actually bread and wine at the level of being. The elements remain as accidents only and thus lose their essential "breadness" and "wineness."[68]

The Winter's Tale represents the exact opposite. The "statue" changes in outward appearance but not in substance. When Hermione descends and decides to "be stone no more" (5.3.99), Leontes does not receive Hermione's substance in the form of a stony accident. Instead he receives Hermione as she is, her substance made known through the very accidents Leontes discerns earlier: her breath, her veins and blood, the color of her lips, her wrinkles, the movement of her eyes. Shakespeare thus makes Hermione present in substance while also manifesting her body physically, in a way that can be apprehended by the senses through the accidents. By contrast, such sensory apprehension of Christ's physical body is not possible in the consecrated host, and it is an issue Aquinas cannot quite accommodate in his theology. In transubstantiation, Aquinas says, "the dimensions of the bread or wine are not changed into the dimensions of the body of Christ, but substance into substance."[69] While Christ's Galilean body is technically present, it cannot be revealed as bones, blood, and flesh to the recipient.[70] Thus the paradox on which the doctrine rests: what can be apprehended by the senses as bread and wine is not such, even though it looks, feels, and tastes like it. Conversely, what *cannot* be apprehended by the senses as the flesh and blood of Christ *is such*, insofar as it is made substantially present under bread and wine, which are accidents without substance.[71]

Unlike Christ's presence in the consecrated host, Hermione's bodily presence can be seen with the bodily eye. Leontes can perceive her physical qualities with his senses. Hermione then reaches out to Leontes with youthful vigor, and he receives her physical body when "she embraces him" (5.3.111) and "hangs about his neck" (5.3.112). Though the specter of transubstantiation looms over this final scene, Hermione's transformation does not fulfill either its theological or its semiotic demands. Unlike Christ in the consecrated host, Hermione is not made present miraculously at the level of substance. When she descends and becomes "stone no more" (5.3.99), we are urged to see what Leontes sees: the flesh that is always present and the stone that is never really there.

By evoking Eucharistic semiotics in order to complicate Eucharistic physics, Shakespeare does not evacuate or extinguish the sacramental energies elicited by *The Winter's Tale*. Rather, he reconceives the semiotics of transubstantiation so that Leontes can receive what the consecrated host does not provide at a sensory level. If transubstantiation fails to explain the bodily communion Leontes experiences, the doctrines of sacramental participation promulgated by the Church of England offer some insight into the interpretive process by which Leontes acknowledges and then receives Hermione's real presence. Sacramental participation, as John Jewel and Richard Hooker conceive it, locates the sacrament's spiritual reality within the recipient and also makes the sacramental encounter contingent on the recipient's interpretation of bread and body. As Torrance Kirby aptly describes it, "Presence is an act of interpretation. . . . Sacraments become necessarily dynamic events where the instrumentality of signs works through the act of interpretation on the part of the receiver."[72] Leontes, who initially reduces Hermione to the status of a stranger in her own court, eventually interprets her as more than an icon etched in stone. He receives Hermione in the flesh because he interprets that reality, and in interpreting that reality he acknowledges Hermione as the friend, mother, and wife she always has been. Insofar as "Leontes experiences not the resurrection moment itself, but rather a post-resurrection appearance," as Marsalek argues, he also enters into the semiotics of presence that defines the Emmaus plays.[73] It is through his interpretive labor that the meaning of Hermione's statue is best realized in its etymological sense: to "establish," "resolve," "determine," or "decide," all derived from the Latin *statutere*.[74] Hermione's revelation in the gallery resolves, establishes, and indeed completes Leontes's own re-creation (3.2.237).

The dramas studied in this chapter illustrate the process of coming to know the presence of a body—Christ's, Careaway's, or Hermione's—as that which requires participation in interpretive acts. At Emmaus, Christ's vanishing forges an interpretive community among the disciples, who in their shared struggle to interpret Christ's body and its signs form the ecclesial body of Christ, the church. In *Jack Juggler*, bodies do not vanish or feign death but are instead dissimulated through disguise and renaming. Careaway, who is less keen a reader than the disciples or Leontes, cannot read the body's signs properly and as a result loses himself. In *The Winter's Tale*, Leontes resignifies Hermione not as a cold adulteress but as his virtuous wife. This is less a conversion of Hermione and more Leontes's own revision of his false understanding. Hermione does not change except in Leontes's signification of her. He corrects the public shaming of Hermione during the trial scene (3.2) with an equally public admission of his guilt followed by a reparative act of right interpretation, which allows him to participate fully in the revelation of her real presence.[75] Indeed, without such a public admission by Leontes, Hermione's real presence cannot be received.

As we recall from chapter 1, both John Jewel and Richard Hooker hold fast to a version of the real presence understood not through a change in substance but through the communicant's bond with Christ's mystical body. Through this reception in faith, the sacrament changes the recipient and effects what Hooker calls "a kinde of transubstantiation in us, a true change both of soule and body, an alteration from death to life."[76] Jewel, who influenced Hooker, expresses the efficacy of the Eucharist in terms of a similar conversion: "We doe expressly pronounce, that in the supper, unto suche as doe beleve, there is truly delivered the Body & Bloude of the Lord, the flesh of the son of God . . . by the partaking whereof we are quickened, we are nourished, & fed unto immortalitie, and by the which we are coupled, we are united, & grafted into the body of Christ, that we might dwell with him and he in us."[77] Jewel's chiasmus indicates rhetorically the reciprocity that defines Eucharistic participation sacramentally. Jewel figures the sacrament as grafting the recipient onto Christ, a Christ made present through the faith of the communicant rather than by means of priestly confection or vicarious reception. Such a mystical union in no way undermines the reality of Eucharistic presence but transposes its efficacy from the change of substance in the elements to a change of heart in the communicant.[78]

Hooker also emphasizes that the participatory encounter is both intimate and efficacious. Christ's body and blood, he says, "are life in particular by being particularly received."[79] The final movement of *The Winter's Tale* models such a participatory logic in reuniting Leontes, Perdita, and Hermione. When Leontes and Perdita reach out to touch the statue, they do so not like Doubting Thomas, who requires tactile proof to shore up his faith, but as confirmed believers who already know that Hermione is living flesh. Perdita, whose own noble identity has been obscured, reaches out to Hermione first: "Lady, / Dear queen, that ended when I but began, / Give me that hand of yours to kiss" (5.3.44–45). She meets Paulina's immediate rebuke: "O patience! / The statue is but newly fixed; the colour's not yet dry" (5.3.46–47). Perdita does not approach Hermione with idolatrous intent; this statue is not, from Perdita's vantage, akin to statues and icons of the Virgin Mary that wept tears or shed blood. To the contrary, Perdita says, "Do not say 'tis superstition, that / I kneel and then implore her blessing" (5.3.43–44). Rather than kneeling before the statue and gazing at it idolatrously, Perdita is unsatisfied by visual communion and seeks tactile contact instead: "Give me that hand of yours to kiss" (5.3.46). Leontes then follows suit, approaching Hermione with the same desire for physical reunion: "Let no man mock me; / For I will kiss her" (5.3.79–80). Paulina must likewise reject his advance: "Good my lord, forbear; / the ruddiness upon her lip is wet. You'll mar it if you kiss it, stain your own / with oily painting" (5.3.80–83). In spite of Paulina's protestations to the contrary, Perdita and Leontes reject visual reception in the name of a more intimate participation. They seek to encounter Hermione as life in particular, particularly received.

However resonant Jewel's and Hooker's theologies of Eucharistic participation are in the context of Hermione's transformation, Shakespeare's dramaturgy proves still too delicate for the import of these theologies to go unchallenged. While transubstantiation and participation ground Christ's real presence on different theological, philosophical, and semiotic premises, they both deny the recipient access to Christ's body in flesh and blood. Transubstantiation locates sacramental presence in the consecrated host; participation displaces it onto spiritual reception in faith. In both cases, Christ is present, but his divine presence is never tangible as body and blood. As Hooker writes, "These holy misteries received in due manner doe instrumentally both make us partakers of the grace of that body and bloud which were given for the life of the world, and besides also imparte unto us even in true and real though misticall manner the very person of our Lorde himselfe whole perfect and intire."[80] The grace of the sacrament is real, as is Christ's involvement in it. Yet sacramental presence and its effects are mystical rather than physical. Cranmer expresses this point in a slightly different manner when he says, "And this greate benefite of Christe, the faithfull man earnestly considereth in his mynde, chaweth and digesteth it with the stomake of his harte, spiritually receavyng Christe wholly into hym, and gyvynge agayne hym selfe wholly unto Christe."[81] Reception is of the heart and not the body;

the change is spiritual and not ontological. While the grace of Christ's passion is truly received, Christ's Galilean body is not there.

Is this the form of participation we see reflected in *The Winter's Tale*? Not exactly. While Leontes participates actively in the interpretive process necessary to receive Hermione anew, he obtains Hermione in the flesh—physically, not mystically—at the end of that process. Unlike Christ's body in the host, moreover, Hermione reveals herself as body and sign, substance and accident joined together. Leontes, in turn, does not have to reconcile to faith the ontological reality of Hermione that his senses cannot perceive. Hermione clasps her hands around Leontes's neck and then beseeches the gods to "pour your graces / upon my daughter's head" (5.3.123–24).[82] There is no *noli me tangere* here. Leontes and Perdita do not only interpret what they receive; they also receive what they interpret, the living Hermione present in the flesh.

In a final echo of the Emmaus plays, Hermione asks Leontes and Perdita to share their story. Once again, the acknowledgment of presence is contingent on a narrative act. "Tell me, mine own," she says, "Where hast thou been preserved? Where lived? How found / Thy father's court?" (5.3.123–25). But Hermione, unlike Christ, legitimately does not know the story. As she meets Leontes and Perdita in flesh and blood, she also participates in the corrective act of storytelling—an act that will repair all that has filled "this wide gap of time since first / We were dissevered" (5.3.154–55).[83] Shakespeare uses language to repair a dismembered social body, and he does all this without making a profession of faith, creating an enchanted miracle, or relying on supernatural agents.

Taken together, the Emmaus plays, *Jack Juggler*, and *The Winter's Tale* show that whether religious or secular, drama is a literary form deeply tied to the twinned semiotic and sacramental energies that stem from the *Quem quaeritis* trope. Drama introduces time and again a quest for presence situated at the nexus of actor and character, word and flesh, sign and thing signified. In both liturgical and dramatic contexts, to ask, "Whom do you seek?" is to put pressure on the identity of whom (or what) is sought in the process. It is also to pursue the endless work of the seeking, which emerges at the intersection of words and the world.

Afterword

As I reflect on the writing of this book, I am reminded that it took shape amid a reformation in twenty-first-century Roman Catholicism. Granted, this reformation was not in the style of the sixteenth-century Council of Trent, nor did it sound the call for *aggiornamento*—a "bringing up to date"—as did the Second Vatican Council in 1962–65. Instead, this reformation took as its focus the language and texts of the liturgy. In particular, it called for a revision of the vernacular liturgical books authorized in the wake of Vatican II—a revision that would hew more closely to a literal rendering of the Latin Rite. Rather than a reformation of doctrine, this was to be a reformation of language and one conducted by means of translation.

We recall from earlier chapters that the Council of Trent streamlined various local liturgical uses into one uniform text, the *Missale Romanum*.[1] The recommendations for the first vernacular translations of this Latin text were issued on December 4, 1963, during the Third Session of the Second Vatican Council. In its landmark document, *Sacrosanctum concilium*, the Council declared, "The church wishes to make strenuous efforts at a general reform of the liturgy itself," explaining that "in the course of this renewal, the texts and rites must be organized so as to express more clearly the holy things which they represent, and so that thus the Christian people ... will be able to understand these things easily."[2] Toward that end, the Council advocated for "a practice of using the local language" and approved vernacular translations of the Latin books used for the Mass, sacraments, and other liturgies.[3] The first English translation of the *Missale Romanum* was authorized by Pope Paul VI and published in 1969.

In 2002, toward the end of the pontificate of John Paul II, the Congregation for Divine Worship and Discipline of the Sacraments (one of several congregations of the Roman Curia) published an official instruction, *Liturgiam authenticam: On the Use of Vernacular Languages in the Publication of the Books of the Roman Liturgy*. This instruction set forth 133 guidelines for a new vernacular translation of the *Missale Romanum* in which "certain expressions that belong to the heritage of the whole or of a great part of the ancient Church, as well as others that have become part of the general human patrimony, are to be respected by a translation that is as literal as possible."[4] This literal translation was to "maintain the identity and unitary expression of the Roman Rite," with the implication that the vernacular translations written in the half century following Vatican II had somehow compromised the liturgy's linguistic, hermeneutic, and ecclesiastical unity by obscuring particularities in the Latin text.[5]

Liturgiam authenticam insists on literal translation as a way to produce a stable, monosemous liturgical text. As we have seen throughout this book, such a commitment is hardly new. In the Church of Rome as in the Church of England, dogma and doctrine have always been framed according to a specific definition of the literal sense—that is, the idea of a fixed, unwavering, "unitary expression" that does not leave liturgical or scriptural texts open to interpretations other than those authorized by the ecclesiastical institution itself. Such a point is evident in *Liturgiam authenticam*'s principal justification for a new vernacular translation: "It seems necessary to consider anew the true notion of liturgical translation in order that the translations of the Sacred Liturgy into the vernacular languages may stand secure as the authentic voice of the Church of God."[6] Moreover, even when the instruction addresses the literary textures of liturgical translation—and it does so in several sections dedicated to "vocabulary" (secs. 49–56) and "syntax, style, and literary genre" (secs. 57–62)—it restricts the play of meaning to an original Latin Rite: "The translator should strive to maintain the denotation, or primary sense of the words and expressions found in the original text, as well their connotation, that is, the finer shades of meaning or emotion evoked by them, and thus to ensure that the text be open to other orders of meaning that may have been intended in the original text."[7] While the instruction addresses both the denotative and connotative planes of meaning in the liturgical texts, it mandates that all figurative expressions be rendered as literal translations of the original Latin. What emerges throughout *Liturgiam authenticam*, then, is a vision of ecclesiastical unity moored in the linguistic and semiotic stability of the literal sense, which produces a liturgical text that can "stand secure as the authentic voice of the Church of God." Such an argument is not all that different in principle from the positions staked out by William Tyndale and sixteenth-century evangelicals who advocated for the literal sense as the only true sense in which the scriptures could be interpreted.

The newly revised English translation of the *Roman Missal* was published and implemented in November 2011. For the first time in over four decades, churchgoers heard and read a Mass that, while still presented in English, was stylistically and linguistically different from the vernacular translations published after the Second Vatican Council. For example, whereas generations of Catholics responded to "The Lord be with you" by saying "And also with you," the new translation reads, "And with your spirit," a word-for-word translation of the Latin "Et cum spiritu tuo."[8] In like manner, "oblation" became the new "offering"; "incarnate" replaced "made flesh"; and "from east to west" was rendered "from the rising of the sun to its setting." In the Nicene Creed, moreover, the phrase that describes Christ as "one in being with the father" now reads "consubstantial with the father," a more literal sense of the Latin "consubstantialem Patre." The final line of the Mass, translated previously as "The Mass is ended, go in peace," now follows the Latin "Ite, Missa est," foregrounding the imperative: "Go forth, the Mass is ended." And, while the words of Christ's Eucharistic institution—"Hoc est enim corpus meum"—have always been translated in the vernacular as "This is my body," much of the language surrounding the Eucharistic rite has been altered. The earlier English translation of the Roman Canon reads, "Through him we ask you to accept and bless these gifts we offer you in sacrifice." Compare this to the 2011 translation: "We make humble prayer and petition through Jesus Christ, your son, our Lord: that you accept and bless these gifts, these offerings, these holy and unblemished sacrifices," which constitutes, again, a more literal translation of the Latin "Uti accepta habeas et benedicas haec dona haec munera, haec sancta sacrificia illibata."[9]

As the above examples illustrate, these changes to the Mass text were made mostly at the level of word and phrase. They did not alter the church's dogmatic teaching on the Mass, nor did they make the language of the Mass any more efficacious or its rites any more sacred. But they did constitute a more literal translation of the Latin Rite. Many defended these translations, while others saw them as arcane, trivial, and alienating. As

James Martin, S.J., puts it, "In short—depending on who you read—it's a beautiful translation that preserves the majesty of the original Latin; or it's not much of a change at all; or it's an overly literal translation that sounds clunky."[10] Martin's assessment, especially its attention to the range of opinion expressed within different liturgical camps, illustrates how debates over revised vernacular translations of the Mass unleash many of the basic semiotic issues that constellate around the Eucharist itself, namely the relationship between sign and thing signified, the meaning of liturgical rites and gestures, and ideas about literal and figurative interpretation.

It is worth noting, too, that the Roman Church is not alone in attending to the revisions of its language and rites. *The Book of Common Prayer*, a text that originated in the context of liturgical translation, was revised substantially across its first three editions (1549, 1552, and 1559) and again in 1662, following the Laudian Reforms, the English Civil Wars, and the restoration of Charles II. More recently, the prayer book was revised in the 1960s—around the same time as the Second Vatican Council issued its approval of vernacular liturgical texts—in an effort to present a more modernized liturgy. The publication of *Common Worship* in 2000 ushered in yet another new version of the Anglican texts.[11]

The renewed contemporary interest in the translation of liturgical texts demonstrates how deeply the connections between sacrament and language persist across confessional and historical divides. As I suggested at the outset of this book, sacramental thinking, from its origins in Augustine's definition of a visible sign that communicates an invisible grace, is modeled on particular relations between word and thing, body and text. The very recent debates about rendering the words of the Mass according to a more literal translation of the Latin texts are debates about semiotics and interpretation. They are debates about the place of language in liturgical life. And they are debates that are as tied to literary concerns as to theological concerns. Thankfully, these recent debates did not prove as violent as many of the Eucharistic Controversies did in centuries past. But they serve as a powerful reminder that religious reformations big and small seem always to return to ideas about language, about signs and their meanings, about texts, about bodies human and divine.

The converse is nonetheless true. The twenty-first-century debates over the language of sacramental liturgy illustrate that those discourses often restricted to the domains of religion or theology actively work through the theoretical questions and interpretive protocols that literary scholars tend to claim as unique to both our discipline and our secular age. Throughout *Shadow and Substance* I have endeavored to correct this critical bias, showing instead how Eucharistic theology, liturgy, and controversy both create and divide textual and human networks in the context of England's long reformation. Eucharistic discourse—in the richness of its exegetical traditions and especially in the vigor of its spirited controversies—provided a historically relevant framework for dramatists and audiences to think about semiotic problems at a time in history when the very terms of literary practice were influenced by scriptural exegesis and sacramental theology.

By locating in Eucharistic discourses a way to think about semiotic issues across the long, uneven span of England's religious reformations from the medieval to the early modern, I have advanced a discussion of religion and early English drama beyond the reductive readings that turn to religion in order to piece out a dramatist's spiritual autobiography or a drama's own religio-political arguments. Instead, I offer this study as a book about interpretation—of the word, the flesh, and everything in between. Sacramental liturgy is profoundly dramatic insofar as it establishes a crossroads between embodied ceremony and textual practice. Moreover, the semiotic questions produced by Eucharistic discourse—in the contexts of controversies over transubstantiation, the literal sense, and the translation of biblical and liturgical texts—are questions that can inform literary study, particularly the study of drama. Regardless of their different forms, the dramas studied in this book all take as their driving impetus versions of the interpretive questions that stem from the Eucharistic Controversies. Sometimes declaring "This is," but more often than not asking "Is this?" these dramas reinvigorate the Eucharist's semiotic energies across sacred and secular stages. In doing so, they show that the process of seeking the body is never separable from reading the sign.

NOTES

Introduction

1. The term *Eucharist* (derived from the Greek εὐχαριστία, "thanksgiving") has many applications and references, including "Corpus Christi," "Blessed Sacrament," "the Lord's Supper," "the sacrament of the altar," and "Holy Communion." While I focus on the Eucharist in liturgical, devotional, and ecclesiological contexts, I am chiefly interested in it as a source of theological controversy. These controversies, I argue throughout this book, constitute a domain in which questions about dramatic language, embodiment, and interpretation unfold within the long history of England's religious reformations.

2. Brian Cummings lays important groundwork for such a discussion in *The Literary Culture of the Reformation: Grammar and Grace* (Oxford: Oxford University Press, 2002): "The historical events now known as the Reformation are bound up at every level with acts of literature both spoken and written, with the interpretation of language and with the practice of literary culture" (5–6). The crucial relationship of the Eucharist to issues of language, textual representation, and embodiment has been formatively established in medieval contexts by David Aers, *Sanctifying Signs: Making Christian Tradition in Late Medieval England* (Notre Dame, IN: University of Notre Dame Press, 2004), and Sarah Beckwith, *Signifying God: Social Relation and Symbolic Act in the York Corpus Christi Plays* (Chicago: University of Chicago Press, 2001). See also Michal Kobialka, *This Is My Body: Representational Practices in the Early Middle Ages* (Ann Arbor: University of Michigan Press, 1999); Cristina Maria Cervone, *Poetics of the Incarnation: Middle English Writing and the Leap of Love* (Philadelphia: University of Pennsylvania Press, 2012); Tamara Atkin, *The Drama of Reform: Theology and Theatricality, 1461–1533* (London: Brepols, 2013); and Margaret E. Owens, *Stages of Dismemberment: The Fragmented Body in Late Medieval and Early Modern Drama* (Newark: University of Delaware Press, 2005). Though Owens's book covers medieval and early modern contexts, it reproduces a firm narrative of periodization with respect to both drama and religious history and grounds its claims about dismemberment principally in trauma theory. For work focused exclusively on early modern or "post-Reformation" contexts, see Stephen Green-

blatt, "Remnants of the Sacred in Early Modern England," in *Subject and Object in Renaissance Culture*, ed. Margreta de Grazia, Peter Stallybrass, and Maureen Quilligan (Cambridge: Cambridge University Press, 1996), 337–45; Stephen Greenblatt and Catherine Gallagher, "The Wound in the Wall" and "The Mousetrap," in *Practicing New Historicism* (Chicago: University of Chicago Press, 2000), 75–109 and 136–62; Regina Schwartz, *Sacramental Poetics at the Dawn of Secularism: When God Left the World* (Stanford, CA: Stanford University Press, 2007); Judith Anderson, *Translating Investments: Metaphor and the Dynamics of Cultural Change in Tudor-Stuart England* (New York: Fordham University Press, 2005), 36–60; W. J. Torrance Kirby, *Persuasion and Conversion: Religion, Politics, and the Public Sphere* (Leiden: Brill, 2013); Timothy Rosendale, *Liturgy and Literature in the Making of Protestant England* (Cambridge: Cambridge University Press, 2007); Sophie Read, *Eucharist and the Poetic Imagination in Early Modern England* (Cambridge: Cambridge University Press, 2013); and Kimberly Johnson, *Made Flesh: Sacrament and Poetics in Post-Reformation England* (Philadelphia: University of Pennsylvania Press, 2014). See also Debora Kuller Shuger, *Habits of Thought in the English Renaissance: Religion, Politics, and the Dominant Culture* (Toronto: University of Toronto Press, 1997), 17–68; Evelyn B. Tribble, "The Partial Sign: Spenser and the Sixteenth-Century Crisis of Semiotics," in *Ceremony and Text in the Renaissance*, ed. Douglas F. Rutledge (Newark: University of Delaware Press, 1996), 23–34; David Coleman, *Drama and the Sacraments in Sixteenth-Century England* (Houndmills, Basingstoke: Palgrave Macmillan, 2007); and Jennifer Waldron, *Reformations of the Body: Idolatry, Sacrifice, and Early Modern Drama* (Houndmills, Basingstoke: Palgrave Macmillan, 2012). For an approach to hermeneutics outside a Eucharistic context, see Ruth Nisse, *Defining Acts: Drama and the Politics of Interpretation in Late Medieval England* (Notre Dame, IN: Notre Dame University Press, 2005). For a discussion of more modern and postmodern approaches, see *The Poetics of Transubstantiation: From Theology to Metaphor*, ed. Douglas Birnham and Enrico Giaccherini (Houndmills, Basingstoke: Palgrave Macmillan, 2005).

3. These periodic divisions have been championed by E. K. Chambers, *The Mediaeval Stage*, 2 vols. (Oxford: Clarendon Press, 1903), 2:68–105; Harold Gardiner, *Mysteries' End: An Investigation of the Last Days of the Medieval Religious Stage* (New Haven, CT: Yale University Press, 1946); and Louis Adrian Montrose, *The Purpose of Playing: Shakespeare and the Cultural Politics of the Early Elizabethan Theater* (Chicago: University of Chicago Press, 1996). Such arguments have been critiqued by Lawrence M. Clopper, *Drama, Play, and Game: English Festive Culture in the Medieval and Early Modern Period* (Chicago: University of Chicago Press, 2001); Paul Whitfield White, "Reforming Mysteries' End: A New

Look at Protestant Intervention in English Provincial Drama," *Journal of Medieval and Early Modern Studies* 29, no. 1 (1999): 121–47; and John Parker, "Who's Afraid of Darwin: Revisiting Chambers and Hardison . . . and Nietzsche," *Journal of Medieval and Early Modern Studies* 40, no. 1 (2010): 7–35. For recent studies addressing connections between medieval and early modern drama, see T. G. Bishop, *Shakespeare and the Theatre of Wonder* (Cambridge: Cambridge University Press, 1996); Sarah Beckwith, *Shakespeare and the Grammar of Forgiveness* (Ithaca, NY: Cornell University Press, 2011); John Parker, *The Aesthetics of Antichrist: From Christian Drama to Christopher Marlowe* (Ithaca, NY: Cornell University Press, 2007); Heather Hirschfeld, *The End of Satisfaction: Drama and Repentance in the Age of Shakespeare* (Ithaca, NY: Cornell University Press, 2014); Kurt A. Schreyer, *Shakespeare's Medieval Craft: Remnants of the Mysteries on the London Stage* (Ithaca, NY: Cornell University Press, 2014); Ruth Morse, Helen Cooper, and Peter Holland, eds., *Medieval Shakespeare: Pasts and Presents* (Cambridge: Cambridge University Press, 2014); and Katherine Steele Brokaw, *Staging Harmony: Music and Religious Change in Late Medieval and Early Modern English Drama* (Ithaca, NY: Cornell University Press, 2016).

4. See Jay Zysk, "The Last Temptation of Faustus: Contested Rites and Eucharistic Representation in Marlowe's *Doctor Faustus*," *Journal of Medieval and Early Modern Studies* 43, no. 2 (Spring 2013): 335–36. Throughout this book, I use *semiotics* (along with the related terms *sign*, *signifier*, and *signified*) in the general sense of sign theory, as developed in both structuralist and poststructuralist contexts, to address how textual signs—verbal and nonverbal, written and performed—are created, manipulated, and interpreted in both sacramental and dramatic contexts. As I discuss in chapter 1, a "Eucharistic semiotics" uniquely emphasizes the overlap between corporeal and linguistic signs and, especially in the context of theological controversy, illustrates how different religious confessions seek to assert a definite meaning between the sacramental signs (bread and wine) and the divine thing signified (Christ's body). At the same time, however, the very texts that shape these controversies illustrate just how indeterminate and polysemous the semiotics of the Eucharist can be. Insofar as I am interested in how bodies operate as signs in drama, I draw on Keir Elam, who in *The Semiotics of Theater and Drama* (1980; repr., London: Methuen, 2002) extends semiotics (as Roman Jakobson and others do) to include stage properties, material objects, and the actor's body. In individual chapters I draw on more specific semiotic concepts such as J. L. Austin's theory of the performative utterance, which I relate to Eucharistic speech acts in chapter 4, as well as Derrida's idea of the *supplement* and C. S. Peirce's definition of the sign as icon, index, and symbol, both of which I use in my discussion of relics and bodily fragmentation in chapter 5. On the rela-

tions between medieval sign theory and contemporary literary theory, see Theresa Coletti, *Naming the Rose: Eco, Medieval Signs, and Modern Theory* (Ithaca, NY: Cornell University Press, 1988); for a recent discussion of semiotics as an approach to understanding material performances on the early modern stage, see Erika Lin, *Shakespeare and the Materiality of Performance* (Houndmills, Basingstoke: Palgrave Macmillan, 2013).

    5. While confessional markers such as *traditional*, *reformed*, and *evangelical* are admittedly fraught, they remind us that the broader terms *Catholic* and *Protestant* are more complex than commonly understood, not least because *Protestant* applies to many different reformed positions ranging from Lutheranism to Calvinism to the Church of England. It was not until the mid-sixteenth century that the term *Catholic* was used to refer specifically to the Church of Rome over against the Church of England and other reformed churches (see "Catholic," *OED*, 7a). Peter Marshall, *Religious Identities in Henry VIII's England* (Aldershot: Ashgate, 2006), 1–14, offers a useful distillation of the problems with such nomenclatures and decides on *evangelical* to describe reformed religions in the sixteenth century. Furthermore, the term *orthodox* refers not to a particular church or confession but to a doctrine (or set of doctrines) regarded as the authoritative and correct position, as with transubstantiation in the context of Roman Catholicism. Orthodoxy, David Aers reminds us, "may describe an explicitly formulated set of beliefs at a particular historical moment," but the term also refers to "the complex modes in which the Church maintained such beliefs, together with a wide range of practices (from liturgy to Church courts), modes that varied in response to different pressures in different circumstances" (*Sanctifying Signs*, ix). Finally, when speaking specifically of the English Reformation, I prefer *Church of England* to *Anglican*, for the latter term did not enter the lexicon until 1598, when it began to refer to the church as an institution, and was not used to refer to individual members of such a church until the early eighteenth century (cf. *OED*, 1a).

    6. I use *early English drama* in the sense adopted by John D. Cox and David Scott Kastan, who in their introduction to *A New History of Early English Drama* (New York: Columbia University Press, 1997) state, "We intend *early* in the same sense as it has been used in the Records of Early English Drama, which considers the beginnings of dramatic performance in England to 1642, when Parliament ordered the theaters closed.... *Early* also works to erase the sharp distinction between *Medieval* and *Renaissance* that has traditionally been used to mark a period boundary" (2–3; italics in original). The term *drama* itself, moreover, is often used in reference to diverse performative contexts including interludes, mummings, royal entries, performative scripts, dramatic manuscripts,

masques, and stage plays. For recent explorations of such diversity, see Claire Sponsler, *The Queen's Dumbshows: John Lydgate and the Making of Early Theater* (Philadelphia: University of Pennsylvania Press, 2014); Carol Symes, *A Common Stage: Theater and Public Life in Medieval Arras* (Ithaca, NY: Cornell University Press, 2007); Carol Symes, "The Medieval Archive and the History of Theatre: Assessing the Written and Unwritten Evidence for Premodern Performance," *Theatre Survey* 52.1 (May 2001): 29–58; and Bruce W. Holsinger, "Medieval Literature and Cultures of Performance," *New Medieval Literatures* 6 (2003): 271–311.

7. The term *Eucharistic Controversies* is often used in reference to the sixteenth-century debates between Martin Luther, Ulrich Zwingli, Andreas Karlstadt, and Johannes Oecolampadius. I use it more broadly to describe controversies that arise from the high Middle Ages through the seventeenth century. For general histories of Eucharistic controversy, see Lee Palmer Wandel, *The Eucharist in the Reformation: Incarnation and Liturgy* (Cambridge: Cambridge University Press, 2006); Stephen Merriam Foley and Clarence H. Miller, "The Shape of the Eucharistic Controversies," in Thomas More, *The Answer to a Poisoned Book*, ed. Stephen Merriam Foley and Clarence H. Miller, The Yale Edition of the Complete Works of St. Thomas More 11 (New Haven, CT: Yale University Press, 1985), xvii–lxi; Gary Macy, *The Banquet's Wisdom: A Short History of the Theologies of the Lord's Supper* (Collegeville, MN: OSL Publications, 2005); Gary Macy, *Treasures from the Storeroom: Medieval Religion and the Eucharist* (Collegeville, MN: Liturgical Press, 1999); Amy Nelson Burnett, *Karlstadt and the Origins of the Eucharistic Controversy: A Study in the Circulation of Ideas* (Oxford: Oxford University Press, 2011); and Jaroslav Pelikan, *The Christian Tradition: A History in the Development of Doctrine*, vols. 3 and 4 (Chicago: University of Chicago Press, 1985).

8. Richard Hooker, *Of the Lawes of Ecclesiastical Polity: Eyght Bookes*, 5.57 (London: John Windet, 1597), sig. M4r.

9. Aers, *Sanctifying Signs*, 1.

10. Greenblatt, "Remnants of the Sacred," 342. Cf. Johnson, *Made Flesh*, 2, 14–15; Read, *Eucharist*, 2–3. While I agree with Greenblatt's general argument, I wish to point out that what he ascribes to a distinctly "early modern" moment—the problem of Eucharistic leftovers, the words of institution, the sublimity of the host as object, the difference between figural and carnal eating—are everywhere evident in earlier theological and literary writings from Augustine to Wyclif. Likewise, the characterization of the host as "the most significant and endlessly fascinating of Early Modern objects" (337) mutes the point that the host had been the subject of fascination and controversy for centuries prior.

11. Hooker, *Laws*, 5.67, sig. Q6r.

12. Kirby notes that the sheer volume of writings produced on the subject of the Eucharist was so great that "for England, such a sustained spate of printed works devoted to a single scholarly disputation was wholly without precedent" (*Persuasion and Conversion*, 126–27).

13. James Simpson, "Tyndale as Promoter of Figural Allegory and Figurative Language: *A Brief Declaration of the Sacraments*," *Archiv für das Studium der Neueren Sprachen und Literaturen* 245 (2008): 41.

14. In their introduction to *Shakespeare and Early Modern Religion* (Cambridge: Cambridge University Press, 2015), David Loewenstein and Michael Witmore write, "If Shakespeare participated in the religious culture of which he was a part, then his mode of participation may have been to compose rich and nuanced plays that provoke his audience and readers *to think* in a more open-minded way about religious issues—including religious disputes, ambiguities, and contradictions stimulated by the upheavals of the protracted Reformation—rather than nail things down" (11; italics in original). Peter McCullough, "Christmas at Elsinore," *Essays in Criticism* 58, no. 4 (2008): 311–32, notes that "Shakespeare was textually promiscuous, and responded just as creatively to pre-Reformation sources such as liturgies and mystery plays as he did to Protestant ones such as Foxe, or, for that matter, to classical ones such as Plutarch or Ovid" (312). On the argument that Shakespeare may have seen religious drama, see Stephen Greenblatt, *Will in the World: How Shakespeare Became Shakespeare* (New York: W. W. Norton, 2004), 32–40; Michael O'Connell, "Vital Cultural Practices: Shakespeare and the Mysteries," *Journal of Medieval and Early Modern Studies* 29, no. 1 (1999): 149–68; and Beatrice Groves, *Texts and Traditions: Religion in Shakespeare, 1592–1604* (Clarendon: Oxford University Press, 2007). On the "incarnational aesthetic" of late medieval religious drama, see Gail McMurray Gibson, *The Theater of Devotion: East Anglian Drama and Society in the Late Middle Ages* (Chicago: University of Chicago Press, 1989).

15. Bishop, *Shakespeare*, 60.

16. Anthony Dawson, "Performance and Participation," in *The Cultures of Playgoing in Shakespeare's England*, by Anthony B. Dawson and Paul Yachnin (Cambridge: Cambridge University Press, 2001), 28.

17. William Shakespeare, *Titus Andronicus*, 3.2.36, ed. Jonathan Bate (London: Methuen Drama, 1996). All references are to this edition and will be cited parenthetically by act, scene, and line. Jennifer R. Rust, *The Body in Mystery: The Political Theology of the Corpus Mysticum in the Literature of Reformation England* (Chicago: Northwestern University Press, 2014), reads Lavinia's "martyr'd signs" as part of "a language saturated with religious trauma" and notes the violence in Titus's "effort to make Lavinia legible within a sacramental system" (89).

18. *Crucifixio Christi*, in *The York Plays: A Critical Edition of the York Corpus Christi Play as recorded in British Library Additional MS 35290*, ed. Richard Beadle, 2 vols., Early English Text Society, Supplementary Series 23 and 24 (Oxford: Oxford University Press, 2009), 1:223–24; *Incredulity of Thomas*, in *York Plays*, ed. Beadle, 1:50–51, 57. All future citations are to this edition and will be given parenthetically by line number.

19. *Crucifixio*, in *The Towneley Cycle: A Facsimile of Huntington MS HM 1*, ed. A. C. Cawley and Stanley Ellis (Leeds: Leeds Texts and Monographs, 1976), fol. 87r. All future citations are to this edition and will be given parenthetically by folio number.

20. For readings of Lavinia in a religious context, see Rust, *Body in Mystery*, 67–102; Nicholas Moschovakis, "'Irreligious Piety' and Religious History: Persecution as Pagan Anachronism in *Titus Andronicus*," *Shakespeare Quarterly* 53, no. 4 (2002): 460–86; Lukas Erne, "'Popish Tricks' and a Ruinous Monastery: *Titus Andronicus* and the Question of Shakespeare's Catholicism," in *The Limits of Textuality*, ed. Lukas Erne and Guillemette Bolens (Tubingen: G. Narr, 2000), 135–55; and Helga L. Duncan, "'Sumptuously Re-edified': The Reformation of Sacred Space in *Titus Andronicus*," *Comparative Drama* 43, no. 4 (Winter 2009): 425–53.

21. Coppélia Kahn, *Roman Shakespeare: Warriors, Wounds, and Women* (London: Routledge, 1997), 60. See also Douglas E. Green, "Interpreting 'Her Martyr'd Signs': Gender and Tragedy in *Titus Andronicus*," *Shakespeare Quarterly* 40, no. 3 (Fall 1989): 317–26, and Jay Zysk, "Shakespeare's Rich Ornaments: Style and Study in *Titus Andronicus*," in *Rapt in Secret Studies: Emerging Shakespeares*, ed. Darryl Chalk and Laurie Johnson (Newcastle-upon-Tyne: Cambridge Scholars, 2010), 269–86.

22. Bate notes that the "shadow/substance" "is one of Shakespeare's favorite antitheses" (Shakespeare, *Titus Andronicus*, ed. Bate, 210n). Thomas Dekker uses the terms in *The Pleasant Comedie of Old Fortunatus* (London: S. S[tafford], 1600) when the character Shadow puns on his own name: "Ile goe to Court in this attire, for apparell is but the shaddow of a man, but shaddow is the substance of his apparel" (sig. Kiir). In Robert Greene's *The Honourable Historie of Frier Bacon and Frier Bongay* (London: [Adam Islip], 1594), Edward says that the conjuror's circle "made me think the shadows substances" (sig. Civv). Steven Mullaney, *The Reformation of Emotions in the Age of Shakespeare* (Chicago: University of Chicago Press, 2015), 120–26, reads the shadow/substance pairing in *1 Henry 6*.

23. William Shakespeare, Sonnet 53, in *The Complete Sonnets and Poems*, ed. Colin Burrow (Oxford: Oxford University Press, 2002), 487.

24. William Shakespeare, *Richard III*, 5.3.229–32, in *The Norton Shakespeare*, 2nd ed., ed. Stephen Greenblatt et al. (New York: W. W. Norton, 1997).

Stephen Greenblatt, *Hamlet in Purgatory* (Princeton, NJ: Princeton University Press, 2001), analyzes this particular reference at 216–17.

25. William Shakespeare, *The Merchant of Venice*, 3.2.130–34, in *Norton Shakespeare*.

26. William Shakespeare, *Richard II*, 2.2.14–15, in *Norton Shakespeare*.

27. Anderson, *Translating Investments*, 44.

28. Thomas More, *The Answere to the fyrst parte of the poysened booke* (London: W. Rastell, 1533?), bk. 4, sig. Kii*v*. The charge is leveled by the anonymous author of the "poisoned book," whom More suggests could be George Joye or William Tyndale. The book in question is *The Souper of the Lorde* (Nornburg: Niclas Twonson, 1533), now attributed to Joye, and takes a distinctly Zwinglian approach to the Eucharist. On Joye's authorship, see Michael Anderegg, "The Probable Author of *The Souper of the Lorde*: George Joye," in More, *Answer*, ed. Foley and Miller, 343–74.

29. Stephen Gardiner, *An explication and assertion of the true Catholique faith, touching the moost Blessed Sacrament of the aulter* (Rouen: Robert Caly, 1551), sig. Diii*v*. Anderson offers an astute gloss on this passage, suggesting that Gardiner does not so much oppose as relate figure and reality: "The word 'substance' refers equally well to the substance (subject matter) of the words or of the sacraments (material reality) and in this way mirrors the real relation he sees between them" (*Translating Investments*, 47).

30. Edward Reynolds, *Meditations on the Holy Sacrament of the Lords Last Supper* (London: Felix Kyngston, 1638), sig. M1r.; Edmund Gurnay, *Corpus Christi* (Cambridge: Cantrell Legge, 1619), sig. B*iv*.

31. Brian Cummings, introduction to *The Book of Common Prayer: The Editions of 1549, 1552, and 1662*, ed. Brian Cummings (Oxford: Oxford University Press, 2011), xxv. Kimberly Johnson likewise notes, "Seemingly from the moment of this ritual's institution, interpreters have disagreed about the precise meaning of Jesus's words, and that history of controversy and division regarding the nature of sacramental worship has ensured that the Eucharist is experienced primarily as a ritual engagement with signs" (*Made Flesh*, 8).

32. Williams, "Nature of a Sacrament," 203. Williams goes on to say that "the Last Supper is not a simple, primitive fellowship meal; as far back as we can go in the tradition about Jesus, it is seen as 'intending,' meaning, the event that finally sets Jesus and his followers apart from the continuities of Israel and makes the beginnings of a new definition of God's people" (203).

33. Greenblatt, "Remnants of the Sacred," 339.

34. Catherine Pickstock, *After Writing: On the Liturgical Consummation of Philosophy* (Oxford: Blackwell, 1998), xv.

35. Beckwith, *Signifying God*, 60. Lowell Gallagher, introduction to *Redrawing the Map of Early Modern English Catholicism*, ed. Lowell Gallagher (Berkeley: University of California Press, 2012), argues that the Eucharistic Controversies "encode diverse perceptions of the ambiguous interface of sacramental and symbolic agency and of the uncertain relation between language and event" (7–8). Paul Strohm, "The *Croxton Play of the Sacrament*: Commemoration and Repetition in Late Medieval Culture," in *Performances of the Sacred in Late Medieval and Early Modern England*, ed. Susanne Rupp and Tobias Döring (Amsterdam: Rodopi, 1994), 33–44, also notes that the consecrated host is "always sought but completely inaccessible . . . an enigma which functions at once as pure symbol and pure presence, as vacant and as utterly productive place" (36).

36. See Read, *Eucharist*, and Johnson, *Made Flesh*, in addition to Robert Whalen, *The Poetry of Immanence: Sacrament in Donne and Herbert* (Toronto: University of Toronto Press, 2002); Richard Strier, *Love Known: Theology and Experience in George Herbert's Poetry* (Chicago: University of Chicago Press, 1983); Gary Kuchar, *Divine Subjection: The Rhetoric of Sacramental Devotion in Early Modern England* (Duquesne, PA: Duquesne University Press, 2005); and Ryan Netzley, *Reading, Desire and the Eucharist in Early Modern Religious Poetry* (Toronto: University of Toronto Press, 2011). On the Eucharist and early modern romance, see Christina Wald, *The Reformation of Romance: The Eucharist, Disguise, and Foreign Fashion in Early Modern Prose Fiction* (Berlin: Walter de Gruyter, 2014). Read contends "that particularities of belief can be made manifest in the verbal texture of a poem, and that rhetorical and theological planes of understanding are linked by a common mental framework" (*Eucharist*, 7) and asserts the "absolute interdependence between theological belief and the form of words in which it is expressed" (8, 10). Johnson claims that "in the period following the religious Reformation of the sixteenth century, the lyric poem becomes a primary cultural site for investigating the capacity of language to manifest presence" and describes the religious lyric in terms of a "poetics that foregrounds the ritual's inherent tensions between material surface and imperceptible substance, between sign and signified, between flesh and spirit, a poetics remarkably attuned to the complicated interdependence of the body and the word" (*Made Flesh*, 6, 27). While I share these interests in the relationship between the sacramental and the literary, I focus on drama rather than poetry and take a broader historical approach that moves across the periodic borders of medieval and early modern. Moreover, I focus less on poetics and more on semiotics, less on the devotional properties and embodied acts associated with poetic creation and more on the interpretive chasms that emerge when textual and corporeal signs are divorced from their referents in drama.

37. On the relation between religion, liturgy, and dramatic performance, see O. B. Hardison Jr., *Christian Rite and Christian Drama in the Middle Ages: Essays on the Origin and Early History of Modern Drama* (Baltimore: Johns Hopkins University Press, 1965); Beckwith, *Signifying God*, 59–71 and 121–57; Dawson, "Performance and Participation"; Jane Hwang Degenhardt and Elizabeth Williamson, eds., *Drama and Religion in Early Modern England: The Performance of Religion on the Renaissance Stage* (London: Routledge, 2011); Atkin, *Drama of Reform*; and Andrew Sofer, *The Stage Life of Props* (Ann Arbor: University of Michigan Press, 2002), chap. 1.

38. For strictly Protestant readings of early modern literature, see Huston Diehl, *Staging Reform, Reforming the Stage: Drama and Protestantism in Post-Reformation England* (Ithaca, NY: Cornell University Press, 1997); Adrian Streete, *Protestantism and Drama in Early Modern England* (Cambridge: Cambridge University Press, 2011); Ramie Targoff, *Common Prayer: The Language of Public Devotion in Early Modern England* (Chicago: University of Chicago Press, 2001); John N. King, *English Reformation Literature: The Tudor Origins of the Protestant Tradition* (Princeton, NJ: Princeton University Press, 1986); Linda Gregerson, *The Reformation of the Subject: Spenser, Milton, and the English Protestant Epic* (Cambridge: Cambridge University Press, 1995); and Barbara Kiefer Lewalski, *Protestant Poetics and the Seventeenth-Century Religious Lyric* (Princeton, NJ: Princeton University Press, 1995). For studies of heterodoxy and early modern drama, see Maurice Hunt, *Shakespeare's Religious Allusiveness: Its Play and Tolerance* (Aldershot: Ashgate, 2004); Jeffrey Knapp, *Shakespeare's Tribe: Church, Nation, and Theater in Renaissance England* (Chicago: University of Chicago Press, 1997); and Peter Lake, "Religious Identities in Shakespeare," in *A Companion to Shakespeare*, ed. David Scott Kastan (Oxford: Wiley Blackwell, 1999), 57–84. On Shakespeare's relation to recusant culture, see E. A. J. Honigmann, *Shakespeare: The Lost Years* (Manchester: Manchester University Press, 1985); Richard Wilson, *Secret Shakespeare: Studies in Theater, Religion, and Resistance* (Manchester: Manchester University Press, 2004); Richard Dutton, Alison Findlay, and Richard Wilson, eds., *Theater and Religion: Lancastrian Shakespeare* (Manchester: Manchester University Press, 2004); Richard Wilson, Richard Dutton, and Alison Findlay, eds., *Lancastrian Shakespeare: Region, Religion, and Patronage* (Manchester: Manchester University Press, 2004); and Claire Asquith, *Shadowplay: The Hidden Beliefs and Coded Politics of William Shakespeare* (New York: PublicAffairs, 2005).

39. On the concept of ritual "evacuation"—the idea that sacred rituals, objects, and discourses are sapped of their efficacy and replaced with secular forms of ritual, art, and knowledge—see Stephen Greenblatt, "Shakespeare and the

Exorcists," in *Shakespearean Negotiations* (Berkeley: University of California Press, 1988), 94–128; Schwartz, *Sacramental Poetics*; Montrose, *Purpose of Playing*; Richard C. McCoy, *Faith in Shakespeare* (New York: Oxford University Press, 2012); and Katherine Eggert, *Disknowledge: Literature, Alchemy, and the End of Humanism in Renaissance England* (Philadelphia: University of Pennsylvania Press, 2015), 55–110. On the religious turn more generally, see Loewenstein and Witmore, *Shakespeare and Early Modern Religion*; Ken Jackson and Arthur F. Marotti, eds., *Shakespeare and Religion: Early Modern and Postmodern Perspectives* (Notre Dame, IN: University of Notre Dame Press, 2009); Arthur F. Marotti and Ken Jackson, "The Turn to Religion in Early Modern English Studies," *Criticism* 46, no. 1 (2004): 167–90; Alison Shell, *Shakespeare and Religion* (London: Bloomsbury, 2010); and David Scott Kastan, *A Will to Believe: Shakespeare and Religion* (Oxford: Oxford University Press, 2013).

40. Theresa Coletti, *Mary Magdalene and the Drama of Saints: Theater, Gender, and Religion in Late Medieval England* (Philadelphia: University of Pennsylvania Press, 2004), 201.

41. Kastan, *Will to Believe*, 9.

42. Exceptions include Michael C. Schoenfeldt, *Bodies and Selves in Early Modern England: Physiology and Inwardness in Spenser, Shakespeare, Herbert, and Milton* (Cambridge: Cambridge University Press, 1999); Owens, *Stages of Dismemberment*; and Mullaney, *Reformation of Emotions*. The connection between religion and embodiment is clearly pronounced in the field of medieval studies, as represented in Caroline Walker Bynum, *Holy Feast and Holy Fast: The Religious Significance of Food to Medieval Women* (Berkeley: University of California Press, 1987) and *Fragmentation and Redemption: Essays on Gender and the Human Body in Medieval Religion* (New York: Zone Books, 1992); Sarah Beckwith, *Christ's Body: Identity, Culture, and Society in Late Medieval Writings* (London: Routledge, 1992); Barbara Newman, *From Virile Woman to WomanChrist: Studies in Medieval Religion and Literature* (Philadelphia: University of Pennsylvania Press, 1995). For representative studies of early modern embodiment, see Gail Kern Paster, *The Body Embarrassed: Drama and the Disciplines of Shame in Early Modern England* (Ithaca, NY: Cornell University Press, 1993); Jonathan Sawday, *The Body Emblazoned* (London: Routledge, 1997); David Hillman and Carla Mazzio, eds., *The Body in Parts: Fantasies of Corporeality in Early Modern Europe* (London: Routledge, 1997); and Bruce R. Smith, *Phenomenal Shakespeare* (London: Wiley Blackwell, 2009).

43. For the revisionist historiography, see Eamon Duffy, *The Stripping of the Altars: Traditional Religion in England, 1400–1580* (New Haven, CT: Yale University Press, 1992); Christopher Haigh, *English Reformations: Religion, Politics, and Society under the Tudors* (Oxford: Oxford University Press, 1993); and Ethan

Shagan, ed., *Catholics and the "Protestant Nation" in Early Modern England* (Manchester: Manchester University Press, 2009).

44. Such arguments for secularization, advanced by Michel Foucault, Max Weber, and Charles Taylor, are challenged by Brian Cummings, *Mortal Thoughts: Religion, Secularity, and Identity in Shakespeare and Early Modern Culture* (Oxford: Oxford University Press, 2013). See also Brad S. Gregory, *The Unintended Reformation: How a Religious Revolution Secularized Society* (Cambridge, MA: Belknap, 2012), a book that has garnered significant critical response and disagreement, as reflected in "Unintended Reformations," a special issue of *Journal of Medieval and Early Modern Studies*, ed. David Aers and Russ Leo, 46, no. 3 (September 2016). On early modern drama and secularization, see Anthony B. Dawson, "Shakespeare and Secular Performance," in *Shakespeare and the Cultures of Performance*, ed. Paul Yachnin and Patricia Badir (Aldershot: Ashgate, 2008), 83–100, and Anthony B. Dawson, "Claudius at Prayer," in Degenhardt and Williamson, *Religion and Drama*, 235–48.

45. See David Bevington, *From "Mankind" to Marlowe* (Cambridge, MA: Harvard University Press, 1962), for such a history. On periodization and early modern literature, see Gordon McMullan and David Matthews, eds., *Reading the Medieval in Early Modern England* (Cambridge: Cambridge University Press, 2012); Thomas Betteridge, *Literature and Politics in the English Reformation* (Manchester: Manchester University Press, 2004), 1–43; David Aers, "A Whisper in the Ears of Early Modernists, or Reflections on Literary Critics Writing the 'History of the Subject,'" in *Culture and History, 1350–1600: Essays on English Communities, Identities, and Writing*, ed. David Aers (Detroit, MI: Wayne State University Press, 1992), 177–202; David Aers, "New Historicism and the Eucharist," *Journal of Medieval and Early Modern Studies* 33, no. 2 (Spring 2003): 241–59; James Simpson, "The Reformation of Scholarship: A Reply to Debora Shuger," *Journal of Medieval and Early Modern Studies* 42, no. 2 (2012): 249–68; James Simpson, *Reform and Cultural Revolution*, The Oxford English Literary History 2 (Oxford: Oxford University Press, 2004); Richard K. Emmerson, "Dramatic History: On the Diachronic and Synchronic in the Study of Early English Drama," *Journal of Medieval and Early Modern Studies* 35, no. 1 (Winter 2005): 39–66; Margreta de Grazia, "The Modern Divide: From Either Side," *Journal of Medieval and Early Modern Studies* 37, no. 2 (2007): 453–67; and Lee Patterson, "On the Margin: Postmodernism, Ironic History, and Medieval Studies," *Speculum* 65 (1990): 87–108.

46. On the endurance of religious drama into the late sixteenth century, see Alexandra F. Johnston, "An Introduction to Medieval English Theatre," in *The Cambridge Companion to Medieval English Theatre*, 2nd ed., ed. Richard Beadle and Alan J. Fletcher (1994; repr., Cambridge: Cambridge University Press, 2008), 1–25.

47. In both medieval and early modern contexts, the representation of religious content was challenged. A Wycliffite condemnation of "miraclis pleyinge" stated that "no man shulde usen in bourde and playe the myraclis and workis that Crist so ernystfully wrought to our helth." Anyone who does so "errith in byleve, reversith Crist, and scornyith God." Quoted in *Selections from English Wycliffite Writings*, ed. Anne Hudson (Toronto: University of Toronto Press for the Medieval Academy of America, 1997), 97. An Elizabethan injunction issued by the Privy Council in 1576 declared that "no pageant be used or set furthe wherein the Ma[jes]tye of God the Father, God the Sonne, or God the Holie Ghost or the administration of either the Sacraments of baptisme or of the Lordes Supper be counterfeyted or represented" (quoted in H. Gardiner, *Mysteries' End*, 78).

48. Though she is writing in the context of devotional poetry and not drama, Johnson rejects the notion "that post-Reformation poetry exhibits a distinctly Protestant poetics in its word-centered pieties, or that it clings bravely to an imperiled Catholic system of valorized materiality," and finds instead that "in the devotional lyric of the English seventeenth century, poets confront directly and explicitly the presence-making capacities of the tangible sign, and probe the relationship between the unstable materiality of the text and its potential as an instrument of referentiality" (*Made Flesh*, 21–22).

49. On the Communion service as revised in the 1549, 1552, and 1559 editions of the *Book of Common Prayer*, see Rosendale, *Liturgy and Literature*, and Alec Ryrie, *Being Protestant in Reformation Britain* (Oxford: Oxford University Press, 2013), 336–51.

50. On Eucharistic ceremony in Laud's theology and writings, as well as Puritan opposition to Laud, see Achsah Guibbory, *Ceremony and Community from Herbert to Milton: Literature, Religion, and Cultural Conflict in Seventeenth-Century England* (Cambridge: Cambridge University Press, 1998), 20–23. Eucharistic discourse proliferated widely at the time the commercial theaters were in operation and well beyond their closing in 1642. For example, the Jesuit Thomas Wright, along with Bishop Edward Reynolds and the Protestant clergyman Thomas Tuke, continued to pen treatises that either defended Catholic doctrines or called for their reform. Moreover, an English translation of Ratramnus (ca. 868), who challenged Paschasius Radbertus in the first official Eucharistic Controversies, was published as *The boke of Bertam the priest* (London: Thomas Raynalde, 1549) in several different printings as late as 1688 in England and 1753 in Dublin (according to the *STC*). In the eighteenth century, Jonathan Swift parodies debates over transubstantiation in *Gulliver's Travels* (1726), where "Little-endians" and "Big-endians" spar over the proper way to crack an egg.

51. *The text of the new testament of Jesus Christ, Translated out of the vulgar Latine by the Papists of the traitorous Seminarie at Rheims . . . Whereunto is added*

the Translation out of the Original Graeke, commonly used in the Church of England, with a Confutation of all such Arguments, Glosses, and Annotations as Conteme manifest impietie, of Heresie, Treason, and Slander, against the Catholike Church of God, and the true Teachers thereof, of the Translations used in the Church of England... The Whole Worke, perused and enlarged... by W. Fulke, D. in Divinitie (London: Deputies of Christopher Barker, 1589). The Bible was reprinted with Fulke's annotations in three subsequent editions (1601, 1617, and 1633).

52. For example, Michael O'Connell, *The Idolatrous Eye: Drama and Iconoclasm in Early-Modern England* (Oxford: Oxford University Press, 1996), argues that the Reformation indicates a transition from "sacramental Christ to Christ as text" (38), and Schwartz claims that "Reformers chipped away at sacramentality until the body of sacramental experience was reduced beyond recognition, and for some, this meant that God might be leaving the world—yet once more" (*Sacramental Poetics*, 11).

53. For such oppositional readings, see Groves, *Texts and Traditions*, 6, and Read, *Eucharist*, 17–19, 29. Rosendale connects differences in liturgy and worship to differences in reading and interpretation, and he asserts these differences stringently: "The differing logics of Catholic and Protestant, Latin and English, worship play out into—or are perhaps derived from—differing views of signification: one opaque and self-enclosed, the other transparently referential; one, therefore, which in a sense resisted reading, while the other demanded it; one, finally, which enhanced institutional authority, while the other enhanced the authority and role of the individual. . . . What ultimately emerges from the Reformed understandings of the Eucharist . . . is a figurative, interpretive, *readerly* conception of the sacrament" (*Liturgy and Literature*, 88, 107; italics in original). And though she otherwise testifies to a profound overlap of flesh and sign in the Eucharist, Johnson concludes that "the Reformation drives, and is driven by, an unprecedentedly vigorous and systemic public discussion about signification," such that "the model of devotion that emerges out of sixteenth century theology is, finally, textual" (*Made Flesh*, 21). *Shadow and Substance* does not think in terms of such dichotomies nor does it reach such conclusions about the movement from literal to figurative or body to text. Rather, it argues that traditional and reformed Eucharistic theologies, however different, *both* advance particular understandings of semiotic reference, readerly activity, and institutional politics. Cummings offers helpful insight into such a mediating position—"Before any rush to see the sixteenth century as a textualization of religion, it should be remembered how textual medieval religion is"—and adds, "Catholic writing is as caught up in the conflicts surrounding language as protestant" (*Literary Culture*, 18, 26).

54. Andrew Cole, *Literature and Heresy in the Age of Chaucer* (Cambridge: Cambridge University Press, 2008), 146.

55. Thomas Cranmer, *A Defence of the true and catholike doctrine of the sacrament of the body and bloud of our savior Christ* (London: Reynold Wolfe, 1550), sig. Yiiiv. For an excellent discussion of Cranmer's negotiation of body and language, see Sarah Beckwith, "Stephen Greenblatt's *Hamlet* and the Forms of Oblivion," *Journal of Medieval and Early Modern Studies* 33, no. 2 (Spring 2003): 261–80, and Anderson, *Translating Investments*, 45–60.

ONE. Eucharistic Semiotics

1. Torrance Kirby states that the sixteenth century gave rise to a "hermeneutics of sacramental presence" based on "how rightly to interpret the relation between a sacramental sign (*signum*) and the mystical reality signified by that sign (*res significata*)" (*Persuasion and Conversion*, 114). Kimberly Johnson makes a similar claim: "The Eucharist is after all a ritual fundamentally involved with the mechanisms of representation, and the question of how exactly Christ is presented in the bread and wine is one of the animating debates of the Reformation" (*Made Flesh*, 2). She goes on to say that "the Sacrament of the Altar is treated as an event in which corporeal experience is not extricable from hermeneutic activity" and that debates over the Eucharist "focus precisely on the relationship between signs and signifieds, presence and representation, materiality and tropology. To put it another way, the history of Eucharistic theology in the sixteenth century is a history of theories about the operations of signification and figuration" (14–15). While Kirby and Johnson focus exclusively on sixteenth-century contexts, this chapter will illustrate how such pressing semiotic and hermeneutic issues play out within a longer history of Eucharistic theology and controversy, one that spans the medieval/early modern divide and proves consequential for the study of English dramas written and performed across it.

2. Henri de Lubac, *Corpus Mysticum: The Eucharist and the Church in the Middle Ages*, trans. Gemma Simmonds, S.J. (Notre Dame, IN: University of Notre Dame Press, 2007), 194–95; italics in original.

3. John Jewel, *Apologie of the Church of England* (London: Reginald Wolfe, 1562), sig. Fir–Fiv.

4. Aers uses the term *Galilean body* to indicate the natural, physical body of Christ born of the Virgin, crucified on Calvary, and made present during the Mass: "At the words of consecration, words spoken by a duly ordained priest, the body of Jesus that had lived in Galilee became present under what had become the appearance of bread and wine lacking their proper substance. The body now present was the tortured, torn, bleeding, sacrificial, and life-giving body crucified

on Calvary. Such was the presence of Christ elevated in the priest's hands for the faithful to gaze at in adoration, the presence processed through the streets of medieval towns on Corpus Christi Day and around the church on Palm Sunday" (*Sanctifying Signs*, 2).

5. For excellent surveys of Eucharistic theology in the English Reformation context, see Rosendale, *Liturgy and Literature*, 25–115; Read, *Eucharist*, 8–39; and Johnson, *Made Flesh*, 1–16. For a history of Eucharistic liturgy, see Joseph A. Jungmann, S.J., *The Mass of the Roman Rite: Its Origins and Development (Missarum Sollemnia)*, 2 vols. (1956; repr., Notre Dame, IN: Ave Maria Press, 2012); Dom Gregory Dix, *The Shape of the Liturgy* (London: Dacre Press, 1945); Paul F. Bradshaw, *The Search for the Origins of Christian Worship: Sources and Methods for the Study of Early Liturgy* (1992; repr., Oxford: Oxford University Press, 2002); and Edward Foley, *From Age to Age: How Christians Have Celebrated the Eucharist* (1989; repr., Collegeville, MN: Liturgical Press, 2008).

6. Johnson, *Made Flesh*, 10–13, surveys the theology of Ambrose and Augustine. On the debates between Radbertus and Ratramnus, see Macy, *Banquet's Wisdom*, 82–128, and Miri Rubin, *Corpus Christi: The Eucharist in the Later Middle Ages* (Cambridge: Cambridge University Press, 1993), 14–18.

7. On Berengerian heresies, see Kobialka, *This Is My Body*, 68–70, 100–105; Rubin, *Corpus Christi*, 16–25; and Macy, *Treasures from the Storeroom*, 20–80.

8. Johnson, *Made Flesh*, 17. See also Rosendale, *Liturgy and Literature*, 90–91 and 102–3.

9. See Wandel, *Eucharist in the Reformation*, 46–138; Burnett, *Karlstadt*; and Carlos M. N. Eire, *War against the Idols: The Reformation of Worship from Erasmus to Calvin* (Cambridge: Cambridge University Press, 1986), 54–104.

10. For an overview of Wyclif's Eucharistic theology, see Aers, *Sanctifying Signs*, 53–65; Anne Hudson, *The Premature Reformation: Wycliffite Texts and Lollard History* (Oxford: Clarendon Press, 1988); Anthony Kenny, *Wyclif* (Oxford: Oxford University Press, 1985); and G. W. Bernard, *The Late Medieval English Church: Vitality and Vulnerability before the Break with Rome* (New Haven, CT: Yale University Press, 2012). On rebuttals to Wyclif's Eucharistic theology, many of which aligned Wyclif with the Berengarian heresy, see Margaret Aston, "*Corpus Christi* and *Corpus Regni*: Heresy and the Peasants' Revolt," *Past and Present* 143 (May 1994): 32–47.

11. On Jewel's debates with Harding and Cole, see Kirby, *Persuasion and Conversion*, 114–43; Lucy E. C. Wooding, *Rethinking Catholicism in Reformation England* (Oxford: Oxford University Press, 2000); and Gary W. Jenkins, *John Jewel and the English National Church* (Aldershot: Ashgate, 2006). For an excellent account of Smith's retractation sermon at Paul's Cross (1547) and the politics

governing his professorship under Edward and Mary, see Kirby, *Persuasion and Conversion*, 99–113. On Hooker's theology and ecclesiastical politics, see Shuger, *Habits of Thought*, and Kirby, *Persuasion and Conversion*, 161–85.

12. Peter the Lombard, *Sententiae*, 4.1.2, trans. Giulio Silano, *The Sentences: Book 4, On the Doctrine of Signs* (Toronto: Pontifical Institute of Mediaeval Studies, 2010), 3.

13. Thomas Aquinas, *Summa theologiae* [hereafter *ST*] III.60.2, ans.; III.63.2, ans., ed. John Mortensen and Enrique Alarcon, trans. Laurence Shapcote, O.P., *Summa theologiae: Tertia pars* (Lander, WY: Aquinas Institute for Sacred Doctrine, 2012). All future citations are to this edition. For a discussion of Augustine's sacramental semiotics, particularly as they differ from a Scholastic understanding of efficacy, see Philip Cary, *Outward Signs: The Powerlessness of External Things in Augustine's Thought* (Oxford: Oxford University Press, 2008).

14. Jewel, *Apologie*, sig. Div.

15. Cranmer, *Defence*, sig. Siiv.

16. Anderson, *Translating Investments*, 60.

17. See Slavoj Žižek, *The Monstrosity of Christ: Paradox or Dialectic?* (Cambridge, MA: MIT Press, 2009); Giorgio Agamben, *The Signature of All Things: On Method*, trans. Luca D'Isanto with Kevin Attell (New York: Zone Books, 2009); Jean-Luc Nancy, *Corpus*, trans. Richard Rand (New York: Fordham University Press, 2008); Maggie Kilgour, *From Communion to Cannibalism: An Anatomy of Metaphors of Incorporation* (Princeton, NJ: Princeton University Press, 2014); and William T. Cavanaugh, *Torture and Eucharist* (Oxford: Blackwell, 1998). Owens, *Stages of Dismemberment*, uses trauma theory to describe religious idioms of dismemberment.

18. Greenblatt, "Remnants of the Sacred," 339.

19. Strohm, "Croxton *Play of the Sacrament*," 35–36; Aers, *Sanctifying Signs*, 5; Johnson, *Made Flesh*, 9; Agamben, *Signature of All Things*, 50; Beckwith, *Signifying God*, 71.

20. Fourth Lateran Council, Constitution 1: "On the Catholic Faith," in *The Decrees of the Ecumenical Councils*, ed. and trans. Norman P. Tanner, S.J., 2 vols. (Washington, DC: Sheed and Ward, 1991), 1:230.

21. Council of Trent, Session 13: "Canons on the Most Holy Sacrament of the Eucharist," in Tanner, *Decrees*, 2:698. Edward Schillebeeckx, *The Eucharist* (1968; repr., London: Sheed and Ward, 2005), argues that the chief goal of the Council of Trent was to assert transubstantiation as "the unique and distinctive character of the eucharistic presence as an inviolable datum of faith" (53), suggesting that transubstantiation is a comparatively new doctrine when we consider that it was introduced over a thousand years after the Eucharistic practices of the early church.

22. The Six Articles (1539), in *Documents of the Christian Church*, 4th ed., ed. Henry Bettenson and Chris Maunder (Oxford: Oxford University Press, 2011), 249.

23. Read, *Eucharist*, 18.

24. O'Connell, *Idolatrous Eye*, 8–9.

25. For a discussion of the biblical contexts of the words of institution, see Wandel, *Eucharist in the Reformation*, 2–11; on Reformation debates, see Anderson, *Translating Investments*, 36–45.

26. Richard Smith, *The Assertion and Defence of the Sacrament of the Aulter* (London: John Herforde, 1546), sig. Bviir.

27. Stephen Gardiner, *A Detection of the Devils Sophistrie* (London: John Herforde, 1546), sig. Cviiiv. Gardiner's confessional identity is somewhat complex. Though his episcopacy is technically within the Church of England, his position on the Eucharist aligns with Catholic orthodoxy. James Kearney, "Reformed Ventriloquism: *The Shepheardes Calender* and the Craft of Commentary," *Spenser Studies* (26) 2011: 111–51, suggests that Gardiner was "considered by most to be a Catholic in everything but name" (119); Anderson is more cautious, preferring the term "conservative" to "catholic" in her discussion of Gardiner (*Translating Investments*, 232n19).

28. Thomas Cranmer, *An aunswere by the Reuerend Father in God Thomas Archbyshop of Canterbury, primate of all England and metropolitane, vnto a craftie and sophisticall cauillation, deuised by Stephen Gardiner Doctour of Law, late Byshop of Winchester agaynst the true and godly doctrine of the most holy sacrament, of the body and bloud of our sauiour Iesu Christ* (London: Reynolde Wolfe, 1551), sig. Dvr.

29. Ibid., sig. Eir.

30. Writing from a Catholic perspective, Robert Sokolowski, *Eucharistic Presence: A Study in the Theology of Disclosure* (Washington, DC: Catholic University of America Press, 2004), says, "Besides being a true sacrifice, the Eucharist is also essentially a sign. While it would be theologically incorrect [for Catholics] to deny the sacrificial character of the Eucharist and the real presence of Christ in the sacrament, it would be no less incorrect to deny its character as a sign. . . . The Eucharist accomplishes what it signifies, but this accomplishment does not eliminate its being as a sign. . . . Even an ontological reflection on the Eucharist would have to take into account its mode of presentation" (31).

31. Aers, *Sanctifying Signs*, 11. Aers discusses the ways in which orthodox Christianity was constructed in the late Middle Ages (1–28), paying particular attention to the role played by signs in the construction of Aquinas's Eucharistic theology. For an extended discussion of the philosophical, theological, and semiotic intricacies of transubstantiation and its opponents, see P. J. FitzPatrick, *In*

Breaking of Bread: Eucharist and Ritual (1993; repr., Cambridge: Cambridge University Press, 2006).

32. *ST*, III.65.3, rep. 3.

33. Peter the Lombard, *Sententiae* 4.8.7.1, trans. Silano, *Sentences*, 44. Lombard goes on to say that the sacrament also includes "the thing signified and not contained," which is Christ's mystical body, the church (4.8.7.1). Andrew Cole accounts for Lombard's emphasis on spiritual reception, noting that for Lombard "all inquiries into sacramental presence are in the name of what he gives as the second, more 'real,' and efficacious attribute of this sacrament—the spiritual, 'true' body of Christ" (*Literature and Heresy*, 138).

34. *ST* III.60.6, ans.

35. Thomas Aquinas, "Lauda Sion Salvatorem," in *One Hundred Latin Hymns: Ambrose to Aquinas*, ed. and trans. Peter G. Walsh with Christopher Husch (Cambridge, MA: Harvard University Press, 2012), 356–57. The translation is Walsh's. On "Lauda Sion" in the Roman liturgy, see Hugh Henry, "Lauda Sion," in vol. 9 of *The Catholic Encyclopedia* (New York: Robert Appleton, 1910), www.newadvent.org/cathen/09036b.htm.

36. See *ST*, III.60.2, ans.; III.61.4, rep. 1.

37. Aers discusses how Aquinas's argument against cannibalism constitutes a deception, insofar as the recipient technically eats flesh and drinks blood (at least at the level of substance), even though flesh and blood are not present in their physical forms (*Sanctifying Signs*, 20–23).

38. *ST*, III.75.1, rep. 3.

39. *ST*, III.75.2, rep. 3.

40. Cole, *Literature and Heresy*, 147. Also relevant is Johnson, *Made Flesh*, 13–14.

41. R. Smith, *Assertion and Defence*, sig. Oviir–Oviiv.

42. Ibid., sig. Oviiv.

43. S. Gardiner, *Detection*, sig. Kvir–Kviv. In his *Answer to a Poisoned Book*, Thomas More likewise writes, "Consyder that that brede that we eate in the sacrament, is not onely a figure of the fleshe of our lorde / but it is also the fleshe of our lord it self" (G3r). He then paraphrases Theophylactus, the eleventh-century church father: "The brede that we receive in the misteries or sacrament, is not onely a certayne figure of the fleshe of our lorde, but it is also the fleshe of our lord it self. But than expresseth he [Theophylactus] plainely that though he [Christ] calleth it brede, he meneth not that it is very materyall brede styll as it was / but that the brede ys transformed, gone, and changed into the very fleshe of Chryste" (G4v–G5r).

44. S. Gardiner, *Explication and assertion*, sig. Ciiiir.

45. On transubstantiation and the issue of "dimensiveness," see FitzPatrick, *In Breaking of Bread*, 108–16.

46. Aston writes that lay Christians "were required to believe that the host which they saw the priest elevating at the altar, and which they occasionally received and ate, was other than what their eyes saw, and their lips and teeth touched, and their mouth tasted. Bread was not bread; wine was not wine" ("*Corpus Christi*," 44).

47. As Aquinas explains, "Christ's body cannot begin to be anew in the sacrament except by change of the substance of bread into itself [i.e., Christ's body]. But what is changed into another thing, no longer remains after such change. Hence the conclusion is that, saving the truth of this sacrament, the substance of bread cannot remain after the consecration" (*ST* III.75.2, ans.).

48. Aers, *Sanctifying Signs*, 21.

49. On Aquinas's appropriation (or misappropriation) of Aristotelian metaphysics, see FitzPatrick, *In Breaking of Bread*, and Eggert, *Disknowledge*, 55–109.

50. *ST* III.75.5, rep. 2.

51. The idea here is that transubstantiation does not come about because substance is merely taken away from the bread and wine but rather that the bread and wine are changed miraculously, through God's power, into Christ's body and blood. Cf. Aquinas: "The substance of the bread and wine, after the consecration, remains neither under the sacramental species, nor elsewhere; yet it does not follow that it is annihilated; for it is changed into the body of Christ; just as if the air, from which fire is generated, be not there or elsewhere, it does not follow that it is annihilated" (*ST* III.75.3, rep. 1).

52. John Wyclif, *De Eucharistia* (*Tractatus maior*), ed. J. Loserth (London: Wyclif Society, 1892), 132. Wyclif writes elsewhere that "the moste heresy that God suffred cum to his Chirche, is to trowe [believe] that this sacrament is accydent withouten subgett ['subject' or 'substance']." "Concerning the Eucharist II," in *Miscellaneous Works*, vol. 3 of *Selected English Works of John Wyclif*, ed. Thomas Arnold (Oxford: Clarendon Press for the Early English Text Society, 1869), 502.

53. Wyclif, *De Eucharistia*, 21.

54. "Et sic patet de corpore Christi, quod est dimensionaliter in celo et virtualiter in hostia ut in signo" (Wyclif, *De Eucharistia*, 271; And thus it is evident concerning the body of Christ, which is dimensionally in heaven and virtually in the host, as in a sign).

55. Aers, *Sanctifying Signs*, 32.

56. Wyclif, "Concerning the Eucharist II," 502.

57. See Aers, *Sanctifying Signs*, 58–59.

58. Wyclif, *De Eucharistia*, 161.

59. On variations within Catholic Eucharistic doctrine, see Mary McCord Adams, *Some Later Medieval Doctrines of the Eucharist: Thomas Aquinas, Giles of Rome, Duns Scotus, and William of Ockham* (2010; repr., Oxford: Oxford

University Press, 2012); Rubin, *Corpus Christi*, 12–82; and Macy, *Treasures from the Storeroom*, 81–120. Cole argues that Peter the Lombard, for example, hews closely to an ecclesiological understanding of Christ's Eucharistic presence and emphasizes points of theology that reflect a "post-Wycliffite context in which ideas about sacramental language were various and not limited to the words of consecration—'Hoc est enim meum corpus'—that were, from the 'Hoc' to the 'corpus,' interpreted widely among Wycliffite and orthodox parties" (*Literature and Heresy*, 148).

60. Jewel, *Apologie*, sig. Diiiir.

61. Cranmer, *Aunswere*, sig. Diiiiv–Dvr.

62. Hooker, *Of the Lawes*, 5.58, sig. Q4v. Shuger reads Hooker's sacramental theology as a shift from the institutional to the individual, suggesting that "it is now the recipient and not the sign that transubstantiates" (*Habits of Thought*, 39–40).

63. Hooker defines sacramental participation as "that mutall inward hold which Christ hath of us and we of him, in such sort that each possesseth other by way of speciall interest, propertie, and inherent copulation" (*Of the Lawes*, 5.56, sig. L6v). Beckwith, *Shakespeare and the Grammar*, writes, "Reformed sacramental theology, to make complex things simple, situates the efficacy of the sacrament in the transformation of the one receiving communion, in the subjective faith—and knowledge—of the worshiper rather than the objective (*ex opere operato*) work of the priest" (27). The idea of the communicant becoming what he receives is an Augustinian concept, discussed by David Aers and Sarah Beckwith, "The Eucharist," in *Cultural Reformations: Medieval and Renaissance in Literary History*, ed. Brian Cummings and James Simpson (Oxford: Oxford University Press, 2010), 153–65.

64. Dawson, "Performance and Participation," 26, italics in original.

65. Cranmer, *Defence*, sig. Ciiv. My reading of Cranmer differs somewhat from the recent studies of Read and Rosendale, which emphasize the figurative dimensions of Cranmer's theology. For an extended discussion of this passage and of Cranmer's adherence to the real presence, see Beckwith, "Stephen Greenblatt's *Hamlet*," 264–67.

66. Article 29 of the Thirty-Nine Articles declares that anything other than spiritual reception is a grave sin: "The wicked, and such as be void of a lively faith, although they do carnally and visibly press with their teeth (as S. Augustine saith) the sacrament of the body and blood of Christ, yet in no wise are they partakers of Christ, but rather to their condemnation do eat and drink the sign or sacrament of so great a thing" (quoted in Cummings, *Book of Common Prayer*, 682). That said, it is also important not to oversimplify Catholic Eucharistic the-

ology. While Gardiner, More, and Harding all aver that Christ's body and blood are present substantially in the sacrament, they state that such reception is decidedly not carnal (or worse, cannibalistic). Harding, for example, states that while Christ's body is present in substance, it is present "not after corporal, carnal, or natural wise, but invisibly, unspeakably, miraculously, supernaturally, spiritually, divinely, and by way to him onely knowen." By using terms like *real, substantial,* and *carnal,* Harding claims, the patristic fathers "have meant onely a truth of being and not a waye or meane of being." *An Answere to M. Jewelles Challenge* (London: John Bogard, 1564), sig. CCiv–CCiir.

67. Hooker, *Of the Lawes*, 5.67, sig. R1r.
68. Shuger, *Habits of Thought*, 77; italics in original.
69. Hooker, *Of the Lawes*, sig. Q3v.
70. For an examination of Calvin's influence on Hooker, see David Neelands, "The Use and Abuse of John Calvin in Richard Hooker's Defence of the English Church," *Perichoresis* 10, no. 1 (2012): 3–22.
71. Jean Calvin, *Institutes of the Christian Religion* [1559], 4.17.10, ed. Henry Beveridge (Grand Rapids, MI: Wm. B. Eerdmans, 1989).
72. Ibid.
73. Read, *Eucharist*, 17.
74. Calvin, *Institutes*, 4.17.30–31.
75. In responding to the sacramental signs in this way, the recipient evinces what Netzley calls "the affective disposition within reception at the centre of the ritual event" (*Reading, Desire*, 13). On Calvin's theology of presence, see Randall C. Zachman, *Image and Word in the Theology of Jean Calvin* (Notre Dame, IN: University of Notre Dame Press, 2009); Thomas J. Davis, *This Is My Body: The Presence of Christ in Reformation Thought* (Grand Rapids, MI: Baker Academic Press, 2008); Christopher Elwood, *The Body Broken: The Calvinist Doctrine of the Eucharist and the Symbolization of Power in Sixteenth-Century Europe* (Oxford: Oxford University Press, 1999); and Waldron, *Reformations of the Body*, 58–66.
76. Joye, *Souper of the Lorde*, sig. Liiiiv.
77. Ibid., sig. Liiiv.
78. Thomas Wright, *A Treatise, shewing the possibilitie, and conueniencie of the reall presence of our Sauiour in the blessed Sacrament* (London: Joachim Trognesius [Valentine Simmes], 1596), sig. A2v.
79. Ibid.
80. Martin Luther, *Confession Concerning Christ's Supper* [1528], vol. 37 of *Luther's Works*, ed. Robert H. Fischer (Philadelphia: Muhlenberg Press, 1961), 238.
81. Tanner, *Decrees*, 2:695.
82. Cranmer, *Aunswere*, sig. Dvv.

83. The Thirty-Nine Articles of Religion (1563, rev. 1571), quoted in Cummings, *Book of Common Prayer*, 681.

84. Beckwith, *Signifying God*, 59.

85. Harding, *Answere*, sig. CCiv. Martin Luther, *Confession Concerning Christ's Supper* (1528), in *Luther's Works*, ed. Fischer, inveighs in a similar fashion against Zwingli. "If it is proper for him to invent tropes and play around with figures as he pleases, and still be right in all he says, is it surprising that he ultimately makes a Belial out of Christ? . . . For what we want is Scripture and sound reasons, not his snot and slobber" (263).

86. Calvin, *Institutes*, 4.17.20, ed. Beveridge, 572.

87. John Foxe, *Actes and Monuments* (London: John Day, 1563), sig. PPpi-iir. For a discussion of Foxe's relationship to sacramental liturgy, particularly the Mass, see Jennifer R. Rust, "Reforming the Mystical Body: From Mass to Martyr in John Foxe's Acts and Monuments," *ELH* 80, no. 3 (Fall 2013): 627–59.

88. Ibid.

89. The Douay-Rheims gloss identifies this passage as "The Gospel upon Corpus Christi day," and its annotation cites Augustine and Leo to interpret Christ's reference to meat and drink as evidence for transubstantiation. *The Holy Bible Faithfully Translated into English out of the authentical Latin, diligently conferred with the Hebrew, Greek, & other Editions in divers languages* (Douay: John Cousturier, 1635), 236. The Geneva gloss, by contrast, asserts spiritual eating: "As our bodies are sustained with meat & drinke: So are our soules nourished with the bodie and blood of Jesus Christ." *The Geneva Bible*, 1560 ed. (Peabody, MA: Hendrickson, 2007).

90. Here I focus on More's debate with Frith; for an extended discussion of More's debate with Joye, particularly over the Eucharistic narrative in John 6, see Jay Zysk, "John 6, *Measure for Measure*, and the Complexities of the Literal Sense," in *The Bible on the Shakespearean Stage*, ed. Thomas Fulton and Kristen Poole (Cambridge: Cambridge University Press, forthcoming).

91. Thomas More, *A letter of syr Tho. More knight impugnynge the erronyouse wrytyng of John Fryth against the blessed sacrament of the aultare* (London: W. Rastell, 1533), sig. Biiiv.

92. Ibid., sig. Diiv.

93. Ibid., sig. Ciiv. More makes a similar claim in his answer to Joye, written in the same year: "I shewed also that I would in allegoricall exposycyons fynde no faute, but be well content with them, so that men mysse use them not, to the takynge away of the trew literall sense bysyde" (*Answer*, sig. A5v).

94. On the fourfold model, see Henri de Lubac, *Medieval Exegesis: The Four Senses of Scripture*, 3 vols. (1959; repr., Grand Rapids, MI: Wm. B. Eerdmans,

2000), and Beryl Smalley, *The Study of the Bible in the Middle Ages* (Notre Dame, IN: University of Notre Dame Press, 1989). Peter Harrison, *The Bible, Protestantism, and the Rise of Natural Science* (Cambridge: Cambridge University Press, 1998), 19–27, explains medieval biblical hermeneutics beginning with Origen, who advocated for three senses (literal, moral, allegorical), and then moving to the Augustinian expansion into four senses. On the literal sense in the Reformation, see James Simpson, *Burning to Read: English Fundamentalism and Its Reformation Opponents* (Cambridge, MA: Harvard University Press, 2007), 106–15; Cummings, *Literary Culture*, 190–96; Brian Cummings, "Protestant Allegory," in *The Cambridge Companion to Allegory*, ed. Rita Copeland and Peter T. Struck (Cambridge: Cambridge University Press, 2010), 177–89; and Thomas Fulton, "Shakespeare's *Everyman*: *Measure for Measure* and English Fundamentalism," *Journal of Medieval and Early Modern Studies* 40, no. 1 (Winter 2010): 125–26. On the tropological sense, see Ryan McDermott, *Tropologies: Ethics and Invention in England, c. 1350–1600* (Notre Dame, IN: University of Notre Dame Press, 2016).

95. See Simpson, *Burning to Read*, 106–41.

96. Simpson, "Tyndale," 48.

97. Ibid.

98. Ibid., 50.

99. William Tyndale, *A Brief Declaration of the Sacraments* (London: Robert Stoughton, 1548 [?]), sig. Biv*v*–B*v*r. For a brief reading of this passage see Rosendale, *Liturgy and Literature*, 104–5.

100. Anderson, *Translating Investments*, 53. For a further discussion of Cranmer's use of metonymy and other rhetorical figures, see Read, *Eucharist*, 13–15 and 19–30; and Julia Houston, "Transubstantiation and the Sign: Cranmer's Drama of the Lord's Supper," *Journal of Medieval and Renaissance Studies* 24 (1994): 113–30.

101. Cranmer, *Defence*, sig. Qiii*r*.

102. Cranmer, *Aunswere*, sig. Miii*r*–Miii*v*. More makes a similar point when he describes the misinterpretation of Christ's flesh and blood in John 6. He paraphrases Christ's teaching as follows: "You must understand [my words] not so fleshely as you do, that I wolde geve you my flesh in gobbettes dede, / but you must understand them spyrytually, that you shall eate it in an other maner animated with my soule, and joined with the spyrite of my godhed" (*Answer*, sig. M5r).

103. In an earlier phase of religious reformation, Wyclif took up a similar argument about the devil's influence on theological argument, suggesting, "It was not trowid [believed] bifor the fend was losid [loosed], that this worthi sacrament was accident withouten suget [accident without subject]." Sermon XLVI, "The Gospel on Eestir Day," in *Sermons on the Gospels for Sundays and Festivals*, vol. 1 of

Selected English Works of John Wyclif, ed. Thomas Arnold (Oxford: Clarendon Press, 1869), 133.

104. Anderson summarizes Gardiner's complex position in the context of sixteenth-century theological controversy: "The reformers are the ones who open a (pre)Cartesian chasm between the mind's figures and a world that is materially real. Oddly, for Gardiner they do so because they are materialists. For him, their understanding is 'carnall' since it answers to the testimony of their senses raegarding the bread. To Gardiner's adversaries, of course, his literal understanding of *est* is carnal because it requires material presence to be real and therefore impervious to the truth of the spirit" (*Translating*, 47).

105. S. Gardiner, *Detection*, sig. Bii*v*.

106. Harding, *Answere*, sig. Bbiiii*r*–Bbiiii*v*.

107. Cummings, *Book of Common Prayer*, xxiii.

108. Agamben, *Signature of All Things*, 50.

109. *ST* III.60.3, rep. 2.

110. Peter the Lombard, *Sententiae* 6.1.4. See also *ST* III.62.1, ans., for a similar position on the sacrament as an efficacious sign. Beckwith offers an eloquent paraphrase of this concept: "It is in the very signing that a sacrament causes, and it is in the causing that a sacrament signs" (*Signifying God*, 71).

111. Ibid.

112. S. Gardiner, *Explication and assertion*, sig. Ciiii*v*–Cv*r*.

113. Fourth Lateran Council (1215), Constitution 1 "On the Catholic Faith," quoted in Tanner, *Decrees*, 1:231. On the doctrine of the keys in medieval Catholicism, see Beckwith, *Shakespeare and the Grammar*, 37–42.

114. Peter the Lombard, *Sententiae* 8.4, trans. Silano, 42–43. Aquinas is equally clear on this point: "Since the minister works instrumentally in all the sacraments, he acts not by his own but by Christ's power" (III.64.9, ans.).

115. There are a few exceptions. Compared to later reformers like Cranmer and Jewel, and especially to evangelicals like Zwingli, Wyclif argues that the signs of bread and wine could remain along with Christ's presence in the sacrament. Aers summarizes Wyclif's position on confection as follows: "The priest blesses, consecrates, and confects the sacrament, the efficacious sign of Christ's body, but he does not confect the body of Christ" (*Sanctifying Signs*, 61). In addition, Martin Luther regards Christ's words as spoken at the Last Supper as efficacious, though he does not subscribe to the notion of a confecting priesthood. In *Confession Concerning Christ's Supper*, ed. Fischer, Luther notes that Zwingli divides linguistic utterances into two categories: "action words" (which make events happen by means of their utterance) and "declaratives" (which refer to or report events). But he says that Zwingli errs in failing to read *est* in "Hoc est enim corpus meum" as an action

word. Speaking of Christ's Eucharistic institution, Luther argues that "everything that the words declare does take place, by the power of this divine imperative through which they are spoken" (182–83). Luther then concludes, "With the word, 'Thus (or this) do,' Christ commands not the eating of the bread alone but the whole ordinance of the supper" (190). Thomas Davis provides an extended reading of Luther's theology of Eucharistic language (*This is My Body*, 41–63).

116. Cranmer, *Defence*, sig. Eiir–Eiiv.

117. *ST* III.75.7, rep. 1.

118. Anderson, *Translating Investments*, 43.

119. S. Gardiner, *Detection*, sig. Oiiiiv. See also FitzPatrick's extensive discussion of "transsignification" in relation to Scholastic theologies of the Eucharist (*In Breaking of Bread*, 49–107).

120. Calvin, *Institutes*, 4.17.5, ed. Beveridge, 559.

121. Hooker, *Of the Lawes*, 5.58, sig. M5r.

122. Ibid., sig. M4v.

123. Gazing upon the host provided a wealth of graces, for "to see the Host, however fleetingly, was a privilege bringing blessing. . . . Grace came by seeing the Host: to see it was to be blessed" (Duffy, *Stripping of the Altars*, 95). See also Rubin, *Corpus Christi*, 54–63.

124. Jewel, *Apologie*, sig. Diir–Diiv. As stipulated in the Order of Communion in the *Book of Common Prayer*, those who come to the table must also be free of sin and make a proper general confession to God and neighbor.

125. Ibid., sig. Diiiv.

126. Cranmer, *Defence*, sig. Ziiiv.

127. Jewel, *Apologie*, sig. Diiiv.

TWO. Words and Wounds

1. John Fisher, "A sermon . . . Preached upon a good Friday, by the same John Fisher, Bishop of Rochester," in *The English Works of John Fisher*, ed. John E. B. Mayor (Ludgate Hill: N. Trubner, for the Early English Text Society, 1876), 395. The comparison of Christ's body to a text is a topos common to English and Continental iconography, as discussed by Jodie Enders, *The Medieval Theater of Cruelty* (Ithaca, NY: Cornell University Press, 1999), 109–10. I learned of Fisher's sermon from Lowell Gallagher's essay, "The Place of the Stigmata in Christological Poetics," in *Religion and Culture in Renaissance England*, ed. Claire McEachern and Debora Shuger (Cambridge: Cambridge University Press, 1997), 93–115. Gallagher writes about Fisher's figuration of Christ's crucified body as a book in the context of temporality at 101–5.

2. David Aers, "The Humanity of Christ: Reflections on Orthodox Late Medieval Representations," in *The Powers of the Holy: Religion, Politics, and Gender in Late Medieval English Culture*, ed. David Aers and Lynn Staley (University Park: Pennsylvania State University Press, 1996), 15–42, writes of the affective piety tradition, "The humiliated, tortured, whipped, nailed-down, pierced, dying but life-giving body of Christ, the very body literally present in the Eucharist—this body became the dominant icon of the late medieval church and the devotion it cultivated and authorized" (17). Aers focuses on an alternative version of Christ's humanity offered in Wycliffite writings, which emphasized Christ's pastoral care for the sick and poor as recorded in the gospels.

3. On the *Stanzaic Life* and *Northern Passion* in relation to biblical drama, see Rosemary Woolf, *The English Mystery Plays* (Berkeley: University of California Press, 1972), and V. A. Kolve, *The Play Called Corpus Christi* (Stanford, CA: Stanford University Press, 1966). On representations of Christ's humanity in vernacular literature, see Aers, "Humanity of Christ," and Nicholas Watson, "Conceptions of the Word: The Mother Tongue and the Incarnation of God," *New Medieval Literatures* 1 (1998): 85–124. On Christ's wounds and the Eucharist, see Rubin, *Corpus Christi*, 302–6, and Anne W. Astell, *Eating Beauty: The Eucharist and the Spiritual Arts of the Middle Ages* (Ithaca, NY: Cornell University Press, 2004), 99–135.

4. Gallagher elaborates the connection between flesh and text in the context of *stigmata*, or the crucifixion wounds miraculously impressed on the bodies of saints: "As marks that both ratify and probe (*probare*, to test) the stigmata figure identity as an interrogative relation of inside and outside. By wounding a body they both reveal and produce its interior; that is, they disclose the body-as-text. The body thus becomes a corpus-text structured as a paradoxical relation of coherence and dispersal, of continuity and mutation" ("Place of the Stigmata," 95).

5. York, *Christ before Pilate II*, line 431, *Crucifixio Christi* (*Crucifixion*), line 43, and *Mortificatio Christi*, line 253, all in *York Plays*, ed. Beadle, vol. 1. All future citations of the York plays are to this edition and volume and will be given parenthetically by line number.

6. William Shakespeare, *Coriolanus* 1.6.22, 2.2.107, ed. Peter Holland (London: Bloomsbury, 2013). All future citations to the play are from this edition and will be given parenthetically by act, scene, and line number. Cynthia Marshall, "Wound-Man: Coriolanus, Gender, and the Theatrical Construction of Interiority," in *Feminist Readings of Early Modern Culture*, ed. Valerie Traub, M. Lindsay Kaplan, and Dympna Callaghan (Cambridge: Cambridge University Press, 1996), 93–118, reads Coriolanus's flaying in the context of the "wound-man" topos common to anatomical discourse. Editors including Holland have

routinely noted the Ovidian context of Marsyas but have not related it to earlier dramatic representations of Christ in biblical drama. Hannibal Hamlin, *The Bible in Shakespeare* (Oxford: Oxford University Press, 2013), argues that parallels between Christ and Coriolanus are evident throughout the play and are "indicated by specific verbal allusions, and by visual allusions in the play's staging, costume, and gesture" (204), though he is right to suggest that these allusions also mark out critical differences between the two figures.

7. On *pietas*, or "filial piety," see C. Kahn, *Roman Shakespeare*, 47–48, 156.

8. Loewenstein and Witmore, introduction to *Shakespeare and Early Modern Religion*, 12. Kurt Schreyer takes a more performance-oriented approach to examining Shakespeare's recycling of religious drama, arguing that "the materiality of the mysteries continued to influence and inspire post-Reformation theatrical production" (*Shakespeare's Medieval Craft*, 6).

9. Those unfamiliar with REED, its aims, and the arguments it has made possible will find some orientation in John Wasson, "Records of Early English Drama: Where They Are and What They Tell Us," in *Records of Early English Drama: Proceedings of the First Colloquium* (Toronto: Records of Early English Drama, 1979), 128–44, and Theresa Coletti, "Reading REED: History and the Records of Early English Drama," in *Literary Practice and Social Change in Britain: 1380–1530*, ed. Lee Patterson (Berkeley: University of California Press, 1990), 248–84.

10. William Shakespeare, *The First Part of King Henry the Fourth*, 1.1.22–27, ed. David Scott Kastan (London: Methuen Drama, 2008).

11. Michael O'Connell suggests that "blood and the torture that it draws forth are a significant legacy of the mystery theater to its Elizabethan and Jacobean successor—and in Shakespeare's case, of a particular potential signification" ("Blood Begetting Blood: Shakespeare and the Mysteries," in *Medieval Shakespeare: Past and Present*, ed. Ruth Morse, Peter Holland, and Helen Cooper [Cambridge: Cambridge University Press, 2013], 177).

12. For such arguments, see Chambers, *Mediaeval Stage*; H. Gardiner, *Mysteries' End*; and Montrose, *Purpose of Playing*. By contrast, O'Connell argues that "there is—indeed, there must be—a relation between the vigorous theater that existed prior to the decade between 1569 and 1579 and the theater that emerged after 1576" ("Vital Cultural Practices," 158). Schreyer likewise argues that religious dramas, such as the Chester cycle, were "vital and direct agents, not rude precursors, in the production of some of the most famous places in the Shakespeare canon" (*Shakespeare's Medieval Craft*, 4).

13. Even the term *mystery play*, which has often been used as a conceptual alternative to *morality play* (and is still employed in much critical scholarship,

including that cited in this book) is fraught. In "A History of 'The Mysteries'" (*Early Theatre* 19.1 [2016]: 9–36), Emma Maggie Solberg assesses the critical history surrounding the terms *mystery* and *mystery play*, traces how such terms came into and fell out of use in the field, and elaborates on related problems of taxonomy and nomenclature in early English drama studies at present.

14. See Clopper, *Drama, Play, and Game*; and Paul Whitfield White, *Drama and Religion in English Provincial Society, 1485–1660* (Cambridge: Cambridge University Press, 2008). For a useful overview of the diversity of dramatic performance in the late Middle Ages, see Jessica Brantley, "Middle English Drama beyond the Cycle Plays," *Literature Compass* 10.4 (2013): 331–42.

15. Alexandra F. Johnston, "The Feast of Corpus Christi in the West Country," *Early Theatre* 6, no. 1 (2003): 16. The argument for an organic relationship between cycle drama and the Corpus Christi feast was made influentially by V. A. Kolve, *The Play Called Corpus Christi* (Stanford, CA: Stanford University Press, 1966).

16. Ibid., 18. While Johnston's argument goes a long way to revise our understanding of biblical drama and the vocabularies we use to talk about it, it is worth pointing out that for those plays that *were* performed on or near the feast of Corpus Christi (a claim that can be made at least about the York cycle, as well as the early Chester plays prior to their shift to Whitsun in the early 1520s), Kolve's suggestion about the relationship between biblical narrative and sacramental feast still commands attention: "The Eucharist serves to recall both the Last Supper and the flesh and blood of Christ offered on the cross—events about which it is possible to rejoice only when they are related to man's fall, Christ's Resurrection, and the Last Judgement.... To play the whole story, then, is in the deepest sense to *celebrate* the Corpus Christi sacrament, to explain its necessity and power, and to show how that power will be made manifest at the end of the world.... The power of the Sacrament must be understood as well as believed in, and this requisite understanding is centered on a narrative. Because the Corpus Christi feast is fixed to a date outside the regular liturgical 'anniversary' time, and because it enjoins a *celebration* of the Eucharistic gift, the English Middle Ages played the whole story, from man's fall to the salvation of the blessed at the Judgement, to reveal the central episode—the Passion—as joyful in meaning" (48–49; italics in original). While the documentary evidence gathered by REED has sufficiently corrected Kolve's position with regard to the influence of the feast on the drama, Kolve's eloquent description of how such a drama could serve to explicate the theology of the feast and its central sacramental mystery remains persuasive still.

17. Theresa Coletti and Gail McMurray Gibson, "The Tudor Origins of Medieval Drama," in *A Companion to Tudor Literature*, ed. Kent Cartwright

(London: Wiley Blackwell, 2010), 229. On the periodization of late medieval religious drama, see also Emmerson, "Dramatic History"; Richard K. Emmerson, "Eliding the 'Medieval': Renaissance 'New Historicism' and Sixteenth-Century Drama," in *The Performance of Middle English Culture: Essays on Chaucer and the Drama in Honor of Martin Stevens*, ed. James J. Paxson, Lawrence M. Clopper, and Sylvia Tomasch (Cambridge: D. S. Brewer, 1998), 25–41; and David Mills, *Recycling the Cycle: The City of Chester and Its Whitsun Plays*, Studies in Early English Drama 4 (Toronto: University of Toronto Press, 1998).

18. Coletti and Gibson, "Tudor Origins," 228.

19. Clopper, *Drama, Play, and Game*, 269.

20. Barbara D. Palmer, "'Towneley Plays' or 'Wakefield Cycle' Revisited," *Comparative Drama* 21 (1988): 319. See also Martin Stevens, *Four Middle English Mystery Cycles: Textual, Contextual, and Critical Interpretations* (Princeton, NJ: Princeton University Press, 1987), 14–15.

21. Richard Beadle, "The York Cycle," in *The Cambridge Companion to Medieval English Theatre*, 2nd ed., ed. Richard Beadle and Alan Fletcher (Cambridge: Cambridge University Press, 2008), 102. On the dating of the York cycle, see Beckwith, *Signifying God*, xv. In addition to the York Register, another civic document, the *Ordo paginarium*, was created in 1415 and contained in the York Memorandum Book. This document contained a list of the craft guilds that sponsored pageants along with very short descriptions of the plays, though Beadle advises, "Since the *Ordo* descriptions are so brief and the pageants are based on standard biblical and apocryphal subjects, scripts could be revised or entirely rewritten without calling for any alteration to the relevant *Ordo* entry" ("York Cycle," 111).

22. Beadle, "York Cycle," 113.

23. Lawrence Clopper, "The History and Development of the Chester Cycle," *Modern Philology* 75, no. 3 (1978): 219–21. See also Clopper, *Drama, Play, and Game*, 181–85; Peter W. Travis, *Dramatic Design in the Chester Cycle* (Chicago: University of Chicago Press, 1982), 30–69; Theresa Coletti, "The Chester Cycle in Sixteenth-Century Religious Culture," *Journal of Medieval and Early Modern Studies* 37, no. 3 (Fall 2007): 531–47; Mills, "The Chester Cycle," in Beadle and Fletcher, *Cambridge Companion*, 125–51; Richard K. Emmerson, "Contextualizing Performance: The Reception of the Chester *Antichrist*," *Journal of Medieval and Early Modern Studies* 29, no. 1 (1999): 89–120; and Schreyer, *Shakespeare's Medieval Craft*, 43–72. The late copying of the plays, notes Mills, could index "the strong antiquarian movement in Chester, which valued the plays as part of the city's history and traditions" ("Chester Cycle," 111).

24. Clopper, *Drama, Play, and Game*, 145–46. See also Coletti and Gibson, "Tudor Origins," 230–33.

25. Clopper explains the shift to Whitsuntide as reflective "of the city's desire to separate its play from the ecclesiastical auspices of the Corpus Christi celebrations in order to emphasize civic sponsorship" ("History and Development," 245) as well as to remove the plays from the shadow of the Corpus Christi procession itself. He notes too that the plays drew visitors to the city, and that staging the plays at Whitsun would avoid competition with plays performed in nearby Coventry and thus create an economic boom for the city (245). Johnston provides an extensive account of tensions that arose in Exeter in 1414 when ecclesiastical and civic authorities disagreed over whether to stage plays at Corpus Christi, as preferred by the bishops, or during the civic festivals at Whitsun, as preferred by the mayors ("Feast of Corpus Christi," 21–29).

26. William Shakespeare, *The Winter's Tale*, 4.4.133–34, ed. John Pitcher (London: Methuen Drama, 2010); and *Two Gentlemen of Verona*, 4.4.150–51, in *Norton Shakespeare*. Robert W. Barrett Jr., *Against All England: Regional Identity and Cheshire Writing, 1195–1656* (Notre Dame, IN: University of Notre Dame Press, 2009), 59–95, offers a fuller discussion of the Chester cycle in the context of Whitsuntide.

27. On the inconclusive performance evidence for the Towneley plays, see Peter Happé, *The Towneley Cycle: Unity and Diversity* (Cardiff: University of Wales Press, 2007).

28. Clopper, *Drama, Play, and Game*, 186–87. Gail McMurray Gibson suggests that the N-Town compilation could have emerged in the monastic context of Bury St. Edmunds in East Anglia; see Gibson, *Theater of Devotion*, 117–35, and "Bury St. Edmunds, Lydgate, and the *N-Town Cycle*," *Speculum* 56 (1981): 56–90. For additional studies of N-Town, see Alexandra F. Johnston, "Cycle Drama in the Sixteenth Century: Texts and Contexts," *Acta* 13 (1987): 1–15; Peter Meredith, "Manuscript, Scribe, and Performance: Further Looks at the N. Town Manuscript," in *Regionalism in Late Medieval Manuscripts and Texts*, ed. Felicity Riddy (Cambridge: D. S. Brewer, 1991), 109–25; and Alexandra F. Johnston, "The Puzzle of the N. Town Manuscript Revisited," *Medieval English Theatre* 36 (2014): 104–23.

29. Beadle, *York Plays*, 1:xxxiii–xxxiv.

30. See B. Palmer, "'Towneley Plays,'" 322, 331–35; Barbara D. Palmer, "Recycling 'The Wakefield Cycle': The Records," *Research Opportunities in Renaissance Drama* 41 (2002): 88–130; Clopper, *Drama, Play, and Game*, 173–81; Peter Meredith, "The Towneley Cycle," in Beadle and Fletcher, *Cambridge Companion*, 152–82; and David Mills, "'The Towneley Plays' or 'The Towneley Cycle'?," *Leeds Studies in English* 17 (1986): 95–104.

31. B. Palmer, "Towneley Plays," 319. Meg Twycross, "'They Did Not Come Out of an Abbey in Lancashire': Francis Douce and the Manuscript of the

Towneley Plays," *Medieval English Theatre* 37 (2015): 149–65, states, "It is to Douce that the Towneley manuscript owes much of its reputation, and much of the obfuscation that surrounds its origins" (151). Twycross focuses her argument on correspondence between Douce and the antiquarian Thomas Sharp. This correspondence, she explains, details Douce's doubt over the manuscript's monastic provenance, perhaps as a result of inspecting the manuscript, which may have been brought to him from Lancashire by John Towneley himself. In the 1814 catalog description, however, Douce nonetheless testifies to the manuscript's monastic origins at the Abbey of Widkirk. Twycross hypothesizes that this grandiose description, which was commissioned by the auctioneer Robert Harding Evans, may have been intended to garner a higher selling price: "For Evans, it would have been more important to stress the antiquity of the MS, and a touch of monkish romance did not come amiss" (156–57).

32. B. Palmer, "Towneley Plays," 324.

33. Ibid., 331.

34. On Walker's forgery of the performance evidence, see B. Palmer, "Towneley Plays," 330–33.

35. Coletti and Gibson, "Tudor Origins," 236–37.

36. Ibid., 237.

37. Ibid., 242.

38. On devotional reading as itself a mode of performance in late medieval culture, see Jessica Brantley, *Reading in the Wilderness: Private Devotion and Public Performance in Late Medieval England* (Chicago: University of Chicago Press, 2007).

39. As a counterargument to Coletti and Gibson, consider Murray McGillivray, "The Towneley Manuscript and Performance: Tudor Recycling?" in *Editing, Performance, Texts: New Practices in Medieval and Early Modern English Drama*, ed. Jacqueline Jenkins and Julie Sanders (Basingstoke: Palgrave Macmillan, 2014), 49–69. McGillivray contends that Towneley "is neither a Marian *compilatio* intended for private reading and devotion, nor an early sixteenth-century record of plays as performed during the medieval period in Wakefield, but more likely a quasi-official record of the plays that were performed for no more than a decade or two in the later sixteenth century, in a form assembled in the mid-1550s from various sources in order to create an old-fashioned Corpus Christi 'cycle' for that late revival, but preceding any long experience with performance of its full contents" (65).

40. Clopper rejects Harold Gardiner's thesis that the Protestant clergy suppressed biblical drama, suggesting that the clergy targeted other *ludi inhonesti* including parish ales, Robin Hood plays, and other seasonal merriments as well. The biblical plays, Clopper argues, were revised for several reasons, including

alterations of devotional practice, especially as set forth in the Edwardian and Elizabethan prayer books; the spread of plague, which caused the suppression of many forms of theater; and most importantly the threat of sedition. "None of the acts, proclamations, or other attempts at control are directed at biblical dramas," he says (*Drama, Play, and Game*, 282). In the decades leading up to the suppression of the plays by 1580, Clopper suggests more a conflict between the lay (i.e., guild) administration of the plays and clerical intervention, resulting less in a full-out assault on the plays by the clergy than in a breakdown in cooperation and administration (cf. 291–93). Paul Whitfield White, *Theatre and Reformation: Protestantism, Patronage, and Playing in Tudor England* (Cambridge: Cambridge University Press, 1993), states that "changing religious attitudes combined with less willingness on the part of the guilds involved to finance the civic religious drama led to its cessation in Coventry" (139). See also Peter Happé, "'Erazed in the Booke': The Mystery Cycles and Reform," in *Tudor Drama before Shakespeare, 1485–1590: New Directions for Research, Criticism, and Pedagogy*, ed. Lloyd Edward Kermode, Jason Scott-Warren, and Martine van Elk (Houndmills, Basingstoke: Palgrave, 2004), 15–33.

41. For a comprehensive account of the Passion sequence, see Woolf, *English Mystery Plays*, 238–68. On Christ's wounds in the context of martyrology, see Alice Dailey, *The English Martyr from Reformation to Revolution* (Notre Dame, IN: University of Notre Dame Press, 2012), 10–52. On the tortured body of Christ in Continental Passion plays, see Enders, *Medieval Theater of Cruelty*, and on the representations of physical violence in the English biblical plays, see Claire Sponsler, *Drama and Resistance: Bodies, Gender, and Theatricality in Late Medieval England* (Minneapolis: University of Minnesota Press, 1997), 146–52.

42. Peter W. Travis, "The Semiotics of Christ's Body in the English Mystery Cycles," *Approaches to Teaching Medieval English Literature*, ed. Richard K. Emmerson (New York: Modern Language Association, 1990), 72.

43. Towneley *Crucifixion*, in *Towneley Cycle*, ed. Cawley and Ellis, fol. 103v. All references to the Towneley plays are to this edition and will be cited parenthetically by folio number.

44. Chester *Play XVI: The Passion*, lines 250–53, in *The Chester Mystery Cycle*, ed. R. M. Lumiansky and David Mills, 2 vols., Early English Text Society, Supplementary Series, 3 and 9 (London: Oxford University Press, 1974), 250–53. All future citations of the Chester cycle are to this edition and will be given parenthetically by line number.

45. N-Town *Crucifixion*, 223, and *Harrowing of Hell (I)*, lines 11–13, in *The N-Town Plays*, ed. Douglas Sugano, TEAMS Middle English Texts (Kalamazoo, MI: Medieval Institute Publications, 2007). All future citations of N-Town plays are to this edition and will be given parenthetically by line number.

46. On the influence of the affective piety tradition on religious drama, Woolf writes, "The traditional theological and meditative emphasis upon the sufferings of Christ required that the scenes of the buffeting and scourging should be made as extensive as possible" (*English Mystery Plays*, 253). Beadle also notes that the plays present "a series of devotional icons familiar to the audience from the visual arts of the period—the Man of Sorrows, the lamenting Virgin, the Deposition and so on—[that] are caused to melt into one another through a metrical medium that is best described as lyrical" ("York Cycle," 107). Taking a different approach, Ruth Nisse situates these tortures in the context of the Wycliffite *Tretise of Miraclis Pleyinge*, arguing, "The body being beaten up in the plays of the buffeting of Christ is, as this text emphasizes, *only* a human body; since it cannot represent Christ in his humanity and divinity, it becomes a mockery, a parody of Scripture" (*Defining Acts*, 13; italics in original). On affective piety, see also Kolve, *Play Called Corpus Christi*, 175–205; Richard Homan, "Ritual Aspects of the York Cycle," *Theatre Journal* 33 (1981): 303–15; Clifford Davidson, *From Creation to Doom: The York Cycle of Mystery Plays* (New York: AMS Press, 1984); Pamela M. King, *The York Mystery Cycle and the Worship of the City* (Cambridge: D. S. Brewer, 2006); and Kathleen Ashley, "Sponsorship, Reflexivity, and Resistance: Cultural Readings of the York Cycle Plays," in *The Performance of Medieval English Culture*, ed. James J. Paxson, Lawrence M. Clopper, and Sylvia Tomasch (London: D. S. Brewer, 1998), 9–24. For additional approaches to semiotics in biblical drama, see Ashley, "Sponsorship, Reflexivity, and Resistance"; Travis, "Semiotics of Christ's Body"; Pamela King, "Seeing and Hearing: Looking and Listening," *Early Theatre* 3 (2000): 155–66; and Owens, *Stages of Dismemberment*, 34–35.

47. Beckwith, *Signifying God*, 71.

48. Beadle explicates these speeches in the context of their scriptural references (Ps. 21 and 56) as well as Christ's "seven last words" as recorded in the gospels (*York Plays*, 2:336–39).

49. Beckwith reads the scene as "a grotesque enactment and revision of the act of elevation" in the Mass (*Signifying God*, 66), a point noted also by P. King, *York Mystery Cycle*, 143–45, and Clifford Davidson, *York Corpus Christi Plays*, TEAMS Middle English Texts (Kalamazoo, MI: Medieval Institute Publications, 2011), 60–62.

50. On the adaptation of *O vos omnes* in lyric poetry, see Rosemary Woolf, *The English Religious Lyric of the Middle Ages* (Oxford: Oxford University Press, 1968), 42–44. On the liturgical context, see Beckwith, *Signifying God*, 66; P. King, *York Mystery Cycle*, 144–45, 149; Beadle, "York Plays," 102–3, who assigns the antiphon to the Reproaches used in the Good Friday liturgy; and Woolf, *English Mystery Plays*, 262–64.

51. Coletti and Gibson, "Tudor Origins," 242–43.

52. Beadle, "York Plays," 101.

53. Beadle notes the attribution to Saint Veronica but also states that Towneley attributes the miracle to Mary Magdalene (*York Plays*, 2:314–15).

54. Lancelot Andrewes, *Copie of the Sermon preached on good Friday last before the Kings Majestie* (London: R. Barker, 1604), sig. B3r. Shuger, *Habits of Thought*, provides an extensive analysis of Andrewes's sermons at 47–65 and 142–50.

55. *A Homilie for good Friday, concerning the death and passion of our Savior Jesus Christ*, in *The Second Tome of Homilies, of such matters as were promised and instituted* (London: Richard Jugge and John Cawood, 1563), sig. Aaa8r.

56. The sixteenth-century sermons depart from the Wycliffite Good Friday sermon, which "offers absolutely no focus on Christ's body, none of the traditional late medieval elaborations of the scene and its violence" (Aers, "Humanity of Christ," 52). In place of the wounded body, Wyclif's sermons emphasize the ethical aspects of Christ's teaching in the gospels as a way to criticize the Catholic clergy: "Instead of the Virgin Mary lamenting, swooning, and clinging to the dead body we read reflections on the need to defend Christ's teaching against orthodox priests, the successors of priests who killed Christ, and the need for the help of secular powers to help in this defense" (Aers, "Humanity of Christ," 53).

57. Coletti notes that "Mary Magdalene's scriptural and legendary experiences with sacred corporeality and divine inspiration provide apt material for enacting the dramatic encounter with the sacred" (*Mary Magdalene*, 197) and discusses the Digby *Mary Magdalene*'s engagement with Eucharistic representation (191–204). Bishop discusses N-Town's representation of Mary Magdalene in *Shakespeare and the Theatre*, 58–62; and Beckwith discusses the York play in *Signifying God*, 83–86.

58. On York's treatment of the encounter as compared to other biblical dramas, see Coletti, *Mary Magdalene*, 206–8. On the *noli me tangere* trope in the context of Mary Magdalene, see Patricia Badir, *The Maudlin Impression: English Literary Images of Mary Magdalene, 1550–1700* (Notre Dame, IN: University of Notre Dame Press, 2009), 59–89.

59. Beadle glosses the reference in both instances as "noble childe" (*York Plays*, 2:117) and "young man, noble warrior, an expression often found in chivalric romances" (2:380) but admits the obvious Eucharistic reading as well. For Eucharistic references to Christ as food in other plays, see the Towneley *Crucifixion*, where the Virgin Mary inscribes Christ within a similar Eucharistic context: "Alle blemyshed is thi ble, I se thi body blede, / In warld, son, were never we so wo as I in wede. / My foode that I have fed, / In lyf longyng the led" (87v); the

York *Nativity*, where Joseph says of the newborn Jesus, "Wele is me I bad this day / To se this foode" (90–91); the York *Shepherds*: "And I myght fynde that frely foode" (78); the York *Herod and the Magi*, where the Magi praise Christ, "Hayll, foode that thy folke fully may fede, / Hayll, floure fairest, that never shall fade" (321–22); and the York *Death of Christ*, where Joseph of Arimathea says that the soldiers "Full falsely thei fellid that foode" (372). Beadle notes that this sequence of "Hail" invocations derives from the levation prayers used during the Mass (*York Plays*, 2:135).

60. The phrase "Goddis body" was used by John Wyclif in his sermon written for Easter Day, where he cites Mary Magdalene's encounter with Christ to teach about worthy reception of the Eucharist and to disavow transubstantiation. John Wyclif, Sermon XLVI, "The Gospel on Eestir Day," in *Sermons on the Gospels*, 131–34. Wyclif defines the sacrament according to the cardinal virtues of faith, hope, and charity (as he does in Cap. VI of *De Eucharistia*). First, the receiver (like the three Marys who approach the tomb) should believe that the host "is kyndely [naturally] breed, as Poul seith, but it is sacramentally verre Goddis bodi." That is, he should assert Christ's real presence in the sacrament without subscribing to the change in substance required by transubstantiation. Second, the recipient must dwell in the hope of Christ's promise of eternal life and think "on kyndenes of Crist to maken hem clene in soule." Finally, he should love his neighbor lest he receive the sacrament unworthily. "Men shudlen clothen hem with these thre vertues, bileve, hope, and charite, to resceyve this sacrament," says Wyclif. "And yif we have this clothinge, takinge this mete in figure, it shal brynge us to hevene, there to ete Goddis body goostly withouten ende; and that is mennis blisse" (133–34).

61. Beadle, *York Plays*, 2:377, 380. Coletti notes an additional Eucharistic reference in the Digby *Mary Magdalene* play, where "the hermit priest who discovers Mary Magdalene in the 'wyldyrnessee' brings her the Eucharistic *viaticum*, accompanied by two angels" (*Mary Magdalene*, 200). The requisite lines from Digby are "My body in form of bred that he bere, / Hur for to hossell, byd hym provyde" (2079–80, quoted in Coletti, *Mary Magdalene*, 200).

62. Coletti, "Chester Cycle," 535. In contrast to Coletti, who argues for theological and historical fluidity, Mills argues that once the Chester plays were moved from Corpus Christi to Whitsun in the 1520s they were "enacted not under the sacramental pressure of the Eucharist but in the context of . . . the coming of the Holy Spirit and of the following Trinity Sunday in honour of the triune God" (Mills, "Chester Cycle," 117).

63. The efficacious language of priestly confection is explicitly Roman Catholic and will be discussed in chapter 4.

64. As Coletti and Gibson argue, "In the context of an illegal Catholicism, recusant religion turned even more toward that familial religion of household, to the private chapels and domestic rooms in which the practice of devotion was often shouldered by wives and mothers while husbands and sons either paid huge fines or outwardly conformed to the state religion rather than be imprisoned for refusal to do so" ("Tudor Origins," 242).

65. McGillivray, "Towneley Manuscript," 54.

66. Travis, *Dramatic Design*, 187. "Although Christ's agonies on the cross are powerfully presented," Travis says, "the gruesome effects and pathetic appeals of Chester's Crucifixion are considerably less sensational than those of Wakefield" (187). Woolf also differentiates between "those [plays] which keep closely to the gospels (Chester and the *Ludus Coventriae*), and those which, taking the liturgy as their starting point, ascribe a series of complaints to Christ (York and Towneley)" (*English Mystery Plays*, 260).

67. On Chester's Expositor, see Travis, *Dramatic Design*, 47–48; Coletti and Gibson, "Tudor Origins," 232–33; and Mark Faulkner, "Exegesis in the City: The Chester Plays and Earlier Chester Writing," in *The Chester Cycle in Context, 1555–1575: Religion, Drama, and the Impact of Change*, ed. Jessica Dell, David Klausner, and Helen Ostovich (Aldershot: Ashgate, 2012), 170–76.

68. Travis also reads the Eucharistic idiom in terms of transubstantiation and sees it as verifying the credal tenet of the communion of saints (*Dramatic Design*, 213–17). See also Travis, "Semiotics of Christ's Body," 71–72.

69. Lumiansky and Mills ascribe the emendation to post-Reformation censorship (*Chester Mystery Cycle*, 2:282–83), but Paul Whitfield White notes that the 1572 Chester script *did* include such a reference, whereby Christ says that the bread "becommen is my fleshe, through wordes 5 betwyxt the prestes handes" ("The Chester Cycle and Early Elizabethan Religion," in Dell, Klausner, and Ostovich, *Chester Cycle in Context*, 127).

70. Travis says of the Last Supper pageant, "Rather than a sacramental celebration, it is treated in performance as a happy 'memoriall'" as mandated by the Late Banns (*Dramatic Design*, 64). He notes that the Bakers' Last Supper pageant was also removed from the Chester cycle in 1550 but was then reinstated during an Elizabethan performance and was mentioned again in the Late Banns.

71. The Chester *Antichrist* introduces a similar semiotic instability with regard to the Eucharistic signs. To refute the false signs of Antichrist with the authentic sign of the sacrament, Elijah blesses, consecrates, and elevates bread in what appears to be a scene consonant with a Roman Catholic Eucharistic theology. Yet what appears to support orthodoxy also undermines it, for the words pronounced over the bread are Latin words, but they do not correspond to the words spoken

over the host at Mass. Instead, they are the words of the sign of the cross: "In nomine Patris . . . / et Filii virginis . . . / et Spiritus Sancti" (573–75). Here a reference to the Trinity replaces (or safely stands in for) the language of transubstantiation or the liturgical enactment of the Canon of the Mass. The *Antichrist* pageant also refers to the Eucharistic element not as a "host" but rather as "breadd" (505), a theologically neutral term preferred in post-Reformation contexts like the *Book of Common Prayer*. This is all to say that the Chester *Antichrist*, like the Chester *Resurrection*, figures the Eucharist according to multiple theological and semiotic positions that do not parse out neatly along confessional divides.

72. Mills, "Chester Cycle," 128–29. Coletti takes a different, and I think more persuasive, stance: "The Chester plays' preoccupation with miraculous portents and wonders engages a reanimated early modern interest in providential signs. Both attributes bear witness to the cycle's complex negotiation of religious difference across the medieval and early modern divide" ("Chester Cycle," 534).

73. On Shakespeare's departure from Plutarch with regard to the wounds, cf. Holland's introduction to his edition of Shakespeare, *Coriolanus*, 47–48; 79–82; and Hamlin, *Bible in Shakespeare*, 204–5.

74. Holland reflects on one such connection with religious drama that Shakespeare may have encountered well before his reading of Livy and Plutarch: "Probably even earlier in his life Shakespeare would have known the gospel account of the arrival of the three Marys at Jesus' tomb and perhaps seen a performance or semiperformance of their encounter with the angels ('Whom seek ye?' or as it is known from its Latin form in the Easter liturgy, the *Quem Quaeritis* trope), an event which may be echoed in the arrival of the three Roman women . . . at Coriolanus' camp" (introduction to Shakespeare, *Coriolanus*, 23). Holland admits his own skepticism about such a connection, which is warranted given that the circumstances under which the women approach Coriolanus, not to mention that the aims and consequences of the approach, differ from those in the liturgical drama. With that said, if Jacobean audiences could recall *quem quaeritis* in the context of this scene, it stands to reason that the same audiences could appreciate the more obvious connection between Coriolanus's wounds and the wounds of Christ as staged in biblical dramas, which persisted late into the sixteenth century.

75. Though much has been written about Coriolanus's wounds, only Stanley Cavell, *Disowning Knowledge in Seven Plays of Shakespeare* (1987; repr., Cambridge: Cambridge University Press, 2003), has examined the wounds in a sacramental context. Hamlin briefly references Christ's showing of the wounds in the York cycle and offers a mostly allegorical reading of Coriolanus's Christ-like attributes (*Bible in Shakespeare*, 203–14). Lisa S. Starks-Estes also refers to Christological imagery in "Virtus, Vulnerability, and the Emblazoned Male Body in

Shakespeare's *Coriolanus*," in *Violent Masculinities: Male Aggression in Early Modern Texts and Culture*, ed. Jennifer Feather and Catherine Thomas (New York: Palgrave Macmillan, 2013), 85–106. Gender has been the dominant framework for reading the wounds, as evident in C. Kahn, *Roman Shakespeare*, 144–59; C. Marshall, "Wound-Man"; Phyllis Rackin, "*Coriolanus*: Shakespeare's Anatomy of 'Virtus,'" *Modern Language Studies* 13, no. 2 (Spring 1983): 68–79; Janet Adelman, "'Anger's My Meat': Feeding, Dependency, and Aggression in *Coriolanus*," in *Representing Shakespeare: New Psychoanalytic Essays*, ed. Murray Schwartz and Coppélia Kahn (Baltimore: Johns Hopkins University Press, 1980), 129–49; Gail Kern Paster, "To Starve with Feeding: The City in *Coriolanus*," *Shakespeare Studies* 11 (1978): 123–44. Of greater interest to the present chapter is the body of work that relates Coriolanus's wounds to language: Lawrence Danson, *Tragic Alphabet: Shakespeare's Drama of Language* (New Haven, CT: Yale University Press, 2004); James L. Calderwood, "*Coriolanus*: Wordless Meanings and Meaningless Words," *SEL: Studies in English Literature, 1500–1900* 6 (1966): 211–24; John Plotz, "*Coriolanus* and the Failure of Performatives," *ELH: English Literary History* 63, no. 4 (1996): 809–32; Maurice Hunt, "The Backward Voice of Coriol-Anus." *Shakespeare Studies* 32 (2004): 220–39; Leonard Tennenhouse, "*Coriolanus* and the Crisis of Semantic Order," *Comparative Drama* 10, no. 4 (Winter 1976–77): 328–46; Arthur Riss, "The Belly Politic: *Coriolanus* and the Revolt of Language," *ELH: English Literary History* 59, no. 1 (1992): 53–75; Carol Sicherman, "*Coriolanus*: The Failure of Words," *ELH: English Literary History* 39, no. 1 (1972): 189–207; William W. E. Slights, "Bodies of Text and Textualized Bodies in *Sejanus* and *Corioanus*," *Medieval and Renaissance Drama in England* 5 (1991): 181–93; and Tetsuya Motohashi, "Body Politic and Political Body in *Coriolanus*," *Forum for Modern Language Studies* 30, no. 2 (1994): 97–112.

76. Cavell, *Disowning Knowledge*, 168. While there is much to admire about Cavell's reading, Cavell treats Christ's wounds as an available iconography, if not also as a cultural "given." What he overlooks, however, is that the iconography of Christ's wounds is part of religious dramatic traditions that would have been known to Shakespeare at the time he wrote *Coriolanus*. Thus biblical drama presents itself as one available discourse out of which Coriolanus's wounds are constructed and thus its resonance for Shakespeare is more historical than universal.

77. Cavell, *Disowning Knowledge*, 165.
78. Beckwith, *Signifying God*, 60–61.
79. C. Kahn, *Roman Shakespeare*, 18.
80. Coppélia Kahn discusses the implications of this etymology for a feminist reading of wounds in ibid., 18–19. On the religious significance of the wounded

body as part of the *ostentatio vulnerum* tradition, see Shannon Gayk, *Image, Text, and Religious Reform in Fifteenth-Century England* (Cambridge: Cambridge University Press, 2010).

81. C. Marshall, "Wound Man," 96.
82. C. Kahn, *Roman Shakespeare*, 152.
83. See Holland's introduction to Shakespeare, *Coriolanus*, 78.
84. On the play's engagements with early modern republicanism, see Annabel Patterson, *Shakespeare and the Popular Voice* (Oxford: Basil Blackwell, 1989), 120–53, and James Kuzner, "Unbuilding the City: *Coriolanus* and the Birth of Republican Rome," *Shakespeare Quarterly* 58, no. 2 (2007): 174–99.
85. Plotz, "*Coriolanus*," 825.
86. Hooker, *Of the Lawes*, 5.67, sig. R1r.
87. Anne Barton, "*Julius Caesar* and *Coriolanus*: Shakespeare's Roman World of Words," in *Shakespeare's Craft: Eight Lectures*, ed. Philip H. Highfill Jr. (Carbondale: Southern Illinois University Press, 1982), 35.
88. On the histrionics displayed by the character Christ in religious drama, see Parker, *Aesthetics of Antichrist*, 66–71.
89. Alexandra F. Johnston and Margaret Rogerson, eds., *Records of Early English Drama: York* (Toronto: University of Toronto Press, 1979) [hereafter *REED*], 1:515. Gordon Kipling, *Enter the King: Theater, Liturgy, and Ritual in the Medieval Civic Triumph* (Oxford: Oxford University Press, 1998), notes that "civic triumphs share a common dramatic heritage with the great religious dramas—the continental passion plays and the English *Corpus Christi* cycles—which sprang up throughout Northern Europe at precisely the same period" (6–7).
90. James I, *Two Meditations of the Kings Majestie; the One in the yeere of our Lord God 1618. The other in the yeere 1619* (London: Robert Barker and John Bill, 1619), sig. G7v.
91. Cavell, *Disowning Knowledge*, 167. See also Cathy Shrank, "Civility and the City in *Coriolanus*," *Shakespeare Quarterly* 54, no. 4 (Winter 2003): 406–423, who argues, "Martius is not Christlike. He refuses to be shared. His 'sacrifice,' when it comes, is for the sake of his immediate household alone" (421). Hamlin likewise concludes that "Coriolanus presents a poor imitation of Christ" (*Bible in Shakespeare*, 208).
92. Writing of Calvin's stance on the Lord's Supper, Lee Palmer Wandel says, "The details of the ceremony were things 'indifferent.' . . . [For Calvin] the meaning of the ceremony lay not in 'externals'—all those details that had become so significant for some—because the ceremony was not a reenactment of Christ's gestures, nor of Christ's sacrifice on the cross." She goes on to say that "the emphasis was not on performance per se: the movements of the minister,

the vessels, the table—these had no significance in or of themselves" (*Eucharist in the Reformation*, 165, 171).

93. James Simpson, "John Bale, *Three Laws*," in *The Oxford Handbook to Tudor Drama*, ed. Greg Walker and Thomas Betteridge (Oxford: Oxford University Press, 2012), 109–22, explores the idea of using drama to kill drama in Bale's *Three Laws*—an early Tudor religious play that stresses the interpretation of scripture as the authorized form of spiritual truth. Simpson argues that Bale's dramatic project is necessarily paradoxical, for in order to repudiate the idolatry of the Roman Church Bale must "kill drama stone dead" (109).

94. Hamlin notes that the Suffering Christ is often depicted in a white garment, as is the case in Albrecht Dürer's paintings of the Passion, and this image is one on which Hamlin grounds his analogy between the election ceremony and a different episode from biblical drama: Christ's trial before Pilate (*Bible in Shakespeare*, 205–6).

95. White, *Drama and Religion*, 13.

96. On the social dynamics of the York cycle, see Beckwith, *Signifying God*, chaps. 2 and 3; Stevens, *Four Middle English Mystery Cycles*, 17–87; Ashley, "Sponsorship, Reflexivity, and Resistance"; Kate Crassons, "The Challenges of Social Unity: The *Last Judgment* Pageant and Guild Relations in York," *Journal of Medieval and Early Modern Studies* 37, no. 2 (Spring 2007): 305–34; Beadle, "York Cycle"; and Nicole R. Rice and Margaret Aziza Pappano, *The Civic Cycles: Artisan Drama and Identity in Premodern England* (Notre Dame, IN: University of Notre Dame Press, 2015), 41–81. So important were these dramas to social life that, in 1476, York moved the Eucharistic procession associated with the liturgical feast of Corpus Christi to the following day so that the plays could be performed on the feast (Beadle, "York Cycle," 105). On the social dimensions of Corpus Christi processions, see Rubin, *Corpus Christi*, 243–71, and Mervyn James, "Ritual, Drama, and the Social Body in the Late Medieval English Town," *Past and Present* 98, no. 1 (1983): 3–29.

97. *REED: York*, 1:723.

98. Beckwith, *Signifying God*, xvi.

99. The controversy over the price of corn in the play has often been situated in the context of the Midlands Revolt of 1607–8, during which angry Londoners responded to growing famine, the rising price of corn, and land enclosure. The problems were particularly pressing in places like Stratford-upon-Avon. See Holland's introduction to *Coriolanus*, 56–71.

100. Kate Crassons studies the class stratifications among York's guilds, especially that of the wealthiest group, the Mercers, who staged the *Last Judgment* pageant, which centered on Christ admonishing the people to unqualified charity:

"However needy a particular group of craftsmen may have been, the guild system excluded those individuals who were most poor, the types of people named in the *Last Judgment* who would be desperately in need of food, clothing and shelter perhaps as a matter of survival" ("Challenges of Social Unity," 323). With respect to the Crucifixion pageant, four guilds—the Pinners, Painters, Stainers, and Latteners—orchestrated the play in two pageants (the nailing of Christ on the cross followed by the raising of the cross) until 1422, when the two were combined into a single pageant staged by the Pinners and Latteners (*REED: York*, 1:723).

101. Jean E. Howard and Paul Strohm, "The Imaginary 'Commons,'" *Journal of Medieval and Early Modern Studies* 37, no. 3 (Fall 2007): 549–77, identify *Coriolanus* as an exception to dramas of popular resistance: "As politics was conceived in the tragedies of state that were increasingly popular throughout the first decades of the seventeenth century, the people as such are less frequently imagined as a political force, with *Coriolanus* the somewhat ambivalent exception. Most often they linger on the edges of plays, not as prime movers, but in familiar postures of deference or dissent" (572).

THREE. Sacramental Signs and Mystical Bodies
in Lydgate, Bale, and Shakespeare

1. As used in this chapter, the term *royal presence* comes from Richard McCoy, *Alterations of State: Sacred Kingship in the English Renaissance* (New York: Columbia University Press, 2002), who suggests that "coronation was seen by some as a sacrament, akin to ordination," and that many in Elizabethan England replaced "controversies over the real presence with veneration for the royal presence" (x).

2. Alice Hunt, *The Drama of Coronation: Medieval Ceremony in Early Modern England* (Cambridge: Cambridge University Press, 2011), 32. Hunt notes that Edward VI's coronation witnessed a shift to a reformed coronation service. Hunt also notes that "it is unclear whether Elizabeth's coronation followed the order for a Catholic Mass or reintroduced Protestant coronation" (151); Elizabeth also refused to take the sacrament and may have withdrawn into her closet during the consecration so as to avoid gazing upon the elevated host (152–54).

3. For a discussion of Romans 13 and divine right, see Fulton, "Shakespeare's *Everyman*," 121, 124–29. On sacred kingship and political theology, see Kipling, *Enter the King*; Rust, *Body in Mystery*; Debora Kuller Shuger, *Political*

Theologies in Shakespeare's England: The Sacred and the State in "Measure for Measure" (Houndmills, Basingstoke: Palgrave, 2001); Schwartz, *Sacramental Poetics*, 18–26; and Timothy Rosendale, "Sacral and Sacramental Kingship in Shakespeare's Lancastrian Tetralogy," in *Shakespeare and the Culture of Christianity in Early Modern England*, ed. Dennis Taylor and David N. Beauregard (New York: Fordham University Press, 2004), 121–40. On early modern political theology more generally, see Julia Reinhard Lupton, *Citizen-Saints: Shakespeare and Political Theology* (Chicago: University of Chicago Press, 2005); Julia Reinhard Lupton and Graham Hammill, eds., *Political Theology and Early Modernity* (Chicago: University of Chicago Press, 2012); Victoria Kahn, "Political Theology and Fiction in *The King's Two Bodies*," *Representations* 106, no. 1 (May 2009): 77–101; and Philip Lorenz, *The Tears of Sovereignty: Perspectives of Power in Renaissance Drama* (New York: Fordham University Press, 2013). Leonard Tennenhouse, *Power on Display: The Politics of Shakespeare's Genres* (London: Methuen, 1986), discusses metaphysical kingship in Shakespearean drama but not in a theological context.

4. On the "royal touch," see Marc Bloch, *The Royal Touch: Monarchy and Miracles in France and England* (New York: Dorset Press, 1990) and Stephen Deng, "Healing Angels and 'Golden Blood': Money and Mystical Kingship in *Macbeth*," in *New Essays on Macbeth*, ed. Nick Moschovakis (London: Taylor and Francis, 2008), 163–81.

5. The scriptural foundations for Christ's mystical body are expressed in 1 Corinthians 12, where Paul writes of the church as one body consisting in many members. On the application of a theology of *corpus mysticum* to the metaphysics of kingship, see Ernst Kantorowicz, *The King's Two Bodies: A Study of Mediaeval Political Theology* (1957; repr., Princeton, NJ: Princeton University Press, 1997). On literary representations to the contrary, see Franco Moretti, "The Great Eclipse: Tragic Form as the Deconsecration of Sovereignty," in *Signs Taken for Wonders: Essays on the Sociology of Literary Forms* (London: Verso, 2005), 42–82.

6. Rust, *Body in Mystery*, xiv. Giorgio Agamben, *The Kingdom and the Glory: For a Theological Genealogy of Economy and Government* (Stanford, CA: Stanford University Press, 2011), asserts that modern political systems derive from older concepts of divine administration like the *corpus mysticum*, as evident in the etymological and ideological contexts of *oikonomia* (economy), which originally signified government, administration, and power in the context of liturgy (derived from the Greek λειτουργία, "public worship").

7. When referring specifically to early Christian and late medieval theological contexts, such as those addressed in Lydgate's verses, I prefer to use *orthodox* rather than *Catholic*, given that the latter term is not used to refer to the Church of Rome until the 1550s.

8. For a reprint of Amalarius's early ninth-century text, see Appendix A in de Lubac, *Corpus Mysticum*, 265–78.

9. De Lubac, *Corpus Mysticum*, 29.

10. Rust, *Body in Mystery*, 1–28, surveys the history of *corpus mysticum* as grounded on the different theories of de Lubac, Kantorowicz, and Carl Schmitt. Kantorowicz, *King's Two Bodies*, 194n4, discusses his reliance on de Lubac. See also McDermott, *Tropologies*, 64–68.

11. De Lubac, *Corpus Mysticum*, 23, italics in original.

12. Ibid., 21; italics in original.

13. Rust, *Body in Mystery*, 8.

14. *Book of Common Prayer* (London: Richard Grafton, 1549), sig. Pii*r*, Nviii*v*. The text of this prayer is retained in both the 1552 and 1559 revisions.

15. These questions were at the forefront of political theology in the English Reformation. Shuger notes that English subjects negotiated the relation between the sacral and the political in such a way that "the political thought of the period between the Act of Supremacy and the Restoration revolves around whether the state constitutes the primary locus of the sacred and, if so, in what sense; whether there were other sacral loci (the Church of Rome, for example) through which grace entered the social body, restoring and redeeming it" (*Political Theologies*, 47).

16. Kantorowicz, *King's Two Bodies*, 197. Rust explains that "Kantorowicz is particularly concerned with tracing how the *corpus mysticum* as a figure for the institutional body of the Church was transferred conceptually to figure the institutional body of the state" (*Body in Mystery*, 14–15).

17. Kantorowicz, *King's Two Bodies*, 196. At the outset of his study, Kantorowicz articulates the displacement of a theology of Christ's mystical body onto the secular realm of the state as follows: "It is evident that the doctrine of theology and canon law, teaching that the Church, and Christian society in general, was a *corpus mysticum* the head of which is Christ, has been transferred by the jurists from the theological sphere to that of the state the head of which is the king" (16).

18. Rust, *Body in Mystery*, 16. For de Lubac, Rust claims, "it is precisely the becoming fictive of the *corpus mysticum* that represents the signal disaster of collective spiritual life in the Middle Ages" (5).

19. Gail McMurray Gibson discusses Lydgate's connections to the monastic and devotional culture of Bury St. Edmunds, noting that he both collected a royal pension and acted as "virtual poet laureate for the Lancastrian dynasty" (*Theater of Devotion*, 108). In a related essay, Gibson raises the possibility that Lydgate's *Procession* and his verses written for the 1445 entry of Margaret of Anjou bear "close relationships to the mystery play cycles," the N-Town plays in particular

("Bury St. Edmunds," 81–83). On Lydgate's monastic and courtly involvements, see Derek Pearsall, *John Lydgate* (London: Routledge and Kegan Paul, 1970), 22–48 and 160–91. On Lydgate's civic engagements, see Anne Lancashire, *London Civic Theatre: City Drama and Pageantry from Roman Times to 1558* (Cambridge: Cambridge University Press, 2002), 118–28; C. David Benson, "Civic Lydgate: The Poet and London," in *John Lydgate: Poetry, Culture, and Lancastrian England*, ed. Larry Scanlon and James Simpson (Notre Dame, IN: University of Notre Dame Press, 2006), 147–68; and Maura Nolan, *John Lydgate and the Making of Public Culture* (Cambridge: Cambridge University Press, 2005). James Simpson, *Reform and Cultural Revolution* (34–67), offers a reappraisal of Lydgate in which he challenges Pearsall's reduction of Lydgate to "a comprehensive definition of the Middle Ages" and his ideas to "platitudes of his age ... no more than was being said by a dozen anonymous pamphleteers of his time" (Pearsall, *John Lydgate*, 4, 15).

20. See Kipling, *Enter the King*, 142–69, and Richard Osberg, "The Jesse Tree in the 1432 London Entry of Henry VI: Messianic Kingship and the Rule of Justice," *Journal of Medieval and Renaissance Studies* 16, no. 2 (Fall 1986): 213–32.

21. In *The Queen's Dumbshows*, Claire Sponsler situates Lydgate's dramatic energies in performative contexts ranging from mummings and dumbshows to "subtleties," or foodstuffs inscribed with verses (which he wrote for Henry VI's coronation banquet in 1429), to the royal entry and Eucharistic procession discussed here. Lydgate's dramatic entertainments survive in large part because of the copyist John Shirley, who included Lydgate's entertainments in manuscript anthologies put together between the 1420s and 1440s, as discussed by Sponsler, *Queen's Dumbshows*, 16–34.

22. Ibid., 131. For a description of the entry's course and the seven pageants, see 116–22; see also John Lydgate, *Mummings and Entertainments*, ed. Claire Sponsler, TEAMS Middle English Texts Series (Kalamazoo, MI: Medieval Institute Publications, 2010), 94–95; and Pearsall, *John Lydgate*, 171–72. Pearsall suggests that Lydgate acted as "an artistic director" in scripting some of the pageants (particularly the Westminster scene), though most scholars now agree that Lydgate's poem is not a script for the historical entry but rather a poetic description based on the Carpenter letter. See Sponsler, *Queen's Dumbshows*, 115–16, 131–32; Kipling, *Enter the King*, 142–43; Benson, "Civic Lydgate," 151–52; and Nolan, *John Lydgate*, 233–35.

23. Sponsler, *Queen's Dumbshows*, 131, 133. On Welles's involvement, see Nolan, *John Lydgate*, 235.

24. Cole dates the text between 1427 and 1429 (*Literature and Heresy*, 134).

25. Anne Lancashire posits that the Skinners may have commissioned Lydgate to write the poem as an official record of their procession (*London Civic The-*

atre, 124), which Sponsler notes may have taken shape as early as 1392 and continued through the sixteenth century (*Queen's Dumbshows*, 98–102). While Sponsler is engaged by the possible connection between Lydgate's verses and the Skinners' procession, she ultimately sees the text as "less an official commemoration than an attempt at fusing spectating and reading—and devotional activity—through the mechanisms of exegesis and instruction" (*Queen's Dumbshows*, 105). Cole is more skeptical about the *Procession*'s performativity, suggesting that the "processional form" and not the sacramental performance itself is most relevant to Lydgate's "poetico-theological enterprise" in the verses (*Literature and Heresy*, 135). Other possibilities include the Corpus Christi processions in Bury St. Edmund's, discussed by Gibson, "Bury St. Edmunds," 79–81, and the idea that Lydgate based his text on sermon exempla, discussed by Clopper, *Drama, Play, and Game*, 164–65.

26. Sponsler, *Queen's Dumbshows*, 114; Cole, *Literature and Heresy*, 139.

27. Cole, *Literature and Heresy*, 137–43. Lydgate's treatment of these scriptural and patristic texts—which is at once translation and reinvention—also exemplifies what James Simpson calls the "accretive reception of historical artefacts" by which the "rereading of old texts produces a rewriting" as well as a dissemination of textual and political authority, a practice Simpson associates with reformist culture (*Reform and Cultural Revolution*, 63–65).

28. Benson, "Civic Lydgate," 152. See also Sponsler, *Queen's Dumbshows*, 133, and Nolan, *John Lydgate*, 184–86 and 233–41.

29. Sponsler, *Queen's Dumbshows*, 126–27. In the most extensive assessment of liturgy's importance to the royal entry, Gordon Kipling argues that the medieval liturgies of Advent and Epiphany, which emphasized the public revelation of Christ's divinity, provide a context for the entry whereby Henry "becomes manifest as a type of Christ the king" and emerges as "a messianic ruler" with a "messianic identity" (*Enter the King*, 152, 155, 164). By contrast, Sponsler argues that Lydgate creates "a shift in emphasis from king to Londoners" as well as a "muting of messianic allusions" in his verses, a move likely "aimed at countering objections to the theocracy of paralleling Henry with Christ" (*Queen's Dumbshows*, 133–35).

30. John Lydgate, *Henry VI's Triumphal Entry into London*, in *Mummings and Entertainments*, ed. Sponsler, lines 22–28. All future citations are to this edition and will be given parenthetically by line number. On London as a New Jerusalem, see Kipling, *Enter the King*, 143–44; Nolan, *John Lydgate*, 185; and Osberg, "Jesse Tree," 218–20.

31. Sponsler notes that Lydgate frequently embellishes and vernacularizes the Latin scriptural quotations in Carpenter's letter and that in the Enoch and Elijah episode he specifically re-creates the written mottoes into dramatic speaking parts (*Queen's Dumbshows*, 136–37). See also Nolan, *John Lydgate*, 237–38.

32. John Lydgate, "A Prayer for King, Queen, and People," lines 52–56, in *The Minor Poems of John Lydgate*, ed. Henry Noble McCracken, 2 vols. (London: Early English Text Society, Oxford University Press, 1911–34), 212–16.

33. Sponsler notes that "Archedeclyne" refers to the master of the house at Cana as recorded in John 2:1–10 and referenced in the Towneley plays and several other late medieval sources (Lydgate, *Mummings and Entertainments*, 100).

34. Kipling, *Enter the King*, 163. Kipling contends further that Henry "seems to produce a miracle of transubstantiation" (163), relating the pageant to the medieval epiphany liturgies, which analogized the wedding at Cana to the Mass (131–32). On the secular contexts for the Wells of Paradise pageant, see Benson, "Civic Lydgate," 156–57.

35. John Lydgate, *A Procession of Corpus Christi*, lines 81–88, in *Mummings and Entertainments*. All citations are to Sponsler's edition and will be cited parenthetically by line number.

36. Cole writes that in the biblical stanzas "Lydgate is deploying the usual allegorical methods of pre-figuration, whereby Old Testament sacrifices, bread offerings, and gifts from the divine persons or their angelic mediators stand as indicators of eucharistic foreshadowing" (*Literature and Heresy*, 136). The grinding and milling of grain as a Eucharistic image was common in medieval sermons, as discussed by Aston, "*Corpus Christi*," 27–31, and the image of the grapes may recall the iconography of the "mystical wine-press," also discussed by Aston (29–30).

37. Cole, *Literature and Heresy*, 142.

38. On Lydgate's translation of the *Te Deum*, see Pearsall, *John Lydgate*, 261–63. For a discussion of the *Te Deum* in the context of coronation, see Hunt, *Drama of Coronation*, 30.

39. Cole, *Literature and Heresy*, 137.

40. Ibid., 142.

41. Sponsler glosses the phrase *forreyne damage* as "public compensation" (Lydgate, *Mummings and Entertainments*, 76). *Damage* refers here to Christ's reparation for the sins of humankind; *forreyne*, as Lydgate uses it, means "public." See "forein," *MED*, 4a: "pertaining to the forum, public."

42. Lydgate treats kingship elsewhere in the *Procession*. For example, he refers to "That braunche of Gesse" (37), an image echoed in the Jesse Tree symbolism of the *Triumphal Entry*; he also devotes a stanza to King David (65–72), which links David's defeat of Goliath to Christ's passion.

43. Sponsler finds the form of the *Procession* revelatory of its content: "Lydgate plays at the borderlands of genres and forms, drawing together performed and written representation in a way that is especially apt for a text focused on

the eucharist, which bears a complex material and symbolic status of its own" (*Queen's Dumbshows*, 103).

44. Pearsall, *John Lydgate*, 14.

45. On *King Johan* as history play, see Peter Happé, *John Bale* (Boston: Twayne, 1996); David Scott Kastan, "'Holy Wurdes' and 'Slypper Wit': John Bale's *King Johan* and the Poetics of Propaganda," in *Rethinking the Henrician Era*, ed. Peter C. Herman (Urbana: University of Illinois Press, 1994), 267–82; Cathy Shrank, "John Bale and Reconfiguring the Medieval in Early Modern England," in McMullan and Matthews, *Reading the Medieval*, 179–92; and Deanne Williams, "Medievalism in English Renaissance Literature," in Cartwright, *Companion to Tudor Literature*, 213–27.

46. On the dating of *King Johan*, see John Bale, *King Johan*, ed. J. H. Pafford (Oxford: Malone Society, 1931), and ed. Barry B. Adams (Princeton, NJ: Princeton University Press, 1969), 1–25; Happé, *John Bale*, 89–92, and his introduction to *The Complete Plays of John Bale*, 2 vols. (Cambridge: D. S. Brewer, 1985), 1:2–11; and Greg Walker, *Plays of Persuasion* (Cambridge: Cambridge University Press, 1991), 170–78. *King Johan* exists in a composite manuscript; the revised B text is an expanded version that includes all of the A text and, as Pafford and W. W. Greg have concluded, is written in Bale's hand. A single reference to "our late kynge Henrye" (line 1112) coupled with references at the end to Anabaptism leads Adams to conclude that "we can do no more than locate the bulk of the B-text additions between 1547–1560" (Bale, *King Johan*, 24).

47. Bale's connections to Cromwell are discussed in Happé, *John Bale*, 90; Walker, *Plays of Persuasion*, 170–71; and David Bevington, *Tudor Drama and Politics* (Cambridge, MA: Harvard University Press, 1968), 97–99. On the playing troupe known as "Bale and His Fellows," which was patronized by Cromwell, see White, *Theatre and Reformation*, 12–41. On Bale as polemicist and clergyman, see Leslie Fairfield, *John Bale: Mythmaker for the English Reformation* (West Lafayette, IN: Purdue University Press, 1976), and Oliver Wort, *John Bale and Religious Conversion in Early Modern England* (London: Pickering and Chatto, 2013).

48. On the possible identification of King Johan with Henry VIII, see Bevington, *Tudor Drama and Politics*, 97–105. On the royal supremacy in the context of *corpus mysticum*, Kantorowicz says, "Instead of treating the state as a *corpus mysticum* Henry treated the Church as a simple *corpus politicum* and therefore as part and parcel of the realm of England" (*King's Two Bodies*, 229).

49. On Bale's use of theatrical signs as Protestant propaganda, see Hunt, *Drama of Coronation*, 98–110; Katherine A. Gillen, "From Sacraments to Signs: The Challenges of Protestant Theatricality in John Bale's Biblical Plays," *Cahiers Elisabethans* 80 (2011): 1–11; Coleman, *Drama and the Sacraments*, 35–59; and

Atkin, *Drama of Reform*, chap. 2. On Bale's metatheater, see Beckwith, *Signifying God*, 148–53; on his resistance to drama itself, see Simpson, "John Bale, Three Laws."

50. John Bale, *King Johan*, line 122, in *Complete Plays*, ed. Happé. All future citations are to this edition and will be given parenthetically by line number.

51. Bale's suggestion that scripture will replace a church obsessed with ceremony typifies an evangelical argument as described by Simpson: "Evangelicals reinstituted the True Church by repudiating the Church of the Anti-Christ, and they did so on the basis of their reading: the historical Church could be rejected as a hypocritical Church of the Devil precisely because it had developed nonscriptural traditions. The True Church, by contrast, was designed in exact measure of the text of Scripture, not a word less or more" (*Burning to Read*, 185).

52. Walker, *Plays of Persuasion*, 181.

53. John Bale, *A Declaration of Edmonde Bonners articles* (1554; repr., London: John Tynsdall, 1561), sig. Iviii*v*–K*r*.

54. Betteridge, *Literature and Politics*, 3.

55. Walker notes, "The sprinkling of holy water, giving of holy bread, bearing of candles, creeping to the cross, and 'kissing of it in memory of our redemption by christ,' all practices mocked in *King Johan*, were specifically described in the Articles as 'laudable customs, rites and ceremonies . . . not to be contemned and cast away'" (*Plays of Persuasion*, 214–15). Atkin, *Drama of Reform*, 83–91, notes that much of Bale's anticeremonial rhetoric is inspired by evangelical polemic, especially William Tyndale's *Obedience of a Christian Man* and *Practice of Prelates*.

56. Rainer Pineas, "John Bale's Non-dramatic Works of Religious Controversy," *Studies in the Renaissance* 9 (1962): 218.

57. *The Six Articles* (1539), in Bettenson and Maunder, *Documents*, 249–50.

58. Happé, *John Bale*, 104. For a survey of the play's engagement with Henrician and Cromwellian religious politics, see Walker, *Plays of Persuasion*, 194–221.

59. On Bale's two exiles, see Happé, *John Bale*, 105–7.

60. *The Six Articles* (1539), in Bettenson and Maunder, *Documents*, 249–50.

61. See Katherine Steele Brokaw, "Music and Religious Compromise in John Bale's Plays," *Comparative Drama* 44, no. 3 (Fall 2010): 339–41, for a discussion of Bale's parody of confession; on his liturgical parody more generally, see Edwin Miller, "The Roman Rite in *King Johan*," *PMLA* 64, no. 4 (September 1949): 802–22. Bale's rejection of Popish ceremony was amplified in the context of Mary I's ascent to the English throne. During her coronation procession through Kilkenny, Ireland, on August 20, 1553, Bale rejected Catholic ceremony

with characteristic verve. Writing as the newly appointed bishop of Ossory, he says, "What a do had I that daye with the prebendaryes and prestes abought wearing the cope crosser and myter in procession it were to muche to write.... I toke Christes testament in my hand and went to the market crosse the people in grete nombre folowinge.... In the mean tyme had the prelates goten ii disgysed prestes one to beare the myter afore me and the other the croser making iii procession pageauntes of one." John Bale, *The Vocacyon of Johan Bale to the bishoprick of Ossorie in Ireland* (London, 1553), quoted in Hunt, *Drama of Coronation*, 98–99. On Bale's episcopal tenure in Ossory, see Alan Fletcher, *Drama, Performance, and Polity in Post-Cromwellian Ireland* (Toronto: University of Toronto Press, 2000), 166–74.

62. Coleman, *Drama and the Sacraments*, 53.

63. John Bale, *The Epistle Exhortatorye of an Englysshe Christiane unto his derelye beloved contreye of Englande* (Antwerp: Widow of C. Reremund[?], 1544[?]), sig. Ciiiv.

64. For a reading of spiritual interiority in this scene, see Coleman, *Drama and the Sacraments*, 57.

65. Bale, *Declaration*, sig. Iiiiir.

66. By turning the pope into an allegorical figure for "Usurped Power," Bale echoes the Royal Injunctions of 1536, which called preachers to declare that "the Bishop of Rome's usurped power and jurisdiction, having no establishment nor ground by the law of God, was of most just causes taken away and abolished; and therefore they owe unto him no maner of obedience or subjection, and that the king's power is within his dominion the highest power and potentate under God" (Bettenson and Maunder, *Documents*, 246). In his introduction to Bale's *King Johan* (20), Adams records Robert Ward's reference to "the bysshopys of Rome usurpyd power" in a letter written to Thomas Cromwell in 1538, which Adams sees as a possible allusion to the play.

67. This scene unfolds as a ritualistic un-kinging that reverses some of the major movements of the coronation ceremony as explained by Alice Hunt: "The undressing of the king, the anointing of his bare exposed flesh and the subsequent relocating of him play out a particular logic and process of king-making in the ceremony. He is unmade and rebuilt again" (*Drama of Coronation*, 30). King Johan is unmade, but not rebuilt, in the deposition ritual.

68. For a more heterodox reading of Bale's appropriation of liturgical music, see Brokaw, "Music and Religious Compromise."

69. Bale's treatment of the Eucharist has traditionally been read as far more moderate than I suggest here. Coleman claims that "the references to the sacrament in the drama are much less confrontational" than in Bale's prose works,

and that "there is a sense of conservatism or disengagement with Bale's treatment of the eucharist" (*Drama and the Sacraments*, 45–46). Walker likewise argues that "Bale's uncharacteristic moderation over Transubstantiation is just one illustration of his desire to present the reformers' case in terms likely to appeal to the King" (*Plays of Persuasion*, 221).

70. Bale's description of the papacy as "a cruell sort of disgyused bloud souppers, / Unmercyfull murtherers all dronke in the bloude of marters" (2189–90) is based on Simon Fish: "Your most nobill realme wrongfully (alas for shame) hath stod tributary (not unto any kind of temporall prince but unto a cruell devilisshe bloudsupper dronken in the bloude of the sayntes and marters of Christ) eversins" (quoted in Bale, *Complete Plays*, ed. Happé, 1:150). In another source for the play, *The Obedience of a Christian Man* (Antwerp: Hans Luft, 1528), William Tyndale writes in the context of the death of King John that "the remission of synnes cometh not by faith in the testamente that God hath made in Christes bloude: but by fyghtinge and murtheringe for the popes pleasure" (sig. V5v).

71. William Shakespeare, *Macbeth*, 5.7.99, ed. Nicholas Brooke (Oxford: Clarendon Press, 1990). All future citations are to this edition and will be given parenthetically by act, scene, and line number.

72. Kastan, "Holy Wurdes," 269. See also Bevington, *Tudor Drama and Politics*, 101–7.

73. Walker, *Plays of Persuasion*, 220. See also Happé, *John Bale*, 68, and A. Hunt, *Drama of Coronation*, 99.

74. Walker argues, "The Reformation and the settling of religion was subsequently achieved by their reconciliation with his eventual successor, Imperial Majesty. Yet, as befits a play which was the product of a continuing and only partially complete reformation, the final mood is not one of complacency in a job well done, but of caution and warning" (*Plays of Persuasion*, 177).

75. In the 1549 prayer book, Edward VI is given pride of place in the prayers following the preface and directly prior to the consecration: "Specially wee beseche the to save and defende thy servaunt, Edward our kyng, that under hym wee maie bee Godly and quietly governed." The prayer book further characterizes Edward as the very king who will "truely and indifferently minister justice, to the punishment of wickedness and vice, and to the maintenaunce of Gods true religion and virtue" (sig. Oviir). These prayers for the monarch are retained in the 1552 and 1559 revisions.

76. See Carole Levin, *Propaganda in the English Reformation: Heroic and Villainous Images of King John* (Lewiston, NY: Edwin Mellen Press, 1988) and "'A Good Prince': King John and Early Tudor Propaganda," *Sixteenth Century Journal* 11, no. 4 (Winter 1980): 23–32; and J. H. Morey, "The Death of King John in Shakespeare and Bale," *Shakespeare Quarterly* 45, no. 3 (1994): 327–31.

77. William Shakespeare, *King John*, ed. A. R. Braunmuller (Oxford: Clarendon Press, 1989). I follow Braunmuller's dating for *Troublesome Raigne* and the *Norton Shakespeare* editors in giving *King John* the date of 1596. Shakespeare's *King John* is more sparing in its anti-Catholic polemic than these other plays, a point discussed by Kastan, *Will to Believe*, 62–65.

78. Bale, *Epistle Exhortatorye*, sig. Biiv.

79. Jewel, *Apologie*, sig. Hir.

80. On the Gunpowder Plot in the context of *Macbeth*, see Rebecca Lemon, *Treason by Words: Literature, Law, and Rebellion in Shakespeare's England* (Ithaca, NY: Cornell University Press, 2006), chap. 4; Jonathan Gil Harris, *Untimely Matter in the Time of Shakespeare* (Philadelphia: University of Pennsylvania Press, 2009), 119–39; Maurice Hunt, "Reformation/Counter-Reformation *Macbeth*," *English Studies* 86, no. 5 (October 2005): 379–98; Karin S. Coddon, "'Unreal Mockery': Unreason and the Problem of Spectacle in *Macbeth*," *ELH: English Literary History* 56, no. 3 (Autumn 1989): 485–501; Henry N. Paul, *The Royal Play of "Macbeth"* (New York: Macmillan, 1950), 226–47; Alvin Kernan, *Shakespeare, the King's Playwright: Theater in the Stuart Court, 1603–1613* (New Haven, CT: Yale University Press, 1995); and Robert S. Miola, "Two Jesuit Shadows in Shakespeare: William Weston and Henry Garnet," in Jackson and Marotti, *Shakespeare and Religion*, 25–45. For a broader discussion of the Gunpowder Plot in the context of anti-Catholic discourse, see Arthur Marotti, *Religious Ideology and Cultural Fantasy: Catholic and Anti-Catholic Discourses in Early Modern England* (Notre Dame, IN: University of Notre Dame Press, 2006), 131–47.

81. Thomas Spencer, *Englands Warning-Peece: or The History of the Gunpowder Treason: Inlarged with some Notable Passages not heretofore Published* (London: T. N., 1659), sig. Eviv, italics in original.

82. James I, *His Majesties Speech in this last Session of Parliament* (London: Robert Barker, 1605), sig. B2r.

83. John Donne, *John Donne's 1622 Gunpowder Plot Sermon: A Parallel Text Edition*, ed. Jeanne Shami (Duquesne, PA: Duquesne University Press, 1996), 95.

84. Lancelot Andrewes, *A Sermon Preached Before His Majestie On Sunday the fifth of August* (London: Robert Barker, 1610), sig. A3v. For a discussion of Andrewes's sermons in relation to political theology, see Shuger, *Habits of Thought*, 141–50.

85. Ibid., sig. G4v, italics in original.

86. De Lubac, *Corpus Mysticum*, 56.

87. Richard McCoy, "'The Grace of Grace' and Double-Talk in *Macbeth*," *Shakespeare Survey* 57 (2004): 27–37, notes that compared to other tragedies "*Macbeth* presents even loftier visions of sacred kingship along with some of the ghastliest images of its violation" (27). See also Susan Zimmerman, "Duncan's

Corpse," in *A Feminist Companion to Shakespeare*, ed. Dympna Callaghan (Malden, MA: Blackwell, 2000), 320–41. For readings of *Macbeth* focused on religious topics other than divine kingship, see Kristen Poole, *Supernatural Environments in Shakespeare's England: Spaces of Demonism, Divinity, and Drama* (Cambridge: Cambridge University Press, 2011), chap. 4; O'Connell, "Blood Begetting Blood," 187–88; John D. Cox, "Religion and Suffering in *Macbeth*," *Christianity and Literature* 62, no. 2 (2013): 225–40; Schreyer, *Shakespeare's Medieval Craft*, chap. 5; Daniel Swift, *Shakespeare's Common Prayers: The Book of Common Prayer and the Elizabethan Age* (New York: Oxford University Press, 2012), chap. 5; and Ewan Fernie, "'Another Golgotha,'" in Loewenstein and Witmore, *Shakespeare and Early Modern Religion*, 172–90.

88. Harry Berger Jr., "The Early Scenes of *Macbeth*: Preface to a New Interpretation," *ELH: English Literary History* 47, no. 1 (1980): 17. See also Lemon, *Treason by Words*, 97–100; David Norbrook, "*Macbeth* and the Politics of Historiography," in *Politics of Discourse: The Literature and History of Seventeenth-Century England*, ed. Kevin Sharpe and Steven N. Zwicker (Berkeley: University of California Press, 1987), 95–97; and David Scott Kastan, "*Macbeth* and the Name of King," in *Shakespeare after Theory* (New York: Routledge, 1999), 165–82.

89. McCoy, "Grace of Grace," 29.

90. On the king's power to heal his subjects, see Bloch, *Royal Touch*; Lemon, *Treason by Words*, 101–3; and Susanne L. Wofford, "The Body Unseamed: Shakespeare's Late Tragedies," in *Shakespeare's Late Tragedies*, ed. Susanne L. Wofford (Upper Saddle River, NJ: Prentice Hall, 1996), 1–21.

91. On the banquet as ritual of state, see Chris Meads, *Banquets Set Forth: Banqueting in English Renaissance Drama* (Manchester: Manchester University Press, 2001); on rituals of hospitality in seventeenth-century literature, see Darryl Palmer, *Hospitable Performances: Dramatic Genre and Cultural Practices in Early Modern England* (West Lafayette, IN: Purdue University Press, 1992); Naomi Conn Liebler, *Shakespeare's Festive Tragedy* (London: Routledge, 1995), 214–23; and Douglas M. Lanier, "Cynical Dining in *Timon of Athens*," in *Culinary Shakespeares*, ed. David Goldstein and Amy Tigner (Duquesne, PA: Duquesne University Press, 2016), 135–56.

92. See *OED*, "chalice" (n.), 1a. The *OED* places such secular usage starting in 825; its first entry for religious usage is in the *West Saxon Gospels*, ca. 1000 (2a, 2b).

93. *Chalice* is used in the Canon of the Mass, according to the Sarum Rite: "Simili modo postea que cenatum est accipiens et hunc preclarum calicem in sanctas ac venerabiles manes suas" (In a similar way at the end of the meal he took the chalice in his holy and venerable hands). Likewise, the rubrical instruc-

tions also refer to the vessel as a chalice, as when the priest is directed "Hic elevet calicem" (Here he elevates the chalice) or "Hic reponat calicem et fricet digitas suos ultra calicem" (Here he puts down the chalice and rubs his fingers over the chalice). Cf. *Missale ad usum . . . ecclesiae Sarum* (London: Wolfgang Hapyl, 1515), fols. 46v–47r. In all editions of the *Book of Common Prayer* the term *cup* replaces *chalice*, as in the rubrical instruction, "Here the priest shall take the Cup into his handes" (sig. Oviiv).

94. McCoy, "Grace of Grace," 29. O'Connell, "Blood Begetting Blood," 188, reads Duncan's blood in the context of the Last Judgment plays, as does Schreyer, *Shakespeare's Medieval Craft*, 135–61.

95. See *OED*, "host" (n.), 4. For the secular context of hospitality, see "host" (n.), 2 and 3. The Eucharistic context, according to the *OED*, first enters the lexicon in 1303.

96. Caroline Walker Bynum, *Wonderful Blood: Theology and Practice in Late Medieval Northern Germany and Beyond* (Philadelphia: University of Pennsylvania Press, 2007), 224.

97. Thomas Aquinas, "O salutaris hostia," in Walsh and Husch, *One Hundred Latin Hymns*, 362. On Aquinas's liturgy for Corpus Christi, see Rubin, *Corpus Christi*, 190–92.

98. See *OED*, "host" (n.), 1.

99. James I, *Two Meditations*, sig. C2r.

100. Ibid., sig. D2r–D2v, italics in original.

101. Ibid., sig. D8v.

102. Kastan summarizes James I's position as set forth in *The True Law of Free Monarchies* (1598) that even a tyrannical king is still an anointed king and that consequently violence waged against him is still an assault upon sovereignty ("Holy Wurdes," 176–80). See also Norbrook, "Politics of Historiography," 92–93.

103. Lemon, *Treason by Words*, 86. Lemon notes that Macbeth "betrays a fiendish intensity challenging not only the state that the king had formerly ruled but also the religious faith to which he is expected to turn" (105).

104. On the play's engagement with two models of succession—tanistry, or "indirect inheritance," and the more familiar lineal succession—see Kastan, "Holy Wurdes," 170–73; Lemon, *Treason by Words*, 99; and Norbrook, "Politics of Historiography," 86–89. Norbrook notes that Shakespeare glosses over the early, more positive tenure of Macbeth's reign as described in Holinshed, Boece, and other sources (96–97).

105. Rust, *Body in Mystery*, 27.

106. The term *butcher* is also associated with Christ's passion in biblical drama. While the Pinners staged the Crucifixion pageant in the York cycle, the

Butchers staged the *Mortificatio Christi* pageant, which in the Mercer's Account Rolls of 1550 was also referred to as "The Butcher paggen" (Johnston and Rogerson, *Records of Early English Drama: York*, 1:295). Zimmerman, "Duncan's Corpse," 29, also analogizes Duncan's murder to Christ's sacrifice.

107. Judas was seen as an example of unworthy Eucharistic reception, for while he received Christ's body and blood at the Last Supper, he did so without faith. As Thomas More writes, "He that in suche plyght receyveth the blessed sacrament without purpose of amendment, or without the fayth and bylyefe, that the very flesshe & bloude of Chryste is in it: he receyveth as saynt Austayne sayth notwythstandyng his noughtynesse the very fleshe and bloude of Cryst, the very pryce of our redempcion. But he receyveth them to hys harme as Judas dyd, & eateth and drynketh hys owne judgement & dampnacyon . . . bycause he discerneth not our lordes body" (*Answer*, sig. O4v–O5r).

108. Cranmer, *Defence*, sig. Eeiiiv.

109. *A Homilie of the worthie receyvyng and reverent esteemyng of the Sacrament, of the body and blood of Christ*. In *The second tome of homilies, of suche matters as vvere promised and intituled in the former part of homilies, set out by the aucthoritie of the Queenes Maiestie* (London: Richard Jugge and John Cawood, 1563), sig. Ccc6r.

110. See Robert S. Miola, "'I Could Not Say 'Amen': Prayer and Providence in *Macbeth*," in *Shakespeare's Christianity: The Protestant and Catholic Poetics of* Julius Caesar, Macbeth, *and* Hamlet, ed. E. Beatrice Batson (Waco, TX: Baylor University Press, 2006), 73–90.

111. Swift, *Shakespeare's Common Prayers*, 173. O'Connell situates the banquet scene in the context of the N-Town *Harrowing of Hell*, making "Macbeth into a version of Herod, a strangely self-conscious and self-damning Herod and one whose ultimate victim, like Herod's has also escaped" ("Vital Cultural Practices," 157, 159).

112. *Book of Common Prayer* (1549), sig. Oiiir. This call to worthy reception is also included in the introductory rubrics to the Communion service, discussed by Swift, *Shakespeare's Common Prayers*, 161–63. A description of Christ's mystical body is also foregrounded in the collect for Good Friday: "Almightie and everlasting GOD, by whose spirit the whole body of the Churche is governed and sanctified: receive our supplicacions and praiers, whiche we offre before thee for all estates of menne, in thy holy congregacion, that every membre of the same, in his vocacion and Ministery, maie truly and godly serve thee" (*Book of Common Prayer*, 1549, sig. Fvv).

113. Rust, *Body in Mystery*, xvi. McCoy also notes the implications for the mystical body: "Regicide profanes the whole sacramental system and taints society's common cup for all partakers" ("Grace of Grace," 29).

114. Swift, *Shakespeare's Common Prayers*, 174. Swift relates the breakdown in representation to Banquo's earlier attempt to interpret the witches (180–83). For an analysis of the play's representational issues outside a religious context, see Coddon, "'Unreal Mockery,'" 485–86; M. Hunt, "Reformation/Counter-Reformation *Macbeth*," 289–90; Cavell, *Disowning Knowledge*, 22; Kent Cartwright, "Scepticism and Theatre in *Macbeth*," *Shakespeare Survey* 55 (2002): 219–36; Marjorie Garber, "Macbeth: The Male Medusa," in *Shakespeare's Ghost Writers: Literature as Uncanny Causality* (1987; repr., London: Methuen, 2010), 116–65; and Andrew Sofer, *Dark Matter: Invisibility in Drama, Theater, and Performance* (Ann Arbor: University of Michigan Press, 2014), 8–9.

115. At the elevation of the chalice in the Sarum Rite, the priest says, "In mei memoriam facientis." In the reformed rite, the command to "do this in remembrance of me" is included in the consecratory prayers, after which the priest also says, "The memoriall whiche thy sonne hath willed us to make, having in remembraunce his blessed passion, mightie resurreccion, and glorious ascension" (*Book of Common Prayer*, 1549, sig. Oviiv).

116. Kastan, "*Macbeth*," 178.

117. Lemon, *Treason by Words*, 104. Kastan reads the political implications of the play's ending as ambiguous: "The ending may be seen either to restore the legitimate line of Duncan, redeeming the murderous interlude of Macbeth's tyranny, or merely to repeat the pattern of violent action that Macbeth initiates" ("*Macbeth*," 174). For arguments in favor of political containment, see Norbrook, "*Macbeth*"; Maynard Mack, *Killing the King: Three Studies in Shakespeare's Tragic Structure* (New Haven, CT: Yale University Press, 1973); and Tennenhouse, *Power on Display*, 127–32.

FOUR. Father Faustus?

1. For general readings of religion in the play, see Bevington, *From "Mankind" to Marlowe*; C. L. Barber, *Creating Elizabethan Tragedy: The Theater of Marlowe and Kyd* (Chicago: University of Chicago Press, 1988), 87–130; C. L. Barber, "'The Form of Faustus' Fortunes Good or Bad,'" *Tulane Drama Review* 8, no. 4 (Summer 1964): 92–119; Catherine Belsey, *The Subject of Tragedy: Identity and Difference in Renaissance Drama* (London: Methuen, 1985), 55–92; Jonathan Dollimore, *Radical Tragedy: Religion, Ideology, and Power in the Drama of Shakespeare and His Contemporaries*, 2nd ed. (Durham, NC: Duke University Press, 1993), 109–19; Leah S. Marcus, *Unediting the Renaissance: Shakespeare, Marlowe, Milton* (London: Routledge, 1996), 38–67; Michael Hattaway, "The Theology of Marlowe's *Doctor Faustus*," *Renaissance Drama*, n.s., 3 (1970): 51–78; Adrian

Streete, *Protestantism and Drama in Early Modern England* (Cambridge: Cambridge University Press, 2009), 140–61; James Kearney, *The Incarnate Text: Imagining the Book in Reformation England* (Philadelphia: University of Pennsylvania Press, 2009), 140–77; Waldron, *Reformations of the Body*, 85–116; Parker, *Aesthetics of Antichrist*, 183–245; John Parker, "Faustus, Confession, and the Sins of Omission," *ELH: English Literary History* 80, no. 1 (Spring 2013): 29–59; Angus Fletcher, "*Doctor Faustus* and the Lutheran Aesthetic," *English Literary Renaissance* 35, no. 2 (2005): 187–209; Kristen Poole, "The Devil's in the Archive: *Doctor Faustus* and Ovidian Physics," *Renaissance Drama*, n.s., 35 (2006): 191–219; Kristen Poole, "*Dr. Faustus* and Reformation Theology," in *Early Modern English Drama: A Critical Companion*, ed. Garrett A. Sullivan Jr., Patrick Cheney, and Andrew Hadfield (Oxford: Oxford University Press, 2005), 96–107; Coleman, *Drama and the Sacraments*, 91–110; Diehl, *Staging Reform*, 67–93; Andrew Sofer, "How to Do Things with Demons: Conjuring Performatives in *Doctor Faustus*," *Theatre Journal* 61, no. 1 (2009): 1–21; John D. Cox, *The Devil and the Sacred in English Drama* (Cambridge: Cambridge University Press, 2000); John D. Cox, "Devils and Power in Marlowe and Shakespeare," *Yearbook of English Studies* 23 (1993): 46–64; John D. Cox, "'To Obtain His Soul': Demonic Desire for the Soul in Marlowe and Others," *Early Theatre* 5, no. 2 (2002): 29–46; Marjorie Garber, "'Here's Nothing Writ': Scribe, Script, and Circumscription in Marlowe's Plays," *Theatre Journal* 36, no. 3 (1984): 301–20; Pauline Honderich, "John Calvin and *Doctor Faustus*," *Modern Language Review* 68, no. 1 (1973): 1–13; Clifford Davidson, "*Doctor Faustus* at Rome," *SEL: Studies in English Literature, 1500–1900* 9, no. 2 (1969): 231–39; and Sara Munson Deats, "*Doctor Faustus*: From Chapbook to Tragedy," *Essays in Criticism* 76, no. 3 (1976): 3–15. For two omnibus reviews of *Faustus* scholarship that treat such religious engagements, see Bruce E. Brandt, "The Critical Backstory," in *Doctor Faustus: A Critical Guide*, ed. Sara Munson Deats (London: Continuum, 2010), 17–40; and Sara Munson Deats, "*Doctor Faustus*," in *Christopher Marlowe at 450*, ed. Sara Munson Deats and Robert A. Logan (Aldershot: Ashgate, 2014), 71–99.

2. Keith Thomas, *Religion and the Decline of Magic* (New York: Charles Scribner's Sons, 1971), 32–33.

3. Christopher Marlowe, *Doctor Faustus: A Two-Text Edition*, ed. David Scott Kastan (New York: W. W. Norton, 2005), A 1.3.15. There are two extant versions of the play: the A text, which as Bevington and others have claimed, is closer to the manuscript version of the play, and the B text, which is based on the performance history and incorporates several stage revisions. While I use both the A and B texts, I will rely on the A text in cases where A and B are identical or only marginally different and will note important differences as they affect my argu-

ment. All future citations are to Kastan's edition and will be given parenthetically by act, scene, and line number. On the differences between the A and B texts, see, in addition to Kastan, David Bevington's edition, *Doctor Faustus*, Revels Plays ed. (Manchester: Manchester University Press, 1993); Marcus, *Unediting the Renaissance*, 38–67; and Eric Rasmussen, *A Textual Companion to "Doctor Faustus"* (Manchester: Manchester University Press, 1993).

4. Euan Cameron, *Enchanted Europe: Superstition, Reason, and Religion, 1250–1750* (Oxford: Oxford University Press, 2010), 74.

5. See Darryl Grantley, *English Dramatic Interludes, 1300–1580* (Cambridge: Cambridge University Press, 2004), 94–5, and Charlotte Steenbrugge, *Staging Vice: A Study of Dramatic Traditions in Medieval and Sixteenth-Century England and the Low Countries* (Amsterdam and New York: Rodopi, 2014). John Wasson calls the entire genre of "morality play" into question. On the basis of his survey of the dramatic records for the Records of Early English Drama, he claims that he has "not found a single reference to a performance of a morality play and . . . that despite all the recent books about them and their later influence, moralities were never part of the main stream of British drama" ("Records of Early English Drama," 140).

6. On the performance history of *Everyman*, which includes highly successful performances in North America beginning in 1902, see Claire Sponsler, *Ritual Imports: Performing Medieval Drama in America* (Ithaca, NY: Cornell University Press, 2004), 156–57, 163–66.

7. On dating and textual history, see *The Summoning of Everyman*, in *Everyman and Mankind*, ed. Douglas Bruster and Eric Rasmussen (London: Methuen Drama, 2009), 1–5, 41–42, 67–76, and Bevington, *Medieval Drama*, 939–40. Bruster and Rasmussen suggest that the play was printed around 1518–19, while Bevington cites four extant versions of the play printed from 1508–37. All references to *Everyman* are to the Bruster and Rasmussen edition and will be given parenthetically by line number.

8. Bruster and Rasmussen, *Everyman and Mankind*, 181.

9. Critical attention to the Eucharist, and specifically to Eucharistic confection, in *Everyman* has been scant, except for Thomas Betteridge, *Writing Faith and Telling Tales: Literature, Politics, and Religion in the Work of Thomas More* (Notre Dame, IN: University of Notre Dame Press, 2013), 25–27. On *Everyman* and broader liturgical concerns, see Murdo William McRae, "Everyman's Last Rites and the Digression on Priesthood," *College Literature* 13 (1986): 305–9; John Conley, "The Phrase 'The Oyle of Forgyvenes' in *Everyman*: A Reference to Extreme Unction," *Notes and Queries* 22 (1975): 105–6; John Cunningham, "Comedic and Liturgical Restoration in *Everyman*," *Comparative Drama* 22 (1988): 162–73; and

Donald F. Duclow, "*Everyman* and the *Ars Moriendi*: Fifteenth-Century Ceremonies of Dying," *Fifteenth-Century Studies* 6 (1983): 93–113.

10. Caroline Walker Bynum, *Jesus as Mother: Studies in the Spirituality of the High Middle Ages* (Berkeley: University of California Press, 1982), 11.

11. On the power of the keys, see Beckwith, *Shakespeare and the Grammar*, 38–42. The priest's power to absolve sins as grounded in apostolic succession is also referenced by Confescio in *The Castle of Perseverance*, in Bevington, *Medieval Drama*, 1494–99.

12. On the importance of the priesthood, sacraments, and performative language to Everyman's salvation, see Bevington, *Tudor Drama and Politics*, 35–37, and Lawrence V. Ryan, "Doctrine and Dramatic Structure in *Everyman*," *Speculum* 32, no. 4 (1957): 722–35.

13. Thomas Aquinas, *Summa theologiae* [hereafter *ST*], III.62.1, rep. 2, ed. Mortensen and Alarcon, trans. Shapcote. All future citations are to this edition.

14. Charles Zika, "Processions and Pilgrimages: Controlling the Sacred in Fifteenth-Century Germany," *Past and Present* 118 (Feburary 1988): 31.

15. The priest's "mumbling" of the Latin words of consecration was a ubiquitous target of sixteenth-century reformers, as discussed by Carla Mazzio, *The Inarticulate Renaissance: Language Trouble in an Age of Eloquence* (Philadelphia: University of Pennsylvania Press, 2009), 28–34.

16. J. L. Austin, *How to Do Things with Words* (1962; repr., Cambridge, MA: Harvard University Press, 1975), defines the performative utterance as a speech act that does not merely refer to or describe something but makes it happen materially in the world. It is worth noting Austin's reliance on ceremony and ritual as a key context for explaining the performative utterance. Lecture II establishes ritual and ceremony (especially marriage and baptism, including the wonderful example of baptizing penguins) as an overarching context for speech acts, and in Lecture VI Austin cites ritual and ceremony when he describes "non-verbal" speech acts like bowing as "similar to performative utterances in that they are the performance of a conventional action (here ritual or ceremonial)" (69).

17. *ST* III.64.1, cont.

18. *ST* III.64.5, ans. In an earlier passage, Aquinas states, "God is the principal cause of grace and sacraments the instrumental cause.... The interior sacramental effect can be the work of man, in so far as he works as a minister. For a minister is of the nature of an instrument, since the action of both is applied to something extrinsic, while the interior effect is produced through the power of the principal agent, which is God" (III.64.1, ans.).

19. *ST*, III.83.3, rep. 8.

20. Tanner, *Decrees*, 2:686. Aquinas discusses *ex opere operato* further in *ST* III.64.5–10 and III.82.1–10.

21. Thomas Tuke, *Concerning the Holy Eucharist and the Popish Breaden-God* (Amsterdam: [successors of] G. Thorp: 1625), sig. Br. In *Wycklifes Wycket* (London: J. Daye [?], 1546), John Wyclif is also recorded as saying, "Thou then that art an earthely man by what reason maist thou saye that thou makest thy maker?" (sig. aiiii*v*).

22. Elizabeth I, *Queen Elizabeth's Opinion Concerning Transubstantiation*, Folger MS 260-135b (London: F. E., 1688).

23. Rosendale discusses in detail the revisions to the words and rubrics of the 1549 Order of Communion, noting that the 1549 edition "provides an ambivalent articulation of eucharistic theology" that brought about significant reforms to the Eucharistic liturgy in 1552 (*Liturgy and Literature*, 96–102).

24. Aers and Beckwith, "Eucharist," 155.

25. *Homilie of the worthie receyvyng*, sig. Cccviiv–Cccviiir.

26. Bruce Holsinger, "Liturgy," in *Middle English*, ed. Paul Strohm (Oxford: Oxford University Press, 2009), 299–300.

27. Such an argument complicates a reading of the play that displaces Marlowe's own reputed atheism onto his travestying of religious rituals. Marlowe's atheism was recorded in a letter written by Richard Baines in 1593, which catalogued Marlowe's blasphemies and concluded that "almost into every Company he Cometh he perswades men to Atheism" (quoted in Marlowe, *Doctor Faustus*, ed. Kastan, 127–28). On Marlowe's own religious beliefs, see David Riggs, *The World of Christopher Marlowe* (New York: Faber and Faber, 2004); and Park Honan, *Christopher Marlowe: Poet and Spy* (Oxford: Oxford University Press, 2005).

28. The B text reads "tire thy brains" (1.1.63) instead of "try thy brains." Both connotations are relevant here.

29. Tom Rutter, *The Cambridge Introduction to Christopher Marlowe* (Cambridge: Cambridge University Press, 2012), notes that a Privy Council document dated June 29, 1587, responded to rumors that Marlowe had left Cambridge for Rheims, the site of a newly established Catholic seminary. While Rutter concludes that it was unlikely that Marlowe actually did go to Rheims, he says that "the reason why any young man in the 1580s would want to go to Rheims would be to attend the English Catholic seminary there which trained up young men for the priesthood, preparing them to return to England in secret with the ultimate aim of converting the country back to Catholicism" (8–9). Again, this is not to say that either Marlowe or his protagonist desires priesthood, only to admit it was hard not to be aware of priestly authority given the religious tensions in England and on the Continent at the time of the play's performance.

30. "Scenes" is included only in the A text. In B, the line reads, "Lines, circles, letters, and characters" (1.1.50).

31. Kearney argues for the importance of the material text to the spiritual concerns of *Doctor Faustus* when he suggests that "to be converted by a text is to give yourself over to the affective experience of reading" and that Faustus is "frustrated, bored, and ultimately seduced by text" and later is "undone by his faith in text" (*Incarnate Text*, 158).

32. On the *grimoire*, see Barbara Mowat, "Prospero's Book," *Shakespeare Quarterly* 52, no. 1 (2001): 1–33.

33. The missal has a complicated history that originates with the earliest liturgical books called *libelli*, proceeds through various *sacramentaries*, and terminates with the missals. The two missals I study in this chapter are the Missal of Sarum Use (*Missale ad usum Ecclesiae Sarum*), which was used through the reign of Henry VIII, and the Missal of Roman Use *(Missale Romanum)*, which was introduced after the Council of Trent in large part to streamline the liturgical variants under a single, uniform Roman rite. For a comprehensive history of the missal, see Eric Palazzo, *A History of Liturgical Books from the Beginning to the Thirteenth Century* (Collegeville, MN: Liturgical Press, 1993); John Harper, *The Forms and Orders of Western Liturgy from the Tenth to the Eighteenth Centuries: A Historical Introduction and Guide for Students and Musicians* (Oxford: Clarendon Press, 1991); Andrew Hughes, *Medieval Manuscripts for Mass and Office: A Guide to Their Organization and Terminology* (Toronto: University of Toronto Press, 1982); and Wandel, *Eucharist in the Reformation*, 231–51.

34. Marcus, *Unediting the Renaissance*, 62.

35. As Targoff notes, clerical texts like the missals were not owned or read by the laity. This led to the publication of companion texts like the *Lay Folks' Mass Book*, which included "not translations from the clergy's Missal, but instead ... separate if often compatible texts for occupying the worshipper's attention" (*Common Prayer*, 22). Duffy suggests otherwise, at least in the context of Masses for the dead: "Lay people frequently showed a remarkable familiarity with the fine detail of the missal, specifying in addition to the votive Masses variant collects and other prayers to be used by their chantry priests and annualers" (*Stripping of the Altars*, 370). An "annualer" is a cleric who offers memorial Masses to mark anniversaries for the deceased.

36. Sarah Wall-Randell, "*Doctor Faustus* and the Printer's Devil," *SEL: Studies in English Literature, 1500–1900* 48, no. 2 (2008): 266–67.

37. Palazzo, *History of Liturgical Books*, 61. Palazzo also notes that the missal "was one of the earliest books to be adorned, at first by a simply ornamental decoration and later on by iconographic cycles" (57). In *Used Books: Marking Readers in Renaissance England* (Philadelphia: University of Pennsylvania Press, 2008), William H. Sherman discusses a unique manuscript version of the *Book of*

Common Prayer, a 1562 edition that displays decorated initials and rubrications that include "a small O with a bust of Christ displaying his wounds." Sherman argues, "The most uncommon feature of all in the volume is the illuminated initials harking back to the aesthetic and devotional models of the medieval manuscript prayer book" (101).

38. The illuminated Crucifixion portraits appear in both the Sarum and Roman missals. See, for example, *Missale ad usum insignis ac preclare Ecclesie Sarum* (London: Richard Pynson, 1520), Houghton Library f Typ 505.20.262, fol. 77v, as well as *Missale Romanum* (London, ca. 1240–60), Huntington Library HM 26061, fols. 178v–79r.

39. Agostino Mainardi, *An Anatomi, that is to say a parting in Peeces of the Mass* (Strasbourg: [heirs of] W. Kopfel, 1556), sig. D8v.

40. For a critique of the New Historicist misreading of images as necessarily opposed to the body and the Eucharist, see Aers, "New Historicism."

41. Mainardi, *Anatomi*, sig. D7v.

42. Ibid., sig. D8r.

43. The scene depicted in the historiated initial is not always that of a priest at Mass, though the iconography is usually Eucharistic. For example, the *Gower Missal of Sarum Use* (15th c.) uses the iconography of Abraham and Isaac to establish a typological relation between an Old Testament covenant and its New Testament analogue. For a discussion of this initial, see Jay Zysk, "Melting Flesh, Living Words," *postmedieval: a journal of medieval cultural studies* 4, no. 4 (December 2013): 404–8. That said, the Sarum missal does not always provide such a richly illustrated *T*. Some editions provide no illustration, while others include a decorated (or floriated) *T* as opposed to the historiated letter that illustrates a liturgical or biblical scene. Palazzo notes that the *T* of the *Te igitur* was more consistently illustrated in missals from the tenth century on. I add that its prominence in post-Tridentine missals may coincide with the Council of Trent's reaffirmation of the doctrine of transubstantiation.

44. Sokolowski, *Eucharistic Presence*, 15.

45. The fractioning of the host also figures the Mass as a sacrifice implicated within the dynamic of social union and division. See John Bossy, "The Mass as Social Institution," *Past and Present* 100 (1983): 29–61.

46. Rosendale, *Liturgy and Literature*, 96–97. The black crosses can also be found in the Great Bible of 1539–40, though they do not signal the need to make a physical sign of the cross as they do in the missal. Cf. *The Byble in Englyshe, that is to say the content of all the Holy Scripture both of ye olde and newe testament, truly translated after the veryte of the Hebrue and Greke textes* (London: Richard Grafton and Edward Whitchurch, 1539).

47. Rosendale, *Liturgy and Literature*, 98.

48. Jean Calvin, *A faythful and moost Godlye treatyse concernynge the most sacret sacrament of the blessed body and bloude of oure sauioure Christe* (London: John Daye and William Seres, 1548[?]), sig. Avr.

49. Schwartz, *Sacramental Poetics*, 7.

50. Piero Camporesi, "The Consecrated Host: A Wondrous Excess," in *Fragments for a History of the Human Body, Part One*, ed. Michael Feher (New York: Zone Books, 1989), 225.

51. Ibid.

52. Ibid., 224–25.

53. Austin, *How to Do Things*, 14.

54. Ibid., 16.

55. Ibid., 36.

56. Ibid. Austin also discusses other infelicities called "abuses" in which the act *does* take hold despite some aberration. In an "abuse" (as opposed to a "misfire"), the act may be "insincere" but is not rendered void. The speech act is carried off despite the private intentions, thoughts, or feelings of the actor, just as in the Eucharistic context of *ex opere operato* the priest's moral condition or personal motivations would not negatively affect the validity of his consecration and confection. Aquinas writes that the moral disposition of the priest would not invalidate the sacrament: "The minister of a sacrament acts in the person of the Church by whose faith any defect in the minister's faith is made good" (III.64.9, rep. 1). See also Aquinas's discussion of the possible defects in the Eucharistic rite (including the death of a priest during Mass, a spider that flies into the chalice before consecration, the absence of the water or wine from the chalice, and the priest's failure to say the words of consecration) at III.83.4–6.

57. *ST* III.60.8, ans.; see also III.60.8, rep. 2 and 3, and III.83.6, rep. 5.

58. Hughes, *Medieval Manuscripts*, 148. Wandel, *Eucharist in the Reformation*, 233–39, surveys some key missal rubrics.

59. *Missale Romanum ad usum sacrosancte Romane ecclesiae* (Venetiis, 1546), Houghton Library f Typ 525 46.262, fol. 127r; my translation.

60. *Missale Romanum ex decreto sacrosancti Concilii Tridentini restitutum* (Antverpiae, 1700), fol. 286r; my translation.

61. Joye, *Souper of the Lorde*, sig. Avv.

62. Calvin, *Institutes* 4.17, ed. Beveridge, 567.

63. Calvin, *Faithful and moost Godlye treatyse*, sig. Dvir.

64. Mainardi, *Anatomi*, sig. Q1v–Q2r.

65. Austin, *How to Do Things*, 22.

66. See Hattaway, "Theology of *Doctor Faustus*," and Sofer, "How to Do Things," 8–9. On the use of church vestments and props in the commercial theater, see Greenblatt, "Shakespeare and the Exorcists," 94–128.

67. Parker, *Aesthetics of Antichrist*, 241.

68. Christopher Haigh, *The Plain Man's Pathway to Heaven: Modes of Christianity in Post-Reformation England, 1570–1640* (Cambridge: Cambridge University Press, 2007), notes that the sign of the cross was a contested gesture in Reformation culture. "Some ministers refused to cross a baby at baptism," he writes, for the gesture was tantamount to "popish idolatry" (32).

69. Faustus's reference to the saints alludes to the long catalog of saints' names included in the text of the *Canon Missae* just prior to the consecration. In the *Missale Romanum ex decreto sacrosancti Concilii Tridentini restitutum*, we read: "Communicantes & memoriam venerantes in primis gloriosae semper virginis Mariae, genitricis Dei & Domini nostri Jesu Christi: sed & beatorum Apostolorum ac Martyrum tuorum, Petri & Pauli, Andreae, Jacobi, Joannis, Thomae, Jacobi, Philippi, Bartholomaei, Mathhaei, Simonis, & Thaddei: Lini, Cleti, Clementis, Xysti, Cornelli, Cypriani, Laurentii, Chrysogoni, Joannis & Pauli, Cosmae & Damiani, & omnium Sanctorum tuorum" (fols. 285v–286r). Though this specific quotation comes from a post-Tridentine missal, all missal texts included (and still include) this catalog in the *Canon*.

70. Reformers from the late medieval period through the sixteenth century discounted such ritual performances as mere magic, as evident in the fourteenth-century *Lollard Conclusions*: "Exorcisms and blessings performed over wine, bread, water and oil, salt, wax and incense, the stones of the altar, and church walls, over clothing, mitre, cross, and pilgrims' staves, are the genuine performance of necromancy rather than sacred theology." *The Lollard Conclusions* (1394), in Bettenson and Maunder, *Documents*, 187.

71. Parker, *Aesthetics of Antichrist*, 241.

72. Belsey, *Subject of Tragedy*, 73. Coleman argues that the play represents "an initiation of Faustus into an anti-church" and concludes with Faustus's "exile from the 'true' church" (*Drama and the Sacraments*, 106).

73. Harris, *Untimely Matter*, 124. In Harris's concept of "palimpsested time," "past and present work together" and "are reworked by the imagination of the theorist to produce the temporalities of matter" (16).

74. Both Parker and Sofer have commented on Faustus's complex relationship to linguistic performativity, though not in an explicitly sacramental context. Parker writes of Faustus as approximating the *magus*, or "wise interpreter," who uses spectacle and deception to win over an audience. Faustus does the same even if his *magus*-like behavior witnesses "the special power of professedly empty

speech" and "promote[s] a kind of grace that cannot match its appearance because such grace appears to exist but does not" (*Aesthetics of Antichrist*, 234). For Sofer, *Doctor Faustus* "probes the uncertain boundary between hollow performatives and magical performativity" ("How to Do Things," 20). Against Austin's dividing line between fictional and nonfictional venues for the performative utterance, Sofer reveals theater to be a more fluid domain in which a purportedly fictive utterance could take hold. "On the Elizabethan stage," he writes, "the term *conjure* always carries a whiff of danger about it, for to adjure something—to address or call upon it solemnly—is to risk calling that thing into existence, just as to perform any act onstage—a laugh, a belch, a curse, a consecration—is to risk actually doing it" ("How to Do Things," 9–10).

75. The failure of Faustus's performatives is indicated further when Mephistopheles admits, "I am servant to great Lucifer / And may not follow thee without his leave. / No more than he commands must we perform" (1.3.41–43). Thus both the magical performances and the magical performatives are governed by Lucifer, and Faustus cannot enact them on his own volition. For a more positive reading of Faustus's speech act, see Sofer, "How to Do Things," 15.

76. Bevington, *Tudor Drama and Politics*, 217.

77. Farce was not always opposed to, but had a place within, liturgical performance, as illustrated by the medieval Feast of Fools and Feast of Asses. Chambers notes that the ritual provided a form of festive release that offered low-ranking clerics "an ebullition of the natural lout beneath the cassock," suggesting that it was "almost an obvious sport to burlesque the sacred and tedious ceremonies with which they were already too familiar" (*Mediaeval Stage*, 1:325).

78. Faustus's arrival at Rome is yet another indication of his limited agency. He says to Mephistopheles, "But tell me now what resting place is this? / Hast thou, as erst I did command, / Conducted me within the walls of Rome?" (A 3.1.21–23). The command is Faustus's, but it is effected by Mephistopheles.

79. Garber, "'Here's Nothing Writ,'" 315. At the same time that she attends to the Eucharistic parody, Garber admits that "for Marlowe, the invisible presence of Faustus at the Pope's feast . . . provides a telling, and, at the same time, safely comic, commentary on presence and absence in the Mass" (315).

80. These mockeries corroborate Clifford Davidson's suggestion about the B text, which elaborates the scene in the context of papal corruption such that "Marlowe's portrait of Pope Adrian is consistent with contemporary Protestant statements on the Papacy." Consequently, he reads Faustus's liberation of Pope Bruno, who defies Pope Adrian's authority in the B text, as "a victory for Protestantism" ("*Doctor Faustus* at Rome," 234–35). The B text has Faustus and Mephistopheles assuming the role of the cardinals of France and Padua and in-

criminating the rival Pope Bruno (a character not found in the A text) as a Lollard. Bruno is then defeated by Pope Adrian, who sees the banquet in question as a confirmation of a political victory: "Go presently and bring a banquet forth / That we may solemnize Saint Peter's feast / And with Lord Raymond, King of Hungary, / Drink to our late and happy victory" (B 3.1.198–201).

81. Deats, "From Chapbook to Tragedy," 15. See also Garber, "'Here's Nothing Writ,'" 312, and Dollimore, *Radical Tragedy*, 115.

82. On Old Testament covenantal ritual, see *The New Oxford Annotated Bible*, ed. Michael D. Coogan et al., 4th ed. (Oxford: Oxford University Press, 2001), HB 116–17; and Michael D. Coogan, *The New Testament: A Historical and Literary Introduction to the Hebrew Scriptures* (Oxford: Oxford University Press, 2005), 138–53.

83. Bynum, *Wonderful Blood*, 224–25.

84. Waldron writes that Marlowe's use of *propitious* calls to mind "a term central to Protestant condemnations of the Mass as a sacrilegious human invention." At the same time, she says that the scene "offers the audience a double perspective, heightening the contrast between Faustus's view of this event and the sacred dramatic tradition of sacrifice that he echoes" (*Reformations of the Body*, 93).

85. Austin writes that one version of the performative utterance is "a written utterance (or inscription)" that the writer carries out "*by appending his signature.*" Austin speaks of a more conventional signature (as in an inscription of a name on paper), which he deems necessary "because, of course, written utterances are not tethered to their origin in the way that spoken ones are" (*How to Do Things*, 60–61). Faustus complicates even this notion of the written utterance, for one might say that when he signs the deed not on paper but in his own flesh and blood his complete speech act yokes a written performative to a spoken performative. That said, he does provide Mephistopheles with an actual signature, "By me, John Faustus" (A 2.1.110), which appears on the signed scroll that Mephistopheles brings onstage at A 2.1.88.

86. Lowell Gallagher, "Faustus's Blood and the (Messianic) Question of Ethics," *ELH: English Literary History* 73, no. 1 (2006): 10.

87. Deats links Christ's blood streaming in the firmament to the religious symbolism of blood in the contract scene. "The use of the word 'streams' implicitly associates the vision of the ensanguinated heavens with the earlier miracle of the coagulated blood," she writes. "Earlier, divine grace impeded the stream of Faustus's blood that he might not endanger his salvation; now divine grace sends another miracle ... to remind him that he is not irrevocably damned" ("From Chapbook to Tragedy," 16n5). James Kearney similarly argues, "Both the congealed blood and the inscribed flesh seem to be examples of divine intervention,

and both interventions are equally ineffective in persuading Faustus to turn away from the contract" (*Incarnate Text*, 170). Moreover, Adrian Streete views the scene as an "imitation of Christ" that is carried out when Faustus performs his "role as devilish parodist prepared for him by Mephistopheles" (*Protestantism and Drama*, 159).

88. *ST*, III.62.5, ans.
89. Marcus, *Unediting the Renaissance*, 51.
90. Ibid.
91. Ophelia's suspected suicide is enough to give the Priest pause:

> Her obsequies have been as far enlarged
> As we have warranty. Her death was doubtful;
> And but that great command o'ersways the order
> She should in ground unsanctified been lodged
> Till the last trumpet: for charitable prayers,
> Flints and pebbles should be thrown on her.
> Yet here she is allowed her virgin crants,
> Her maiden strewments, and the bringing home
> Of bell and burial.
>
> (5.1.215–23)

Offering the full range of obsequies to a suspected suicide would violate canon law and also profane the liturgical rite itself. For this reason the Priest says, "No more be done. / We should profane the service of the dead / To sing a requiem and such rest to her / As to peace-parted souls" (225–28). William Shakespeare, *Hamlet*, ed. Ann Thompson and Neil Taylor (London: Cengage Learning, 2006).

92. John Bale also refers to "Bell, book, and candle" pejoratively in *King Johan*, 1034–45.

93. The manuscript under discussion here is the Knollys Family Psalter, currently housed in the Transylvania University Library, Lexington, KY. The catalog entry traces the manuscript's provenance to John Welles, who apparently gave the Latin psalter to Thomas Knollys. In a recent examination of the manuscript, Lisa Fagin Davis notes that there are actually two members of the Knollys family named Thomas. The elder Thomas Knollys was lord mayor of London in 1399 and 1410 and died in 1435. Davis has found in John Welles's will (dated to 1442) a reference to "meum psalterium in Latinis discriptum" bequeathed to one "Thome Knolles." Davis suggests that this is Thomas Knollys the son, who then inscribed his father's name next to the date of his death in the psalter's calendar (fol. 1). For the catalog entry, see http://transy.worldcat.org/title/knollys-family-psalter/oclc/904990773&referer=brief_results. See also Lisa Fagin Davis's "The

Knollys Psalter," *Transylvania Treasures* 8, no. 2 (2016), http://www2.transy.edu/about/treasures.htm, and "Manuscript Road Trip: Knoxville, Nashville, and a Knollys," *Manuscript Road Trip* (blog), August 23, 2014, https://manuscriptroadtrip.wordpress.com/2014/08/23/manuscript-road-trip-knoxville-nashville-and-knollys/. I am grateful to B. J. Gooch of Transylvania University for her kind assistance with this manuscript.

FIVE. Relics and Unreliable Bodies in the Croxton *Play of the Sacrament*, *The Duchess of Malfi*, and *The Changeling*

1. The earliest extant printed account of the Cannobio miracle is published in the eighteenth-century *Relazione de' Miracoli Avvenuti nel borgo di Cannobio Sopra il Lago Maggiore, l'anno 1522* (Milan: Federico Bianchi, 1718), which is likely based on an earlier unrecovered *relazione*. The cited *Relazione* contains a representation of the miraculous image on page 5.

2. On the Mass of Bolsena and related Eucharistic miracles, see Rubin, *Corpus Christi*, 114–15. See also Steven Justice, "Did the Middle Ages Believe in Their Miracles?," *Representations* 103 (2008): 1–29, and "Eucharistic Miracle and Eucharistic Doubt," *Journal of Medieval and Early Modern Studies* 42, no. 2 (2012): 307–22.

3. Caroline Walker Bynum, *Christian Materiality: An Essay on Religion in Late Medieval Europe* (New York: Zone Books, 2011), 154. In their introduction to *The Body in Parts: Fantasies of Corporeality in Early Modern Europe*, David Hillman and Carla Mazzio argue that early modern formations of the body "are in many ways most powerfully encoded by the symbolics of any given part, where the tensions between the metaphoric and the metonymic, between the floating and the firmly contextualized, or more generally between conditions of autonomy and dependence are powerfully articulated" (xii–xiii). Despite their emphasis on bodily fragmentation, neither the editors nor the contributors to this volume consider the literary aspects of sacred relics. In a more recent study, *Relics and Writing in Late Medieval England* (Toronto: University of Toronto Press, 2013) Robyn Malo argues that relic discourse provides "an avenue for exploring the tenuous relationship between a metaphorical vehicle and its tenor—and the degree to which the vehicle might obscure, rather than illuminate, the tenor" (186).

4. As was the case in chapter 3, I prefer the term *orthodox* to *Catholic* when referring to the doctrine of transubstantiation in the context of the Croxton *Play of the Sacrament*. This is not to suggest that the two terms are synonymous, only that

the use of *Catholic* as a confessional marker is a sixteenth-century development and therefore postdates the play's performance context.

5. John Donne, "The Funeral," in *The Major Works*, ed. John Carey (Oxford: Oxford University Press, 2000), 130.

6. Peter Brown, *The Cult of the Saints: Its Rise and Function in Latin Christianity* (Chicago: University of Chicago Press, 1982), 88. The religious historiography of relics has been well documented by Bynum, *Christian Materiality*; Caroline Walker Bynum, *The Resurrection of the Body in Western Christianity, 200–1336* (New York: Columbia University Press, 1995); Patrick J. Geary, *Furta Sacra: Thefts of Relics in the Central Middle Ages* (Princeton, NJ: Princeton University Press, 1991); and G. J. C. Snoek, *Medieval Piety from Relics to the Eucharist: A Study of Mutual Interaction* (Leiden: Brill, 1995). See also Thomas, *Religion*; Ronald Finucane, *Miracles and Pilgrims: Popular Beliefs in Medieval England* (New York: Palgrave, 1995); John Dillenberger, *Images and Relics: Theological Perceptions and Visual Images in Sixteenth-Century Europe* (Oxford: Oxford University Press, 1999); and Sarah Stanbury, *The Visual Object of Desire in Late Medieval England* (Philadelphia: University of Pennsylvania Press, 2008). For readings of relics in early modern literary contexts, see Elizabeth Mazzola, *The Pathology of the English Renaissance: Sacred Remains and Holy Ghosts* (Leiden: Brill, 1998); Susan Zimmerman, *The Early Modern Corpse and Shakespeare's Theater* (Edinburgh: University of Edinburgh Press, 2007), 24–89; and Richard C. McCoy, "The Tragedy of the Handkerchief: Objects Sacred and Profane in Shakespeare's *Othello*," in *Medieval and Early Modern Devotional Objects in Global Perspective: Translations of the Sacred*, ed. Elizabeth Robertson and Jennifer Jahner (New York: Palgrave, 2011), 155–65.

7. C. S. Peirce, *Collected Papers, 1931–1958*, vol. 2, *Elements of Logic*, 143, quoted in Elam, *Semiotics of Theater*, 19.

8. Terence Hawkes, *Structuralism and Semiotics* (London: Methuen, 1977), 129.

9. From both psychoanalytic and anthropological perspectives, fetishes are objects that acquire power from something external to them. William Pietz, "The Problem of the Fetish, I," *Review of English Studies* 9 (Spring 1985): 5–17, argues, "The truth of the fetish resides in its status as a material embodiment; its truth is not that of the idol, for the idol's truth lies in its relation of iconic resemblance to some immaterial model or entity" (7). C. David Benson, "The Past, the Present, and the Future in Medieval Surveys of Roman Relics," in Robertson and Jahner, *Medieval and Early Modern Devotional Objects*, 115–34, further differentiates between secular ruins or remains and holy relics: "Instead of simply providing the impetus for the memory of former magnificence, relics grant tangible

rewards: the hope of eternal salvation rather than the melancholy recollection of ruin" (125). On trinkets and fetishes in the reformist imagination, see Kearney, *Incarnate Text*, chap. 4.

10. Thomas Aquinas, *Summa theologiae* [hereafter *ST*], III.76.1, rep. 2, ed. Mortensen and Alarcon, trans. Shapcote. All future citations are to this edition. Wycliffites charged that it was impossible for Christ to be fully contained in the host and the chalice: "Ye saye under the hoost of breade is the full manhode of Christe, then by youre owne confession muste it nedes be that we worshyppen a fallse god in the chalice" (*Wyclyfes Wyckett*, sig. Aviiir). The *Wicket* was not a text written by Wyclif himself but rather a later compilation that summarizes Wyclif's teachings on scripture and transubstantiation. As Alec Ryrie, *The Gospel and Henry VIII: Evangelicals in the Early English Reformation* (Cambridge: Cambridge University Press, 2003), notes, it was not printed until 1546 and it influenced such reformers as George Joye (235–37).

11. Richard Crashaw, "Lauda Sion Salvatorem: The Hymn for the Blessed Sacrament," in *The Complete Poetry of Richard Crashaw*, ed. George Walton Williams (Garden City, NY: Anchor Books, 1970), 183.

12. Bynum, *Resurrection of the Body*, 108.

13. Taking a different perspective, Malo argues that the late Middle Ages recognized "hierarchies of devotional objects," which "moved in descending order from large bodily relics to smaller objects and images" (*Relics and Writing*, 41). "In the context of relic discourse," she notes, "size matters," and "Not all relics were viewed equally—not every part was understood to be as good as the whole" (42).

14. Aston, "Corpus Christi," 44.

15. Aers, *Sanctifying Signs*, 11. Sarah Beckwith, "Ritual, Church, and Theater: The Croxton *Play of the Sacrament*," in Aers, *Culture and History*, 65–90, adds, "It is against the competing claims of other images, relics, and icons that the Church is anxious to assert the centrality of the eucharist—the only relic, after all, which doctrinally endorses clerical power and centralizes it, rather than diffusing it to popular or other control" (67).

16. Thomas Cranmer, *Defence*, sig. Miiir.

17. Ibid.

18. S. Gardiner, *Explication*, Div. Gardiner also says, "In the booke of commen prayer . . . It is ordred to teache the people, that in eche parte of the bread consecrate, broken, is the holy body of our Christ, which is christene to the Catholique doctrine" (*Explication*, sig Dvr). Gardiner refers to the rubrics of the 1549 edition, which say as much but are then removed from all subsequent editions. Cranmer answers the charge by transposing his use of *pars pro toto*

into a spiritual, as opposed to carnal, register: "And as for the Booke of common prayer . . . as in baptisme we receave the holy ghost, and put Christ upon us, as well if wee be christened in one dysh full of water taken out of the fonte, as if it were christened in the whole fonte, or river, so we be as truly fed, refreshed, and comforted by Christ receavyng a peece of bread at the Lords holy table, as if we dyd eat an whole loaf. For as in every part of the water, in baptisme is wholl Christ and the holy spirit, sacramentally, so be they in every part of the bread broken, but not corporally as the Papists teach" (*Answer*, sig. Gvi*r*).

19. R. Smith, *Assertion and Defence*, sig. Lviii*r*–Lviii*v*.

20. Elizabeth Williamson, *The Materiality of Religion in Early Modern English Drama* (Aldershot: Ashgate, 2009), 101. On the same point, see also Kenneth Fincham and Nicholas Tyacke, *Altars Restored: The Changing Face of English Religious Worship, 1547–1700* (Oxford: Oxford University Press, 2008). Wandel notes that at the turn of the eighth century separate reliquaries were constructed in which saints' remains would be housed along with fragments of the consecrated host (*Eucharist in the Reformation*, 27). For an account of the entombment and enshrinement of relics, see Malo, *Relics and Writing*, chaps. 1 and 2.

21. B. G. (Bernard Garter), *A newyeares gifte, dedicated to the Popes Holinesse, and all Catholikes addicted to the Sea of Rome* (London: Henry Bynneman, 1579), sig. Hii*r*. On the placement of relics in superaltars, see W. H. Sewell, "On Sealed Altar Slabs," in *Norfolk Archaeology: Or Miscellaneous Tracts Relating to the Antiquities of the County of Norfolk* (Norwich: Miller and Leavins, 1879), 87–118: "The super altar contained relics between the marble and its wooden or other base, and the portable altar contained relics within it" (100–101).

22. Garter, *Newyeares gifte*, sig. Hii*r*.

23. Ibid., sig. iiii*v*–iv*r*.

24. John Foxe, *A Sermon Preached at Paules Crosse the Friday before Easter, commonly called Goodfryday* (London: John Daye, 1570), sig. Aiii*v*.

25. Alexandra Walsham, "Skeletons in the Cupboard: Relics after the English Reformation," *Past and Present Supplements* 5 (2010): 141. Walsham surveys some key relics and their cults, including nails from the Crucifixion purportedly discovered by Joseph of Arimathea, blood relics of Thomas Becket, and the head of Thomas More.

26. Quoted in Eire, *War against the Idols*, 91.

27. William Tyndale, *An answere unto Sir Thomas Mores Dialoge* (Antwerp: S. Cock, 1531), sig. G*v*.

28. Titus Oates, *The Popes Ware-house, or the Merchandise of the Whore of Rome* (London: Tho. Parkhurst, Dorman Newman, Thomas Cockerill, and Tho. Simmons, 1679), sig. C2*r*. Commercial terms like *warehouse, merchandise, goods,*

trinkets, and *wares* were often used in reformist satires on relics, as evident in the anti-Laudian poem *Lambeth faire* (London: s.n., 1641), which details a rummage sale of Catholic goods. "Come, customers, see what you lack and buy, / Heres vestments consecrate, all sorts and sizes," proclaim the sellers. "Buy a crucifix, another loud doth call, / 'Twill scare the Devil and will preserve your soul" (sig. A2v–A3r). An equally forceful satire of relics appears in John Bale's *King Johan*, where the anti-Papist character Sedition offers the following catalog, the hyperbole of which drives its reformist charge:

> Here is first a bone of the blessed Trinity.
> A dram of the turd of sweet Saint Barbabas ...
> A maggot of Moses, with a fart of Saint Fandigo;
> Here is a fig leaf, and a grape of Noah's vineyard,
> A bead of Saint Blythe with the bracelet of a berewarde ...
> Besides other bones and relics many one.
> (1215–16, 1228–30)

The banality and vulgarity of these relics testify to the apparent absurdity with which Bale regards relics and their ties to material devotion. Happé provides a thorough gloss on these rather obscure saints, each of whom was associated in a particular way with relics (Bale, *Complete Plays*, ed. Happé, 1:123–24).

29. Quoted in Eire, *War against the Idols*, 96–97. In addition to these sixteenth-century reformers, earlier reformers repudiated relics with equal fervor. The Lollard Conclusions of 1394 state: "Pilgrimages, prayers, and offerings made to blind crosses or roods, and to deaf images of wood or stone, are pretty well akin to idolatry and far from alms. . . . We ask you, pilgrim, to tell us when you offer to the bones of saints placed in a shrine in any spot, whether you relieve the saint who is in joy, or that almshouse which is so well endowed and for which men have been canonized" (Bettenson and Maunder, *Documents*, 188).

30. Geoffrey Chaucer, *Canterbury Tales*, 6.347–49, in *The Riverside Chaucer*, ed. Larry D. Benson (Boston: Houghton Mifflin, 1987). The Host rebukes the Pardoner thus: "Thou woldest make me kisse thyn olde breech, / And swere it were a relyk of a seint, / Though it were with thy fundement depeint!" (6.948–50). On the Pardoner and relics, see Stanbury, *Visual Object of Desire*, 50–56; Malo, *Relics and Writing*, 125–47; Alastair Minnis, *Fallible Authors: Chaucer's Pardoner and the Wife of Bath* (Philadelphia: University of Pennsylvania Press, 2007); and Carolyn Dinshaw, *Chaucer's Sexual Poetics* (Madison: University of Wisconsin Press, 1989), 159–68.

31. John Calvin, *A very profitable treatise, made by M. Ihon Caluyne, declarynge what great profit might come to al christendome, yf there were a regester made of all sainctes bodies and other reliques* (London: Rouland Hall, 1561), sig. Aviir.

32. Jacques Derrida, *Of Grammatology*, trans. Gayatri Chakravorty Spivak (Baltimore: Johns Hopkins University Press, 1997), 145, italics in original.

33. Caesarius of Heisterbach, *The Dialogue of Miracles* (*Dialogus miraculorum*), 2 vols., trans. H. Von E. Scott and C. C. Swinton Bland (London: George Routledge and Sons, 1929), 2:71. On the miraculous transformation of false relics, see also Robert Bartlett, *Why Can the Dead Do Such Great Things? Saints and Worshippers from the Martyrs to the Reformation* (Princeton, NJ: Princeton University Press, 2013), 328–29.

34. Caesarius of Heisterbach, *Dialogue of Miracles*, trans. Scott and Bland, 2:72.

35. Ibid.

36. On contact relics, see Bynum, *Christian Materiality*, 131–39, and Bartlett, *Why Can the Dead*, 244–50. The Scottish loyalist John Barclay (1582–61) writes of contact relics in *Vindication of the Intercession of Saints, the Veneration of Relics, and Miracles against the Sectaries of the Times* (London: Mary Thompson, 1688): "We diligently and devoutly apply our Handkerchiefs and Garments to the Coffin, or Bier, in or on which these sacred bones are laid, that secret Blessings may flow upon us" (11).

37. Bynum reminds us that there were no actual blood or bone relics of Christ on the grounds that "Christ's whole body had already ascended into heaven, so no part could be left behind without threatening his perfection" (*Christian Materiality*, 155).

38. Calvin, *Very profitable treatise*, sig. Ciir–Ciiv.

39. Ibid., sig. Cvv.

40. Bynum, *Christian Materiality*, 154–55.

41. On the play's connections to East Anglia, which was a center for dramatic activity in the late Middle Ages, see Gibson, *Theater of Devotion*, 32–41. On the host miracles attributed to Aragon and Rome in the late fifteenth century, see John T. Sebastian's introduction to *The Croxton Play of the Sacrament*, ed. John T. Sebastian, TEAMS Middle English Texts Series (Kalamazoo, MI: Medieval Institute Publications, 2012), 65–68.

42. See Tamara Atkin, "Playbooks and Printed Drama: A Reassessment of the Dating and Layout of the Croxton *Play of the Sacrament*," *Review of English Studies*, n.s., 60, no. 244 (2008): 194–205, and Seth Lerer, "'Representyd Now in Yower Syght': The Culture of Spectatorship in Late-Fifteenth-Century England," in *Bodies and Disciplines: Intersections of Literature and History in Fifteenth-Century England*, ed. Barbara A. Hanawalt and David Wallace (Minneapolis: University of Minnesota Press, 1996), 29–62.

43. Beckwith, "Ritual, Church, and Theater," synthesizes many of these topics into a remarkably cogent reading of the play. On physical violence, see Ann

Eljenholm Nichols, "The Croxton Play: A Re-reading," *Comparative Drama* 22 (Summer 1988): 117–37; Jodi Enders, "Dramatic Memories and Tortured Spaces in the *Mystere de la Sainte Hostie*," in *Medieval Practices of Space*, ed. Barbara A. Hannawalt and Michal Kobialka (Minneapolis: University of Minnesota Press, 2000), 199–222; Enders, *Medieval Theater of Cruelty*; Victor Scherb, "Violence and the Social Body in the Croxton *Play of the Sacrament*," in *Violence and Drama*, ed. James Redmond (Cambridge: Cambridge University Press, 1991), 69–78; and Owens, *Stages of Dismemberment*, 48–49 and 70–77. The play's engagement with transubstantiation and theatricality has been noted by Beckwith, "Ritual, Church, and Theater"; David Lawton, "Sacrilege and Theatricality: The Croxton *Play of the Sacrament*," *Journal of Medieval and Early Modern Studies* 33, no. 2 (Spring 2003): 281–309; Atkin, *Drama of Reform*; Strohm, "Croxton *Play of the Sacrament*"; Greenblatt and Gallagher, "Wound in the Wall"; Cameron Hunt McNabb, "*Hocus Pocus* and the Croxton *Play of the Sacrament*," *Early Theatre* 17.2 (2014): 11–33; and Christina Fitzgerald, "Performance Anxiety and the Passion in the Croxton *Play of the Sacrament*," *Journal of Medieval and Early Modern Studies* 46.2 (2016): 315–37. On the play's relation to Lollardy, see Gibson, *Theater of Devotion*, 34–36; Cecilia Cutts, "The Croxton Play: An Anti-Lollard Piece," *Modern Language Quarterly* 50, no. 1 (1944): 45–60; and Michael Jones, "Theatrical History in the Croxton *Play of the Sacrament*," *ELH: English Literary History* 66, no. 2 (Summer 1999): 223–60. For pushback on the Lollard argument, see Hudson, *Premature Reformation*, 445. On the blood libel and anti-Semitism, see James Shapiro, *Shakespeare and the Jews* (New York: Columbia University Press, 1996), 89–112; Lawton, "Sacrilege and Theatricality," 289–97; Claire Sponsler and Robert Clark, "Othered Bodies: Racial Cross Dressing in the *Mistére de la Sainte Hostie* and the Croxton *Play of the Sacrament*," *Journal of Medieval and Early Modern Studies* 29, no. 1 (Winter 1999): 61–88; and Nisse, *Defining Acts*, chap. 5.

44. Beckwith, "Ritual, Church, and Theater," 68. On the host as prop, see Sofer, *Stage Life of Props*, chap. 1, and Atkin, *Drama of Reform*, chap. 1; on the host as object, see C. J. Gordon, "Bread God, Blood God: Wonderhosts and Early Encounters with Secularization," *Genre* 44, no. 2 (Summer 2011): 105–28.

45. Sebastian, *Croxton Play of the Sacrament*, 16.

46. Simpson, *Reform and Cultural Revolution*, 557.

47. *Croxton Play of the Sacrament*, ed. Sebastian, lines 38 and 45. All future references are to this edition and will be cited parenthetically by line number.

48. *Merchandise* was a common pejorative used by reformers. In his *Apologie of the Church of England*, John Jewel rejects "the Marchaundyses and open saales of masses, and the bearing up and downe and worshiping of bread" as "abuses of the Lords supper" that are analogous to the idolatry of pagans. He says that Papists "doe not onely sette forth to the people the sacramental breade

to be worshypped with godly honoure, but also thei carry it about upon an ambelinge horse, where so ever thei ride themselves, as in times past the Persians did fier, and the Egyptians the relikes of Isis" (sig. Diiii*r*). Likewise, in a preface to his translation of Jean Calvin's *A faythful and moost Godlye treatyse concernynge the most sacret sacrament of the blessed body and bloude of oure sauioure Christe* (London: John Daye and William Seres, 1548[?]), Miles Coverdale describes how Catholics treat the host in similar manner: "Therefore to hoyse it over theyr heads, to daunce it over the cuppe, to carye it in the stretes, with a great pompe and glorye, to bowe theyr knees and to knocke theyr breastes before it, and to locke it up in a pix to have it ready to serve at all hours, all such chapmen as shal call for it: is but a polytyke caste of the marchayntes whyche displeye and set abrode to be sene such marchaundyse as thay would faynest sel" (sig. Avii*r*–Avii*v*).

49. Malo discusses how "material treasure was supposed to affirm the spiritual value of authentic relics" but also notes that Guibert of Nogent and others rejected such opulence (*Relics and Writing*, 7, 49–52).

50. For readings of the play in an economic context, see Lawton, "Sacrilege and Theatricality," 299; Parker, *Aesthetics of Antichrist*, 126–35; Derek Higgenbotham, "Impersonators in the Market: Merchants and the Premodern Nation in the Croxton *Play of the Sacrament*," *Exemplaria* 19, no. 1 (Spring 2007): 163–82; and Alexandra Reid-Schwartz, "Economies of Salvation: Commerce and the Eucharist in *The Profanation of the Host* and the Croxton *Play of the Sacrament*," *Comitatus: A Journal of Medieval and Renaissance Studies* 25, no. 1 (1994): 1–20.

51. In the fifteenth and sixteenth centuries, *cake* refers to any small piece of baked bread and not necessarily to a sweet confection as modern usage suggests. Cf. *OED*, "Cake" (n.), 1a.

52. "Alle ye moven," quoted in David Williams, "'Lo How I Vanysshe': The Pardoner's War against Signs," in *Chaucer and Language: Essays in Honor of Douglas Wurtele*, ed. Robert Myles and David A. Williams (Quebec: McGill-Queens University Press, 2001), 220n53.

53. Other references include "smyte ye in the myddys of the cake" (457), "bryng that ylke cake here" (495), "fast fetche hether that ylke cake" (700), and "The cake I have cawght here" (705). Such anti-Catholic repudiations of the host persist into the sixteenth century. In his answer to Bishop Bonner, for example, John Bale charges that Catholic priests "saye to the people, that there white coloured Cake, is their maker, their redeemer, their savior" (*Declaration*, sig Ivi*v*). A century later, Thomas Tuke derides the fetishization of the consecrated host in similar terms: "Priests make their maker Christ, yee must not doubt, / They eat, drink, box him up, and beare about . . . / They eat him whole: whole they suppe; / Whole i'th'cake, and whole i'th'cuppe" (*Concerning the Holy Eucharist*, sig. A3r).

54. Cf. Wycliffite rejections of images: "Dere Lord! What almes is it to peynte gayly dede stones and rotun stokkis with sich almes that is por mennus good and lyfelode?" (quoted in Hudson, *Selections*, 85). For a discussion of Wycliffite rejections of relics and images in the name of repurposing such wealth for the care of the poor, see Malo, *Relics and Writing*, chap. 5.

55. On the play's staging, see Elisabeth Dutton, "The Croxton *Play of the Sacrament*," in Betteridge and Walker, *Oxford Handbook*, 55–71; and Donalee Dox, "Theatrical Space, Mutable Space, and the Space of Imagination: Three Readings of the Croxton *Play of the Sacrament*," in Hanawalt and Kobialka, *Medieval Practices of Space*, 167–98.

56. On host desecration narratives in anti-Jewish literature, see Miri Rubin, *Gentile Tales: The Narrative Assault on Late Medieval Jews* (Philadelphia: University of Pennsylvania Press, 2004). Cf. Sebastian, *Croxton*, 7–10.

57. Aers, *Sanctifying Signs*, 20; Cutts, "Croxton."

58. John Wyclif, *Prima Confessio Wyclyf de Sacramento*, in Hudson, *Selections*, 17.

59. Aquinas reconciles the gap between visible matter and invisible substance to a matter of faith. "There is no deception in the sacrament," he says, "for the accidents which are discerned by the senses are truly present. But the intellect, whose proper object is substance . . . is preserved by faith from deception" (*ST* III.75.5., rep. 2). Aers analyzes this argument in *Sanctifying Signs*, 21–23.

60. Parker, *Aesthetics of Antichrist*, 131; italics in original.

61. In this scene Christ also illustrates the *Christus medicus* topos, common to late medieval devotion, as he resets Jonathas's dismembered arm, something the quack doctor Brundyche cannot accomplish. On the *Christus medicus* topos, see Scherb, *Staging Faith*, 75–76, and Atkin, *Drama of Reform*, 27–30.

62. Gibson, *Theater of Devotion*, 40.

63. On the composition of *O sacrum convivium*, see Rubin, *Corpus Christi*, 191–92.

64. *A Manual of Prayers* (ca. 1685), Folger Shakespeare Library, MS V.a.488, fol. 38r.

65. Gibson reads this line as a probable reference to the Guild of the Holy Name of Jesus, an influential college of priests and lay members in Bury St. Edmund's (*Theater of Devotion*, 38–40).

66. Beckwith, *Signifying God*, 142–43.

67. Johnston and Rogerson, *Records of Early English Drama: York*, 2:735.

68. Ibid., 2:858–59.

69. The term *waxworks* was first used by Inga-Stina Ekeblad, "The 'Impure Art' of John Webster," *Review of English Studies* 9, no. 35 (1958): 253–67, who dismissed the scene as "a horror-show" with "no other function than Madame

Toussauds" (253–54). More recently, Margaret Owens, "John Webster, Toussaud Laureate: The Waxworks in *The Duchess of Malfi*," *ELH: English Literary History* 79, no. 4 (Winter 2012): 851–77, and David Bergeron, "The Wax Figures in *The Duchess of Malfi*," *SEL: Studies in English Literature* 18, no. 2 (1978): 331–39, have offered fresh interpretations in the context of monuments, funerary effigies, and sculptures. See also Brian Chalk, "Webster's 'Worthyest Monument': The Problem of Posterity in *The Duchess of Malfi*," *Studies in Philology* 108, no. 3 (Summer 2011): 379–402; Michael Neill, "Monuments and Ruins as Symbols in *The Duchess of Malfi*," in *Drama and Symbolism*, ed. James Redmond (Cambridge: Cambridge University Press, 1982): 71–87; and Lynn Maxwell, "Wax Magic and *The Duchess of Malfi*," *Journal of Early Modern Cultural Studies* 14, no. 3 (Summer 2014): 31–54.

70. John Webster, *The Duchess of Malfi*, 3.2.135–38, ed. Leah S. Marcus (London: Methuen Drama, 2009). All references are to this edition and will be cited parenthetically by act, scene, and line number. Webster uses the term *relic* in the dedicatory epistle to *The Duchess of Malfi*, written to a would-be patron, George Harding. He also uses it in *A Monumentall Column* (London: N. O, 1613), written upon the death of Prince Henry, the heir apparent to James I. He says of the deceased prince, Slander "shall never dare / To approach his Tombe, be she confined as farre / From his sweete reliques as is heaven from hell" (sig. B4v).

71. On reliquaries, see Malo, *Relics and Writing*, 7–9, 47–56; Bartlett, *Why Can the Dead*, 272–82; Cynthia Hahn, *Strange Beauty: Issues in the Making and Meaning of Reliquaries, 400–ca. 1204* (College Park: Pennsylvania State University Press, 2013); and Seeta Chaganti, *The Medieval Poetics of the Reliquary: Enshrinement, Inscription, Performance* (New York: Palgrave Macmillan, 2008).

72. Thomas Rist, *Revenge Tragedy and the Drama of Commemoration in Reforming England* (Aldershot: Ashgate, 2008), 136–37, reads the passage as a rejection of Catholicism. For additional anti-Catholic interpretations, see Diehl, *Staging Reform*, 182–212, and Owens, "John Webster," 863–64. For a more nuanced reading of religion in the play, see Williamson, *Materiality of Religion*, 54–61. The Duchess also uses the relic to assert her sexual will in the face of patriarchy, and such assertions have shaped a number of feminist readings of the play, including Wendy Wall, "Just a Spoonful of Sugar: Syrup and Domesticity in Early Modern England," *Modern Philology* 104, no. 2 (2011): 149–72; Theodora A. Jankowski, "Defining/Confining the Duchess: Negotiating the Female Body in John Webster's *The Duchess of Malfi*," *Studies in Philology* 87, no. 2 (Spring 1990): 221–45; Catherine Belsey, "Emblem and Antithesis in *The Duchess of Malfi*," *Renaissance Drama*, n.s., 11 (1980): 115–34; and Maurizio Calbi, *Approximate Bodies: Gender and Power in Early Modern Drama and Anatomy* (London: Routledge, 2005), chap. 1.

73. Incidentally, one of the Duchess's brothers is a cardinal and would have some authority over the cult of relics as decreed in the Council of Trent: "Not any new miracles [are] to be accepted, or new relics recognized, without the bishop similarly examining and approving them. And as soon as he learns of something of this kind, he should consult with theologians and other devout men and decide as truth and devotion suggests" (Session 25, December 3–4, 1563, in Tanner, *Decrees*, 2:776).

74. The description of the Virtuous Widow is original to Overbury. On Webster's additions to Overbury, who died in 1613, see Marcus's introduction to Webster, *Duchess of Malfi*, 5.

75. Thomas Overbury, *Characters, or witty descriptionns of the properties of sundry persons* (London: Edward Griffin, 1616), sig. L3r–v.

76. OED, "relict" (n.), 1a. I am grateful to Gail Gibson for this suggestion.

77. Malo, *Relics and Writing*, 185.

78. Katherine Rowe, *Dead Hands: Fictions of Agency, Renaissance to Modern* (Stanford, CA: Stanford University Press, 2000), reads this scene in terms of the "Hand of Glory," which "evokes the manufacture of false relics and the corrupted interests they serve" (101). Though he does not discuss the hand in the context of relics, see Albert Tricomi, "Historicizing the Imagery of the Demonic in *The Duchess of Malfi*," *Journal of Medieval and Early Modern Studies* 34, no. 2 (Spring 2004): 345–82, and Albert Tricomi, "The Severed Hand in Webster's *The Duchess of Malfi*," *SEL: Studies in English Litearture* 44, no. 2 (Spring 2004): 347–58.

79. On the scene as a parody of marriage, see Belsey, "Emblem and Antithesis," and Frank Whigham, *Seizures of the Will in English Renaissance Drama* (Cambridge: Cambridge University Press, 1996). Marcus notes that the ring is meant to be the same one given by the Duchess to Antonio in act 1 and then surrendered to the Cardinal during her excommunication (*Duchess of Malfi*, 261).

80. Sheetal Lodhia, "'The House Is Hers, the Soul Is But a Tenant': Material Self-Fashioning and Revenge Tragedy," *Early Theatre* 12, no. 2 (2009): 135–61, is right to suggest that "when Ferdinand reveals the wax figures to the Duchess, both the play in production and the play as a reader's text must be considered," in that the revenge plot "is contingent on the Duchess's inability to distinguish between the wax figures and real people" (152). Huston Diehl also states, "What [the Duchess] gazes upon is itself only a picture fashioned out of wax, and its power to harm her lies in its capacity to deceive her into confusing the representation for the reality" (*Staging Reform*, 197).

81. Marcus, *Duchess of Malfi*, 262. On the staging, see Owens, "John Webster," 861, and Zimmerman, *Early Modern Corpse*, 149.

82. False relics, says Rowe, "pervert[] the actual synecdoche, *pars pro toto*, inherent in a true relic" (*Dead Hands*, 101). Such forgery and perversion were

cited in the decrees of the Fourth Lateran Council (1215), where it was stated that "prelates... should not in future allow those who come to their churches, in order to venerate, to be deceived by lying stories or false documents, as has commonly happened in many places on account of the desire for profit" (Fourth Lateran Council, Constitution 62, in Tanner, *Decrees*, 1:263).

83. John Frith, *Boke answeringe unto M. Mores lettur* (Munster [Antwerp]: Conrade Willems [i.e., H. Peetersen van Middelburch?], 1533), sig. G1r.

84. Richard Smith, *A Defence of the sacrifice of the Masse* (London: John Herforde, 1546), sig. Giv.

85. Edmund Gurnay, *Corpus Christi*, sig. A4r.

86. Diehl, *Staging Reform*, 184.

87. *Liber Eliensis (The Book of Ely)*, ed. and trans. Janet Fairweather (Woodbridge: Boydell and Brewer, 2005), 163.

88. Ibid.

89. Calvin, *Very profitable treatise*, sig. Br–Bv.

90. Ibid., sig. Aviiiv. For similar warnings against false relics in the High Middle Ages, see Malo, *Relics and Writing*, 50–52, and for the Reformation context see Walsham, "Skeletons in the Cupboard."

91. The Duchess fits within the literary and religious discourses of martyrology as described by Alice Dailey, who notes that physical pain often fails to kill the martyr, with figures like St. Laurence and St. Christina repeatedly surviving even the most abhorrent of punishments (*English Martyr*, 14–42).

92. Seven of the ten echoes are identical in form, content, and register: "Like death that we have" (5.3.19), "Deadly accent" (5.3.21), "A thing of sorrow" (5.3.24), "That suits it best" (5.3.25), "Do not" (5.3.29), "Be mindful of thy safety" (5.3.31), "Thou art a dead thing" (5.3.38). Two others—"I, wife's voice" (5.3.26) and "Oh, fly your fate" (5.3.34)—change the content, and one—"Thou art a dead thing" (5.3.38)—changes Antonio's question into a statement.

93. Bynum, *Fragmentation and Redemption*, 85.

94. Belsey, "Emblem and Antithesis," 133. Neill sees the voice as "an echo of the Duchess's voice sounding defiantly over the ruins of time," one consonant with the "Triumph of Fame through Fame's agent, Poetry" ("Monuments and Ruins," 73).

95. *ST* III.5.72, rep. 3.

96. For readings of embodiment in the context of anatomy and gender, see Calbi, *Approximate Bodies*, esp. chap. 2; Deborah Burks, "'I'll Want My Will Else': *The Changeling* and Women's Complicity with Their Rapists," *ELH: English Literary History* 62, no. 4 (1995): 759–90; Sara Eaton, "Beatrice-Joanna and the Rhetoric of Love in *The Changeling*," *Theatre Journal* 36, no. 3 (October 1984):

371–82; Christina Malcolmson, "'As Tame as the Ladies': Politics and Gender in *The Changeling*," *English Literary Renaissance* 20, no. 2 (1990): 320–39; Michael Neill, "Hidden Malady: Death, Discovery, and Indistinction in *The Changeling*," *Renaissance Drama*, n.s., 22 (1991): 95–121; Judith Haber, "'I(t) Could Not Choose but Follow': Erotic Logic in *The Changeling*," *Representations* 81 (2003): 79–98; Marjorie Garber, "The Insincerity of Women," in *Desire and the Renaissance: Psychoanalysis and Literature*, ed. Valeria Finnuci and Regina Schwartz (Princeton, NJ: Princeton University Press, 1994), 19–38; Naomi Liebler, "A Woman Dipped in Blood: The Violent Femmes of *The Maid's Tragedy* and *The Changeling*," in *Women and Violence in English Renaissance Literature*, ed. Linda Woodbridge and Sharon Beehler (Tempe, AZ: Medieval and Renaissance Texts and Studies, 2003), 361–78; and Gail Kern Paster, "The Ecology of the Passions in *A Chaste Maid in Cheapside* and *The Changeling*," in *The Oxford Handbook to Thomas Middleton*, ed. Gary Taylor and Trish Thomas Henley (Oxford: Oxford University Press, 2012), 148–63.

97. The play's "madhouse" subplot, attributed to Rowley, lies outside the scope of this chapter. While it is rife with idioms of physical fragmentation, it does not cast them in terms of relics. I also want to note that *The Changeling* has not been a stranger to religious issues. A recurring topic in the criticism on the play is the religious and political anxiety of the "Spanish Match"—the marriage of Prince Charles to the Spanish Infanta—that Middleton addresses in *A Game at Chess* (1624). This union was unpopular because it brought the prospect of a Catholic queen even as it promised better political and economic relations between England and Spain. See A. A. Bromham and Zara Bruzzi, *The Changeling and the Years of Crisis, 1619–1624: A Hieroglyph of Britain* (London: Pinter, 1990). In the introduction to the play in Thomas Middleton, *The Complete Works*, ed. Gary Taylor and John Lavagnino (Oxford: Oxford University Press, 2008), Annabel Patterson qualifies Bromham and Bruzzi's position by citing "ethical undecidability" as preferable to political allegory. "The most that can be argued from this collage of internal signposts and stage historical details," she argues, "is that *The Changeling* permitted its original audiences to intuit a connection between Spanish/Catholic interests, crimes of violence, and sexuality out of control" (1635).

98. Thomas Middleton and William Rowley, *The Changeling*, 1.1.1, ed. Michael Neill (London: New Mermaids, 2006). All future references are to this edition and will be cited parenthetically by act, scene, and line number.

99. Laura Gowing, *Common Bodies: Women, Touch, and Power in the English Renaissance* (New Haven, CT: Yale University Press, 2003), 53.

100. Thomas More, *A dyaloge of syr Thomas More knyghte: one of the counsayll of oure souerayne lorde the kyng [and] chauncellour of hys duchy of Lancaster.*

Wherin be treated dyuers maters, as of the veneration [and] worshyp of ymages [and] relyques, prayng to sayntys, [and] goyng o[n] pylgrymage (London: J. Rastell, 1529), sig. Hiiiv. On saintly friendship, see Janel Mueller, "The Saints," in Cummings and Simpson, *Cultural Reformations*, 166–87.

101. The exchange between DeFlores and Beatrice-Joanna inverts the conventional interplay between pilgrim and saint in a devotional context. In a dramatic context, moreover, it likewise reverses the scene between Romeo and Juliet in which Romeo memorably compares his lips to the hands of pilgrims: "My lips, two blushing pilgrims, ready stand / To smooth that rough touch with a tender kiss." Juliet replies coyly, "Good pilgrim, you do wrong your hand too much, / Which mannerly devotion shows in this; / For saints have hands that pilgrims' hands do touch, / And palm to palm is holy palmers' kiss." *Romeo and Juliet*, 1.5.90–107, in *Norton Shakespeare*. Unlike Beatrice-Joanna, Juliet accepts the worship and requites the gesture.

102. Peter Stallybrass and Ann Rosalind Jones, "Fetishizing the Glove in Renaissance Europe," *Critical Inquiry* 28, no. 1 (Autumn, 2001): 127–28.

103. On the role of touch as physical sensation in the play, see Patricia Cahill, "The Play of Skin in *The Changeling*," *postmedieval: a journal of medieval cultural studies* 3 (2012): 391–406.

104. George Puttenham, *The Art of English Poesy*, ed. Frank Whigham and Wayne E. Rebhorn (Ithaca, NY: Cornell University Press, 2009), aptly calls metonymy "the Misnamer": "You take . . . the thing containing for that which is contained, and in many other cases do, as it were, wrong name the person or the thing" (265–66). The idea that the glove stands in for the hand and the hand for the body recalls the idea of giving and taking one's "hand" in marriage, which also renders the encounter between DeFlores and Beatrice-Joanna as an inverted marriage ritual.

105. On the materiality of *spiritus* in early modern physiology, see Gail Kern Paster, *Humoring the Body: Emotions and the Shakespearean Stage* (Chicago: University of Chicago Press, 2004), and Bruce R. Smith, "Mona Lisa Takes a Tike, Hamlet Goes for an Ocean Dip," in *Center or Margin: Essays in Honor of J. Leeds Barroll*, ed. Lena Cowen Orlin (Cranbury, NJ: Associated University Press, 2006), 238–53.

106. Stallybrass and Jones, "Fetishizing the Glove," 127.

107. Quoted in Hudson, *Selections*, 84.

108. Tyndale, *Answer*, sig. E3v. It is also worth noting that some of the same idioms were used by those such as Thomas More, who defended relics, to characterize the reformers: "Now [they] neyther crepe to the crosse, nor set by any halowed thynge, dispute pylgrymages, and set holy sayntes at nought, no more

reverence their images than a horse of wax, nor reken theyr relykes any better than shepys bones" (More, *Answer*, bk. 4, sig. Fviiv).

109. Tyndale, *Answer*, sig. G2v.

110. Calvin, *Very profitable treatise*, sig. Avr–Avv.

111. *The Royal Injunctions*, 1536, 1538, in Bettenson and Maunder, *Documents*, 246–48.

112. Council of Trent (1563), Session 25, "On Invocation, Veneration and Relics of the Saints, and on Sacred Images" (Tanner, *Decrees*, 2:776–77).

113. The connection between ring and flesh has been written about by Bynum in the context of religious mysticism: "When Catherine of Siena spoke of the foreskin of Christ, as a wedding ring, she associated that piece of bleeding flesh with the Eucharistic host and saw herself appropriating the pain of Christ" (*Fragmentation and Redemption*, 86).

114. Calbi, *Approximate Bodies*, 53.

115. I offer a longer reading of the chastity test in Jay Zysk, "Relics and Unreliable Bodies in *The Changeling*," *English Literary Renaissance* 45, no. 3 (Autumn 2015): 417–19. On the metatheatricality of the chastity test, see Garber, "Insincerity of Women," and Paster, *Body Embarrassed*, 99–101.

116. William Shakespeare, *Love's Labour's Lost*, 5.2.894, 902, in *Norton Shakespeare*.

117. O'Connell, *Idolatrous Eye*, 58.

six. Conjured to Remembrance

1. *Incredulity of Thomas*, lines 175–78, in *York Plays*, ed. Beadle, vol. 1. All future citations to the York plays are to this edition and volume and will be given parenthetically by line number.

2. The Emmaus story is recorded biblically in Luke 24:13–35, and parts of the story including the Doubting Thomas episode are also referenced in the Gospel of John and the Acts of the Apostles.

3. Luke 24:30–32, in *Holy Bible Faithfully Translated* (Douay: John Cousturier, 1635).

4. On the liturgical trope of the *peregrini*, see Chambers, *Mediaeval Stage*, 2:36–40, and Karl Young, *Drama of the Medieval Church*, 2 vols. (Oxford: Oxford University Press, 1933), 1:451–89. For an overview of *quem quaeritis* as a dramatic form, see Bevington, *Medieval Drama*, 3–8; 21–24; Chambers, *Mediaeval Stage*, 2:1–36; and Young, *Drama*, 1:201–491. Richard Beadle describes the dramatic pageant as a "recognition scene" as well as "an encounter between pilgrims,

as it were on the road to a shrine, with the role of the disciples understood in spiritual terms: they are still on a journey or quest, not fully enlightened as to the significance of the momentous events of the previous days" (*York Plays*, 2:387).

5. On the drama of the sepulcher, see Young, *Drama*, 112–48; Pamela Sheingorn, *The Easter Sepulchre in England* (Kalamazoo, MI: Medieval Institute Publications, 1987); Duffy, *Stripping of the Altars*, 29–35; and Beckwith, *Signifying God*, 76–83.

6. On sixteenth-century Resurrection plays, see Alexandra F. Johnston, "The Emerging Pattern of the English Resurrection Play," *Medieval English Theatre* 20 (1998): 3–23, and Karen Sawyer Marsalek, "'Awake Your Faith': English Resurrection Drama and *The Winter's Tale*," in *Bring Furth the Pagants: Essays in Early English Drama Presented to Alexandra F. Johnston*, ed. David Klausner and Karen Sawyer Marsalek (Toronto: University of Toronto Press, 2007), 271–91.

7. On the staging of the liturgical trope, Karl Young says: "We can only surmise that the meal is enacted at a table in front of the altar. The rubric '*dividit Dominus hostiam inter illos*' shows that during the supper Christ distributes a wafer among those present. It has been suggested that this wafer is a consecrated host from Holy Thursday, previously used in the *depositio* on Good Friday and in an *elevation* early Easter morning" (*Drama*, 1:455). Young concludes that such hosts would have already been used at an early Easter Mass, making it more likely that the Emmaus host would be unconsecrated. In the York cycle, Beadle states, "[Christ's] nature is implicitly disclosed by his assuming the role of host at table, and in his eucharistic gestures of blessing, breaking, and distributing bread in a manner reminiscent of the Last Supper" (*York Plays*, 2:387). See also King, *York Mystery Cycle*, 164–65.

8. Beckwith, *Signifying God*, 88.

9. Coletti, *Mary Magdalene*, 204.

10. Bishop, *Shakespeare and the Theater*, 57–58.

11. Chester *Emmaus*, lines 37–38, in *Chester Mystery Cycle*, ed. Lumiansky and Mills. All future citations to the Chester plays are to this edition and will be given parenthetically by line number.

12. N-Town *Cleophas and Luke*, lines 49–50, in *N-Town Plays*, ed. Sugano. All future citations to N-Town plays are to this edition and will be given parenthetically by line number.

13. Beckwith, *Signifying God*, 89.

14. Towneley *Peregrini*, fol. 109r, in *Towneley Cycle*, ed. Cawley and Ellis. All future citations to the Towneley plays are to this edition and will be given parenthetically by folio number.

15. Coletti and Gibson, "Tudor Origins," 232.

16. de Lubac, *Corpus Mysticum*, 69.

17. *N-Town*'s emphasis on typological reading may distinguish it from the York cycle and the Towneley plays. James Simpson notes, "Chester and the N-Town plays are much more clearly aligned with an academic and clerical posture of lay instruction. This is evident not only in their very explicit teaching on the sacraments, but also in their much more consistently underlined typology" (*Reform and Cultural Revolution*, 534). On Chester's attention to biblical typology, see Coletti and Gibson, "Tudor Origins," 231–32, and Travis, *Dramatic Design*, 79–80; on typology in the plays generally, see Kolve, *Play Called Corpus Christi*, 57–100. Typological readings of the Eucharist went back to patristic writers like Origen and Cyprian; they were also included in Peter Lombard's distinctions on the sacrament in his *Sententiae*; and they are the subject of William Tyndale's *Briefe Declaration*, where Tyndale reads circumcision as an Old Testament prefiguration of baptism and also the Hebrew Passover or "Pesah" as "a very prophesy of the passion of christ, describing the very maner & facyon of hys death, and the effect and virtue thereof also, in whose steade is the sacrament of the body and bloude of Chryst commen as baptesme in the roume or stead of the cyrcumcyson" (sig. Aviiiv).

18. *The Resurrection of Our Lorde* (ca. 1530–60), Folger MS V.b.192, fol. 47. All future citations will be given parenthetically by folio number. For modern editions, see *The Resurrection of Our Lorde*, ed. J. Dover Wilson and Bertram Dobell (Oxford: Oxford University Press, 1912), and Karen Sawyer Marsalek, "*The Resurrection of Our Lord*: A Study and Dual-Text Edition" (PhD diss., University of Toronto, 2001), which includes an extensive and erudite introduction. In a more recent essay, Marsalek provides a hypothetical model for what the complete play (now lost) might have looked like ("'Doctrine Evangelicall' and Erasmus's *Paraphrases* in *The Resurrection of Our Lord*," in Kermode, Scott-Warren, and van Elk, *Tudor Drama before Shakespeare*, 57–58). Wilson and Dobell tentatively suggest John Bale as a potential author. Paul Whitfield White does not discount the possibility but also notes the play's dependence on William Tyndale's New Testament. He notes that the play's "harsh criticism of those authorities who oppose Bible reading . . . suggests that the play, or at least this version of it, dates from around the time of Cromwell's 1536 and 1538 Injunctions, when the order for a Bible to be placed in every parish church throughout the realm provoked vehement protest from religious conservatives" ("Reforming Mysteries' End," 132). The play's attention to spiritual versus carnal interpretation may also suggest a later date of composition, perhaps Edwardian, which would align it with the spiritual hermeneutics expressed by Thomas Cranmer in his *Defence*.

19. Marsalek discusses various details of the play's performance, including possible venues ranging from a royal chapel script to closet drama ("'Doctrine Evangelicall,'" 54–57).

20. On Appendix as expositor, see Marsalek, "*Resurrection of Our Lord*," 117–20, and O'Connell, *Idolatrous Eye*, 98–99; on Appendix's relation specifically to Chester's Expositor, see K. Janet Ritch, "The Role of the Presenter in Medieval Drama," in Klausner and Marsalek, *Bring Furth the Pagants*, 241–43.

21. I am grateful to Gail Gibson for helping me think through this point.

22. Whereas I situate the play in the context of Cranmer's Eucharistic theology, which allows for a greater dynamic between body and spirit as well as retains a notion of Eucharistic presence, Marsalek, by contrast, argues for a dominantly Zwinglian reading of the play's Eucharistic material, one in which "Christ reemphasizes the memorial nature of the sacrament" ("'Doctrine Evangelicall,'" 49). Though Marsalek rightly identifies strands of Zwingli's theology in the speeches by Appendix and Christ, she tends to equate "spiritual" almost exclusively with "memorial," concluding that "Christ's speech on the road to Emmaus replaces the corporeal understanding of the sacrament with a doctrine of spiritual and memorial presence" ("'Doctrine Evangelicall,'" 50–51). Marsalek elaborates the connections with Zwingli's Eucharistic theology in "*Resurrection of Our Lord*," 133–39.

23. S. Gardiner, *Explication and Assertion*, sig. Oviiiv. FitzPatrick notes that Aquinas uses the Emmaus story to explain transubstantiation and that such a connection was picked up again in the seventeenth and eighteenth centuries (*In Breaking of Bread*, 223).

24. Cranmer, *Defence*, sig. Fiir.

25. Ibid., sig. Biiiiv.

26. Such a claim is consistent with Marsalek's characterization of the play as "an evangelical answer to the traditional Easter liturgical drama" ("'Doctrine Evangelicall,'" 57).

27. In the Douay-Rheims (1635) annotations to Luke 24:30 (where Christ takes bread, breaks it, and blesses it), it is stated, "The Fathers in divers places take this to be meant of the B. Sacrament. . . . And that if it should be meant of the holy Sacrament, the forme of solemne taking the bread into his hands, blessing it, breaking it, and reaching it to his disciples (exceeding proper to the consecration, and common to none other vulgar benediction, nor any where used but in Christs miraculous multiplying the loaves), and the singular effect in notifying Christ unto them, do prove" (213). While the liturgical movement parallels the consecration and the Mass, it also recalls the Eucharist of the early church, in which the Christians performed the ritual of the Last Supper in community and in their homes. See Aers, *Sanctifying Signs*, 57–58.

28. Beckwith, *Signifying God*, 86.

29. Writing in the context of his own controversy with George Joye over John 6, Thomas More speaks to the work required for belief: "Cryste here for the

gettynge of that spyrituall meate, setteth them about a spyrituall wurke / bydynge them labour to byleve. Why is it any labour to byleve? Ye verily good readers to byleve wel is no litell work / and so greate a wurke, that no man can do it of his owne strength without the specyall helpe of god" (*Answer*, sig. D3r–D3v).

30. Rowan Williams relates Christ's vanishing at Emmaus to the Eucharist: "The Eucharist—apart from its actual penitential episodes—identifies the worshipers with the unfaithful disciples at table with Jesus, and enacts (again in muted and barely visible form in much of our liturgical practice) a breaking which is seen as signifying the 'cost' to God of our restoration to wholeness, and so, obliquely, the moment of our own loss of God (the loss of a God whose power answers to our perceived needs and definitions)" (*On Christian Theology*, 10).

31. On visual reception, see Duffy, *Stripping of the Altars*, 91–116.

32. Aers, *Sanctifying Signs*, 32.

33. John Jewel, *A sermon pronounced by the Byshop of Salisburie at Paules Crosse the second sondaye before Ester in the yere of our Lord, 1560. Wherupon D. Cole first sought occasion to encounter, shortly setforthe as nere as the author could call it to remembrance* (London: John Daye, 1560), sig. Fir.

34. Ibid., sig. Hvr–Hvv.

35. In N-Town and Chester, the Doubting Thomas episode is included as part of the Emmaus play; in York and Towneley, the episode is presented independently in a subsequent play.

36. Hooker, *Of the Lawes*, 5.67, sig. Q4v.

37. *Homilie of the worthie receyvyng*, sig. Cciiiiir.

38. On Udall's authorship, see Marie Axton's introduction to *Three Tudor Interludes*, ed. Marie Axton (Suffolk: Boydell and Brewer, 1982); White, *Theatre and Reformation*; and Grantley, *English Dramatic Interludes*, 154–55. The dating of the play, like its authorship, is subject to critical debate. Axton and Grantley agree that the play was entered in the Stationer's Register between 1562 and 1563, and White suggests a performance date of 1555. Tamara Atkin argues for an Edwardian date based on the play's appropriation of Cranmerian theology (*Drama of Reform*, 135–46), and Bevington argues that the Epilogue was an Elizabethan interpolation (*Tudor Drama and Politics*, 126).

39. White, *Theatre and Reformation*, 125–27. White also notes that the actor playing Jack Juggler may have donned a clerical surplice for the role, as depicted on the title page of the 1562 quarto. For an excellent appraisal of Udall's religious moderation in *Ralph Roister Doister* and *Respublica*, see Brokaw, *Staging Harmony*, 86–121.

40. *Jack Juggler*, in *Three Tudor Interludes*, ed. Axton, 118, 127. All future citations are to this edition and will be given parenthetically by line number. While the play's Plautine sources and conventions have been duly noted, the term *requite* also

recalls the Chaucerian *fabliaux* in which farcical plots of disguise and mistaken identity were executed in the name of retribution, usually for cuckoldry.

41. White uses the phrase "educational drama" (*Theatre and Reformation*, 125), and Anne Lancashire refers to *Jack Juggler* as "a children's piece" intended for performance in the grammar schools (*London Civic Theatre*, 114).

42. Kent Cartwright, *Theater and Humanism: English Drama in the Sixteenth Century* (Cambridge: Cambridge University Press, 1999), 68.

43. On the play's critique of multilocationism, see Atkin, *Drama of Reform*, chap. 4; Paul Dean, "'Nothing That Is So Is So': *Twelfth Night* and Transubstantiation," *Literature and Theology* 17, no. 3 (2003): 281–97; Tracey Sedinger, "'And Yet Woll I Stiell Saye That I Am I': *Jake Juggler*, the Lord's Supper, and Disguise," *ELH: English Literary History* 74 (2007): 239–69; and William N. West, "What's the Matter with Shakespeare? Physics, Identity, Playing," *South Central Review* 26, nos. 1 and 2 (2009): 103–26.

44. Luther takes up multilocationism in *Confession Concerning Christ's Supper* (1528), in *Luther's Works*, ed. Fischer.

45. Atkin, *Drama of Reform*, 129.

46. Axton, *Three Tudor Interludes*, points out that the term was favored by Thomas Cranmer but also traces it back to the fourteenth century, where the phrase "Jack the juggler" was used in a similar vein by William Langland in *Piers Plowman* (A, B, and C texts). Shakespeare also uses the word *juggler* pejoratively in *A Midsummer Night's Dream* when Hermia says to Helena, "Oh, me, you juggler, you canker-blossom, / You thief of love!" (3.2.282–83), as well as in *The Comedy of Errors*, when Antipholus of Syracuse says, in reference to Ephesus, "this town is full of cozenage, / As, nimble jugglers that deceive the eye / Dark-working sorcerers that change the mind" (1.2.97–99).

47. John Jewel, *Apologie*, sig. Riiii*v*; John Bale, *The Resurrection of the Masse* (Strasburgh: J. Lambrecht [?], 1554), sig. Liiii*v*, Biiii*r*.

48. Cranmer, *Defence*, sig. Fiii*r*.

49. Cranmer, *Answer*, sig. Diii*v*. On the relation of "juggling" to the drama of the Mass, see Atkin, *Drama of Reform*, 136–39.

50. Tyndale, *Obedience of a Christen Man*, sig. Bvi*v*. The term *juggler* is included in the extended title of Tyndale's manual: *The Obedience of a Christen man and how Christen rulers ought to governe where in also (yf thow marke diligently) thou shalt fynde eyes to perceive the crafty conveyaunce of all jugglers* (Air).

51. Ibid., Viii*r*.

52. More, *Answer*, sig. V8*v*.

53. For a discussion of Jack Juggler as a Vice, see Axton, *Three Tudor Interludes*; Bevington, *Tudor Drama and Politics*; and Sedinger, "*Jack Juggler*."

54. See *Jack Juggler*, 918–24. Axton sees these pronouns as evidence of Careaway's creation of "a compound personality" (*Three Tudor Interludes*, 195); Atkin discusses the pronouns in *Drama of Reform*, 132–33.

55. Cranmer, *Defence*, sig. Pir.

56. Shakespeare, *Winter's Tale*, 5.2.87–89, ed. Pitcher. All future citations are to this edition and will be given parenthetically by act, scene, and line number.

57. On the addition of the statue scene, see William Shakespeare, *The Winter's Tale*, ed. Stephen Orgel (Oxford: Oxford University Press, 1996), 63, and *Winter's Tale*, ed. Pitcher, 91–102. Steven R. Mentz, "Wearing Greene: Autolycus, Robert Greene, and the Structure of Romance in *The Winter's Tale*," *Renaissance Drama*, n.s., 30 (1999–2001): 73–92, makes a case that the final scene is based on Greene's own *The Repentance of Robert Greene*, published posthumously in 1592 (73, 85–86).

58. On Resurrection drama and *The Winter's Tale*, see Beckwith, *Shakespeare and the Grammar*, chap. 6; Marsalek, "'Awake Your Faith'"; Alice Dailey, "Easter Scenes from an Unholy Tomb," in *Marian Moments in Early British Drama*, ed. Lisa Hopkins and Regina Buccola (Basingstoke: Palgrave, 2007), 127–41; Glynne Wickham, *Shakespeare's Dramatic Heritage* (London: Routledge, 1969); and Darryl Grantley, "*The Winter's Tale* and Early Religious Drama," *Comparative Drama* 20, no. 1 (1986): 17–37. For additional readings of the play in religious contexts, see Phebe Jensen, "Singing Psalms to Horn-Pipes: Festivity, Iconoclasm, and Catholicism in *The Winter's Tale*," *Shakespeare Quarterly* 55, no. 3 (Autumn 2004): 279–306; Andrew Moran, "Eating, Synaesthesia, and *The Winter's Tale*," *Religion and the Arts* 9, nos. 1 and 2 (2005): 38–61; Anthony Dawson, "The Distracted Globe," in Dawson and Yachnin, *Cultures of Playgoing*, 88–110; Gloria Olchowry, "The Issue of the Corpus Christi Cycles, or 'Religious Romance' in *The Winter's Tale*," in *Staging Early Modern Romance: Prose Fiction, Dramatic Romance, and Shakespeare*, ed. Mary Ellen Lamb and Valerie Wayne (New York: Routledge, 2009), 145–62; Waldron, *Reformations of the Body*, 78–83; Walter S. H. Lim, "Knowledge and Belief in *The Winter's Tale*," *SEL: Studies in English Literature* 41, no. 2 (2001): 317–34; Gareth Roberts, "'An Art Lawful as Eating': Magic in *The Tempest* and *The Winter's Tale*," in *Shakespeare's Late Plays: New Readings*, ed. Jennifer Richards and Richard Knowles (Edinburgh: Edinburgh University Press, 1999), 126–42; Susanna Brietz Monta, "'It Is Required You Do Awake Your Faith': Belief in Shakespeare's Theater," in Degenhardt and Williamson, *Religion and Drama*, 115–38; and McCoy, *Faith in Shakespeare*, 113–45.

59. Jensen, in "Singing Psalms to Horn-Pipes," argues that "if it is Eucharist" that we have in the final scene, "then it is a Catholic one. Instead of simply commemorating Hermione, the theatrical/religious position makes her miraculously

present, in a ceremony presided over by a Pauline practitioner, during which stone is transformed to flesh just as bread and wine becomes body and blood in the Catholic Mass" (303–4). In her later book, *Religion and Revelry in Shakespeare's Festive World* (Cambridge: Cambridge University Press, 2008), Jensen revises the claim: "The fictional transformation of stone into flesh further recalls the [Eucharistic] ritual, though given the subtleties of Eucharistic debates, and the middle road taken by the English prayer books, it would be a simplification to claim that transformation in the Eucharist always signals Catholic transubstantiation" (226), though she does not develop this claim any further and continues to insist that Shakespeare's representation of "festive play can function as a sign of inclination toward religious traditionalism" (230). Dailey writes, "The way in which Hermione is displayed is similar not only to saint's statues but to the consecrated Corpus Christi, which was elevated on an altar and often hidden by a curtain or screen" ("Easter Scenes," 134). Diehl, by contrast, takes a hard Protestant line: "Shakespeare wrests [the statue] from its popish associations and locates it, and the wonder it elicits, in the representational practices of early Protestantism" (*Staging Reform*, 80).

60. In arguing for the importance of language to Leontes's transformation at the end of the play, Carol Thomas Neely, "The Triumph of Speech in *The Winter's Tale*," *SEL: Studies in English Literature* 15.2 (Spring 1975): 321–28, likewise focuses on Leontes's attention to the fleshly body of Hermione but does so in a strictly linguistic, not a theological or sacramental, context.

61. By adding the resurrection scene to his source text, Shakespeare creates an opportunity for such semiotic repair to occur. In Greene's *Pandosto*, Bellaria (the Hermione figure) dies as a result of Pandosto's rash behavior toward her and Pandosto eventually kills himself in order redress his misdeeds. Shakespeare redeems Greene's tragic vision by affording Leontes the opportunity to acknowledge his tyranny and seek repentance.

62. Julia Reinhard Lupton, *Afterlives of the Saints: Hagiography, Typology, and Renaissance Literature* (Stanford, CA: Stanford University Press, 1996), adopts a strong iconoclastic stance in relation to this scene: "The play's rationalizing deflation of its carefully staged mystery definitively undercuts the Catholic iconography the scene so powerfully evokes, enacting the movement from the Church to its Reform" (216). See also O'Connell, *Idolatrous Eye*; and Lowell Gallagher, "'This Seal'd Up Oracle': Ambivalent Nostalgia in *The Winter's Tale*," *Exemplaria* 7, no. 2 (1994): 465–98.

63. On the Catholic (and specifically Marian) contexts of the chapel, see Wilson, *Secret Shakespeare*, chap. 11; and Lupton, *Afterlives of the Saints*, 212. On the religious connotation of the supper, see Jensen, "Singing Psalms to Hornpipes," 303–4, and Gallagher, "Ambivalent Nostalgia," 485–86.

64. Gillian Woods, *Shakespeare's Unreformed Fictions* (Oxford: Oxford University Press, 2013), 169.

65. Paul Strohm, *England's Empty Throne: Usurpation and the Language of Legitimation, 1399–1422* (1998; repr., Notre Dame, IN: Notre Dame University Press, 2006), 47.

66. Paulina's verbal efficacy has been attributed to her priestlike (or Pauline) functions by Diehl, *Staging Reform*, 135ff.; Marsalek, "'Awake Your Faith,'" 282; and Dailey, "Easter Scenes," 135.

67. Bishop, 161–62, 166. Bishop's reading here is supported by the punctuation of the scene in the First Folio (1623), which sets off each imperative with a colon, creating a kind of gestural force to accompany each utterance.

68. For Cranmer, the idea that accidents could remain without substance confounds reason: "There remayneth whitenes, but nothing is white: there remaineth colours, but nothyng is coloured therewith: there remaineth roundness but nothyng is round: and there is bygness, and yet nothing is bygge: there is swetenes, withoute any swete thyng: softnes, without any soft thyng: breakyng without any thyng broken: division without any thyng devided, and so other qualities & quantities, without any thyng to receive them" (*Answer*, sig. Eiii$v$). On the contradiction in Aquinas's permission of accidents without substance, see FitzPatrick, *In Breaking of Bread*, chaps. 1 and 2, and for a summary of the Aristotelean foundations of transubstantiation, see Kobialka, *This Is My Body*, 106–9.

69. Thomas Aquinas, *Summa theologiae* [hereafter *ST*] III.76.1, rep. 3, ed. Mortensen and Alarcon, trans. Shapcote. All future citations are to this edition.

70. Transubstantiation offers Christ's Galilean body and blood wholly and completely in substance but without the burden of ingesting that body *as body* and that blood *as blood*, which would amount to cannibalism. Aquinas writes, "Because it is not customary, but horrible, for men to eat human flesh and drink human blood . . . Christ's flesh and blood are set before us to be partaken of under the species of those things which are more commonly used by men, namely, bread and wine" (*ST* III.75.5, ans.). Peter the Lombard similarly argues that the accidents of bread and wine are necessary as "an aid to taste and faith." "Christ gave us his body, not torn into parts . . . but whole," he says. "Christ does not appear in human form but is veiled by the form of bread and wine. That is why his flesh is called invisible: it is truly on the altar, but because it does not appear in its own species it is called invisible" (*Sentences*, 50–51). Aers states that Aquinas views transubstantiation as an "act of divine condescension which in no way diminishes the presence of Christ in his full humanity," yet also he points out that Christ's "plenitudinous presence, although 'in the mode of substance,' and although disguised from our carnal eyes, is such that we are indeed eating human flesh and drinking human blood" (*Sanctifying Signs*, 4–5). Eucharistic

cannibalism has been widely noted in the context of *The Winter's Tale* when Leontes reacts to Hermione's revelation saying, "If this be magic, let it be an art lawful as eating" (5.3.110–11). See Marsalek, "'Awake Your Faith,'" 281, and Lupton, *Afterlives of the Saints*, 216–17.

71. Aquinas addresses this point as well: "Christ's body as it is in the sacrament cannot be seen by any bodily eye. . . . Christ's body is substantially present in the sacrament. But substance, as such, is not visible to the bodily eye, nor does it come under any one of the senses, nor under the imagination, but solely under the intellect" (*ST* III.76.7, ans.).

72. Kirby, *Persuasion and Conversion*, 140–41. Kirby offers a fine summation of Hooker's position, which is derived from Jewel: "There is, he says, a sacramental change of substance, but the transubstantiation is not to be found outwardly in the physical elements of the sacrament, but rather within the conscience of the faithful participant in the sacramental action. Signs and things signified are 'distinct'; nonetheless, the mystical substance of the sign is not to be 'separated' from the sign" (139). On the importance of interpretation to the reformed Eucharist, see also Rosendale, *Liturgy and Literature*, 102–8.

73. Marsalek, "'Awake Your Faith,'" 284.

74. "Statue" (n.), *OED*. It is in 1597, according to the *OED*, that the sense of being silent or motionless comes into usage.

75. Beckwith reads Leontes's acknowledgment as Shakespeare's re-envisioning of the medieval sacrament of penance: "The statue gives him a view of Hermione, but it is in the felt presence conjured by her likeness, in the sheer promise and gratuity of her return, in the self-forgetful yearning and love conjured into being by the statue, that he can also bear the thought of being seen by her, and so bear his shame" (*Shakespeare and the Grammar*, 141). For an alternate reading that locates the penitential agency in Hermione, see Lupton, *Afterlives of the Saints*, 214.

76. Hooker, *Of the Lawes*, 5.67, sig. Q6r.

77. Jewel, *Apologie*, sig. Div–Diir. For a discussion of Jewel's influence on Hooker, see Kirby, *Persuasion and Conversion*.

78. As discussed in chapter 1, the idea that Eucharistic transformation occurs in the believer as opposed to the elements is expressed formatively by Augustine. As Philip Cary writes of Augustine's sacramental semiotics, "Those who receive these things well—which clearly means in faith and charity—*are* what they have received, which is to say, they are the Body of Christ, the church. It is as if, for the purposes of piety at least, the flesh of Christ has suddenly dissolved into an inner unity" (*Outward Signs*, 247). See also Aers and Beckwith, "Eucharist."

79. Hooker, *Of the Lawes*, 5.67, sig. Q4r.

80. Ibid., sig. Q5r.

81. Cranmer, *Defence*, sig. Ziiir. For the Wycliffite versions of this idea, see Aers, "The Humanity of Christ," 53–55.

82. The reconciliation is somewhat complicated because Hermione does not speak directly to Leontes as she does to Perdita. As Lynn Enterline, *The Rhetoric of the Body from Ovid to Shakespeare* (Cambridge: Cambridge University Press, 2001), points out, "Paulina's intervention tells us that if Hermione is to be restored to Leontes and not fade away again before the force of fantasy and doubt, it is on the condition that she *not* respond to his words only, that she not conform utterly to his language and his desire" (224, italics in original).

83. Polixenes also asks Paulina to "make it manifest where she has lived, / Or how stolen from the dead" (5.3.113–14). His suggestion that Hermione may have been "stolen" echoes the concerns raised by Annas, Caiphas, and Pilate in the Resurrection plays, especially the York *Resurrection*, which focuses on the political anxiety that washes over Pilate's court after the Crucifixion.

Afterword

1. See chapter 4 for this discussion in the context of the Council of Trent. For a longer history leading up to the new English translation, see Edward Foley, ed., *A Commentary on the Order of Mass of the Roman Missal: A New English Translation* (Collegeville, MN: Liturgical Press, 2011), as well as US Council of Catholic Bishops, "The Roman Missal," n.d., accessed January 9, 2017, www.usccb.org/prayer-and-worship/the-mass/roman-missal.

2. Second Vatican Council, *Sacrosanctum concilium*, Third Session, December 4, 1963, III. 21, in Tanner, *Decrees*, 2:825.

3. Ibid., in Tanner, *Decrees*, 2:828.

4. Holy See, Congregation for Divine Worship and the Discipline of the Sacraments, *Liturgiam authenticam: On the Use of Vernacular Languages in the Publication of the Books of the Roman Liturgy* (Rome: Holy See, Congregation for Divine Worship and the Discipline of the Sacrament, 2002), www.vatican.va/roman_curia/congregations/ccdds/documents/rc_con_ccdds_doc_20010507_liturgiam-authenticam_en.html, sec. 56. All future references will be made parenthetically by section number.

5. Ibid., 7.

6. Ibid.

7. Ibid., 52.

8. On this specific revision and its history, cf. US Council of Catholic Bishops, "And with Your Spirit," n.d., accessed January 9, 2017, www.usccb.org/prayer-and-worship/the-mass/roman-missal/and-with-your-spirit.cfm#_ftnref1. This essay points out that in other vernacular languages, such as French and Italian, the Latin *spiritus* was translated into those vernacular equivalents of "spirit" in a way that English was not.

9. *The Roman Missal*, 3rd ed. (Vatican City State: Libreria Editrice Vaticana, 2008, Latin text; 2010, English text).

10. James Martin, S.J., "An Elegy for the Sacramentary," *America: The National Catholic Review*, November 21, 2011, http://americamagazine.org/content/all-things/elegy-sacramentary.

11. Brian Cummings notes that "in 2000, to mark the millennium, *Common Worship* finally marked the real end for [the prayer book of] 1662, although in many churches diehards and enthusiasts are still allowed their regular dosage of sixteenth-century prose at least once a week" (*Book of Common Prayer*, xlvii).

BIBLIOGRAPHY

Primary Sources

Andrewes, Lancelot. *Copie of the Sermon preached on good Friday last before the Kings Majestie.* London: R. Barker, 1604.

———. *A Sermon Preached Before His Majestie On Sunday the fifth of August.* London: Robert Barker, 1610.

Aquinas, Thomas. "Lauda Sion Salvatorem." In Walsh and Husch, *One Hundred Latin Hymns*, 356–57.

———. "O salutaris hostia." In Walsh and Husch, *One Hundred Latin Hymns*, 362.

———. *Summa theologiae: Tertia pars.* Edited by John Mortensen and Enrique Alarcon. Translated by Laurence Shapcote, O.P. Lander, WY: Aquinas Institute for Sacred Doctrine, 2012.

Axton, Marie, ed. *Three Tudor Interludes.* Suffolk: Boydell and Brewer, 1982.

Bale, John. *The Complete Plays of John Bale.* Edited by Peter Happé. 2 vols. Cambridge: D. S. Brewer, 1985.

———. *A Declaration of Edmonde Bonners articles.* 1554. Reprint, London: John Tynsdall, 1561.

———. *The Epistle Exhortatorye of an Englysshe Christiane unto his derelye beloved contreye of Englande.* Antwerp: [Widow of C. Reremund?], 1544[?].

———. *King Johan.* Edited by Barry B. Adams. Princeton, NJ: Princeton University Press, 1969.

———. *King Johan.* Edited by J. H. Pafford. Oxford: Malone Society, 1931.

———. *King Johan.* In *The Complete Plays of John Bale*, vol. 1, edited by Peter Happé. 2 vols. Cambridge: D. S. Brewer, 1985.

———. *The Resurrection of the Masse.* Strasburgh: [J. Lambrecht?], 1554.

———. *The Vocacyon of Johan Bale to the bishoprick of Ossorie in Ireland.* Rome [i.e., Wesel?]: by J. Lambrecht? for Hugh Singleton, 1553.

Barclay, John. *Vindication of the Intercession of Saints, the Veneration of Relics, and Miracles against the Sectaries of the Times.* London: Mary Thompson, 1688.

Beadle, Richard, ed. *The York Plays: A Critical Edition of the York Corpus Christi Play as recorded in British Library Additional MS 35290.* 2 vols. Early English Text Society, Supplementary Series, 23 and 24. Oxford: Oxford University Press, 2009.

Bettenson, Henry, and Chris Maunder, eds. *Documents of the Christian Church.* 4th ed. Oxford: Oxford University Press, 2011.

Bevington, David, ed. *Medieval Drama.* Boston: Houghton Mifflin, 1975.

B. G. (Bernard Garter). *A newyeares gifte, dedicated to the Popes Holinesse, and all Catholikes addicted to the Sea of Rome.* London: Henry Bynneman, 1579.

The Book of Common Prayer. London: Richard Grafton, 1549.

The Book of Common Prayer: The Editions of 1549, 1552, and 1662. Edited by Brian Cummings. Oxford: Oxford University Press, 2011.

Bruster, Douglas, and Eric Rasmussen, eds. *Everyman and Mankind.* London: Methuen Drama, 2009.

The Byble in Englyshe, that is to say the content of all the Holy Scripture both of ye olde and newe testament, truly translated after the veryte of the Hebrue and Greke textes. London: Richard Grafton and Edward Whitchurch, 1539.

Caesarius of Heisterbach. *The Dialogue of Miracles (Dialogus miraculorum)* [ca. 1220–35]. Translated by H. Von E. Scott and C. C. Swinton Bland. 2 vols. London: George Routledge and Sons, 1929.

Calvin, Jean. *A faythful and moost Godlye treatyse concernynge the most sacret sacrament of the blessed body and bloude of oure sauioure Christe.* Edited and translated by Miles Coverdale. London: John Daye and William Seres, 1548[?].

———. *Institutes of the Christian Religion* [1559]. Edited by Henry Beveridge. Grand Rapids, MI: Wm. B. Eerdmans, 1989.

———. *A very profitable treatise, made by M. Ihon Caluyne, declarynge what great profit might come to al christendome, yf there were a regester made of all sainctes bodies and other reliques.* London: Rouland Hall, 1561.

Cawley, A. C., and Stanley Ellis, eds. *The Towneley Cycle: A Facsimile of Huntington MS HM 1.* Leeds: Leeds Texts and Monographs, 1976.

Chaucer, Geoffrey. *The Riverside Chaucer.* Edited by Larry D. Benson. Boston: Houghton Mifflin, 1987.

Coogan, Michael, ed. *The New Oxford Annotated Bible.* 4th ed. Oxford: Oxford University Press, 2001.

Cranmer, Thomas. *An aunswere of the most reuerend father in God Thomas Archebyshop of Canterburye, primate of all Englande and metropolitane vnto a crafty and sophisticall cauillation deuised by Stephen Gardiner doctour of law, late byshop of Winchester agaynst the true and godly doctrine of the most holy sacrament, of the body and bloud of our sauiour Iesu Christ.* London: Reynolde Wolfe, 1551.

———. *A Defence of the true and catholike doctrine of the sacrament of the body and bloud of our savior Christ.* London: Reynolde Wolfe, 1550.

Crashaw, Richard. *The Collected Poems of Richard Crashaw.* Edited by George Walton Williams. New York: Anchor Books, 1970.

Davidson, Clifford, ed. *The York Corpus Christi Plays.* TEAMS Middle English Texts. Kalamazoo, MI: Medieval Institute Publications, 2011.

Dekker, Thomas. *The Pleasant Comedie of Old Fortunatus.* London: S. S[tafford], 1600.

Donne, John. *John Donne's 1622 Gunpowder Plot Sermon: A Parallel Text Edition.* Edited by Jeanne Shami. Duquesne, PA: Duquesne University Press, 1996.

———. *The Major Works.* Edited by John Carey. Oxford: Oxford University Press, 2000.

Elizabeth I. *Queen Elizabeth's Opinion Concerning Transubstantiation.* [Folger MS 260-135b]. London: F. E., 1688.

Fisher, John. "A sermon . . . preached upon a good Friday, by the same John Fisher, Bishop of Rochester." In *The English Works of John Fisher*, edited by John E. B. Mayor. Ludgate Hill: N. Trubner, for the Early English Text Society, 1876.

Foxe, John. *Actes and Monuments.* London: John Day, 1563.

———. *A Sermon Preached at Paules Crosse the Friday before Easter, commonly called Goodfryday.* London: John Daye, 1570.

Frith, John. *Boke answeringe unto M. Mores lettur.* Munster [Antwerp]: Conrade Willems [i.e., H. Peetersen van Middelburch?], 1533.

Gardiner, Stephen. *A Detection of the Devils Sophistrie.* London: John Herforde, 1546.

———. *An explication and assertion of the true Catholique faith, touching the moost Blessed Sacrament of the aulter.* Rouen: Robert Caly, 1551.

The Geneva Bible. 1560 ed. Peabody, MA: Hendrickson, 2007.

Greene, Robert. *The Honourable Historie of Frier Bacon and Frier Bongay.* London: Adam Islip, 1594.

———. *The Repentance of Robert Greene.* London: [J. Danter], 1592.

Gurnay, Edmund. *Corpus Christi.* Cambridge: Cantrell Legge, 1619.

Harding, Thomas. *An Answere to M. Jewelles Challenge.* London: John Bogard, 1564.

The Holy Bible Faithfully Translated into English out of the authentical Latin, diligently conferred with the Hebrew, Greek, & other Editions in divers languages. Douay: John Cousturier, 1635.

The Holy Bible Translated from the Vulgate and Diligently Compared With Other Editions in Divers Languages (Douay, AD 1609, Rheims, AD 1582). New York: Benzinger Brothers, 1994.

A Homilie for good Friday, concerning the death and passion of our Savior Jesus Christ. In *The Second Tome of Homilies, of such matters as were promised and instituted in the former part of homilies, set out by the aucthoritie of the Queenes Maiestie*. London: Richard Jugge and John Cawood, 1563.

A Homilie of the worthie receyvyng and reverent esteemyng of the Sacrament, of the body and bloud of Christ. In *The second tome of homilies, of suche matters as vvere promised and intituled in the former part of homilies, set out by the aucthoritie of the Queenes Maiestie*. London: Richard Jugge and John Cawood, 1563.

Hooker, Richard. *Of the Lawes of Ecclesiastical Polity: Eyght Bookes*. London: John Windet, 1597.

Hudson, Anne, ed. *Selections from English Wycliffite Writings*. Toronto: University of Toronto Press for the Medieval Academy of America, 1997.

James I. *His Majesties Speech in this last Session of Parliament*. London: Robert Barker, 1605.

———. *Two Meditations of the Kings Majestie; the One in the yeere of our Lord God 1618. The other in the yeere 1619*. London: Robert Barker and John Bill, 1619.

Jewel, John. *Apologie of the Church of England*. London: Reginald Wolfe, 1562.

———. *A sermon pronounced by the Byshop of Salisburie at Paules Crosse the second sondaye before Ester in the yere of our Lord, 1560. Wherupon D. Cole first sought occasion to encounter, shortly set forthe as nere as the author could call it to remembrance*. London: John Daye, 1560.

Johnston, Alexandra F., and Margaret Rogerson. *Records of Early English Drama: York*. 2 vols. Toronto: University of Toronto Press, 1979.

Joye, George. *The Souper of the Lorde*. Nornburg: Niclas Twonson, 1533.

Knollys Family Psalter. Manuscript. [Winchester?], ca. 1430. Transylvania University Library. Lexington, KY.

Lambeth faire, vvherein you have all the bishops trinkets set to sale. London: s.n., 1641.

Liber Eliensis (Book of Ely). Edited and translated by Janet Fairweather. Woodbridge: Boydell and Brewer, 2005.

Liturgiam authenticam: On the Use of Vernacular Languages in the Publication of the Books of the Roman Liturgy. Rome: Holy See, Congregation for Divine Worship and the Discipline of the Sacrament, 2002.

Lumiansky, R. M., and David Mills, eds. *The Chester Mystery Cycle*. 2 vols. Early English Text Society, Supplementary Series, 3 and 9. London: Oxford University Press, 1974.

Luther, Martin. *Confession Concerning Christ's Supper* [1528]. Vol. 37 of *Luther's Works*, edited by Robert H. Fischer. Philadelphia: Muhlenberg Press, 1961.

———. *Confession Concerning Christ's Supper* [1528]. In *Martin Luther's Basic Theological Writings*, edited by Timothy F. Lull, 2nd ed. Minneapolis, MN: Fortress Press, 2005.

Lydgate, John. *The Minor Poems of John Lydgate*, 2 vols. Edited by Henry Noble McCracken. London: Early English Text Society, Oxford University Press, 1911–34.

———. *Mummings and Entertainments*. Edited by Claire Sponsler. TEAMS Middle English Texts Series. Kalamazoo, MI: Medieval Institute Publications, 2010.

Mainardi, Agostino. *An Anatomi, that is to say a parting in Peeces of the Mass*. Strasbourg: [heirs of] W. Kopfel, 1556.

A Manual of Prayers. ca. 1685. Folger MS V.a.488. Folger Shakespeare Library. Washington, DC.

Marlowe, Christopher. *Doctor Faustus*. Edited by David Bevington. Manchester: Manchester University Press, 1993.

———. *Doctor Faustus: A Two-Text Edition*. Edited by David Scott Kastan. New York: W.W. Norton, 2005.

———. *The Tragicall Historie of the life and death of Doctor Faustus*. London: John Wright, 1631.

Middleton, Thomas. *Thomas Middleton: The Complete Works*. Edited by Gary Taylor and John Lavagnino. Oxford: Oxford University Press. 2008.

Middleton, Thomas, and William Rowley. *The Changeling*. Edited by Michael Neill. London: New Mermaids, 2006.

Missale ad usum insignis ac preclare Ecclesie Sarum. London: Richard Pynson, 1520. Houghton Library f Typ 505.20.262.

Missale Romanum. London, ca. 1240–60. Huntington Library HM 26061.

Missale Romanum. Saragossa, 1511. Houghton Library Typ 560.11.262.

Missale Romanum ad usum sacrosancte Romane ecclesiae. Venetiis, 1546. Houghton Library f Typ 525 46.262.

Missale Romanum ex decreto Sacrosancti Concilii Tridentini Restitutum. Antverpiae: 1700.

More, Thomas. *The Answer to a Poisoned Book*. Edited by Stephen Merriam Foley and Clarence H. Miller. The Yale Edition of the Complete Works of Thomas More 11. New Haven, CT: Yale University Press, 1985.

———. *The Answere to the fyrst parte of the poysened booke*. London: W. Rastell, 1534.

———. *A dyaloge of syr Thomas More knyghte: one of the counsayll of oure souerayne lorde the kyng [and] chauncellour of hys duchy of Lancaster. Wherin be treated dyuers maters, as of the veneration [and] worshyp of ymages [and] relyques, prayng to sayntys, [and] goyng o[n] pylgrymage.* London: J. Rastell, 1529.

———. *A letter of syr Tho. More knight impugnynge the erronyouse wrytyng of John Fryth against the blessed sacrament of the aultare.* London: W. Rastell, 1533 [?].

Oates, Titus. *The Popes Ware-house, or the Merchandise of the Whore of Rome.* London Tho. Parkhurst, Dorman Newman, Thomas Cockerill, and Tho. Simmons, 1679.

Overbury, Thomas. *Characters, or witty descriptionns of the properties of sundry persons.* London: Edward Griffin, 1616.

Peter the Lombard. *The Sentences: Book 4, On the Doctrine of Signs.* Translated by Giulio Silano. Toronto: Pontifical Institute of Mediaeval Studies, 2010.

Puttenham, George. *The Art of English Poesy* [1589]. Edited by Frank Whigham and Wayne E. Rebhorn. Ithaca, NY: Cornell University Press, 2009.

Relazione de' Miracoli Avvenuti nel borgo di Cannobio Sopra il Lago Maggiore, l'anno 1522. Milan: Federico Bianchi, 1718.

The Resurrection of Our Lorde (ca. 1530–60). Folger MS V.b.192.

The Resurrection of Our Lorde. Edited by J. Dover Wilson and Bertram Dobell. Oxford: Oxford University Press, 1912.

Reynolds, Edward. *Meditations on the Holy Sacrament of the Lords Last Supper.* London: Felix Kyngston, 1638.

The Roman Missal. 3rd ed. Vatican City State: Libreria Editrice Vaticana. 2008, 2010.

Sebastian, John T., ed. *Croxton Play of the Sacrament.* TEAMS Middle English Texts Series. Kalamazoo, MI: Medieval Institute Publications, 2012.

Shakespeare, William. *The Comedy of Errors.* In *Norton Shakespeare.*

———. *The Complete Sonnets and Poems.* Edited by Colin Burrow. Oxford: Oxford University Press, 2002.

———. *Coriolanus.* Edited by Peter Holland. London: Bloomsbury, 2013.

———. *The First Part of King Henry the Fourth.* Edited by David Scott Kastan. London: Methuen Drama, 2008.

———. *Hamlet.* Edited by Ann Thompson and Neil Taylor. London: Cengage Learning, 2006.

———. *King John.* Edited by A. R. Braunmuller. Oxford: Clarendon Press, 1989.

———. *Macbeth.* Edited by Nicholas Brooke. Oxford: Clarendon Press, 1990.

———. *The Merchant of Venice.* In *Norton Shakespeare.*

———. *A Midsummer Night's Dream.* In *Norton Shakespeare.*

———. *The Norton Shakespeare.* Edited by Stephen Greenblatt. New York: W.W. Norton, 1997.

———. *Richard II.* In *Norton Shakespeare.*

———. *Richard III.* In *Norton Shakespeare.*

———. *Titus Andronicus.* Edited by Jonathan Bate. London: Methuen Drama, 1996.

———. *Two Gentlemen of Verona.* In *Norton Shakespeare.*

———. *The Winter's Tale.* Edited by Stephen Orgel. Oxford: Oxford University Press, 1996.

———. *The Winter's Tale.* Edited by John Pitcher. London: Methuen Drama, 2010.

Smith, Richard. *The Assertion and Defence of the Sacramente of the Aulter.* London: John Herforde, 1546.

———. *A Defence of the sacrifice of the masse.* London: John Herforde, 1546.

Spencer, Thomas. *Englands Warning-Peece: or The History of the Gun-powder Treason: Inlarged with some Notable Passages not heretofore Published.* London: T. N., 1659.

Sugano, Douglas, ed. *The N-Town Plays.* TEAMS Middle English Texts. Kalamazoo, MI: Medieval Institute Publications, 2007.

Tanner, Norman, S.J., ed. and trans. *The Decrees of the Ecumenical Councils.* 2 vols. Washington, DC: Sheed and Ward for Georgetown University Press, 1991.

The text of the new testament of Jesus Christ, Translated out of the vulgar Latine by the Papists of the traitorous Seminarie at Rheims... The Whole Worke, perused and enlarged ... by W. Fulke, D. in Divinitie. London: Deputies of Christopher Barker, 1589.

Tuke, Thomas. *Concerning the Holy Eucharist and the Popish Breaden-God.* Amsterdam: [successors of] G. Thorpe, 1625.

Tyndale, William. *An answer unto Sir Thomas Mores dialoge.* Antwerp: S. Cock, 1531.

———. *A Brief Declaration of the Sacraments.* London: Robert Stoughton, 1548[?].

———. *The Obedience of a Christen Man.* Antwerp: Hans Luft, 1528.

Walsh, Peter G., with Christopher Husch, eds. *One Hundred Latin Hymns: Ambrose to Aquinas.* Cambridge, MA: Harvard University Press, 2012.

US Council of Catholic Bishops. "And with Your Spirit." n.d., accessed January 9, 2017. www.usccb.org/prayer-and-worship/the-mass/roman-missal/and-with-your-spirit.cfm#_ftnref1.

———. "The Roman Missal." n.d., accessed January 9, 2017. www.usccb.org/prayer-and-worship/the-mass/roman-missal.

Webster, John. *The Duchess of Malfi.* Edited by Leah S. Marcus. London: Methuen Drama, 2009.

———. *A Monumentall Column*. London: N. O., 1613.

Wright, Thomas. *A Treatise, shewing the possibilitie, and conueniencie of the reall presence of our Sauiour in the blessed Sacrament*. London: Joachim Trognesius [Valentine Simmes], 1596.

Wyclif, John. "Concerning the Eucharist II." In *Miscellaneous Works*, vol. 3 of *Selected English Works of John Wyclif*, edited by Thomas Arnold, 3 vols. Oxford: Clarendon Press for the Early English Text Society, 1869.

———. *De Eucharistia (Tractatus maior)*. Edited by J. Loserth. London: Wyclif Society, 1892.

———. *Sermons on the Gospels for Sundays and Festivals*. Vol. 1 of *Selected English Works of John Wyclif*, edited by Thomas Arnold, 3 vols. Oxford: Clarendon Press for the Early English Text Society, 1869.

———. *Wycklifes Wycket*. London: J. Daye [?], 1546.

Secondary Sources

Adams, Mary McCord. *Some Later Medieval Doctrines of the Eucharist: Thomas Aquinas, Giles of Rome, Duns Scotus, and William of Ockham*. 2010. Reprint, Oxford: Oxford University Press, 2012.

Adelman, Janet. "'Anger's My Meat': Feeding, Dependency, and Aggression in *Coriolanus*." In *Representing Shakespeare: New Psychoanalytic Essays*, edited by Murray Schwartz and Coppélia Kahn, 129–49. Baltimore: Johns Hopkins University Press, 1980.

Aers, David, ed. *Culture and History: Essays on English Communities, Identities, and Writing*. Detroit, MI: Wayne State University Press, 1992.

———. "The Humanity of Christ: Reflections on Orthodox Late Medieval Representations." In *The Powers of the Holy: Religion, Politics, and Gender in Late Medieval English Culture*, edited by David Aers and Lynn Staley, 15–42. University Park: Pennsylvania State University Press, 1996.

———. "New Historicism and the Eucharist." *Journal of Medieval and Early Modern Studies* 33, no. 2 (Spring 2003): 241–59.

———. *Sanctifying Signs: Making Christian Tradition in Late Medieval England*. Notre Dame, IN: University of Notre Dame Press, 2004.

———. "A Whisper in the Ears of Early Modernists, or Reflections on Literary Critics Writing the 'History of the Subject.'" In Aers, *Culture and History*, 177–202.

Aers, David, and Sarah Beckwith. "The Eucharist." In Cummings and Simpson, *Cultural Reformations*, 153–65.

Aers, David, and Russ Leo, eds. "Unintended Reformations." Special issue, *Journal of Medieval and Early Modern Studies* 46, no. 3 (September 2016).

Agamben, Giorgio. *The Kingdom and the Glory: For a Theological Genealogy of Economy and Government*. Translated by Lorenzo Chiesa with Matteo Mandarini. Stanford, CA: Stanford University Press, 2011.

———. *The Signature of All Things: On Method*. Translated by Luca D'Isanto with Kevin Attell. New York: Zone Books, 2009.

Anderson, Judith. *Translating Investments: Metaphor and the Dynamics of Cultural Change in Tudor-Stuart England*. New York: Fordham University Press, 2005.

Ashley, Kathleen. "Sponsorship, Reflexivity, and Resistance: Cultural Readings of the York Cycle Plays." In *The Performance of Medieval English Culture*, edited by James J. Paxson, Lawrence M. Clopper, and Sylvia Tomasch, 9–24. London: D. S. Brewer, 1998.

Asquith, Claire. *Shadowplay: The Hidden Beliefs and Coded Politics of William Shakespeare*. New York: PublicAffairs, 2005.

Astell, Anne W. *Eating Beauty: The Eucharist and the Spiritual Arts of the Middle Ages*. Ithaca, NY: Cornell University Press, 2004.

Aston, Margaret. "*Corpus Christi* and *Corpus Regni*: Heresy and the Peasants' Revolt." *Past and Present* 143 (May 1994): 3–47.

Atkin, Tamara. *The Drama of Reform: Theology and Theatricality, 1461–1533*. London: Brepols, 2013.

———. "Playbooks and Printed Drama: A Reassessment of the Dating and Layout of the Croxton *Play of the Sacrament*." *Review of English Studies*, n.s., 60, no. 244 (2008): 194–205.

Austin, J. L. *How to Do Things with Words*. 2nd ed. 1962. Reprint, Cambridge, MA: Harvard University Press, 1975.

Badir, Patricia. *The Maudlin Impression: English Literary Images of Mary Magdalene, 1550–1700*. Notre Dame, IN: University of Notre Dame Press, 2009.

Barber, C. L. *Creating Elizabethan Tragedy: The Theater of Marlowe and Kyd*. Chicago: University of Chicago Press, 1988.

———. "'The Form of Faustus' Fortunes Good or Bad.'" *Tulane Drama Review* 8, no. 4 (Summer 1964): 92–119.

Barrett, Robert W., Jr. *Against All England: Regional Identity and Cheshire Writing, 1195–1656*. Notre Dame, IN: University of Notre Dame Press, 2009.

Bartlett, Robert. *Why Can the Dead Do Such Great Things? Saints and Worshippers from the Martyrs to the Reformation*. Princeton, NJ: Princeton University Press, 2013.

Barton, Anne. "*Julius Caesar* and *Coriolanus*: Shakespeare's Roman World of Words." In *Shakespeare's Craft: Eight Lectures*, edited by Philip H. Highfill Jr., 24–47. Carbondale: Southern Illinois University Press, 1982.

Beadle, Richard. "The York Cycle." In Beadle and Fletcher, *Cambridge Companion*, 99–124.

Beadle, Richard, and Alan J. Fletcher, eds. *The Cambridge Companion to Medieval English Theatre*. 2nd ed. Cambridge: Cambridge University Press, 2008.

Beckwith, Sarah. *Christ's Body: Identity, Culture, and Society in Late Medieval Writings*. London: Routledge, 1992.

———. "Ritual, Church, and Theater: The Croxton *Play of the Sacrament*." In Aers, *Culture and History*, 65–90.

———. *Shakespeare and the Grammar of Forgiveness*. Ithaca, NY: Cornell University Press, 2011.

———. *Signifying God: Social Relation and Symbolic Act in the York Corpus Christi Plays*. Chicago: University of Chicago Press, 2001.

———. "Stephen Greenblatt's *Hamlet* and the Forms of Oblivion." *Journal of Medieval and Early Modern Studies* 33, no. 2 (Spring 2003): 261–80.

Belsey, Catherine. "Emblem and Antithesis in *The Duchess of Malfi*." *Renaissance Drama*, n.s., 11 (1980): 115–34.

———. *The Subject of Tragedy: Identity and Difference in Renaissance Drama*. London: Methuen, 1985.

Benson, C. David. "Civic Lydgate: The Poet and London." In *John Lydgate: Poetry, Culture, and Lancastrian England*, edited by Larry Scanlon and James Simpson, 147–68. Notre Dame, IN: University of Notre Dame Press, 2006.

———. "The Past, the Present, and the Future in Medieval Surveys of Roman Relics." In Robertson and Jahner, *Medieval and Early Modern Devotional Objects*, 115–34.

Berger, Harry. "The Early Scenes of *Macbeth*: Preface to a New Interpretation." *ELH: English Literary History* 47, no. 1 (1980): 1–31.

Bergeron, David. "The Wax Figures in *The Duchess of Malfi*." *SEL: Studies in English Literature* 18, no. 2 (Spring 1978): 331–39.

Bernard, G. W. *The Late Medieval English Church: Vitality and Vulnerability before the Break with Rome*. New Haven, CT: Yale University Press, 2012.

Betteridge, Thomas. *Literature and Politics in the English Reformation*. Manchester: Manchester University Press, 2004.

———. *Writing Faith and Telling Tales: Literature, Politics, and Religion in the Work of Thomas More*. Notre Dame, IN: University of Notre Dame Press, 2013.

Betteridge, Thomas, and Greg Walker, eds. *The Oxford Handbook to Tudor Drama*. Oxford: Oxford University Press, 2012.

Bevington, David. *From "Mankind" to Marlowe: The Growth of Structure in the Popular Drama of Tudor England*. Cambridge, MA: Harvard University Press, 1962.

———. *Tudor Drama and Politics*. Cambridge, MA: Harvard University Press, 1968.
Birnham, Douglas, and Enrico Giaccherini, eds. *The Poetics of Transubstantiation: From Theology to Metaphor*. Houndmills, Basingstoke: Palgrave Macmillan, 2005.
Bishop, T. G. *Shakespeare and the Theatre of Wonder*. Cambridge: Cambridge University Press, 1996.
Bloch, Marc. *The Royal Touch: Monarchy and Miracles in France and England*. New York: Dorset Press, 1990.
Bossy, John. "The Mass as Social Institution." *Past and Present* 100 (1983): 29–61.
Bradshaw, Paul F. *The Search for the Origins of Christian Worship: Sources and Methods for the Study of Early Liturgy*. 2nd ed. Oxford: Oxford University Press, 2002.
Brandt, Bruce E. "The Critical Backstory." In *Doctor Faustus: A Critical Guide*, edited by Sara Munson Deats, 17–40. London: Continuum, 2010.
Brantley, Jessica. "Middle English Drama beyond the Cycle Plays." *Literature Compass* 10, no. 4 (2013): 331–42.
———. *Reading in the Wilderness: Private Devotion and Public Performance in Late Medieval England*. Chicago: University of Chicago Press, 2007.
Brokaw, Katherine Steele. "Music and Religious Compromise in John Bale's Plays." *Comparative Drama* 44, no. 3 (Fall 2010): 325–49.
———. *Staging Harmony: Music and Religious Change in Late Medieval and Early Modern English Drama*. Ithaca, NY: Cornell University Press, 2016.
Bromham, A. A., and Zara Bruzzi. *The Changeling and the Years of Crisis, 1619–1624: A Hieroglyph of Britain*. London: Pinter, 1990.
Brown, Peter. *The Cult of the Saints: Its Rise and Function in Latin Christianity*. Chicago: University of Chicago Press, 1982.
Burks, Deborah. "'I'll Want My Will Else': *The Changeling* and Women's Complicity with Their Rapists." *ELH: English Literary History* 62, no. 4 (1995): 759–90.
Burnett, Amy Nelson. *Karlstadt and the Origin of Eucharistic Controversy: A Study in the Circulation of Ideas*. Oxford: Oxford University Press, 2011.
Bynum, Caroline Walker. *Christian Materiality: An Essay on Religion in Late Medieval Europe*. New York: Zone Books, 2011.
———. *Fragmentation and Redemption: Essays on Gender and the Human Body in Medieval Religion*. New York: Zone Books, 1992.
———. *Holy Feast and Holy Fast: The Religious Significance of Food to Medieval Women*. Berkeley: University of California Press, 1987.
———. *Jesus as Mother: Studies in the Spirituality of the High Middle Ages*. Berkeley: University of California Press, 1982.

———. *The Resurrection of the Body in Western Christianity, 200–1336*. New York: Columbia University Press, 1995.

———. *Wonderful Blood: Theology and Practice in Late Medieval Northern Germany and Beyond*. Philadelphia: University of Pennsylvania Press, 2007.

Cahill, Patricia. "The Play of Skin in *The Changeling*." *postmedieval: a journal of medieval cultural studies* 3 (2012): 391–406.

Calbi, Maurizio. *Approximate Bodies: Gender and Power in Early Modern Drama and Anatomy*. London: Routledge, 2005.

Calderwood, James L. "*Coriolanus*: Wordless Meanings and Meaningless Words." *SEL: Studies in English Literature, 1500–1900* 6 (1966): 211–24.

Cameron, Euan. *Enchanted Europe: Superstition, Reason, and Religion, 1250–1750*. Oxford: Oxford University Press, 2010.

Camporesi, Piero. "The Consecrated Host: A Wondrous Excess." In *Fragments for a History of the Human Body, Part One*, edited by Michael Feher, 220–37. New York: Zone Books, 1989.

Cartwright, Kent, ed. *A Companion to Tudor Literature*. London: Wiley Blackwell, 2010.

———. "Scepticism and Theatre in *Macbeth*." *Shakespeare Survey* 55 (2002): 219–36.

———. *Theater and Humanism: English Drama in the Sixteenth Century*. Cambridge: Cambridge University Press, 1999.

Cary, Philip. *Outward Signs: The Powerlessness of External Things in Augustine's Thought*. Oxford: Oxford University Press, 2008.

Cavanaugh, William T. *Torture and Eucharist: Theology, Politics, and The Body of Christ*. Oxford: Blackwell, 1998.

Cavell, Stanley. *Disowning Knowledge in Seven Plays of Shakespeare*. 2nd ed. Cambridge: Cambridge University Press, 2003.

Cervone, Cristina Maria. *Poetics of the Incarnation: Middle English Literature and the Leap of Love*. Philadelphia: University of Pennsylvania Press, 2012.

Chaganti, Seeta. *The Medieval Poetics of the Reliquary: Enshrinement, Inscription, Performance*. New York: Palgrave Macmillan, 2008.

Chalk, Brian. "Webster's 'Worthyest Monument': The Problem of Posterity in *The Duchess of Malfi*." *Studies in Philology* 108, no. 3 (Summer 2011): 379–402.

Chambers, E. K. *The Mediaeval Stage*. 2 vols. Oxford: Clarendon Press, 1903.

Clopper, Lawrence M. *Drama, Play, and Game: English Festive Culture in the Medieval and Early Modern Period*. Chicago: University of Chicago Press, 2001.

———. "The History and Development of the Chester Cycle." *Modern Philology* 75, no. 3 (1978): 219–46.

Coddon, Karin S. "'Unreal Mockery': Unreason and the Problem of Spectacle in *Macbeth*." *ELH: English Literary History* 56, no. 3 (Autumn 1989): 485–501.

Cole, Andrew. *Literature and Heresy in the Age of Chaucer*. Cambridge: Cambridge University Press, 2008.

Coleman, David. *Drama and the Sacraments in Sixteenth-Century England*. Houndmills, Basingstoke: Palgrave Macmillan, 2007.

Coletti, Theresa. "The Chester Cycle in Sixteenth-Century Religious Culture." *Journal of Medieval and Early Modern Studies* 37, no. 3 (Fall 2007): 531–47.

———. *Mary Magdalene and the Drama of Saints: Theater, Gender, and Religion in Late Medieval England*. Philadelphia: University of Pennsylvania Press, 2004.

———. *Naming the Rose: Eco, Medieval Signs, and Modern Theory*. Ithaca, NY: Cornell University Press, 1988.

———. "Reading REED: History and the Records of Early English Drama." In *Literary Practice and Social Change in Britain: 1380–1530*, edited by Lee Patterson, 248–84. Berkeley: University of California Press, 1990.

Coletti, Theresa, and Gail McMurray Gibson. "The Tudor Origins of Medieval Drama." In Cartwright, *Companion to Tudor Literature*, 228–45.

Conley, John. "The Phrase 'The Oyle of Forgyvenes' in *Everyman*: A Reference to Extreme Unction." *Notes and Queries* 22 (1975): 105–6.

Coogan, Michael D. *The New Testament: A Historical and Literary Introduction to the Hebrew Scriptures*. Oxford: Oxford University Press, 2005.

Cox, John D. *The Devil and the Sacred in English Drama*. Cambridge: Cambridge University Press, 2000.

———. "Devils and Power in Marlowe and Shakespeare." *Yearbook of English Studies* 23 (1993): 46–64.

———. "Religion and Suffering in *Macbeth*." *Christianity and Literature* 62, no. 2 (2013): 225–40.

———. "'To Obtain His Soul': Demonic Desire for the Soul in Marlowe and Others." *Early Theatre* 5, no. 2 (2002): 29–46.

Cox, John, and David Scott Kastan, eds. *A New History of Early English Drama*. New York: Columbia University Press, 1997.

Crassons, Kate. "The Challenges of Social Unity: The *Last Judgment* Pageant and Guild Relations in York." *Journal of Medieval and Early Modern Studies* 37, no. 2 (Spring 2007): 305–34.

Cummings, Brian, and James Simpson, eds. *Cultural Reformations: Medieval and Renaissance in Literary History*. Oxford: Oxford University Press, 2010.

———. *The Literary Culture of the Reformation: Grammar and Grace*. Oxford: Oxford University Press, 2002.

———. *Mortal Thoughts: Religion, Secularity, and Identity in Shakespeare and Early Modern Culture*. Oxford: Oxford University Press, 2013.

———. "Protestant Allegory." In *The Cambridge Companion to Allegory*, edited by Rita Copeland and Peter T. Struck, 177–89. Cambridge: Cambridge University Press, 2010.

Cunningham, John. "Comedic and Liturgical Restoration in *Everyman*." *Comparative Drama* 22 (1988): 162–73.

Cutts, Cecilia. "The Croxton Play: An Anti-Lollard Piece." *Modern Language Quarterly* 50, no. 1 (1944): 45–60.

Dailey, Alice. "Easter Scenes from an Unholy Tomb." In *Marian Moments in Early British Drama*, edited by Lisa Hopkins and Regina Buccola, 127–41. Houndmills, Basingstoke: Palgrave, 2007.

———. *The English Martyr from Reformation to Revolution*. Notre Dame, IN: University of Notre Dame Press, 2011.

Danson, Lawrence. *Tragic Alphabet: Shakespeare's Drama of Language*. New Haven, CT: Yale University Press, 2004.

Davidson, Clifford. "*Doctor Faustus* at Rome." *SEL: Studies in English Literature, 1500–1900* 9, no. 2 (1969): 231–39.

———. *From Creation to Doom: The York Cycle of Mystery Plays*. New York: AMS Press, 1984.

Davis, Lisa Fagin. "The Knollys Psalter." *Transylvania Treasures* 8, no. 2 (2016). Transylvania University Library, Lexington, KY. http://www2.transy.edu/about/treasures.htm.

———. "Knoxville, Nashville, and a Knollys." *Manuscript Road Trip* (blog), August 23, 2014. https://manuscriptroadtrip.wordpress.com/?s=kentucky.

Davis, Thomas J. *This Is My Body: The Presence of Christ in Reformation Thought*. Grand Rapids, MI: Baker Academic Press, 2008.

Dawson, Anthony. "Claudius at Prayer." In Degenhardt and Williamson, *Religion and Drama*, 235–48.

———. "The Distracted Globe." In Dawson and Yachnin, *Culture of Playgoing*, 88–110.

———. "Performance and Participation." In Dawson and Yachnin, *Culture of Playgoing*, 11–37.

———. "Shakespeare and Secular Performance." In *Shakespeare and the Cultures of Performance*, edited by Paul Yachnin and Patricia Badir, 83–100. Aldershot: Ashgate, 2008.

Dawson, Anthony, and Paul Yachnin. *The Culture of Playgoing in Shakespeare's England: A Collaborative Debate*. Cambridge: Cambridge University Press, 2001.

Dean, Paul. "'Nothing That Is So Is So': *Twelfth Night* and Transubstantiation." *Literature and Theology* 17, no. 3 (2003): 281–97.

Deats, Sara Munson. "*Doctor Faustus*." In *Christopher Marlowe at 450*, edited by Sara Munson Deats and Robert A. Logan, 71–99. Aldershot: Ashgate, 2014.

———. "*Doctor Faustus*: From Chapbook to Tragedy." *Essays in Criticism* 76, no. 3 (1976): 3–15.

Degenhardt, Jane Hwang, and Elizabeth Williamson, eds. *Religion and Drama in Early Modern England: The Performance of Religion on the Renaissance Stage.* London: Routledge, 2011.

de Grazia, Margreta. "The Modern Divide: From Either Side." *Journal of Medieval and Early Modern Studies* 37, no. 2 (2007): 453–67.

———. "World Pictures, Modern Periods, and the Early Stage." In Cox and Kastan, *New History*, 7–24.

Dell, Jessica, David Klausner, and Helen Ostovich, eds. *The Chester Cycle in Context, 1555–1575: Religion, Drama, and the Impact of Change.* Aldershot: Ashgate, 2012.

de Lubac, Henri, S.J. *Corpus Mysticum: The Eucharist and the Church in the Middle Ages.* Translated by Gemma Simmonds, S.J. Notre Dame, IN: University of Notre Dame Press, 2007.

———. *Medieval Exegesis: The Four Senses of Scripture.* 3 vols. 1959. Reprint, Grand Rapids, MI: Wm. B. Eerdmans, 2000.

Deng, Stephen. "Healing Angels and 'Golden Blood': Money and Mystical Kingship in *Macbeth*." In *New Essays on Macbeth*, edited by Nick Moschovakis, 163–81. London: Taylor and Francis, 2008.

Derrida, Jacques. *Of Grammatology.* Translated by Gayatri Chakravorty Spivak. Baltimore: Johns Hopkins University Press, 1997.

Diehl, Huston. *Staging Reform, Reforming the Stage: Drama and Protestantism in Post-Reformation England.* Ithaca, NY: Cornell University Press, 1997.

Dillenberger, John. *Images and Relics: Theological Perceptions and Visual Images in Sixteenth-Century Europe.* Oxford: Oxford University Press, 1999.

Dinshaw, Carolyn. *Chaucer's Sexual Poetics.* Madison: University of Wisconsin Press, 1989.

Dix, Dom Gregory. *The Shape of the Liturgy.* London: Dacre Press, 1945.

Dollimore, Jonathan. *Radical Tragedy: Religion, Ideology, and Power in the Drama of Shakespeare and His Contemporaries.* 2nd ed. Durham, NC: Duke University Press, 1993.

Dox, Donalee. "Theatrical Space, Mutable Space, and the Space of Imagination: Three Readings of the Croxton *Play of the Sacrament*." In Hanawalt and Kobialka, *Medieval Practices of Space*, 167–98.

Duclow, Donald F. "*Everyman* and the *Ars Moriendi*: Fifteenth-Century Ceremonies of Dying." *Fifteenth-Century Studies* 6 (1983): 93–113.

Duffy, Eamon. *The Stripping of the Altars: Traditional Religion in England, 1400–1580*. New Haven, CT: Yale University Press, 1992.

Duncan, Helga L. "'Sumptuously Re-edified': The Reformation of Sacred Space in *Titus Andronicus*." *Comparative Drama* 43, no. 4 (Winter 2009): 425–53.

Dutton, Elisabeth. "The Croxton *Play of the Sacrament*." In Betteridge and Walker, *Oxford Handbook*, 55–71.

Dutton, Richard, Alison Findlay, and Richard Wilson, eds. *Theater and Religion: Lancastrian Shakespeare*. Manchester: Manchester University Press, 2004.

Eaton, Sara. "Beatrice-Joanna and the Rhetoric of Love in *The Changeling*." *Theatre Journal* 36, no. 3 (October 1984): 371–82.

Eggert, Katherine. *Disknowledge: Literature, Alchemy, and the End of Humanism in the Renaissance*. Philadelphia: University of Pennsylvania Press, 2015.

Eire, Carlos M. N. *War against the Idols: The Reformation of Worship from Erasmus to Calvin*. Cambridge: Cambridge University Press, 1989.

Ekeblad, Inga-Stina. "The 'Impure Art' of John Webster." *Review of English Studies* 9, no. 35 (1958): 253–67.

Elam, Keir. *The Semiotics of Theater and Drama*. 1980. Reprint, London: New Accents, 2002.

Elwood, Christopher. *The Body Broken: The Calvinist Doctrine of the Eucharist and the Symbolization of Power in Sixteenth-Century Europe*. Oxford: Oxford University Press, 1999.

Emmerson, Richard K. "Contextualizing Performance: The Reception of the Chester *Antichrist*." *Journal of Medieval and Early Modern Studies* 29, no. 1 (1999): 89–120.

———. "Dramatic History: On the Diachronic and Synchronic in the Study of Early English Drama." *Journal of Medieval and Early Modern Studies* 35, no. 1 (Winter 2005): 39–66.

———. "Eliding the 'Medieval': Renaissance 'New Historicism' and Sixteenth-Century Drama." In *The Performance of Middle English Culture: Essays on Chaucer and the Drama in Honor of Martin Stevens*, edited by James J. Paxson, Lawrence M. Clopper, and Sylvia Tomasch, 25–41. Cambridge: D. S. Brewer, 1998.

Enders, Jodie. "Dramatic Memories and Tortured Spaces in the *Mystere de la Sainte Hostie*." In Hanawalt and Kobialka, *Medieval Practices of Space*, 199–222.

———. *The Medieval Theater of Cruelty: Rhetoric, Memory, Violence*. Ithaca, NY: Cornell University Press, 2002.

Enterline, Lynn. *The Rhetoric of the Body from Ovid to Shakespeare*. Cambridge: Cambridge University Press, 2001.

Erne, Lukas. "'Popish Tricks' and a Ruinous Monastery: *Titus Andronicus* and the Question of Shakespeare's Catholicism." In *The Limits of Textuality*, edited by Lukas Erne and Guillemette Bolens, 135–55. Tubingen: G. Narr, 2000.

Fairfield, Leslie. *John Bale: Mythmaker for the English Reformation*. West Lafayette, IN: Purdue University Press, 1976.

Faulkner, Mark. "Exegesis in the City: The Chester Plays and Earlier Chester Writing." In Dell, Klausner, and Ostovich, *Chester Cycle in Context*, 161–77.

Fernie, Ewan. "'Another Golgotha.'" In *Shakespeare and Early Modern Religion*, edited by David Loewenstein and Michael Witmore, 172–90. Cambridge: Cambridge University Press, 2015.

Fincham, Kenneth, and Nicholas Tyacke. *Altars Restored: The Changing Face of English Religious Worship, 1547–1700*. Oxford: Oxford University Press, 2008.

Finucane, Ronald. *Miracles and Pilgrims: Popular Beliefs in Medieval England*. New York: Palgrave, 1995.

Fitzgerald, Christina. "Performance Anxiety and the Passion in the Croxton *Play of the Sacrament*." *Journal of Medieval and Early Modern Studies* 46.2 (2016): 315–37.

FitzPatrick, P. J. *In Breaking of Bread: Eucharist and Ritual*. 1993. Reprint, Cambridge: Cambridge University Press, 2006.

Fletcher, Alan. *Drama, Performance, and Polity in Post-Cromwellian Ireland*. Toronto: University of Toronto Press, 2000.

Fletcher, Angus. "*Doctor Faustus* and the Lutheran Aesthetic." *English Literary Renaissance* 35, no. 2 (2005): 187–209.

Foley, Edward, ed. *A Commentary on the Order of Mass of the Roman Missal: A New English Translation*. Collegeville, MN: Liturgical Press, 2011.

———. *From Age to Age: How Christians Have Celebrated the Eucharist*. 1989. Reprint, Collegeville, MN: Liturgical Press, 2008.

Fulton, Thomas. "Shakespeare's *Everyman*: *Measure for Measure* and English Fundamentalism." *Journal of Medieval and Early Modern Studies* 40, no. 1 (Winter 2010): 119–47.

Gallagher, Lowell. "Faustus's Blood and the (Messianic) Question of Ethics." *ELH: English Literary History* 73, no. 1 (2006): 1–29.

———. "The Place of the Stigmata in Christological Poetics." In *Religion and Culture in Renaissance England*, edited by Claire McEachern and Debora Shuger, 93–115. Cambridge: Cambridge University Press, 1997.

———, ed. *Redrawing the Map of Early Modern English Catholicism*. Berkeley: University of California Press, 2012.

———. "'This Seal'd Up Oracle': Ambivalent Nostalgia in *The Winter's Tale*." *Exemplaria* 7, no. 2 (1994): 465–98.
Garber, Marjorie. "'Here's Nothing Writ': Scribe, Script, and Circumscription in Marlowe's Plays." *Theatre Journal* 36, no. 3 (1984): 301–20.
———. "The Insincerity of Women." In *Desire and the Renaissance: Psychoanalysis and Literature*, edited by Valeria Finnuci and Regina Schwartz, 19–38. Princeton, NJ: Princeton University Press, 1994.
———. "Macbeth: The Male Medusa." In *Shakespeare's Ghost Writers: Literature as Uncanny Causality*. 1987. Reprint, London: Methuen, 2010.
Gardiner, Harold. *Mysteries' End: An Investigation of the Last Days of the Medieval Religious Stage*. 1946. Reprint, Hamden, CT: Archon, 1967.
Gayk, Shannon. *Image, Text, and Religious Reform in Fifteenth-Century England*. Cambridge: Cambridge University Press, 2010.
Geary, Patrick J. *Furta Sacra: Thefts of Relics in the Central Middle Ages*. Princeton, NJ: Princeton University Press, 1991.
Gibson, Gail McMurray. "Bury St. Edmunds, Lydgate, and the *N-Town Cycle*." *Speculum* 56 (1981): 56–90.
———. *The Theater of Devotion: East Anglian Drama and Society in the Late Middle Ages*. Chicago: University of Chicago Press, 1989.
Gillen, Katherine A. "From Sacraments to Signs: The Challenges of Protestant Theatricality in John Bale's Biblical Plays." *Cahiers Elisabethans* 80 (2011): 1–11.
Gordon, C. J. "Bread God, Blood God: Wonderhosts and Early Encounters with Secularization." *Genre* 44, no. 2 (Summer 2011): 105–28.
Gowing, Laura. *Common Bodies: Women, Touch, and Power in the English Renaissance*. New Haven, CT: Yale University Press, 2003.
Grantley, Darryl. *English Dramatic Interludes, 1300–1580*. Cambridge: Cambridge University Press, 2004.
———. "*The Winter's Tale* and Early Religious Drama." *Comparative Drama* 20, no. 1 (1986): 17–37.
Green, Douglas E. "Interpreting 'Her Martyr'd Signs': Gender and Tragedy in *Titus Andronicus*." *Shakespeare Quarterly* 40, no. 3 (Fall 1989): 317–26.
Greenblatt, Stephen. *Hamlet in Purgatory*. Princeton, NJ: Princeton University Press, 2001.
———. "Remnants of the Sacred in Early Modern England." In *Subject and Object in Renaissance Culture*, edited by Margreta de Grazia, Peter Stallybrass, and Maureen Quilligan, 337–45. Cambridge: Cambridge University Press, 1996.
———. "Shakespeare and the Exorcists." In *Shakespearean Negotiations*, 94–128. Berkeley: University of California Press, 1988.
———. *Will in the World: How Shakespeare Became Shakespeare*. New York: W. W. Norton, 2004.

Greenblatt, Stephen, and Catherine Gallagher. "The Mousetrap." In *Practicing New Historicism*, 136–62. Chicago: University of Chicago Press, 2000.

———. "The Wound in the Wall." In *Practicing New Historicism*, 75–109. Chicago: University of Chicago Press, 2000.

Gregerson, Linda. *The Reformation of the Subject: Spenser, Milton, and the English Protestant Epic*. Cambridge: Cambridge University Press, 1995.

Gregory, Brad. *The Unintended Reformation: How a Religious Revolution Secularized Society*. Cambridge, MA: Harvard University Press, 2012.

Groves, Beatrice. *Texts and Traditions: Religion in Shakespeare, 1592–1604*. Oxford: Oxford University Press, 2007.

Guibbory, Achsah. *Ceremony and Community from Herbert to Milton: Literature, Religion, and Cultural Conflict in Seventeenth-Century England*. Cambridge: Cambridge University Press, 1998.

Haber, Judith. "'I(t) Could Not Choose but Follow': Erotic Logic in *The Changeling*." *Representations* 81 (2003): 79–98.

Hahn, Cynthia. *Strange Beauty: Issues in the Making and Meaning of Reliquaries, 400–ca. 1204*. College Park: Pennsylvania State University Press, 2013.

Haigh, Christopher. *English Reformations: Religion, Politics, and Society under the Tudors*. Oxford: Oxford University Press, 1993.

———. *The Plain Man's Pathway to Heaven: Modes of Christianity in Post-Reformation England, 1570–1640*. Cambridge: Cambridge University Press, 2007.

Hamlin, Hannibal. *The Bible in Shakespeare*. Oxford: Oxford University Press, 2013.

Hanawalt, Barbara A., and Michal Kobialka, eds. *Medieval Practices of Space*. Minneapolis: University of Minnesota Press, 2000.

Happé, Peter. *Cyclic Form and the English Mystery Plays: A Comparative Study of the English Biblical Cycles and Their Continental and Iconographic Counterparts*. Amsterdam: Rodopi, 2004.

———. "'Erazed in the Booke': The Mystery Cycles and Reform." In Kermode, Scott-Warren, and van Elk, *Tudor Drama before Shakespeare*, 15–33.

———. *John Bale*. Boston: Twayne, 1996.

———. *The Towneley Cycle: Unity and Diversity*. Cardiff: University of Wales Press, 2007.

Hardison, O. B. *Christian Rite and Christian Drama in the Middle Ages: Essays on the Origin and Early History of Modern Drama*. Baltimore: Johns Hopkins University Press, 1965.

Harper, John. *The Forms and Orders of Western Liturgy from the Tenth to the Eighteenth Centuries: A Historical Introduction and Guide for Students and Musicians*. Oxford: Clarendon Press, 1991.

Harris, Jonathan Gil. *Untimely Matter in the Time of Shakespeare.* Philadelphia: University of Pennsylvania Press, 2009.

Harrison, Peter. *The Bible, Protestantism, and the Rise of Natural Science.* Cambridge: Cambridge University Press, 1998.

Hattaway, Michael. "The Theology of Marlowe's *Doctor Faustus.*" *Renaissance Drama*, n.s., 3 (1970): 51–78.

Hawkes, Terence. *Structuralism and Semiotics.* London: Methuen, 1977.

Heinemann, Margot. *Puritanism and Theater: Thomas Middleton and Opposition under the Early Stuarts.* Cambridge: Cambridge University Press, 1982.

Henry, Hugh. "Lauda Sion." In vol. 9 of *The Catholic Encyclopedia.* New York: Robert Appleton, 1910. www.newadvent.org/cathen/09036b.htm.

Higgenbotham, Derek. "Impersonators in the Market: Merchants and the Premodern Nation in the Croxton *Play of the Sacrament.*" *Exemplaria* 19, no. 1 (Spring 2007): 163–82.

Hillman, David, and Carla Mazzio, eds. *The Body in Parts: Fantasies of Corporeality in Early Modern Europe.* London: Routledge, 1997.

Hirschfeld, Heather. *The End of Satisfaction: Drama and Repentance in the Age of Shakespeare.* Ithaca, NY: Cornell University Press, 2014.

Holsinger, Bruce. "Liturgy." In *Middle English*, edited by Paul Strohm, 295–315. Oxford: Oxford University Press, 2009.

———. "Medieval Literature and Cultures of Performance." *New Medieval Literatures* 6 (2003): 271–311.

Homan, Richard. "Ritual Aspects of the York Cycle." *Theatre Journal* 33 (1981): 303–15.

Honan, Park. *Christopher Marlowe: Poet and Spy.* Oxford: Oxford University Press, 2005.

Honderich, Pauline. "John Calvin and *Doctor Faustus.*" *Modern Language Review* 68, no. 1 (1973): 1–13.

Honigmann, E. A. J. *Shakespeare: The Lost Years.* Manchester: Manchester University Press, 1985.

Houston, Julia. "Transubstantiation and the Sign: Cranmer's Drama of the Lord's Supper." *Journal of Medieval and Renaissance Studies* 24 (1994): 114–30.

Howard, Jean E., and Paul Strohm. "The Imaginary 'Commons.'" *Journal of Medieval and Early Modern Studies* 37, no. 3 (Fall 2007): 549–77.

Hudson, Anne. *The Premature Reformation: Wycliffite Texts and Lollard History.* Oxford: Clarendon Press, 1988.

Hughes, Andrew. *Medieval Manuscripts for Mass and Office: A Guide to Their Organization and Terminology.* Toronto: University of Toronto Press, 1982.

Hunt, Alice. *The Drama of Coronation: Medieval Ceremony in Early Modern England.* Cambridge: Cambridge University Press, 2011.

Hunt, Maurice. "The Backward Voice of Coriol-Anus." *Shakespeare Studies* 32 (2004): 220–39.

———. "Reformation/Counter-Reformation *Macbeth*." *English Studies* 86, no. 5 (October 2005): 379–98.

———. *Shakespeare's Religious Allusiveness: Its Play and Tolerance*. Aldershot: Ashgate, 2004.

Jackson, Ken, and Arthur F. Marotti, eds. *Shakespeare and Religion: Early Modern and Postmodern Perspectives*. Notre Dame, IN: University of Notre Dame Press, 2009.

James, Mervyn. "Ritual Drama and the Social Body in the Late Medieval Town." *Past and Present* 98, no. 1 (1983): 3–29.

Jankowski, Theodora. "Defining/Confining the Duchess: Negotiating the Female Body in John Webster's *The Duchess of Malfi*." *Studies in Philology* 87, no. 2 (Spring 1990): 221–45.

Jenkins, Gary W. *John Jewel and the English National Church*. Aldershot: Ashgate, 2006.

Jensen, Phebe. *Religion and Revelry in Shakespeare's Festive World*. Cambridge: Cambridge University Press, 2008.

———. "Singing Psalms to Horn-Pipes: Festivity, Iconoclasm, and Catholicism in *The Winter's Tale*." *Shakespeare Quarterly* 55, no. 3 (Autumn 2004): 279–306.

Johnson, Kimberly. *Made Flesh: Sacrament and Poetics in Post-Reformation England*. Philadelphia: University of Pennsylvania Press, 2014.

Johnston, Alexandra F. "Cycle Drama in the Sixteenth Century: Texts and Contexts." *Acta* 13 (1987): 1–15.

———. "The Emerging Pattern of the English Resurrection Play." *Medieval English Theatre* 20 (1998): 3–23.

———. "The Feast of Corpus Christi in the West Country." *Early Theatre* 6, no. 1 (2003): 15–34.

———. "An Introduction to Medieval English Theatre." In Beadle and Fletcher, *Cambridge Companion*, 1–25.

———. "The Puzzle of the N. Town Manuscript Revisited," *Medieval English Theatre* 36 (2014): 104–23.

Jones, Michael. "Theatrical History in the Croxton *Play of the Sacrament*." *ELH: English Literary History* 66, no. 2 (Summer 1999): 223–60.

Jungmann, Joseph A., S.J. *The Mass of the Roman Rite: Its Origins and Development (Missarum Sollemnia)*. 2 vols. 1956. Reprint, Notre Dame, IN: Ave Maria Press, 2012.

Justice, Steven. "Did the Middle Ages Believe in Their Miracles?" *Representations* 103 (2008): 1–29.

———. "Eucharistic Miracle and Eucharistic Doubt." *Journal of Medieval and Early Modern Studies* 42, no. 2 (2012): 307–22.

Kahn, Coppélia. *Roman Shakespeare: Warriors, Wounds, and Women*. London: Routledge, 1997.

Kahn, Victoria. "Political Theology and Fiction in *The King's Two Bodies*." *Representations* 106, no. 1 (May 2009): 77–101.

Kantorowicz, Ernst. *The King's Two Bodies: A Study of Mediaeval Political Theology*. 1957. Reprint, Princeton, NJ: Princeton University Press, 1997.

Kastan, David Scott. "'Holy Wurdes' and 'Slypper Wit': John Bale's *King Johan* and the Poetics of Propaganda." In *Rethinking the Henrician Era*, edited by Peter C. Herman, 267–82. Urbana: University of Illinois Press, 1994.

———. "*Macbeth* and the Name of King." In *Shakespeare after Theory*, 165–82. New York: Routledge, 1999.

———. *A Will to Believe: Shakespeare and Religion*. Oxford: Oxford University Press, 2013.

Kearney, James. *The Incarnate Text: Imagining the Book in Reformation England*. Philadelphia: University of Pennsylvania Press, 2009.

———. "Reformed Ventriloquism: *The Shepheardes Calender* and the Craft of Commentary." *Spenser Studies* 26 (2011): 111–51.

Kenny, Anthony. *Wyclif*. Oxford: Oxford University Press, 1985.

Kermode, Lloyd E., Jason Scott-Warren, and Martine van Elk, eds. *Tudor Drama before Shakespeare, 1485–1590: New Directions for Research, Criticism, and Pedagogy*. Houndmills, Basingstoke: Palgrave Macmillan, 2004.

Kernan, Alvin. *Shakespeare, the King's Playwright: Theater in the Stuart Court, 1603–1613*. New Haven, CT: Yale University Press, 1995.

Kilgour, Maggie. *From Communion to Cannibalism: An Anatomy of Metaphors of Incorporation*. Princeton, NJ: Princeton University Press, 2014.

King, John N. *English Reformation Literature: The Tudor Origins of the Protestant Tradition*. Princeton, NJ: Princeton University Press, 1986.

King, Pamela M. "Seeing and Hearing; Looking and Listening." *Early Theatre* 3 (2000): 155–66.

———. *The York Mystery Cycle and the Worship of the City*. Cambridge: D. S. Brewer, 2006.

Kipling, Gordon. *Enter the King: Theater, Liturgy, and Ritual in the Medieval Civic Triumph*. Oxford: Oxford University Press, 1998.

Kirby, W. J. Torrance. *Persuasion and Conversion: Religion, Politics, and the Public Sphere*. Leiden: Brill, 2013.

Klausner, David, and Karen Sawyer Marsalek, eds. *Bring Furth the Pagants: Essays in Early English Drama Presented to Alexandra F. Johnston*. Toronto: University of Toronto Press, 2007.

Knapp, Jeffrey. *Shakespeare's Tribe: Church, Nation, and Theater in Renaissance England*. Chicago: University of Chicago Press, 1997.

Kobialka, Michal. *This Is My Body: Representational Practices in the Early Middle Ages*. Ann Arbor: University of Michigan Press, 1999.

Kolve, V. A. *The Play Called Corpus Christi*. Stanford, CA: Stanford University Press, 1966.

Kuchar, Gary. *Divine Subjection: The Rhetoric of Sacramental Devotion in Early Modern England*. Duquesne, PA: Duquesne University Press, 2005.

Kuzner, James. "Unbuilding the City: *Coriolanus* and the Birth of Republican Rome." *Shakespeare Quarterly* 58, no. 2 (2007): 174–99.

Lake, Peter. "Religious Identities in Shakespeare." In *A Companion to Shakespeare*, edited by David Scott Kastan, 57–84. Oxford: Wiley Blackwell, 1999.

Lancashire, Anne. *London Civic Theatre: City Drama and Pageantry from Roman Times to 1558*. Cambridge: Cambridge University Press, 2002.

Lanier, Douglas M. "Cynical Dining in *Timon of Athens*." In *Culinary Shakespeares*, edited by David Goldstein and Amy Tigner, 135–56. Duquesne, PA: Duquesne University Press, 2016.

Lawton, David. "Sacrilege and Theatricality: The Croxton *Play of the Sacrament*." *Journal of Medieval and Early Modern Studies* 33, no. 2 (Spring 2003): 281–309.

Lemon, Rebecca. *Treason by Words: Literature, Law, and Rebellion in Shakespeare's England*. Ithaca, NY: Cornell University Press, 2006.

Lerer, Seth. "'Representyd Now in Yower Syght': The Culture of Spectatorship in Late-Fifteenth-Century England." In *Bodies and Disciplines: Intersections of Literature and History in Fifteenth-Century England*, edited by Barbara A. Hanawalt and David Wallace, 29–62. Minneapolis: University of Minnesota Press, 1996.

Levin, Carole. "'A Good Prince': King John and Early Tudor Propaganda." *Sixteenth Century Journal* 11, no. 4 (Winter 1980): 23–32.

———. *Propaganda in the English Reformation: Heroic and Villainous Images of King John*. Lewiston, NY: Edwin Mellen Press, 1988.

Lewalski, Barbara Kiefer. *Protestant Poetics and the Seventeenth-Century Religious Lyric*. Princeton, NJ: Princeton University Press, 1995.

Liebler, Naomi Conn. *Shakespeare's Festive Tragedy*. London: Routledge, 1995.

———. "A Woman Dipped in Blood: The Violent Femmes of *The Maid's Tragedy* and *The Changeling*." In *Women and Violence in English Renaissance Literature*, edited by Linda Woodbridge and Sharon Beehler, 361–78. Tempe, AZ: Medieval and Renaissance Texts and Studies, 2003.

Lim, Walter S. H. "Knowledge and Belief in *The Winter's Tale*." *SEL: Studies in English Literature, 1500–1900* 41, no. 2 (2001): 317–34.

Lin, Erika. *Shakespeare and the Materiality of Performance*. Houndmills, Basingstoke: Palgrave Macmillan, 2013.

Lodhia, Sheetal. "'The House Is Hers, the Soul Is But a Tenant': Material Self-Fashioning and Revenge Tragedy." *Early Theatre* 12, no. 2 (2009): 135–61.

Loewenstein, David, and Michael Witmore, eds. *Shakespeare and Early Modern Religion*. Cambridge: Cambridge University Press, 2015.

Lorenz, Philip. *The Tears of Sovereignty: Perspectives of Power in Renaissance Drama*. New York: Fordham University Press, 2013.

Lupton, Julia Reinhard. *Afterlives of the Saints: Hagiography, Typology, and Renaissance Literature*. Stanford, CA: Stanford University Press, 1996.

———. *Citizen-Saints: Shakespeare and Political Theology*. Chicago: University of Chicago Press, 2005.

Lupton, Julia Reinhard, and Graham Hammill, eds. *Political Theology and Early Modernity*. Chicago: University of Chicago Press, 2012.

Mack, Maynard. *Killing the King: Three Studies in Shakespeare's Tragic Structure*. New Haven, CT: Yale University Press, 1973.

Macy, Gary. *The Banquet's Wisdom: A Short History of the Theologies of the Lord's Supper*. Collegeville, MN: OSL Publications, 2005.

———. *Treasures from the Storeroom: Medieval Religion and the Eucharist*. Collegeville, MN: Liturgical Press, 1999.

Malcolmson, Christina. "'As Tame as the Ladies': Politics and Gender in *The Changeling*." *English Literary Renaissance* 20, no. 2 (1990): 320–39.

Malo, Robyn. *Relics and Writing in Late Medieval England*. Toronto: University of Toronto Press, 2013.

Marcus, Leah S. *Unediting the Renaissance: Shakespeare, Marlowe, Milton*. London: Routledge, 1996.

Marotti, Arthur F. *Religious Ideology and Cultural Fantasy: Catholic and Anti-Catholic Discourses in Early Modern England*. Notre Dame, IN: University of Notre Dame Press, 2006.

———. "The Turn to Religion in Early Modern English Studies." *Criticism* 46, no. 1 (2004): 167–90.

Marsalek, Karen Sawyer. "'Awake Your Faith': English Resurrection Drama and *The Winter's Tale*." In Klausner and Marsalek, *Bring Furth the Pagants*, 271–91.

———. "'Doctrine Evangelicall' and Erasmus's *Paraphrases* in *The Resurrection of Our Lord*." In Kermode, Scott-Warren, and van Elk, *Tudor Drama before Shakespeare*, 35–66.

———. "*The Resurrection of Our Lord*: A Study and Dual-Text Edition." PhD diss., University of Toronto. 2001.

Marshall, Cynthia. "Wound-Man: Coriolanus, Gender, and the Theatrical Construction of Interiority." In *Feminist Readings of Early Modern Culture*, edited by Valerie Traub, M. Lindsay Kaplan, and Dympna Callaghan, 93–118. Cambridge: Cambridge University Press, 1996.

Marshall, Peter. *Religious Identities in Henry VIII's England*. Aldershot: Ashgate, 2008.

Martin, James, S.J. "An Elegy for the Sacramentary." *America: The National Catholic Review*, November 21, 2011. http://americamagazine.org/content/all-things/elegy-sacramentary.

Martz, Louis. *The Poetry of Meditation: A Study in English Religious Literature in the Seventeenth Century*. New Haven, CT: Yale University Press, 1973.

Maxwell, Lynn. "Wax Magic and *The Duchess of Malfi*." *Journal of Early Modern Cultural Studies* 14, no. 3 (Summer 2014): 31–54.

Mazzio, Carla. *The Inarticulate Renaissance: Language Trouble in an Age of Eloquence*. Philadelphia: University of Pennsylvania Press, 2009.

Mazzola, Elizabeth. *The Pathology of the English Renaissance: Sacred Remains and Holy Ghosts*. Leiden: Brill, 1998.

McCoy, Richard C. *Alterations of State: Sacred Kingship in the English Renaissance*. New York: Columbia University Press, 2002.

———. *Faith in Shakespeare*. New York: Oxford University Press, 2012.

———. "'The Grace of Grace' and Double-Talk in *Macbeth*." *Shakespeare Survey* 57 (2004): 27–37.

———. "The Tragedy of the Handkerchief: Objects Sacred and Profane in Shakespeare's *Othello*." In Robertson and Jahner, *Medieval and Early Modern Devotional Objects*, 155–65.

McCullough, Peter. "Christmas at Elsinore." *Essays in Criticism* 58, no. 4 (2008): 311–32.

McDermott, Ryan. *Tropologies: Ethics and Invention in England, c. 1350–1600*. Notre Dame, IN: University of Notre Dame Press, 2016.

McGillivray, Murray. "The Towneley Manuscript and Performance: Tudor Recycling?" In *Editing, Performance, Texts: New Practices in Medieval and Early Modern English Drama*, edited by Jacqueline Jenkins and Julie Sanders, 49–69. Houndmills, Basingstoke: Palgrave Macmillan, 2014.

McMullan, Gordon, and David Matthews, eds. *Reading the Medieval in Early Modern England*. Cambridge: Cambridge University Press, 2012.

McNabb, Cameron Hunt. "*Hocus Pocus* and the Croxton *Play of the Sacrament*." *Early Theatre* 17.2 (2014): 11–33.

McRae, Murdo William. "Everyman's Last Rites and the Digression on Priesthood." *College Literature* 13 (1986): 305–9.

Meads, Chris. *Banquets Set Forth: Banqueting in English Renaissance Drama.* Manchester: Manchester University Press, 2001.

Mentz, Steven R. "Wearing Greene: Autolycus, Robert Greene, and the Structure of Romance in *The Winter's Tale.*" *Renaissance Drama*, n.s., 30 (1999): 73–92.

Meredith, Peter. "Manuscript, Scribe, and Performance: Further Looks at the N. Town Manuscript." In *Regionalism in Late Medieval Manuscripts and Texts*, edited by Felicity Riddy, 109–25. Cambridge: D. S. Brewer, 1991.

———. "The Towneley Cycle." In Beadle and Fletcher, *Cambridge Companion*, 152–82.

Miller, Edwin. "The Roman Rite in *King Johan.*" *PMLA: Publications of the Modern Language Association* 64, no. 4 (September 1949): 802–22.

Mills, David. "The Chester Cycle." In Beadle and Fletcher, *Cambridge Companion*, 125–51.

———. *Recycling the Cycle: The City of Chester and Its Whitsun Plays.* Studies in Early English Drama 4. Toronto: University of Toronto Press, 1998.

———. "'The Towneley Plays' or 'The Towneley Cycle'?" *Leeds Studies in English* 17 (1986): 95–104.

Minnis, Alastair. *Fallible Authors: Chaucer's Pardoner and the Wife of Bath.* Philadelphia: University of Pennsylvania Press, 2007.

Miola, Robert S. "'I Could Not Say 'Amen'': Prayer and Providence in *Macbeth.*" In *Shakespeare's Christianity: The Protestant and Catholic Poetics of "Julius Caesar," "Macbeth," and "Hamlet,"* edited by E. Beatrice Batson, 73–90. Waco, TX: Baylor University Press, 2006.

———. "Two Jesuit Shadows in Shakespeare: William Weston and Henry Garnet." In *Shakespeare and Religion: Early Modern and Postmodern Perspectives*, edited by Ken Jackson and Arthur F. Marotti, 25–45. Notre Dame, IN: University of Notre Dame Press.

Monta, Susannah Brietz. "'It Is Required You Do Awake Your Faith': Belief in Shakespeare's Theater." In Degenhardt and Williamson, *Religion and Drama*, 115–38.

Montrose, Louis Adrian. *The Purpose of Playing: Shakespeare and the Cultural Politics of the Early Elizabethan Theater.* Chicago: University of Chicago Press, 1996.

Moran, Andrew. "Eating, Synaesthesia, and *The Winter's Tale.*" *Religion and the Arts* 9, nos. 1–2 (2005): 38–61.

Moretti, Franco. "The Great Eclipse: Tragic Form as the Deconsecration of Sovereignty." In *Signs Taken for Wonders: Essays on the Sociology of Literary Forms*, 42–82. London: Verso, 2005.

Morey, J. H. "The Death of King John in Shakespeare and Bale." *Shakespeare Quarterly* 45, no. 3 (1994): 327–31.

Morse, Ruth, Helen Cooper, and Peter Holland, eds. *Medieval Shakespeare: Pasts and Presents*. Cambridge: Cambridge University Press, 2014.

Moschovakis, Nicholas. "'Irreligious Piety' and Religious History: Persecution as Pagan Anachronism in *Titus Andronicus*." *Shakespeare Quarterly* 53, no. 4 (2002): 460–86.

Motohashi, Tatsuya. "Body Politic and Political Body in *Coriolanus*." *Forum for Modern Language Studies* 30, no. 2 (1994): 97–112.

Mowat, Barbara. "Prospero's Book." *Shakespeare Quarterly* 52, no. 1 (2001): 1–33.

Mueller, Janel. "The Saints." In Cummings and Simpson, *Cultural Reformations*, 166–87.

Mullaney, Steven. *The Reformation of Emotions in the Age of Shakespeare*. Chicago: University of Chicago Press, 2015.

Nancy, Jean-Luc. *Corpus*. Translated by Richard Rand. New York: Fordham University Press, 2008.

Neelands, David. "The Use and Abuse of John Calvin in Richard Hooker's Defence of the English Church." *Perichoresis* 10, no. 1 (2012): 3–22.

Neely, Carol Thomas. "The Triumph of Speech in *The Winter's Tale*." *SEL: Studies in English Literature* 15.2 (Spring 1975): 321–28.

Neill, Michael. "Hidden Malady: Death, Discovery, and Indistinction in *The Changeling*." *Renaissance Drama*, n.s., 22 (1991): 95–121.

———. "Monuments and Ruins as Symbols in *The Duchess of Malfi*." In *Drama and Symbolism*, edited by James Redmond, 71–87. Cambridge: Cambridge University Press, 1982.

Netzley, Ryan. *Reading, Desire and the Eucharist in Early Modern Religious Poetry*. Toronto: University of Toronto Press, 2011.

Newman, Barbara. *From Virile Woman to WomanChrist: Studies in Medieval Religion and Literature*. Philadelphia: University of Pennsylvania Press, 1995.

Nichols, Ann Eljenholm. "The Croxton Play: A Re-reading." *Comparative Drama* 22 (Summer 1988): 117–37.

Nisse, Ruth. *Defining Acts: Drama and the Politics of Interpretation in Late Medieval England*. Notre Dame, IN: Notre Dame University Press, 2005.

Nolan, Maura. *John Lydgate and the Making of Public Culture*. Cambridge: Cambridge University Press, 2005.

Norbrook, David. "*Macbeth* and the Politics of Historiography." In *Politics of Discourse: The Literature and History of Seventeenth-Century England*, edited by Kevin Sharpe and Steven N. Zwicker, 78–116. Berkeley: University of California Press, 1987.

O'Connell, Michael. "Blood Begetting Blood: Shakespeare and the Mysteries." In *Medieval Shakespeare: Past and Present*, edited by Ruth Morse, Peter Holland, and Helen Cooper, 177–89. Cambridge: Cambridge University Press, 2013.

———. *The Idolatrous Eye: Drama and Iconoclasm in Early-Modern England.* Oxford: Oxford University Press, 1996.

———. "Vital Cultural Practices: Shakespeare and the Mysteries." *Journal of Medieval and Early Modern Studies* 29 (1999): 149–68.

Olchowry, Gloria. "The Issue of the Corpus Christi Cycles, or 'Religious Romance' in *The Winter's Tale*." In *Staging Early Modern Romance: Prose Fiction, Dramatic Romance, and Shakespeare*, edited by Mary Ellen Lamb and Valerie Wayne, 145–62. New York: Routledge, 2009.

Osberg, Richard. "The Jesse Tree in the 1432 London Entry of Henry VI: Messianic Kingship and the Rule of Justice." *Journal of Medieval and Renaissance Studies* 16, no. 2 (Fall 1986): 213–32.

Owens, Margaret E. "John Webster, Toussaud Laureate: The Waxworks in *The Duchess of Malfi*." *ELH: English Literary History* 79, no. 4 (Winter 2012): 851–77.

———. *Stages of Dismemberment: The Fragmented Body in Late Medieval and Early Modern Drama.* Newark: University of Delaware Press, 2005.

Palazzo, Eric. *A History of Liturgical Books from the Beginning to the Thirteenth Century.* Collegeville, MN: Liturgical Press, 1993.

Palmer, Barbara D. "Recycling 'The Wakefield Cycle': The Records." In *Research Opportunities in Renaissance Drama* 41 (2002): 88–130.

———. "'Towneley Plays' or 'Wakefield Cycle' Revisited," *Comparative Drama* 21 (1987–88): 318–48.

Palmer, Darryl. *Hospitable Performances: Dramatic Genre and Cultural Practices in Early Modern England.* West Lafayette, IN: Purdue University Press, 1992.

Parker, John. *The Aesthetics of Antichrist: From Christian Drama to Christopher Marlowe.* Ithaca, NY: Cornell University Press, 2007.

———. "Faustus, Confession, and the Sins of Omission." *ELH: English Literary History* 80, no. 1 (Spring 2013): 29–59.

———. "Who's Afraid of Darwin: Revisiting Chambers and Hardison . . . and Nietzsche," *Journal of Medieval and Early Modern Studies* 40, no. 1 (2010): 7–35.

Paster, Gail Kern. *The Body Embarrassed: Drama and the Disciplines of Shame in Early Modern England.* Ithaca, NY: Cornell University Press, 1993.

———. "The Ecology of the Passions in *A Chaste Maid in Cheapside* and *The Changeling*." In *The Oxford Handbook to Thomas Middleton*, edited by

Gary Taylor and Trish Thomas Henley, 148–63. Oxford: Oxford University Press, 2012.

———. *Humoring the Body: Emotions and the Shakespearean Stage.* Chicago: University of Chicago Press, 2002.

———. "To Starve with Feeding: The City in *Coriolanus*." *Shakespeare Studies* 11 (1978): 123–44.

Patterson, Annabel. *Shakespeare and the Popular Voice.* Oxford: Basil Blackwell, 1989.

Patterson, Lee. "On the Margin: Postmodernism, Ironic History, and Medieval Studies." *Speculum* 65 (1990): 87–108.

Paul, Henry N. *The Royal Play of "Macbeth."* New York: Macmillan, 1950.

Pearsall, Derek. *John Lydgate.* London: Routledge and Kegan Paul, 1970.

Pelikan, Jaroslov. *The Christian Tradition: A History in the Development of Doctrine.* Vol. 3. *The Growth of Medieval Theology (600–1300).* Chicago: University of Chicago Press, 1980.

———. *The Christian Tradition: A History in the Development of Doctrine.* Vol. 4. *The Reformation of Church and Dogma (1300–1700).* Chicago: University of Chicago Press, 1985.

Pickstock, Catherine. *After Writing: On the Liturgical Consummation of Philosophy.* Oxford: Blackwell, 1998.

Pietz, William. "The Problem of the Fetish, I." *Review of English Studies* 9 (Spring 1985): 5–17.

Pineas, Rainer. "John Bale's Non-dramatic Works of Religious Controversy." *Studies in the Renaissance* 9 (1962): 218–33.

Plotz, John. "*Coriolanus* and the Failure of Performatives." *ELH: English Literary History* 63, no. 4 (1996): 809–32.

Poole, Kristen. "The Devil's in the Archive: *Doctor Faustus* and Ovidian Physics." *Renaissance Drama*, n.s., 35 (2006): 191–219.

———. "*Dr. Faustus* and Reformation Theology." In *Early Modern English Drama: A Critical Companion*, edited by Garrett A. Sullivan Jr., Patrick Cheney, and Andrew Hadfield, 96–107. Oxford: Oxford University Press, 2005.

———. *Supernatural Environments in Shakespeare's England: Spaces of Demonism, Divinity, and Drama.* Cambridge: Cambridge University Press, 2011.

Rackin, Phyllis. "*Coriolanus*: Shakespeare's Anatomy of 'Virtus.'" *Modern Language Studies* 13, no. 2 (Spring 1983): 68–79.

Rasmussen, Eric. *A Textual Companion to "Doctor Faustus."* Manchester: Manchester University Press, 1993.

Read, Sophie. *Eucharist and the Poetic Imagination in Early Modern England.* Cambridge: Cambridge University Press, 2013.

Reid-Schwartz, Alexandra. "Economies of Salvation: Commerce and the Eucharist in *The Profanation of the Host* and the Croxton *Play of the Sacrament*." *Comitatus: A Journal of Medieval and Renaissance Studies* 25, no. 1 (1994): 1–20.

Rice, Nicole, and Margaret Aziza Pappano. *The Civic Cycles: Artisan Drama and Identity in Premodern England.* Notre Dame, IN: University of Notre Dame Press, 2015.

Riggs, David. *The World of Christopher Marlowe.* New York: Faber and Faber, 2004.

Riss, Arthur. "The Belly Politic: *Coriolanus* and the Revolt of Language." *ELH: English Literary History* 59, no. 1 (1992): 53–75.

Rist, Thomas. *Revenge Tragedy and the Drama of Commemoration in Reforming England.* Aldershot: Ashgate, 2008.

Rist, Thomas, and Andrew Gordon, eds. *The Arts of Remembrance in Early Modern England: Memorial Cultures of the Post-Reformation.* Aldershot: Ashgate, 2016.

Ritch, K. Janet. "The Role of the Presenter in Medieval Drama." In Klausner and Marsalek, *Bring Furth the Pagants*, 230–70.

Roberts, Gareth. "'An Art Lawful as Eating': Magic in *The Tempest* and *The Winter's Tale*." In *Shakespeare's Late Plays: New Readings*, edited by Jennifer Richards and Richard Knowles, 126–42. Edinburgh: Edinburgh University Press, 1999.

Robertson, Elizabeth, and Jennifer Jahner, eds. *Medieval and Early Modern Devotional Objects in Global Perspective: Translations of the Sacred.* Houndmills, Basingstoke: Palgrave Macmillan, 2011.

Rosendale, Timothy. *Liturgy and Literature in the Making of Protestant England.* Cambridge: Cambridge University Press, 2007.

———. "Sacral and Sacramental Kingship in Shakespeare's Lancastrian Tetralogy." In *Shakespeare and the Culture of Christianity in Early Modern England*, edited by Dennis Taylor and David N. Beauregard, 121–40. New York: Fordham University Press, 2004.

Rowe, Katherine. *Dead Hands: Fictions of Agency, Renaissance to Modern.* Stanford, CA: Stanford University Press, 2000.

Rubin, Miri. *Corpus Christi: The Eucharist in the Later Middle Ages.* Cambridge: Cambridge University Press, 1993.

———. *Gentile Tales: The Narrative Assault on Late Medieval Jews.* Philadelphia: University of Pennsylvania Press, 2004.

Rust, Jennifer R. *The Body in Mystery: The Political Theology of the Corpus Mysticum in Post-Reformation England.* Evanston, IL: Northwestern University Press, 2014.

———. "Reforming the Mystical Body: From Mass to Martyr in John Foxe's *Acts and Monuments.*" *ELH: English Literary History* 80, no. 3 (Fall 2013): 627–59.

Rutter, Tom. *The Cambridge Introduction to Christopher Marlowe.* Cambridge: Cambridge University Press, 2012.

Ryan, Lawrence V. "Doctrine and Dramatic Structure in *Everyman.*" *Speculum* 32, no. 4 (1957): 722–35.

Ryrie, Alec. *Being Protestant in Reformation Britain.* Oxford: Oxford University Press, 2013.

———. *The Gospel and Henry VIII: Evangelicals in the Early English Reformation.* Cambridge: Cambridge University Press, 2003.

Sawday, Jonathan. *The Body Emblazoned.* London: Routledge, 1997.

Scherb, Victor. "Violence and the Social Body in the Croxton *Play of the Sacrament.*" In *Violence and Drama*, edited by James Redmond, 69–78. Cambridge: Cambridge University Press, 1991.

Schillebeeckx, Edward. *The Eucharist.* 1968. Reprint, London: Sheed and Ward, 2005.

Schoenfeldt, Michael C. *Bodies and Selves in Early Modern England: Physiology and Inwardness in Spenser, Shakespeare, Herbert, and Milton.* Cambridge: Cambridge University Press, 1999.

Schreyer, Kurt. *Shakespeare's Medieval Craft: Remnants of the Mysteries on the London Stage.* Ithaca, NY: Cornell University Press, 2014.

Schwartz, Regina. *Sacramental Poetics at the Dawn of Secularism: When God Left the World.* Stanford, CA: Stanford University Press, 2007.

Sedinger, Tracey. "'And Yet Woll I Stiell Saye That I Am I': *Jake Juggler*, the Lord's Supper, and Disguise." *ELH: English Literary History* 74, no. 1 (2007): 239–69.

Sewell, W. H. "On Sealed Altar Slabs." In *Norfolk Archaeology: Or Miscellaneous Tracts Relating to the Antiquities of the County of Norfolk.* Norwich: Miller and Leavins, 1879.

Shagan, Ethan, ed. *Catholics and the "Protestant Nation" in Early Modern England.* Manchester: Manchester University Press, 2009.

Shapiro, James. *Shakespeare and the Jews.* New York: Columbia University Press, 1996.

Sheingorn, Pamela. *The Easter Sepulchre in England.* Kalamazoo, MI: Medieval Institute Publications, 1987.

Shell, Alison. *Shakespeare and Religion.* London: Bloomsbury, 2010.

Sherman, William H. *Used Books: Marking Readers in Renaissance England.* Philadelphia: University of Pennsylvania Press, 2008.

Shrank, Cathy. "Civility and the City in *Coriolanus.*" *Shakespeare Quarterly* 54, no. 4 (Winter 2003): 406–23.

———. "John Bale and Reconfiguring the Medieval in Early Modern England." In *Reading the Medieval in Early Modern England*, edited by Gordon McMullan and David Matthews, 179–92. Cambridge: Cambridge University Press, 2007.

Shuger, Debora Kuller. *Habits of Thought in the English Renaissance: Religion, Politics, and the Dominant Culture*. Toronto: University of Toronto Press, 1997.

———. *Political Theologies in Shakespeare's England: The Sacred and the State in "Measure for Measure."* Houndmills, Basingstoke: Palgrave, 2001.

Sicherman, Carol. "*Coriolanus*: The Failure of Words." *ELH: English Literary History* 39, no. 1 (1972): 189–207.

Simpson, James. *Burning to Read: English Fundamentalism and Its Reformation Opponents*. Cambridge, MA: Harvard University Press, 2007.

———. "John Bale, *Three Laws*." In Betteridge and Walker, *Oxford Handbook*, 109–22.

———. *Reform and Cultural Revolution*. The Oxford English Literary History 2. Oxford: Oxford University Press, 2004.

———. "The Reformation of Scholarship: A Reply to Debora Shuger." *Journal of Medieval and Early Modern Studies* 42, no. 2 (2012): 249–68.

———. "Tyndale as Promoter of Figural Allegory and Figurative Language: *A Brief Declaration of the Sacraments*." *Archiv für das Studium der Neueren Sprachen und Literaturen* 245 (2008): 37–55.

Slights, William W. E. "Bodies of Text and Textualized Bodies in *Sejanus* and *Coriolanus*." *Medieval and Renaissance Drama in England* 5 (1991): 181–93.

Smalley, Beryl. *The Study of the Bible in the Middle Ages*. Notre Dame, IN: University of Notre Dame Press, 1989.

Smith, Bruce R. "Mona Lisa Takes a Tike, Hamlet Goes for an Ocean Dip." In *Center or Margin: Essays in Honor of J. Leeds Barroll*, edited by Lena Cowen Orlin, 238–53. Cranbury, NJ: Associated University Press, 2006.

———. *Phenomenal Shakespeare*. London: Wiley Blackwell, 2009.

Snoek, G. J. C. *Medieval Piety from Relics to the Eucharist: A Study of Mutual Interaction* Leiden: Brill, 1995.

Sofer, Andrew. *Dark Matter: Invisibility in Drama, Theater, and Performance*. Ann Arbor: University of Michigan Press. 2014.

———. "How to Do Things with Demons: Conjuring Performatives in *Doctor Faustus*." *Theatre Journal* 61, no. 1 (2009): 1–21.

———. *The Stage Life of Props*. Ann Arbor: University of Michigan Press, 2002.

Sokolowski, Robert, S.J. *Eucharistic Presence: A Study in the Theology of Disclosure*. Washington, DC: Catholic University of America Press, 2004.

Solberg, Emma Maggie. "A History of 'The Mysteries.'" *Early Theatre* 19.1 (2016): 9–36.

Sponsler, Claire. *Drama and Resistance: Bodies, Gender, and Theatricality in Late Medieval England*. Minneapolis: University of Minnesota Press, 1997.

———. *The Queen's Dumbshows: John Lydgate and the Making of Early Theater*. Philadelphia: University of Pennsylvania Press, 2014.

———. *Ritual Imports: Performing Medieval Drama in America*. Ithaca, NY: Cornell University Press, 2004.

Sponsler, Claire, and Robert Clark. "Othered Bodies: Racial Cross Dressing in the *Mistére de la Sainte Hostie* and the Croxton *Play of the Sacrament*." *Journal of Medieval and Early Modern Studies* 29, no. 1 (Winter 1999): 61–88.

Stallybrass, Peter, and Ann Rosalind Jones. "Fetishizing the Glove in Renaissance Europe." *Critical Inquiry* 28, no. 1 (Autumn 2001): 114–32.

Stanbury, Sarah. *The Visual Object of Desire in Late Medieval England*. Philadelphia: University of Pennsylvania Press, 2008.

Starks-Estes, Lisa S. "Virtus, Vulnerability, and the Emblazoned Male Body in Shakespeare's *Coriolanus*." In *Violent Masculinities: Male Aggression in Early Modern Texts and Culture*, edited by Jennifer Feather and Catherine Thomas, 85–106. New York: Palgrave Macmillan, 2013.

Steenbrugge, Charlotte. *Staging Vice: A Study of Dramatic Traditions in Medieval and Sixteenth-Century England and the Low Countries*. Amsterdam: Rodopi, 2014.

Stevens, Martin. *Four Middle English Mystery Cycles: Textual, Contextual, and Critical Interpretations*. Princeton, NJ: Princeton University Press, 1987.

Streete, Adrian. *Protestantism and Drama in Early Modern England*. Cambridge: Cambridge University Press, 2009.

Strier, Richard. *Love Known: Theology and Experience in George Herbert's Poetry*. Chicago: University of Chicago Press, 1983.

Strohm, Paul. "The Croxton *Play of the Sacrament*: Commemoration and Repetition in Late Medieval Culture." In *Performances of the Sacred in Late Medieval and Early Modern England*, edited by Susanne Rupp and Tobias Döring, 33–44. Amsterdam: Rodopi, 1994.

———. *England's Empty Throne: Usurpation and the Language of Legitimation, 1399–1422*. 1998. Reprint, Notre Dame, IN: Notre Dame University Press, 2006.

Swift, Daniel. *Shakespeare's Common Prayers: The Book of Common Prayer and the Elizabethan Age*. New York: Oxford University Press, 2012.

Symes, Carol. *A Common Stage: Theater and Public Life in Medieval Arras*. Ithaca, NY: Cornell University Press, 2007.

———. "The Medieval Archive and the History of Theatre: Assessing the Written and Unwritten Evidence for Premodern Performance." *Theatre Survey* 52.1 (May 2001): 29–58.

Targoff, Ramie. *Common Prayer: The Language of Public Devotion in Early Modern England*. Chicago: University of Chicago Press, 2001.

Tennenhouse, Leonard. "*Coriolanus* and the Crisis of Semantic Order." *Comparative Drama* 10, no. 4 (Winter 1976–77): 328–46.

———. *Power on Display: The Politics of Shakespeare's Genres*. London: Methuen, 1986.

Thomas, Keith. *Religion and the Decline of Magic*. New York: Charles Scribner's Sons, 1971.

Travis, Peter W. *Dramatic Design in the Chester Cycle*. Chicago: University of Chicago Press, 1982.

———. "The Semiotics of Christ's Body in the English Mystery Cycles." In *Approaches to Teaching Medieval English Literature*, edited by Richard K. Emmerson, 67–78. New York: Modern Language Association, 1990.

Tribble, Evelyn B. "The Partial Sign: Spenser and the Sixteenth-Century Crisis of Semiotics." In *Ceremony and Text in the Renaissance*, edited by Douglas F. Rutledge, 23–34. Newark: University of Delaware Press, 1996.

Tricomi, Albert. "Historicizing the Imagery of the Demonic in *The Duchess of Malfi*." *Journal of Medieval and Early Modern Studies* 34, no. 2 (Spring 2004): 345–82.

———. "The Severed Hand in Webster's *The Duchess of Malfi*." *Studies in English Literature* 44, no. 2 (Spring 2004): 347–58.

Twycross, Meg. "'They Did Not Come Out of an Abbey in Lancashire': Francis Douce and the Manuscript of the Towneley Plays." *Medieval English Theatre* 37 (2015): 149–65.

Wald, Christina. *The Reformation of Romance: The Eucharist, Disguise, and Foreign Fashion in Early Modern Prose Fiction*. Berlin: Walter de Gruyter, 2014.

Waldron, Jennifer. *Reformations of the Body: Idolatry, Sacrifice, and Early Modern Drama*. Houndmills, Basingstoke: Palgrave Macmillan, 2012.

Walker, Greg. *Plays of Persuasion*. Cambridge: Cambridge University Press, 1991.

Wall, Wendy. "Just a Spoonful of Sugar: Syrup and Domesticity in Early Modern England." *Modern Philology* 104, no. 2 (2011): 149–72.

Wall-Randell, Sarah. "*Doctor Faustus* and the Printer's Devil," *SEL: Studies in English Literature 1500–1900*. 48, no. 2 (2008): 266–67.

Walsham, Alexandra. "Skeletons in the Cupboard: Relics after the English Reformation." In *Relics and Remains*, edited by Alexandra Walsham. *Past and Present Supplements* 5 (2010): 141–63.

Wandel, Lee Palmer. *The Eucharist in the Reformation: Incarnation and Liturgy*. Cambridge: Cambridge University Press, 2007.

Wasson, John M. "The English Church as Theatrical Space." In Cox and Kastan, *New History*, 25–38.

———. "Records of Early English Drama: Where They Are and What They Tell Us." In *Records of Early English Drama: Proceedings of the First Colloquium*, edited by Joanna Dutka, 128–44. Toronto: Records of Early English Drama, 1979.

Watson, Nicholas. "Conceptions of the Word: The Mother Tongue and the Incarnation of God." *New Medieval Literatures* 1 (1998): 85–124.

West, William N. "What's the Matter with Shakespeare? Physics, Identity, Playing." *South Central Review* 26, nos. 1 and 2 (2009): 103–26.

Whalen, Robert. *The Poetry of Immanence: Sacrament in Donne and Herbert.* Toronto: University of Toronto Press, 2002.

Whigham, Frank. *Seizures of the Will in English Renaissance Drama.* Cambridge: Cambridge University Press, 1996.

White, Paul Whitfield. "The Chester Cycle and Early Elizabethan Religion." In Dell, Klausner, and Ostovich, *Chester Cycle in Context*, 111–32.

———. *Drama and Religion in English Provincial Society, 1485–1660.* Cambridge: Cambridge University Press, 2008.

———. "Reforming Mysteries' End: A New Look at Protestant Intervention in English Provincial Drama." *Journal of Medieval and Early Modern Studies* 29, no. 1 (1999): 121–47.

———. *Theatre and Reformation: Protestantism, Patronage, and Playing in Tudor England.* Cambridge: Cambridge University Press, 1993.

Wickham, Glynne. *Shakespeare's Dramatic Heritage.* London: Routledge, 1969.

Williams, David. "'Lo How I Vanysshe': The Pardoner's War against Signs." In *Chaucer and Language: Essays in Honor of Douglas Wurtele*, edited by Robert Myles and David A. Williams, 143–73. Quebec: McGill-Queens University Press, 2001.

Williams, Deanne. "Medievalism in English Renaissance Literature." In Cartwright, *Companion to Tudor Literature*, 213–27.

Williams, Rowan. "The Nature of a Sacrament." In *On Christian Theology*, 197–208. London: Wiley Blackwell, 2000.

Williamson, Elizabeth. *The Materiality of Religion in Early Modern English Drama.* Aldershot: Ashgate, 2009.

Wilson, Richard. *Secret Shakespeare: Studies in Theater, Religion, and Resistance.* Manchester: Manchester University Press, 2004.

Wilson, Richard, Richard Dutton, and Alison Findlay, eds. *Lancastrian Shakespeare: Region, Religion, and Patronage.* Manchester: Manchester University Press, 2004.

Wofford, Suzanne L. "The Body Unseamed: Shakespeare's Late Tragedies." In *Shakespeare's Late Tragedies*, edited by Susanne L. Wofford, 1–21. Upper Saddle River, NJ: Prentice Hall, 1996.

Wooding, Lucy E. C. *Rethinking Catholicism in Reformation England*. Oxford: Oxford University Press, 2000.

Woods, Gillian. *Shakespeare's Unreformed Fictions*. Oxford: Oxford University Press, 2013.

Woolf, Rosemary. *The English Mystery Plays*. Berkeley: University of California Press, 1972.

———. *The English Religious Lyric of the Middle Ages*. Oxford: Oxford University Press, 1968.

Wort, Oliver. *John Bale and Religious Conversion in Early Modern England*. London: Pickering and Chatto, 2013.

Young, Karl. *Drama of the Medieval Church*. 2 vols. Oxford: Oxford University Press, 1933.

Zachman, Randall C. *Image and Word in the Theology of Jean Calvin*. Notre Dame, IN: University of Notre Dame Press, 2009.

Zika, Charles. "Processions and Pilgrimages: Controlling the Sacred in Fifteenth-Century Germany." *Past and Present* 118 (February 1988): 25–64.

Zimmerman, Susan. "Duncan's Corpse." In *A Feminist Companion to Shakespeare*, edited by Dympna Callaghan, 320–41. Malden, MA: Blackwell, 2000.

———. *The Early Modern Corpse and Shakespeare's Theater*. Edinburgh: University of Edinburgh Press, 2007.

Žižek, Slavoj. *The Monstrosity of Christ: Paradox or Dialectic?* Cambridge, MA: MIT Press, 2009.

Zysk, Jay. "John 6, *Measure for Measure*, and the Complexities of the Literal Sense." In *The Bible on the Shakespearean Stage*, edited by Thomas Fulton and Kristen Poole. Cambridge: Cambridge University Press, forthcoming.

———. "The Last Temptation of Faustus: Contested Rites and Eucharistic Representation in *Doctor Faustus*." *Journal of Medieval and Early Modern Studies* 43, no. 2 (Spring 2013): 335–67.

———. "Melting Flesh, Living Words." *postmedieval: a journal of medieval cultural studies* 4, no. 4 (2013): 1–15.

———. "Reforming Corporeality: Eucharistic Semiotics in Early Modern English Drama." PhD diss., Brown University, 2011.

———. "Relics and Unreliable Bodies in *The Changeling*." *English Literary Renaissance* 45, no. 3 (Autumn 2015): 401–24.

———. "Shakespeare's Rich Ornaments: Style and Study in *Titus Andronicus*." In *Rapt in Secret Studies: Emerging Shakespeares*, edited by Darryl Chalk and Laurie Johnson, 269–86. Newcastle-upon-Tyne: Cambridge Scholars.

INDEX

Aers, David
    on the Eucharist, 3, 30, 32, 34, 125, 158, 230n.2, 244n.4, 247n.31, 250n.63, 254n.115, 256n.2, 319n.70
    on Galilean body, 244n.4
    on orthodoxy, 233n.5
    on relics and consecrated host, 158
    Sanctifying Signs, 230n.2, 233n.5, 247n.31
    on transubstantiation, 32, 34, 319n.70
    on Wyclif, 34, 168, 254n.115, 264n.56
affective piety tradition, 53
Agamben, Giorgio, 47, 272n.6
Alleyn, Edward, 141
Amalarius of Metz, 85
Ambrose, St., 22, 48, 85, 172
Anderson, Judith, 24, 49
    on Gardiner, 247n.27, 254n.104
    on *substantiam* in Eucharistic debate, 7, 237n.29
Andrewes, Lancelot
    on Christ's wounds, 65–66
    on divine kingship, 107–8
Aquinas, Thomas
    on doctrine of *pars pro toto*, 158
    on errors in rituals, 139
    on the Eucharist, 4, 11, 16, 22, 29–31, 33, 49, 124, 139, 149–50, 158, 172, 219, 247n.31, 248n.37, 249n.47, 249n.51, 254n.114, 288n.18, 292n.56, 305n.59, 319n.70, 320n.71
    on faith, 33
    on God's agency, 124, 288n.18
    on Incarnation, 30
    "Lauda Sion Salvatorem," 30–31
    "O sacrum convivium," 172, 173
    "O salutaris hostia," 111
    on sacraments and Christ's Passion, 149–50
    on sacraments as signs, 23, 29–31, 47, 123
    on substance and accidents, 33, 181, 219, 305n.59, 320n.71
    Summa theologiae, 29–30, 124, 139, 249n.47, 249n.51
    on transubstantiation, 4, 22, 30, 47, 49, 158, 219, 249n.47, 249n.51, 305n.59, 314n.23, 319n.70, 320n.71
Askew, Anne, 4
Aston, Margaret
    on Corpus Christi feast, 158
    on the Eucharist, 249n.46
Atkin, Tamara, 165, 208, 315n.38
Augustine, St.
    on the Eucharist, 11, 22, 35, 86, 234n.10, 250n.63, 252n.89, 320n.78
    on faith, 35
    on sacraments and signs, 23, 228

auricular confession, 95, 97–98
Austin, J. L.
   speech-act theory of, 24, 47, 124, 138–39, 144, 232, 292n.56
   How to Do Things with Words, 138–39, 288n.16
   on infelicities in speech acts, 138–39, 144, 292n.56
   on performative utterance, 124, 141, 232n.4, 288n.16, 292n.56, 293n.74, 295n.85
Axton, Marie, 315n.38, 316n.46, 317n.54

Baines, Richard, 289n.27
Bale, John, 56, 198, 313n.18
   as anti-Catholic, 95–101, 102–4, 106, 278n.61, 280n.70
   on auricular confession, 97–98
   The Epistle Exhortatorye of an Englysshe Christiane, 99
   and the Eucharist, 12, 84, 98–99, 100–101, 102, 105, 117, 209, 278n.51, 278n.55, 279n.69, 304n.53
   and sacred kingship/*corpus mysticum*, 12, 82, 84, 87, 94, 95–96, 98–99, 100, 101, 102, 105, 108, 117
   on scriptural and royal authority, 95, 96, 97
   Three Laws, 270n.93
   on Word of God, 95
   See also King Johan
baptism, 150, 313n.17
Barclay, John, 302n.36
Barton, Anne, 77
Bate, Jonathan, 236n.22
Beadle, Richard, 58, 59, 68, 259n.21, 263n.46, 263n.48, 264n.59, 311n.4, 312n.7
Becket, Thomas, 104, 162

Beckwith, Sarah, 62, 194–95, 320n.75
   on biblical drama, 72–73, 80, 165, 172, 201, 263n.49, 264n.57
   on the Eucharist, 8, 41, 125, 250n.63, 254n.110, 263n.49, 299n.15
   Signifying God, 230n.2, 263n.49, 264n.57
Belsey, Catherine, 143, 181, 307n.79
Benson, C. David
   on Lydgate, 89
   on relics, 298n.9
Berengar of Tours, 22, 86, 245n.10
Berger, Harry, Jr., 108
Bergeron, David, 305n.69
Betteridge, Thomas, 96
Bevington, David, 144, 286n.3, 287n.7, 315n.38
biblical dramas, 55–58, 151, 197, 269n.89
   adaptability to religious changes, 60–61
   Christ's wounds as readable text, 2, 53–54, 61–72, 73, 75, 170, 255n.1
   and *Coriolanus*, 11, 53–55, 71, 72, 74–75, 77, 79–82, 267nn.74–75
   Doubting Thomas in, 64, 191, 193, 194, 197, 204, 206, 210, 215, 315n.35
   and the Eucharist, 1, 2–3, 9, 61, 62, 64, 66–71, 75, 82, 191, 192, 193–94, 196, 199–202, 203–6, 207–8, 212–13, 264n.59, 265n.61, 266nn.68–69, 266n.71, 297n.4, 312n.7, 314n.27
   and feast of Corpus Christi, 14, 56, 58, 77, 80, 89, 92, 94, 158, 172, 244n.4, 258nn.15–16, 260n.25, 270n.96
   and Shakespeare, 5, 53–54, 55, 59–60, 61, 71, 235n.14, 257n.8, 257nn.11–12, 267n.74, 268n.76, 283n.106, 284n.111, 321n.83

and social community, 11, 54, 56–57, 71, 72, 79–80, 202, 203, 204, 205, 270n.96
  suppression of, 56, 58
  variety of, 56–57
  at Whitsunday (Pentecost), 58–59, 258n.16, 260n.25, 265n.62
  See also Chester plays; Emmaus plays; N-Town plays; Towneley plays; York plays
biblical hermeneutics
  allegorical interpretation, 43, 44
  anagogical interpretation, 43
  literal interpretation, 43–47, 227
  tropological interpretation, 43
Bishop, Thomas, 5, 194, 218, 264n.57, 319n.67
Boece, Hector, 283n.104
Bonaventure, St., 172
Bonner, Edmund, 96, 99
Book of Common Prayer, 25, 105, 284n.112, 290n.37
  Eucharist in, 15, 16, 51–52, 71, 86, 115, 125, 137, 266n.71, 282n.93, 285n.115, 299n.18
  Order of Communion, 71, 86, 115, 125, 255n.124, 289n.23
  revisions, 15, 105, 115, 137, 228, 280n.75, 282n.93, 322n.11
Borromeo, San Carlo, 155
Braunmuller, A. R., 105
Brokaw, Katherine Steele, 315n.39
Bromham, A. A., 309n.97
Brown, Peter, 157
Bruster, Douglas, 287n.7
Bruzzi, Zara, 309n.97
Bucer, Martin, 137, 160–61
Bury St. Edmunds, 171, 260n.28, 273n.19, 305n.65
Bynum, Caroline Walker, 111, 122, 147, 311n.113
  on relics, 156, 164, 181, 302n.37
Byrhtnoth, 179

Caesarius of Heisterbach: *Dialogus miraculorum*, 161–62
Calbi, Maurizio, 187
Calvin, John
  on the Eucharist, 11, 37–38, 39, 41–42, 50, 137, 140, 269n.92
  on false relics, 161, 163, 179–80, 185
  Institutes of the Christian Religion, 37–38, 41
  on predestination, 146
  on transubstantiation, 41–42, 140
  A Very Profitable Treatise on Relics, 179–80
  vs. Wyclif, 38
Cameron, Euan, 121
Campion, Edmund, 4
Camporesi, Piero, 138
Cannobio: *sacra costa* (holy rib) miracle in, 155–56, 297n.1
Carpenter, John, 88, 274n.22, 275n.31
Cartwright, Kent, 207
Cary, Philip, 320n.78
Castle of Perseverance, The, 121
Catesby, Robert, 106
Catherine of Siena, St., 311n.113
Cavell, Stanley
  on *Coriolanus*, 72, 78, 267n.75, 268n.76
  Disowning Knowledge in Seven Plays of Shakespeare, 267n.75
Chambers, E. K., 294n.77
charity, 33, 34, 265n.60, 270n.100, 320n.78
Chaucer's *fabliaux*, 315n.40
Chaucer's Pardoner, 161, 301n.30
Chester plays, 69–70, 266n.66, 267n.72
  Antichrist, 266n.71
  Ascension, 205
  Emmaus, 193, 194, 196, 202, 204, 315n.35

Chester plays (*cont.*)
  and the Eucharist, 61, 68, 70, 71, 196, 201, 266nn.68–69, 266n.71, 313n.17
  Passion, 62
  performed as civic cycle, 54, 58–59, 60, 61, 79–80, 257n.12, 258n.16, 260n.25, 265n.62, 266n.70
  Resurrection, 69–71, 266n.71
  suppression of, 56
Chrysostom, John, 22
Church of England
  Eucharistic participation in, 10, 35–36, 37, 51, 125–26, 191, 202–3, 213, 217, 220, 221–22
  Good Friday sermons, 53, 65–66
  See also Book of Common Prayer
Clopper, Lawrence M.: on biblical dramas, 56, 57, 58, 59, 260n.25, 261n.40
Cole, Andrew, 16, 31, 89, 93, 248n.33, 249n.59, 274n.24, 275n.25, 276n.36
Cole, Henry, 23
Coleman, David, 98, 279n.69, 293n.72
Coletti, Theresa, 9, 266n.64
  on Chester plays, 265n.62, 267n.72
  on Emmaus plays, 194
  on Mary Magdalene, 68, 264n.57, 265n.61
  "The Tudor Origins of Medieval Drama," 57
  on Towneley plays, 60, 64, 261n.39
commedia dell'arte, 207
Common Worship, 228, 322n.11
confession, 95, 97–98
Congregation for Divine Worship and Discipline of the Sacraments, 225–26
1 Corinthians 12, 272n.5

Coriolanus
  Aufidius, 81, 82
  and biblical drama, 11, 53–55, 71, 72, 74–75, 77, 79–82, 267nn.74–75
  Brutus, 78, 79, 81
  death of Coriolanus, 81–82
  and the Eucharist, 72, 73, 76, 77, 82
  grain riots in, 80, 270n.99
  iconoclasm of Coriolanus, 11–12, 74–79, 80–82, 269n.91
  Menenius, 73, 74, 75
  Sicinius, 81
  and social community, 11–12, 72, 73–74, 76, 77, 78, 82
  Volumnia, 73, 74, 75
  wounds of Coriolanus, 11–12, 53–55, 61, 71–82, 256n.6, 267nn.74–75, 268n.76
Corpus Christi plays. *See* biblical dramas
Council of Constance, 5
Council of Trent, 225, 290n.33
  on *ex opere operato*, 124
  on relics, 157, 186, 307n.73
  on transubstantiation, 25, 40–41, 246n.21, 291n.43
Counter-Reformation, 25
Coventry plays, 56
Coverdale, Miles, 137, 303n.48
Cox, John D.: on early English drama, 233n.6
Cranmer, Thomas, 4, 95, 96, 316n.46
  Defence of the True and Catholike Doctrine of the Sacrament of the Body and Blood of Our Saviour Christ, 36, 48, 313n.18
  on the Eucharist, 16, 23, 27, 28, 35, 36, 38, 41, 42, 45–46, 48–50, 51, 99, 113–14, 158–59, 198, 199, 209, 212, 222, 250n.65, 254n.115, 299n.18, 314n.22

on sacraments as signs, 24
on substance vs. accidents,
   319n.68
on transubstantiation, 35, 41,
   45–46, 48–50, 158–59, 212
on words of consecration, 48–49
Crashaw, Richard, 8
   on the Eucharist, 158
   "Lauda Sion Salvatorem," 158
Crassons, Kate, 270n.100
Cromwell, Thomas, 95, 96, 97, 118,
   279n.66, 313n.18
Croxton *Play of the Sacrament*, 57,
   111, 164–74, 297n.4, 302n.43
   Aristorius, 166
   Episcopus, 166, 170–72, 189
   and Eucharistic Controversies, 166,
      167, 169
   image of Christ in, 169–70, 177,
      188
   Jasdon, 169, 170
   Jason, 169
   Jonathas, 166–69, 170–71, 177,
      188, 305n.61
   Malchus, 170
   Masphat, 168, 169
   and Middleton and Rowley's
      Changeling, 13, 156, 164, 174,
      188, 189–90
   skepticism of Jews in, 156, 164,
      166–71, 177
   violence in, 165–66, 167–70, 174,
      188
   and Webster's *Duchess of Malfi*, 13,
      156, 164, 174, 177–78, 189–90
Cummings, Brian, 243n.53, 322n.11
   *The Literary Culture of the
   Reformation*, 230n.2
   on Protestant Reformation, 47,
      230n.2
cycle plays. *See* biblical dramas
Cyprian, St., 313n.17

Dailey, Alice, 308n.91, 317n.59
Davidson, Clifford, 294n.80
Davis, Lisa Fagin, 296n.93
Dawson, Anthony, 5, 35–36
Deats, Sara Munson, 146
Dekker, Thomas: *Pleasant Comedie of
   Old Fortunatus*
   Shadow in, 236n.22
de Lubac, Henri
   Corpus Mysticum, 85
   on the Eucharist, 20, 87, 93, 95, 99,
      108, 254n.115
   on supper at Emmaus, 196
Derrida, Jacques: on *supplement*, 161,
   164, 232n.4
Diehl, Huston, 179, 307n.80, 317n.59,
   319n.66
Digby *Mary Magdalene*, 264n.57,
   265n.61
divine right, 83, 107–8, 112
Dobell, Bertram, 313n.18
Doctor Faustus
   A text vs. B text, 130, 148, 149, 150,
      151–52, 154, 286n.3, 289n.28,
      289n.30, 294n.80
   Bad Angels, 153
   conjuror's circle in, 130, 141–44,
      146
   and Eucharistic confection, 12, 13,
      119, 120–21, 126, 128–30,
      131–41, 143, 145–46, 147–48,
      153
   and *Everyman*, 12–13, 118, 119,
      120–21, 126, 128, 150, 154
   Faustus as magician, 118, 120–22,
      126, 128–29, 130–31, 137, 138,
      140, 141–44, 148, 152, 154,
      290n.31, 293nn.72, 74, 294n.75
   Faustus's salvation, 120, 128, 145,
      146, 149, 150, 151–52, 153
   Good Angel, 151
   Lucifer, 152

Doctor Faustus (cont.)
  Mephistopheles, 129, 130, 144, 145, 146–47, 149, 294n.75, 294n.78, 295n.85
  and missals, 13, 119–20, 126, 128, 129–40, 143, 148, 152, 293n.69
  Old Man, 150, 153
  scene at Rome, 141, 144–45, 152, 294nn.78–80
  Second Scholar, 151, 152
  signing of the deed of gift/contract scene, 3, 141, 146–49, 150, 295n.85, 295n.87
  Valdes, 129
  vision of Christ's blood in the firmament, 141, 145, 146, 149, 150, 152, 295n.87
Donatist Controversies, 124
Donne, John, 8
  on divine kingship, 107–8
Doubting Thomas, 6, 67, 221, 311n.2
  in biblical dramas, 64, 191, 193, 194, 197, 204, 206, 210, 215, 315n.35
Douce, Francis, 59, 260n.31
Duffy, Eamon, 255n.123, 290n.35

Edward VI, 23, 52, 61, 104, 271n.2, 280n.75
  Edwardian Reforms, 95, 208
Ekeblad, Inga-Stina, 305n.69
Elam, Keir, 232n.4
Elckerlijc, 121
Elizabeth I, 61, 105, 271n.2
Elizabethan Settlement, 51, 126
  Thirty-Nine Articles, 25, 41, 250n.66
  Opinions Concerning Transubstantiation, 125
embodiment studies, 9–10
Emmaus plays, 170, 191–206, 215, 311n.2, 311n.4
  and the Eucharist, 3, 13, 14, 61, 64, 68, 70, 71, 191, 192, 193–94, 196, 199–202, 203–6, 207–8, 212–13, 266nn.68–69, 266n.71, 270n.96, 312n.7, 313n.17, 314n.27
  and *Jack Juggler*, 13–14, 192, 206, 207, 210, 211, 212–13, 220, 223
  and *Winter's Tale*, 206, 214, 216, 220, 223
  See also Chester plays; N-Town plays; Towneley plays; York plays
Enders, Jodie: *The Medieval Theater of Cruelty*, 255n.1
Enterline, Lynn, 321n.82
Eucharist, the
  Christ's institution of, 4, 7–8, 19–21, 26–28, 30, 33, 39, 44, 46, 50, 90, 99, 125, 177, 210, 212, 227, 237n.31, 254n.115
  doctrine of *pars pro toto*, 158–59, 163, 186, 299n.18
  and ecclesiastical community, 19, 25, 35, 56, 80
  fractioning of the host, 136, 291n.45, 299n.18
  levation prayers, 68, 69, 265n.59
  memorialism, 3, 22–23, 36, 44
  miracula related to, 155–56
  multilocationism regarding, 33, 208, 316n.44
  as *mysterium tremendum*, 8
  reformed views regarding, 4–5, 7, 9, 11, 15–16, 20–21, 22–23, 27, 33–39, 40–42, 44–46, 48–51, 68, 69, 70–71, 86, 97, 98–99, 115, 118, 125–26, 137, 139–40, 141, 142, 143, 158, 198, 202–3, 208–9, 212, 217, 220, 221, 222, 242n.50, 243nn.52–53, 250nn.62–63, 250n.66, 252n.85, 253n.103, 254n.115, 265n.60, 278n.51, 278n.55, 279n.69, 289n.23, 295n.84, 299n.18, 303n.48, 304n.53, 317n.59, 320n.72

relationship to drama, 1–3, 4, 5–6,
8–9, 10–12, 13–14, 16–17
relationship to religious poetry,
8–9
relationship to religious violence,
4–5
relationship to scriptural
interpretation, 28, 29, 39, 41,
43–44
relationship to semiotics, 8, 26, 28,
30, 31–32, 38, 228, 232n.4,
244n.1, 248n.33, 320n.72
role of faith in, 33, 34, 35, 37, 39,
41, 42, 50, 51, 71, 125–26, 146,
167, 203, 221, 222, 250n.63,
284n.107, 305n.59, 320n.72,
320n.78
and sacramental grace, 28, 37, 50,
124
and sin, 115
traditional/orthodox views
regarding, 4–5, 7, 9, 15–16,
20–21, 22, 25–26, 27, 31–33,
34, 35, 40–43, 45–46, 47–48,
49–50, 68, 69, 70–71, 89, 95, 97,
99, 100, 118, 121–23, 126, 137,
139–40, 141, 142, 143, 157–59,
198–99, 202, 208–9, 211–12,
217, 219, 242n.50, 243n.53,
246n.21, 247n.30, 249nn.46–47,
249n.51, 250n.66, 252n.93,
266n.71, 291n.43, 297n.4,
299n.15, 314n.23, 317n.59,
319n.70
typological readings of, 30, 91, 111,
196–97, 313n.17
See also Croxton *Play of the
Sacrament*; Eucharistic
confection; Eucharistic
Controversies; Eucharistic
participation; flesh and spirit;
missals; semiotics;
transubstantiation

Eucharistic confection, 47–52, 126,
159, 170, 221, 254nn.114–115,
265n.63, 288n.15
defined, 39, 47, 208
and *Doctor Faustus*, 12, 13, 119,
120–21, 126, 128–30, 131–41,
143, 145–46, 147–48, 153
and *Everyman*, 119, 120–22,
123–24, 125, 128
and *Jack Juggler*, 208, 211–12
and *Winter's Tale*, 215, 217–18
and words "hoc est enim corpus
meum," 21, 37, 47, 69, 139, 208,
218
Eucharistic Controversies, 1, 2, 3–5,
7, 9, 10, 15–16, 17, 20–29, 76,
93, 228, 229, 230n.1, 242n.50
semiotics in, 11, 20, 22, 24, 26,
27–28, 29–35, 201–2
and Croxton *Play of the Sacrament*,
166, 167, 169
defined, 234n.7
and *Doctor Faustus*, 128
and doctrine of *pars pro toto*,
158–59
and Emmaus plays, 199–203
flesh and spirit in, 11, 28, 35–39,
84
and *Jack Juggler*, 192, 207, 208,
211–12
literalism and figuralism in, 11, 28,
39–47
role of metaphysics in, 20, 22, 23,
27, 29, 32–34, 49–50, 51
and Webster's *Duchess of Malfi*, 178
and *Winter's Tale*, 192
words and deeds in, 11, 28, 29, 39,
47–52
Eucharistic participation, 9, 29,
34–37
in Church of England, 10, 35–36,
37, 51, 125–26, 191, 202–3, 213,
217, 220, 221–22

Eucharistic participation (*cont.*)
  Hooker on, 4, 35, 36–37, 50, 51, 200, 204, 220, 221, 250n.63, 320n.72
  Jewel on, 51, 200, 203, 220, 221
  Wyclif on, 34, 200, 202–3
Everyman
  clerical authority in, 119, 121–24, 126
  and *Doctor Faustus*, 12–13, 118, 119, 120–21, 126, 128, 150, 154
  and Eucharistic confection, 119, 120–22, 123–24, 125, 128, 287n.9
  Five Wits, 122, 123, 125
  performance history, 287n.6
  printing history, 287n.7
Exodus 3:14, 210

faith
  Aquinas on, 33
  Augustine on, 35
  Jewel on, 35, 71
  role in the Eucharist, 33, 34, 35, 37, 39, 41, 42, 50, 51, 71, 125–26, 146, 167, 203, 221, 222, 250n.63, 265n.60, 284n.107, 305n.59, 320n.72, 320n.78
  Wyclif on, 265n.60
Fawkes, Guy, 106
feminism, 268n.80, 306n.72
Fish, Simon: *Supplicacyon for Beggars*, 101, 280n.70
Fisher, John: on Christ's body and blood, 53, 66, 255n.1
FitzPatrick, P. J., 314n.23
flesh and spirit
  in Eucharistic Controversies, 11, 28, 35–39, 84
  relationship to *corpus mysticum*, 85–86, 109, 113, 117, 118

Fourth Lateran Council
  on Eucharistic confection, 48
  on relics, 157, 307n.82
  on transubstantiation, 25–26, 89
Foxe, John
  Actes and Monuments, 101, 103
  on the Eucharist, 42
  on poisoning of King John, 101–2, 110
  on relics, 159–60
  A Sermon of Christ Crucified, 159–60
Frith, John: on the Eucharist, 42, 43, 178, 252n.90
Fulke, William, 15

Gallagher, Lowell, 148, 255n.1
  on the Eucharistic Controversies, 238n.35
  on stigmata, 256n.4
Garber, Marjorie, 145, 294n.79
Gardiner, Harold, 261n.40
Gardiner, Stephen
  Detection of the Devils Sophistrie, 46
  on doctrine of *pars pro toto*, 159
  on the Eucharist, 7, 16, 23, 27, 28, 31, 32, 41, 42, 45–46, 48, 49–50, 159, 198–99, 237n.29, 247n.27, 250n.66, 254n.104, 299n.18
  on reason, 32
  on shadow and substance, 7, 237n.29
  on transubstantiation, 23, 27, 31, 32, 41, 45, 46, 48, 49–50, 159, 198–99
Garter, Bernard, 159, 160
Genesis 2:21, 190
Gibson, Gail McMurray, 266n.64, 305n.65
  on Bury St. Edmunds, 171, 273n.19, 274n.25
  on N-Town plays, 260n.28

on Towneley plays, 60, 64, 261n.39
"The Tudor Origins of Medieval Drama," 57
God's agency, 123, 124, 288n.18
God's creation of Eve, 190
God's grace, 185, 288n.18
God's miracles, 162
Gower Missal of Sarum Use, 291n.43
Gowing, Laura: on "politics of touch," 183
Grantley, Darryl, 315n.38
Great Bible of 1539–40, 291n.46
Greenblatt, Stephen, 3–4, 8, 24, 234n.10
Greene, Robert
  The Honourable Historie of Frier Bacon and Frier Bongay, 236n.22
  Pandosto, or the Triumph of Time, 213, 318n.61
  The Repentance of Robert Greene, 317n.57
grimoire, 129
Guibert of Nogent, 304n.49
Gunpowder Plot of 1605, 105, 106–7, 112
Gurnay, Edmund
  Corpus Christi, 179
  on the Eucharist, 7, 179

Haigh, Christopher, 293n.68
Hamlet: Ophelia's burial, 152, 296n.91
Hamlin, Hannibal, 256n.6, 267n.75, 269n.91, 270n.94
Happé, Peter, 97, 105, 300n.28
Harding, Thomas
  on the Eucharist, 16, 23, 41, 46, 250n.66, 252n.85
  on transubstantiation, 23, 41, 46
Harris, Jonathan Gil, 143, 293n.73
Harrison, Peter: *The Bible, Protestantism, and the Rise of Natural Science*, 252n.94

Harrowing of Hell pageants, 151
  Anima Christi in, 62
Helena, St., 163
Henry VIII, 105, 209, 290n.33
  Act of Supremacy of 1534, 95
  break with papacy, 96
  coronation of, 83
  on the Eucharist, 4, 25–26, 35, 97
  Royal Injunctions of 1538, 185–86
  Six Articles, 25–26, 95, 97, 278n.55
  on transubstantiation, 4, 25–26, 35, 97
Herbert, George, 8
Hillman, David, 297n.3
Holinshed's *Chronicles*, 105, 283n.104
Holland, Peter, 267n.74
Holsinger, Bruce: on liturgical books, 126, 128
Homilie for Good Friday, 66
Homilie of the worthie receyvyng and reverent esteemyng of the Sacrament, 114, 125–26, 205
Hooker, Richard, 11, 16
  on the Eucharist, 4, 35, 36–37, 38, 50, 51, 71, 76, 99, 200, 204, 220, 221, 222, 250nn.62–63, 320n.72
  on Eucharistic participation, 4, 35, 36–37, 50, 51, 200, 204, 220, 221, 250n.63, 320n.72
  on interpretation of sacraments, 3
  on transubstantiation, 4, 35, 221, 320n.72
  on word of God and wounds of Christ, 36–37, 76–77
hope, 33, 34, 265n.60
Howard, Jean E., 271n.101
Hunt, Alice, 271n.2, 279n.67

iconic signs, 176, 178
indexical signs, 157–58, 176, 178, 184

Jack Juggler, 207–13
  Buongrace, 207, 208, 211, 212
  Dame Coy, 207
  and Emmaus plays, 13–14, 192, 206, 207–8, 210, 211, 212–13, 220, 223
  and the Eucharist, 192, 207, 208–9, 211–13
  Jack Juggler, 207, 208–12, 315n.39
  Jankyn Careaway, 192, 206, 207–12, 213, 216, 220–21, 317n.54
  performance history, 315n.38, 316n.41
  term *juggler*, 139–40, 316n.46
  and *Winter's Tale*, 13–14, 192, 206, 210, 213, 216, 220–21, 223
James I
  on divine right, 112, 283n.102
  on Gunpowder Plot, 106–7
  progress to York in 1603, 77–78
  The True Law of Free Monarchies, 283n.102
  Two Meditations of the Kings Majestie, 112
Jensen, Phebe, 317n.59
Jeremiah's chalice, 91
Jerome, St., 89
Jesus Christ
  as bread of life, 42–43, 50, 69, 70, 253n.102
  as *Christus medicus*, 305n.61
  Crucifixion, 2–3, 5–6, 19–20, 36–37, 53–54, 55, 61–66, 74–75, 79, 80, 81, 82, 131–32, 147, 148, 149, 150, 154, 169, 170, 195, 197, 244n.4, 256n.4, 258n.16, 266n.66, 283n.106, 291n.38, 321n.83
  Eucharistic body of, 1, 7–8, 12, 28, 30–31, 39, 45–46, 47, 80, 83, 84–87, 88, 89, 93–94, 95, 99, 101, 102, 108, 117, 132, 166, 167, 168, 170, 172, 174, 178–79, 189, 193, 201, 205, 208, 244n.4
  Eucharistic institution, 4, 7–8, 19–21, 26–28, 30, 33, 39, 44, 46, 90, 99, 125, 177, 210, 212, 227, 237n.31, 254n.115
  Galilean body of, 12, 21, 23, 32, 34, 76–77, 83, 84–85, 86, 93–94, 102, 108, 125, 137, 168, 170, 191, 192, 204–5, 219, 223, 244n.4, 319n.70
  Incarnation, 19, 30, 31, 34, 74, 84, 91, 169, 194, 196, 197
  Last Judgment, 258n.16
  mystical body (*corpus mysticum*)/ecclesial body of, 4, 5, 12, 28, 34–35, 51, 75, 76–77, 81, 83, 84–87, 88, 90, 92–94, 95, 98–99, 101, 102, 105, 107–8, 109, 111, 112–13, 114, 117, 123, 171–72, 174, 201, 202, 205, 220, 221, 248n.33, 272nn.5–6, 273nn.16–18, 277n.48, 284nn.112–13, 320n.78
  Passion, 5, 6–7, 11–12, 19, 55, 61, 62, 63, 64, 65, 66–68, 70, 71–72, 74–75, 91, 111, 112, 147, 148, 149–50, 194, 195–96, 197, 258n.16, 263n.46, 270n.94, 276n.42, 313n.17
  Peter appointed as first pope, 122
  Resurrection, 2–3, 5, 13, 19–20, 53, 54, 55, 61, 62, 67–68, 69–70, 82, 192–206, 211, 258n.16
  and salvation, 63, 64, 65, 66, 67, 71, 74–75, 81, 111, 112
  sweating blood at Gethsemane, 147
  water changed into wine, 90
  words at Last Supper, 4, 7–8, 20–21, 26–27, 28, 33, 39, 40, 41–42, 44, 45–46, 48, 49, 50, 99, 115, 116, 210, 212, 227, 249n.51, 254n.115
  wounds of, 2, 11–12, 36–37, 53–54, 61–72, 73, 74–75, 76, 79, 81, 82, 131, 170, 255n.1, 256n.2,

256n.4, 263n.46, 263n.48, 267n.75, 268n.76
See also biblical dramas; Eucharist, the; Eucharistic confection; Eucharistic Controversies
Jewel, John
  Apologie of the Church of England, 20–21, 106, 303n.48
  on the Eucharist, 11, 20–21, 23, 35, 41, 51, 71, 99, 139, 200, 203, 208–9, 220, 221, 222, 254n.115, 303n.48, 320n.72
  on Eucharistic participation, 51, 200, 203, 220, 221
  on faith, 35, 71
  on sacraments, 23–24
  A Sermon Pronounced at Paul's Cross, 203
  on transubstantiation, 20–21, 221, 320n.72
John 6:53–57, 42–43, 70, 252n.89, 253n.102
John Paul II, 225
Johnson, Kimberly, 23, 237n.31, 238n.36, 242n.48, 243n.53, 244n.1
Johnston, Alexandra F., 56–57, 258n.16, 260n.25
Jones, Ann Rosalind, 183, 184
Joye, George
  on the Eucharist, 29, 38–39, 42, 139, 140, 209, 237n.28, 252n.93, 299n.10, 314n.29
  The Souper of the Lorde, 237n.28
Judas, 284n.107
Julius Caesar
  Caesar's wounds in, 74
  Octavius, 74

Kahn, Coppélia, 6, 73, 75, 268n.80
Kantorowicz, Ernst, 85, 95, 273nn.16–17, 277n.48
  The King's Two Bodies, 87

Karlstadt, Andreas, 22, 34, 234n.7
Kastan, David Scott, 9, 118, 233n.6, 285n.117
Kearney, James, 247n.27, 290n.31, 295n.87
King Johan, 95–105, 277n.46, 278n.55, 280n.70
  Dissymulacyon, 100, 101, 102
  Imperiall Majestye, 12, 102–5, 117, 280n.74
  King Johan, 12, 94, 95, 97, 100–102, 104, 106, 110, 117, 279n.67
  and Lydgate's *Procession of Corpus Christi*, 95, 101
  and Lydgate's *Triumphal Entry*, 100, 101, 104
  and *Macbeth*, 12, 82, 87, 94, 108, 109, 110, 117–18
  Nobylyte, 96, 98, 101, 102
  relics in, 300n.28
  sacred kingship/*corpus mysticum* in, 12, 82, 84, 87, 94, 95–96, 98–99, 100, 101, 102, 105, 108, 117
  Sedicyon, 97–98, 100, 101, 300n.28
  and Shakespeare's *King John*, 105
  Usurped Power, 100, 279n.66
  Veritas, 96, 102–3
Kipling, Gordon, 88, 90, 269n.89, 275n.29, 276n.34
Kirby, Torrance, 220, 235n.12, 244n.1, 320n.72
Knollys Family Psalter, 153, 296n.93
Kolve, V. A.: on feast of Corpus Christi, 258nn.15–16

Lambeth faire, 300n.28
Lamentations 1:12, 63
Lancashire, Anne, 274n.25, 316n.41
Langland, William: *Piers Plowman*, 316n.46
Late Banns (Chester plays), 266n.70
Laud, William, 15

Lemon, Rebecca, 112, 118, 283n.103
Lerer, Seth, 165
Liber Eliensis, 179
Liturgiam authenticam, 226–28
Livy, 267n.74
Lollard Conclusions, 293n.70, 301n.29
Love, Nicholas: *Mirror of the Blessed Life of Jesus Christ*, 53
Loewenstein, David: *Shakespeare and Early Modern Religion*, 235n.14
Ludus Coventriae, 266n.66
Luke
  24:13–35, 311n.2
  24:30, 314n.27
  24:35, 202
Lumiansky, R. M., 266n.69
Lupton, Julia Reinhard, 318n.62
Luther, Martin, 11, 43
  Confession Concerning Christ's Last Supper, 40, 254n.115, 316n.44
  on the Eucharist, 23, 40, 208, 234n.7
  on multilocationism, 316n.44
Lydgate, John, 272n.7, 273n.19
  and the Eucharist, 12, 84, 87, 89, 90–91, 92–94, 95, 110, 118, 276n.34, 276n.36, 276n.43
  Henry VI's Triumphal Entry into London, 12, 82, 84, 88–90, 91–92, 94, 100, 101, 104, 108, 109, 152, 274nn.21, 22, 275nn.29, 31, 276nn.34, 36, 42
  on Jacob, 92–94
  on Jeremiah's chalice, 91
  "A Prayer for King, Queen, and People," 90
  A Procession of Corpus Christi, 12, 82, 84, 88, 89, 91, 92–94, 95, 101, 118, 273n.19, 274n.21, 274n.25, 275n.27, 276nn.41–43
  and sacred kingship/*corpus mysticum*, 12, 82, 84, 87, 88, 90–91, 92–93, 94, 101, 108
  and social community, 88, 90, 93, 94

Macbeth, 9, 108–18, 281n.87
  Banquo's Ghost, 109, 113, 114–17, 285n.114
  Duncan's murder, 12, 87, 105, 108–13, 115, 117–18
  and the Eucharist, 84, 113–14
  and *King Johan*, 12, 82, 87, 94, 108, 109, 110, 117–18
  Lady Macbeth, 110, 116
  Macbeth, 109–11, 112–13, 114, 115–17, 283n.103, 284n.111, 285n.117
  Macduff, 102
  Malcolm, 109, 117–18
  sacred kingship/*corpus mysticum* in, 12, 82, 84, 87, 94, 108–9, 111, 112–13, 114, 116–18, 281n.87, 285n.117
Mainardi, Agostino
  An Anatomi, that is to say a parting in Peeces of the Mass, 131–32
  on the Eucharist, 140
Malo, Robyn, 176, 299n.13, 304n.49
Mankind, 121
Marburg Colloquy of 1529, 23
Marcus, Leah, 130, 151, 177, 307n.79
Marlowe, Christopher, 289n.29
  atheism of, 17, 289n.27
  and the Eucharist, 1, 120–21
  as rejecting Catholic ritual, 143
  See also Doctor Faustus
Marsalek, Karen Sawyer, 220, 313nn.18–19, 314n.22, 314n.26
Marshall, Cynthia, 75, 256n.6
Martin, James, 228
Mary I, 23, 52, 60, 61, 208, 278n.61
Mary Magdalene, 9, 64, 67–68, 193, 196, 264n.57, 265nn.60–61
Mass of Bolsena, 155, 168
Mayer, Sebastian: on relics, 161
Mazzio, Carla, 297n.3
  The Inarticulate Renaissance, 288n.15

McCoy, Richard
  on *Macbeth*, 108, 110, 281n.87, 284n.113
  on royal presence, 271n.1
McCullough, Peter, 235n.14
McGillivray, Murray, 69, 261n.39
memorialism, 3, 22–23, 36, 44
Mentz, Steven R., 317n.57
metaphor, 24, 34, 40, 87
metonymy, 45, 156, 184, 310n.104
Middleton, Thomas, and Rowley, William: *The Changeling*, 182–90
  Alonzo de Piracquo, 182, 186–87, 190
  Alsemero, 182, 183, 187–89
  Beatrice-Joanna, 182–85, 186–89, 190, 310n.101, 310n.104
  chastity test, 182, 187–88
  and Croxton *Play of the Sacrament*, 13, 156, 164, 174, 188, 189–90
  DeFlores, 182–85, 186–87, 188, 190, 310n.101, 310n.104
  and the Eucharist, 1, 186, 189–90
  gloves in, 156, 174, 182–84, 186, 187, 190, 310n.104
  "madhouse" subplot, 309n.97
  and relics, 13, 156, 174, 182, 183, 185, 186, 187, 188, 189–90
  ringed finger in, 174, 182, 186–87, 190, 311n.113
  and Webster's *Duchess of Malfi*, 13, 164, 174, 182–83, 186, 188, 189–90
Middleton, Thomas: *A Game at Chess*, 309n.97
Midlands Revolt of 1607–8, 270n.99
Mills, David, 71, 259n.23, 265n.62, 266n.69
missals, 119, 290n.35, 290n.37
  Canon Missae, 115, 124, 129–36, 266n.71, 282n93, 293n.69
  and *Doctor Faustus*, 13, 119–20, 126, 128, 129–40, 143, 148, 152, 293n.69
  Missale ad usum Ecclesiae Sarum, 290n.33, 291n.38
  Missale Romanum, 129–36, 225–28, 290n.33, 291n.38, 293n.69, 322n.8
Misterie de la sainte hostie, La, 164
Mizaldus, Antonio: *De arcanis naturae*, 187
morality plays, 121, 257n.13, 287n.5
More, Thomas, 209, 253n.102
  on allegorical interpretation, 42–43
  Answer to a Poisoned Book, 42
  on charitable intercession of saints, 183
  on the Eucharist, 7, 11, 16, 29, 42–43, 46, 237n.28, 248n.43, 250n.66, 252n.90, 252n.93, 284n.107, 314n.29
  on relics, 310n.108
Mullaney, Steven: *The Reformation of Emotions in the Age of Shakespeare*, 236n.22
multilocationism, 33, 208

Neely, Carol Thomas, 318n.60
Neill, Michael, 308n.94
Netzley, Ryan, 251n.75
Nicene Creed, 227
Nicholas II, 22
Nisse, Ruth, 263n.46
Norbrook, David, 283n.104
North, Thomas: translation of Plutarch's *Lives*, 72
Northern Passion, 53
N-Town plays, 58, 260n.28, 264n.57, 273n.19
  Cleophas and Luke, 194, 195, 196–97, 204
  Crucifixion, 62

N-Town plays (*cont.*)
  and Emmaus episode, 193, 194, 203, 204, 315n.35
  and the Eucharist, 61, 203, 313n.17
  Harrowing of Hell, 284n.111
  as manuscript compilation, 59, 61

Oates, Titus, 161
O'Connell, Michael, 190, 257nn.11–12, 283n.94, 284n.111
  on religious signs, 26
Oecolampadius, Johannes, 22, 234n.7
Old Law, 19–20, 26, 123
Old Testament, 196–97
  Passover in, 7, 30, 111
Order of Holy Communion (1548), 14–15
Ordo paginarium, 259n.21
Origen, 22, 85, 252n.94, 313n.17
Overbury, Thomas: *Newe and Choice Characters*, 175, 307n.74
O vos omnes hymn, 63–64, 65, 67, 69
Owens, Margaret E., 305n.69
  Stages of Dismemberment, 230n.2

Palazzo, Eric, 131, 290n.37, 291n.43
Palmer, Barbara, 59–60
Palm Sunday, 244n.4
Parker, John, 142, 143, 168, 293n.74
Parkes, Malcolm, 60
Passover, 313n.17
Patterson, Annabel, 309n.97
Paul, St., 272n.5
Paul VI, 225
Peacock, Matthew, 59
Pearsall, Derek, 273n.19, 274n.22
Peirce, C. S.: on indexical signs, 157
Percy, Thomas, 106
periodization, 1–2, 8, 10, 55, 57, 230n.2, 242n.48
Peter, St., 122, 193, 197, 204

Peter the Lombard, 89
  on the Eucharist, 11, 48, 249n.59, 254n.110, 313n.17, 319n.70
  on sacraments as signs, 23, 30, 47, 248n.33
  Sententiae, 23, 30, 47, 313n.17
  on spiritual reception, 248n.33
Pickstock, Catherine, 8
Pietz, William: on the fetish, 298n.9
Pilgrimage of Grace, 105
Pineas, Rainer, 97
Plautus's *Amphitruo*, 207
Plotz, John, 76
Plutarch's *Lives*, 72, 82, 267n.74
poetry, 8, 238n.36, 242n.48
Popish Plot of 1678–79, 161
Protestant Reformation, 8, 9, 10, 11, 21, 24–25, 106, 128, 136–37, 243nn.52–53, 244n.1, 293n.68
  and *corpus mysticum*, 109, 117, 273n.15
  Cummings on, 47, 230n.2
  and *Doctor Faustus*, 148, 149
  iconoclasm of, 157, 190
  misrepresentations of, 15–16, 99, 126
  and suppression of biblical drama, 56
Puritans, 15
Puttenham, George, 310n.104

quem quaeritis, 2, 56, 193, 197, 214, 223, 267n.74

Radbertus, Paschasius, 22, 85, 242n.50
Rasmussen, Eric, 287n.7
Ratramnus, 22, 85, 86, 242n.50
Read, Sophie, 26, 38, 238n.36, 250n.65
Records of Early English Drama (REED), 55, 258n.16, 287n.5

relics, 11, 153, 297n.3, 299n.13
    Catholic views of, 157–61, 163
    Christ's true cross, 163
    contact relics, 162–63, 164, 183, 184, 302n.36
    as containing fullness of saint's holy presence, 157–58, 162–63, 164, 172, 174, 184
    and doctrine of *pars pro toto*, 158–59, 163
    as false, 13, 161–62, 163, 164, 178, 179–80, 307n.82
    as indexical signs, 157–58
    and Middleton and Rowley's *Changeling*, 13, 156, 174, 182, 183, 185, 186, 187, 188, 189–90
    and part-whole relations, 157
    reformed views of, 157, 158–61, 163, 179–80, 185, 190, 300n.28, 301n.29, 305n.54, 310n.108
    relationship to the Eucharist, 13, 158, 164, 166, 167, 168, 171, 172, 174, 189–90
    and *sacra costa* miracle, 155–56
    and superaltars, 159–60, 300n.21
    and Webster's *Duchess of Malfi*, 156, 174–77, 179–80, 181–82, 189–90, 306n.70, 307n.73, 307n.78
Requiem Mass, 151, 152
Resurrection of Our Lorde, The, 56, 193, 205–6, 313n.18
    Appendix, 198, 199, 206, 215, 314n.22
    Christ, 197–98, 211, 215, 314n.22
    and the Eucharist, 198, 199, 211, 214–15, 314n.22
Reynolds, Edward, 7, 242n.50
Rheims New Testament, 15
Rist, Thomas, 306n.72
ritual evacuation, 239n.39

Rosendale, Timothy, 137, 243n.53, 250n.65, 289n.23
Rowe, Katherine, 307n.78, 307n.82
Rowley, William. *See* Middleton, Thomas, and Rowley, William
Royal Injunctions of 1536, 279n.66
Rust, Jennifer, 84, 87, 113, 115, 273n.16
Rutter, Tom, 289n.29
Ryrie, Alec, 299n.10

sacra costa (holy rib) miracle, 155–56, 190
sacred kingship
    and Bale, 12, 82, 84, 87, 94, 95–96, 98–99, 100, 101, 102, 105, 108, 117
    and Lydgate, 12, 82, 84, 87, 88, 90–91, 92–93, 94, 101, 108
    relationship to *corpus mysticum*, 83–84, 87, 88, 92
    and Shakespeare, 12, 82, 84, 87, 108–9, 111, 112–13, 114, 116–18, 281n.87, 285n.117
salvation, 119, 123, 126
    and Christ's passion, 63, 64, 65, 66, 67, 71, 74–75, 81, 111, 112
    in *Doctor Faustus*, 120, 128, 145, 146, 149, 150, 151–52, 153
Sarum Rite, 282n.93, 285n.115, 290n.33, 291n.38, 291n.43
Saussure, Ferdinand de, 26
Schillebeeckx, Edward
    on Council of Trent, 246n.21
    The Eucharist, 246n.21
Scholasticism, 21, 22, 23, 32, 34, 35, 45, 48
Schreyer, Kurt, 257n.8, 257n.12, 283n.94
Schwartz, Regina, 137, 243n.52
Sebastian, John T., 165
Second Vatican Council, 85, 227, 228
    Sacrosanctum concilium, 225

semiotics, 1–4, 5–6, 9, 15, 17, 19–20, 223, 229, 232n.4, 249n.54
   in Eucharistic Controversies, 11, 20, 22, 24, 26, 27–28, 29–35, 201–2
   instability of, 2, 7–8, 13–14, 16, 26, 32–33, 88, 201–2, 214–15
Sewell, W. H., 300n.21
Shakespeare, William
   All's Well That Ends Well 2.3.1, 9
   and biblical dramas, 5, 53–54, 55, 59–60, 61, 71, 235n.14, 257n.8, 257nn.11–12, 267n.74, 268n.76, 283n.106, 284n.111, 321n.83
   Catholicism of, 17
   Comedy of Errors, 207, 316n.46
   and the Eucharist, 1, 12, 84, 109, 110–11, 112, 113–16, 118, 213, 214–15, 216–20, 221–23, 282n.93, 285n.115, 317n.59, 319n.70
   1 Henry 4, 55
   1 Henry 6, 236n.22
   King John, 105, 281n.77
   Merchant of Venice, 7
   Midsummer Night's Dream, 316n.46
   Richard II, 7
   Richard III, 7
   Romeo and Juliet, 310n.101
   and sacred kingship/*corpus mysticum*, 12, 82, 84, 87, 94, 108–9, 111, 112–13, 114, 116–18, 281n.87, 285n.117
   on shadow and substance, 6–7, 236n.22
   Sonnet 53, 6–7
   Titus Andronicus, 5–6, 235n.17
   Two Gentlemen of Verona, 59
   See also Hamlet; Julius Caesar; Macbeth; Winter's Tale, The
Sharp, Thomas, 260n.31
Sherman, William H., 290n.37
Shirley, John, 274n.21

Short Title Catalogue, 126, 128
Shrank, Cathy, 269n.91
Shuger, Debora, 37, 250n.62, 273n.15
Simpson, James, 165, 270n.93, 313n.17
   on Croxton *Play of the Sacrament*, 165
   on evangelicals, 278n.51
   on literal sense of scripture, 43–44, 45
   on Lydgate, 273n.19, 275n.27
   on semiotics and the Eucharist, 4
Smith, Richard
   Assertion and Defence of the Sacrament of the Aulter, 27
   on doctrine of *pars pro toto*, 159
   on the Eucharist, 23, 26, 28, 31–32, 159, 178–79
   on transubstantiation, 23, 178–79
social community
   and biblical dramas, 11, 54, 56–57, 71, 72, 79–80, 202, 203, 204, 205, 270n.96
   and *Coriolanus*, 11–12, 72, 73–74, 76, 77, 78, 82
   ecclesial community and the Eucharist, 19, 25, 35, 56, 80
   and king's sacred body, 82
   and Lydgate, 88, 90, 93, 94
   and *Winter's Tale*, 192, 206
Sofer, Andrew, 293n.74
Sokolowski, Robert, 136, 247n.30
Solberg, Emma Maggie, 257n.13
Southwell, Robert, 4
Spanish Match, 309n.97
Spencer, Thomas
   Englands Warning-Peece, 106
   on King John, 106
Sponsler, Claire, 88, 89, 274n.21, 274n.25, 275n.29, 275n.31, 276n.33, 276n.41, 276n.43
Stallybrass, Peter, 183, 184
Stanzaic Life of Christ, 53

Streete, Adrian, 295n.87
stigmata, 256n.4
Strohm, Paul, 217, 238n.35, 271n.101
substance, 20, 44, 116, 186, 250n.66
   vs. accidents, 21, 32–33, 36, 51, 163, 181, 191, 217, 218–19, 223, 244n.4, 249n.52, 253n.103, 319n.68, 319n.70, 320n.71
   Aquinas on, 33, 181, 219, 305n.59, 320n.71
   See also transubstantiation
Swift, Daniel, 114, 115, 284n.112, 285n.114
Swift, Jonathan: *Gulliver's Travels*, 242n.50
synecdoche, 156, 158–59, 163, 185, 307n.82

Targoff, Ramie, 290n.35
Te Deum, 92, 100
Te igitur prayer, 131, 132, 133, 134, 135
Test Act of 1673, 15
Theophylactus, 248n.43
Thomas, Keith, 120
Towneley plays, 58, 266n.66, 276n.33
   Crucifixion, 5, 64, 75, 264n.59
   and Emmaus episode, 193, 195, 203–4, 315n.35
   and the Eucharist, 61, 64, 68, 70, 71, 200–201, 203–4, 313n.17
   Coletti and Gibson on, 60, 64, 261n.39
   as manuscript compilation, 59–60, 61, 260n.31
   Peregrini, 195, 200–201, 205
   Resurrection, 62, 64–65, 69, 70, 74–75
transubstantiation, 2, 3, 9, 15, 32–33, 38, 76, 85, 93, 99, 100, 198, 242n.50, 249n.46, 252n.89, 266n.68
   Aers on, 32, 34, 319n.70
   Aquinas on, 4, 22, 30, 47, 49, 158, 219, 249n.47, 249n.51, 305n.59, 314n.23, 319n.70, 320n.71
   and biblical plays, 69, 70–71, 200, 202
   Calvin on, 41–42, 140
   Council of Trent on, 25, 40–41, 246n.21, 291n.43
   Cranmer on, 35, 41, 45–46, 48–50, 158–59, 212
   in Croxton *Play of the Sacrament*, 156, 164, 165–66, 168, 171
   defined, 21, 22, 191
   Fourth Lateran Council on, 25–26, 89
   Gardiner on, 23, 27, 31, 32, 41, 45, 46, 48, 49–50, 159, 198–99
   Harding on, 23, 41, 46
   Henry VIII on, 4, 25–26, 35, 97
   Hooker on, 4, 35, 221, 320n.72
   Jewel on, 20–21, 221, 320n.72
   Smith on, 23, 178–79
   and *Winter's Tale*, 213, 214, 216–20, 222, 317n.59
   Wyclif on, 23, 29, 34, 86, 168, 254n.115, 265n.60, 289n.21
   See also Eucharistic confection
Travis, Peter, 62, 69, 266n.66, 266n.68, 266n.70
Tretise of Miraclis Pleyinge, 263n.46
Troublesome Raigne of King John, The, 105
Tuke, Thomas, 242n.50, 304n.53
   Concerning the Holy Eucharist and the Popish Breaden-God, 125
Twycross, Meg, 260n.31
Tyndale, William, 4, 42, 237n.28, 313n.18
   on baptism and circumcision, 313n.17
   A Briefe Declaration of the Sacrament of the Altar, 44, 313n.17

Tyndale, William (*cont.*)
  on the Eucharist, 16, 29, 38, 44–45, 46, 139, 313n.17
  on literal sense of scripture, 43, 227
  The Obedience of a Christian Man, 209, 278n.55, 280n.70, 316n.50
  Practice of Prelates, 278n.55
  on relics, 161, 185

Udall, Nicholas
  Ralph Roister Doister, 207, 315n.39
  Respublica, 207, 315n.39
  See also Jack Juggler

Virgin Mary, 22, 62, 64, 91, 214, 264n.59

Waldron, Jennifer, 295n.84
Walker, Greg, 96, 105, 278n.55, 279n.69, 280n.74
Walker, John, 59–60
Wall, Wendy, 306n.72
Wall-Randell, Sarah, 131
Walsham, Alexandra, 160, 300n.25
Wandel, Lee Palmer, 269n.92, 300n.20
Ward, Robert, 279n.66
Wasson, John, 287n.5
  Webster, John: *The Duchess of Malfi*, 174–82
    Antonio, 175–76, 177, 179, 180–81, 307n.79, 308n.92
    Bosola, 180
    Cariola, 178
    and Croxton *Play of the Sacrament*, 13, 156, 164, 174, 177–78, 189–90
    Duchess, 3, 164, 174–77, 178, 179, 180–82, 190, 306n.72, 307nn.79–80, 308nn.91–92, 308n.94
    and the Eucharist, 1, 175–76, 178–79, 181, 189–90
    Ferdinand, 176–77, 178, 179, 180, 181, 188, 307n.80
    and Middleton and Rowley's *Changeling*, 13, 164, 174, 182–83, 186, 188, 189–90
    and Overbury's *Newe and Choice Characters*, 175
    and relics, 156, 174–77, 179–80, 181–82, 189–90, 306n.70, 306n.72, 307n.73, 307n.78
    wax figures in, 3, 156, 164, 174, 176–77, 178, 179, 180, 181, 190, 305n.69, 307n.80
Welles, John, 88, 152, 296n.93
Whigham, Frank, 307n.79
White, Paul Whitfield, 56, 261n.40, 266n.69, 313n.18, 315nn.38–39, 316n.41
Williams, Rowan
  on Christ as sign-maker, 7–8, 237n.32
  on the Eucharist, 315n.30
Williamson, Elizabeth, 159
Wilson, J. Dover, 313n.18
Winter's Tale, The
  and Emmaus plays, 206, 214, 216, 220, 223
  and the Eucharist, 192, 213, 214–15, 216–20, 221–23, 317n.59, 319n.70
  Hermione, 3, 14, 180, 213–17, 218–20, 221–22, 223, 317n.57, 317n.59, 318n.60, 319n.70, 320n.75, 321n.82
  and *Jack Juggler*, 13–14, 192, 206, 210, 213, 216, 220–21, 223
  Leontes, 3, 14, 192, 213, 214–17, 219–20, 221, 222, 223, 318nn.60–61, 319n.70, 320n.75, 321n.82
  Paulina, 192, 213, 215–16, 218, 219, 222, 319nn.66–67, 321nn.82–83

Perdita, 59, 213, 216, 221–22, 223, 321n.82
Polixenes, 216, 321n.83
and social community, 192, 206
Steward, 213
Witmore, Michael: *Shakespeare and Early Modern Religion*, 235n.14
Woods, Gillian, 216
Woolf, Rosemary, 263n.46, 266n.66
Wright, Thomas, 242n.50
  on the Eucharist, 40
  The Passions of the Minde in Generall, 39–40
  A Treatise, shewing the possibilitie, and conveniencie of the reall presence of our Sauiour in the blessed Sacrament, 40
Wyclif, John, 5, 34, 38, 253n.103, 256n.2, 263n.46, 264n.56
  on cardinal virtues, 265n.60
  on Christian virtue, 34
  on the Eucharist, 11, 23, 29, 33–35, 38, 86, 126, 137, 167, 168, 200, 202–3, 234n.10, 245n.10, 249n.52, 249n.54, 254n.115, 265n.60, 289n.21, 299n.10
  on Eucharistic participation, 34, 200, 202–3
  on faith, 265n.60
  on transubstantiation, 23, 29, 34, 86, 168, 254n.115, 265n.60, 289n.21

York Memorandum Book, 80
York plays, 69, 259n.21, 266n.66, 267n.75, 283n.106, 312n.7, 315n.35
  Christ's Appearance to Mary Magdalene, 67–68
  Crucifixion, 5, 61–62, 64, 67, 270n.100
  Death of Christ, 63, 263nn.48–49
  Emmaus, 193, 195, 200, 202
  and the Eucharist, 61, 71, 191, 200, 270n.96, 313n.17
  Herod and the Magi, 264n.59
  Incredulity of Thomas, 191, 206
  Last Judgment, 63, 270n.100
  Nativity, 264n.59
  performed as civic cycle, 54, 58, 59, 61, 79–80, 258n.16, 270n.96
  Resurrection, 321n.83
  Road to Calvary, 65, 79
  Shepherds, 264n.59
  suppression of, 56, 58
York Register, 58, 259n.21
York's Corpus Christi guild, 172
Young, Karl, 312n.7

Zika, Charles, 123
Zimmerman, Susan, 283n.106
Zwingli, Ulrich, 11, 209
  on the Eucharist, 4, 22–23, 34, 38, 39, 40, 42, 44, 234n.7, 252n.85, 254n.115, 314n.22
  vs. Wyclif, 34

JAY ZYSK
is assistant professor of English
at the University of Massachusetts Dartmouth.

www.ingramcontent.com/pod-product-compliance
Lightning Source LLC
Chambersburg PA
CBHW071358300426
44114CB00016B/2096